Who cares who's 3RD?

(or 2nd for that matter)

John Philips

AuthorHouse™
1663 Liberty Drive
Bloomington, IN 47403
www.authorhouse.com
Phone: 1-800-839-8640

© 2012 by John Philips. All rights reserved.

No part of this book may be reproduced, stored in a retrieval system, or transmitted by any means without the written permission of the author.

Published by AuthorHouse   06/15/2012

ISBN: 978-1-4685-7790-7 (sc)
ISBN: 978-1-4685-7789-1 (e)

Any people depicted in stock imagery provided by Thinkstock are models, and such images are being used for illustrative purposes only.
Certain stock imagery © Thinkstock.

This book is printed on acid-free paper.

Because of the dynamic nature of the Internet, any web addresses or links contained in this book may have changed since publication and may no longer be valid. The views expressed in this work are solely those of the author and do not necessarily reflect the views of the publisher, and the publisher hereby disclaims any responsibility for them.

. . . Katie Walsh (on *Seabass*—8-1 jt fav) for starters, but way back in our 'National' history, when *Red Alligator*—"owned by J. Manners, trained by D. Smith and ridden by Brian Fletcher," got up at Aintree—(1 horse died—*"bred for the job"*—hmm), Mrs. John Sherwood, could, justifiably, have had the serious hump that her husband's high-altitude efforts (over hurdles, admittedly) had not been duly recognised on telly.

More, on that, and more, anon.

A few years ago—in the absence of a pre-nupt—the BBC and *Grandstand* were divorced, without fuss and spoil-sharing, two short of a 'gold,' as in that anniversary bash for making it to fifty years together . . . which *Sports Report* (on 'steam radio') has already celebrated, commendably (*"one dimensional, see"*).

We on 'Bairdview' had to settle for a 'ruby' and bits.

In its death throes, Lynam D.M.,—a stalwart of both leviathans—called the big *G*, "*a dinosaur,*" that, lest he forgets, provided him with a posh car for each foot, an O.B.E., and us with the best years of our working lives.

So here—in a ramble akin to a David Vine link—are those ball-grabbing times, in no kind of order.

Remember 'Di-Vine?'
. . . from *Superstars* and *The World's Strongest Man*, via *Question of Sport*, *Ski Sunday* and all things show jumping, to the green room at the snooker . . . a *seriously under-rated pro*.

He'd take a pinch of practically anything, wrap it round a verb, add an object to fit, we'd ease it on down with a little bitty bit of *poptastic*, and if he felt he were about to dry . . . *why, he'd start over* (doddle to write, tough to do).

In the melting pot of 'live' telly, 'Viney' could fill for hours.

Listen closely to the voice-over on the BBC recording of the Eurovision Song Contest from Brighton in 1974—the year *Waterloo* got most votes and AββA were launched into popular music's exosphere: none other.

From Mexico to Macclesfield . . . and beyond, it won't be Route 1 exactly, but, hopefully, you'll remember some of it from your front-rooms, kirks, sun-beds, cells or boozers (*is that about everybody?*).

This *ain't no text book*, so if there's stuff herein that's factually challengeable, or other grammatical own-goals appear . . . . *call somebody else*.

John Campbell—from Cupar in Fife—the Member for Edinburgh in the 1830s and soon to be Lord High Chancellor under Victoria Hanover, wrote:

'I propose to bring a bill into Parliament to deprive an author who publishes a book without an index of the privilege of copyright, and, moreover to subject him for his offence to a pecuniary penalty.'

Propose away, Johnboy.

Now you've invested (and eternal thanks for that), best you read the lot, if you can.

Who do I think I am?

Well, I'm not related to the poor sod of a telegraph officer who came close to surviving the *Titanic* catastrophe (his had two '*ll*'s . . . or •—•• x 2) . . . nor am I <u>that</u> keen on being associated with 'Papa John' (Phillips) of the *Mamas and Papas* (much as I enjoyed the tunes) . . .

. . . no—and I'm guessing here—it all began for me one night in May 1943.
My Mama and Papa loved each other . . . but the Germans were playing nasty buggers . . . the Japs were just hideous . . . nobody trusted the Italians . . . so, if they were going to add to David (aged 2½), it had better be before Dad and his potent spermatozoons were dispatched back to the fray.

If mine were an exact term, the egg in Mum's tubes got the needle around the time the Yanks were bombing Sardinia . . . for reasons best known to them (they tend not to be long on geography).

On February 25th 1944 the world continued to fight and took no notice whatsoever of John Grant Gordon, born with dimples and curly blond hair, to Enid Jessie Bain (née Grant) and David Philips—in my Granny's 'hoose' at 161 Glasgow Road in the Royal Burgh of Perth (now Scotland's 7th city, *so there*) at 0530hr (in the new money)—and, very possibly, to wee Davie's chagrin (heir to bugger all, materially).

The journey from there to the showers on the Ladies European Golf tour has happened, not without incident.

Curriculum vitae (potted)

<u>The</u> *School in Scotland*—Morrison's Academy, Crieff *"Ad Summa Tendendum"*—Philips J.G.G., capable at sport, the embodiment of the camel in the eye of the scholastic needle, but not thick altogether—3 Highers 3 Lowers . . . *result!*

Airdrie and Coatbridge Advertiser—half-baked 'reporter'

BBC Scotland—news sub-editor/assistant floor manager rising to f.m. (*gosh*), thence to stage manager (outside broadcasts* viz., *on the road*)

BBC London—*OBSM/production assistant/director/producer/editor

Trans World International—golf, golf and more golf, for men (only)

Sunset & Vine—cricket, lovely cricket to *Mambo No. 5*

Ark Production—golf, female golfers, lovely female golfers (gays and straights)

. . . *now this.*

"... We're Starting Now!"

September 11th (*that* one): Dave the cameraman—beautifully formed but with no obvious route to a career in basketball being several inches shorter than Alton Byrd probably the most famous US point guard to rebound round the courts of Crystal or any other UK palace (*breathe*), his chiseled assistant, Damian—shit on sound, the embodiment of babe-bait . . . the crew's angler fish—and I, were on board a B.A. flight to Greece, bemoaning our slightly late take-off and, in my case, the leg-room.

Moi? . . . a lanky Scotsperson abroad, with two marriages to date . . . made either side of the divide . . . four regular, and five grand children—the helplessly cute and tiny variety being the only category that can be improved upon decently—25 years loyal to Auntie, with a tiny BBC camera on a plinth to prove it, and a modest, suspended pension to come . . . . *so, if you enjoy this, even in bits, phone a friend, please.*

On 9/11, of expediency, I was sleeping with my auld enemy (ITV) albeit on a short term contract, about as precarious a tenancy as any Premiership manager's outside 'The Big Four.'
The following evening Manchester United were to play a tie in Athens.

'The Bhoys'—my team for as long as She (QE II) has reigned—had failed to qualify that year, so Mr. Ferguson was "da man," the patriotic link for the '01/'02 UEFA Champions League campaign . . . *Govan's brawest* (finest), *made frae (*from*) gurders* (large steel beams) . . . . *scum* (a Hun) *to Celtic fans, but <u>Scottish</u> scum*: "see <u>you</u> Fergie!"
More fantasy than fact, but 34 years earlier, the bookies in Glasgow were gleefully accepting bets that the big Royal Mail Ship—job No.736 . . . all chained up and waiting to go on Clydeside that September . . . would be named the *Sir JOCK STEIN*; not a bad shout if you had any escudos and brains cells left after staggering home from Lisbon four months earlier (1967 and all that), and a disregard for traditional (sexist) maritime gender rules.
Neither honour was bestowed on the Big Man.

More recently, Cunard missed another trick by failing to name their new flagship liner (built in France) the *Sir ALEX FERGUSON*, opting for the unimaginative *QUEEN MARY II*, not, apparently, after (sexy) King Billy of Orange's child bride . . . with more of a Hollywood sequel feel to it than that.
Govan—where *scally* (impish) wee Fergie was brought up—doesn't do big boats anymore.

Our place, and cyberspace, abound with conspiracy—Marilyn and J.F.K., the dodgy wee Russian linesman in 1966 (wonder what Gray and Keys would have made of him), *J.R. Ewing, Nessie,* and Diana . . . they all need clearing up . . . *or do they?* And what of that most famous of Englishmen (after James Corden), Willm Shakspere and his sonnets and plays, and "Virgin" (?) Queen Lizzie, slimy Robbie Dudley and Amy his "suicidal"(?) missus?
Nessie being utter bollocks of course.

P.S. We were just about over Culloden, when that seminal Act of 1966 shut Scottish faces, tight.

A *Not Proven* theory that rankles still north of Hadrian's, is that the English—unseen by 97,350 of us inside Old Wembley—had spiked big Frank Haffey's half-time brew (our national drink has a 'b,' an 'r' and a 'u'), resulting in a 9/3 humiliation on 15/4/61 (. . . we were only 3-zip adrift after 45 minutes).

Glen Chandler—*Taggart's* creator—might have seen it thus:
"Jackie (Blythe Duff—what a crackin' name), *get on to forensics . . . Stuart, check the CCTV in both changing rooms . . . Robbie, you're on a house-tae-house of possible witnesses"* . . . (pause) . . . *"You're havin a fucking laugh, Boss!!"*

My brother, three mates and I, all recent, teenage recruits to the travelling Tartan Army, were brought up to take a shot, but this simply *wasnae* fair . . . . a *'pick up the baw, here's the big yins'* scenario.
The year before, we'd all been at Hampden for a squeaky draw; the on-the-line/over-the-line incident in that one, was less convincing—by a couple of feet—than the Blatter blooper in Bloemfontein(*never mind, eh?*).

Here we were, buoyed from a night on the Glasgow sleeper (*The Insomniac Express*), in hats and scarves be-decked, ready for the fray:
"Bring on the English"
. . . Bob Bruce . . . penicillin . . . Davie Baird . . . tarmac . . . *"wee-r-ra pee-pelle!"*

None, with gonococci in the genital tract, waiting in line at Glasgow's Black Street clap clinic, would question Alexander Fleming's role in the discovery of the wonder drug; had it been available 600 years earlier, even 'the mighty Bruce' (more than a *bit* of ladies' man) would have queued up (possibly in disguise); such was the claim, that he could have been back in the saddle within four hours . . . *nice one Alex* . . .
. . . *and where would we be without the box—or the M8 for that matter?*

Alas, it was to be Flodden Field revisited: September 3rd 1513 . . . by which time, we were already one down . . .

Robson 9' (*"ach"*) . . . Greaves 21' (*"come on Scotland"*) . . . Greaves 30' (*"he was miles aff, ref"*) . . . Douglas 55' (*"it's only 4-2, boys"*) . . . Smith 73' (*"five!—now we are in the shit"*) . . . Haynes 78' (*"the game's a bogey"*) . . . Haynes 82' (*"let's get pished"*) . . . Greaves 83' (*"ya wee poachin' bastard"*) . . . Smith 85' (*"for fuck's sake Frank!"*)

Forty years, four months and twenty-eight days on, our mission—considered impossible by all at ITV, and ludicrous by the BBC, who hadn't been able to get a word out of Man. U.'s guv'nor since Lineker turned gamekeeper—was to secure an interview with 'Sir' Alex as he was by then, for the brand new Terry *Venables* show on the terminally ill sister channel, ITV Digital—death by hacking on an industrial scale.

What a start for the inaugural . . . a chat with the bold Fergie, first up.
We hadn't given DNA samples before requesting an audience with 'His Loftiness,' but we guessed 'Telboy' wouldn't be perceived as a threat . . . and thus, miraculously, it came to pass.
The one absolute, hand on heart, *cut my dyed* (blue)*-in-the-wool throat if I-fib-to-a-Tim* (Celtic fan) definitive from Alex the Unimpeachable was:

"I WILL retire from the job at the end of the season (2002), *oh yes"*
. . . and *nothing* would dissuade him (*yeah right, Eck*).

As he struggled, in driving rain, for a double-bogey in the British Par 3 golf championship celeb-am we were filming for BSkyB at Nailcote Hall Golf Hotel and Country club in 2009 (it was a *two*-shot hole for him), *bugger me* if the bedraggled knight wasn't STILL boss at Old Trafford.

The drape from the posh seating, up front, was thrown aside:

"You never phone, you don't write . . . God knows the messages I've left . . ."

There in person, 'Lyners', the greying eminence (save for the 'tache)—a close season signing by ITV three years back . . . for plenty.
Any name that worked became an *'-ers'* in radio sport, courtesy of the origin of the species, Brian 'Johnners' *"do stop it Aggers"* Johnston (*Test Match Special* 1966-1994, deceased—the man, sadly . . . thankfully, not the show).

'Lyners' had come up the same, tough way . . . through the wireless, and the sternest of taskmasters in grumpy old *Sports Report* programme boss Angus MacKay; like his namesake—*'Mister MacKay'* at *Slade* prison, Angus was a fierce, Scottish disciplinarian—his was not an act.

Des curled into the vacant seat beside me as we hurtled towards Hellas. Once upon a time (1984-1990), we worked together pretty harmoniously at BBC Sport . . . should the April Fool's day 'fight' in the *Grandstand* studio, and his opening of a Cup Final edition from a dressing-room bath (*him* in the good Armani) be measures.

'Don't recall Peter Dimmock doing too much of this!'
"Dim," who'd directed the EIIR's Coronation for the "Beeb," begat "Colemanballs" on *Grandstand* in 1958, and was double-breasted—a Savile Row man, with pocket handkerchief; D.C. was more *Burton's* . . . *"the window to watch"*—mohair suits, not a turn-up in sight.

As a prologue to our first *Venables* show, Des agreed to write and recite, a very short, pre-title soliloquy, extolling the virtues of the host; pure hyperbole of course, amplified off-camera by the Dagenham diva, who could—asked or not—do an implausible 'Tony Bennett' of a karaoke evening at *ScribesWest* speak-easy; strong men and music lovers did their best to prise the mic from him, but it was *his* gaff. One of many 'requests' to be avoided was *My Way,* sung in Catalan, to celebrate Barca's La Liga title in 1985.

Never one to miss a paying trick, Venables latched on to several commercial opportunities during the last World Cup, concurrently waging ecological warfare on the villagers of Penaguila in southern Spain, where he plans to build a multi-million pound sports complex:
"Hold on, the latest odds are coming up on the screen . . . NOW!"

On the subject of slashing wrists, in 1978 Willie Todd (no relation of the demon barber of Fleet Street)—then chairman of St. Mirren F.C—in a move akin to 'The Hoff' buzzing ingénue Beyoncé in an early round of *America's Got Talent*, got rid of Alex Ferguson as his manager.
N.B. 'The Buddies' of Paisley have played in Europe several times . . . . *"yous didn't expect that did ya? . . . no!"* (Ant declares on 'SuBo').

Terry would then to fly to Holland to talk to Rinus Mikels, legendary mentor to Cruyff and co., in the 70s and architect of 'Total Football,' an attacking style of play the former Wimbledon F.C. never quite mastered at Plough Lane . . . or anywhere else.

One of the Crazy Gang (whilst at SW17), prodigious striker John Fashanu tried to impose those 'Mikelsian' principles . . . and a touch of ingrained bish, bash, bosh . . . on his own hand-picked, TV-contrived side, Fash F.C.—in the Hendon and District Sunday league—without notable success.
Hendon wasn't built in a day.
We were *Zig Zag* productions acting on behalf of *Bravo Televison*.
Knocks came from dressing-room rather than pitch battles; the groin strain was regularly featured as reality T.V. went clubbing with handsome, Welsh, Gary Speed look-a-like, Jason Phillips and his team of wannabes (*looks,* in Jason's case, being everything).

Our lady-in-waiting/presenter, Caroline Flack (*a-ha*) was on several wanted lists but remained dispassionate throughout, riding toilet-talk from the boys' showers with a captivating smile . . . an Ann Boleyn figure, if you're following my train. (Harry Mountbatten-Windsor was into Chelsy, whereas his good friend 'Flackie' is known to favour Spurs).

Zig Zag were toying with candidates to manage F.F.C. so I dropped Venables in as being fit for purpose: coach at Crystal Palace, Queen's Park Rangers, Barcelona, Spurs, England . . . a spot of bother with the judiciary . . . Australia, Portsmouth, Crystal Palace II, Middlesbrough, Leeds, back to England again <u>under</u> (as if) Steve 'Wally with the Brolly' McLaren; he even tried it on with Scotland—*'yer havin' a giraffe, Tel.'*

Terry could have matched any amateur clubber on *Fash's Football Challenge* . . . but early Sunday mornings in North London in the pissing rain for a pittance and no favourable press coverage . . . *eh? no!*
Without Tel's managerial pedigree—or any delusions about his own singing voice—the Millwall and Wimbledon hitman got the nod . . . as did Andy(s) Burton and Goldstein, as commentators.

'F' list humpers, big (Abe) Titmus and her tall boy John Leslie (née Stott) were cast in the floodlit finale . . . an am/celebrity, end-of-season clash—'live,' if you will—on *Bravo*.
The ex-(rated) night nurse was gagged in a manner so as not to speak by a popular Sunday paper; her beau (between sticks and sheets) was substituted by Fash in the second half.

Boots and trackies by Adolf Dassler had given way to suits by Calvin Klein, and correspondent shoes; the dude manager's FA Cup winner's medal (for 'The Wombles' against Liverpool in 1988) and England caps (2—same as Terry) lost some of their shine, courtesy of some unsavory antics given large by the gutter press (same as Terry . . . *same as Stott*).

Not sure if T.V.'s up for presenting *Deal or No Deal*—as Fash has . . . albeit in Nigeria—but Edmonds came back didn't he?
(by the by, what were *Setanta* and Des thinking with their cardboard cut-out initiative—*all doomed, that's what?!*).

Shortly afterwards, it went tits up for long John Leslie (rough justice for supporting Hibs); busty Abs (be grateful) endures, as does *Bravo* (be ambivalent) . . . but isn't it odd how things connect: Fashanu worked on *Gladiators* with Ulrika . . . Ulrika was mentioned in despatches with Leslie . . . Leslie played pantomime with Andy Gray . . . and Andy Burton got yellow from Sky to Gray's straight red.

Where was I? . . . Oh yes . . . our inaugural.
The opening and closing links for Programme 1 of a promised 20 (this was an ITV Digital contract, negotiated in the crotch-protecting, folded-arms, fingers-crossed, penalty area-wall stance) we'd shoot in the northern French village of VENABLES . . . *cunning, eh?*
(*if it was good enough for Richie chez BENAUD on Channel 4 cricket* . . . and Leonardo in VINCI . . .)

VENABLES <u>could</u> have been built in a day.

More tortured links were squeezed out of Tel the Talent midst the wisteria and peachy nymphea of Claude Monet's gardens at Giverny, which we happened upon (with our rushes) *en route* to de Gaulle airport.

'*The old impressionist would be spinning in his grave, Harry*' (Carpenter*). Georges Carpentier—'The Orchid Man'—one of France's greatest boxers (*go on, name me another*), who'd have the living crap beaten out of him by Jack Dempsey in the first ever million dollar heavyweight championship of the World fight in 1914, used to own a bistro in Paris called, creatively, *Chez Carpentier*; shooting in there, one felt, would be a tad lateral for Brian Barwick, Digital's programme boss (*yes, the very ex-F.A. fellow*).

* 'Little H.' (Carpenter) would assume the soubriquet at BBC Sport for patently obvious reasons. While I refer to him here in the vertically challenged position, I'll hint at him, later, horizontally . . . *reading on is a must, fight fans.*

An archive feature on the Brazilians of 1970 viz. Tostao, Rivelinho, Gerson and Jairzinho, plus token appreciations of pre-lunatic 'Zizou,' and pre-'Macca' 'Becks', made for not a bad start-up half-hour (if a smidgin on the expensive side).

Shrewdly, Michelle Williams, the Scottish chancellor of our budgets, had kept some back for the imminent wrap party; a Carpentier-style collapse was just around the corner with all souls lost—bar the officers . . . *naturally*.

Not without conditions did the great Lynam BBC→ITV defection come; on-screen the Brighton fan's performances were constantly monitored by Brentford's Greg Dyke, and off-piste, the red tops were on round-the-clock alert, after all, this was as near a 'Towerable' offence as one could get in peace-time England.

Then, so help us, didn't the Dykemeister do the very same thing a year or so later . . . *football folk, eh?*
Each, in his own way, was hugely popular at the Beeb; pity their times hadn't coincided—we'd certainly have had a longer laugh.

Tush, a man in a mack couldn't take a (shag) break to Paris without someone poking around in the laundry . . .

SEVEN TIMES A NIGHT . . .

. . . the banner in one of the tabloids proclaimed, after the great communicator had (allegedly) strayed away in the romantic French capital. Secretly, 'shoulders' Lynam loved the idea of it; his stunning, long-suffering Rose probably fell about like the rest of us.

Many a fun soirée we had picking the bones out of Diamond's barbecued sardines (Rose Diamond—lovely name, lovely girl . . . lovely cook) as glass by glass of the brutally chilled, we mapped out the way forward for BBC Sport:

'The figures are great . . . we're having a gas . . . nae bother. Sláinte.'

Dessie's was not a contra-deal made in the plush lounges of a five-star hotel on the Marylebone Road; 'bung' talk was rife in football (and athletics), but perish the thought that ITV's negotiator, who'd go on to such high office in Soho's ancient Golden Square (and beyond the scandals), would expose himself, unnecessarily.
'Bazzer' Barwick came on board during my time as *Grandstand* boss, but he too sold out and wandered off down Devil Gate Drive.
My position near the top of Lynam's Christmas card list came under threat as Barwick's stock grew by the dollar.

Famous as they both were, neither was responsible for unearthing Pavarotti's belting version of *Nesun Dorma* and putting football pictures to it; that was my sidekick Philip Bernie's idea first, on *Football Focus*—the other two naughty boys just hi-jacked it for World Cup '90 . . . and grabbed the credit of course.
Dutifully, without protest, Phil B. remained at his post and is now, most deservedly, head honcho of BBC Sport. (more anon of "my mate" Pav)

Gone, in the transfer window, the urbane indulgences, the wispy one-liners—in their stead, unpalatable hyperbole for the B.B.C. Old Boy, plus tiresome commitment to the commercial break:

'Auntie, Auntie, why hast thou forsaken me?' he cried, from his second home in Sussex, as Diamond waxed the beamer and Mellors pruned her roses.

In the mayhem of what would become Ground Zero, none of it mattered.

Although they were only highlights, our two hour, in-flight reminisce en route to the Grecian capital, affected our fellow travelers much as *Striker's* winges had in *AIRPLANE*.
Moderately trousered, we became infuriatingly hysterical . . .
. . . but how were we to know?

The baggage hall at Athens was teeming.
Every ear had a mobile phone attached, every face incredulous.
On T.V. sets in shop windows and cafés, replays of the jets smashing into the towers and the innocent.
Folk drifted along . . . in slow-motion.
Now what?

Bobby Charlton and I waited for our bags in silence—*what could he be thinking?*
The recurring nightmare of surviving a plane crash . . . making a miraculous escape . . . no way—*this was horrific.*
When United's B.E.A. Ambassador crashed on take-off on February 6th 1958 in Munich, after United had qualified in Belgrade for that season's European Cup, Bobby's was one of the lucky ones.

Scots of all tribal persuasions respected *The Busby Babes*, drawn to them, probably through Sir Matt, much as we were to Liverpool under 'Shanks.'

My brother and I had pictures in our scrapbooks of Roger Byrne, Duncan Edwards—Bobby, naturally—and big Frank Swift, the former Manchester City and England keeper who also died in the aftermath: he was an anathema to Scottish international strikers, and supporters, for years, either side of the Second World War.

It was in Munich too that I first experienced terror.

We were working in the International Broadcast Centre at the 1972 Olympics, my first 'major.' Security was always central to our preview film; not one went by without a barking Alsatian . . . the muzzle of a semi-automatic rifle, shot through de-focused barbed wire . . . water-canon trucks and drilling riot police.

The Black September gunman in his balaclava, appearing on the balcony of the Israeli athletes' apartment block, within a short ride of our complex, changed everything.

David Coleman, essentially, was there as our track and field commentator and linkman, as he'd been for several Games previously, but nothing could have prepared anyone for this.

It was very early in the morning of the scheduled tenth day of competition that word of the unbelievable sequence of events began to filter through to us.
Coleman threw himself into the challenge, his choice of words befitting, unerringly, the whole chilling episode—seat of the pants reporting.

These were the wished for "Happy Games" and those who took part did so outstandingly: Mark Spitz and his seven golds . . . Olga Korbut and her clashes with moody Ludmilla Tourischeva . . . <u>her</u> future intended, Valery Borzov's duel for sprint headlines with East Germany's 'prop forward' Renate Stecher . . . the seemingly indestructible Cuban fighting machine Teofilio Stevenson . . . 'Lazarus' Lasse Viren's amazing distance double . . . our own Mary Peters:

"Come on Mary, gets those legs going!"

The unfolding drama at the Olympic village beggared belief.

Our recording machines, preserving those sporting moments forever, were hastily re-plugged to news feeds from all points, as the kidnap and planned escape evolved.

It was reported than ten thousand police had been deployed round the village; for once, our preview film was lop-sided and inadequate. Helicopters buzzed above . . . the world's press got as close as they dared.

Two Israelis—one a wrestling coach, the other a weightlifter—had been killed instantly when the terrorists burst into their quarters, spraying bullets from sub-machine guns . . . *AT THE FUCKING OLYMPICS?!*

In all, eighteen team members managed to get away, but nine didn't, and until such time as 200 Palestinians being held in Israeli jails were released and the kidnappers given free passage out of Germany, hostage they'd remain.

The West German Chancellor, Willie Brandt, flew in to make the big decisions. After protracted negotiations, it was agreed that the terrorists would be flown by helicopter to an airport outside Munich, where a jet would be waiting to take them to a safe Arab haven.

The plan seemed to be working, the getaway was almost complete.

Suddenly all the airport lights went out and security forces were given the command to *"open fire."*

More madness.

The sheer size of the Olympic infrastructure exuded its own confidence—*it couldn't happen to us* . . . the plane crash syndrome; for nine hostages, five terrorists and a German policeman on the tarmac, it did.

9/11 was 29 years and 6 days away—as inconceivable then, as it continues to be.

The thrust of Steven Spielberg's *Munich* (the movie, released in 2005) was about vengeance and the systematic extermination of surviving terrorists, but his reconstruction of events leading up to, during and in the immediate aftermath of the massacre, graphically demonstrated how close we'd come to real and present danger in 1972.

A few days before the shootings, I'd been sent out to get an interview with Jesse Owens, one of the International Olympic Committee's guests of honour in Munich—a far cry from Berlin 1936 and his slighting by Germany's most celebrated homophobe.
This mission, by the Ferguson/Venables scale of one-to- improbable, was eleven plus.

Why me, I'm the new kid here?

Knowingly (should the joker fail), they threw in an ace.

Ian Wooldridge ticked all media boxes: great voice, vast reservoir of words fuelling flawless syntax, an inherent feel for sport and sportspeople, sound opinions, fearless in their expression, be they written in *The Daily Mail* or in his many tomes, or spoken on telly . . . and he wasn't bad looking in a Jeremy Clarkson sort-of-a-way—chinos not jeans . . . grown man not boy-racer.

When he died in 2007, 'Woolers' O.B.E., had more ribbons than Monty (the soldier): columnist of several years, sportswriter of many, a Hall of Famer and, in this apology of a book, is, was, and forever shalt be to journalism what Tiger would become to four footers . . . *unrivalled*.

Talk about zones and comfort.

Black and white stills of Owens's winning long jump—the third of four slingshots suffered by the Aryans—were amazing; the soaring height off the board was something our coach at school banged on about, ambitiously, as he coaxed us white-trash towards the 20ft mark.
Jesse did just over 26 feet in Berlin . . . today's pros are knocking on the 30ft door (*imagine if Usain St. Leo Bolt got hopping mad*).

The BBC Head of Sport decreed that someone should go out with the single camera unit—our news gathering truck—and track down the great man, who was on an ambassadorial tour of the sites with Vera Caslavska, the normally-built Czechoslovakian, forerunner to the emaciated elves, Korbut and Comaneci. As good gymnasts tend to, Caslavska won stacks of gongs: three golds in Tokyo in 1964, and four more in Mexico (plus three silvers).
The city's thin air could have had little bearing on any of those, but you wonder what Jesse Owens would have made of it, considering Bob Beamon's so-called 'jump into the 21st century (nearly two <u>feet</u> further than Owens in '36).

Blimey, the son of a humble Scottish newspaper proprietor from sleepy old Crieff in Perthshire, off with one of Fleet Street's finest, in pursuit of arguably the greatest Olympian thus far, for an interview that would be broadcast that night to millions on BBC1 . . . . ?

G'on yersel' big man!

The wherewithal for our recording was a van, not dissimilar to those appearing in the title sequence of the SATURDAY NIGHT OUT programme, which those of you non-bungalow dwellers using dinky funiculars Dame Thora Hird used to encourage senior citizens into, might remember.
S.N.O. was a lifestyle-magazine-current affairs type of show, in the halcyon days of monochrome telly, hosted by Canadian actor and broadcaster, Robert Beatty—'The Man with the Mike.' Bob was a contemporary of Dame Thora's, whose own gorgeous daughter Janette (Scott), in a tight-fitting, if throat-hugging cardy, aroused the senses of many a spotty teenager. Certain thumb-worn passages from my older brother's copy of *Lady Chatterley's Lover* had a similar affect, I can now own up to.

Anyway, the phone would ring . . . . a hand, in close-up, picked the black enamel receiver from its cradle . . . then Beatty exclaimed, dramatically:

"Outside Broadcasts? . . . we're starting now!"
. . . as a precursor to the wagons (*The Roving Eyes*) rolling off into the metropolis, crashing, on their way, through a paper hoarding bearing the show's title and thence to the programme location . . . all to a dodgy theme tune, and always 'live.'
Exciting, ground-breaking stuff.

'See things happen, when they happen, where they happen' (*very good . . . bit of work to do there, then*).
In 1956, S.N.O. created 'a first' by transmitting pictures and sound from a submarine on exercise under the English Channel—testament to future amazing deeds by BBC engineers.

Co-incidentally, my boss in Munich was one of the production assistants on *Saturday Night Out* . . . so there was hope.

(should you survive the present struggle, there's an irony about me chasing after an Olympic champion in a van, which will become clear, presently)

Inexorably, we were closing on the fleet-footed biped.
Scandalously, after those seminal acts of 1936, Owens had to put his great speed to the test racing *horses* for a living; disgracefully, Marion Jones got rich, infamous, time, and sympathy I can't fathom—Ben Johnson just wrecked it for everyone.

Although it took us a while, the dapper dress, glowing ebony skin and flashing smile, discernable at a hundred metres, and closing fast, soon betrayed his whereabouts; me, being a shy drip, Ian asked if an interview might be possible.
Owens beamed . . . . quarry No.1 was secure.

Alas, the blonde gymnast had given us a high-tariff swerve of her still lithesome body—Jesse would do famously as mitigation.

Just as Tommie Smith and Juan Carlos had done raising their gloved fists to the Black Power movement during their medal ceremony in the National Auditorium in Mexico City, Čáslavská bowed her head and turned away from the podium when the Soviet anthem was played at a couple of hers.
(for the pub quizmasters/anoraks amongst you, Peter Norman of Australia got silver in the 200m and <u>Natalia Kuchinskaya</u> of U.S.S.R. won the beam. P.S. Juan Carlos may have been left-handed).

Prior to the Games, the Soviets had invaded Czechoslovakia; being a signatory to a petition denouncing the communist regime in her country, Prague wasn't a great place for Věra to be, so she repaired to a remote village and began lifting sacks of potatoes for her strength work.
Much later in life, her son was accused of murdering her husband during a family row; understandably depressed she all but vanished . . . for *ten years*. The son was convicted of murder, but pardoned, eventually.

My earliest recollection of the Olympics was 'Chaplinesque' footage of Harold Abrahams winning the 100 metres in Paris in 1924, accompanied by a 'Chumley-Warner' commentary, and something pacy on the 'Aunt Joanna.'
As I watched the crew scurry about, I imagined how my Dad might have felt had he been sent out as cub reporter on the *Strathearn Herald* (our family newspaper) to interview Eric Liddell (after church) in Edinburgh. But that never happened.
"J.C." however, was right in front of me.

Gushing sycophancy, I ushered the golden one to a grassy knoll; Owens was a hero . . . to me . . . to most of black America . . . and to any wretched Semite with a sixth sense that all was not well in the Fatherland. Ironic then, that Leni Reifenstahl's propaganda film of the Games would only serve to exhalt the modest Owens . . . at once powering his way on the cinder tracks of the Berlin stadium . . . then, by way of sixteen equally toned facial muscles, radiating uninhibited glee at her camera.
None could fail to be be-dazzled at his achieving so much in front of so many would-be hostiles . . . not even the petrified.

It was kicking off all over the place in '36 . . . in Italy with Mussolini, in Spain with Franco, in France with Blum . . . . but from London came the exciting news that Leslie Mitchell was to be the BBC's first television announcer!
"This is Movietone, Leslie Mitchell reporting" . . . coming on in the newsreels

"Good night and good luck" . . . Ed Murrow, legendary US broadcaster/journalist . . . going off at CBS

"Hello . . . good evening . . . and welcome" . . . the incomparable David Frost

Signature catch-phrases, like:

"Outside Broadcasts . . . we're starting now."

We had . . . . started.

The geometric wonder that is the roof of the Olympiastadion made for the perfect backdrop. We ran out some cable and rigged the less than portable camera. 'The Wordsmith' had a good handle on his line of questioning, so I simply co-ordinated (i.e. *watched*) the recording and thought about what to 'paint' with library footage.
The 'plumbers' in the truck—about the size of Jones the butcher's wagon in *Dad's Army*—declared sound and pictures "stable," so off we went.

Twenty minutes later—job done . . . *or so I thought.*

Jesse (I'm taking *real* liberties here) was on a schedule made tighter by us over-running (*"your indulgence is much appreciated"*—*I could get a gold for this one*). As you'd imagine, the content was spellbinding. Ironically, the little moustachioed swine in the officer's hat came out of it rather better than the racist regime of President F.D. Roosevelt, but Owens remained the personification of dignity and diplomacy . . . back then, and now. Germany's Lutz Long, who came second in the jump of the same name, was privately received by Hitler, but by day two of the Games, the "black mercenaries"—Goebbel's considered take on Owens and the brothers—were spared an audience with the little turd; not without justification, he felt he was bigger than any Olympics.

Stand back to be amazed further: in1936, Great Britain were Olympic ice hockey champions . . . which is akin to the ladies of Chad winning synchro gold in 2012. Check the odds on Stenhousemuir ever winning the S.P.L., . . . then switch your alarm to doze.

Excitedly—the kid with the prototype toy—I sped back to base.

They're going to absolutely <u>love</u> this one.

"J.P., ma man, your career's *off and running!*"

Like *Pike*, I'd been a *"stupid boy."*

The newsreels of the '24 Games headlined Abrahams and Liddell, but others, like Johnnie Weissmuller, and the incredible (*an inadequate adjective*) Pavvo Nurmi, had several moments. Neither is it unusual for swimmers to win lots of medals at major championships, but for a runner to bag *nine* Olympic golds—five in Paris alone—<u>and</u> come second in three other finals, is phenomenal . . . ridiculous . . . *extra-terrestrial*.

Weissmuller was <u>the</u> swimmer of the French Games, in the dodgiest trunks imaginable: an ugly covering, certainly, but more palatable than the white *Speedos* which barely did the job for Tom 'The Voice' Jones in an early video . . . one that ought be destroyed to protect future generations.
'The Groin' never had much trouble attracting the ladies, nor, apparently, did Johnny-boy, whose marriage tally—up there with Henry Tudor's—fell a couple short of Liz Taylor's and three of Zsa Zsa's nine.

I was chatting on the pool deck in Sydney, with Bud Greenspan, the man responsible for the official Olympic film, almost since Reifenstahl. 'Thorpedo'—like croc-killing 'Tarzan'—was expected to clean up in the pool (*real* sharks patrol Harbour Bay . . . but then the tri-athlete is a very particular kind of nutter). Aqua-dynamics, rather than modesty, put the big Aussie in an all-black (*oops*) outfit for his swims, possibly, with no *Speedos* on at all (*struth*).
His three golds at home, and two more away—in Athens, next time round—matched Johnny's in Paris and Amsterdam.

The official films, for anyone interested in the greatest sports event on Earth, are a cinematographic joy and an editorial nightmare. Nowadays, nothing is left uncovered (should sumo ever be accepted as an Olympic sport, the girls will have to cover their mighty hips and thighs—fact, not sexist). There are cameras and microphones everywhere—gyroscopically mounted javelin chip-cams with pentagonic sound are but a spear-chuck away. Bullet tracking in hi-motion—from any position and in close-up—will get ballistics manufacturers with product placement in mind, very excited.

Sumptuous though the images were, the much decorated Greenspan's relatively limited resources meant it wasn't possible to be in the right place all of the time . . . *and some of the voice-over scripts:*

They'd return, older, and wiser, those men of steel, to stir the Gods of Ancient Athena and make safe treasured dreams of gold and glory.

Wouldn't knock the man (nor was that ↑ verbatim): in 1976, Bud won an Emmy for *The Olympiad*—his epic, twenty-two, hour-long documentaries, one of which—entitled *Jesse Owens returns to Berlin*—he'd shot in 1964 (*ok, ok, way before us, and in Berlin, but ours was on swanky two-inch <u>videotape</u> . . . .* I prayed).

In Reifenstahl's case, she <u>had</u> to cover Owens; he was the far-from politically correct star, but imagine the outcry had his efforts ended up as mere captions . . . . *people have gone to war for less.*

Eventually, Messrs Puttnam (producer, who—*let me tease you with a starter*—told me he'd secretly been 'in love' with an Olympian himself), & Hudson (director) latched on to the Abrahams/Liddell saga in *Chariots of Fire*.
Now those <u>were</u> irresistible scripts, with as haunting a theme as Puccini (*Nesun Dorma*) or Fleetwood Mac (*The Chain*) could muster, fully deserving of the Oscars that would follow . . . *four of the little beauties.*
When *Chariots* premiered in 1981—the year Charles and Diana tied their (slip) knot—the film's executive producer, the late Dodi Fayed (something to do with the finances, one suspects) and Miss Spencer (not suspecting Camilla, one suspects) were in the same room; that is neither pro-Egyptian nor anti-Grecian propaganda.

Plagiarism being the highest form of flattery, for our closing title sequence at the Alfred Dunhill Cup one year, I ordered white T-shirts and shorts for the crew, and sent them skipping through the surf, on the very St Andrews beach Ben Cross, Ian Charleson and Nigel Havers had trod for Hudson and Puttnam . . . to Van Gellis of course. Verily, the seas had been warmer.
One of our golf carts doubled as a dune buggy, with the crew and "wannabe Hugh," clinging on; shockingly, we weren't nominated in any category, for *anything*, but Ken Brown, that most excellent of golf commentators and citizens, got our unanimous vote as most promising newcomer in the role of Eric Liddell, bursting through the pack, head back, invoking a greater power than Palmer, as he sprinted towards the spires of the ancient burgh.

A film by Quentin Tarantino, with original soundtrack by Puff Daddy or P.Diddy (*whatever*), and there you have X-rated *Seoul '88*.

Had Peter Jackson not already been working on his Tolkien trilogy when the best Games, ever, happened in Australia, it would have been Hobson's in Oz—no sleepless nights working on a title for that one.

And for *Sherlock Holmes* alone, it should be Guy 'Madonna' directing in London 2012 . . . voiceover by former Wimbledon F.C. enforcer and Hollywood hardman, V.P. Jones; tragic little Amy would have been perfect for the title song.

Re-WIND.

You know the delicate little tape in Walkman cassettes—prior to the digital pods with Dolby all-round global positioning and hyper-motion Champions League goals—well, ours in Munich were the 2 inch wide, forerunning monsters by Ampex (catch this for an acronym: **A**lexander **M**. **P**oniatoff **Ex**cellence—an American, strangely) . . . videotape, FOR MEN.

With me dribbling over his shoulder about taking maximum care, one of the VT engineers, in sandals, with no discernable passion for anything other than bargains in *Exchange & Mart* and the latest gear offers in *SCUBA Monthly*—no student of Olympic history this one—wound the shiny brown tape round a myriad of spindles, took up the slack, and pressed PLAY.

"There, see, told you . . . . JESSE bloody OWENS, in living colour."

Senior production eggs gathered to watch and listen, hating my success, as I sat, smugly, if a tad tight-arsed, in the corner. The four videotape machines, alone, were bigger than wardrobes, so to proffer cat swinging, in a technical area the size of a fifth bedroom in a Victorian terraced house, was to be impractical rather than offensive to the Royal Society for the prevention of; windowless with neighbours from hell in the unforgettable shape of the assassin at Apartment 1 in the Olympic village and his murderous cohorts in dirty underpants.

The overnight shift was to be avoided.
Principal among the mundane tasks was to organize all recordings from the previous day into a readily accessible library, sport by sport—drying paint, but vital.

For example, the boxing ended up as an unstable, mini-high-rise of tape spools, each 2 inches deep, wide as steering wheels, with "hot-end" recordings of bouts in varying lengths.
The best of 357 boxers, from 12 weight divisions, might have to fight five times for a gold and we'd have versions of the lot of them.
Depending on the quality of the contest, there'd be a heavyweight fight—rounds 1 and 3 only—balancing on a 2nd round featherweight knock-out, above a three round middleweight classic, each marked with the protagonists' names, their countries

and corners, who the commentator was, the fight durations etc., so they could be accessed quickly whenever a hole appeared in the aertex 'live' schedule.
All that tape-to-tape malarkey has given way to non-linear editing by computer; none of the chaos and uncertainty we pioneers endured . . . the guaranteed volley for loading the wrong fight . . . the laborious re-stacking of the leaning tower.
On the final day of competition, September 10th 1972, our edifice was topped out when Teó Stevenson walked-over in the Heavyweight final.

Compared to ABC—the American network held bullshit rights to the Games—our section of the Broadcast Centre was tiny, yet size would matter in the middle of the night, when I found myself on the phone to a frantic colleague from their ponderosa *'Did we* (the BBC) *have the freestyle eliminator between Fandango from California* (no great memory for the giants of freestyle wrestling) *and Grapplelbollocks of Austria?'*
Actually, I do remember their main guy as being the biggest son'bitch Olympian, ever, at very nearly 30 stone; none but Chris Taylor's family would remember his coming 3rd.

We had *it* of course, we had everything; our man, Huw Jones, head of all things pugilistic, curator of the leaning tower of head-bash, was on the case. In an inter-round flash, two of the eternally grateful in dazzling yellow blazers appeared . . . bearing gifts—ABC pin badges and pens, the currency of the I.B.C., sufficient, they hoped, with which to barter.

As they left, fight of the century in hand, and clearly free of the hook, one quipped, in that *sota voce* style:

"Sh-oooot . . . d'y'all see the size of that dump, Chuck?"

"Mm . . . mm, but they do kiss-ass stuff."

Spot on, we had the Olympische Spiele Munchen 1972 covered.

The post-war 'special relationship' we had with the Yanks had been invoked the previous year at Royal Birkdale.

The 72nd hole at the Open Golf Championship.

Lu Lian Huan from Taiwan—aka the more commentator-friendly 'Mr. Lu'—had just holed out for a final round of 70, leaving Lee Trevino a two-footer for the first of his back-to-back titles.
Scunthorpe's Tony Jacklin, the holder, was a shot further adrift in 3rd (where he'd end the following year, at Muirfield, courtesy of a poor 71st and some phenomenal 'Supermex' luck/skill along the way).

As the packed grandstands rose to a person in appreciation, the director cut up the dapper little man from the Orient in mid-shot, blue canvas trilby held high, beaming acknowledgement to the masses.

While the viewers at home watched his reverential bowing, Trevino stepped up and holed the putt that won the Championship.

Oops! . . . we'd missed it . . . the BBC had f—missed it!

Greg Rusedki's outburst at Wimbledon, some years back, was PG rated compared to our Head of Sport's evaluation of the fuck-up. He summoned the press officer, metaphorically splattering the director's entrails against the walls of the scanner (the mobile control room, or MCR).
Ere long they'd produced this masterpiece—the 'official' BBC line:

"*Someone walked in front of our camera at the precise moment . . .*"
(*what?!* . . . nine, simultaneous, miraculous perpetrations—*the dirty, lying, free-to-air bastard!*).

Sharp as a tack, Huwie—the very same man who'd save yellow men's skins in Munich a year on—was out the door of our van, cap in hand, and into the American's tape truck, bringing to the table nothing other than the reputation of BBC sport and his Welsh gift of the gab . . . plus a MENSA score in the early hundreds . . . *the havering smart arse Taff.*

So remember as you look over those "*final scenes*"—as dear old Henry Longhurst would annually describe the denouement of the Championship—that the Trevino putt in 1971 is not a BBC original . . . *but keep it to yourselves, would you?*

I'll build the Owens saga to fever pitch by *di*—or *pro*-gressing, rather, to 1984 . . . briefly; for a bonus point, name the winner of the women's 3,000m in Los Angles.
The Olympics is a protracted affair for BBC Sport—the L.A. Games especially with the eight-hour time difference.
We were at it round the clock, from the moment ten gallon Ronnie Reagan fluffed his opening remarks, to Lionel Richie's closing rendition of the apposite "*All Night Long.*" They were having a seriously good party out there, but around 0500hr BST, midst pyrotechnics and mild substance abuse on the floor of the Memorial Coliseum, we were commanded (prematurely, in my exhausted view) to come off air . . . *talk about leaving a party at the wrong time.*
The Games had been covered 'for the world' by an American network—*well they covered the Americans anyway, excessively.* Broadcasters, like 'the Beeb,' could isolate home runners using a 'unilateral' camera mounted on a very busy communal rostrum, just

beyond the finish line; *but what to do . . . who to follow, were there three Brits in a final,* as in Moscow and Los Angeles?
In '84, we had a fix on Kathy Cook in the 800m; she came third, a 'British' position I'll get back to, lest my title continues to bamboozle.
Down below, trackside reporters operated from a small pen where the breathless and exhausted were pulled for the *"how do you feel?"* / *"now you ask . . . fucked actually!"* post-race interview.

In Moscow, our bosses flipped over who should get to Coe and Ovett *first*—ITV or us—and our guys knew how to lose it *big time*.
Covert (*get it?*) operations were mounted in hotel corridors, where Seb and Steve shouldn't have been, and in the village where even Sebastian the Great had a four-poster with warming pan.
Ensuring their verbal commitment in advance of battle was no guarantee post heat of it.
Call me complacent—then check the figures—but most viewers were watching us anyway, so who came to chat first was of no import, in fact, the longer they had to compose themselves, the more illuminating the athlete's analysis might be (possibly). Ramming a mic under the eloquent Coe's nose after the 800, would have been as disrespectful as his condescending handshake had been to Ovett from the second step of the podium in 1980.
Contrast the emotions of Steve, signaling an inverted I.L.Y—*I Love You*—to his Rachel after the 800m, with Seb's demonic, sinew-straining, self-exonerating, press-baiting celebration, on winning the first leg of his amazing 1500m Olympic double.

Many years later, I was making a series called *Olympic Reflections*—an inspired title—with some famous folk looking back over their favourite memories. The now deceased, Cardinal 'Basil' Hume of Westminster Cathedral (and Newcastle United F.C.), a man who had as much chance of being Pope as Cardinal Wolsey, selected the Coe-Ovett duelling in Moscow for his appreciation. As you'd expect from a Christian soul, gentle Basil was more sympathetic to Coe's sulking than most others, identifying the deep disappointment he must have felt at *a)* cocking up the 800 metres tactically, and *b)* knowing he was the quicker man over the distance. *No excuse, your Grace.*

The records are littered with tales of the unexpected: Hicham El Guerrouz in Sydney, and Herb Elliott all over the place, but man, were we lucky to see Steve and Seb in their pomp, and what a nice old cardinal Basil was. His Scottish, heart specialist Dad was a Protestant, but young George plumped for his French Mum's religion . . . and it worked out almost perfectly. In 1976, Pope Paul VI made him Archbishop of Westminster—the UKs top Catholic—just reward, I'm sure, for 25 years devoted service.

I'm not huge on religion—and the priesthood has its scandals—but had I been, Basil Hume was the kind of guy I'd have wanted on the other side of the kiss-and-tell gauze. Like the man Shakespeare wrote . . . *'some are born great, some achieve greatness and others have greatness thrust upon them'* . . . and if I'm reading the Bard right, George Haliburton Hume qualified on all three counts.

Far from wishing harm on the opposition, not even divine intervention from their most deified fan could bring the First Division title to St. James' during his tenure . . . *nor perhaps, <u>ever</u> again, Kevin.*
If they've gone in the same direction, you'd imagine 'Archbish Bazz' and Sir Bobby Robson spending hours together in their celestial quarters, extolling 'Wor Jackie,' the Robledos and 'Supermac' and baulking at the Carroll and Barton excesses.

The English were never very kind to Ulrika's Sven, and we Jocks didnae fancy the wee German full back that much either, but I'll bet Basil would have made a canny Pope. The Vatican's loss.
Three years after he died, his statue was unveiled by the Queen in Newcastle.

Why-Aye George.

We had deployed four mobile units in '84 to make features, pointing up things to come, mini-adverts to excite the senses and keep our nocturnal Olympic audience from hitting on the birth-rate; no kind of promise should take precedence over the old *faster, higher, stronger* ethos.

The tangled web of the 1500 metres was an obvious topic: where would Cram, Coe and Ovett finish? . . . Would Ovett finish at all, in the smog?
He, Steve, was now the good guy to the British public, but Seb was the race favourite; Cram was slightly off their blistering pace and would only spoil the cosy dichotomy.

For years, Brendan Foster had been one of the bigger cheeses at *Nike,* the sports clothing and shoe giants in the U.S; he knew everyone, he could run a bit, and he was on our payroll. Getting to super-humans like Carl Lewis and Ed Moses, one-to-one, did not present 'Big' Bren with a problem (actually he's not *that* big; in much later life, when the brown ales had kicked in and the punishing training runs stopped . . . . perhaps then).

The shy, retiring Francis Morgan Daley Thompson—*"I've got the big G boys, the big G"*—constantly offered himself up for interview. Adodele, or Dele, or Daley as he settled for, was an *Adidas* man who 'snook-cocked' formality and convention; look at the medals, the world records, the hero worship, the trail of exhausted decathletes in his wake, and you wonder if his non-conformity was worth it. *Each to his own, I guess.*

As so many disparate stories were being beamed back on the satellite link from the BBC offices in L.A., our vertically challenged leader, to whom 't' crossing and 'i' dotting seemed as crucial as medals, demanded that all incoming items should be written up on a chalkboard: what was due . . . its title . . . who, if necessary, would add the words . . . its proposed duration . . . the date of transmission . . . which show it should go into *etcetera, etcetera, et-<u>bloody</u>-cetera, with a side order of nauseum.*

Drastic tactics were required.
Coleman had christened our leader 'midge' to his face, as in small and irritating—*he could get away with it.* The little southpaw's version of Domesday Book was a large, black ledger, where every event result was recorded—a Book of Kells, in English, without the pictures.
It had to be 'mislaid,' put out of harm's way.
The lighting grid, high above the studio floor was the very spot.

I set to work on his poxy chalkboard.

Two late entries in the features column:
a) *Pork Sword Swallowing* (due today) b) *Horizontal Jogging* (Richard to voice)

Spiffing 'Richard' Meade, a horseman of two Olympiads and countless three-day trials, was commentating on the equestrian events. He seemed the most inappropriate man for such prurience . . . together with the fact that he was in L.A., well out of harm's (and a lawyer's) way. I <u>think</u> he'd have been mortified, but you never know with these horsey types.

Items came and went and were duly wiped from the board, but to our continued amusement and, it has to be said, gathering disquiet, *a)* and *b)* survived; more's the worry that one so elevated in the Corporation hadn't sussed out the St. Trinian's mentality.
We expected to be carpeted like the errant school boys and girls, stress and lack of sleep had turned us into. Instead, the boss demanded to know when the pieces would be ready and why we hadn't given them a transmission date . . . *JEE-zuss, "Jonty," get out more!*

The man he trained under at the '60s school of screaming and shouting, was in his pomp back in Olga's Munich, reaching new heights of preposterous behaviour, hiring and firing as he went, falling in love at once with the skinny little Sparrow of Minsk, then with her better-developed, surly team-mate:

'Oh, *Tourischeva*,' he'd moan, as once more the judges fell for Korbut's theatrics.

But that would come after my Owens exclusive.

None of us, least of all 'Mr. Big,' was to know that the lovely Ludmilla was herself 'on the covet.' The loins in question were Valeri Fillipovich Borzov's, tagged by the cynics as Ukraine's Frankenstinian *Six Million Dollar Man*—a champion made in the laboratory.

Howard *'tell it like it is'* Cosell, the follicly-challenged voice of ABC sports—the man who brought news of John Lennon's death to the American nation in 1980 (well, those watching ABC's *Monday Night Football* anyway)—was also the man I hold responsible for introducing the ridiculous full-frontal three-shot interviewing technique: guest to left of him, guest to right of him, volleyed and thundered—with the viewer, seemingly, fielding the questions . . . . *bizarre*.

Do you mean to tell me, coach White, he drawled, in his yellow blazer, *that two of our Olympic athletes didn't make the heats of the 100metres . . . . because they missed the bus?!*

I'm paraphrasing here before Howie's estate attorneys pounce, but he was referring to Eddie Hart and Reynaud Robinson's failure to make it to the Olympic stadium on time, thereby missing out on the shorter sprint final.
Spicing it up, they vowed to run Valeri Fillipovich 'into the ground' in the 200, but all they saw was his *"cute ass"* and No.932 speeding to the line, and a sprint double.
I was lucky enough to get time off and a seat in the stadium for that race, but never at any time was I pre-occupied with his butt.
As a sprinter of sorts at school, I was fascinated by his control and technique.
Twelve years on it got better, as smiling Frederik Carlton Lewis set up as a one-man gold standard; only he, Owens, Borzov and Bolt have managed the double, thus far; the Jamaican, you imagine, might have the final say on that one.

When I got back to the Black Hole at the I.B.C., one of the inmates put the race on for me. The isolated shot of Borzov pinging down the straight in super-slow-motion was stunning. Only trainee astronauts, under several Gs, were depicted thus. Though Borzov wasn't going quite that fast, his cheeks did billow and flap in the turbulence, and, if you looked closely (*steady*), you could see many of his muscles in a high state of excitement, yet relaxed, somehow.
A still picture from one of the heats was sent whirling into space in a box of 'golden records,' aboard *The Voyager* in 1977.

Tourischeva and Borzov didn't get hitched for another five years, still, four golds 'in the family' wasn't too shabby. Ludmilla might have had more, had everyone, including the judges, and Alan Weeks, our gymnastics commentator, not fallen under the spell of the technically less able Korbut.

Checking for lip-readers, I mumbled:
. . . . *"wait till the ginger-haired bastard sees this baby."*

Producer by 30, I predicted for myself, and the final end-of-show credit—*Executive in Charge of Production, J.P.*—by Moscow 1980, at the latest.

I'd launch my campaign, for real, in Montreal.

"Ginger" . . . a.k.a. Bryan Cowgill, Head of BBC Sport—tyranny personified.

In 1958, when I was reading D.H. Lawrence, selectively, and pondering girls' parts, "Ginger" launched *Grandstand*. Saturday 11th October, at two o'clock in the afternoon, the famous tune (*not* the one we died to) introduced the very first edition of a strand that almost made it to a 'golden' record itself, falling short by some 21 months, on 28th January 2007 *(boo-hoo)*.
Roger Mosey, Head of Sport at the time of the '*murrdarr*' did not face any charges—*'he may not have acted alone, surr'*.

As stated at bath-time, Peter Dimmock—"Dim"—was the first presenter. His three-piece pinstripe, Windsor knot and poppadom-crisp white shirt-front were about as far removed from Max Rushden on *Soccer AM,* as Trinny and Susannah could contemplate.
Back then, the West Indies were really good at cricket—Sobers, alone, made 365 against Pakistan in Kingston, Jamaica—Brazil continued to be brill at footie.

Grandstand edition 1—in black and white—offered:
The World Amateur Team Championship of Golf for the (first) Eisenhower Trophy, 'direct' from the Old Course at St. Andrews, Henry Longhurst and Michael Henderson commentating (Australia winning) . . . Horse racing with Peter O'Sullevan and Clive Graham, featuring the 3 o'clock at Ascot, The Diadem Stakes (first won in 1946, by the unfortunately named 3 year old *The Bug*) . . . and the Horse of the Year Show from Harringay (it moved to Wembley the following year) Dorian Williams on mic . . . plus a full results service.
Dorian and Peter went to the same prep school, the incredibly posh Hawtrey's; Cowgill didn't. He did the studio presentation i.e. he was the show's director, and the editor was Paul Fox, both of whom were with me (they'd have seen it differently) in Munich.
Cowgill had been Head of Sport since '63 (it seemed like <u>18</u>63) and I think Fox was Controller of BBC 1, a post "Ginger" aspired to and *got* the following year.
I must have helped . . . but would he remember?

You may not have caught Christopher Lee in the '50s re-make of Bram Stoker's *Dracula,* but the scenes leading up to *Incisorman*'s first appearance are etched, forever, on my sub-conscious; a night on the port and stilton can still bring them on.

23

Night time, obviously, otherwise the old boy would have been tucked up in his satin-lined coffin dreaming of Peter Cushing, or some unsuspecting sleeping beauty with outstanding veins and heaving mammaries. The howling wind whistled through the dingy old house, sending leaves cascading across a moonlit archway.
Suddenly, the shot changed: b.b.c.u.(bloody big close-up) "Dracs" . . . eyes, bloodshot as Bestie's on a bender . . . fangs dripping as Iron Mike's would at the feast of Holyfield's ear—The Count of Transylvania—a countenance less oily than Michael Howard's yet just as off-putting.

Momentarily, bums and hearts left stall and circle seats in unison . . . all sorts took flight.

Even out of make-up, Christopher Lee cut a frightening figure. In not too dissimilar fashion, he burst into the pro-shop as I was collecting cards for a celebrity golf event we were televising at Turnberry and gruffly ordered a *Mars Bar,* for which, in the absence of any move on his part so to do, I offered to pay (great voice, mind). Despite his tiff with *Lord of the Rings* director Peter Jackson, Lee's *Saruman* was thought to be his finest role, even by scared-shitless horror buffs.

We were five or six minutes into a sneak preview of our Owens scoop, when the adjoining door to the production gallery crashed open, and *there he was.* Take away the setting, sound effects, 'Hampstead heaths' and 'mince pies,' add an Oliver (stone) or two, some waspish red hair and a strong northern accent, and there you have "Ginger" at the point of entry.

Bearing in mind his running mate was Jewish, all comparisons with the aforementioned, Austrian-born corporal were plain silly and over the top . . . *or were they?*

"Ginge" wasn't evil. Loud? . . . yes—arrogant as Clough? . . . close.
Few found him friendly, or fun. Minus the sychophants and plain terrified, you'd never voluntarily pop over the top for him. Ridiculous though it may be, he was frightening to some, and though I wasn't laced with 'Boom-Boom' Minter's courage, it seemed so unnecessary to be barking at everyone all the time.
That said, Bryan Cowgill (and one or two other notables) laid the foundations of a sports organization that had no peer (till the Sky train came along), one that opens doors still from Bala to Beijing—*but easy on the dictatorial bullshit* . . . this was *sport* in peace-time, mostly.

A countryman of mine was 'fired' on the spot at the Commonwealth Games in Edinburgh in 1970 because "The Clitheroe Kid" claimed—in his own whining dialect—that he couldn't understand a word the Scottish person was saying:

'Get back to Glasgow' "Ginge" roared, *'and travel <u>second</u> class!'*
My old mate Bill Malcolm—the mildest of men—was re-instated the following Monday and given a volley for wasting the head's time; there's a syndrome in there, but for the life of me I can't place it legally.

Anyway, down onto a low stool slumped Iron Man, right in front of the videotape machine where "Woolers" and I had been clutching knees for the last five minutes—nothing untoward, just genuine pleasure at making a killing . . . . *but had we?!* (cue foreboding music).

Now, another attractive feature of Mr. Cowgill's was his propensity, consciously or not, to probe—normally with the index finger of the right hand (some had evidence of his ambi-dexterity)—the hidden recesses on his proboscis for detachables, real or imaginary. Had it not been disgusting, he could have profited from an instructional guide for schools and big business: from classroom to boardroom, he had a best seller at his fingertips. On experience, technique and dogged determination, he was matchless—a role (roll) model with hours and hours of solo exploration behind him.

No hint of any need, as Wooldridge began interrogating "J.C." on screen.
B.C. watched the first few minutes, gratified, murmuring that we'd run *'the whole foockin' shooting match'* at the top of our peak-time show, along with his darling Tourischeva and her battles with Valentinovna Korbut:

'O-h-h Olga! . . . show me Olga!'

Hold on "Ginge," you had the hots for Ludmilla a minute ago!

He may have *coveted* Ludmilla, but he *loved* Olga; with her undoubted prowess and pert, anorexic, Belarussian look, she duped the judges into believing her more worthy than *'bitch-face Tourischeva'* (now, now, calm down girls . . . taking part, remember?). She was simply irresistible, certainly to my man and, no doubt, to millions tuned to BBC 1.

The thing was, Olga could do a somersault on the beam . . . *backwards!*

Next time you've had a few, draw a couple of lines on the floor, 5m long—they have to be 4" (10cm) inches apart . . . *and no cheating*.
Get on the sofa, cross yourself, then pitch it with all your worth backwards, in the tucked position. If you land with both feet on the strip, then Gunga Din to you . . . you've just done a version of the Korbut Flip . . . if you can't, you'll never be a gymnast.
Now get down to A&E.

On the floor, with her white leotard gathered at the waist Simon Cowell style, she was nimble and jaunty—the punters went crazy for her . . . . and so did 'Weeksie':

'*Ho-ho-ho, how can you take it away from her,*' he squealed at the end of her routine (*whatever that meant?*).

But it was the ratings policeman in him that exposed "Ginger," not as a d.o.m., but as a chartbuster on the audience research Richter scale—figures compiled by BARB, the British Audience Research Board—by which all programmes and their makers by association, were judged.
(like Cyclops at Wimbledon, some years later, there were grave doubts about the accuracy of the whole exercise).

The Olympics never needed measuring.

I swear there was a swelling in B.C.'s great big Y-fronts at the mention of Olga's name, and "Woolers" and I were pretty happy too . . . about Jess.

But then, without warning, the probe stiffened . . . his finger I mean; with a few snorts to lubricate the way, in it went, down went the head—the masterclass was *on*.
I tell no lie, at that precise moment, the picture on our monitor went to *shash*—technical slang-speak to describe the snowstorm-look your T.V. got (circa 1950) after the white dot (*'the what?'*) had disappeared, signaling transmitter shut-down.

'*A very good night from all of us here at BBC Television . . . and if you're living alone . . . DON'T LOOK ROUND!!!*'

Shut-downs don't happen now; whither the lowlights of the latest bunch of deeply unattractive attention seekers, upstaging, perchance 'rogering' one another, 'live' in some squalid reality house . . . porn marginally too soft for the adult channels?

Don't ask me how it happened, only the geeks would know, but there had been some kind of electrical blip during our recording which threw the pictures off lock.
As you'd expect, Jesse disappeared in a flash.

Oh, sweet Jesus . . . are you in, my friend?

The totally uninitiated, *id est* every production person from the Head of Sport down to mole level (mine), would use the expression '*sound in syncs*' as the reason for any technical hiccup, with absolutely no idea of what it meant. On this occasion, the sound was fine.

The bogie miner hadn't been distracted—a big prize was just out of reach—but my life had already started to unravel:

There am I, a tiny blonde thing of three summers, being returned to Gran's house in Perth as, "your little girl," by two kind, old (blind) biddies

. . . there too, my brother, shutting his cock in Dad's desk drawer—what a laugh!

. . . me again, panic stricken, and knickerless, as a swarm of wasps crawl over my red kilt at a family picnic . . . .

. . . and, some time later, that first erection: WOW! what's that?

I wanted death to come quickly.

. . . would the engineers stop the tape to investigate?

. . . would "Ginger" stir and order me back home, steerage?

. . . would the others ever hold their gesticulating?

Like some crazed, Chinese, chicken-sexer on crack, my gaze darted back and forth from the monitor to the top of Ginger's head.

"Bugger, he's got one!"

Was it a roll-up and flick, or one to keep back for later?

"It's a flick—seal the lunch boxes!"

Simultaneously—otherwise I wouldn't be putting you through this—the gaffer looked up, and there, restored to all his beautiful black beauty was my new mate, speaking passionately about jackboots and jumping . . . . and big Joe Louis.

Mein Führer was orgasmic: . . . *OWENS* . . . *OLGA* . . . *oh-h-h-h* . . . (BARBtastic). We covered up the hole in the tape with vintage footage from Reifenstahl's film, and, as promised, "Ginger" ran the whole *'fookin'* feature at six. If he hadn't been in '36, Jesse Owens was sanctifiable now: I felt the earth move a little.

One Christmas I was given Donald McRae's excellent tome, *In Black & White*, 'the untold story' *of Joe Louis and Jesse Owens*, which I commend to you—you'd wish for a better end for "Becks" and Jonny Wilkinson.

A brief spar with Muhammad Ali, a Pelé signature, plus one of Tiger's balls, leaves only Mr. Mandela from preventing me ever bathing again.

However the 19 year old U.S. Amateur Champion was less than accommodating when we first met at Carnoustie in 1995. Clearly young Woods was unaware that his inquisitor would be none other than Eton College boy and former Walker Cup teamster (1969), Bruce Critchley of Sunningdale parish—a man swathed in 'A' levels and exceptionally good manners, and, in Hazel, a winning choice of lifetime companion (*it's not all buggery and beatings at Windsor*).

'Give me golf clubs, fresh air and a beautiful partner . . . . and you can keep my golf clubs and the fresh air.'

In the end 'The Colonel' (as he'd become at Sky) had to settle for three minutes with Gordon Sherry (Gordon *who?*). In the wake of Tiger's imprint, the gigantic Sherry won the '95 Amateur at Royal Liverpool . . . and promised much. The year before, he'd helped Great Britain and Ireland finish 2nd in the Eisenhower trophy; the inaugural event was featured on that first *Grandstand* in 1958.

Whisper this lest the R&A have ears, but big Gordy took a quid off Tiger by finishing higher up the amateur leaderboard at the 124th Open at H.Q., and, a couple of months later, he put another one over him when G.B. & Ireland snatched the Walker Cup from the jaws of a U.S.A. hat-trick, at Royal Porthcawl.
6ft 8in Gordon—"mind your head"—would stay home with his wife and children, while Tiger conquered the World.

My own little boy Jamie—then aged four—did better with Tiger.

During practice for the World Matchplay at Wentworth, Kenny Brown took the wee man under the ropes at the 18th tee as M.F. O' Meara and E.T. Woods waited to play.

Ken was *deliberate* as a player, dragging controversy round with him—not unlike his opponent one day at Sunningdale.
At times, Gregory John Norman, the big blond, gauche Australian, was more of a raging bull than the multi-millionaire statesman he'd become. A couple of months earlier, he'd tamed tempest and Turnberry's Ailsa course to win what many believed would be a hatful of majors.

The two were in a play-off . . . *not*, as it would prove subsequently, Greg's ideal place to be. The green on the first extra hole of the 1986 Panasonic European Open at the fabulous Old Course was just a lob wedge over Hazel and Bruce's hedge.

"Brownie" had a stinker of a putt first, for a birdie, and a possible 6th win on tour.

Hunched over the ball in a stance that had brought a high conversion rate on Ryder Cup dance-floors, he slowly righted himself:

"It's all gone terribly quiet."
The gallery laughed . . . Ken missed, Greg didn't.

"What tiger?!" Jamie hollered, down the road at Wentworth . . .
"I can't see a tiger?"

Somewhat embarrassingly, it wouldn't be his only such cry—my boy was no quitter.

Tiger flashed his gnashers as Fluff Cowan—the young master's bag-man at the time . . . he of the Jimmy Edwards moustache—reached in for a new balata with TIGER emblazoned across its belly and handed it to a bemused hunter.

Now . . . *we've started, so I'll finish:*

Maricica Puica of Romania won the 3,000 metres in L.A.

"... Here is the Shipping Forecast"

Everyone—even *Superman*—stumbles on an asshole in the work place: fictitious *Clark Kent, Lois Lane*, even his long suffering missus, were fodder for *J.J. Jameson*'s excesses at *The Daily Bugle*. In the offices of *The Airdrie and Coatbridge Advertiser*, just outside Glasgow, where my great media adventure began, we took the lead from a *real* Clark (Hunter), an editor with a bit of a past, brought in from the *Scottish Daily Mail* to gee up our circulation, but of more concern was his own; his blood had undergone a thinning process over the years, and acute though his undoubted news sense was, the proximity of the local boozer meant it was seldom tested undiluted.

His predecessor, shifted sideways to make room, stank (no charity there: a personal hygiene by-pass). The old boy knew plenty and had an enviable, parochial touch in his *Notes and Comments* column . . . but give us an admittedly rare, hot summer's day . . . in a nylon shirt and . . . *phew*, sick-bag time (couldn't happen now—Health and Safety would be on to him).

Airdrieonians F.C. were in the Scottish First Division, and Albion Rovers, down the road in the Iron Burgh of Coatbridge, weren't; how the auditors got the figures to work for the Second Division side, only a 'compleat' banker of Fred Goodwin's calibre would know, with stewards and household pets often outnumbering the fans.

After hanging up his boots, the leggy Lisbon Lion, Tommy Gemmell, whose bared shins bemused and baffled the Inter Milan defence in Celtic's epoch making European Cup win in 1967, took on an even bigger challenge at Rovers' sprawling theatre of impossibilities (the classic leveling effect of the beautiful game). The razing of Cliftonhill was a popular, recurring thought amongst a long-suffering support.

Airdrie by comparison, was Real Madrid; there was none between their place, Broomfield Stadium (now, sadly, a *Morrisons*) and the Santiago Bernabéu (forever *holy* ground). Playing Rangers or Celtic came within a few miles of being a local derby, with lorry loads of sectarians making the short trip from Glasgow to away games; Airdrie . . . where Cistercian monks once ruled, *OK?*.

Our owners and editors perceived sports reporting as journalism's lowest form, but when the big boys came to town, front pages were held; advance bookings for the civil court, shot up.

Well-stocked shelves and pub cellars were hoovered dry, as densely populated streets became awash with regurgitated pies and fish suppers—hardly money well spent. One was advised never to wear a 'Monty coat' (that soldier fella, again) on match days, as the duffle hood presented ravenous spendthrifts with the ideal vomit receptacle . . . murder, in memory lapses, if the rains came . . . <u>when</u> *the rains came.*

It took several wage packets—just over seven quid a week in the hand—to get the editor's confidence, but when the opportunity came to report my first match—'The Diamonds' against 'The Gers,' no less—I was over-ripe and *"over the Moon, David."* The fiver in the trilby and the green eyeshade? . . . *taking the piss*, but you went along with it, if only to appease our saddo, wannabe 'sunshine boys.'

The smelly one—Archie Charteris—was the doyen. He could write alright, but shunned roll-ons and contemporary technology—cranky old *Olivettis* with carriage bells and jamming '*Ys*'—preferring to pen his copy in longhand. He didn't go out much—he'd kinda done the streets—but were there gaps on any page, Archie could contrive something from his intimate knowledge of the hinterland. I learned plenty from him . . . at shouting distance.

Here was Clark's ideal boozing mate; the two were often to be found, hunched over the bar next door (great planning for a newspaper office), with half pints of heavy and pernicious chasers aplenty, point-scoring as they supped. Inevitably, it turned ugly, poor Archie fielding the brunt of the seldom justified vitriol from an embittered Hunter.

Our chief reporter, Bob Sutter—an ugly version of Hank Marvin, the opaque, guitar playing genius in *The Shadows*—had limited musical talent. He could sing a bit (more Nelson Eddy than Cliff), and was always well turned-out, in shades of brown and tan, selected from the local 'window to watch.' He liked the coat collar, *up*; bottle-bottom glasses and finger nails, bitten to the quick, spoiled the image, completely, were Bogart the intention.

Remarkable to libelous—as he spent much of his time in the local courts (reporting)—our head hack didn't do shorthand. What he did have, was a bespoke portable which he played at deceptive speed with long, padded, index fingers . . . and, fortunately, quite a good memory. Up at full tilt, the ambient noise from our pool of assorted typists was deafening. Only Archie, and his retractable biro, would have had a prayer amongst the Trappists.

To Bob's right, crashing keys (sticking Ys notwithstanding)—Bobby Crush at a Liberace tribute night—was Malcolm Speed, a 'choochter,' a country bumpkin from one of the 36 inhabited islands in Scotland's Inner Hebrides. "Malky" quickly adapted to big burgh life, swopping kilt and woad for sharp suits and kipper ties. As the name implied, he could do *Pitman's* at a whore-of-a-clip—100 words per minute, and type in the 80s, which tended to make his stories a tad on the long-winded side, yet enormously valuable on 'slow' weeks.

On an adjoining desk to mine was David Kerr, a well-educated, properly groomed, bit of a lazy bastard. He was red hot on modern English usage and would quote *Fowler* at you, should any of his prose be contested as verbose or fundamentally lacking in structure. His jousts, round the table, with hard-nosed Hunter, were Arthurian.

And there you had it, a smelting pot of motleys, and a weekly tabloid to fill, with all life's human and inhumane diversity: murders, burglaries, G.B.H., A.B.H., fires and storms, love stories and sob stories, sex and sedition (football), hatches, matches and dispatches.

The compressed press box at Broomfield was alive with nicotine and jabber. Morning 'dailies' needed constant servicing, re-writes and updates. Juniors dictated opening salvos down permanent phone lines, as their masters assimilated play and prepared to sacrifice their next offerings to ruthless sub-editors at base.

"*Smith, you say? . . . how are we spelling that?*" . . ."45 minutes . . . *is that four five minutes?*" from adenoidal amoebas, with in-store tannoy voices, taking copy on the other end. Social intercourse with the un-dead.

We, at least, had a day's grace; a Wednesday under lights gave us until midnight the following day, before the Advertiser 'went to bed,' so, time to reflect . . . get the scorers right (a constant worry for grown-up reporters on deadline, with no TV crib) . . . glean opinion from players, management and fans—"*it was a great comeback by the lads*" . . . "*I was pleased with the commitment and energy levels*" . . . "*they were shite!*"—something considered and unpredictable.

Unsurprisingly, Rangers, the league champs, won my debut match ('Big Jock' and his all-conquering Celts—circa1965-74—were lurking round the corner). Forty years or so later, having lost twice in the Cup Final (to the '92 Bears and the '95 Bhoys), and making it *in*, and swiftly *out* of the Cup Winners Cup, the grim receiver caught up with Airdrieonians F.C.

The former Excelsior Football Club was around in eighteen hundred and frozen solid, when Queen's Park started the whole F.C. thing off in Scotland. Following some acrimonious shenanigans, and gnashings of ancient teeth, Airdrieonians—via Clydebank (who were also skint) and the league's constitutional lawyers—became Airdrie United, to the town's undying relief. They've dropped into Scottish II now, and only a few months ago went down 7-2 to Albion Rovers . . . of all neighbours. The struggle continues (*if not in Rangers' league, circa 2012*).

Others played their part on that floodlit night, but Jim Baxter starred.
He was Cruyff and Beckenbauer in one, with time, in the less competitive Scottish First, to spare. James Curran Baxter was a Fifer, and though he only spent five tumultuous years at Ibrox, he'll forever be synonymous with Glasgow Rangers.

"Slim Jim" could well have been the template for the bad-boy-genius of the working man's game. He liked booze, birds and bookmakers in descending order, but *man* could he play. At Wembley in '63, and '67, when we walloped the English, Baxter was transcendental, scoring two in the first game, and completely orchestrating the second. Scotland played most of the '63 game without Jim's Rangers teammate, Eric Caldow—our left back and penalty taker, who broke a leg (in the non-theatrical sense)—so it fell upon the nerveless No.6 to slot his, and our second, from the spot, right in front of where we were swaying.

No subs in them dark days, so, lest I over-gloss the folklore, the World Champions had to play most of the '67 game with Charlton the Elder hobbling about up front. Injured or not, big Jack was a bloody pest in front of goal—their best striker in fact; still, *we battered them*.

Early in that First Division piece, Jim Storey, Airdrie's inside right (i.e.—for planet *Zorg* guests—to the *right* of the centre forward as you look towards the enemy goal) pulled off the perfect nutmeg, leaving 'Slim' humiliated, temporarily, and at the mercy of a small pocket of suicidal, home supporters (the touts knew Rangers travelled in vast numbers).

I spoke to Jim (Storey) after the match—doubt if I could have untied my tongue to ask anything sensible of the slender one, keeping me in the good company of my new-found brethren—and wanted to know what Baxter had said, having suffered thus . . . *something about the healing time for fractured fibulae and tibiae*. Storey had an unusually quiet match.

In my final year on the paper, a Ranger from the Henderson, McMillan, Miller, Brand and Wilson, forward line—Scottish internationals all—re-routed to Broomfield; local boy, Ian McMillan—'the wee Prime Minister'—played hundreds of times for the Diamonds, and scored plenty. In the early 70s, he became club manager of the Waysiders.
A prerequisite for any fledgling reporter with Woodward/Wooldridge ambition, was a decent turn of speed at shorthand and typing. Personally, the prospect of night classes, after thirteen years of day school, had little attraction when clubs needed visiting and inter-gender offers, honouring.

The quick brown fox jumped over the lazy dog.

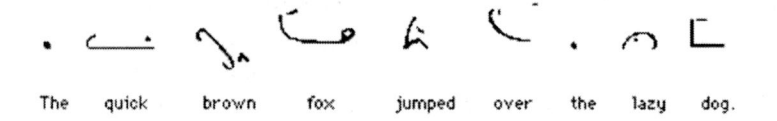

. . . was as far as I got. The absence of any form of dependable Gregg's or Pitman's—or the instant whip of shorthand, *Speedwriting*—made sloppy court reporting an expensive bullet to dodge; lying to one's editor about competence levels was one thing, being dragged before 'Hanging Judge' Tommy Young was to appreciate *all* freedoms.

Correctly, he was Sheriff Thomas Young, and the office was a vast, foosty (musty) courtroom, just off Main Street. Glasgow—McArthur and Long's *No Mean City*—was ten miles to the west, but the Monklands had its fair share of bad guys, and girls.

Banish the idea of some black dude in shades, shiny tin star on his chest, ivory-handled six-guns on his hips, bestride a palomino—*Blazing Saddles* style—Sheriff Young was your regular judge: black robes, silly wig and half-moon specs, ideal for the disdainful, disbelieving, withering glare, and he *could* wither . . . sentence enough.

Respect for the law was quite trendy in the mid-Sixties, unless you were a Great Train robber, or a petty, thieving 'scuzzbag' from Leith or the Gorbals. Sheriff courts—about fifty of them in Scotland—handled the more serious offences; getting a Sheriff's appointment was a cinch compared to seeing a quack today. Unlike the in-vogue, fictional *Dr. Finlay*, Sheriff Young didn't do house calls. Plaintive cries from the hard done-by were nothing to the trials and tribulations of the Arden House doctors (and their ubiquitous receptionist) in *Doctor Finlay's Casebook*.

A.J. Cronin's tales of a country practice, set in *Tannochbrae*—whose co-ordinates do not appear on any sat-nav service—evolved into one of the BBC's longest running series, amidst a pandemic of sanitised soaps. The Yanks would send us *Doctor Kildare* (Richard Chamberlain)—for the girls to swoon at—and *Ben Casey* (Vince Edwards) . . . strong . . . dark . . . silent.

Our lives were placed in the hands of couthie (sympathetic) *Dr. Finlay*, played by hook-nosed Bill Simpson, whose real-time bride was English actress, Tracy Reed, whose great uncle was Compton Mackenzie, whose step cousin was Oliver Reed and whose first of four husbands, was Edward Fox . . . the abridged Reed tree.

We'd speed for a good seat in BBC Scotland's canteen at lunch, should statuesque Mrs. Simpson be on set. Alexandra Bastedo was an added bonus for front-row lechers, She was a 'doll' of the Sixties who, I submit (and apologies to all if I'm wide of the mark) was having 'a thing' with occasional *Casebook* cast member, Anthony Valentine. Grub missed mouths by fork-widths as 'La Bastedo' bent to check the salad bar; *little things, small minds . . . as charged.*

Finlay's mentor was thrawn (contrary) *Doctor Cameron*—the magnificent Andrew Cruikshank; his American equivalents were *Dr. Gillespie* (Raymond Massey) in *Kildare*, and *Dr. Zorba* (Sam Jaffe) in *Ben Casey*—there was no equivalent for *Janet*, the devoted housekeeper at *Arden House,* portrayed, incomparably, by Barbara Mullen: *"will you no be takin' a wee scone with your tea, Doctor?"*

According to the village gossip, *Mistress Niven*—Effie Morrison's character—the wonderfully named *Doctor Snoddy* (Eric Woodburn) 'had the hots' for Janet. Aside from fending *him* off, and her domestic duties, *Janet* refereed regular bouts of black-bagging between the partners: *Finlay,* the whipper-snapper, rich in bedside manner, ever abreast of *The Lancet's* latest . . . *Cameron* old-school, immovable, iconic.

Like *Miss Hoolie's Balamory* in the early Noughties, *Tannochbrae* wasnae real—the village elders would never have condoned technicolour housing—no, it was all Archibald Joseph Cronin's fault. 'A.J.' and pals—Ms. Reed's great uncle Compton(*Monarch of the Glen,* etc.,) amongst them—kept their respective publishers, and BBC Scotland's drama department, constantly supplied (disappointing he had to be English, with a name like Mackenzie; maybe his Mum was visiting in West Hartlepool when her waters broke, but clues aplenty that Edward Montague Compton was no clansman).

The official shorthand writer at Airdrie Sheriff Court was intriguing—not entirely out of envy, and conscience about lessons skipped, but for the celerity of it. *Perry Mason* and *Hamilton Burger* had their stenographer, but give me Pitman's, at speed, from our man, any day. He'd turn it round in an instant . . . every bullshit lie, 'um,' 'ah,' grunt, fart, burp, . . . *verbatim.*

Although not black-capped for Scotland, the Sheriff could hand down some ferocious sentences. It would depend, obviously, on the evidence and the law, but the accused and their representatives were well-advised not to get cute with 'His Honour.'

From the steps of the civil court—home to the altogether less heinous crimes, and pansy in comparison to the heavyweight stuff heard before "Thomas le Terrible"—habitual shoplifters would give daily performances of the mis-understood and framed:

"Goanae keep ma name oot o' the paper, Jim?"
The name's John . . . keep your fiver.

One needed to be firm and not succumb to the routine rounds of bribery, even though acceptance, in the long term, could mean the difference between a second hand Mini, and a brand new, two-stroke Saab 96, in white, one of the *'it'* cars of the time, and the first of their models to be imported to the UK; *if it was good enough for Erik Carlsson, at Monte Carlo and the RAC, it was just the kiddie for me.*

I enjoyed the Mini; alas, back-seat action, for one so tall, was to invite disc trouble in future, but she (the Mini) had a good motor and kept me safely under the built-up area speed limit, even on motorways.

Not so for the well-kempt figure arraigned before Sheriff Young, one dreary Monday morning in North Lanarkshire. We'd failed to recognize him at first in his Bogart-style Mac (a much better effort than our Bob's).

Collar in the prescribed *up* position, blond locks, slicked . . . head bowed.

The clerk rose:
"State your full name"

"Ronald David Bell Mitchell Shade"

Mumble, mumble in the galleries . . . . *could it be?*

Even without a gloved left hand, harlequin jumper by Jaeger (*Christ, they were awful*), checked slacks (*worse*) and noisy shoes, here was the much decorated Scottish amateur golfer . . .

Right **D**own the **B**loody **M**iddle Shade . . . *It's him!*

Non-driver Young wouldn't like *any* motorist, but could he be one of that rare breed of Scotsperson who didn't give a monkey's about golf?

Tred carefully, Ronnie, we beseeched, silently.

Gazing down at his papers, presumably to remind himself of the limits of his sentencing powers, and now in full possession of the facts about the Duddingston man's (golfing) previous—a result of some animated whispering in his shell-like by the Clerk of the Court—and without raising his be-wigged head, he ventured:

"Are you the Ronnie Shade?"

. . . of course he is, Hanging, I mumbled to blinkered heed-the-ba' Bob Sutter, sat next to me . . . genuinely clueless.

(pause)

(The reply came proudly, *too* proudly, even for an M.B.E.)

"Indeed I am, your Honour"

If Ronnie had sensed empathy in the tone of the Sheriff's brief cross examination, he was to be horribly mistaken; made a good front-pager for me though (*who needed shorthand? . . . you've seen the telling quotes*).

Ronnie kopped a maximum, I think for driving without due care or attention, something he rarely did at work. Only Sir Michael Bonnallack achieved as much from the unpaid ranks in Britain. R.D.B.M. Shade played in four Walker Cup teams, and won the Scottish Amateur Championship five times . . . *in a row*. Died of cancer in 1986, aged 47.

The Airdrie and Coatbridge Advertiser was not of *'The News of the Screws'* genre. The paucity of celebrity scandal meant relying on lineage for 'luxury' items such as *Brut* after-shave—as pedaled by Henry Cooper, Barry Sheene and J.K. Keegan—and condoms by *Durex*—"**D**urability, **R**eliability, and **Ex**cellence" . . . . a big ask, lingering doubt.

I'd been paying minimum rent to live, cushily, in my boss, Jack Crichton's house in Airdrie, with his redoubtable wife Berta, and their two grown-up children; Mrs. C. often hung her sheets on the line on windy Mondays with no knickers on, which certainly livened up her ageing bachelor neighbour's day, and, ultimately, probably did for him.

The Crichtons' son, Alan, spent rather too much time, alone, in a dark room. He was one of the paper's snappers: hands permanently stained, reeking of developing fluid. Al's big sister, Lesley, was a physiotherapist at a Glasgow hospital: *she* smelt divine. My feigned, weekly, groin-strain-injury performance—following our Friday night five-a-side—was of Premiership quality, yet never once did she offer relief.

That apart, I was seriously anxious about my long term prospects.

The surface of my ambitious plan to infiltrate the ovas of babeworld, had barely been scratched, and here they were threatening to blow the bugger up. Nikita Khrushchev, the shoe-tapping potato-head, often seen applauding himself from behind those *very* high balconies in Mockba, was becoming a pain in every Westerner's butt, shipping all kinds of illegal 'nasties' to the Caribbean. Fidel Castro—he of the jump suit and huge stogies—was hell bent on turning Cuba into an island of mass destruction in a sea of global hysteria, into which we could all soon be plunged. On the other side (*ours*), J.F.K. was tooled up and spoiling—Gary Cooper in *High Noon*. A showdown—be it with his own government and the CIA, or with the Reds—was at DEFCON 3 . . .

and rising. Meanwhile, his headstrong kid brother Bobby was trying to comfort scrumptious Miss Monroe (a mutual friend), and keep Mr. Hoover (a mutual enemy) out of all their faces; eyes and ears followed them everywhere.

October '62: Bono was 2½ . . . U-2 was a spy plane . . . *we* were shitting ourselves. No need to sex up any of this, the newsreels had irrefutable evidence—*these big Russian cigars could seriously damage your health* . . . . we could be toast at any minute.

One WMD, President Castro was keeping to himself, however, was still in short pants; Teofilio Stevenson was a lad of 10 (albeit a tough one) at the time of all this lethal posturing, and would only become a threat should anyone call him '*a big Jessie*' at break-time. With the bell to end the Cold War still some 12 years off, Cuba's greatest peacetime export was sent on a search and destroy mission to Russia in 1980.

Everything put in front of him was smashed. And not just Moscow; he'd done untold damage in Montreal and Munich. His fantastic three round quarter final win over Duane Bobick had pride of place on our fistic tower in '72. All big threats were removed, and still he had appetite for more. Alas, Fidel funked the trip to L.A. Were proof needed that Teo could have coped with bare-chested fighters, several months before Tyrell Biggs became the 1984 Olympic heavyweight champ, he thumped him too. Perhaps the pros might have rearranged his handsome features, slightly, but we'll never know.

It was mildy incestuous—if harmless—at the admirable Crichtons. Much as I fancied the landlady's daughter, there was no future in it. We did a mean jive to the Shadows' *Foot-tapper,* but in truth, she flirted more with my father. In the end, the physio married a sleepwalker who once pissed in Dad's wardrobe (*that's Highland hospitality for you*). Lesley's old man and mine (his suits were *ruined*) were members of the Scottish Newspaper Proprietors' Association, and between them managed to get me a job on *The Advertiser*, tenuous though my qualification was; had Scottish Highers (better than English As, *obviously*) in History, French and English, but if there were journalistic genes, they'd yet to be tested.

After three years, the occasional by-line and an all-digit typing p.b. in and around (a windy) 50 w.p.m., it was time to rise and twitch my mantle (*blew*) . . . *tomorrow to fresh woods and pastures new.*

See, I was paying attention; he being my chosen poet to cram (along with the obligatory Shakespeare), I was ecstatic when John Milton's *Lycidas* leapt off my final English exam paper. I'd blindly memorized huge tracts of 'the Scottish play,' which, on the day, I managed to work into a plausible answer to a question that had nothing to do with ghosties and walking trees:

*I will not be afraid of death and bane,
Till Birnam forest come to Dunsinane*

Makes no sense, but young Rabbie Burns never got a shout at school—our most famous rhymer kept on the bench for the duration, yet they made us sing *Jerusalem* in the school choir, <u>and</u> *Swing Low Sweet* bloody *Chariots*—not an anthem to sing in praise of big strapping Englishmen in tight lycra, I'll be bound . . . . bloodied or otherwise.

More strings—Rotarian ones this time—were pulled, and under the auspices of an executive friend in the A.A. (the Automobile Association), I was given an audience with *his* close buddy, James Kemp, Head of BBC Scotland's News and Current Affairs Department . . . oddbollocks personified.

Dad had been a Rotarian for years, and Mum was huge in the (wives only) Inner Wheel ('inner' the Rotarian's wheel, *savvy?*) the caring, sharing, equivalent for well-intentioned business and professional ladies.

Concurrently—hundreds of miles away, at Ambleside Avenue, Streatham—Madame Cynthia and *her* pros were doing their bit for the common man, albeit uncharitably; there was no such thing as a free ride at a Payne and pleasure party.

If D.H. Lawrence had sent blood south in my schoolboy shorts, the handiwork of one our hometown residents would—had *Blockbuster* been around in the 60s—have provided thrills on demand . . . in the absence of any kind of teenage night life in Crieff. The film adaptation of Neil Patterson's steamy novel, *Room at the Top*, with cheating bastard *Joe Lampton* (Lawrence Harvey) shagging all-comers (unprotected, as far as I could make out), may not have been the author's initial intention, but it worked for us. Being a highly successful writer, Patterson lived in the swanky part of town—in "the terraces"—along with doctors, dentists, and lawyers, and ex-city-dwellers in search of tranquility.

*"Ye lovers of the picturesque, if ye wish to drown your grief,
Take my advice, and visit the ancient town of Crieff."*

. . . . was how our 'adopted' Scottish 'poet,' William McGonagall, put it, succinctly (his folks were Irish).

On week-ends off, I'd approach—by Mini—down the bottom end, where hardy folk lived. 'Your Are Now Entering Crieff'—the road-sign bade no welcome, as one decelerated to 30 on the Muthill Road, and prepared to swing 90° right, over the River Earn, at Bridgend. Up through a little chicane, with houses built tight to the roadside, to the first of few choices in a town of only 5,000 or so, souls. Fork left, and head up Burrell Street . . . choose right and prepare to use everything your gearbox had, with the Drummond Arms Hotel the target, many feet above.

I'd pass Crieff Earngrove F.C.'s ground on my right.

At this juncture I want to send you off on a 'Roy of the Rovers' journey . . .
. . . to the Cup Winners Cup final, at De Kuip (The Tub) in Rotterdam. In goal for Tottenham Hotspur, a former Crieff High schoolboy (whose parents sacrificed so much) dives to his weaker, left side, and tips the deciding penalty round the post. The travelling fans, among 49,000 packed into Feijenoord Stadion, go wild, and in front rooms across Perthshire, families unite in patriotic fervour . . .
. . . but I can't.

Spurs won the 3rd CWC final in southern Holland in 1963, by five goals to one, thereby preventing an Atlético Madrid hat-trick. Tottenham's goalkeeper played 222 league games for the double winners, was capped 28 times by Scotland, and seldom made the English laugh. Bill Brown was born in Arbroath (*close*—30 miles away—*but not close enough*).

One year after that 'actual' match, Crieff's junction railway station—a few hundred yards on from Market Park 'stadium'—was closed down. Established in the glory days for steam—when Victoria was Queen and IK Brunel civil engineered Britain—it fell victim to Doc Beeching's Axe.

On a bit more—still glancing right—Donald Sorley's barber shop, where schoolboy heads were shorn for a few pence. Nothing demonic about Donald, though his wooden leg did have lasting fascination, as we sat motionless on his 'booster' plank. It was very off-putting, for nit conscious parents, when he'd run his 'operating' comb through his own greasy locks, mid cut, but you couldn't fault his back and sides for value. On past the cop shop and Johnny Grilli's Scoto-Italian chippie, and into second gear for the climb to the Square—the meeting point for local thrill seekers most evenings, and all-of-a-bustle on Thursdays . . . market day.

Historically, cattlemen—Rob Roy MacGregor amongst them—would come to town to trade and drink. Where men and cattle and whisky were gathered, during the October Tryst (market), things often got completely out of hand; the Kind Gallows lay in wait for miscreants.

To the best of my knowledge there wasn't a brothel, certainly not when I was interested. My brother and I were aware of clandestine meetings in the house, and of Dad not being at lunch one day a week, but it could have been *The Skull and Bones,* or *The Klan,* for all we cared. Neither did I know what to make of Grandpa's apron 'thingy' with the big badge on the front, and the silly little hat, which I spotted Gran laying out, lovingly, on the master bed.

Rolled-up trouser legs, goats and compasses, telling handshakes and signet rings, became tittle-tattle for we early, innocent, playground conspiracy theorists. (Hoover was a Mason, so was Don Bradman . . . and Harry Houdini—*a lot of good it did him*).

Rotary started in the States at the beginning of the 20th century, and gradually made its way across 'The Pond.' The Masons go back to the Middle Ages, and whilst professing not to be secretive, no one shows you anything until you join . . . bit like a brothel (I'm told).

I was still under age when I discovered *Smirnoff* (and lime), necking copious amounts whilst out with my brother and his 'legal' friends. The Perthshire village of Comrie, nine miles west of Crieff, lies on a geological fault line, so either the tectonic plate was on the move or I was wankered. Teetering into yet another Burrell Street, outside the crime scene (the owner of the offending hotel bar was *still* a friend of the family *Oh. My. God.*), the ensuing collision of vodka fumes and fresh air demanded a standing count. I passed on the blotting paper effect of a battered fish supper, without words. *How come the stars were at my feet?* Just as suddenly, they were gone, in a splash, as the wheels of the bus shocked some sense back at me.

Having troubled the driver to make countless, unscheduled stops on the journey home (terribly unsatisfactory trying to chuck on 'empty'), I fancied I was in for flying lessons from Dad, should I make it home, alive. He was enormously supportive, sitting me down and challenging me to down a huge whisky, in one.

It might all have been my brother's devilish work, either way, I was happy to wait for legitimacy. Boldly, one grew from a lime mix, into full-on (*none of your slim-line-diet-shit*) tonic, as pimples—or 'plukes' as we Scots called the be-puss ridden, anti-girl afflictions—raged across our faces, curiously, on the eve of something very promising.

My weekly wage of £7.10s. on the paper—essentially, reciprocal hospitality to Mr. Hunter—got bumped to a staggering £32 at Broadcasting House, Glasgow, with mohair suits and silk ties to follow. A brand, spanking new Saab 96, in white—with space and possibilities—was the first of many indulgences (*got one! ya beauty!*). The transition from Clark Hunter to Jim Herd, my immediate boss in the Scottish newsroom, was unnerving. Jim, the most agreeable of news editors, did the job without pretence and fist-banging. He'd sample the news and then distribute it to us sub-editors for pruning, in broadcast English.

There were three senior subs, each commanding an eight hour shift within the cycle. Bill Gilchrist was archetypically BBC—cautious, accurate, and uninspiring . . . "*alleged*" and "*it's believed*" and "*unconfirmed sources report*" were hallmarks of his copy. John Fairgrieve took a slightly more lyrical line, and was always on hand to help juniors with our composition. Goatee-bearded John's back trouble was so acute that he once turned up for his shift, completely doubled over—*Catweazle* with tuck—as if the kitchen chair he'd been in when the disc slipped, was soldered on, invisibly. Whilst accepting our sympathies, politely, as was his way, he refused to go for treatment. With no noticeable change in posture, he settled down to work.

The noisy arse opposite was Eric Moncur—ex-*Scottish Daily Express*—a no-frills newsman with a permanent sniff, that would make his nose hair lean to, as if being hit by a cyclone. We put the affliction down to something untoward buried in his black, bushy moustache. Designer drugs were still some way off challenging booze in the profession, and little was known of pneumonoultramicroscopicovolcanoconiosis, other than it was endemic to Icelanders living near Eyjafjallajökull, and to others living in unstable surroundings, duped by their estate agents into viewing at night.

Had 'Eric the Irascible' not opted for journalism—at which he was mightily good—testing telephone sets to destruction could have been an option. His draw was lightning: dial and bell housing would arrive on his lap, half a second after the handset wire had re-coiled. His probing "*NEWSROOM?!*" was more a threat, than an enquiry.

As he wound up a call, we went to "*brace!*" "*brace!*" mode. With one parting, nostril-clearing inhalation, instantly consigning lingering, dried nasal mucus to the lower recesses of his breath sacks, via Route 1—i.e. 'keeper to 'keeper—big Eric would bring handset to cradle with such ferocity, it was as if he'd just been jilted . . . again. The cell phone would change his life forever.

First up, television news had priority: there were bulletins on radio . . . re-writes for the Gaelic speaking minority (*helicopter* and *hovercraft* were untranslatable) . . . film stories to organize . . . and the shipping forecast to prepare . . .

. . . . *ah*, the shipping forecast.

Every week night, at about eight minutes past eleven, BBC (radio) Scotland would broadcast a protracted, jargon-filled Met Office epistle, warning brave sea-farers of possible storms, their force, and conditions that might prevail in specific coastal waters.

Our Scottish news followed a two minute national summary. There was nothing for the lowly sub-editor to do, but add the tightly-typed, prediction to the back of the news bulletin (which we'd prepared earlier), and stick it under the newsreader's nose. Bill Jack's, on this special occasion, *was* that proboscis. He had the most glorious voice . . . you could taste the fruit in it, deep, resonant, loaded with *basso profondo*. He was a 'Jock' Jack, a bit on the plumy side, but in no way too handsome for the wireless . . . and he liked his dram—neat, and plenty of them.

In other cities and towns, the BBC club—the much-abused staff facility—was often in-house. In Glasgow, it was a stiff walk from the main block—time to refresh, yet more than enough to compound.

As the clock ticked nearer our on-air time (2302 in the new money), still no sign of the newsreader—*was this to be my big break?* . . . the news I could handle, but the old, punctuation-free shipping forecast was a career buster:

'*Lundy Fastnet Shannon Rockall Bailey* (over we go) *Fair Isle Cromarty Forth Tyne Dogger* (aye, aye) *Humber Thames* (and back) *Hebrides Rhum* coke *Eigg* bacon beans chips *Muck* . . . . *visibility ten* (yuck) *closing* . . . . *winds Nor'—Nor' East storm force 9 gusting to gale force 10 imminent* (oh, fuck!)' . . . plus lots of *'occasionallys'* and *'moderates . . .'*

. . . meteorological mumbo-jumbo, but vital to those in peril.

At one and a half minutes past eleven, with the network news in its final throe, the familiar whistle of the sound-proofed studio doors announced that William Jack was '*in da house.*'

Bums!

Red light on, cough, (fart, perhaps), face-stretch, fader open . . .

"*Cue Bill.*"

How on blue planet Earth he managed to get through the news beats me. "BJ" was 'blootert' . . . . and the 'big yin' was nigh:

"It's 2308 GMT—here is the shipping forecast for in<u>door</u> fishermen."
(*oops . . . that should have been 'in<u>shore</u>' Billy-boy, but press on*).

Flawless delivery followed. The last two paragraphs were all about fierce storms, high 10s, mountainous seas, night-marish conditions for all afloat, many of whom—certainly amongst trawlermen—couldn't swim (*no point . . . the sea's bloody freezing*).

"Well, there we are . . . have a great night, and good fishing gentlemen!"
(*. . . as he handed in his notice*).

Amazingly, Bill survived the ad-libbed postscript, but a contemporary wasn't treated with *any* understanding . . . probably because *his* was peak-time porridge, and he *did* make a meal of it.

Bruce McKenzie was an actor-turned-newsreader, soon to be on his way back to the boards. The news item that would send him there, referred to a contentious policy, amongst Water Boards in Scotland, of adding fluoride to domestic supplies. I hadn't written it, but it was as clear as H²0 that the process was called 'fluoridation' (just the *five* syllables).

Bruce's first crack came out as 'fluori*diza*tion' (up to *six*, suddenly) . . . and the second, and the third.

"I'll leave that one, shall I, and come back to it a bit later?"
(*a smidgen on the frivolous side for BBC Radio, Brucie old love*)

Even if he'd had an offer from Drama or L.E., why risk permanent scarring? BBC News was sacrosanct—not be messed with, nor commented on; good job big John Reith, the first general manager of the newly-formed (1922) British Broadcasting Company, was well in with the maggots by then.

James Kemp's office (where Brucie was certainly heading), was on the top floor of North Park House, Queen Margaret Drive, premises pre-dating BBC Scotland's decant to their glass box on Clydeside's grandly named, Pacific Quay, near the long defunct graving docks of scally, wee Fergie's Govan (*you don't get that kind of information with Tom-Tom*).

There's a gang of powerful, top guns at the BBC in London, known as 'The St John's Wood mafia' (no names, no decapitated horses)—*cos* that's where they live, and how they are perceived by the embittered. Mr. Kemp, however, came from Stonehaven, a little fishing village on the North Sea coast, birthplace too, you'll be astounded to learn, of Mr. Reith. Where the former stalled at department-head level, the latter went stratospheric, clutching his *educate, inform, entertain* mantra to his bosom, until baronetcy was secured and Churchill put in his place viz. told to keep his nose out of BBC business! *Say what you think, John boy!*

Mr. Kemp never talked religion to us (one of the more delicate issues in Glasgow), but on the idiosyncratic, he was fearless. I recall being summoned—I assumed for a bollocking for my 'assist' on the shipping forecast—only to be confronted, straight-faced, with: "Would you say these are black or brown shoes?" (*tricky one, could be a trap . . . certainly look black . . . if I get this wrong, one or other could be heading for my bum crack*). The answer was . . . . they were brown shoes which he'd used black polish on (*right . . . will that be all Mr. Kemp?*) because, apparently, brown leather is softer (*in the heed*).

John Reith's father, the reverend Doctor George, was a 'wee Free' minister—that's the United Free Church of Scotland—and after an extraordinary career in the army, the BBC and Government, his boy, John Charles Walsham, became Lord High Commissioner to the General Assembly of the Church of Scotland (*tricky one for the caption artist, given the space allowed*). Reith jr., was a throwback to John Knox, another fiery Jock, who, posthumously, qualified for the Glasgow Rangers' Supporters Club. Five hundred years earlier, his *The First Blast of the Trumpet against the Monstrous* (unnatural)*Regimen of Women* (women's lib coming to a town near you) had inadvertently kick-started *The Spice Girls'* movement. Fuck knows (if I can put it that way), what he and J.R. would have made of young Ramsay—no series on 'the Beeb,' for starters.

Intriguing times, with Knox getting everyone at it—the feminists, the French, the Catholics. I remember a photograph of Mum, dressed as Mary Stewart—the Queen of Scots—who ticked all those boxes . . . she played golf, *with men* . . . she was virtually French . . . and, doubtless, would have supported Celtic. Ma's elegant look served as a reminder of how delicate a woman's neck can be (not unlike Mrs. Beckham's), and I've been fascinated by that period—and women's golf—ever since. Full marks to Posh and Mel and Mel and Geri and Emma for their far reaching contribution to global history—*no shit*—but none to the axeman of Fotheringhay for missing such a simple target.

That was at Reformation time—way before the flat back four and Ally McCoist. No question, Knox would have had to have been a 'Teddy Bear' and, very possibly, a Mason, though the fraternity "it's believed" is non-religious
(note well: *Archie* Knox—*who does he think he is?*—was assistant manager at Rangers from 1991-1997—'Coisty time'—if you're keeping up with the ecumenical, club connections . . . plus, there is no 'f' in Ramsay, nor, apparently, any record of his playing for Glasgow Rangers F.C.).

We'd passed on all that was new in Scotland, including the sport, leaving only the headlines for young Mackenzie to re-cap. You'll have noticed how 'anchors'—i.e. 'newsreaders' to those of us weaned on Sylvia Peters and MacDonald Hobley (go on, *Google* them)—*smile* when they arrive at the sports section, as if relieved that the latest on the Afghanistan catastrophe and the seemingly fruitless search for 'pimpernelian' O.b.Laden, were over for another day.

"Come on" said Bruce, as last rites were prepared, "let's be having another crack at that fluoridisation shall we?
"Oh, oh . . . said it again . . . *fluoridation*."

"Got it!"

"Am I glad I cleared that up . . . so that now is the very end of the Scottish News!" *(and of you too, cock . . . break a leg).*

There's a famous *Panorama* clip—*clip? . . .* more like a *lifetime for* the eldest of the Dimbleby boys, as images of family holidays and memorable moments from Dad Richard's Remembrance Day commentaries and General Election marathons, flashed before him—when every attempt to call up taped inserts for the show, failed, leaving a half a dozen free-rangers on David's face—with which he just about coped.

It's all very well for a famous footballer, or Olympic oarsperson to re-train as a media bod, but when the brown stuff gets airborne, and you're 'live,' an intimate knowledge of potato crisps, or crabs and square feathering, ain't gonna help a bunch. Vocabulary's the key. Lynam was best of the lot, because, like any gifted sportsperson, his grey matter was ordered—he made room for most eventualities. He'd done the 'hard yards' (*hate myself for that one*) on steam radio, where you simply have to keep talking or someone will phone in. Like I.V.A. Richards hooking a 95m.p.h. beamer, 'Dessie' was always able to ease his way out of a crisis; sure, Viv made a duck or two, and the former amateur boxer from Ennis dried once *(after I'd gone)*—but you can't teach class . . . nh-nn.

Production meltdown for two very different presenters on our early evening current affairs magazine, *A Quick Look Round*—following the national news, and its *very* large audience; Dimbleby only had a telephone to go with his seeming unflappability . . . our pair had props and stuff, when the shit hit.

Presenter 1: Leonard McGuire—no film, no taped inserts, no guidance from above, and none from the production gallery. As they froze and cussed, I hid in the shadows of the fiercely lit studio, pretending my floor manager's talkback had gone down. Leonard, a distinguished actor, with three *Fringe First* awards to his name, arose from the electric chair. Glancing comfortingly at the camera, betraying none of our panic, he reached into the well-stocked bookshelf, forming part of the set, for something by Scott (Walter) or Buchan (John) or Mackenzie (Compton), and began to read . . . and read . . . and read. Fuelled by sorely disappointed ghouls, and perennial writers-in, the show rated better than normal.

Presenter 2: the Queen diva—Mary Marquis—the show's first choice 'front person.' John Knox appeared to have a problem with the name Mary—Mary Tudor, Mary of Guise and Mary Stuart (as she'd become) were anathemas—but it was a Barbara (Mandell) who'd rattle his rusting cage in the 1950s by becoming the first female newsreader on telly. Now chauvinists would have a hard time getting back in.

Mary Marquis had oodles of mystique, a handsome husband, and a make-up pack to rival Nancy Dell Ollio's, with whom she might be compared favourably, in all but the arse and leg departments. Where she scored massively over the Italian, was in her choice of bedfellow; appearances can often deceive, but Sven would have needed to have been a right animal between the sheets to compete.

When *Reporting Scotland*—the regional *Newsnight* of its time—began in 1968, out of our offices, it was a step-up in gravitas for her ladyship . . . from *The Daily Record* (handy red top) to *The Scotsman* (unmanageable on the underground) say, but first she had to take one for the team.

You can just hear Knox: "Pride goeth before destruction, and a haughty spirit before a fall." *(*Proverbs 16:18).

When Mary's *A.Q.L.R.* house came tumbling down, in Studio B, she opted to interview the camera crew; high marks for artistic impression, but the surly judge in the fur coat and daft boots, gave her a poor set for technical merit.

The cameramen—Ian Turner, Doug Hammond, Alistair Scott and Gordon Penfold—had seen and done plenty, but revealed little. The ring*leader* or 'father' of that particular Association of Cinematograph, Television and Allied Technicians 'chapel,' Charlie Ring*land*, was probably hatching a cunning plan to get the brothers some time off—this being a blatant contravention of their job description.

The 1st Director of the BBC, John Reith, defender of our faith in independent broadcasting, had locked horns and appeared to prevail over Churchill—some feat; its 10th—Indian born Scot, Alasdair Milne's nemesis was Mrs. Thatcher—"15 all."

Straight-talking Milne started out as programme director of *Tonight*, an early evening magazine show, hosted by Cliff Michelmore and produced by Donald Baverstock. D.B. would eventually become Controller of BBC One, but left in the huff the year I joined (irrelevant). Among the *Tonight* reporters were Alan Whicker, Trevor Philpott and a wafer-thin Scotsman, Fyffe Robertson (odd spelling—same as the bananas). The redoubtable Fyffe was on a round-Scotland tour when he rode into "ancient" Crieff, on horseback He was the embodiment of the outdoor feature maker: craggy face, wispy beard, sensible shoes, and a deliberate delivery, full of nasal intonation and fascinating fact.

When the filmed piece was all joined up, you could not but admire the pentagenarian's staying power; what the public didn't see, off camera, were the horsebox and *Land Rover* (*all in the editing—nothing terribly wrong with that*—Top Gear *do it all the time, Ma'am*).

Fyffe and 'Monty' (*him* again—a.k.a. Field Marshall Bernard Law Montgomery, 1st Viscount Montgomery of Alamein, KG GCB DSO PC) were my banker impressions in times when Halloween was a trick or *no* treat experience—not the smash n grab of the pick n mix it is today. The Everly brother's *Bye Bye Love* and *Dream* were seldom enforced encores . . . my brother on melody, me with the dodgy descant.

Fyffe's equivalent north of the border was Jameson Clark, a far-from-hungry, character actor (*The 39 Steps/ Geordie/ Tunes of Glory/ The Ring of Bright Water* etc.,) turned newsreader/reporter/presenter. He was a *Look Round* stalwart. I was fazed more than a touch, when I caught a whiff of his 'water,' just prior to going 'Red' in the radio newsroom; catch it late of an evening, and you'd swear his hooter was on fire. One of his most memorable appearances was in the film version of Compton Mackenzie's *Whisky Galore*, released in 1949 (I rest my case).

Jimmy Clark was a lovely bloke, not investigative like Bernstein, nor biting like Muggeridge. He didn't offend anyone. As a result, he could pull even the most recalcitrant types for the show; for the egomaniac, hot on style, devoid of substance, celebrity rather than star, he was an easy ride on either outlet—wireless or telly.

After the show one evening, Mary Marquis's co-presenter, Alex McIntosh, and I went into town; handy man to have in a crisis—not that we were expecting one. Although he looked demure and sounded gracious, he was a 10th Dan judo player . . . *and a very, very good friend*.

The restaurant he'd chosen for dinner (presenter's money then, as now, was a zillion times better than the string-puller's) had partitioned booths down either side of the main room. As he was quite famous, the patron put Alex on pole *a)* to afford him catchment for name-dropping . . . as T.V. types tend to in public places, and *b)* and more importantly, to have first and uninterrupted sight of any incoming babes.

Our neighbours—one booth up—seemed like any normal couple on a night out; as the house wine kicked in, we sensed they might be married. The bloke became belligerent. His tirade had his companion reeling, not unlike the scene in the iconic rugby league film *This Sporting Life* when nasty bastard loose forward, and canon, *Frank Machin* (Richard Harris) set about publically humiliating *Mrs. Hammond* (Rachel Roberts) during dinner in a posh restaurant.
Only our stone-sub on the paper in Airdrie could have competed with the dialogue.

Picture this: the local minister comes in, humbly, with his church notices, a tad on the tardy side of a Thursday evening, as wee Andy Collins and his mates lock down the remaining pages:
"*Jesus f—Christ reverend, what the f—time is this to bring in your bits and f—pieces?*
"*Aw' the pages is away, for f—'s sake.*

"Yoozehavenae got a a f—hame to gae to, right—we f—have
"Get tae f—!"

"Bless you, Andrew" normally did the trick.

Satiated, our space invaded, our senses sullied, time for Alex and me to take our leave. The anchorman stooped over the distressed diner, and whispered: "Tell me, my dear, is that divine smell *Coco?*" (a safe bet at the time, even if he wasn't 100% sure).

Flabbergasted by one so indentifiable's identification:
"Aye, it is" she replied, coyly.
Before the curmudgeon could make a fist, 'The Charmmeister' followed up:
"Suits you *perfectly*."
Undetectable courage would have been foolhardy.

Mr. McIntosh, by the way, did the voice-over on ITV's very first advert (in 1955) for *Gibb's SR "tingling fresh"* toothpaste

You had a sense of being in the big time at BBC Scotland. Our industrial correspondent, John Hossack, was forever doing pieces from Fairfield's ailing shipyard on the Clyde for the national news bulletin at six.
There were serious assaults and murders . . . Jim Clark died . . . and way before Scotland's own Parliament sent house prices soaring in Edinburgh, weighty pro-devolution debates and demos to report.

One (whole) week in May, in the capital, the General Assembly synod sits. Back in my newspaper days, editor Hunter had sent me to follow up a parochial issue, due for debate at a mid-week session of the Presbyterian Church's rulers. If the House of Lords ever gets to stimulating, *this* was the dead rubber of a Test match series, with Trevor 'Boiley' Bailey and K.F. 'slow-coach' Barrington at the crease on a 'flattie.'

The omnipotent, Christian God would have his hands full, fending off appeals and referrals from all sides, so no point enquiring of him.

In theory, Mr. Knox was the Assembly's first Moderator, so if all else failed (*no shorthand, remember*) I had plenty with which to pad: the Right Reverend James Stewart was the incumbent . . . Hollywood legend Jimmy Stewart's antecedents had Scottish Presbyterian connections . . . the complex love life of James Stewart—the Black Knight of Lorn—would add spice . . . and Arthur's seat, where I'd take lunch most days, had long been connected with religion in Scotland. Make antecedents work for you.

The Reverend E.G. "Eggy" Balls, from Hamilton, was our regional rep (*couldn't forget that one . . . nor would his schoolmates: "Claude," one hopes, was never considered an option at birth*).

Off he went with a discourse that was way too long, even for the devout and conscious, and delivered at ball-bursting speed.

"*Pitman, Gregg and Speedwriting . . . I denied thee thrice.*"

Speculative prayers, on the train home, from a known trespasser, were answered with the spike. Next day 'Malky' Speed went one-on-one with 'Eggy,' on the blower, and painlessly nailed the local slant (*why hadn't Hunter thought of that, the bastard?*).

Depending on how you could cope with sleeping during the day, the overnight shift in the BBC newsroom was the best. The day-shift afforded time to 'bevvy' and scavenge—the back-shift (1430 to 2230) made phone sex, at worst, a possibility. Apart from the boilerman, and the nightwatchman/fireman patrolling the offices, the overnight sub was on his tod. Extra curricula bonking in vacant dressing rooms was punishable by medieval quartering by horse. Reithian statutes were only reviewed every fifty years or so.

Having seen to the transmission at 2302hr, the hours of darkness were devoted to gathering stories from freelance agencies and wire services, and hourly trawling of police, fire and ambulance contacts in the City, ahead of the 0710 and 0810 bulletins.

I'd become restless again, and decided to apply for a job as a BBC presenter/reporter in Bristol. Much to my amazement and amusement, they invited me to attend an interview. *I could, conceivably, squeeze the trip in between shifts—finish at 2230 on Wednesday . . . take various rattlers South . . . dazzle and amaze, and be back in time for 'nights' on Sunday.* Sorted.

Hugh Moran, out of network news in London, who'd replaced John Hossack as Industrial Correspondent, gave me one of his old Fairfield TV scripts, and coached me on delivery . . . should I make the short list for the in-vision auditions. I came second; pity, as Bristol, with its boob tubes and VPLs, seemed like a fun town—the Newcastle of the South-West.

The journey back took forever. I knew I had to be in for 2200hr, but not having slept the night before, with nerves, I was cream-crackered by the time I got to my digs in Glasgow. *I'll just have a quick kip* (mistake).

'Sniffer' Moncur, who was on the outgoing tour, called to enquire after my health, and *"when the f—"* I was going to show; the only blessing was, I missed the hang-up. Grabbing my instant snack—no fizzy drinks and fatty crap dispensers in those days—I made it to the newsroom, about half an hour late. Eric was *not* happy to see me.

I lasted till about two in the morning—consciousness lost, finally. Not even the explosion of the boil-in-the-bag rice I'd attempted to prepare in the electric kettle in the copy room, stirred me. More career threateningly, a huge fire had broken out on board a ship in the docks at Greenock. Crewmen, fully clad, were jumping into the chilly, if still waters, below, as fire engines, police units and ambulances roared about—a scene from any of the *Lethal Weapons* (apparently).

Nutty Nero might have empathized, but I knew Eric wouldn't; to be fair, this information hadn't been forthcoming from the City emergency services, as it was deemed to be outside their area of responsibility (*sound*). Nonetheless, it was headline news on the early editions of all the Scottish evening papers (*Kemp: "... a word, John"*). No one had been seriously hurt, but it must have been quite a spectacle in the night sky—not one to miss, ideally

Three years in, having fallen out of love with the Scottish Newsroom, and never having felt much for the weird, head honcho, I took a financial hit of the gravest proportion and slid, metaphorically, down a massive constrictor to the bottom of the ladder—'trainee floor assistant,' about as low as one could go in production.

The Procurator Fiscal is an official in the Scottish judiciary, a coroner with nobs on; should you turn out to be a bent copper, or try to dodge the Excise Man, or blow a jumbo jet out of the sky, he tended to be on your case. The 'procurer physical,' in TV studio-land, was the said floor assistant.

More background info: 'stramash' (the word) means 'a bit of bother' or 'a racket'—*Stramash* (the show) was *Top of the Pops* come North, enacted, on the pale blue floor of BBC Scotland's Studio A, by the likes of Marie Lawrie, Thomas Woodward and Clive Powell . . . to name but three.

The inspirational director/producer, David Bell, who'd go on to great things down south—spectacular variety shows, tedious awards evenings . . . and many same-gender alliances—was a man way ahead of his time at work, and promiscuous plus, at rest and play. Forty years ago the sight of grown men touching each other in a pubic place, publically, would have Mrs. Whitehouse beating a path to the Board of Governors. But it was no big deal. Stay light on your feet, dodge attempted assaults, and accept them as '*poofery*'—as onomatopoeically sound a word as there's ever been—and think vaginal.

One of David's lovers was the show's choreographer, Bruce McClure; their monumental, petulant, rows were conducted in full gaze, and earshot, of all and sundry . . . *and boy could these girls scream.* Every control gallery has a system whereby the production team can talk to the studio floor, via a loudspeaker . . . for extra bite; for privacy, there's also person-to-person talkback. David <u>loved</u> to blast Bruce to hell and back over the P.A. They'd make up later, in a flurry of male bits.

Not for the first time, I was asked by an artiste in the 'star' dressing room, (*narrowing the field a touch*) to invite a member of the chorus to while away the time between takes; a mild form of procurement, but exciting stuff for the pub—nothing for the Fiscal to get het up about.

Gays—or 'queers' as they were back then—from 'The Lady with the Lamp' to Leonardo di Ser Piero da Vinci would know the signs, as we 'straights,' in the night spots of Glasgow, believed *we* did.

"*Erra-herry-ova-rerr*" or "*that wee burd has some paps on her*"— meaning, in essence . . . "*the buxom wench at the bar is looking this way.*"

David's other great collaboration was with Stanley Baxter, whose own extravagances got him the boot, uniquely, from the <u>two</u> major channels. Some of his production numbers were as lavish, proportionately, on the small screen, as Cecil B. de Mille's were on the big silver one, the difference being, it was *your* cash they were splashing; perhaps ITV didn't think his genius merited their loyalty.

The afternoon educational show, *Parliamo Italiano* or *'Let's Speak Italian'* (*bene*) was a cheesey attempt at 'learning' those with time-share intentions, 'the lingo.' Day-time actors searching for peak-time breaks would enact everyday scenario, in Italian, and then repeat it in English. In-your-face, hand-held caption cards pointed up key-words and phrases. Enter the undisputed master of pastiche with . . . *Parliamo Glasgo.*

(a market stall in the city) Stanley approaches:
'IzatamarraonyerbarraClara?'
Caption.
Is that a marrow on your barrow, Clara?

Betty Marsden, and my first wife's wheelchair-bound drama producer boss's actress wife, Doris McLatchie (*following?*), and the legendary Una McLean, were willing accomplices in skits that were prescribed viewing for any who wanted to talk proper Glaswegian.

The coming together of Baxter and Bell was magical . . . *and it didn't half piss Bruce off.* David's camera plans for *Stramash* could have been choreographed by his petulant partner; tripods, Heron cranes, boom trolleys, swept across the studio floor in beautifully orchestrated manoeuvres, as possessed youngsters, some in multi-coloured flares, others in shorts and knee-high boots (the girls looked just as daft) gyrated to Lulu, Tom Jones and Georgie Fame (as previously mentioned at the foot of page 51). It was mini-skirt time. *Come on!* As ever, the lads were left trailing in the fashion stakes, though up top—<u>right</u> up top—there wasn't much to choose, the crusty mullet giving fragile bee-hives a good run for time spent on lacquer and gell. Visible panty line concerned boys too.

"Go COMMANDO"—or, as they say in Chile: *"Andar a lo gringo"*

The main objective for risking life and limb at *Barrowland* in Glasgow's notorious east end, was to exercise one's social skills, and, if possible, get the old leg across. Eye-wateringly tight *Farahs* and skinny ties were *de riguer* for us wolverines. A swirling mass of flightless, hopping 'burds' holding tight formation in an impenetrable Catherine wheel, guarded a giant pile of abandoned handbags in the centre of *le palais de dance*.
Who knew what a girl kept in her purse—war-paint, illicit miniatures, flick-knives, perhaps a second hand Glock, re-cyclable *lettres de France* should the whim or the voddie take them there.

Several laps on, I'd narrowed my choice to a pair of cuties, one steaming along backwards, in the girlie position, as her slightly fitter partner led her through the most basic of quicksteps . . . . *one-two-three hop—nae turns . . . take it or leave it*. In the dervish community, the trance-like state is induced by the speed of the dancers' revolutions; for the 'Barrowlander' monotony, and the leniency of the 'offie' owner, were key.

My old man had been a pretty cool hoofer in his day, not in the Donald O'Connor/ Gene Kelly class, but way better than Gough or Dawson. He could Viennese waltz my little Ma, in either direction, i.e. normal (to the left) and reverse (clockwise), his size ten patents nimble and precise as an Indian elephant. My quarry could only gain from such inherent expertise.

I upped my speed: "Excuse me" . . . as I drew alongside, much as a *Walzter* employee would at the fair, "would either of you ladies like to dance?" (*best they had an option*)

"We <u>are</u> fuckin' dancin' . . . *piss aff*" as they continued apace round *The Barras*.

Lezzers . . . <u>had</u> to be . . . *from the Dark Side . . . the boys would need to know.*
It could have been that they weren't familiar with the phrase "excuse me," or had abandoned all hope of finishing school, but my ego wouldn't entertain such errant nonsense. At the point of departure, the package had been simply irresistible:

a generous splash of 'The Essence of Man' (by *Fabergé*), a see-through floral shirt, suffocating strides, and just enough gell to keep the duck's-arse in check on the walk from the car . . . *yup, Lezzers* . . . but one had to persevere . . . procreation was a heterosexual's duty.

One of the more mundane jobs I, as a newly promoted *assistant* floor manager (*respect*), had to tackle was the *Autocue* machine—the teleprompter. Later, mains-driven models used a succession of cunningly placed mirrors through which the presenter's scripts were displayed, smack on his/her eye-line . . . but 'twas not always thus. The early versions were mounted <u>above</u> the camera lens—a good six to eight inches—and had to be operated with a hand-cranking device; optically challenged presenters in bi-focals had no chance.

There were two basic components: the bit that fitted on the camera—'the slave'—was the size of a take-away pizza box, with a little strip-light on top, and the operator (*je*) controlled 'the master.' By rolling a wheel to its side, you could alter the speed the words rolled through, your text and the presenter's crib in sync—perfectly straightforward . . . idiot-proof.

We hired the equipment from the company of the same name (typist included). Using a 36-point font, the scripts were reproduced onto an 8" wide roll of paper that even a fully grown lab would struggle with; thence round a number of spindles, and Bob was very nearly your uncle.

That was the rig . . . bring on the talent(?) viz., men of the cloth with their five minute epistles for the all-singing, all-dancing *Epilogue* show.

Not much of a floor plan with this one—devout bloke, chair, mic, camera, mid-shot (zooming to close up), done. You knocked off a week's worth at one sitting. Although they were used to public speaking—more often than not to limited numbers—their lack of control of the prompter put their considerable faith to the test.

The star of this particular episode, key lit and resplendent in flowing coat of many colours, was right out of Monty Python and *The Spanish Inquisition*; long, Knoxian, greying beard, an ornate version of the Highland shepherd's crook by his side, and an embroidered tea cosy you wouldn't wear for a bet.

Glasgow, after closing time, (or any time), wasn't renowned for religious tolerance; requesting that he do his *Epilogue* 'live' meant the cleric might have to run the sectarian gauntlet on the late bus home, for these were not big budget productions.

The operator's position was downstage, close enough to sense, or smell, discomfort, should the unthinkable happen.

'Cue' the Unthinkable.
Maybe it was a power surge, or divine retribution from a rival camp, but the machine went off in my hand like Bernhard Langer's putter. We'd nipped from *Genesis* to *Revelation* to a place of no consequence, pissing past *The Epistles*, much as Stanley Matthews did, down the right, to Banks, Barrass and Bell of Bolton in the '53 Cup Final.

Here was man and Maker in a moment of mortal need; the audience hadn't tuned in to see him pray.
Time for the cowboy hero—a Tom Mix . . . a Gene Autrey . . . leaping from his galloping steed to arrest the helpless heroine's bolting six-*out*-of-hand.

The seconds seemed like minutes.
I found His Grace's place, but the damage had been done—he'd been made to look a right prat 'n' fanny.

We gave corporate thanks for his mercies, and the double strength of autocue paper. *(I needed to see his lips immediately after he'd blessed and forgiven me).*

New Year was always a busy time at BBC Scotland with the Old Firm game, the Hogmanay show and bags of 'specials' to produce.
The chestnut about the woman who goes to the doctor and asks if she can get pregnant from anal sex, shouldn't make you laugh: *"Where do you think Auld firm fans come from?"* . . . it does me.

According to those who bother to research such nonsense, the surname 'Thomson' or 'Thompson' (the 'p' is silent as in the sea off any of the Costas), is the 16th most common in Britain.

Everyone in Scotland knew about John Thompson, Celtic's keeper, who died after colliding with Sam English in a derby match, but households knew little of Bobby Thomson.

It's 1951, at Polo Grounds IV. The New York Giants are playing Brooklyn Dodgers for the National Baseball League Pennant. The Giants are 4-2 down in the play-offs, when Glasgow-born batter, Bobby Thomson, smacks a home run over the left-field fence: *"The Giants win the pennant! . . . The Giants win the pennant!"* roared the announcer, barely containing his bias. It became known as '*the shot that was heard round the world*,' as many US battle troops were presumed to have been 'all ears' by the killing fields of Korea.

It would have fitted my story better, diametrically, had the match been between the Giants and the Yankees, but at least the World Series came home to the Big Apple that year, furthermore, it's probably gilding the patriotic lily to claim Bobby as one of 'ours,' yet, equally, it's tough to forge a birth certificate.

P.S. Scotland's football team—when Dally Duncan (Derby County) and Tommy Walker ('The Jambos' of Midlothian) were in their pomps—played at the Polo Grounds, N.Y. N.Y., in 1935 and 1939, winning twice against an all-star US team, and drawing once. More than 25,000 turned up to watch.

It's 1967, the remains of New Year's Day, Studio B Glasgow; I'm still a bit pissed but someone has to floor manage *Sportsreel*. At stake, the career of our leading football commentator and studio presenter, Peter Thomson. That afternoon, his team and mine had fought out their customary Ne'er Day battle. The Gers were leading, with minutes to go, when one of the Celtic forwards broke through what "Thommo" described as ". . . <u>our</u> magnificent defence" for the equalizer, "totally against the run of play." My elation gave way to gutted, then incense, in the 'not happy' sense; with a little poetic licence, his live commentary went on:

"Rangers pressing forward for the winner they certainly deserve . . . Wilson dances round Young . . . inside to Brand . . . that's a brilliant ball. Alex Scott now . . . he's tormented Gemmell all day . . . . Ralphie (*hel-lo?*) a wee one into Millar . . . Millar to McMillan . . . McMillan back to Miller—Jimmy shoots (*"Jimmy" is it?!*) . . . . <u>we've</u> scored (*whit?*) . . . . Rangers have done it . . ." (*for any in doubt*).
We couldn't have been taken further aback—*2-1 to 'The Huns.'*

Peter's co-presenter, Sandy McLeish, was only part-time on *Sportsreel*; his proper job was to manage the Renfield Street branch of *Hector Powe*—the gent's outfitters—deep in the heart of the city, and equidistant from the cauldrons of partiality at Ibrox and Parkhead.

George Davidson—our second match commentator—was very probably inclined towards 'The Blues' too, but Sandy kept his colours close to his well-tailored chest. What better shop window than the popular Saturday night football show to display H.P.'s full range of snappy suits, shirts and ties? Inadvertently exposing the inside label of his jacket, in mid-shot, whilst pretending to search for an imaginary pen, was taking the product placement piss, altogether.

By the time transmission came round, the bold Thomson had all but lost the power of intelligible speech. He had 'nasals' peculiar to many homo sapiens from that part of God's country, but its clarity in sobriety, had been eroded beyond an instant fix by caffeine. It was a worry . . . but hey, it was New Year's Day, his team had done 'The Bhoys,' at Parkhead—reasons *(for them)* to be cheerful.

The blow-up picture of skipper John Greig, suspended to Peter's right (camera left), slightly behind the raised, presenter's podium, had turned his workplace into Valhalla . . . were it not for the corresponding one of Celtic's skipper to his left—in his blind spot.

As the titles to the show ran down, I bundled Peter to his studio throne.

Missed his footing didn't he?. Arse over tit, and five seconds to go.

'Ready' is Rangers' motto, but I'd be lying if I said he made it in time.
As they cut to him, he looked as *Capt'n Mainwaring* would after failing to negotiate a carefully laid trip-wire on a *Dad's Army* night exercise . . . glasses askew, hair ski-whiff, and startled . . . as in headlights and rabbit.

He managed the opening gambit word perfectly:

"Hello there, and a Guid New Year to ain and a'."

The director—the very fellow whom "Ginger" Cowgill would send packing, 'second class' from the Edinburgh Commonwealth Games, three years later on a trumped-up foreign language charge—sensed there was little more than solids to come, so, at the first sign of cat-gagging, he ran in the highlights tape of the big game

Full time, and the jinx of Studio B. was about to strike again. Just as Peter closed in on his pay-off, Greig's picture broke free of its moorings, partially, lurching on to its bottom left-hand corner in a surreal tackle on upstanding Billy McNeill. To a pervading groan . . . like tug hawsers re-straining a newly launched liner at John Brown's yard . . . down came John, cable and all. It could have been the work of known Celtic subversives in the long suffering stage crew; notwithstanding, the old pro in Peter, plus the remnants of craitur-spiked adrenalin, got us to his parting shot:

"A Happy New Year."

Rest the old boy . . . he was a one-off.

Purely on account of spending all but three years of my working life in London, I miss the Hogmanay show. Jules Holland's *Hootenanny* is more fun than BBC Scotland's recent efforts, but we had some great laughs north of the wall, in days gone by.

Knowing when to leave a party is about timing and opportunity, and maybe the BBC's centralised governors decided enough was enough, but for those of us who worked on it, that last show of the year was a special event. Chic Murray—Scotland's Tommy Cooper—was a shoo-in.

"I met this chap at the Olympics.
'Excuse me,' I said, 'but are you a pole vaulter?'
'No,' he replied, 'I'm German, but how did you know my name was Walter?'"

Chic, like his young disciple, Billy Connolly, began life in the shipyards, and grew into an international star. He was a pussycat to work with. Hours and hours he'd spend in the production office, trying out his monologues on the first Mrs. Philips, her boss, Pharic McLaren, and Haldane Duncan, a burgeoning talent in BBC Scotland's light entertainment department. Hal would direct all the major, network soaps and episodes of *The Bill* and *Taggart*. He and Chic became bosom buddies and at the boozing, Chic was different class.

"I've just been to the doctor and he told me that the only known cure for my condition is to drink mother's breast milk."
Having had a slap from Mum, she sent him upstairs to a young neighbour, recently released—and lactating—with her new baby. As her husband was away, he asked if he could have a drink from one of her swollen boobs—*"for medicinal purposes?"*

The young Mum was a bit of a sort, and after a few minutes was beginning to warm to her task:

"Will there be anything else while you're here?"

"Well . . ." he said, unlatching himself . . . "*a wee Abernathy biscuit would be nice.*"

Big Chic—'The Tall Droll'—and his diminutive wife Maidie—'The Small Doll'—had been huge in Scottish vaudeville; they'd have been on the bill at the Royal Variety, but their show had to be called off when Nasser got possessive and aggressive about the Suez Canal in the 50s.

Backstage, after one such command performance, Tommy Cooper famously tried to negotiate with the Queen for her Cup Final tickets.

Around 1956-57, anyone in a fez, far less the big Welsh magician, was a target; Tommy had served with Montgomery's Desert Rats in Egypt during the Second World War, and now here we were scrapping over the Canal with those very Egyptian soldiers; for years, they'd worn the little red Turkish hat as part of their uniform.

It would have been chaos . . . Cooper and Murray on the same bill . . . <u>and</u> in the same bar.

Chic once phoned Liverpool F.C. using Bill Shankly's voice; the Anfield receptionist on hearing the great man again 'from beyond the grave,' burst into tears.

Bill had been dead for years.
Chic was in the middle of rehearsing the musical *You'll Never Walk Alone*, as "Shanks" (*"if Everton were playing at the bottom of my garden, I'd close the curtains"*).
He apologised for any distress he may have caused.

N.B. Gerry Marsden's hit version of Rodgers and Hammerstein's song was originally from *Carousel* (1945) as any 'Koppite' or 'Jungle' inhabitant at 'Parkheid' will tell you.

Then there was that other bachelor of the comedic art, Rikki Fulton . . . . as the motor cycle copper.

Having just pulled over a speeding motorist, he dismounts the machine he'd been on for too long. Nonchalantly flicking his right leg to free-up tangled short and curlies, he slowly and deliberately unfixes his Biggles-style goggles, pulls hard on their elastic straps, and let's go, expecting them to snap back on his helmet. He's non-plussed as they fly off into the bushes.
Quickly gathering himself, he licks the tip of his pencil:
"Right Stirling, oot the motor"
(it was ↑ of course—*you had to be there*).

That sketch did for many, what *Delboy* and the open bar-hatch and French and Saunders' dirty fat bastards at *Miss World* do for everybody . . . comedy classics, beautifully observed, timed to perfection.

Rikki and partner, Jack Milroy—at once '60s teddy-boys (Jack's *Francie* to Rikki's *Josie*) in fluorescent frock-coats, brothel creepers and bootlace ties—the next, over-fed, heavily plumed, talking pigeons peering over a ledge in George Square, assessing who best for a bowelful of guava, as Hogmanay revelers below begin counting down to the bells.

On 'educated' trombone, funny man George Chisholm—a stalwart of *The Black and White Minstrel Show* (they got away with blacking-up in those days)—and glaikit Duncan Macrae (also of *Whisky Galore* fame . . . and practically every other film that required a Scottish character actor in it). Duncan's hardy annual rendition—in rhyme—about an audacious male sparrow, his tormentor and a near fatal case of mistaken identity, brought the house down.
If you're singing along, repeat the first line of each stanza three times—there's no way to describe the tune:

A wee cock sparra sat on a tree (x 3)
Chirpin awa as blithe as could be.

Alang came a boy wi'a bow and an arra (x3)
And he said: 'I'll get ye, ye wee cock sparra.'

The boy wi' the arra let fly at the sparra (getting the hang of it?),
And he hit a man that was hurlin' a barra.

The man wi' the barra cam owre wi' the arra,
And said: 'Ye take me for a wee cock sparra?'

The man hit the boy, tho he wasne his farra
And the boy stood and glowered; he was hurt tae the marra.

And a' this time the wee cock sparra
Was chirpin awa on the shank o' the barra.

Here's the key:

sparra = sparrow
arra = arrow
farra = father
hurlin = pushing
barra = barrow

owre = over
wasnae = wasn't
tae = to
marra = marrow (as previously stated)
shank = handle

Rab C Nesbitt's 'network' success is interesting, bearing in mind the breadth of naked Glasgwegian accents therein.
Rab—another man of Govan at the top of his profession (benefit cheat)—was disgusting to look at, so half the job done.
It mattered not a jot that few south of the Wall had a Scooby Doo what he was on about.

When King Kenny Dalglish took over as Liverpool manager in 1985, we sent our very own psychophantic redhead, Alan Parry, home for a chat:

"Don't the players find it difficult to understand your accent at times, Kenny?"

(pause)

"Pardon?" says the Weedgie (right back atcha).

Nothing the Romans built could stem the tide as northern expeditionary forces rallied round the piano: beardy Robin Hall and his partner, Jimmy McGregor (who'd find greater fame writing calypsos for BBC *Nationwide*) were in the vanguard; *The Corries*—a duet in the end—with Ronnie Browne and his buddy Roy Williamson, who could play anything with strings and was the power behind '*Flower of Scotland,*' which Ronnie, to this day, belts out before big games at Hampden, and to which Ken Buchanan, the world flyweight champ used to make his entrances; *The Humblebums*—Gerry Rafferty, Tam Harvey and Billy Connolly.

The Bums (Tam had gone by then) often gigged at the *Green Restaurant* folk club in Crieff, before setting off separately—*one* down the A41 to *Baker Street* and a No. 3 spot in the UK singles chart in 1978, *the other* to make the planet laugh.

I'd risen to outside broadcast stage manager by now, and the stage I had to manage on December 31st 1968 was the bar at The Aviemore Centre, Inverness-shire . . . . *starring, for one night only* . . . . '*Mr. Jimmy 'sausages are the boys' Logan,*' brother of magnificent Annie Ross, actress and jazz singer (same genes, widely differing talents).

It'd been snowing, and now it was freezing. The approved way of keeping warm was to get into the Scottish firewater or beer or vodka or gin or lager, anything that would make you feel like shit thro' January 3rd.

Dixie Ingram and his *White Heather Club* dancers (four of the girls <u>were</u> 'Heathers') attracted the odd snowball in Allander Square, that bitter night, as they reeled around to Jimmy Shand and his country dance band.

The White Heather Club was one of the first shows to be 'taped' by the BBC, following their invention, in 1958, of VERA, a primitive video recording device, which, half a century on (with one or two refinements like freeze-frames, high speed scene searching, duplex recordings, stability and colour), makes light of tough Saturday evening choices . . . *Strictly Come Dancing* or *X Factor* . . . or the pub?

They weren't the world's slickest shows, but on Hogmanay the kilt was our delight. Overt 'Scottishness' gets on even the most impassioned tits, but this was the way to go on 'oor nicht' (you could almost forgive Andy Stewart . . . *almost*).

One Hogmanay, we were sitting at home having a dram. As midnight approached Mum flicked on the telly; in fifteen minutes the network would switch to BBC Scotland to bring in the new year.
My parents and their friends—the Kyles family, from affluent Whitecraigs in Glasgow—waited as the set flickered into life.

Jimmy (Kyles) was like an uncle to us, always good for a laugh . . . but that was about to change:

"Ladies and gentlemen . . . the legend that is Monsieur Maurice Chevalier."

Well, it could have been a bomb at Abbotsinch. No sooner had the Frenchman launched into the opening line of *"Thank Heaven for Little Girls"* (his signature song from *Gigi*), than Jimmy was roaring down the phone at the BBC switchboard, demanding that he be removed from our screens (so much for the Auld Alliance) *". . . zank heaven, for lee-tal girls."*

Back in Aviemore, we'd done lots of day-time shooting up on the White Lady—Cairngorm's answer to the *Streif* on the Hahnenkamm in Kitzbühel (the black sections on the Invernesian version were rocks . . . *but who was having more fun?*).

Not the hardy bagpipers and drummers for sure; missiles that started not unreasonably as *bone fide* snowballs, had assumed the density of meteors in the frozen air as they crunched home, wedging nippy fingers to chanters and disrupting all forms of syncopation (don't see Albert Hall 'prommers' behaving like that . . . *but those dopey flags and streamers, and all that bouncing up and down malarkey . . . give it a rest, eh?*).

On the subject of pomp (and Paxman), what are they're on about in *Newsnight Review?!*

Big 'Jez,' addressing a gathering of TV types at the Edinburgh Festival, said he felt the industry had lost its sense of purpose (how was he to know *Big Brother* was on the verge of implosion), but you do wonder why creative people bother when you listen to the assassins at review. Paxman had strongs views too on Scottish country dancing, but as he might well be getting upsides 'Sir' Robin Day soon (and we all know how HMQ likes to strip-the-willow at Balmoral) I'll spare him one debate he'll never win.

Remaining mounted on my high horse . . . . I tuned in to watch an 'arts and farts' production on Andrea Bocelli, the hugely popular, blind tenor from Italy.
As kids in the school choir, we were mesmerised by the power of Caruso and Mario Lanza, and, later on, by the big goalkeeper himself, 'lucky Luciano'—as 'laddy-da' critics go, the man in the Bocelli film took the biscuit . . . *the tin.*
Choking on self-importance, he decreed that *Bocelli would never be a true star of opera . . . he didn't have the voice.*
Bit of a party-pooper and clearly not one of the 60 million or so who've bought his records; it's like saying Nige Kennedy of Aston Villa isn't a proper fiddler.

Be Lara, then criticise Tendulkar . . . . *pillock!*

Really, the Hogmanay show was terribly good natured, end-of-term frivolity . . . *if you weren't on stage*, and that very ambition was nagging away at some of the daredevils. Towards the end of their gigs, as euphoria and amphetamines kick in, rock band frontmen have a tendency to do trusting falls into the fanatics' midst; at ours, those who managed to slip security (their occupations plastered across their backs lest they forgot under questioning) and made it, briefly, on stage, were returned to the masses in free-fall. Not quite the surfing technique in which Axel Rose and the mighty fliers of rock believed, nor the kind of thing you'd expect from imperious Iberian matadors like *El Cordobés* or the mounted *Peralta Brothers*.

Hemingway's *Death in the Afternoon* was all about the dubious practice of bull fighting . . . about courage and fear; at Spey Valley's amphitheatre, respect for doomed opponents was the lowest priority—pantomime horses, not picadors (*what a disgusting line of work that is*).

In synchronised acts of simulated cape waving, to cries of '*olé*' and the colloquial '*die ya bastard,*' the short assisted, flights of the *espontáneos* (intruders) came to dramatic ends. Good job it was 'Baltic' and most were bladdered; even so, the cushioning effect of the slush and snow couldn't save some from Aviemore's health centre and *Auld Lang Syne*.

The Scottish Variety Orchestra, a non-temperance collective, shielded from the elements, and the hooligans in the square, sawed away at their accompaniment from a neighbouring hall, while artistes did battle with inadequate fold-back on stage.

As for Mr. Logan, his was an improvised end: despite my attentions, each of his props—'Jags' scarves and rosettes, hats, bells and whistles, the lot—had been purloined by souvenir hunters and saboteurs (*make that "drunks . . . children and animals"*).

Drawing on years of sticky, stand-up audiences and annual panto 'pish,' plus clever-dick gleanings from Firhill's terraces—home of his beloved *Maryhill Magyars*—Jim gained safe passage (I got a volley).

"I thought they were actually *called* 'Patrick Thistle Nil'" said Connolly.

That was January 1st 1968.
A few months later, I tied a speckled bag to a stick, swung it on my shoulder and made a progress to London . . .
. . . *where I await my fortune.*

"Forfar 5 East Fife 4"

Not a great endorsement for my chosen career path that booze should once again be the catalyst, but when they amended the expression to . . . *a legend in his own <u>lunch hour</u>,* they must have had Ronnie Pantlin in mind. Ron was the next man to whom one paid undivided attention, in the BBC Kensington House bar, if any kind of career were to burgeon.

It wasn't corruption, just a very expensive way to get the old boy 'trousered,' on the off chance he'd remember next morning who'd helped him to the last train home and that monumental hangover.

Pantlin was a rear gunner during the Second World War, which he told us about every day around noon, about the sixth pink g & t (large) in:

"I'll leave the size entirely up to you old boy"

. . . viz four fingers, if you wanted to get on *MISS WORLD*, three were it *JAZZ NIGHT* at Ronnie Scott's in Soho, a couple for *TOP OF THE FORM* . . . but you could forget racing at Newbury—or anywhere else—that was off limits—Pantlin's preserve—not even a two-handed horse-measure could get you on that one.

Every outside broadcast, be it *The Farnborough Air Show, The Grand National, It's A Knockout* or Chelsea in full bloom, had to have a floor manager—or stage manager as we were called—and Ronnie, *in imperio,* was the guv'nor . . . the *Senior* S.M. He ruled his little basement Empire with a light touch, sat beneath an enormous blackboard; the names of his charges went down one side—Pantlin at the top, of course (Philips constantly in the drop zone) with our wide ranging assignments across the length of one wall.

His absolutely-no-nonsense-assistant, Gail, bestrode the master's desk monthly, as fresh jobs hit the schedules. In truth, she *ran* the office; many tried to curry favour, but her loyalty was incorruptible . . . plus she vetted expenses before submission to the treasury above, so it was prudent to stay just behind the back four at all times.

The best jobs—the money spinners—involved mileage and overnights. The boys (there were about twenty of us at any one time) had the claiming process down to a fine art. In retrospect that was the toughest part . . . mis-time your run and you could be on the bench forever.

Match of the Day was for the favoured few.

Stage managers came with earphones or 'cans' for listening to the director/producer, a 'lazy' microphone, so they could talk back (in the nicest way possible), and a hard skin. As go-betweens, we'd catch it from all sides . . . from 'the bridge' of the mobile control room, or MCR, as the main truck, or 'scanner,' was abbreviated to . . . from the artistes and crew on stage . . . and, at times, from the public who, less increasingly, were falling for the TV bullshit.

The *events* side of BBC TV Outside Broadcasts (anything other than *sport*), took us to Covent Garden of a summer's evening. Ballet is not my thing but neither is appreciating its grace and athleticism the connoisseurs' prerogative . . . try as they might to keep the shop closed.

I would have remembered Nureyev—*his* was the complete package: the Christiano Ronaldo of the grande jeté (stepover) . . . the Lionel Messi of the pas de basque (indescribable) . . . the Tim Cahill of the soubresaut (sudden leap) . . . the George Farm—Blackpool's keeper in that Matthews final—of the ballotté (balloon).
(*how dangerous is a little knowledge?*).

Reigate's Margot Fonteyn and the big Russian toy-boy (18 years her junior) had perfect *vertical* alignment and, some said, were far from shabby when *horizontal*; they were to ballet what Astaire and Rogers were to most other forms of the medium.
Torvill and Dean would add another layer to cutting edge balance and poise—Widdecombe was stomach-churning.

Ronnie—on point(e), in a box, high above the stage—was charged with cueing the presenter into inter-act links, and keeping safe, bunches of flowers, which, at the end of the performance (regardless of its quality . . . not that we peons would be any the wiser) were to be thrown 'spontaneously' on stage; at their peak, Fonteyn and Rudi could wipe out the Garden's stocks in a night.
It was just something one did, like cutting off a bull's ears in appreciation of a good kill, or moving slightly backwards when the Queen was about.

Mike Begg, Pantlin's constant running mate—due to his ability to drink the old boy under any table, any*where*, any*time*—was backstage, regaling the chorus of his oily repartee, home phone number and cure for tendonitis. I shadowed the boss in the presenter's nest, manning the roller caption for the end-of-show credits: cerebral stuff.

I'd spent thirteen years at school squeezing out a University qualification, and three more in newspapers skimming over Constitutional Law and avoiding Pitman's to reach this pinnacle of achievement, but none at home need know.

Come on, I was at the ballet in Covent Garden with Richard Baker . . . I could touch him. Mum would be so proud.

It was hard (give thanks *it* wasn't) not to notice much other than the danseur's enhanced endowment as the prima ballerina assoluta was hoisted towards the lighting gallery in the grandest of finales . . . . like Ben 'Whopper' Kay in a Tiger or Lion line-out.

'Standby with the flowers' came the director's voice in our ears, as the room erupted. Similar to the echo in a courtroom as a new witness is called to the stand, Ronnie re-iterated *"standby with the flowers"*—pointless, as he would be the one doing the throwing, and rather too loudly to make it any kind of surprise below.

I sensed the rap would be coming my way, when, right on cue, Ronnie lobbed the flowers towards the bowing, curtseying duo. Having omitted, in the pressure of the moment, to take the rubber bands off, two random bundles thudded onto the stage like giraffe shit.

In a flourish, with supreme elan, *'the bloke with no strides on'* swept what he could from the floor and the two, balancing bouquets and rogue roses like *Crackerjack* contestants (*"CRACK-ER-JACK!"*) with prizes and cabbages ("three-and-out"), sashayed off stage right, beaming.

'Seemed to go alright, Ron?'

Apart from shooting Fokkers out of the sky, Ronnie's passion was horse racing . . . not in the Peter O' Sullevan, Clive Graham, Julian Wilson sense of knowing the business backwards, but for his implicit understanding of the power of the T&D—the almighty travel and duty allowance, cash for the keeping of slates, at BBC bars (various) between Oxford Circus and Shepherd's Bush, to manageable levels.

"*Put a few more expenses in there, old boy*" he'd beseech, as the remaining traces of another 'pink' faded from his tumbler.
He used the wide-open-mouth technique of the porn star to suck the life out of his *Gordon's* and angostura bitters—a committed, swallow-but-never-spit man.

For the number of days Ron spent *in* the office scheduling his minions and agonising over his latest works of fiction, he spent double *out* on the road with his good buddy Dennis Monger, the BBC's racing producer, and *his* trusty assistant, Pam Guyler . . . a threesome you had to be in training for, come yardarm (1100hr at sea); talking was deemed to be wasting time.

Peter O'Sullevan wasn't seen much in the TV compound; he lived at a more rarified altitude, amongst owners, trainers, countesses (belters), earls (belted) and minted Sheikhs in civvies. His seeming mystique belied a sense of fun and mischief; Pete was always up for a ruse, and you'd never be disappointed to have him sat next to you at dinner . . . that is *after* you'd negotiated the learning curve.

The stage manager got to the racecourse well in advance.
The commentary position had to be *just so*.
There were special, free-standing binoculars—'half inched' from a German sub during the War (not by Sir Peter, you understand)—a sophisticated version of the-penny-a-go (circa 1950) numbers on sea-front promenades . . . heavy, yet perfectly balanced, operated by the forehead . . . and a cunningly designed lip-microphone which had been built into a harness . . . akin to a busker's harmonica rig.

'Pozz' (several laps of curves were required to get on *those* terms) would slip it over his camel coat—the meaning of *'coming in his (coat)'* I was only guessing at—leaving hands free for his notes . . . racing colours, jockeys, trainers, owners, sires, dames, who covered who with what, the odds, the going, who had the cough, which had blinkers, what weights were being carried, etc., etc., priceless information two-quid-each-way Hillman Hunters (punters) without a chanty to piss in, ignored at their cost ('chanty' being a Scottish word meaning chamber pot).

'Mr.' O'Sullevan, as he was on debut (mine), handed me his portable television (tuned to ITV . . . . sound down):

"Watch the Cesarewitch and give me the 1-2-3 as soon as it's over, would you?" he asked, rhetorically, not remembering any part of my name.

If you're not familiar with this race, it's a stampede, a sprint over the Rowley mile at Newmarket with stacks of runners—the commentator's nightmare, the field, throughout, using '*the full width of the pitch, Ron.*'

As the pepped-up three year olds tumbled across the line in a blanket finish, I faked a conversation with my colleague in the parade ring commentary box until I saw ITV's Starting Price graphic flash on screen.
Legibly scribbling the details down, I slipped them to our esteemed race caller; he waved me away, dismissively
Read it in between times, *off* the muted, black and white monitor, hadn't he? . . . working it seamlessly into his BBC commentary.
RE-SPECT!

Formulaic isn't a fair description of the O'Sullevan creed, but there was a 'jump'-to-SPs template:

'*And they're off* . . .' other than the order and casualties, he never said much between fences . . . '*all safely over the first*' he'd purr, like a Silver Cloud in top . . . '*coming to the last of the open ditches on the final circuit* . . . *Moorhen pecks at that one*' (slight gear change there) . . . '*two left to jump and it's still anyone's race* . . . (yeah sure—you know it's not).

As they charged into the final straight, 'The Voice' moved up through the box, imperceptibly, just as his good mate Piggott might on a patient challenger from the other code.

Heresy I know, and I'm surmising (a writ may follow), but the smooth-talking Irishman appeared to favour the Sport of Kings in its intended form, rather than National Hunt, which some snooty bastards perceived as a 13 rather than a 15-a side thing, more Harris than Ellis, more Hanley than Guscott, more Waring than West. Cheltenham and Aintree may unify hunters, chasers, sprinters and stayers . . . but there's only *one* Ladies Day.

In 1668 George Villiers, the 2nd Duke of Buckingham came up with the obnoxious idea of fox-hunting, but in the O'Sullevan filofax, BUCKINGHAM was for the Palace, first, and *Foinavon*'s famous pilot, John, second.

Breeding was paramount. Racing 'royalty'—from the O'Briens of Coolmore to Sheikh Mohammad al Maktoum, Ruler of Dubai—were big mates. His own 'sire,' Colonel John Joseph O'Sullevan, handed down the law to wrong uns in southern Ireland, and his 'dame'—Vera—was a knight's daughter.

Peter's manner, and grammar, said Epsom rather than Leopardstown . . . Charterhouse School rather than Killarney comp, or maybe it was indeed how he 'came in his coat' . . . the bespoke tailoring, the Swiss finishing school, the perspicacity of the prep(aration), the measured economy of one of broadcasting's most distinctive voices.

Were you to trawl the BBC archives, you'd find David Coleman's voice on *every* meaningful Olympic and World Championship final—from 100m to the Marathon . . . Rome 1960 to Sydney 2000—*he saw to it*.

And so it *ought* to have been for Peter: he is synonymous with horses.

As the Derby was considered a 'national' event, rights were shared by ITV and us from the outset (1960—St. Paddy . . . "*owned by Sir Victor Sassoon, trained by Noel Murless and ridden by Lester Piggott*").

Ever since, it's been tossed back and forward across the Downs amongst the two big boys and Channel 4, and for now, rests in the incomparable hands of *Mill Reef* (1971)—"*owned by Paul Mellon, trained by Ian Balding and ridden by Geoff Lewis*"—trainer's daughter, Clare, the excellent (for a Victorian) Jim McGrath, and whichever independent production company the BBC have deemed fit to do their bidding.

But frankly, His Master's Voice *should* be on all the classics, those in 1969-70 won by the incomparable *Nijinsky*—"owned by Charles W. Englehard jr., trained by Vincent O'Brien and ridden by Lester Piggott," and the epic at Epsom in 1981with *Shergar*—"owned by HH Aga Khan IV, trained by Michael Stoute and ridden by Walter Swinburn" . . . but it isn't.

Peter's identification was legendary; compute the margin of error—the foreshortening effect of the binoculars and the angle of his commentary position to the course—and still he'd know precisely who was in front, be they on the rails, the grandstand side, or—like Eric Liddell or Bryan Robson—bursting through the middle, unannounced.

If *Shergar's* 10 lengths win was the largest margin in the Derby—and it certainly was/is (at the time of printing)—Robbo's opener against France, in Spain 1982, had been the fastest goal ever scored in the World Cup finals . . . 27 seconds, if memory serves me (*it emerged that Vaclav Masek of Czechoslovakia had done one quicker—in 15"—against Mexico, in Chile, twenty years earlier, but that's fact interfering, again*).

I just made it to my seat at Stadio San Mames in Bilbao—the row behind Ron Greenwood and the England bench—to see Robson's spectacular lunge; with the bladder and enlarged prostate I have now, I would have missed it.

P.S. all you anoraks (*please, let me be right*) . . . the fastest goal in the final stages of the competition was scored by Turkey's Hakan Sükür, after 11 seconds, against South Korea, in 2002 . . . so 'Robbo' drops to 3rd.

P.P.S. (for Jocks, and any anorak not already writing) who could forget San Marino 1993 . . . . 8.3. secs wasn't it, when 'Psycho' Pearce put David Seaman right in it—a qualifier 'the enemy' won 7-1 in the end.

Ronaldhino <u>was</u> shooting in 2002—live with it.

Footballers' nags are high-maintenance, risk-laden investments.
Jim Baxter's long running affair with turf accountancy ended in tears; Michael Owen's must have too, though, unlike Baxter, there's plenty more where that came from.

Were Mick Channon to get it even *slightly* wrong with a godolphin, he could forget his 185 goals for Southampton and 46 England caps—Mohammed Bin Rashid Al Maktoum would be on his case . . . and you know how close Bedouins are to their Arabians.
Channon has trained some good sorts—perhaps not in Vincent O'Brien's class, yet—but who'd you rather have at your back: Robert Sangster, who certainly knew where the next punt was coming from . . . or the <u>Ruler of Dubai</u>; *could there ever be a grander title?*

Other owners with 'boarders' at Mick's school of equine excellence, down Newbury way, have included Line-acre's mate Sir Alex . . . the late Alan Ball, and *'the boy Seven'*—Kevin Keegan.

Mick was infectiously popular as an ITV pundit, regularly clashing on-screen with Brian Clough; his lack of research reminded me of Cliff Morgan towards the end of his commentary days: *". . . what a score by the big man"* he'd give it were an instant ident not forthcoming. If Mick got stuck he'd favour: *". . . the boy TEN done brilliant"* (Pelé included) in his Wiltshire twang.
Coleman favoured *"ONE-NIL"* for openers, covering all fuck-up possibilities.

With a couple of furlongs to go—in deference to the race sponsor, and conscious that the *Six O'Clock News* would pick up his commentary from precisely that point—Peter would launch the highlight with:
". . . so as they enter the final furlong of the Going for a Song Bargain Hunters Selling Platers' Hurdle, it's Willow Pattern going on from The Auctioneer with Kiln Fire in third . . . and making a run on the rails, Brass Monkey . . . . Brass Monkey goes on . . . two hundred yards left to run, he's going to get up (meaning it's 'nailed on') *. . . at the line, <u>BRASS MONKEY</u> wins the Going for a Song Bargain Hunters Selling Platers' Hurdle"* . . . and so on, tailing off into all the significant finishers and re-capping the fates of ante-post fancies . . . in one breath
(Eminem and Jeff Stelling were watching and listening).

Were the win outright—no photos, no objections, no stewards' (enquiry)—Peter would process *". . . that's the one-two-three-four, now, let's review the closing stages with* (cuddly) *Richard Pitman* (over the sticks, or the equally engaging, if more snappily turned out) *Jimmy Lindley* (on the flat)."

Thereafter, it might be a throw to the winning connections, with Swindon Town F.C.s most loyal and misguided fan, Julian Wilson. 'Winning' and 'Swindon' seldom appeared in the same sentence . . . until 1986, when they went utterly barmy, amassing 102 points in a season—albeit in the Fourth Division (*wash your mouth out, they're now in League One!*).

And thence to Tim Gudgin or Len Martin for the starting prices.
Len's voice was the more recognizable; for as long as I could remember, his was the one we listened to at football results time on *Grandstand*, my grandfather, pen poised, coupon in hand, awaiting the familiar intonation of the 'score' draw, giving him 8 from 10, and me, at least a new bike (*I got the bike alright*).

"Forfar 5, East Fife 4" from Len, didn't have the public school resonance of his radio counterpart, James Alexander Gordon's, but 'Len the Lip' (heard, but seldom seen) never missed a beat, and very few *Grandstands* between the first, in 1958, and his death

in '95—nor was it <u>ever</u> *"High* (phonetic) *bernian"* when *"Hib* (as in 'bib') *ernian"* is proper.
Good bloke Leonard . . . for a Queenslander.

What would Sir Stanley Rous, former boss of FIFA, have given for a couple of minutes with him before presenting the top prize at *Sports Review* in 1985, the year Barry McGuigan—*'The Clones Cyclone'*—won the WBA World featherweight boxing Championship at Queen's Park Rangers' ground in London; put an ear to the sod at Loftus Road today, and you'd probably still hear it rumbling . . . *what a night, what a fantastic, awesome, dangerous night*; Des Lynam was commentating for the wireless, so Brian Barwick and I nabbed the ringside complimentaries—*outstanding value.* Unaminous in 15.

The presentations were largely unscripted affairs, and because time was always at a premium, we'd ask the 'honoured guest' not to indulge in a great soliloquy about the year we'd just spent two hours or so unraveling . . . but to press on with the 3-2-1—Eric Morley style.
To be fair, Sir Stan did (press on) but he made a right 'cauli' of the main name: *". . . and the winner is the excellent Irish boxer, Barry McCorcharin"*—near enough for sport, I guess, and it made the affable Finbar smile.

A couple of days before the Pedroza fight, Des and I went to meet Barry and his manager, Barney Eastwood, at a pub in St. John's Wood (*"sin gas, all round . . . . and make it snappy"* I demanded, with confidence).
Stats will show that Sonny Liston's 15" sledge-hammer fists were probably the biggest in the pro-game, but then he was a heavy; for a feather (said Henry), Barry's were *"like bleedin' shovels, they was, Harry."*

Seventeen year old Boris Becker won Wimbledon that year, and Mrs. Miriam Francome's husband was champion 'jump' jockey for the *seventh* time (*she* remaining gorgeous, throughout).

A Duke by any other name, Miles Francis Stapleton Fitzalan-Howard—"Norfolk" to his mates—was another great fan of the flat.
On non-race days, he was Earl Marshal of England with an all-expenses-paid seat at Arundel Castle in Sussex, and a blood line as long as the thoroughbred pedigree database.

The 17th Duke was responsible for organising all major state occasions—*noblesse oblige*—so, best be on one's game when the old soldier was about; whether *he* was on *his*, was none of one's business.

First on parade . . . rear gunner Pantlin.

Not sure how many he had, but the RAF silk tie was an ever-present, even in tails. The unsaddling at Ascot heaved with privilege and the over-bred. Elegant necks, in wide-brimmed monstrosities, craned for a clear view through graceless tenements of hired toppers, as His (Grace) was led out.

There's always a Royal flunky or two directing affairs, and between them and the BBC's Senior Stage Manager, it was agreed—after lengthy deliberation—that the best place to see and hear the old boy was from *the very middle of the enclosure* (loving your work). A microphone was hooked up to the public address system, and since the Duke's speech was to be broadcast 'live' on our mid-week racing show, we (Ronnie) would be cueing Norfolk: *listen up, this will be inconsequential to all but the Illuminati and half a per cent of the population.*

Picture a Fairbanks jr. or *Zorro* movie, as a sparkling flame speeds irreversibly along a fuse wire towards the gunpowder cache stacked high in the vaults of the baddie's castle . . .

His 'Dukeship' was speaking alright, but only his ghost writer knew the thrust of it. As producer Monger politely enquired of the audio department as to *"what the f—k"* was going on, one of the cameras zoomed in on the mic.
Very slowly, it tracked the cable across turf trodden by equine stars and rich bitches, pausing at Ronnie's well-buffed Veldtschoens, one of which, metaphorically, was already heading north towards his gob.

In the truck, those brave enough joined in whistling the cracking *Mission Impossible* theme as the camera panned up Ron's trousers.

Rolled neatly round his left hand were loops of the microphone extension cable, whilst casually draped in his right was the female connector socket; agonisingly, the male end was fifty feet away. Oblivious.

In Tudor times, it would have been the Bloody Tower for the senior O.B.S.M; fortunately the 3rd Duke's less influential descendant—14 times removed—was none the wiser . . . and nothing of note escaped the great British unwashed.

I mentioned Charlie Liston, a page or two ago, and if you look closely at *Sgt. Pepper's Lonely Hearts Club Band* album sleeve you'll see him in the crowd (*"where's Wally/ Sonny?"*—extreme left . . . in white and gold).

Whether it was the result of my inordinate spending, or an administrative oversight, I found myself on the list for Ronnie Scott's. The boss, on sax, was a member of The Kenny Clarke-Francy Boland Big Band, plus he had his own quartet, quintet and octet (<u>and</u> he played the solo on The Beatles' *Lady Madonna*).

He and co-founder Pete King would meet and greet all sorts at one of the great jazz venues, originally set in London's Gerrard Street; on the night our big green trucks stopped by, the club was in Frith Street, Soho.

Because he was into music—and fags (*Benson's*) and booze (the lot) and birds—Mike Begg was given responsibility for the ever-changing cast: *one band off . . . spin the stage . . . next band on . . . like clockwork.*
I was typecast—*back on the bloody captions.*
Had my career stalled or peaked?

Over afternoon 'scotch' at her tiger-skin-clad gaff in North London, the formidable Doris Troy—jazz singing diva and Scott's regular—whispered that she thought 'Beggie' was as '*a real purrtie drinker*' . . . praise indeed. The 'gold watch' we liked, but neither of us risked the questionable cake.

Sharing afternoon delights were a few session players and American soul songbird Madeline Bell. She—and the Bronx's 'Mama Soul' (Doris)—had been in Dusty Springfield's backing group, and later on would hook up with Rogers Coulam and Cook, Herbie Flowers and Barry Morgan in *Blue Mink* . . . "*Melting Pot,*" "*Banner Man*" and all those huge hits of the late Sixties.
Maddy was from Newark, New Jersey and was a fabulous chanteuse in her own right . . . tombstone teeth, humungus lungs, "qualité" as *Le Professeur* might say, if asked.
(dig out Joe Cocker's *"With A Little Help From My Friends"* and you'll be blown away—bit like Arsenal on song).

Having filmed with the SAS . . . gone gorge-fishing with rock-climber-supreme, Joe Brown . . . man-handled *Miss Nicaragua* (allegedly) . . . Mike would later produce and direct 'the Master' in *Wooldridge and Whisky*—a documentary that took *months* of research and site visits, arguably more life-threatening than running with the bulls in Pamplona or hurtling down the Cresta Run on a tray—a couple of Ian's other ventures in the name of his glorious brand of journalism.

"Soho, we have a problem . . ."
Jazz Scene on BBC 2 was 'live' and the headliners—the Oscar Peterson trio—were *one* light:
". . . *just the fucking pianist !*" . . . replied 'Beggie' to a polite.
. . ."*who are we missing, Mike?*" from producer Terry Henebery.

For a long time, the U.S. federation of musicians had banned American artistes from travelling to the U.K. to play, but now that the path had been cleared, we could marvel at the Maharaja in the flesh . . .
. . . *or would we?*

Mr. P. wasn't thrilled about the terms and conditions (<u>now</u> *you tell us*), and refused to budge from his pram, leaving bassist Sam Jones and fabulous Bobby Durham (on skins) to a roomful of devotees. You'd think there'd only be so much drums, cymbals and bass could do, but that would be to underestimate Durham and Jones; for what seemed like an eternity (to us), they performed improvised miracles—relieved, no doubt, to be out of the big guy's reflection for a while. The Steinway awaited.

Midway through 'our' eternity—midst frenzied finger-plucking and paradiddling—the great Canadian slid, deftly (for one so large) onto his stool as the now elated room warmly acknowledged his pals' efforts.

In seconds we were in wonderland; the hiatus had been worth every chewed nail, every . . . "*is he there yet?*"
My chest of names-for-the-dropping-of was lined with pure gold (ebony and ivory having long since been discontinued for keyboards).
They (the experts) say Oscar Emmanuel Peterson was the greatest pianist . . . EVER; he (and Victor Borge) 'll do for me Arsene, though I *love* Johnny Parker's riff in Humph's *Bad Penny Blues* . . . and now that I mention *him*, Alfred Lyttleton—the late Etonian trumpet player's great uncle—was the first to play cricket and football for England . . . and, recklessly whizzing forward to Soho again, you can still catch the Lyttleton band at the famous old club from time to time, sadly without the main man.

It's not such a great distance, musically, from Ronnie Scott's to Fairfield Hall; the acts at both tend to be "world class" . . . as they give it (often without justification) in 'footie' . . . so, south of the river our units went.

I'm window dressing (this is pre-Oyster), but the name of the conductor from whom I obtained a cheap day-return on boarding the routemaster to Croydon, was never sought; however, the 'frontman' of the Royal Philharmonic was most certainly Rudolf Kempe—as different a man from my old newsroom boss at BBC Scotland, as Dresden is from Stonehaven.
Kempe was a legend in the world of classical music . . . much as Best, Law and Charlton were (with justification).
Herr Kempe's baton technique gave great scope to our close-up cameras (nowadays, given the right gear, you can access Maestro-cam throughout, much as you can the ubiquity of Messi).

As a director of sorts myself, I loved the deep access big lenses gave: to Connors' twirling racquet as he set himself for a Tanner 'bomb' . . . to Trevino's grip for a looping fade, feet at ten to one (B.S.T.) . . . to Sheene's gloved throttle-hand, winding it to 'max' out of Copse, with sufficient time, cheek, balls and flex to give Kenny Roberts the 'V' with his left.

No doubt James Last and Victor Silvester had their own schematics (*I know, I know, it isn't the same—posh smart arses!*), but the boy Kempe was very particular about laying out RPO members (*not* for notes bummed): strings, brass and percussion had their appointed spots . . . woodwind found their own seats when the music stopped . . . the 'trianglist' stood throughout, lest the moment were missed.
Call it a power surge, or a fun-size, standing before so many musicians' union members at the London Lyceum, as iridescent sequins of light burst from the spinning glitter ball, was an awesome experience.

Down the road, in Covent Garden, Arlene Phillips was teaching jazz dance at the Pineapple Club . . . out east, Len Goodman was putting Dartford on the hoofing map . . . and I had Ray McVay's 'Band of the Day' in the palm of my hand.
"Raymondo" had nipped off for a gypsy's (kiss=piss) during a *Come Dancing* rehearsal, and *("nudge nudge, wink, wink")* had left me 'in charge.'
The normally militant brothers and sisters of the M.U. were at their most accommodating and promised not to spoil my big moment:
"*A-one, two, a-one-two-three-four*" . . . and as if by magic . . .

Having listened to the rehearsal of the first act in Croydon, and *not* to my after-school, sado-masochistic, piano teacher, Mrs. "Bobo" Fletcher, my dread was that Kempe could stop proceedings at any time for adjustments, and enquire of me '*from which letter*' we'd like to re-start?

'What? . . . you never mentioned this in the NAAFI, Uncle Ron!'

Eccentric "Bobo" Fletcher taught me a special brand of geography at school . . . by strap, and his missus compounded the felony, after hours, by taking a round ruler to my stubby fingers for failing to achieve an octave span they were never built for, at seven.

Look, I knew . . . . how to re-set American pool balls . . . my side-outs from hand-outs in badminton . . . a salchow from a lutz on ice . . . an entrechat from a chateaubriand at dinner . . . . a blend from a malt, anytime . . . blindfolded; even the change-over craziness at ice hockey was kinda clear. Scoring a trick-run on water-skis or identifying a high tariff dive from 34ft 6in were comparative cake—and, at a push, I could follow the shipping forecast . . . but *"from which letter?"*
Jesus Sebastian!!

N.B. Reverse swing was a mystery in the making.

It only happened once: I just repeated, parrot fashion, what the director was saying in my ear.

The Kempemeister never looked at me . . . *why would he?*
Meeting Jesse and Pelé, breathing the same smog as Oscar at Scott's, mattered not a crotchet in the great canvas of classical music.
I was unworthy: gum on the soles of his shoes
(. . . but would *he* know St. Johnstone's *goal difference after 14 matches played? NO . . . so*).

There's an illustrated instruction in Barbara Cartland's *Etiquette Handbook* (essential reading for the baby boomer) showing a household lacky losing control of a salver of crockery, right behind the Lady in Pink's dining-room chair:
. . . . *carry on regardless . . . retain one's poise . . . ignore, ignore, ignore.*

Tough titties were the hapless, inadequately remunerated, serving wench—with no apparent Christian name—to twist an ankle and suffer first degree soup-burns in the fall.

George, (forgotten his surname) the reasonably-paid rigger who lost control of a heavy loop of 2" thick, co-axle camera cable, sending it crashing to the resonant parquetry of the Festival Hall, countless, frenetic sheet-turns into the piece, and precisely at the string section's highest register (if that's the right expression for barely audible) just went red . . . *guilty . . . arrowed.* A room trembler.

"Ignore, ignore, ignore"

Beethoven and Pete Townshend of *The Who* managed their deafness . . . *was 'Kempy' a bit mutton too?*
No sign of the leviathan slowing down . . . we might just be getting away with this . . . had Babs' wee book not been published in German?
(I'm struggling with one—the 'Queen of Romance' wrote hundreds from her chaise longue; *that* could be the answer).

Several minutes later, like a Sea Hawk in the clutches of a carrier's restraining wire, the great orchestra slithered to a halt.
George was 'on a break'—nowhere to be seen.

". . . ve vill pick up, laydees unt gentleherren, from zee lettar F."
(the perfect letter, Maestro, good thinking).

By the way, I know a man who's Dad has fallen off an aircraft carrier *twice*. William Scott Dyke* had found himself working on the Ladies European Golf Tour (**catch me falling into a non-p.c. trap*). He's a wizard engineer who can build an edit suite in half the time it takes Laura Davies to shoot 70. Dad Dyke was a ground crew member in the Fleet Air Arm, and very lucky to still be with us, having falling off *separate* carriers, once at sea—when, miraculously, he was spotted by a ship's helicopter—and a second time in dock . . . not *dry* dock, for he lives on, *but what a careless bugger.eh?*

Command of the language, and confidence to address large groups of paying customers—other than at *Songs of Praise*—were not prerequisites for the stage manager. Moving through a church, full of attention-seeking non-attendees at the regular Sunday morning service during a recording of *S. o. P.*—headphones on, clipboard in hand, talking back to the director like *you* were in charge—was great for nailing eye-contact, and possible sequels with daughters of the devout. They'd succumbed to three-line, parental whips, and dressed up for the gig . . . thereby demonstrating to God-slot viewers, that belief pulsed through the hearts and minds of the designated parish . . . *but would they come across?*

As a rule, the cameramen (and they were all men in those dark ages) did much better than the F.M.s; they had added mystique, bags of front, plus, they had the power of the big close-up.

Look away, dear, they're all nasty, corrupt television people—there's no future in it for you. You'll meet a nice accountant, one day. Look away!

Just another quick aside: it was Rudolf Kempe (above) who was responsible for breaking Sir Thomas Beecham's 'men only' credo at the RPO. Imagine what the founding father would have made of *Escada's* legs (or Sian Massey and her orange and yellow flag).

Now, spot the grammatical gaffs in this sentence:

"*Youzell have tae wait . . . the guitar strings have gone and went.*"

Despite my Scottish colleague's retreat into the vernacular— baffling as it was to the clean and polished in the good seats of the London auditorium at which Manitas de Plata was playing stunning flamenco guitar—the *Little Hands of Silver* had contrived to pop a G-string . . . *so there would be a delay.*
The recital was worth waiting for: de Plata is *"world class."*

I was a little harsh a moment ago on my pal Beggie; one thing he did do 'pretty well' was play guitar, but, like lots with gifts, he was a reluctant performer.

Mike, Ronnie and I were continuing with a 'wet' lunch in a cellar club, just off Shepherd's Bush Road in West London.
The big two were drawn there by the extended licensing hours afforded to members—a small price to pay.
My 'sponsoring' of the boss, after hours, meant many Brownie points.

Ron and Mike set a cracking pace, but for those of a more fragile constitution wishing to limit damage to brain cells (and one's oscillating current account), there was a decent little combo, tinkering away in a corner, to enjoy.

Fuelled by several too many, an aspiring drummer-boy asked if he could 'do a number' with the band. Drummers, the world over, are seldom shrinking violets—Keith Moon and Buddy Rich spring to mind. Most know which end of the bottle the sauce comes from, so any break, was welcomed . . . *no harm in it.*

What the new kid must have known, was *his* ability far out-weighed the incumbent's . . . over-staying his welcome would be a risk.

A risk? . . . Christ!

Cymbals and mic stands went flying as the humiliated resident drummer returned to claim his rightful place. Others joined in for the hell of it, Wild Western style.

The BBC trio checked for egress, but there were bodies everywhere; not good to be grabbed by the fuzz . . . less so 'at work.'

Va-*moose*.

(segue to Paddy *Feeny*, who used to present TELEVISION TOP OF THE FORM in his slippers—and not a lot of people knew *that*).

"*Right*" said the cheery inquisitor, armed with another batch of 'cinchy' Boswell Taylor questions ". . . let's move on to the picture round."

"*Sh-h-it!*"

. . . forgotten to put them out, hadn't I?

Incredulous, horrified expression, palms up, head-pointing like a demented wood-pecker to the table in front of me and the sealed brown envelopes containing those very pictures.

My colleague Paddy *Hughes* was on the case in a trice.

Once upon a time, "Pads" flew Phantoms very quickly, but kept blacking out at crucial times . . . like take-offs and landings. By kicking him out, the M.o.D. was spared a monumental bill (around £5m a pop for a showroom model), and the family Hughes, unimaginable grief.

Swiping the evidence from my frozen grasp, and with no regard for his own new-found reputation (*in the carelessness stakes, trashing a Phantom ranked considerably higher than getting 'in shot'*), he dropped to the floor and set off commando style—envelopes clenched firmly between his teeth—to talking-Paddy's desk.

In that moment, airman Hughes may just have saved my stuttering career.

The Mods and the Rockers differed from the clever-dick contestants on *TOP OF THE FORM* in that they'd o.d'd. on theory and were now hell bent on regular practice; that's not to say there weren't grammar school boys and girls amongst them.
The Mods were clean-cut scooter freaks—the Rockers were Angels . . . *'but Made in Britain, yeah?'*

Normally they'd meet by the seaside to knock the shit out of each other—Brighton, Hastings, Clacton and Margate being among their favourite spots for a day out. Stabbing, slashing, nutting, gouging were allowed, with bonus points for good clean breaks.

Ah, the English coast—can't be beat . . . if only the weather were better.

No volunteers from the community programme unit for this potential *Razzie*, and way too toxic for Esther 'no nicks' Rantzen's *That's Life* show; alternate-shot sentence construction, endless vox-popping in Shepherd's Bush market, and dogs with big teeth who could say "sausages," were cozier by half.

I can't come down too hard on Esther and her boys.
After a shocking family holiday on Menorca, I'd sought their help in retrieving some wedge from the travel company who'd dumped on us.

Wee Grant, our toddler, was asthmatic and our 'dream villa' had damp mattresses and something other than yoghurt living in the fridge.
We coped with the daily, sheer, drop down to the beach *('a stone's throw'*—no argument there) but when the ground transfer failed to materialise on the way home, it was time to act.

Amazing the power of the old BBC letterhead, and a Kierin Prendiville signature.

Esther (allegedly) was 'having it off' with the boss (*man alive!*), which was very 'non you' at the BBC; fine for we scruff in the trenches, but Wilcox and Rantzen were pillars.

'*No nicks*,' by the way—as in *sin panties*—came from a corroborated sighting in the BBC club, as her worthiness perched on a bar stool in a most un-lady-like pose; her breast-feeding at work was one thing . . . but please, Est . . . the pussy . . . we're having our lunch!
(she was a revelation on *I'm a Celebrity* . . . fair dos).

Back to maming business . . . at a hall, out in the sticks, some distance from the nearest emergency services.

As our wagons were counted out of their Acton base in London, on one of their more precarious missions, three of Ronnie P.'s finest prepared to boldy go where no man in his right mind would—even the SAS may have hesitated.

There's a word rhyming with 'canker'—to accompany a gesture irate drivers and opposing football fans have perfected—for our field producer.

He'd decided on a bridge-building exercise: "it might help."

How's that for underestimating a national blight?

All manner of contagion had rendered the stage manager's office a wilderness . . . Asian, African and American 'flus struck, simultaneously . . . cholera, malaria and syphilis were rife . . . periods—normally a 'woman thing'—crossed genders . . . sudden deaths in families . . . . unseemly cases of stage fright . . . dental appointments from nowhere . . . leaving the experienced, the stupid and a Boy Scout to cope.
In order, Terry Learner, me and Harry Coventry; happy to admit to the 'stupid' tag, but having spent a little time in Glasgow, I was aware of gang culture, without ever having the bottle (a poor choice), nor the need, to enlist.

Intrepid Ross Kemp would sooner be riding out of Sydney with *Notorious,* and, for all his bravery and good intent, 'Stevo' Irwin, the engaging (and ex) Australian crocodile hunter, might have had better odds on Batt reef.

Nervously clutching our triple X British Board of Film Censors' certificate, I awaited the arrival of the cast . . . *and waited . . . and waited* . . . much as *Flik* and the ants had in *A BUGS LIFE*, knowing that *Hopper* and co., were on their way.
Being punctual would have been pansy, and though the Mods weren't averse to *some* social graces, giving ground this early would be poor form.

It wasn't hard to distinguish the waspish hum of the *Lambrettas* from the predatorial roar of the *Matchlesses.*
The cacophony suggested that quite a few had decided to turn up.
(brown trouser time . . . Cuba revisited)

In one of his better moves, the 'wanker' had arranged access for the armies through separate doors (the way *out* might not be so orderly).

To the left, came the lightweight suits and polo-necks of the Mods, abandoning their US Army parkas in a heap, as they took up station; to the right, in jeans of course, winkle-picker shoes and an abundance of studs, were the Rockers.

"*Mingle with them boys, . . .*" came the command from old dopey-bollocks, playing with himself in the safety of the production truck . . .
. . ."*get a few stories together, and we'll record in a jiffy.*"

"*So which side are you from?*" proffered the worthy member of our volunteer force to a veritable giant in leathers, holding a chicken.
(which side? . . . this wasn't a fucking wedding . . . we could die here!).

As if to confirm their handprint in Rocker folklore, the big geezer pulled an egg from his *Levi's*, dropped it on the floor of the ring (*'hall'*), and without hesitation, his female companion went down on her knees (*surely not*) and licked it up, sealing it with a 'mucusy' French kiss.

Nice.

"*Could you do that again when we start recording?*"

Spare me . . . . my man Harry (the boy scout) <u>did</u> have the death wish;
I won't tell you what happened to the chicken.

The Mods were much more forthcoming.

A 'Malky' McDowell look-a-like peeled up his yellow polo-neck, on request, revealing a chest Doctor Frankenstein might have operated on *pissed* . . . dozens of times. The big 'zip' went from crotch to Adam's apple; the most recent incision was still leaking.

Well hard, and proud.

Prior to this session of *The Brains Trust*, we'd asked that all weaponry be left outside as frisking would be impractical for so few petrified stewards.

You got the feeling the moratorium option was not universally acclaimed—not that we were questioning anyone.

In the end, we got a few quotes, the odd stage-managed stunt, and miles of vacant *what the f—are we doing here when there's carnage to be done* kind of expressions from both sub-cultures.

Oh, and the rescue?

Harry—the 'Baden-Powellist'—felt the experiment was lacking spontaneity, so, using the trusted symbol of police control, law and order—the megaphone—he screeched at the assembly:

"*On behalf of BBC Television* (error), *would you boys and girls* (another) *mind getting together* (<u>what</u>!!!) *in the middle of the hall so we can get this show on the road.*"

I believe I saved Harry's life that night.

Mods 0   Rockers 0
. . . shame really, as therein lay some very unusual talents.

Ronnie Pantlin's empire went the way of all things imperial, down the tubes (hatch); the intrepid rear-gunner gave King, Queen and country his best shots, and kept his Lancaster crew's spirits up, high over Dresden.

We certainly enjoyed him.

'Chocks away, "Ronaldo."'

". . . Who Cares Who's Third"

"Sport and Leisure, please . . . ."

Big Brian Barnes's father-in-law, Herbert Gustavus Max Faulkner, got 300 quid for winning The Open Championship at Royal Portrush in 1951 (the only time it's been played outside Britain), but do you know who came third?

Save yourselves . . . . I'll tell you: it was Charlie Ward from Little Aston (had to search for that one—Antonio Cerda from Argentina ran-up); Percy Alliss's 20 year old son Peter (*ich bin Berliner*) missed the cut.

Back in the tome, I tried to prise the gold medallist in the women's 3K in Los Angeles from your memories; in the protracted aftermath of the Decker/Budd distraction, Romania's Maria Puica—one of the pre-race favourites—became Olympic champ, with Zola's team-mate (if not *country*woman, exactly) Wendy Sly, second.
How much do you care—unless you're related, a pal or a native—that Lyn Williams of Canada was 3rd?

Mary Teresa Decker-Slaney-Tabb—currently, as far as I can take her genealogy—lost a bundle of dollars, and quite a few fans, with her histrionics at the Coliseum, yet 16 years on she was still active, trying, but not making, the US team for Sydney—*could she run or what?*.

Now, here's an easy one for you:

"Hemery takes the gold . . . . *who cares who's third*"

Not so much a question, more a partial jingoistic haemhorrage (*and, I contend, a cracking good title for a book that's bound to do well*).

It wasn't a *COLEMANBALLS* as such, but it caused a stir; nor did Gerhard Hennige from West Germany, who was second, get a mention for some time. Just seeing a Boston, Mass., alumni (out of St Catherine's, Oxford), in a GBR vest, winning gold (in 48.12—a N.W.R) in the rarified atmosphere of Mexico City was to concentrate even the most agile of minds, singularly, but it probably made Mrs. John Sherwood blanch and rage (they do blanching and raging particularly well in Yorkshire).

She—long jumping Shelia Parkin—and *he*—hurdling John Sherwood—had sworn to put their differences on hold and married the year before.

'68 had been a lousy one for Martin Luther King, Bobby Kennedy, and thousands upon thousands in Vietnam, but here was I, six years out of school—the new recruit on the BBC videotape team—working on the Olympics, and not in any way anxious for my ex-form mates fretting over thirds and re-sits at uni.

None of our women had won on the track (or in the field) at an Olympics, until 1964 (in Tokyo) when Britain's blonde bombshell—sculling Sid Rand's missus—No. 59 (*her* competition number)—flew across our screens (in black and white) and landed a world record long jump (22ft 2¼), much to the particular delight of Hilda and Eric Bignal; doubtful if the 'live' signal (by satellite—for the first time) was available in the tiny cathedral city of Wells, Somerset, home to Wells City FC funnily enough.
(Sheila P. made the final but didn't get anywhere near a gong).
In the second week, Mary's room-mate Ann Packer (fiancée of British team captain Robbie Brightwell) put the other British 'omission' right by winning the 800 metres—*"quite remarkable"* (a Coleman catchphrase).

Mrs. Rand won *Sports Personality of the Year* in 1964 (the third dame in a row, succeeding Anita Lonsborough and Dorothy Hyman), *and guess who was 3rd?*—Why, the imminent bride-to-be Miss. P., *of course.*

Some supplementals from that night in Shepherd's Bush Theatre: it was Nesta Bough's Frank's first crack at introducing the show, which Polly Dimmock (née Elwes)'s old man Peter had hosted for a decade, and it was he who introduced Prince Charles's great uncle Dickie (Mountbatten) to present the trophy to Mary; no extra points for knowing that Cliff Morgan of Wales edited the show (in black and white), and that Fred Trueman—"the greatest living Yorkshireman" according to Harold Wilson—had come 4th in the postal vote (Neil Hawke of Australia being his 300th Test victim at the Oval in August—caught Colin Cowdrey for 14; Ashes lost).

But for Irina Press—and feckless, gender policing—Mrs. Rand might have won the pentathlon too in '64; we boys all fancied her (Mary) . . . and we were not alone (*quite remarkable,* indeed).

Unless the I.O.C. relax their rules on hermaphrodites, and easy-to-swallow male hormone becomes available on the National Health, we won't see the likes of 'the Press brothers' again; they left 'the west behind' alright, with gold medals and world records for all to savour 'back in the USSR'. Irina Natanovna and Tamara Natanovna had been Bats at their Mitvahs but—according to reliable sources . . . *allegedly . . . it's claimed . . . very probably*—they were nearer to being Bars in the field.

Amidst a glut of world records and political protest in Mexico, the jumpers again caught the attention . . . for the right reasons: Mrs. Sherwood won silver in the long jump (to add to Lilian Board's in the 400 flat) but—at roughly two and a half thousand metres up from the ocean's surface (between tides)—it was Dick Fosbury (on his back) and Bob Beamon (feet first) who brought sea change to the worlds of high and long jumping in Mexico City—'attatood' at altitude

Squash-playing fitness fanatic, Jonah Barrington, 'juicy' Brian Jacks (*loved* his oranges) and Hemery—the flaxen-haired, golden boy—brought signature precision and dedication . . . professionalism, almost . . . to *Superstars,* when all that running and jumping for fun nonsense stopped (in the nick of time for David, as Edwin Moses was beginning to get the hang of it; *his* winning, nine year 'streak' lasted just the 122 consecutive races—not the greatest dynasty in which to be fancying oneself as a one-lap hurdler).
My former boss on the Ladies European (golf) Tour—Scottish all-comers champion and all-round good egg, Mark Fulton—was a sub-53 second man over the lower barriers (*says he can still remember the whiff of Edwin's after-shave*).

The idea for *Superstars* came from an American figure skater, Dick Button* (the first male to land a triple loop in competition), who won Olympic golds at consecutive Games after the Second World War.
In the first of those—in Switzerland—the skating was held outdoors, and despite a thaw, all three events were completed . . . *and we got a big B* (for bronze).
Don't be misled by the Germanic sounding name (or the spelling of 'misled' which confused many in primary), our medallist was as British as Hemery.
Bronze, in ladies singles figure skating: Jeanette Altwegg (born in India, raised in Liverpool)—silver: war-torn Eva Pawlik (later of the Austrian Broadcasting Corporation . . . and one or two forgettable movies)—gold: Barbara Ann Scott "Canada" (the first woman/girl 13, *Dick, to land a double lutz in competition, six years previously).

Here's another corker:
Who, in 1904, won the last Olympic gold medal for golf?
Why, George Seymour Lyon of Canada, no less; bit of a sporting smart arse was our George, having been good at bloody everything . . . . once scoring 238 not out for his club cricket side in Ontario . . . winning the Canadian Amateur golf title 8 times, and the Olympic final 3&2 in St. Louis.

Altwegg was GBR's only winner at the next Winter Games, in Norway; and to labour a point to *Viva la Vida*, the dominant French champion, Jacqueline de Bief was 3rd.
P.S. David Coleman would have been 22, and already editor of *The County Press* newspaper in Cheshire.

P.P.S. (partially quoting Brian Clough) whoever thought of *Celebrity Dancing on Ice* "needs shooting!"

Nearly half a century later, in that very Bislett stadium where the Olympic flame had burned those twelve threateningly mild days in February 1952, tell-tale cracks were beginning to appear in the great commentator's armory.
Back at Television Centre in London we were about to transmit the annual IAAF meet from Oslo; along with similar events in Rome, Zurich, Monaco, Brussels, Paris and Berlin, they'd become known as 'golden meets' in a league of the same currency—big money spinners for professional athletes (and the occasional cheat).
Famously (for those lucky enough to get the nod), Norwegian promoter Arne "with the straw hat" Haukvik would hold a strawberry party for the competitors in his back garden (free berries, unlike at London SW19).

In order to get ahead, we asked that David send down his sound-only, opening link as a 'wildtrack'—as they say in the trade—prior to the start of the cash flow.

What a fucking drama that turned out to be.

'Welcome to Islo and the Boslett Games' . . . . the first of several tongue-tied conundrums.
Exasperated, running out of prep time and risking all that I'd been building towards, I suggested he throw a bunch of syllables at us and we'd join them up later: *attack* was always best with D.C.

The late (defamation, therefore, not being an issue) Alan Weeks whose wife, Jane Huckle, had been an ice skater . . . *"quite remarkable"* . . . was thick with Coleman . . . *so quickly*, another from the record books.

I was sat next to 'whispering Al' as he commentated a world championship swimming final in Yugoslavia ('whispering' Ted Lowe just talked *quietly* for added drama . . . should a frame-risking, three-cushion snooker-escape be required . . . or, with pink and black remaining, a 'live' 147 be on).

In a flurry of arms, like an orca pod out to baby seal-lunch, the winner's touch lit up 'lane 5' on the big electronic scoreboard:

"*(Shamu) wins, and I guess Hammy* (Hamilton Bland, co-commentator) *in a pretty good time?* (Bland remonstrates in pantomime fashion, tapping his stop-watch) . . . *er, in fact his personal best* (tapping is now slapping, plus muted cussing) . . . *and a . . . championship record* (face and arms are thrown skywards in despair) . . . *no, it's a new <u>WORLD</u> RECORD!* (paramedics rush to Bland).
Not as easy as it sounds, this commentary malarkey.

Daley Thompson might view *Superstars* as a poor man's decathlon, but Hemery and co., took it very seriously; the audience figures proved it a popular format. Compared to cricket's Duckworth Lewis system, the handicapping for the gym tests—at which judoka Jacks excelled—required more than a working knowledge of parametrics.

One who took full advantage—and of many other half-openings in life—was the vaultingly ambitious (and hugely successful at everything he touched . . . from forelock to skeets of clay) was Royalist supreme, dead-eyed Jackie Stewart . . . or "wee Jackie" as he was known to all but Helen, his lady wife.
The net result was a triumph for the racing drivers: skill, timing, strength and endurance, in exact proportions. Jody Schekter also did pretty well, so no fluke that the G-force F1 brigade were to be reckoned with on the multifarious test track.

An 'unworthy' of mention—O.J. Simpson—won an American version of the show, but when soccer 'star' Brian Budd (*who?*) made it three-in-a—row, he was asked to leave (*showing off, clearly*). Ex-pole vaulter, Brian Hooper'man'—a Superstar across Europe, way back then—was still up for it aged 50, when the call came for more, in 2003 (that's not showing off . . . *that's daft*; you'll be telling me next that four-time Olympic champion Al Oerter would throw a personal best in the discus at 43, and that 59 year old Tom Watson would nearly win another Open at Turnberry, Scotland . . . *get real, people*).

Lesley Crichton, the landlady's daughter during my spell on the Scottish newspaper, was a driver you'd not be nervous to sit with: she'd do amazing things in her Dad's red Humber were he unconscious with the drink, in the back
Not so, the poor lass assigned to take 'The Flying Scot' to a recording of *Superstars* at Crystal Palace.

Our chauffeuse was to be pitied rather than pilloried.
She confided, anxiously, that her framed, pink slip ('*Pass*') had only recently been mounted on her kitchen wall, and now here she was—at green minus 3 or so—courteously awaiting the three-time World Formula1 Champion (*bricking it*, she was).
With a nervous giggle . . . offering to let Jackie drive . . . ha, ha, ha . . . we leapt away (*oops!*—manual shift); I suppressed a titter, as unfit, she was not.

When Ron Dennis offered my petrol-head pal, Murray Walker, a spin round Silverstone in a pukka McLaren bullet, he was like a pig in poop; BBC *Sportsnight* crews (and 'The Shunt') were there to bear witness.

Stalled the bugger, didn't he?
That's one small stall for a man . . . . one giant finger from the ladies.

(more's the pity Neil Armstrong hadn't run his lunar touchdown speech by his module mate . . . still, it's *nearly* a great quote.

"*I felt a lump in my f(th)roat as the ball went in*"
. . . now that (from Venables) is clear thinking.

There'd been a 'knobby do' in London town—a penguin suit and far too much foundation affair—for the celebrated and their proxies. As the free grape took effect, my colleague waded in with an ice-breaker, asking his immediate dinner companion—a distinguished man of some 45 summers—what his 'line of work' was (obviously having only read his *own* name on the seating plan). The mystery man thought for a second, turned his inquistor's gaze to the curtain-less window (how fortunate) and pointed to the (full) Moon (*some guys, eh?*):
'See that old fellow?
'Been there!
'Buzz Aldrin . . . nice talkin' witcha.'
The clanger had landed . . . and he wouldn't be the first.

There's a doubting Thomas in most of us: in the absence of DNA from the Turin shroud or CCTV at Joseph's sepulcher, I'll never be 100% behind the gospels and that second coming, but surely it's irrelevant where those digital-quality pictures of Neil and Buzz originated—they'd been to the Moon . . . they brought rocks back to prove it.

Cold Play—the band—came faces-to-faces with Melvyn 'Gooner' Bragg recently, in one of those irritating pieces which allowed for only snatches of my favourite tracks, midst the crack and meaningful cutaways of his grinning Lordship.

Chris Martin recounted a dinner his Dad had gone to.

Having given the weather—*et les hors d'oeuvres*—a seeing to, up next was family:
'And what do your sons do, Mr. Martin?'
'One's a banker, the other's a rock star,' said Dad
"Really . . . which bank?"

Ultimately, the Mods and Rockers of the '60s would give way to hippies and skinheads: entire wardrobes had to be made-over.
No-one, not even Dr. King would know for sure where Black Power was heading . . . a *black* President by 2009? . . . *Dream on, Doc*; the Rev. Jesse Jackson's chances were about as good as Calvin Peete's—the African American golfer who once tied 3rd in the USPGA.
Tiger blew it altogether . . . *or someone did* . . . but where does it say cunnilingus is undemocratic in the Bill of Rights . . . or the Rules of Golf?

Tommie Smith (gold) and John Carlos (bronze) stood on the medal rostrum in Mexico, shoeless, in long black hose, heads bowed, their black-gloved fists raised defiantly, symbolising something bigger than either could have imagined at the time. Medal ceremonies came at us 'loggers' thick and fast, but this one would need a star or two in the margins; deep in the bowels of TVC, thousands of miles away, my priorities were the 'out-words' and duration of the 200 metres package.
Smith's leading role had taken a fraction under 20 seconds—the presentation was about to 'shake up the world' . . . again.
Even Australia's Peter Norman—white as 'The Shark' himself—who'd split the American flyers, joined in with his O.P.H.R (Olympic Project for Human Rights) badge (Smith was a founding member of the movement).

The repercussions hit far and wide: crusty I.O.C. President Avery Brundage ordered the sprinters to be suspended from the U.S. team and kicked out of the Olympic village.
Deaths threats would follow, but massive support too, for their conviction . . . and talent.

James Peters was the first black man to play rugby for England (against Scotland in 1904: we lost), nor were there many black faces around in BBC sports department when I came South with my accent.
The management was in a time warp: the only P.C. they appreciated was *Dixon of Dock Green*, and he was rapidly becoming anachronistic.
(Norwell Roberts would become London's first black 'copper' in 1967).

Four decades on, social adjustments have been made; correct boxes haven't just been ticked, they've been filled in: blacks, whites, coloureds, Scotspersons, catholics, proddies, muslims, hindus, atheists, agnostics, lezzers, homos, heteros, undeclared druggies and boozers—many with smashing ideas and sound opinions—have served to level Lord John Reith's playing field at last.

It's 2012, and lesbians are 'sick'; should they come over moody and menstrual, the world's great sports circuits and tours would implode, flying up their collective orifices in a seepage of essential body fluids—*then where would we be for light relief on a dull night on telly?*

On the subject of omissions/irate women/superstars/and all blacks, anyone caring a jot about rugby, will remember, or at least should have seen highlights by now of *The Barbarians v. New Zealand* match at Cardiff Arms Park in 1973 . . . if not, put this down, go on *You Tube* or order a copy of the 'revised' version from *Amazon*—you won't find *my* name on the production credits, but "I was there" in spirit (with Max Boyce & Co).

Phil Bennett's twinkled-toed, triple side-step *"oh, that's brilliant"* . . . J.P.R. Williams resisting a forearm smash from namesake Bryan to keep the move alive . . . John Dawes (on the wrong camera, in my view) *"what a dummy"* ghosting past his markers . . . . uncapped *"David, Tom David"* at his shoulder, linking with countryman Derrick Quinnell . . .

. . . then (continued Morgan the Organ on commentary):
"This is Gareth Edwards . . ." as Cardiff's pocket battleship burst through Grant Batty's despairing tackle; the pugnacious ginger Tom—who'd later have the gall to square up to Goliath (*"David, Tom David"*) in the black and white hoops—had made his way, blisteringly, from the opposite wing.
"A dramatic start . . . what a score!"
. . . followed by:
"Oh, that fellow Edwards."

At one stage, England hooker John Pullin got in the way of this free-spirited *Welsh* theme (John Bevan's time was to come).

I was editing the match highlights for *Rugby Special* later that evening . . . make that <u>extra</u> special. My fellow production assistant, Paul Lang and I had a half each—I, the first, with that fabulous opening moment, but really the whole thing was one long, priceless highlight: simply the best rugby match you could ever imagine.

(I'm getting in a lather thinking about it)
Not long to go before transmission, Paul, looking appositely green about his Irish gills, stood frozen in the doorway of my channel: his part was a minute too long . . . somehow, he'd cocked up his timings . . . *could I lose a minute from my half?*
"Not a problem," says I (*big Dick*).

I scanned my detailed log sheets and found a line-out on the far side of the pitch, just inside the metric '22,' and another, almost in the same place, one minute later.
That'll do nicely.
"Cut <u>there</u>, please" I said, unhesitatingly, to my videotape editor . . .
"and come back in . . . <u>there</u>," pointing to a series of numbers on my clipboard.

Neil Pittaway's razor blade sliced through the delicate brown tape with the kind of conviction and accuracy the Queen of Scots could have done with; the deleted minute slithered on the floor.

Moments later, the join had been made good . . . no Scot was injured . . . *yet*. Marking the re-edited tape with a big 'Q' (for cue-point) in white chinagraph pencil, ten seconds back from the first usable picture, and Cliffie's recorded introductory words, we were ready to go.

The mercurial Morgan had been the first star in my firmament since arriving from God's country with my little bag on a stick. The English were still banging on about '66, so by biding my time for a couple of years before making a transfer request to BBC Sport in London, some of the heat would be taken out of the reception.
I'd been down on what they described as 'attachments' before, but, until now, hadn't managed to nail down anything stable enough for the RBS . . . long term.

They described me—to my face—as an acting, assistant stage manager, and paid me accordingly; more of an assist towards my rent than mortgage fodder, still, to sit next to such a hero in the commentary box was a huge post-pubescent turn-on.
I played at stand-off for my school and, risking the stake, took Richard Sharp as my role model . . . a Cornishman, but one with silky running skills, ball in both hands, never one to get tangled up in all that violent, macho behaviour around the scrums—much as Barry John, 'little Benny,' Bob Burgess (of those 7th All Blacks) and John Rutherford of Selkirk and Scotland all managed to do so appealingly.

"You are no good to me, Philips, lying under sixteen forwards . . . stay on your feet," Brigadier Alston, our coach in the Colts would command.
Bearing only a couple of facial scars (one from a golfing mis-hit, the other from a brush with the rockery in my grandparents' garden) and harbouring fanciful intent towards Claudia Cardinale and/or Sophia Loren (depending on *their* availability), I obeyed.
The American contenders for my virginity were: Natalie Wood, whose classy cleavage I should have mentioned earlier, Connie Stevens (great cupids), Debbie Reynolds (*l*-oved her) and (big breaths) swimming actress, Esther Williams—the older woman—just right for a dithering Piscean. Marilyn was spoken for, over and over, and Jayne Mansfield—the prodigious, tissue-filler—had her hands full with boyfriend Micky Hargitay, who out-chested her by 11" (. . . then I'd wake up in a mess).
Excellent quip attributed to Jayne 'the Bomb' at a Mae West revue; having watched Hargitay's muscles perform, she was asked what she was having for dinner: '*Steak, and the man on the left.*'

Our school—Morrison's Academy in Crieff—was pretty tasty in the rugby department, despite having no formal coaching; our arch rivals—Dollar Academy . . . just up the road—were guided by 'gentleman' Adam Robson, many times capped at wing forward for Scotland.
Robson, an author and artist of some repute, born in the Borders (where selectors were often to be seen skulking), spent much of his time in the windy wastes of the Shetland Isles, from whence his Mama came, and *to* whence we Morrisonians would gladly have consigned him.

Nairn McEwan, Lewis Dick and Simon Taylor (who made Lion status) got to wear the blue (and occasional white) of Scotland, from my *alma mater*; having come a less than robust 2nd in a schoolboys' trial, I reverted to those other kinds of dreams.

My brother played on the wing at school, and dashed nippy he was for a long, skinny drink-of-water, yet it was a shot of C.I. Morgan—lord of the stand-offs—cut from the front cover of *World Sports,* that adorned his bedroom wall (*. . . ball tucked under one arm, cheeks puffed, eyes fixed, sensing a dummy coming on, quick as you like . . . lovely*).

Others in the gallery were Lawrie Reilly of Hibernian and Scotland (of the fabled Smith, Johnstone, Reilly, Turnbull and Ormond forward line, for club and country); England and Bolton Wanderers' 'Lion of Vienna,' Nat Lofthouse, caught in mid-strike on Harry Gregg in the 1958 Cup Final; Geoff Duke (on *Norton* and *Gilera*) and—more stylishly—Bob McIntyre (the first man to lap the Isle of Man at 100m.ph. in the Senior TT) representing the bikers, one of which *he* (my sibling) would become, in a strictly social sense . . . *it got him to the burd's house, rapido.*

Cliff was never huge on research; I guess when you've done what he had, finding out about the donkey at tight head for Ebww Vale (*no offence lads, any of you surviving former incumbents . . . I'm comparatively little*), wasn't huge on his list of 'must-dos.' Being Welsh, and a bit of an old tart (in thespian parlance), his real gift was for the prosaic: Dylan Thomas, with a dash of Burton gravitas, on very special legs . . . bandy as a cowpoke's.

He was, is, ever shalt be, world without blood replacements, a diamond geezer . . . as you'd *never* hear said in the Rhonnda . . . and a clue to his magnanimity was heading my way, one wintry Saturday on *Rugby Special*: it was tipping down, and by the time my big moment was upon us, every shirt, sock, short and hair-do looked the same.

There was a break inside the Bath '25' (*told you it was a while back*—David Vine was our anchorman), ending with Richmond's stand-off (*see . . . ages ago*) diving over for a three-pointer (*blimey*).

Brian Bennett (no relation of Llanelli's Phil), the drummer in *The Shadows* (Cliff's band—*RICHARD! . . . keep up*) wrote the theme tune for *Special* ('*Special,*' like '*Strictly*' *. . . hate that*); now you'll know, if quizzed at *Trivial*.

Looking to ingratiate myself with the well-connected wizard (not only would he go on to head-up BBC Outside Broadcasts and become Royal Liaison Officer, but his best mate was 'Mr. Baked Beans' himself, Tony O'Reilly of Ireland . . . of the British Lions . . . of the World, in truth), I thrust my finger at the No. 10 on the team sheets—*the Bath No 10!*

Their names were as different as Catt and Dallaglio, so, with a mental shimmy sending me reeling for the sick-bag, the bow-legged outside-half called on his stock '*what a score by the big man*' bale-out phrase.

He squeezed my jellied knee, and winked.

I would sooner have been at the base of the next ruck (*well, maybe not that drastic*).

'The Organ' was forever doing charitable deeds, and to my knowledge—unlike Clinton, Thatcher and Tony Gubba (in dramatic, descending order)—never took a shilling for his personal appearances.

Next to Thomas the poet (and Mrs. Michael Douglas), Mervyn Davies is high among Swansea's best kent faces.
'The Swerve' was teetering on the brink, after one kick to the head too many, so when Cliff said he was going to visit at the University Hospital of Wales, I asked if we could take a film crew along.
It hosed down (and Cliff talked) the whole way from London to Cardiff.

Not really knowing what to expect, we were shocked to see the big No.8 swathed in bandages where his solitary trademark sweatband would have been, his Zapata 'tache barely visible through the mask. He couldn't say much . . . . he didn't have to; Cliff kept everyone entertained—surgeons, doctors, nurses, orderlies, receptionists and, most importantly, big Merv, who duly recovered from an inter-cranial haemorrhage, but would never play again.
Under Capt'n Davies, Wales seldom lost, in fact very few sides from Swansea to the Lions and back, did.

Argentina, 1978: we were short of vital supplies and equipment; word went back to Blighty.
The International Broadcast Centre in Buenos Aires was a forbidding place, not that the folk weren't friendly to the cosmopolitan masses who'd flooded their capital for football's World Cup, but the military were in charge, and several of the armed and unpredictable were stationed, strategically, about the building.
It wasn't one of our sound supervisor's better calls to pipe Elaine Page's *'Don't Cry for Me Argentina'* through the PA system at our pre-fabricated suite of offices; it seemed to make 'the uniforms' very restless.

I felt a tap on my shoulder: a gaucho-in-fatigues poked at my BBC pin badge; the little trinkets were legal tender for all kinds of favours amongst broadcasters, and sought-after souvenirs everywhere you went (*you could probably get laid for one . . . but we were there to work*).
I say the soldier 'tapped' me on the shoulder . . . . what I didn't say was that he used the barrel of his semi-automatic rifle for that purpose, grinning in a '*do-as-I-say-asshole—or I'll-blow—your pale-faced—mother-f—g head off*' sort of a way (in Spanish).
I shook my *p.f.m.f.* head in English (not present), and thought of Scotland (qualified: *beauties!*).

"No more left mate."

Absolutely lost on the old boy.

The tapping and poking, next time, was firmer . . . the smile— gone, *nada*.

I unpinned my only remaining badge and handed it over; off he went, content as an Argentinian butcher's dog . . . and they *love* their meat out there.

Packed in the consignment Cliff had agreed to accompany from London, were more badges, in a bloody great wooden box full of spares for cameras and recording machines and things—a Red Cross parcel for desperate engineers.
There were 'ciggies' and 'hooch'—no doubt bought from his own pocket and for which, he would not seek recompense.

Most of the bags from the London flight had been re-claimed.
Through the glass wall I spotted a lone figure, appearing slightly worse for the wear; he teetered a while, then sat, peering into the carousel for sight of his cargo.
Suddenly, he was up and darting away (I think off the *right* foot), grabbing at the twine binding our vitals. Rather than pull it from the conveyor, he yelped, dived onto the moving belt and disappeared through the rubberised flaps, as if Colin Meads had him by the throat.
Moments later he emerged, perched on top of the box—*The Cat in the Hat*—smoking a fag.
The soldiers had to laugh.
A senior BBC executive breaking the mould—bit like Dyke and Attenborough . . . rare.

The National stadium in Cardiff—City of Arcades, the fort on the Taff, where the sun shines rightly on Cliff and Gareth's bike-racks—is 'The Baa-Baas' spiritual home.
A try was now worth 4 points, so you'll appreciate that to see the score jump that precise amount, without any discernable line-crossing, came as a bit of a shock.

"Holy Mary Mother of God, Langers, I've left out a try!"
(the 'home' team's 3rd)

After the show had gone off air, Paul peeled me, paralysed, from the wall of the edit suite and dragged me to the bar, to meet up with our Executive Producer, Alan Mouncer.

"Mounce," in my opinion, was the best outside broadcast director of his, or any other's time: he had an uncanny knack . . . Marty Feldman eyes—not to look at, but for their ability to see in all directions, simultaneously (Mr. Lu at Birkdale, excepted) . . . and a flamboyant dress sense.
Michael Flatley was asked how, as an American, he'd managed to win over the troupe of sceptical Irish dancers assembled for the first *Riverdance* production: he replied by *showing* them—much as Douglas Bader (legs or no legs) had done when his flying

ability was called into question. The sceptics had never seen dancing (nor flying) like it.

I was never party to a Mouncer shasse or lockstep, but his vision, his ability to scan a 'live' scene and direct his cameras—sometimes thirty or more—to precisely the point of interest, was legendary. Listening to what was being said on commentary was paramount, and often as not, he prompted it—a genius . . . like Morgan, and Flatley, and Feldman.

Behind shut the postern, the lights sank to rest,
And into the midnight we gallop'd abreast.

The *"we"* were three Belgian 'despatch' riders—Dirck, Joris and the narrator of Robert Browning's seemingly meaningless poem—as they set off from Ghent, at moonset, to ride, hell for leather, across the kingdom, apparently with some cracking news for the folks of Aix . . . though no one has been able to find out what it was: very probably, nothing other than a good excuse for writing a poem about road testing horses—a 19th century spin on a *Top Gear* feature.
On the way, two of them dropped dead, presumably leaving Dirck (Hammond) and Joris (May) stranded in the night, while the rhymer (Clarkson) and Roland—his one-break-horse-power, wine drinking steed—galloped on.

Our news—awaiting Alan Mouncer's return from the Horse of the Year show at Wembley (one of his other jobs) to White City, and the bar at Television Centre—was very real . . . *and very bad indeed.*

Show jumping had always been a huge part of sports department's portfolio, from the days of Harry Llewellyn and *Foxhunter*, to David Broome and practically anything he chose to throw a leg over.
Disregard the innuendo for now; concentrate on Anneli Drummond-Hay, a mounted version of Grace Jones (*are you forming a picture?*).
She wasn't black, and, as far as I know, didn't sing much, but she was tall, straight and sexy in an upper crust, 'horsey' sort of way: like Ms. Jones, she didn't do *shy*.

I was trailing David Coleman round the collecting ring at Wembley Pool, picking up interviews for *Sportsnight*.
The purple drapes separating the warm-up ring from the main arena were pulled back, and there—back lit and magnificent, astride her gleaming, steaming, red nostril-flaring steed *Xanthos*—was A.D-H.

"*Quick, Philipo, the mic*" barked Coleman, speeding towards the towering animal.

"Sweating up a bit, Annie, isn't he?" the typically aggressive, if slightly familiar interrogation began.

It wasn't a long interview, but it was 'live.'

"You'd be too, David darling, had you had the good fortune of being between my thighs for the last three minutes."

There was a stirring in the Whitehouse family's front room.

Alan Mouncer (1929-1997) was as colourful an individual as you might wish to find; his bigamistic inclinations brought an armed father to his door on one tricky occasion—*how grateful am I that he was able to disarm* (as in charm) *the shootist?*
"Mounce" was rogue and maverick, and brilliant as both; knobbing it with the horsey elite (and Stephen Hadley) at chateau Bunn in Sussex—overlooking the All England course, the self-appointed 'home' of British show jumping—was a plan coming together; by Derby day, he had them eating metaphoric carrot.
A bolt hole, in the east wing of the big hoose, for himself and Linda—the legitimate, unmarried daughter of the irate parent above—was icing.

Eddie Waring knew his beloved rugby league inside out, and for a non-participant "Mounce" could talk-the-equestrian-talk; be it a pint of bitter at the Queen's Hotel in Leeds for Ed, or *ze cointreau* by an open fire at Bunn manor for Al, the wild ambition was palpable: make television work, take it to the limits of your talents, and see if it doesn't lead to success for all. Neither was cut out for accountability, but north and south of the class divide, their passion was irresistible, their contributions immeasurable.

Harvey Smith embodied both cultures— *'Heathcliff on horseback.'*
His hunting pink didn't fit like Anneli's shapely black number, but set 'em up anywhere . . . in Aachen, München, Bradford or Bingley, and be prepared for fireworks . . . and very few jumping, or time, faults

Imagine the great Scouse philander, W.M. Rooney, crashing in the winner against Arsenal in extra-time (when Sir Alex is at his best), then sweeping past his exultant, masticating boss with a 'wanker' gesture (a long-time favourite among off-duty priests at Parkhead on derby day). The only possible explanation would be that wayward Wayne was finally ready for a crack at the pros of Madrid and Colleen had grown bored of his excuses.

Harvey Smith's tale was similarly flawed.

Smith snr., would win the prestigious Hickstead Derby *seven* times altogether.

Mouncer was directing, as usual, in 1971.
The story goes that Harvey, who'd won for the first time the previous year on *Mattie Brown*, hadn't brought the pot back when he came to defend; *he* said he'd forgotten it . . . Bunn didn't buy it . . . fur flew.
Was he so arrogant to believe that he'd win again and hadn't bothered? The boss's view in a nut-shell.
The two heavyweights would bitch about prize money, stabling fees, and the price of fish, but this was something else.

With no faults to spare, *Mattie* cleared the final spread to bag successive Derbys, the trophy, sash and that irritating bridle rosette.

But *"hold . . . wait one."*

As the vast crowd applauded horse and rider, Smith—retaining control with his right hand—looked up and sent a swift 'V' (presumably for 'fuck you') sign with his left, in the direction of Dougie B.'s box.
Raymond Brooks-Ward, commentating, laughed nervously:
"I don't know what that sign meant . . ."
(*we* did—and so, of course, did he).

Stand-off: the establishment versus the workers, a precursor to Scargill v Heath in '74: 'Grocer' Heath lost that one, but at Hickstead, 'Lord' Bunn dug in for conservatism and common decency
Insulted or miffed, he came over all unnecessary: Harvey's cheque was stopped . . . Bunn 'clyped' to the beak at B.S.J.A.H.Q . . . *"disgusting behavior"* he reported . . . Harvey appealed . . . Harvey was re-instated . . . Harvey won.

We thought it a riot, a tape that would get played and played—which we did, and has.

"Mary Whitehouse holding for you, Alan . . ."

One of the ground level cameras, positioned by the last element of the final treble, began waving around, violently.

A placid operator normally, Mouncer let rip.
His bollockings were preceded by a sustained inhalation through the nose, as if hoovering up a line
(bigamy, prodigality . . . fine, but he was my mentor: *I won't hear another slanderous word or see libel written*).

Sure he could, and did, splash the BBC's cash; what with tight-fisted licence holders regularly moaning about paying the price of a daily paper for a service that was second to none, worldwide (with the wireless thrown in), you couldn't appear to be spending big or recklessly.

Our office at the 'Weiskopf' Open, at Troon in '73, was a caravan, parked on the edge of the 16th fairway, an *'oops, mind your head'* number to get in to, and once there, a warm g. & t. in a paper cup was the best 'honoured guests' could expect.
"Mounce," typically, was for booking a hospitality suite in the Marine Hotel, smack by the links, where he'd been invited to stay for the duration of the Championship by its perspicacious manager.
A second twin was made available which I offered to "Slim" (Wilkinson), my boss, or, should he defer to the talent, little Harry Carpenter, say—but they turned it down, and as no other taker forthcame, yours truly moved in.

Wilkinson derided us for being 'disloyal and divisive.' I was ordered to 'Coventry' with big Al, while the rest of the production crew settled into rented billets, miles from Royal Troon; their loss. Our quarters were luxurious and the isolation, splendid, *thank you very much*—we were able to cope.

"What the f . . . are you doing 14?!" . . . Mouncer exhaled from the control truck at Hickstead.

"A dog just hit me on the head, Mounce!"

Naturally, he—"14"—had a name, but there were two dozen or more of them, surrounding the uprights, water-jump, oxers, Devil's Dyke and the signature Derby Bank with its 10ft drop and rapid re-collection, so "14"—with 3 x "Petes" and 4 x "Johns" on the crew—was deemed a not unreasonable soubriquet for the cameraperson.

The offending canine had slipped through the bars of the box above . . . *or was it kicked, Cruella?'*

Magnanimously, "14" was exonerated at cocktails . . . as I would be over the missing try (*I'll get to the exorcist, one day*).
The dog, a slightly squatter dachshund than hitherto, was returned shaken and visibly stirred, to an owner wasted beyond caring . . . . or remembrance.

Great moment in *A Touch of Class* when George Segal (*Steve Blackburn*) is questioned as to the whereabouts of the family pooch, which he claimed he'd lost on a walk . . . when <u>he</u> knew, and <u>we</u> knew, and even the mutt knew, he'd been bonking (in a manner

of role playing) the future Member of Parliament for Hampstead and Highgate, "Mr. Deputy Speaker"—a post-shag-euphoria memory lapse.
Ms. Jackson (*Vicky Alessio*) got an Oscar for her trouble:
'My God, my one chance to be raped, and you can't get your bloody trousers off!'
(you need to watch it).

Sports department's meaningful programme reviews were done in 'The Club'—a sort of in-house feeder facility for The Priory.

"*Forget it, J.P.,*" Mouncer said, way back at that impromptu *Rugby Special* post-mortem . . . "*have a drink; it's not like you were trying to make a mistake.*"

No, I wasn't, and I'd have been fine had Paul not cocked-up, but we kept our team counsel.

A few weeks past . . . no more had been said or read.

Phew!

We repaired the damage by slotting in the try from a back-up recording, sure in the knowledge that this match was going to have grooves in it by the number of plays it would get over the years.
It's still asked for, regularly, and pops up occasionally on the Sky platform.

There may have been ten British Lions in the 'Baa-Baas' side, but the touring All Blacks had already turned over Scotland, England and Wales—so make no mistake, they wanted to play . . . even if the haka at the start was rubbish.

That second half skirmish between little Batty and large David embodied the competitive spirit, but it was an isolated outburst in an otherwise glorious, breathless exhibition, from both sides.

When did you last see a move where every member of the team touches the ball? . . . where scrums set without prompting? . . . where not everyone was built like a brick shit-house?

The 9s: Gareth Edwards going for the corner—Sid Going going bald; in the centre: free-flowing, blond and extravagant David Duckham in hoops—modest Bruce Robertson for the Blacks; from a standing start (no assists): long tall Peter Whiting—versus Willie John McBride in the line-outs; Joe Karam kicking toe-ended—the dancing cavalier in red socks, Phil Bennett, trusting his instep; the Williams boys: J.P.R. at 15—flying Bryan coming at him (a tad high on occasion) from the 14 berth . . . and all the 7s: "*Slattery of Ireland*"—and Ian Kirkpatrick ("*the big man*") skipper of the mighty 7th All Blacks.

A fairytale (with a double-shite ending).

One Friday, weeks later, I was squinting through the sports pages of a Red Top, and there, tucked away in a corner, a paragraph that sent a shiver through me, sharper that a Bob Burgess break; not verbatim, but it went along the lines of:

One person who <u>won't</u> be watching Rugby Special this week, is Mrs. John Bevan, whose husband's wonderful try, in last month's classic Baa-Baas versus the All Blacks match at the Arms Park, wasn't shown by the BBC in their highlights show . . . for reasons unknown.

Well, you do now.

I spent 26 assorted years at BBC Sport—that was the narrowest of my squeaks

(. . . . wasn't <u>that</u> good a try).

Paul Lang was in his 20s when he dropped dead, out running in Windsor.

Cheeky, Wee Cow...

When company (1922-1927) becomes corporation (1927—present), its parts grow precious and territorial. In a multi-million dollar outfit like 'the Beeb,' one department appeared to know little, and care less, what the other was about; the impact of stepping on toes was not for consideration—the Ferguson family affair on *Panorama*, in 2004, a case in point (*had Querioz and Phelan really been doing the guvnor's bidding all that time?*).

There was pre-meditation (as they say prior to a reverse sweep) and culpability (when K.P. sloggs on 99), but what hacked off many good film makers on our patch, were the occasional sports documentaries which commissioners conceded deserved a place amongst 'proper' issues—like vulture crime in the Serengeti, or buggery on the Isle of Man—but took elsewhere.

Sport had lots of bad boys (and East German girls)—corruption, drugs? . . . . *done those*; Tommy Simpson, who had some bad shit in his system when he died on the Tour (de France), and Boris (dis)Onishchenko—the man with the 'automatic' sword, in Munich—were good enough without cheating; Maradona would claim *his* was a reflex thing, Hanse Cronje was tougher on himself, and though Fred Lorz—'the Marathon man' of the III Olympiad in St. Louis—had hitched a ride for ten miles or so in a car, *his* was nothing to what Canadian athletics would bring from their labs, to edition XXIV in South Korea.

Seldom did the Features mob reveal anything we hadn't alluded to, within our own wide-ranging brief, yet their researchers never called for a steer on which contributors might give credible, articulate evidence to their films. Whether valid points were made, ultimately the damage done to our chances of retaining good relationships with the governing bodies of targeted sports—and the athletes in them—took wasted time to repair. Some properly talented souls left as a result.

Representatives of each department—usually Heads or senior producers—were invited to the weekly Review Board, for a good old inter-departmental bitch. Given the scope, there was never much time for debate, with pressing house notices to get away, and frankly it could have been done by memo . . . but the coffee and digestives were free.

Granted a rare appearance—my boss was out to lunch (receipt)—the recently introduced practice of covering cricket from both ends of the ground came under ferocious attack by one from 'the Arts' (. . . *stand-by*).

No one bothered that Gary Sobers was back-to-camera as he helped all Malcolm Nash could lob at him, over the ropes at Swansea in 1968 (Glamorgan's Roger Davis, fielding on the boundary, should be credited with 'an assist' for punching one—and Sobers—into the record books, once more). Were it today, we'd have, isolated, head-on, hi-motion images of the peerless West Indian to juxtapose with the many faces of a reconciled Nash, much as there are of Herschelle Gibbs and Daan van Bunge from the 2007 World Cup; in his defence, Nash once hit four consecutive sixes in an over and he got Sobers out a few times in his county career, so let's not be taking the piss altogether.

Conversely, it was pure luck for the telly that P.B.H. May decided J.C. Laker should bowl his off-breaks from the Stretford end at Old Trafford in '56. Only three Aussies were leg-before, but had *Hawkeye* been around, the 19 'magic' balls would have made a fascinating, multi-coloured, animating, trace-map for E.W. Swanton to huff and puff about.

I sat back in amazement as pompous 'Mr. Art Farty' began:
. . . *dis-orientating, innovation for innovation's sake . . . would never receive the blessing of those who knew and loved the traditions of the game* . . . blah, blah—he even recorded his son's displeasure!
Hm-mm . . . probably gone by now . . . death by 20/20; good job his specialist subject was the life and times of Malcolm Morley and not Kerry Packer's.
I *liked* Jackson Pollock, and Emin's bed, and the various angles of Gillian Carnegie's arse (and that Jack Russell of Gloucestershire and England and Pat Nevin of Chelsea and Scotland could paint a bit), and though I couldn't hum any of his tunes, I knew Claudio Monteverdi didn't play up front for Inter.
For once, I let the bait go . . . no point, the tablets had been handed down—the Long Room at Lord's was in for an almighty dusting.

I did, however, make a call to Ann Robinson, the morning after one of her *Points of View* performances . . . didn't get through, of course.
Naively, I believed the purpose of the show was to air opinions from the proletariat about BBC programmes, not for Robinson to craft her second coming as odious inquisitor on *The Weakest Link* (*boy, she believes her own stuff that woman*).
Without the benefit of a transcript, I can't quote her directly, but the gist was . . . there had been a complaint about *Grandstand* . . . . fair enough. The voice-over artist read it out, over a caption, presumptuously in the accent of the postcode, but for the autocue reader to then snipe that the very sound of our theme tune had her scurrying for the remote, was, what we 'dopes' in sport would deem, an o.g.

Cheeky, wee cow—don't you wink at me, lady!

Psychologists will tell you that only 10 per cent of the brain works when you're angry, but that was plenty.
Barrels of bile were evacuated into the dog 'n' (bone):

'. . . *and could I take a name, sir?*'

Slamming the thing down, Moncur style, was a futile expression of my feelings, and grossly unfair on the switchboard operator.
My 'greeting' did get through, via 'Urbanityman' Lynam (always one for the older sort), who, in response, was asked to invite me to lunch: no one could be *that* hungry.
The ginger minger pissed a fair few off in *Grandstand*—and Wales—but other people's feelings appeared low on her list of priorities (*some act, if it is one*).

Being a public servant of sorts, you were rightly accountable, even if the majority who could find time to put pen to paper were at the far end of the critical divan. Complainants' views, expressed forcibly to those non-programme making masochists in the Duty office, were passed on, in abridged form, to the relevant departments for action (. . . or shredding).
However, when you get a call to attend a Commons Select Committee to answer for your decision making, the tendency is to doubt it (the decision making) . . . *was this to be a cheap-day-return to Westminster, or a single to Traitor's Gate?*

Rugby League Cup Final day on *Grandstand*—one of our 'majors'—May 3rd 1986: Castleford had just beaten Hull Kingston Rovers by a point, at smelly old Wembley, where the final had been played since 1929. Exhausted winners graciously received a little medal for their graft, and "JJ" Joyner—Tigers' captain—the Challenge Cup; that old baby dated back to 1897 when Batley and Leeds met in the first final at Headingley.
(*not that I'm getting in early with the mitigation, but the FA Cup started in 1872*).
Out of the corner of one eye—there was always a bit going on around final score—I noticed that time was running out in the crucial clash at Stamford Bridge between Chelsea and Liverpool.
Were Liverpool to win, they'd become League champions for the 16th time, giving them a chance, the following week-end—on the very turf chewed up by the harder men of 'Cas' and Hull K.R.—of doing 'the double,' thus becoming only the 3rd side in the 20th century so to do *"Mister Chairman of the Select Committee on crimes against Ruby League, Sir"*. . . . so quite an important game really.

Alan Hansen—captain, "Lawro"—never far away, the player/manager—'King' Kenny: *Ronnie Whelan heads it on to Jim Beglin* (who'd stayed forward) . . . *the full back flicks it through, and there's Dalglish, calm as you like chesting it down and ramming a right foot volley past Tony Godden, for the only goal of the game* (at around 23 minutes past three): by 4.45, Chelsea hadn't replied.

We stood the OB at the Bridge by, for a report.
John Motson had said on commentary that he couldn't remember a player manager winning the first division championship before, so, were further proof needed that I should be spared quartering-by-horse for my actions, that was it; neither was I about to challenge "Motty"'s fact: pointless . . . heretical, even.

Within seconds of the final whistle, we wound up Ray French and the scenes of celebration at Wembley and cut to Chelsea, as Liverpool players and fans went quite as berserk as Castleford's had ten minutes earlier.

Right choice in my view, obviously, but as far as Rugby League's congregation was concerned, not one with which it could concur; the Cup Final was <u>their</u> day.
Impasse—after the fact, but impasse.

Down the years we'd done our share for the 13-man game on *Grandstand* . . . me and my mate Cowgill; no issues for him, he was a northern boy—I just thought it a cracking sport; its general appeal had everything to do with Eddie Waring, and a lot to do with fictitious *Frank Machin*—a.k.a. Richard Harris (*Prof. Dumbledore*)) in *This Sporting Life,* the movie.

When I took over as editor, our leading man was Ray French, an ever-present in the commentary box, and in the executive dining room for the pre-Cup Final bash at TV Centre (on the licence payer—an above-the-line cost, so no receipt required). A kindlier hunk you couldn't wish to take cheap wine with: played for his country at both codes, and having picked up the ball when uncle Eddie played it back en route to *his* final *"early bath"* in 1981, we got right behind the big forward, heart and soul.

Eddie had bamboozled the nation for decades with his bizarre delivery. No self-respecting member of staff went through life without at least attempting an impersonation (Mike Yarwood *did* him best) . . . but Waring was no joke.

Drop by the Queen's of an evening and there he'd be—the dapper little Messiah—regaling disciples with tales of Billy Boston and Augustus ('Bev' to his pals) Risman . . . of Don Fox . . . and of the Black Knights of Dewsbury.

In the end, having survived petitions from the hoi poloi to 'get rid,' he opted for the jokers of *Jeux sans Frontiere,* having earned his stripes (jacket) on the domestic leagues of *It's A Knockout.*

One of our sports producer's assistants (painted bullies with stopwatches and skinny lattés) was married to a set/games designer on *Knock Out,* which millions bought into. She went by the splendid name of Fanny Cassidy: it was 'standing room only' in the mixed sauna of our team hotels when Irish Fanny decided to cleanse the pores (she was naturally blessed). Coleman and co., lost pounds on tour with the big ones—like the Olympics and World Cups . . . . *come on, leave it!*

It was never easy taking over from an icon as Tony Gubba could attest to after Coleman quit *Sportsnight*—but we always stood '*up*' for Ray '*and*' the big forward from St. Helens, '*under*' my stewardship, never let the Waring legend—or the League—down.

Eddie crumbled, ultimately, with poxy dementia in 1986: they could, and did, take the mick, and many got the hump with him, but he was an exotic bird, a believer; look at the game now—*he'd be lovin' it.*

And then there was 'Murph the Mouth.' Later on, across the divide, the dancing union star—*'The Leicester Lip'*—Austin Healey (save for a hyphen, the vowels and consonants precisely in line with the flash motor) became a pain in a lot of backsides, some towering over his own pert little number (female input)—but he had *nothing* on Murphy. On the pitch—for any number of clubs—Alex was tricky, cheeky, tough as teak; on mic . . . fearlessly opinionated
The light fantastic, with picky Bruno Tonioli, would not have been his fancy.
Grudges endured; Alex had ruffled feathers all over the place, but I thought he and Ray were mustard together, much as Eddie Butler and Brian Moore are today in the ruffian's game (with a little bit of Austin by their side), and Jon Champion and Craig Burley are in the gentleman's.

Rugby league was staple at BBC Sport: there was a week-night floodlit competition which no less a giant than David Attenbrough had given the nod to as Controller of Two, and *Grandstand* went 'live' for a second half of rugged behavior—in groups of six—in any clime . . . they never cancelled.

Apart from the Open, our tournament golf coverage had afternoon slots on Thursdays and Fridays; *early* tended to mean better surfaces, therefore better *numbers*, so it was probable that none of the *late* starters would affect the mid-point leaderboard.
Very unsatisfactory . . . could do better; had my friend from the Arts argued that one, I'd have been right behind him.

Grandstand's 'main events' in the winter had to finish around 4.30, unless BBC 2 were joining in.
Second halves were often anti-climactic: we *did* do better.

Extended highlights of the first half, preceded going live for the second—nothing was missed.

Don Fox's 'sitter' at the Challenge Cup Final:
"He's a poor lad," said Eddie, sincerely, in 1968—and so in the end (1986) was he.

It's ironic that such a big chunk of our Saturday sport came out of BBC Manchester back then; come 2012, it'll be the hub.
We did the Five Nations, the Middlesex Sevens, some domestic cup games and *Rugby Special* out of London, but all technical and production logistics for our extensive coverage of league, were handled, up north, by match-director/producers Nick Hunter, Keith Phillips (two '*l*'s . . . like 'Foggy,' Zara's Dad), and Malcolm Kemp, out of New Zealand, where 'footy' was rapidly gaining ground on all but the Blacks.

Malcolm had been a light-entertainment director before signing with us. He loved 'football' and would batter me, constantly, for more resources, which he got, and used with aplomb. Music was his other passion, and together we managed to combine the two within the coverage; Eddie would have reveled in it—Cowgill wouldn't, and, no doubt, would not have cared for my decision-making on Cup Final Day 1986.
(not interested in the wee cow's point of view)

Would I have done the same had the roles been reversed?
Definitely not.
This was an historical moment in the 'world' game.
Thanks to the pioneers of VERA—the great, great grandmother of Sky Plus—within minutes of winding up the Liverpool story, we were turning round a recording of the lap-of-honour at Wembley . . . . . so, dummies back in, pens down, and on with proper Parliamentary business.

What *was* it about '86?
The Five Nations Championship had reached a crucial stage: were they to beat France at Murrayfield, Scotland would share the title they'd won outright, two seasons previously.

Wallis Willis's Afro-American negro spiritual—*Swing Low Sweet Chariot*—hadn't been wholly adopted by the English, and we natives were still *humming* along to *Scotland the Brave*: Kenneth McKellar 'kent aw the wurds,' but none of *us* did—not even our patron, the Princess of Edinburgh.
Being only 10th in line, Anne Elizabeth Alice Louise wasn't in any real danger of riling her Mum; the snuffing out of royals, by decapitation, died out with Charles I (circa 1649), and the Corries's slightly more inflammatory anthem—*Flower of Scotland*—wouldn't hit Murrayfield till 1990.

(don't see 'organic' Prince Charlie at the rugby anymore; none but the Welsh can cope with *Hen Wylad fy Nhadau*: the tune's a belter tho—makes grown men cry).

It'd be some time before the BBC were forced into a proper evaluation of the Five Nations (Six by 2000) and throw open both channels to 'live' coverage, so on this 'double' day it was Wales v. England for a bit of pride in Cardiff, and the championship decider in Edinburgh, simultaneously. Sky + and the sixth nation were 14 years down the track.

I'd never been in doubt as to where our viewers should be at 2.15p.m., (and it wasn't Cardiff). The Head of Sport thought otherwise.
We locked antlers.

Now, this wee guy could stir my corpuscles like none other.
He knew his business and responsibilities, thoroughly: keep the Department in pole (*loved* Formula 1, and wee Bernie . . . . *to distraction*); invent *Ski Sunday*; win all meaningful contracts for longer and pay less; don't offer to make any controversial documentaries; always respond to the duty log; keep the Governors off our case; continue to fantasise about Virginia Wade; get on J.P.'s tits whenever possible.

No point in having wings if you can't soar; anyone in BBC Sport suspected of flying too close to 'Sun God' Reith was shot down—their preferences being . . . . clement to tropical, cautious to cavalier.
My *Icarus* to Jonathan Martin's *Daedalus* wasn't going to work; we didn't agree on huge amounts . . . . not programmes, not Greek mythology, not on his chances with Virginia.

In the end, he persuaded BBC Two to show the Welsh match 'live,' while *Grandstand* attended to the big issue.
Scotland duly won a thriller by 18 points (against the name of debutante full-back Gavin Hastings) to 17.

I'd moved on from Richard Sharpe:
'I'm ready, Matthew, to become John Rutherford.'

One decision I'm grateful *not* to be associated with—unless there's to be a broad sweep of the tar-brush—was at Lord's in 1990. England were playing India, and Graham Gooch was heading to a colossal personal best of 300.
The match was on BBC Two, who, for reasons best known to Controller Alan Yentob, had begun scheduling news bulletins on the hour, every hour, throughout the afternoon. CNN's rolling 24 hour service had the occasional 'breaking' story barging its way to the top of the running order, but it was often hard to spot the difference, summary to summary . . . *and no bugger was watching anyway.*

Wee Jonathan and I were arguing about something or other in his office much as, I imagine, civil partners might, while the moustachioed man of Essex hammered his way into the 290s. It was Friday—Lord's was full of skivers. As the clock—and Goochie's score—ticked towards the big 3-mark, the lead commentator at the cricket (Benaud, more than likely) announced, chokingly:

". . . we are having (*what? . . . say's who?*) to leave Lord's (*you're jesting, right?*) for a couple of minutes (*why for C—t's sake?*) to bring you (*we only want Gooch*) a summary of the news (*this IS the bloody news!*)."

Two interminable minutes of inconsequential drivel and—would you Adam and Eve it—weather, passed and with them the 300 and its celebration—a milestone, a landmark, a triumph . . . *a fuck-up!*

The presentation announcer who in essence, had sanctioned one of the worst decisions I'd ever come across in my life (save for Jack Kennedy's to travel through Dallas in an open-topped limo, and Neville Chamberlain's to believe anything that slimy little shit Hitler said in Munich) then announced, triumphantly to our folk at Lord's:

"*Standby cricket . . . coming back to you. Cut, and cue.*"

Gooch went on to make 333 (and 123 in the second innings—only an aggregate world bloody record . . . to this day . . . in Tests) and 'yer' actual man with the can—the extremely wealthy, brilliant, if follickly challenged Al 'Botney' (Yentob . . . get it?)—to Controller of BBC 1.
Although culpable by association, I never mentioned it (nor my thinning crown) when—years later—Graham and I worked together on *Channel 4 Cricket*. Hair loss must be down to stress, or too many hours at the crease in a sweaty helmet.
It annoyed the hell out of me when a batsman reached a personal mark—even a third as good as Goochie's—to have the director cut away to applauding hordes.
Vainly, I tried to ban all 'unrelated' crowd shots.
With digital technology, the output of each camera is now recorded separately, so those telling moments of elation or relief can be recalled seconds after the fact, and no one is any the wiser.

In analogue days, the risks were considerably higher: what if the BBC had been showing the billions a group-shot of flag-waving, royalist believers in the holy state of matrimony as Diana planted that cheeky one on her charming prince? Had the director cut away to Mrs. Bowles in close-up, during the swearing and vowing in St. Paul's—*that* would have been *inspirational* . . . treasonable, but inspirational.

In these savage economic times, where greedy politicians and obscenely remunerated, top-flight bankers and footballers are role models for the looters and arsonists—it

might tax even slippery Lord Coe's legendary diplomatic skills to convince those donors still in work, that ludicrous amounts of money spent on opening and closing ceremonies at the Olympics are justifiable.
They've become mega-shows in their own right, markers for national excellence and creativity, spectaculars, each upstaging the next, with tourism at their hearts.
Roll on London 2012, *slowly*, if the trailer in Beijing was anything to go by . . . . *what was that green bus all about?*—maybe they should have fire-bombed it and thrown banana-skins Leona's way for authenticity.
How the Chinese motivated all those folk is nothing short of . . . communism; 'volunteers' danced and waved their arms in the air for hours (*'and look happy about it'*) as endless ranks of foreigners processed round the track . . . *but wasn't that wall-of-death run round the roof, something else and isn't the nest itself a miracle of engineering?*

Barbecued dove of peace, on the wing, was a late addition to the specials menu in Seoul (presumably they'd rehearsed the fly-past *before* the flame reached the city limits).
In Atlanta, we agonised for poor old Muhammad . . . would he ever get the flame lit without torching himself . . . and in Sydney when the whole watery affair came to a shuddering halt around Cathy Freeman's shoulders.
Had Rafer Johnson donned the rocket man's gear and gone flying towards the Coliseum's gas rings—brushed chrome *Zippo* in hand—*that* would have been *sensational* . . . typically excessive, but sensational.

Something radical has to be done with the parade of athletes in Twenty Twelve (a great laugh), "Mr. Mayor."
Should the fleet of revised Routemasters be ready in time, slap country names on the panels where the movie ads would normally go, get the flag bearers—in national costume . . . *if they must*—*on the rear platforms (the buses, therefore, must circulate clockwise), and have the teams follow on bikes . . . . but GET A MOVE ON . . . it's a drag on the box* (Sky + will be 12 years old by then).

Down a league or two from China, the Moscow ceremony in 1980 did little business at the travel agents; one of few in keeping with the *faster, higher, stronger* credo, it was about human tapestry on the stadium floor, and in the bleachers. The giant mosaic of *Miska* the bear—the Games mascot—was seen to shed a tear at the close, probably for the Cold War, or . . . thinking *well* ahead . . . . for Ken Bates at Chelsea.

The technique—honed in the Eastern bloc—was plagiarsied, most effectively, on opening day in L.A . . . . <u>and</u> in our *Match of the Day* titles.

We spoke very nicely to the Board at Queen's Park Rangers F.C., in London, and gained permission to do our shoot at Loftus Road. Local schoolchildren, ever keen to dodge double-science of a Monday morning, volunteered their services and arrived promptly, as instructed by the director—and longest serving *Grandstand* producer in the history of starting prices—Martin Hopkins . . . '*Sir*' for the day (he'd have made a spanking good teacher).

Each bunking student was issued with a seat number and a small piece of cardboard, painted on both sides; despite their legendary reputation for subterfuge, they managed, almost to a blazer, to do as they were asked.

On Martin's "*3-2-1 UP!*" command—he was in the stand opposite, megaphone to mouth (not that he needed it)—the mosaic came together with a ripple, revealing the words *Match of the Day* in our livery.

Then—on the second command "*SPIN*"—there, in all its bearded glory, was the unmistakable mush of ubiquitous James William Thomas Hill—the Sky Blue pimpernel.

Looking down from above at the Bird's Nest, the machinations have moved on a touch, but apart from the hassle of re-takes, and re-positioning of the educationally challenged few, the operation, by modern standards, was cheap, cheerful and effective on screen.

Olympic opening ceremonies, programme title-sequencing, and pop vids are about *impact*.

Incongruously morphing a melanistic leopard (black) into (edelweiss white)Michael Jackson is old hat now, so good are the digital toys, but it was ground-breaking at the time.

One thing on which we were all pretty much agreed, was title music—seldom the original choices, but once adopted, there was folly in change.

Not a lot of people know (or care) that the theme tune for the *Grand Prix* programme came out of a black hole we, my mate Chris Lewis, his girlfriend Jill (of *Leg's&co*) and mine, Dee (of Crockford's casino, London), were slipping into one early Boxing Day morning in the front room of his bachelor flat near Twickenham.

It was the late 70s. Everyone knew about Mick Fleetwood, the McVies and Buckingham-Nicks, but *Rumours*—yet to be released in the UK—was about to send the band stratospheric.

Chris had 'acquired' a copy on a trip to the States.

I'm no musician, but the bars in the middle of "*The Chain*" were hypnotic . . . . from John McVie's bass solo to the instrumental madness that followed. The good (first hand) news was the BBC had a buy-out deal—we could use anything we liked: this particular puppy had motor racing written all over it.

Back and forward it went, until the girls—numbed by repetition—cried out for "*Second Hand News*" or "*Go Your Own Way*."

I was prepared to sacrifice all offers for my art.

The rest (I thought) was history, till a recent obituary for an ex-colleague, erroneously claiming the 'Archimedes moment' had been his.

You are mistaken wee Bob—St. Margaret's not Syracuse—but R.I.P.

So there you have it pop-pickers—might have been just as cool for the cricket, had they not already had their own little rumba (. . . a chain . . . 22 yards . . . *too lateral?*).
On the other hand, Puccini's ode to insomniacs, *Nessun Dorma*, which propelled big Pav into the charts via the BBC's World Cup titles was, as previously stated, an application by one of our assistant producers on *Grandstand*: other claimants can sue and whine in vain . . . Bernie's the name, Philip Bernie (with a little help from opera buff and football commentator, Gerald Sinstadt).
None of us was on a percentage of the box office, but . . . we had each other.

My ears were deceiving me—we were actually discussing dropping Mambo No.5 from Channel 4 cricket!
The Clinton/Lewinsky scandal apart (Monica got an oblique reference in the chorus of the Lou Bega version . . . along with several other little bits on the side), this was the best sports theme, ever.
The Oval Office mess—rather than "needle time"—probably accounted for the US being the only place on the planet where it didn't make No.1., but ad campaigners and TV shows latched on, voraciously.

Nowhere to better effect than in the *The Royle Family's* front room as *Jim* and *Twiggy* got down and dirty with the paper strippers. The *emphasis there was on the tune*—in *Reservoir Dogs, the music and lyrics* of Stealer's Wheel's *Stuck in the Middle with You* suited perfectly, as *Mr. Blonde* set about converting officer *Nash's* hearing to mono, during one of cinema's gorier passages.

When the derisory laughter died down at Sunset + Vine's head office in Piccadilly (S+V were 4's *terribly good* choice of independent cricket producers), their Head of Sport, Jeff Foulser—who'd batted for the other side (in a manner of speaking) at ITV Sport—wisely ruled for retention; sadly, for cricket lovers, he dropped a dolly when the contract came up for renewal, and Sky swanned off with the Test matches.

The London Marathon title music sent goose bumps up the neck every April (by running it, I'd miss the sensation), but that's a comparatively new one (1981). The *Match of the Day* (1970—present) and *Grandstand* (1975—deceased) themes have been re-worked down the years. *Grandstand*'s original version couldn't have survived—a bit Souza for modern tastes—but *Wimbledon* has stayed true, the golf too . . . almost. Can you imagine *Panorama* or *News at Ten*, or *Corrie*, or *Enders* or *Neighbours*, changing scores?

I've no regrets about confessing never to have watched an entire episode of the Aussie soap in the 25 years it's been available over here, yet Jackie Trent's words and Tony Hatch's music say Kylie to me as much as her tight tush and lippied cupids do: top totty . . . brave and beatific.

We got permission to use the opening shot (a solitary, galloping pair skimming the horizon . . . wide as you like) and music from the *Champions* film, for *Grand National Grandstand* in 1983, as much in tribute to Bob Champion and *Aldaniti,* as for its aesthetic value; it was used, somewhere in the show, for years . . . making it synonymous, *right?*

Not a dry eye in the house as *Corbiere* . . . "owned by Bryan Burrough, trained by Jenny Pitman and ridden by Ben de Haan" . . . pulled up next to Lynam in 1983. Mrs. P. was the first woman to train a National winner; not sure she knew at the time, but she too had cancer. She survived. Little Helen Rollason didn't; the year she died (1999), the BBC created a special award "for outstanding achievement in the face of adversity" and Jenny Pitman was recognised first.

What's perceived to be a successful amalgamation of pictures and music, is as subjective in television as it is paramount in the video business.

For a start to any show—or video—you'd be pushed to improve on a windswept Brian May playing our National Anthem on his electric machine, atop 'Buck House' (*who thought of that one?*).

Sports Personality of the Year is nearing its 60th anniversary (2014).
I only directed it once—the year they laid a mini-ice rink in the adjoining studio for Torvill & Dean to do their turns on—and that was by default. I was walking past the boss's office when the regular director (Hopkins) phoned in a 'sickie' . . . *with four days to go!*

On the back of that, amazingly, the Guv'nor let me produce it (once).
I felt the whole thing needed a shake . . . it was predictable, cheesey in many aspects, a critique that would have sent Fox and Cowgill—the founding fathers—spinning on their merry-go-round like *Dougals* on heat.
Fox did . . . *spin.*

A sober gathering of great athletes in smart suits and high heels, under blazing studio lights, might be a lot preferred by a stand-up to a first night at the Glasgow Alhambra, but it was *dull* to look at; not that I was suggesting they all get pissed and fall about the studio (Sky managed to make their award show like happy hour at *Hedonism III* on Jamaica).

Rather than run great edited lumps of individual sports, which only apposite sections appeared remotely excited about, I felt it might be neat to reflect the year, month by month, with an amalgam of sports, using lots of topical music, ending each segment with the outstanding performer gassing, in person, with Des or Steve Rider. Events would spill over inevitably, but they were scriptwriters, storytellers, compéres of genuine class . . . <u>world</u> class, their agents said. Not brain surgery, but a variation on a tired old theme.

There was always a centerpiece: some were a bit daft (glad I'd gone by the duck-shoot) . . . Red Rum on stage in an equine/human 'two-way' with Tommy Stack, the last of his successful jockeys . . . Sandy Lyle, on a near, life-size model of the 18th green, re-enacting his fluffed chip at Sandwich, the year he won the Open (1985) . . . Nash and Dixon (1964) in their two-man bob (*the cut from film to studio—not the most convincing*) . . . that ice-rink, for a bit of rock 'n' roll . . . F1 cars, on 'empty' (*Health & Safety*), in for new wheels from turbo-charged, quick-fit fitters (no dancing) . . . *Scalectrix* cars, tested by idiots (us) and driven by champions . . . . trampolines and high bars . . . snooker tricks and penalty shoot-outs . . . . table football, and so on (*the meetings we had*).

Lynam leaned into the cockpit of Richard Noble's World land-speed-record-breaking car:

"How's it at getting away from the lights?"

Nota bene—(fingers crossed)—*my classical masterstroke will top the lot.*

I rang Mrs. Pavarotti in Italy, and got through (we knew a man, who knew a man, who knew her, pretty well). I told her the story: she promised to put it to Luciano.
How would he receive the news . . . up to his uninsurable neck in a chamomile and peppermint bath, his sweat 'blankie' floating by on a convoy of yellow ducks?

We checked the availability of the BBC Symphony Orchestra and laid plans for a fly-in stage (*this'll waken the starchy bastards up*).

A couple of weeks before the show, Mrs. P. rang:*'Pavarotti'* as she called him, *couldn't do it now*.
"BLAST" (or word to that effect).

R.A.I.—the Italian state broadcaster—had asked him to do something similar and he'd turned it down, so to show up in London would be neither *Calaf* nor cricket.

I paraphrase here, but any way you look at it, it was a bummer (*who thought of fucking Puccini in the first place?*)

A new format and now no lingering *Vincerò* to rattle the roof of the Queen Elizabeth II Conference Centre.

I sensed a sharpening of executive dirks.

The gig, of course, went ahead: it wasn't perfect but at least the studio audience stayed awake.
At drinks and sausage rolls afterwards, my little boss wasn't alone in commending the re-vamp. Paul Fox, the Director General at the time—self-styled inventor of everything in BBC Sport from *Grandstand* (which he did) to fun-filled, laid-back, creative sports broadcasting (which he didn't)—walked out in the huff.

Bless.

Three weeks later, on my return from an extravagant break on that most indulgent of Caribbean islands (miles from Negril), the vaultingly ambitious, second-guessing, middle-management turn-coats rounded on me.
(Bitter? . . . who me?)

My old mate, the Contracts boss—the late David Keir—was the only one who stuck to his story: *"liked it then . . . like it now."*

With higher principles than Fox, I walked too . . . <u>out</u> of BBC Sport.

When the dust settled, I was sent a tiny replica camera on a wooden plinth . . . that after 26 years I wouldn't have missed for the World.

"... There's Been Another Five Murrdurrs, Surr!"

Talk of home-rule for Scotland in the 50s was as rife as Caledonian blue wins at Wembley; the SNP was wasting its money on deposits; the Ryder Cup (one win all decade), compared to the Calcutta Cup, was tight-knit.

A twine-bound, brown-paper package, addressed to my elder brother—he of the staved willy—was delivered to our door in Crieff: he was out, so, being younger and a little shit, I opened it . . . to discover the most enormous football boot I'd every seen in my short life—just one. No white kid-skin, diamante in-layed slipper, as worn by the better-heeled professionals at the Santiago Bernabéu, this . . . it was huge, Gleneagles for a nest of timorous beasties made homeless-by-combine at harvest time; cantilevered sides, bulbous toe-caps on which the bows of nuclear subs, soon to be heading Faslane's way, would be modeled, with outsized solid thimbles for studs: these babies demanded the shin-pad.

The note inside read:
To David,
GOOD LUCK,
F. Martin.
Doc. M.—the good German boot-maker—spelled his with an '*e*' and an '*s*' on the end, and it was '*K*' for Klaus, not '*F*' as in ('get tae') Forgandenny—a village about ten miles away, close to Strathallan School, our arch rivals on the rugby playing fields of Perthshire.

It was appropriate, that early in a sheltered development, my first proper use of the improper '*f*' word would come on my 'blooding' trip to a favoured pool on the River Earn, with Dad and our house-painter friend, Jimmy Innes. In *its* development, the Earn joins up (in the Firth) with Britain's longest river—the salmon-rich (pre netting), silvery Tay.

Excitement levels soared as we lost sight of the sun. The fairly strict bedtime curfew, during school week, came and went. Full body waders, assorted rods, reels and tackle, nets and gaffs (in the event of a salmon)—plus a sumptuous picnic Mum had prepared earlier—were loaded into the boot of our car.
Roll on break-time tomorrow . . . grown-up, night angling was no ordinary brag—we were honour bound to get fish.

Angler there was standing, with rod and line in hand,
Intent upon the fishes, a sportive fearless band,
"'tis vain" said I "good neighbour, to fish a brooklet clear,
The fish will surely see you upon the bank so near.
The fish will surely see you upon the bank so near.

That verse, from one of our school choir 'hits'—I think (not unreasonably) called *The Trout*—reverberated in my sub-conscious as the car's headlights picked out the appointed beat. This was no brooklet clear: if not in spate exactly, the water was running quickly. I imagined hungry, be-speckled, opened-mouthed brown trout, effortlessly knifing through the current in search of a late-night snack: big browns like to feed in the dark.

Jimmy pulled a battered tin from his pooch (pocket).
Ah, mints . . . nice touch.
I was about to reach in, when Dad's torch beam revealed that 'the confection' was *on the move!*
On this auspicious occasion, we weren't to be fishing the traditional, lovingly crafted, artificial fly, favoured by canny, long-casting devotees of this most popular pastime . . .
. . . tonight, gentlemen, the chosen lure is . . . the MAGGOT!.

FUCK me!

The accompanying slap—the first and only disciplinary hand-to-face contact I recall having with my co-creator—was a rap worth taking.

Never before had so many gathered in pursuit of so few; popping re-loads of one of nature's more repulsive creations into the fleshy drawer between his lower, false teeth and bottom lip, Jim deftly armed his and my hook, then splashed off through the shallows:

"*Tight lines.*"

As to the late dining trout? . . . they must have been equally disgusted.

The only other 'Martin' I knew who could possibly fit into such a monster boot, was the right back of our local Earngrove F.C. side . . . but he was a 'J' for Jimmy (*weren't they all?*).
Even were it an initiative test—*find the sister ship*—there was no mileage in being spiteful, so I chucked it under the boy David's bed.

On discovering the prize, and giving me a belt on the way past for opening it—and for abetting the shutting of his tiny member in Dad's desk-drawer—it was as if he'd happened on *Cinders'* glass slipper (*Irina Press, more like*).
"Do you realise, you little fart, (*nice talk to your younger and dearest*) that this boot belonged to Scotland's goalkeeper?"

"*Let me get to the foot of our stairs . . . the Scotland goalkeeper, really?*"
"Bet he's pish on crosses."
I collected a second palm-print, just short of the door.

When Grandpa felt I was big enough to take a punch, he provided boxing gloves for us warring siblings, so the escalating rivalry could be settled once and for all.
The dining room was stripped for action; the factions, to vest and pants.
I lost by TKO.
As Harry Carpenter would say in commentary, especially when 'Cooperman' was atop the bill:
"*Harry Gibbs* (the ref, who all but ended his career) *is going to have to take a long, hard look at that one*". . . reference the trench that regularly opened above Our 'Enry's eyes, sending crimson rivulets into both, and bringing to a premature close, contests he was often controlling—courtesy of some serious hammer.

In my case of aggravated bodily harm, there had been inflammation and a slight depression—nothing lasting—so, with a swift, compounding 'Harvey Smith,' I threw myself at the stairs and made off, three-at-a-time.
It was fair comment mind you: having to hoist two of these beauties (boots) in the air, over a rain-sodden Hampden, with Nat 'The Lion of Vienna' Lofthouse coming at you—his name on a Matthews corner from the right, or a pin-pointer from Finney on the left—plus the extra poundage in the saturated, roll-neck wooly, meant there'd only be one winner . . . and it wouldn't be Fred, long though he was at full stretch.
(imagine were 'lifting' allowed in football—and who says it isn't—
'*Lennon crosses from the right . . . ah, it's too long . . . no hang on, here come King & Crouch . . . One—nil!*'

Early signs that the Union of 1603 was teetering, came with the introduction (in 1879) of the Calcutta Cup matches: up to 1951, we Jocks pretty much held our own (*stop it*)—the rest of the decade was dismal to disastrous, home and away.
The line-out 'power-assist' hadn't been invented in those lean times . . . but Marques and Currie, two upright gentlemen of Oxbridge and Harlequins, were no strangers to us.
Burning leg-curling and bench-pressing in gym greenhouses, would soon be put to spectacular, high altitude effect, come yet more rule changes in the 90s, as boiler-room giants like Johnson and Kay made telescopic reaches for their hooker's balls (were

they to revert to front-row striking, in the modern game, set scrums could recover some of their fascination—too late for Brian Moore and his redundant follicles).

R.W.D. Marques and J.D. Currie—amateur embodiments of 'the rugger bugger' with initials aplenty to intimidate in match programmes and team photos—played against each other in the '54 and '55 Varsity matches; no skin-tight kit and personalised footwear for them . . . it was an altogether purer form of violence.
Manning Scotland's engine room were the upstanding and, therefore, frequently out-jumped, Frans ten Bos (of the little known ten Bos clan), aka *The Flying Dutchman*, from Richmond in Surrey—and Mike Campbell-Lamerton of the Duke of Wellington's Regiment (West Riding) *"sir"*—a Malteser by birth.
The origin of the attacking full-back species, Kenneth James Forbes Scotland, was also capped, by his birth country, at cricket, but wisely chose rugby (our cricket being in the infancy in which it remains).
Slight by modern standards, K.J.F. was good enough to rub shoulders metaphorically with massive A.J.F. ('Tony') O'Reilly, and literally with R.E.G. ('Dickie') Jeeps on the 1959 Lions tour to Australia and New Zealand. M.A.F. English, who was Irish, didn't make the test side.

I too have three initials (m.y.o.b.) but lacked the *dedication, application and embrocation* Alan Hansen deems necessary to succeed in sport *"at this level . . . for me."*

Astonishing co-incidence, but my brother and I met Fred Martin in the locker-room of Crieff Golf Club a few years ago . . . . *Jeez, he'd lasted well*; couldn't stop looking at his frankly, unremarkable feet. Seemed like a decent bloke . . . *but the goals Fred, the bloody goals man* (choked on asking about them).
It grieves me yet. In 6 international appearances for Scotland, Fred let in 20 (not *entirely* on his own): 18 in 3, 14 in 2, viz., 7 against 'the Auld Enemy' in '55 (Lawrie Reilly and Tommy Doc got a couple back for us), and 7 more (without reply) in a World Cup match against Uruguay in 1954. The other 4 came against the Olympic champions (1952) and World Cup finalists (1954), Hungary—Puskas, Kocsis, Hidegkuti *et al*, of *The Magnificent Magyars* . . . . not <u>too</u> bad a result bearing in mind the goulash they made of the English at Wembley, the year before (. . . . *6-3 wasn't it?*)

Dad bought our first television for the Coronation in 1953 (never did get a satisfactory explanation as to what Archbishop Fisher of Canterbury was doing to young Elizabeth under that canopy—*'anointing her'* didn't clear up anything for a nine-year-old, compounded by Mum promising that: *". . . your father will tell you about it later"*).

Just the kind of damaging reaction Churchill was anticipating; he was said to have been against televising the ceremony as he felt 'it would make profane, an otherwise sacred event.'
What a load of old bollocks, Winnie.

Even now, US producers are hoping to mount hot-head (unmanned) cameras *behind* the screens . . . should Charles ever get the call.
Nuttin's sacred no more, bled.
Whether it amounts to profanity, when the US networks transmitted our new Queen's big day, they fell into the traditionalists' lap by nipping off to ad breaks: one was for tea, which was sound imperial placement but for the monkeys therein who, unwittingly, rather let the side down.

Equally stupid were my brother's antics during *God Save the Queen* by the Abbey Church of Saint Peter choir: the *skelping* of his bum certainly counted as a win double for Philips the (oppressed) Younger; had it been 'radio only' as the Prime Minister had argued for, he'd still have qualified for a smack, such was his mischievousness that dank day in June.

Corporal punishment (mild), respect for your elders (siblings excepted) and 'the polis,' were acceptable parts of the process in those days.

As reward for *good* behavior, we were allowed to travel, with the school, to all Scotland's home internationals at Murrayfield. Banish any thought of pitch invasions and, therefore, possible brushes with the authorities. School kids had front row, ground level seats, but as our Morrisonian uniform came with unmistakable bright-red stockings, to be worn knee-length at all times, we'd be guilty by association—instigators or not. The favoured trick, by the less cautious, was to head for the point scorers in sure and certain belief they'd be captured on the telly on the final whistle.

A few weeks prior to E.A.M. ('Lilibet') Windsor's crowning glory as Queen of Great Britain and other Commonwealth domains where Lions trod fearlessly, Celtic—all local lads—had won the special Coronation Cup; hardly got a mention alongside Hillary and Tensing, Richards and *Pinza,* Compton and the Ashes, or Hogan and his alley at Carnoustie, where, incidentally, Fred Martin was born (it's called *following the link* nowadays).
The year after, 'the Tims' played 'the Dons' in the Scottish Cup Final proper.

Dangerous territory, dates, as you <u>know</u> they'll be checked.
Odd the ones that stick:
1594-1632   *Gustavus Adolphus*—bigger than *Abba* in his day
1598   The Edict of Nantes—long-term benefits for Rangers' fans
1618   The Defenestration of Prague—"gardez l'eau"
2006   Walter's boys batter Les Bleus—"one-nil"
1437   James I of Scotland—murrdarrd in the sewers of Perth

Tyrannical King Jimmy the First—great grandson of Robert the Bruce—liked to play tennis but kept losing his balls in the sewers under his house, so he instructed them to

be boarded up; a few days later—his own family having grassed him up and sent the boys in to terminally cure his unreliable first serve—his only route out was blocked.
Long live James II—death to the murderous A(ss)tholl(e)s.
(not sure the storyline's strong enough for Hollywood, but Ewan Gordon McGregor—born just up the road at PRI—would be apposite as the hapless tennis player).

The family seat being just 20 minutes from St. John's toun ('the fair city' of Perth . . . a royal burgh with an eye on promotion), our designated stomping grounds were the cindered terraces of Muirton Park; but on Cup Final day 1954, with the rest of my 'impartial' family rooting for Aberdeen, I decided, defiantly (at 10), to fight Celtic's corner and have remained loyal, if removed, ever since (we liked to have a First Division team to follow and the yo-yos—"The Saintees"—were . . . inconsistent).
Martin (the boot donor) let in two goals, as my new team—Charlie Tully, Willie Fernie, Jock Stein and 'the Bhoys'—ran out 2-1 winners of the Coronation Cup (that kind of slip-up was perfectly fine . . . *but not in the yellow wooly of Scotland, Fred*).

A while after the game, my uncle Gordon, a fanatical Celtic fan (in blinkers) spotted the auction of Cup Final memorabilia in a fitba mag.
Listed among the coveted trophies, and probably still damp and rising, was one of Martin's boots; fortunately—kind soul that he was—'Gogo' thought of David the (favoured) Elder, first.
Much to my house-proud mother's displeasure, the boot came with a distinct bouquet, yet it survived in pride of place in the sad one's bedroom until April 1955, at which point—in the defenestration of Crieff—it was pitched, without warning, from the fourth-floor window of our house above the printing works, into the main street, 50ft below, by person or persons well-known; so good were its fortifications that a passing ten ton lorry barely impressed the toe-cap.

This wanton act of treachery had been provoked by England's annihilation of our brave lads at Wembley; if we suffered in relative silence over that one, the 9 they lashed past Haffey in 1961 (same fixture, same place, same nausea . . . better boots) would have made Fred alone, a wincey bit happier in his skin.

My favourite football club in *England* was Wolverhampton Wanderers—great strip, in black and white. Not sure whether it was the family foot-fettish, but I was fascinated by Johnny Hancocks'—the smallest in top flight football. One misty December night, they worked ever so daintily for Bert Williams, Billy Wright, Ron Flowers and 60,000 packed into Molineux, as the Wanderers (in unfamiliar white shirts) came from two down to beat mighty Honved 3-2 (Hancocks got the first from the penalty spot)—thereby repairing some of the English nation's humiliation.
Small world, but thirty years later I would be working at BBC Sport with Barbara Slater, whose Dad, Bill, was Wolves' captain that foggy, foggy night. A former

gymnast of some repute, little Babs's handstands in the BBC club at Television Centre (in trousers, mostly) abide with me, more than her not inconsiderable contributions to a largely chauvinistic (then) sports department, over which she now appears to have triumphed.

My (fight promoter) grandfather's house on the Glasgow Road was always open—a state taken advantage of by a 'tea leaf,' one warm, summer afternoon. Grandpa Grant was a patron of Perth theatre, so the relatively famous were always coming in and out of our 'second' home. We four cousins, Enid, Hugh, Davie and tiny me—plus *Ben,* our big, soft (as in rideable), black Labrador—would often gather at our 'secret' vantage point, on the first floor landing, to sneak a glimpse, between the banisters, of 'a star'—Scottish actress and comedienne, Janet Brown say, and her actor hubby Peter Butterworth—*Narnia* moments for us (*Ben* knew when to keep his mouth shut).

Auntie Dreda—short, for the much less attractive 'Mildred' (*how could they?*)—was sick, and alone with her misery, in an upstairs bedroom, when a bad guy broke (walked) in for a nose.
Around about the time of this attempt on the forgotten and hardly-worth-risking-porridge-for treasures of No.161, four students—in a bold and provocative act—had nicked the Stone of Scone(or *Stone of Destiny*) from under St. Edward's chair at Westminster Abbey, the very one upon which on June 2nd 1953 our Queen, like so many before, had been crowned, and from which (if the screenplay's to be believed) Edward VI's Aussie voice coach Lionel Logue had disrespectfully challenged its place in our heritage.

They all get a mention in the Stone's eventful history: Dunsinane Hill—of Burnham Woods fame, in 'the Scottish play' . . . William McGonagall's silvery Tay . . . biblical Jacob—he of the Ladder, 12 sons and solitary daughter . . . Columba of Iona—joint patron to Paddies and Jocks . . . and monarchs from Constantine (Kenneth MacAlpin's son) in AD 862, to Queen Elizabeth II, stammering A. F. A. G. Windsor's elder daughter (*four* initials . . . he was monarch after all).

The actual lump (*can we believe this?*) is kept at Edinburgh Castle, where, lest the glorious incumbent abdicates or passes on leaving the way clear for 'Fergie' (Alexander Chapman) to manage the Republic (*like we can afford a Royal Wedding, the Olympics <u>and</u> another Coronation on our wages*), it ought to remain.
Happily, Mr. President is talking to the BBC . . . for now.

Gavin Vernon—my brother's school pal Ward's uncle—was a member of that band of student thieves (or national heroes depending from which side of the old wall you hang), but how brazen to commit robbery of that significance, in broad daylight? Altogether a classier act than the violent, unpredictable, junk-crazed efforts of today's looters.

Apprehending those who would 'burlgalrize,' was a big part of the Bobby's job back then, even if 'police box' didn't *necessarily* mean what it said on the label.

To the Radiophonic Workshop's *musique concréte*, we've slipped on a generation from the reign of William Hartnell (he too was in *This Sporting Life* with Richard Harris & co.,), to a 5th (Peter Davison), or possibly 6th (Colin Baker) *Doctor*—Patrick Troughton and Jon Pertwee having been relieved of their temporary tenancies of the time-Lord's *Tardis*.

We were enjoying a welcome beaker in a north London boozer, after a Denis Waterman XI charity match. 'Diesel'—our inspirational leader—super centre-forward-cum-minder—signed autographs and ordered huge Blue Lable 'voddies,' while our equally-gifted right back—actor cum comedian (come prepared)—Warren Clarke engaged the only fit babe in the pub.
You learned the hard way that when 'His Corpulence' was centre stage, twas best to watch, listen and learn: what he lacked in the chiseled features department, he more than made up for in badinage.
Short-sighted, desperate women, *love* levity.

It transpired that the well-kempt figure to his target's right, was the one she'd sworn to honour and obey, till death (or the nick) did them part.

Ere long, 'Mr. X.'—an extremely well-dressed burglar—excused himself:
"I have to go to work."
Funny, had he been in your hallway, torch and some of your wedding 'prezzies' in hand, you'd happily have taken the sand wedge to him, but here we were chatting away about technique and detection rates (came across as a decent enough cove—a Robin of Croxley—providing it wasn't your stash he was rifling).

The larcenist sifting through my grandparents' drawers (medieval Scone is just a couple of clicks away) would have been well advised to beware the lady in sickness in the adjoining room—Mrs. Mildred Grant Robertson of Granton on Spey . . . *whisky country*.
Dreda's sister—my Mum—had been the (elder) Grant girl to stay home, in fact, she didn't leave Scotland till she was in her fifties, such was the tie of the family in those days . . . meals together, conversation, Caledonian holidays every year, that sort of bizarre behaviour.

Just before World War number two, Dreda had taken her troupe to the Philippines . . . to Manila where her husband, Hugh, had been seconded by *International Harvester*—makers of fine tractors, and things.
When the Japanese invaded, they were among thousands captured and sent to concentration camp.

Reluctantly, she'd tell us of their three years there . . . how Hugh snr., was wounded by mortar shrapnel . . . the hopelessness, the hunger, the disease, the cruelty . . . knowing escape was virtually impossible. The inmates were starving to death, but Dreda wasn't a quitter. She made friends with the villagers, who'd risk much by coming to the barbed-wire fences with scraps of food.
Knowing escape meant death in the jungle, or in seas teaming with things that could really bite for good, the Japs didn't mind that some were given the means to prolong the inevitable—death by starvation, or torture (of which she said little).

One night some Philipinos dragged a tin bath full of ox blood, and worked it through a gaping hole in the defences; the ration of one cup of rice per day per family (four, in my auntie's) would now go a long way. Many stayed alive by communally adding to an unsavoury mix.

She was one tough lady, and no petty criminal was getting the better of her; temperature or no temperature, she tore into the front bedroom, brandishing a shooting-stick, so surprising the intruder that he smashed through the bay window and jumped for it, landing in a flower-bed 15 feet below and making off swag-less, limping.

Dreda's daughter, Enid, introduced me to paper dolls (I was the angelic looking runt of the litter, with curly blonde locks any girl would die for), and to the notion of re-incarnation, as our brothers pursued a plump bumble-bee round the lounge, flailing at it with their tennis raquets (quite put me off the game, for a bit).
Even if Darwin didn't agree, to a Church of Scotland regular like me, these were God's creatures, and none—save the wasp—deserved death by cat gut.
Nowhere in *On the Origin of Species* (nor in Christianity's best seller) is there mention of coming back from a fatal overhead smash—nor are nets and tram lines featured on the lawns of Gethsemane.

The excessive rainfall, during much of my childhood, wasn't down to the North Atlantic drift—arachnid *trial by ordeal* did it: a popular game for two or more players, generally my elder brother and male cousin. Hapless, petrified, disorientated spiders had to anticipate which way the aforementioned sadists would wind the drums of grandma's Victorian mangle, in a game of *no survivors*.

We always had pets in the family—dogs cats, budgies, but so far, no rodents. The whim to change all that took me in an Edinburgh pet shop, as we whiled away the hours before what was to be a one-sided match between Scotland and Wales at Murrayfield.
The delights of Rose Street and its hundred pubs were years from our grasp, as were the prurient offerings from the lady professionals in Leith Walk . . . but there was no harm in window-shopping.

There, on display, like a hooker in Amsterdam (I'd read), was a tiny golden hamster, his cheek panniers loaded with nourishing carry-outs, and by his side a mini-Millennium wheel on which to demonstrate his credentials as an irresistible and entertaining pet (without justification).

At the point of sale, the wee guy was incarcerated in a flimsy cardboard box. He was less than thrilled with a tiny viewing slat. A restricted view of the boring Welsh and their boring nine-man tactics, as they slowly tortured and finally undid Jimmy Greenwood and his team, sent him stir crazy. I name and shame, Clive Rowlands.

I lost my little mate in the crowd—chewed right through one cell wall—so, if anyone remembers seeing a psychologically scarred hamster wandering the streets of Edinburgh one snowy Saturday evening in the early Fifties in the cutest *Timberlands* ever, proudly sporting a saltire transfer on his blown-up face, <u>do</u> get in touch and let me sleep at last.
He could only have lived for three years, max.

Far more mischievous an act—one of which animal 'rightists' would have approved—came with the threat of the sack, legal proceedings, and, quite possibly, terminal illness.
During the school summer holidays, some of us had taken jobs at a mink farm near Comrie, in Perthshire. Not far away was Cultybraggan army camp, where my old man had seen duty during the War, and where many German prisoners had been held, without trial.
The mink at Dalchonzie Farm could have done with their own Geneva Convention, or Great Writ (*habaeus corpus*).
For us, the pay was good, far better than for beating grouse from the comfort of their heathery nests, into speeding grapeshot, in a very one-sided contest; crazy old cocktail of humanity was the shooting party—the idle rich, element-hardened gamekeepers (some on the turn), and barassic schoolboys.

But we'd moved on from that . . . for *BIG MONEY*.

Mink pelts were so valuable that the little critters were constantly being vaccinated against something or other (*women*, basically); that meant sizeable pricks for them and razor sharp teeth for us. Catching a detainee by the thick part of its tail was no easy task, as it careered, in a frenzy, round its wire-mesh prison.
Once arrested, you held the business end with your other hand and the vet gave them the right needle.
Extreme pain creates an overwhelming need to bite back; failing that, get ready for a good dousing of the foulest smelling acid your fellow passengers on the night bus home are ever likely to have to endure . . . nor was it too fabulous for us.

The female mink had to be strapped down for sex . . . nothing kinky, just self-preservation for the guy.
All things considered, it was a shitty life at Scotland's Guantánamo; no swimming facilities . . . dollops of raw grub in the morning (that we risked fingers and forearms picking from cage rooves, at night) . . . rape or be raped now and again . . . . and a horrible death.
And for what, ladies? . . . deadly sin No.8.

Setting the odd one free wasn't part of our brief—and it was rough justice to be bitten for your philanthropy—but having seen how it ended, it was the least we could do.

One of our line managers at the farm had a dreadful stutter, not that he let it bother him (he had absolutely no claim on any throne).
When the ghoulish and well-heeled came to visit—one, provocatively, in a coat of many distant relatives—*T-T-T-Tommy* did his party piece.
He removed a large, male carnivore—two-and-a-half feet long, teeth to tail, and as heavy as six bags of sugar.
'Unusually,' he'd explain (eventually) '*this p-p-p-urple-pelted beauty is . . . t-t-t-t-tame, and likes to b-b-b-b-b-be . . . s-s-s-s-stroked*' (not easy for him to say).
So we swapped him over with old angry bollocks in the next cell, didn't we?
Two potential buyers were rushed off for tetanus shots.
At least *they* lived.

Several 'civilized' farms to the east of Comrie, lived Sir William Patrick Keith Murray—11th Baronet of Ochtertyre . . . cattleman and curling fan; Scotland's gold medal at the Olympics in Salt Lake City would have delighted him—had he lived—as it did all weaned on 'the roaring game.'

We were no strangers to the outdoor bonspiel; a hip flask of the hard stuff, for consenting adults, would keep cockles and muscles warm—sweeping "hard" did it for us minors.

Around Christmas, in times of limited ozone chatter, we'd take to the solid waters of Ochtertyre loch. Team Philips had me as shaky lead, my brother and his unsolicited power-game, second, Uncle 'Gogo' protecting what was left, at third, and Dad, our tactician, skip and saviour.
His stones were two well-hung babies, hewn from Ailsa Craig, an uninhabited, volcanic plug rising from the Irish sea, due west of Turnberry golf course, over which Tom Watson, Greg Norman, Nick Price and Stewart Cink have had the pleasure in recent times.
On a clear day—even if it was *about to rain*—Rhona could see the gannets and puffins from her bedroom window in Ayr; if she couldn't, it would be chucking.

The big house on the estate was a girls' boarding school—Seymour Lodge—in my day, and after we'd scared them off, the Keith-Murray family took over their rightful ownership.

Sir Brian Souter of the *Stagecoach* company—Clause 28 and other queer goings-on—is the present owner.

'Willie' Murray, as you came to know the young Laird after a few soirees, was Scottish aristocracy personified: big spread . . . delightful wife in figure-hugging tweed skirt, twin-set and pearls . . . a liveried nanny to fetch him his son and heir, scrubbed and ready for bed . . . an insatiable appetite for hearty social intercourse, and one even better for *Glenturret* whisky, distilled locally, available at competitive wholesale prices when buying in bulk . . . and a head full of crazy schemes.

W.P.K.M. was patron of our water-ski club, but he never took to it . . . in his malt, nor anywhere else. He had bags of buoyancy in the mid-section, and seldom sat down, preferring to command the open fireplace with an elbow on the mantelpiece, a thumb in the *cratur* and his bollocks a-toasting.

In winter, his estate workers provided tractor power for a t-bar tow, servicing our makeshift ski slope on the hills behind his fabulously appointed house.
None of us showed anything like the potential of Alain Baxter—another Scottish 'success' in 2002 (soon to be stripped of his well won bronze . . . for snorting *Vick*).

Willie tried to start a theatre company in the cellars, enlisting the help of young Denis Lawson, who was treading the boards at Perth and Pitlochry theatres, to great acclaim.

One of my best pals at Morrison's Academy—just a John Daly metal 3 from our house—was Jim McGregor . . . common enough name in these parts; his 'hoose' at the top of the town—when backlit by moonlight—could have doubled for Norman Bates's *mother's* place in *PSYCHO*.

The McGregors were/are a cheery bunch; many a wild Hogmanay party we had in their cluttered front room at *Donavourd*.
But to cut a long story down to fascinating, I was seeing the local jeweler's daughter, Carol (Denis Lawson's sister); quite what 'seeing' her meant, is a hard one, but occasional, tight-lipped necking was all she'd allow. I'd worked steadfastly on my bra-release technique with previous escorts . . . *but there was something about Miss Lawson* . . . and there was definitely something about Larry, her Dad—reminded me a little of the child-catcher in Ian Fleming's *Chitty Chitty Bang Bang* . . . and there was I, in short pants, dating his daughter.

No ambivalence where Phyllis—the mighty, if diminutive, potential mother-in-law (*'in your dreams'*)—was concerned.

One holiday, the Philips family went off to Aberdeen; not being rich (in pounds, shillings and pence), we'd exchange houses with the Christies, our relations in the Granite City.
The Aberdeen buttery—a distant relative of the French croissant, high in fat and bloody gorgeous—and ice-cream from the Washington café on the front (to be taken separately), were to travel long distances in a tiny, leaking, black Austin Standard (registration mark YJ 9427) for; gag reflexes were taken to the edge by a pungent cocktail of Arbroath smokies (haddock with a twist), bought en route, and unascribable human exhaust fumes.
'I Spy'—Gran's cure for motion sickness—had no effect.

This next tangent will be contested, but, following one of his trips to visit his daughter, Dreda—domiciled at Crystal Lake, on the outskirts of Chicago—my grandfather returned bearing gifts, as usual: boxes of bubble-gum for the kids, and for his magnificent Humber Super Snipe—a private limo for the Grant/Philips entourage, and charabanc to 'the stars' of Perth rep—a curious, Perspex device, about 8" x 6" x 4", in clear plastic, shaped like the concave bows of Brunel's *Great Eastern*.

Speeds in excess of all statutory limits were achieved, even on short trips between home and *Fraser's of Perth,* the High Street outfitters managed directly by John Grant (he of the big ring and funny handshake).
Any oncoming bug, flying without due care and attention at precisely its level, would crash into 'the accessory of the century,' mounted externally by the Snipe's radiator cap; at worst, instant death . . . at best (and better for the bug, and the product's UK future) a bounce off, stage left or right, in a hurry, very possibly blinded, with a sore arse, certainly, but no entrail splatter on the windscreen.
Didn't work really, but it was a U.K. 'first,' J.G. claimed, and he was grandpa Grant and we believed <u>everything</u> he said.

Can't say Dad's assertion that he was on the Dons' scouting staff was overwhelmingly convincing. His frequent 'fake' calls to manager Davie Shaw (well before 'Fergie'—circa 1978-86), advising him on team selections and the like, simply stirred we gullible Saints fans up.
Ferguson. A.C., joined *The Muirtonians* in 1960 from Queen's Park F.C., in Glasgow, the oldest club in Scotland.

In 1967, I signed binding forms with Margaret Gordon Nairn Agnew. Her father, Rankine, looked after *The Spiders'* youth team at lesser Hampden (*great, when a plan comes together*).

When we got back from Aberdeen—slightly heavier—two indulgent weeks later, my best mate Jim was 'seeing' my best girl Carol—*the bastard* . . . Jim, I mean (not *my* Carol).

When Carol Diane and James Charles Stuart became the McGregors a few years later, I raised no objection, dispensing my best man duties unquestioningly.
Obi-Wan Kanobi was born in 1971 . . . 'an ugly brother for Colin. Both well.'
(*Ewan Philips* doesn't have the same big-screen ring to it)

Boys being boys, any risque adventure that might endear us (Jim and me) to the young ladies of Seymour Lodge, was to be embraced wholeheartedly. Essentially the plan was to break and enter; thereafter some under-age drinking, plenty giggling, and very possibly, some grappling (minimum).
Carol Lawson—for now—appeared to be off the radar (*the double bastard*).
Stimulating gifts in cans, made the three-mile jog to our targets' dorm, slightly uncomfortable . . . but beers by torchlight, with bored girl boarders in wynsiette nighties . . . *does it get better?*
Trot on!

I had desires for the school's best looker—maid Marion Brown (or her identical twin sister, Helen, in the event of not being over the right bed in the dark) . . . . McGregor wasn't fussy (make that a *triple*).

Detailed plans of the school-house had been smuggled to us during an afternoon of free-skating on the loch below. In a medieval ritual, favours were exchanged . . . ladies to their knights: Marion's scarf was pink—in cashmere if you will—so there were long-term possibilities.

I was never one for 'merchandise'—complimentary or otherwise—but I recall buying two branded towels at Wimbledon: one butch, in All England Club green, the other pink (McEnroe's and Martina's, obviously, should any house guest ask).
This clumsy attempt at arrant gender identification by the Club didn't go down a bundle with the First Lady; only the disparity in prize money, and some dodgy line-calls, displeased 'Her Maj' more.

Checking 'the ageds' were out cold, I donned my *Milk Tray* kit.
Ours was an old house, with unfriendly stairs for burglary and opposite sex sleep-overs. My (reluctantly) complicit brother had mapped each squeaky step over the years, and, for a not inconsiderable wad of pocket money, agreed to share his findings.
Jim, similarly attired, waited in a shop doorway, rucksack bulging.

Entry through the conservatory was facilitated by our co-conspirators latching the *Chubb*. We snuck by the night-matron's open office door in a balletic move, S.A.S.

signaling away in the gloom—*hell, she was 'a big un'* . . . Hattie Jacques proportions, more than a match for any pubescent.

What a rush . . . our hearts were racing. We were up the back stairs like spider-men.

Just the big, padded, fire door left—*fear not, your princes cometh*.

LOCKED, wasn't it?

Inside loos we'd had for years, but mobiles and GPS were yet to reach rural Perthshire. Hell, we'd risked possible criminal charges, and expulsion from a very fine school only to be thwarted, feet from a fumble.
Whatever the inmates did to free the door from its moorings, produced a cadaver-rousing screech, so, rather than wait for a citizen's arrest and a verbal lash by Matron, we were down and out from whence we came, booty intact . . . libido, shot.

Ronnie Steel was the estate gamekeeper on duty that night: he knew his way around in the dark like a Gurkha in Korea.
Within seconds of reaching what we thought was the safety of the rhododendrons, we were rabbits in his flashlight—barn-door syndrome. In his spare time, Ronnie was a crack-shot at our local, small bore, rifle club, and pointing our way at that moment, were twelve of them (bores). He was smart enough not to ask what we were doing; threatening to expose us to our respective fathers, whose own previous (non-criminal) convictions in the irresponsible-teenage-behavioral-stakes were legendary, was an acceptable, almost commendable punishment.

(*My buddy Jim's boy would've got the girl—the producers would've seen to it*).

None of us had any idea of Sir Willie Keith-Murray's finances, except that he'd systematically sold off most of his father's prize herd, and it was increasingly difficult to see how his philanthropy could be sustained.

Charming chap, but he blew his head off in the end . . . at 38.

As crime scenes go, Crieff is a little town (pop. 5,000 odd)—bigger than your average *Midsomer* village . . . but tiny compared to *Morse's* Oxford—yet we did have a grown-up *'murdurr.'* An irate farmer blasted his cheating wife's lover from their marital bed and didn't pass *GO* on his way to Barlinnie jail in Ferris & Thompson's no mean city; she survived . . . just.

My future parents-in-law lived in Burnside on the outskirts of Glasgow, uncomfortably close to where Peter Manuel—'The Beast of Birkenshaw'—had murdered two women and a teenage girl during a killing spree that would end (for him) by rope.

'Bar-L' wasn't just for evil fuckers like Manuel; apparently, big softie, Duncan 'The Dragon' Bannantyne has done a few overnights, as has ex-Everton striker Duncan 'Disorderly' Ferguson (Duncan, in Gaelic, means 'dark-skinned fighter').

We came close, certainly to a good hiding, after five-a-side practice in Glasgow. The team had gone for chips and *Cokes* (we knew about nutrition), to undo that which had gone before; it could have been our final supper on the planet.

The café was empty but for a bunch of no-marks, tucked away in a corner. The only free table was slap bang in the middle of the room, so no cover on any side.
There's always good banter in Glasgow; 'the scuzzers' to our right, alas, had had the by-pass.

I don't recall the key-word that set up our brush with death, but it had at least four syllables, and—as my mate Gordon implied, audibly enough—had it been a spelling bee, the collective capability of our moronic neighbours would have been stretched to breaking point
Not smart, buy *fifteen-love* to the better-schooled.

We tore into our greasy fries and 'juice,' tittering at an early strike for *education, education, education*.

Even in the city, mobiles were rarities.
Whether it was some form of urban bush telegraph, or the whiff of imminent danger that alerted fellow blood-lusty gang members, within minutes, all seats were taken.
Metal ashtrays were ripped into sharp-edged munitions, and surrounding table tops were cleared of drained *Coke* bottles.

Without overstating . . . *it was time to break out the camouflaged trousers.*

Kick-off is usually around the time the first lunge is made; they, judging by some poor quality facial stitching, being infinitely more experienced in armed combat, made it (the opener) . . . but <u>we</u> were in training.
Wearing the odd superficial laceration, and 'lamp,' on the way, we were out the door more efficiently than Celtic's back-line setting an offside trap; our beautifully co-ordinated surge left the opposition in disarray.

Be absolutely clear, this wasn't hand-bagging.

In anticipation of a captive quarry, a rival gang—presumably on the same frequency as those who would do grievous to our bodies—had convened a few yards from the upcoming crime scene.
Their intervention saved us from being scarred for life, at best . . . *'deed'* at worst.

'There's been another _five_ murrdurrs, surr.'

We grew up with *West Side Story*—New York, New York . . . Bernstein and Sondheim . . . Natalie Wood's cleavage (worthy of another mention)—but this was for real . . . *Taggart's* Glasgow, bloody Glasgow.

The two 'tooled' sides squared up as we, bravely, legged it to the getaway car . . . at some pace it has to be said . . . *ventre a terre* i.e. stomach to the ground (get the picture, non?)

How, at that moment, I yearned for the comfort of Nat's bosom, a fantasy I was able to enjoy, alone, for several more nights, thanks to the timely intervention of the U.K. Jets . . . or were they Sharks?—we cared not a jot.

We'd parked our snappy little two-tone Ford Anglia 105E—which could take five sitting, at a push, and ten lying down, comfortably (proven)—in Blythswood Square, a notorious spot, where ladies of the night conducted preliminary interviews.

Yield not to temptation, for yielding is sin;
Each victory will help you, some other to win;
Fight manfully onwards, dark passions subdue,
Look ever to Jesus, he will carry you through.

Those lines from Horatio Palmer's hymn we'd sing, as little innocents, round the fire at Scripture Union camp in Glen Lyon.
The glen—one of Perthshire's finest—is famous for *MacGregor's Leap*, where Gregor MacGregor of Glentrae made a 'Beamonesque' jump across the river (Lyon), pursued by angry Campbells . . . for a *murrdarr* done. Gregor was married to Duncan the Hospitable's daughter (presumably in days when he was, hospitable).

Where was the Big Yin, at this hour of dire consequence?

We'd slowed to a trot; behind us in the street, hell had broken loose.

The occupants of a police panda were less interested in the mayhem caused, than the action they might take against the white-booted lady commandos patrolling the square (*at least I _think_ that's what they were doing*).

I'm not convinced of the second—nor of the facts of the first—but there could be no doubt a third coming was being negotiated, up ahead: there, peering through the rain-swept windscreen of his idling motor, was the very man who preached the perils of the flesh at us from the pulpit of our local kirk, sixty miles to the east (from whence the Magi came).

Normally, his sermons lasted 20 minutes, time enough to suck two of Gran's pan-drops—mint imperials (large)—to saliva, whilst making sporadic eye-contact with the kilted (supposed) maidens of Benheath boarding house sat, alluringly, in the pews below.
Sadly, the aforementioned Seymour Lodgians 'worshipped' elsewhere in town.

Now, the minister <u>could</u> have been there on a mission, offering absolution to the 'prozzies,' or maybe he was just looking for a little light relief from his pastoral duties, miles from a gossiping flock (they were still experimenting with CCTV)

'. . . but, come on Robbie, the open-necked shirt is a bit of a clue!'

We were on an unofficial BBC office outing to a celebrated house of ill-repute in downtown Frankfurt in 1974. The three-storey establishment was listed in the tourist blurb—even so . . . *no names, no law suits*, but one or two very famous faces and associated body parts were exposed that night.
An interesting concept: the tenants on the ground floor got straight to the point, hand on the bollocks . . . base rate; one floor up, more subtlety but nothing to write home about if pissed beyond caring; the greater the climb, the higher the tariff, the fitter the fraulein.
All residents came with state clearance, but we were just looking. *Pussies.*

No cameras!

One of our executives—there to show proclaimed team spirit, yet palpably lacking a fundamental grasp of what was required on a field trip of this nature—declared that <u>his</u> one (bored into keeping the grater *on*, throughout) thought Holland would win the World Cup . . . *not a bad shout at the end of the first group stage.*

The idea of him settling up, then unfurling a BBC wall-chart to hang over her workbench, where—should she find time between fakin' it—the results and scorers could be filled in, was almost plausible: he really was into that kind of anal behavior, and clearly not the other.

WEST GERMANY 2 (finally, before 75,000)
HOLLAND 1
Assuming the butcher of Wolverhampton took note of the scorers (Neeskens, Breitner and Müller) . . . he only booked four* in the game: Bertie Vogts, early on—presumably still pissed about the pen awarded after Uli Hoeness had up-ended the Dutch skipper, right under the future Scotland manager(*"incredible!"*)'s nose, and before anyone had broken sweat . . . and 'the man' himself—the European Footballer of the 20th century elect (ratified in 1999 . . . the same year J. K. Taylor was inducted into FIFA's hall of Fame in Barcelona), and, lest super Leo and the blinding Barca boys forget, not too

dusty at the management game, either——Puma's H.J Cruijff, he of the two 'Adidas' stripes and tiny shorts.

*(Wim van Hanegem and Johann Neeskens were the other two, Magnus).

The great Dutchman and his wife Danny were good mates of Megs and Bob Wilson, maybe from Amsterdam 1971:

NETHERLANDS   2
SCOTLAND   1 (the second of big Bob's 2 caps)
'Willow' presented *Football Focus* throughout my *Grandstand* stewardship . . . look, he *knows* he ought to have covered his near post as Steve Heighway stuck the opener past him in the first period of extra time at the Cup Final earlier that year——enough folk have reminded him . . . *but no harm done, eh?*
LIVERPOOL   1
ARSENAL   2 (and the double).

The shocking story behind Cruyff's 'no-show' at the next World Cup in Argentina was only made known a couple of years ago. He and Danny had been tied up at gunpoint, in front of their children, in their flat in Barcelona, and though undamaged physically, his perspective changed, forever.

N.B. 'Our' pyrrhic victory over the Dutch, and wee Gemmill's 'wonder' goal must <u>never</u> be forgotten.

Should Howard Webb M.B.E. be forced into semi-retirement with a firm of security specialists following a botched operation to remove a perfectly workable whistle from his arse, and Holland . . . or Netherlands . . . whatever, get to their fourth World Cup final in Rio, the Oranje will be praying Sian Massey hasn't trained on (mind you, Howie was unbelievably lenient on Nigel de Jong after his alarming tackle on Xabi Alonso . . . *he could have killed the bugger*).

SPAIN   5 yellows (1 buster)
NETHERLANDS   9 yellows (1 red)

As a postscript to our night of terror in Glasgow, the guy who lit the touch paper in the Byers Road café——which could have led to our disfigurement and/or *murrdurr*——became a top cop in Glasgow city police.

'You just <u>never</u> know, Jackie?'

"... AS LONG AS Z-A-I-R DO"
(AS IN 'HAIR-DO')

26th May 1967: I was dispatched to Abbotsinch—Glasgow airport as it infamously (since the burning car) became—to film Celtic fans' homecoming from Lisbon; many didn't bother . . . for weeks—some didn't bother at all.

The first couple were to type: kilted, booted and minging . . . they'd loved it.

'What a result . . . what a team . . . what aboot the Big Man . . . we-r-ra-peepelle' those sort of considered reactions.

"And what were your seats like?"

"Nae seats in jile, pal!"

Spot of D&D, sadly, but no real bother—there seldom was/is internationally.

I'd missed out on a cracking 3rd/4th place match between Brazil and Italy in Argentina in '78, with an unstemmable attack of the runs, *but how could they get that pissed, knowingly, on such a day?* To be fair, it could have been a 48 hour sentence, yet here we had long standing dipsos, trained for marathons—none of your binge-drinking sprinters' nonsense.

And while I'm on about bears (a Scottish term of endearment for a right, big, hairy-git-of-a-human), Tony Gubba—a tiny English homo sapien—and I volunteered (*he*'d lost his marbles) to visit a Scottish 'township' in Germany during the World Cup in 1974, to get a flavour of what life was like for the travelling Tartan Army.
They'd been allocated a fresh field, where they were at liberty to pitch anything from empty cans of *McEwan's Export* * to tents for the truly posh; there were hundreds of them, sleeping bags and blankets strewn amongst the inevitable clutter of life on the road: high loos, there *were* . . . li-los, there certainly were *not*—these were descendants of fighting men, Gaels and Picts, in kilts and wode . . . pale-skinned 'Duncans.'

Un-phased, Gubbs marched in . . .

*Before *we* do, a footnote on *McEwan's Export*—a libation made in Edinburgh, enjoyed (as encouraged by *The Laughing Cavalier* on the cans) by thousands of football fans, till

1987 when Rangers F.C. signed a sponsorship deal with the then owners, *Scottish & Newcastle*.
Guess who lost the taste for it?
Shame, because it was a decent drop.

For years, *Tennent's Lager* had fit birds down the side of the cans. Grown men—prostrate in the gutter, regretting married life and she who lay in wait should they manage the remaining steps to their back doors and a right battering—could dream of *Ann* (the first), or *Violet* (the last) and all those in between . . . and curse their hastiness.
The series became collectors' items, not just for bin men.

DEFCON 3 at Internierungslager, Frankfurt am Main.

Gubba was immediately surrounded as we set up to start filming. Being of the idiom, I explained that we wanted thoughts on the trip so far, not about the football, more about Germany and German hospitality, which, in spite of all that had gone before, was known to be generous.
I was asking for trouble, but 'the Sweaties' don't have a good reputation for nothing (*Irish, but English can do that sometimes*).
Overnight conditions weren't great . . . but who was sleeping?

We'd had more than enough of the 'vox-popping' when my reporter spotted a caravan, a Romani affair with iron bars on the windows, and substantial locks on the door.
"Dinnae ask," said one of our hosts, spotting Tony's interest, "that's *the Bear* in there."
I quickly translated.
Fair enough, said 'Tone,' thinking clearly, as ever . . . this *is* Germany.

"Gubbs" was cursed with short-man syndrome; his reputation for doggedness, bloody-mindedness, and irritating-bastard-persistence when a good tale was afoot, preceded him like B.O.
By way of illustration (from Hotel Arabella—our BBC base-camp in downtown Frankfurt): a spectacular verbal ruck had occurred, earlier in the week, in one of the boy's bedrooms, over not very much, as usual; couldn't put it down to booze . . . no, it was more of an ego meteor storm, with the talent vying for station as we production 'eggs' worked on a three-week survival strategy.

It may be just a football match—well, dozens of them '*in actual fact*' (one of Brian Clough's favoured expressions . . . a rival, on ITV's panel)—but our shows went on forever: 'live' ones, highlights, re-runs, re-runs of the re-runs, then more 'live' ones, with the inevitable previews and numbing analysis . . . . wall-to-wall, high-class (for the most part) football, with the object, as ever, of '*sticking the ball in the back of the net*' (© A. Hansen of Liverpool, Scotland, M.O.T.D. and *Morrisons*—winner of the silver medal for its onion bhaji dippers in the Frozen Savoury Category of 2010).

The bedroom scene was typical: Coleman at the heart of it, barking out *his* ideas, denouncing all and sundry, and generally being the total knob he could be with next to no provocation; fine, he'd been doing this for years, but that didn't make him omnipotent, *right Tony?*

"Motty"—our debutante—kept his own counsel . . . . Jock Stein and Lawrie McMenemy, some kind of order.

The Rottweiler braced himself as the fearless Yorkie (about as insulting as it gets for a Lancastrian) bared his teeth and prepared a preemptive strike. But "Dave" (Emlyn Hughes was the only man I knew who could get away with that) not known to be a clean fighter, immediately reminded his opponent of his height and standing—I think *"little prat"* was the thrust of it—followed by . . . *"you wouldn't know a story if it bit you in your short arse"* . . . quality, journalistic japing and jousting.

Tony reeled, clearly shaken . . . *would he recover?* He gathered himself and (persisting with issues hirsute) countered that David should *"see someone about a transplant,"* viz. hair from his (arse) to supplement irreversible natural losses on top (not ideal for uber-cool alpha male on the telly) . . . *"and would you ever consider a rug?"* (blimey, pot calling the kettle there . . . but victory to Antonio). Overall, his head-to-heads with 'The Champ' weren't great—but best that he kept sharp and in shape, for re-matches there were bound to be. Cerebral stuff though.

Frank Bough—our studio presenter—would have appreciated the debate: once upon a time, early in his career, the bold boy turned up for work in an unconvincing 'syrup,' drawing the odd gasp and muffled wisecrack, yet insufficient to halt his intention of 'going public' . . . that was until the boss, Mr. Cowgill, saw him: *"What's that foocking thing on your head, Frank!"* (more of an ultimatum than a question).

You've never seen such a gigantic mother in all your life: when the door of the gypsy caravan finally came off its hinges, there, in Hunting Stewart and Scotland top, stood *Sumosorearse Rex*.
Four of his 'keepers' were losing the battle, as he bee-lined the camera.

Invoking the Shakespearian discretion and valour number—as perfected by away fans at Ibrox or Parkhead—we legged it.

Good of the lads to look after 'Duncan the Bear,' who, we'd been assured, was harmless when sober: the embodiment of personal insurance during the day, but a right handful after dark.
His chances of making the final were as slim as Scotland's.

For a decade, Jock Stein's Celtic won the lot playing his brand of pure, beautiful, inventive football: consecutive League titles, the European Cup, Scottish Cups, Cup

Winners' Cups, Glasgow Cups . . . you name it, they'd done it (strange then that club Chairman Bob Kelly got the knighthood, and not the man in charge of the team).

Jock was a great signing at the 1974 Weltmeisterschaft . . . for the BBC and German law enforcement. A terse but friendly *"behave yersels boys,"* from the Big Man, was taken in the intended spirit, as we strolled the straßes of an evening, amidst atheists, agnostics and all who'd otherwise denominate, away from Tartan Army duty.

Jock was a gambler who didn't drink, but his travelling companion Tony Queen did . . . and he was Glasgow's 'King of the Bookies.'
Stein came from the mining village of Burnbank in South Lanarkshire (also home of world flyweight boxing champ Walter McGowan, and the legendary vaudeville turn, Sir Harry Lauder)—Tony would have followed him to the end of the earth . . . and very nearly did when the pair were hit by an oncoming car in 1975, with Jock at the wheel of his pal's car.

The two quickly warmed to us 'weird' TV folk and reveled in the wind-ups; even 'Attila Coleperson' was circumspect about taking on the gaffer and his mate.

We knew plenty about Willie Ormond: after a fantastic playing career at Hibs, he took over as St. Johnstone manager in 1967, taking them to the League Cup final *and* into Europe . . . almost unheard of for a wee club from the sticks. Then, when Tommy Docherty stepped down after a short spell as Scotland boss, Willie was handed the chalice and charged with getting the Jocks to Germany the following year. England hammered them 5-0 in his opening friendly, but Willie had the last laugh when his lot made it to the finals and Alf's didn't. Divine retribution for all the years of piss-taking about our goalkeepers that everything thrown at Jan Tomaszewski (in open play), he managed to keep out somehow. Brian Clough described the Polish keeper as "a clown" (he certainly made us pee our pants).

It was comforting for Ormond to have Jock handy in Frankfurt and they spoke frequently about tactics and team selections.
"Donny"(Osmond↔Ormond)'s squad was a motley group of mullets: opinionated individuals, an ageing superstar, 12 Anglos, 1 Ranger . . . and Kenny Dalglish—one of 4 Celtic players to make the trip.

If Jock's team of '67 had virtually picked itself, Ormond's choices were far from clear cut . . . plus, they had a pig-of-a-draw: Brazil, Yugo-'hard-nuts'-slavia (under mighty Miljan Miljanic) and Zaire (*"cannon fodder—relax, boys"*).

'Crazy Horse' a.k.a. Emlyn Hughes—a Shankly man, but England skipper at the time (of their non-qualification)—was quoted as saying (in his high-pitched, Barrow boy voice):

"I don't mind who beats the Jocks, as long as Z-A-I-R do"

We went scouting to the Scots' training ground—"Queenie," the boss and me.
"Look at them" Jock whinged *"running round cones . . . Christ, if they're no fit by now . . . and whit are aw they hangers-on doing on the pitch . . . those fat buggers in tracksuits . . . and where are the baws?"*
Even I could detect there was room for more purpose and sparkle.

Next on our list were the Slavs.
Miljan and Jock were old adversaries; the Serbian had coached, with huge success, at Red Star Belgrade, Real Madrid and Valencia.
They nodded, respectfully, as training got underway.

"This is a complicated thing they're doing . . . . tough on the players' concentration."
It was as if they were playing three games of one-touch, simultaneously, the outer channels inter-passing across the central group, who were moving in the opposite direction (. . . *saw it all the time at Muirton Park*).

"It's about awareness—watching and listening."
The sage counsellor was taking mental notes . . . . maybe he was fancying another crack at the Scottish job (please)—him or "Fergie."

For many years I was a side-drummer in the school band—right at the back, keeping time, with fast hands, and, in the true spirit of Scotsmen in unbifurcated clothing, nothing on underneath.

There were ten pipers in all, while out front strode our majestic drum-major, Nairn "Ozzie" McEwan, who'd go on to win lots of rugby caps for Scotland (and coach them for a while). He was the only man in the band in a bearskin (*busby* being Sir Matt, or the much smaller headgear worn by Hussars); the rest of us came in the ship-shaped *Glengarry*.

"Oz" cut a spectacular dash in his bright red tunic. Occasionally (when the girls were watching), he'd hurl his silver-crowned mace in the air, catch it on the full in one hand without missing a step, then twirl it faster than your average prancing majorette . . . a great advert for his lecherous corps of six (one bass, two tenors, three sides)in the rear.

Stage left was our lead drummer, Ewan Mac's Dad, Jim—my fellow *Man in Black* from the failed raid on the desperate boarders of Seymour Lodge (*hope you're keeping up*); centre file, Chris Boam—an American, if you will, who could belch the alphabet from a single lungful—with me on the right (A→D was *my* p.b.): Chris and I came in on the second parts, doing in three what Jim had just done on his own; alternate four bars gave the Yank and I extra seconds to clock possible 'follow-ups' lining the route on public march-pasts.

Down the years, Morrison's Academy's combined cadet force band won bags of titles, and we hungered for more; we were the Celtic (circa '64-'74) of Scottish schools' bands (circa '52-'62).
Membership meant being excused tedious drilling and night-time exercises, plus, you got to wear the kilt, white spats and (in the drummers' and drum-major's cases) eye-catching, hunting pink . . . a bigger draw, by far, than the pipers' drab, yet ever-so-co-ordinated black numbers . . . their long, flowing plaids in matching Morrison tartan, gathered at source by a sparkling, jeweled brooch; ours (plaids), of necessity, were shorter, keeping hands free for flamming, rolling, dragging and paradiddling—the dynamics of side-drumming.

Bag-piping is for multi-taskers (*therefore, men shouldn't be able to do it—right, girls?*) . . . blow hard, squeeze, cover and uncover the right holes, march, counter-march in line, and look cool about it . . . a head-tapping-stomach-stroking-plate-spinning-sort-of-thing . . . with big breaths.

Any band, be it at Fairfield Hall, the Locarno, in the Cavern or down Ronnie Scott's, needs to be *tight*—not *wasted*, but *together*—as were Spurs under Billy 'Nic' (Nicholson), Liverpool under Shankly, and Celtic under Stein.

'Pipey' Bob had made it just that little bit more difficult so to be at practice, by scattering us to all points, mixing up drummers and pipers, in a wide circle. Can't do the science but if sound travels at a mile a second, watching Jim's hands in the wind 25 yards away, didn't give you much catch-up time if sync were lost; equally, the pipe-major's fingers were vital clues. On reformation . . . reed and skin in perfect harmony.

We did 'the double' again that year, winning the East <u>and</u> West of Scotland pennant and trophy.

All the Lisbon Lions lived in the Glasgow area; the nearest thing to a 'foreigner' would be Sean Fallon—"The Iron Man"—Jock's assistant, a native of Sligo, birth county of Andrew Kerins, the Marist Brother who founded Celtic F.C. in 1888.
St. Johnstone, on the other hand, was a brood-mare-of-a-club in the Scottish First Division (the S.P.L. of today), when no free-standing room and overflowing toilets were measures of success.
Eighteen year old Sandy McLaren—the youngest goalkeeper to play for Scotland—was capped five times while on the books at Perth, before moving to what would become Gordon Banks country—Leicester City—in 1933.

(*I could get bogged down here*) Billy Taylor was No.1 choice in goal for Saints when I was a teenager, and Bobby Brown—Queen's Park F.C.'s custodian and a clubmate of young Ronnie Simpson's—was the last amateur to be capped for Scotland; Brown became Muirton boss in 1958 and some years later was the first full-time manager of the national side.

Our left half (No. 6) was debonair Ron McInven—the club's pin-up boy—who played for G.B. at the 1960 Olympics . . . the last time Britain entered a team; Yugoslavia won the gold medal.

Manchester United's guv'nor, Matt Busby, had managed the British squad (17 year old Simpson amongst them) at the 1948 Games in London; Sweden gold, Yugolsavia (them again) silver, and Denmark bronze—GB was 4th
. . . might Sir Alex find time in 2012???
The lanky, angular, inside forward was a regular starter in St. Johnstone blue in the early '60s, having also served his 'apprenticeship' amongst the amateurs of Queen's Park.
Very few get away with scoring hat-tricks against Rangers, and thus, following three productive years at Dunfermline, Ferguson signed on for the true Blues of Ibrox.
Gers' current manager, Alistair (as he's known since his elevation) McCoist, maintained his goals-to-games ratio from his Muirton experience (22 in 57) when he fell under Smith & Thornton's spell at Ibrox . . . *and* some (355 bulgers in 581 games for "Coisty").
Jimmy Smith's staggering totals were 225 in 234 (circa 1928-46) and Willie Thornton's 138 in 219, each with a very long half-time break while the whole world kicked-off, and from which Thornton took a Military Medal for *'acts of gallantry and devotion to duty under fire'*.

To extend the link to impatience, Smith once scored six against *The Pars* of Dunfermline, who—betwixt '60 and '64—were managed by Jock Stein.

In order that things don't spiral out of control on the touchline again (till the next time), Kenny Dalglish scored 112 times for Celtic in 204 games, and Neil Lennon was a holding midfielder (. . . *whatever that means*).

On the day war broke out—September 3rd 1939—16 year old Stein was on the books at Albion Rovers in Coatbridge.
The Allies would take the points from the long game, and by 1948 Rovers had won promotion to Division 1.
(*I'm not done with this*).
Alex Ferguson's brother, Martin, is one of a long list (44 to date) of those who've managed at Cliftonhill . . . 'big Tam' Gemmell included: the Lisbon Lion liked it so much he came back for another go . . . as did Joe Baker, the Hibernian, Arsenal,

Nottingham Forest and England striker who was the first player (with a Motherwell accent) to have played for England without having previously played in the English football league: like Stein, Joe survived a serious car crash while on Torino's books with Denis Law

P.S. Jackie Stewart from Dunbartonshire, who won the Italian Grand Prix, twice, and almost single-handedly changed driver and spectator safety in F.1., is not related to Jackie Stewart, football manager . . . at Dumbarton, Coatbridge and Perth.

So there it was: St. Johnstone—small club, big talents, huge losses—whose finest hour was that League Cup final in 1970: I didn't know whether to laugh or cry when Celtic's outside left, Bertie Auld scored the only goal of the game at Hampden.

Uncle 'Go-Go' (the boot benefactor) and my elder brother were minders on *my* first trip to the great arena—aged 12 . . . excited and apprehensive—for a Scotland-England match. I'd heard all about the swirling currents and the spirits of Gallacher and Waddell, but it was the size of the crowd that lowered my jaw; don't know that I counted as I'd been popped over the turnstiles, but if I did, I was the one hundred and thirty-two thousand, eight hundred and seventeenth eye witness to the travesty.

Such was the mass of human kindness that my feet didn't touch the ground till half-time, by which, *we* were ahead.

Without looking it up, all I remember is Johnny Haynes—Fulham and England's answer at inside left, to Tottenham and Scotland's John White at inside right—equalizing late on from a free-kick (*'we wasnae ready ref'*) . . . and a wet coat pocket—my Sunday best, in Tweed, from Grandpa's shop in Perth High Street . . . Mum having gotten me ready.

Getting out for a pie, a pee and a *Bovril* at the break wasn't feasible for everyone packed into the famous old bowl, so the 'done thing' (*says who?*) was to whip out the snake, find the nearest pocket, drop the old man in, and, with an apologetic . . . '*sorry about that, John*' . . . piss on.

The dampness had nothing to do with the euphoria Graham Leggatt's opening goal produced.

I rounded to remonstrate, but at five feet nothing, I had *'nae chance.'*

How did he know my name was John? . . . but then everybody in Glasgow is *'John'* in an emergency.

'I know cos I was there' (© Max Boyce) when we beat the World Cup holders at Wembley in '67, but not another word on the 9-3 lapse, suffice to say, that rounding up strays who'd wandered into the bordellos of Soho—to bury face and sorrow—and getting them to King's Cross and even more, if less well-structured temptation (a

knee-trembler was bargain-of-the-day, *apparently*), was a feat of organizational skill from which Frank Haffey and his defenders could have benefited.

The boys took it pretty well on the way home but . . . *corridor-less trains on a 'football special?'* Not smart to stick your head out for air.

Jimmy Hill introduced me to Johnny Haynes at a book signing in the Café Royal, in central London; largely as a result of Jim's efforts to abolish the £20 maximum wage in 1961, Johnny became the first-ever £100-a-week footballer (THIS IS NOT A MIS-PRINT).
Whether it was the *Brylcreem* he used to advertise (D.C.S. Compton having lost the gig), or just clean living, I swear the No.10 (inside left) shirt of England would still have fitted a very-fit-looking OAP.

Leggatt I never met, nor did I receive any of his vestments or accessories, but Aberdeen's 'finest' was team-mates with and, therefore, bore witness to both F. Martin's boots of a Saturday afternoon
Ultimately, Graham joined Haynes at Craven Cottage and each would go to Sweden as members of their respective World Cup squads in 1958:
(big) early baths for them, but Wales and Northern Ireland made it to the quarters . . . and Pelé (No.10) did quite well, if I remember . . . for a 17 year old.

That was Sweden . . .
. . . back to Deutschland.

The Stein/Queen scouting party had moved on to Camp Brazilia.

"Baws," a more gleeful cry this time from the Big Man—*baws, baws everywhere, and all the goals did shrink*: wrested, hungrily, from their sacks, they were caressed, bent and abused—the Sunshine Boys, the Samba Masters, the Boys from Brazil were back in town.
By then, Pelé, Gerson, Tostao and Carlos Alberto, from the beautiful team of the Azteca in 1970, had retired, but there was Rivelino and Edú and Jairzinho and Paulo Cesar . . . and I could reach out and touch them . . . the W (for WOW) Factor.

You could understand the hiatus had a gaggle of be-thonged Ipanema beach-babes been shipped in as an away-day surprise, but when the 1972 World F1 Champion, who'd been testing his McLaren M23 nearby, dropped in by helicopter . . . training ground to a halt.
Here was the embodiment of national pride—the perfect fillip for Zagallo's men as they prepared to defend their title, and add a brand new FIFA World Cup trophy to the Jules Rimet.

Emerson Fittipaldi won the drivers' championship again that year.
(his Polish Mum would get the drop on his Dad in the play-off final)
Poland   1 (they were *good* . . . Deyna, Domarkski and "the
                                clown")
Brazil   0

Tony was lighting up; a stiff blend lay within easy reach on the bedside table as the phone went in Jock's room:
"*Hullo wee man.*" I motioned to leave but was signaled to stay put.
Right.

Jock Stein was a masterful manager, not in Ron Greenwood's league, tactically, but like Shankly and Nicholson, he knew what the fans expected, and how best to get his players to perform, be it imperious club skipper Billy "Caesar" McNeill, or the little wizard, jinking Jimmy Johnstone.
Celtic Park was no place for moody buggers.

"*Listen, son,*" our end of the conversation began, "*you'll no be talkin' any mair aboot goin' hame—d'ya hear me wee man? He'll pick you soon enough.*"

Jock put the phone down . . . "*Jinky*" (he rolled his eyes).

Only Denis Law, Billy Bremner and David Hay had more caps than Jimmy, and he (Hay), Danny McGrain and the redoubtable Kenny Dalglish—all Celts—were down to play in the upcoming match.

Jock was perplexed, yet inwardly sympathetic.
Scotland always had great wingers . . . from Alex Jackson and Willie Waddell to wee Willie Henderson and the ginger-nut himself; were a vital spark needed to 'turn' a game, "JJ" was the very fellow to provide it . . . but he was easily led. He'd already clashed with the manager for boozing on one of the qualifying trips and was now in danger of shooting himself in the foot (his *left*, preferably).

There were other issues—big ones:
Was 'the King' (Denis Law) *past it at 34?* (the Zaire game was his only appearance in the final stages of a World Cup—Scotland having missed out from 1962-70 . . . his prolific days at Old Trafford)
How many would the Yugoslavs and Brazilians get against the Africans?
Could we qualify from such a tough group?

The concensus was we could—and we bloody nearly did: had Bremner's shin-pad been an inch thicker, it might have deflected a wicked, second-half cross into Brazil's goal . . . then we wouldn't have needed to bother about goal difference.

A meagre 2-0 margin against Emlyn's Z-a-i-r wasn't enough—the Slavs putting 9 past them, and Brazil, 3.
Unbeaten (played 3, won 1, drawn 2) and bowed, my team was on the way home and the bragging had to stop.
An ignominious exit awaited us four years later, under Ally McLeod (*at least we were there*).

No atmosphere rivals an Old Firm game; the World Darts at Frimley Green is wild and raucous, but it lacks that cutting sectarian edge—if *Rocking All over the World* by the Quo impassions . . . *The Sash* and *Hail Hail* rabble-rouse (maybe one year they could try Old Firm rugby . . . then they could all get stuck in . . . Neil and Ally too).

Archie McPherson, an erudite, if somewhat aloof citizen, commentated on many top-end comings-together, for BBC Scotland.

Our TV trucks were parked on the opposite side of the ground from the administrative offices at Celtic Park. Rather than take the 'safe' route, round the exterior roadway, educated 'Arch' proposed a stroll round the cinder track to the manager (Mr. Stein)'s office.
The distance to be covered was around 350 yards, at an average speed of 3 m.p.h. (*you do the maths*), but to appreciate the full force of invective attracted (me by association), you had to be there (or not).

The real fan stood in those days, so they could take a run at it (us).

No-one can enjoy having their legitimacy questioned, even Peter West, the BBC rugby commentator (*yes, someone <u>other</u> than Bill McLaren had done it*); according to the Murrayfield faithful, he was "a biased English bastard" . . . which was rude of course, but mild compared to the baying denunciations from Parkhead's terrraces. Only the knitting hags of Paris (during The Red Terror of the French Revolution) were a match.

Liberté, égalité, fraternité . . . *my arsesity!*

Unlike "Westy," Archie hadn't given in to the ravages of *total* hair loss, so *Weetabix* got a few gratuitous plugs along the way.
Head and shoulders bowed, like 18th century aristocrats rumbling by tumbrel towards the only full-proof dandruff cure, we walked the walk, inexorably. Archie cruised along, as if on roller skates, seemingly oblivious, his wispy strands blowing in the bile.
By the time we reached the safety of the players' tunnel, I was a wreck. Marie Antoinette, allegedly, had gone grey overnight.
(*I'd be taking a close look—back and sides—in the morning*).

We made it, physically unharmed; with his familiar, stooped, shuffling walk—a legacy of playing too long with dodgy ankles and knees—Jock appeared across the hall. Archie called out, confidently:

"See you Archie . . . . your commentary on oor last game was a disgrace; caw canny, or I'll ban you forever" (so *that's* where "Fergie" got the idea).

I returned the hand with which I was planning to greet my old friend to my jacket pocket; odd time to be thinking of *Jock Falstaff*:

"The better part of Valour, is Discretion; in the which better part, I haue saued my life"

(Henry The Fourth, Part 1 Act 5, scene 4 . . . *if I'm not mistaken*)

McPherson wasn't alone when it came to a Stein rollicking: he (Jock) once launched himself into the crowd (the Celtic end) to berate them for singing sectarian songs. Archie contended it was character building for him—not bad from one who'd accede to the office of Lord Rector of Edinburgh University (*wonder if local boy Sir Chris Hoy has a chance in 2012*).

Stein left Parkhead eleven years and eighteen major Scottish titles later; apparently he was offered the job at Manchester United after Matt Busby had called it a day, but he turned it down, opting instead for a spell at (pre-'damned') Leeds.

As it was for the incomparable Tommy Cooper, death came prematurely, publically and suddenly—at work—for Jock Stein; the big fella's heart, that could have burst with pride at any time (Celtic won five cups in '67 alone) gave out during a World Cup qualifier in Cardiff.
Scotland had just scored through a Davie Cooper penalty, and as the manager rose from the team dug-out to remonstrate with a photographer, he stumbled and collapsed . . . much as the iconic Welsh comedian had, mid-performance, at Her Majesty's theatre in London . . . and as the former Rangers and Motherwell striker had while filming a skills show with Charlie Nicholas.
Tommy was 63 when he died, Jock was 62—Davie was only 39 (hundreds of Celtic fans sent messages of condolence).

My biggest regret, other than not being on the terraces in Lisbon, was that a carefully planned television tribute hadn't come off while Jock was alive. On the 10th anniversary of the win in Portugal, I'd contacted all the Lions—Simpson, Craig, Gemmell, Murdoch, McNeill, Clark, Johnstone, Chalmers, Wallace, Lennox and Auld—who played—and Hughes, McBride, O'Neill and Gallagher—who didn't.

We offered to pay for them to travel to a surprise bash at Parkhead, and we'd put it on film for *Sportsnight*.

The players would have come anyway, but it's a close-knit group at Celtic F.C.—word got out:
"Naw, I wouldnae have liked that, John" said Jock.

Bill Shankly's appreciation, on the coach back to the team hotel after Internazionale had succumbed, will do nicely:

'John, you're immortal now.'

I never came across (Sir) Matt—the second member of the great Scottish managerial triumvirate (it's a four-ball now)—but Shanks—the third—I did . . . quite often.

Match of the Day is alive and well, and so too, *Goal of the Month* . . . albeit, "it's not a competition" now.
Back issues . . . like Ronnie Radford's rocket against Newcastle in the Cup for non-leaguers Hereford . . . a fabulous turn and shot by the late Justin Fashanu against Liverpool at Carrow Road . . . . Mickey Walsh for Blackpool against Sunderland in 1975 . . . screamers from Kevin Beattie and Emlyn Hughes . . . had us out of our seats.
The first three made it to *Goal of the Season,* as did Alan
Mullery's volley for Fulham against Leicester in the F.A.Cup on 26th January 1974; it had a long stint as the precursor to the *Match of the Day* titles;

"What a goal, goal, goal, goal . . ."
Motty's commentary, echoing and fading over an exultant "Mullers" in medium close-up.
(I'm happy to retain those bragging rights, to credit—as is the custom—'my' VT editor Neil Pittaway with its construction, and to acknowledge Barry Stoller for writing Britain's most recognisable theme tune).

The prematurely grey (*or were they highlights?*) legend, Roberto Bettega (*what a great name*)—'La Penna Bianca'—hero of Juve and 'the Azzuri,' had scored an absolute belter against England, which, under international rules, made it eligible for consideration; back then—with turgid catenaccio all but dead—a hundred quids' worth of premium bonds wasn't to be sneezed at (I wonder at times if ERNIE* *ever did* swallow my three numbers—*electronic random* number indicator equipment: *random = equally likely.

Each month, a celebrity guest would be filmed making his 3-2-1 choice. I'd drawn 'The Chosen One.'

Clutching my Video Home System copy of the contenders, I travelled to West Derby to seek out William Shankly of Glenbuck Cherrypickers F.C.

Jeff Stelling probably knows a thing or two about Glenbuck's away form in the south Ayrshire junior league in the1890s, but I doubt if your average Scouser did.
Grit and determination, pass and move, the ethos of the Cherrypickers, would soon be Liverpool F.Cs' credo . . . the new manager, its embodiment.

"Shanks"—miner and motivator extraordinaire—was about to make the red faction of Merseyside very happy indeed.

(INTERIOR: *Chez Shanks*. The Manager moves forward to greet his faltering guest, a gnarled hand extended in friendship)

"Come in, son" (or, *put that hand in this vice*).

Apologising to Ness (Mrs. S.) for the disruption, I explained the drill, showed the busters, and left Bill to make his choice.

(*The Manager stands . . . legs part, slightly . . . hands fumble in his pockets*)

"Right, ready when you are, John."

(*Blimey, that was quick*)

(*Camera and recorder reach the required speed . . . the Manager—a twinkle in his eye—peers down the lens, demanding attention; his mouth curls slightly as he begins, confidently, in a rich, melifluous, west coast accent*):

"The winner is Bettega, *Goal of the Month*"

(*. . . dare I?*)

. . . I spluttered, hesitantly:

"Er . . . couple of things Bill . . . you need to mention your <u>third</u> place goal <u>first</u>, <u>then</u> the second, and then . . . '*but the winner is* . . .' and explain why you've picked that particular goal . . . OK?"

"Aye, right."

(*The Manager hardly takes a breath*)

"The winner is <u>Bettega</u> . . . *Goal of the Month,* but it should have been *Goal of the Century* cos he beat <u>Ray</u> the best goalkeeper in the <u>Wurld</u>."

(i.e. Clemence of Liverpool . . . . *not sure 'Shilts' would agree with that bit, William*).

I'd probably still be there if I'd stuck to the principles laid down for other, mortal judges.

Bettega it was.

In February 1967, after a short spell at Blackpool, Emlyn Hughes signed for Liverpool—for just over £60,000 . . . about half a week's worth for Gerrard and co., today.

The story goes that the police had stopped "Shanks" in his car, as he drove the new boy to Anfield for the first time:

"D'y'a know who this young man iz?"

The copper (obviously not a Seasider) didn't have a *Scooby Doo*.

"I'll tell you—he's the future captain of England!"

Spot on there: Joe Mercer gave Hughes the armband in 1974, the year Anfield trembled and bade goodbye to its Messiah . . . not before the two ("Shanks" and "Crazy Horse") had shared in League Championship, FA Cup and UEFA Cup glory.

Emlyn was all over the BBC schedules . . . and Princess Anne in *A Question of Sport* . . . when he stopped playing; were it now, he'd have been a celebrity chef, a beaming ballroom dancer, a clumsy Cousins on ice, a jungle shoo-in . . . *no question*.

Hughes never played in the World Cup finals; his quip about 'Zair' and the Jocks was meant in fun . . . *I think*.

"I think he's up The Dikler"

Style councillors abound amongst the sporting greats.

Radcliffe and Zatopek don't qualify, but Lord Coe, as a lad, and El Guerrouj of Morocco certainly do. Front crawling Bobby McGregor told me in a radio interview, at Bon Accord baths in Aberdeen, that he believed style was key in sport; in track sprinters like Borzov, Lewis, Don Quarrie, Katrin Krabbe, flying housewife 'Fanny' Blankers-Koen, and McDonald Bailey (from bygone days), you'll see his point; Houston McTear and Ben Johnson got there quickly, but it was never pretty (. . . *if only Usain could get his start right*).

The fun and aesthetic of sport are its attractions; as individuals, many disappoint—not everyone's born shy like Christina Kim, or cool as 'Fedex'—but fail to be thrilled by Elkington and Ballesteros with golf clubs . . . Best and Berbatov with 'tied-on' footballs . . . McIntyre and Rossi, at one on their bikes . . . McEnroe (mute key *on*) and Edberg (mute key *unnecessary*)—touch and grace personified . . . the efficacious elegance of either Richards—I.V.A. or B.A. (and D.I. Gower of Leicestershire, England and B.Sky.B.) . . . . talents that aren't unique by definition, but you'd wish to try their way first (even soppy girls would).

One of my good pals in Crieff, Simon Rogerson, jumped for Britain—or his horses did, while he sat quietly: his too, the style-first credo, and he was surrounded by role models . . . Alvin Schockemöhle from Germany . . . . the elegant Brazilian, Nelson Pesoa . . . and Liz Edgar, (David Broome's sister) who clearly didn't attend the same finishing school as her bashful old man.

They'd clear a wide berth, from the collecting ring to the main arena at Wembley Pool when *Uncle Max*'s rodeo round was due (you suspected a little showboating on both their parts). *Max* could dream all he liked, bustling Ted was no 8 stone anorexic—a full English, with chips and a fried slice, meant what it said on the wrapper.

The trailer park at the Horse of the Year Show was a breeding ground. Simon's custom-built box slept six at a push, with hot and cold running water, fridge, cooker, head—the works . . . human quarters similarly.
But it was in the old-fashioned caravans that most business (equine, human, monkey) was done; where dames and sires gathered, trading (and covering) could begin.

There were card-schools and troughs of drink. Stephen Hadley, who handled a running martingale better than most, knew good horseflesh when he saw it, and was always on the look-out for something decent to mount.

Steve was to the novice show jumper, what David Leadbetter would become to Florida's hackers; his counsel was sought, constantly, so little surprise that when he laid his rarely used whip (on horses) down, the BBC offered him a lip-microphone.

The show jumping commentary double act, when I was around, was a 'plummy' affair, viz., Dorian Williams and Raymond Brookes-Ward; eavesdrop any night, in and around the trailer park, and little of their brand of the Queen's was being spoken; some of the behaviour was public school in its cad-and-child-ishness, but most of the jocks/jockettes were down-to-earth (4 faults, under the 1925 rules) folk . . . . more Young Ones than To The Manor Born.

There'd always be some tale to tell, from a night in the (Harvey) Smith family's tender, were you brave enough to attend, far less opine.

The state-sponsored German team, with whom Eddie Macken would become very familiar, often came with horses to sell. Further flung, less affluent jockeys traded out of necessity . . . perhaps to pay for their return trip from the Mecca of jumping, or to settle gambling debts; *when in London, poker is played to U.K. rules, O.K.?*.

We were dining at the Edgars' ranch, which adjoined the Bland estate, in Warwickshire (*obviously, I was in the wrong game*).
After brandy—which, in that company, could come at you any time between the gazpacho and the baked Alaska—Ted promised to demonstrate his great empathy with his horses by inviting those brave, or tanked enough, to join him in the paddock—more of a three-line whip, really. It was snowing, but Ted, held in place by his red braces, shunned a blanket and marched us off into the fields . . . *was this to be another Wild Western collaboration with Max?*

"Take a look at this chap, he's a right sort" . . . his whispered words freezing in a thought bubble. Chubby thumb and forefinger to his lips creating the perfect reed, he sent a faint whistle out towards three barely discernable figures, silhouetted in the moonlight—one, we knew to be his accomplice.
Nothing.
He tried again, with a *"here boy"* on the end.

'KIT'—in the popular *Knight Rider* series—had been wired with in-built voice recognition, but *'Ted no Hoff he was'* (as little Yoda—emerging as a huge force in the movies—might have put it).

'Amateur' jumpers (the horses) now came with sponsors' names in front, requiring more on-screen caption space and totally 'de-humanising' the formerly, instantly recognizable equines.
The Hongkong and Shanghai Banking Corporation's Penwood Forge Mill would have been a time fault on its own had they chosen to invest in the 1973 King George V Gold Cup winner (Paddy McMahon up) . . . but they didn't.

Was the new boy to the yard simply doing as contracted?
"Here boy" was scant recognition, regardless of the audience.

When Ranulph Fiennes' fingers died on him, he hacked them off with a *Black & Decker*, so in advance of ours going black, we abandoned the whisperer-in-Larry King's to his theories, and repaired to his hearth, at the gallop.

David Coleman was great mates with the Edgars; clearly some of Mama Liz's superb technique had rubbed off on D.C.'s daughter, Ann—Eddie Macken's too. At Hickstead Derby time, the Irishman was in his element, stringing four wins in a row together, a couple times on plain *Boomerang*, before *Carroll's* fags took a hold.
Bred in Ireland as *Battle Boy*, his Mum was called *The Girl from Brown Mountain* and his Dad was a well-endowed, randy bugger from Kilkenny. Then the Edgars got him; *they* sold him to the Germans—Paul Schockemöhle riding him for a bit (while)—who gave the re-named *Boomerang* to Eddie—the rest (Mrs. Tindall) is *"amazing."*

Let's hear it for the BBC archive: the inscription, in Irish, by the 16.2 hunter's grave means . . . *you won't see the likes of me again*

Ann's Dad was between jobs, yet he needn't have taken his failure to crack the American television market so seriously. When Charles Sonny Liston destroyed Floyd Patterson in the ring, the humiliation was too much for the former champ, so he put on a fake beard and disappeared for a while. As yet, no one had come along to challenge D.C. as undisputed, undefeated, heavyweight champion of sports broadcasting in the UK; pound for pound, Bough and Carpenter punched their very different weights and the boy Vine was a genuine contender, but if block-busting were required, Davie was your man.

(Worryingly for all of them, the Irish pretender's beard was real.)

'The champ' took to driving his daughter's horse-box, shades on, flat-cap down, keeping his distance from a world he dominated for so long.
He'd be back . . . to collect a hard earned O.B.E. from the Palace, and the Olympic Order from Mr. Samaranch . . . . *but would he stay too long?*

Plenty folk, other than those with an allergic reaction or inherent fear, like horses—some say they help with human depression and anxiety—but when Henry T. Ford set up in competition, their job opportunities diminished, rapidly.

Show jumping took up a lot of winter prime-time on television, basically because the Brits were good at it; houses were always full at Wembley, Olympia and Hickstead.

Can't say I shared our bosses' obsession with horse racing.
Leading lights at the BBC, like Paul Fox and Harry 'the Horse' Middleton, may have felt their fanatical endorsement of the sport of Kings was a fast track to knighthoods, but there was too much of it—too many mediocre races; in any other sport they'd never have had the airtime (the viewing figures supported my view). Happily for those who loved it, the racing contracts weren't down to me.

What *was* within my power (to Mr. O'Sullevan's chagrin) was to cut down the time spent, front and back—certainly of insignificant races—on *Grandstand*. If I could squeeze in three more overs from the Oval, rather than look at rider-less horses, walking round and round like hamsters in a wheel, or listen to a trainer describe how the gallops had gone and hypothesizing on the outcome of the upcoming lottery, then I would.

I like *Radio Five Live's* approach on Saturdays—throw to the racing two furlongs out. That said, there's no greater sight in sport than Piggott on a flying filly at the point of release, the pair hurtling, telepathically, towards the line; John Francome, technically adept and courageous for sure, crafting his way round a glutinous steeplechase course at Chepstow in a biting north easterly, buns tight to the plate, knees in, heels down, stylish as the show jumper he was, was as classic.

But the 'stars' weren't there every week—racing was . . . and so, passionate above and beyond the point of irritation, was McCrirrick . . . in everyone's face, and ear, on the *Grandstand* floor and in the production gallery—a chauvinist with a plan was John (if no great dress sense).
Nothing changes.

What *Channel 4* demonstrated with its racing (and cricket) coverage, was that dedication of effort to one sport allowed for a more consistent and detailed examination of its elements than we were able to achieve on *Grandstand*. We could tell you, with matchless authority, who was running, what their chances were, and show you the races, but resources, and time allowed—certainly at week-ends—left room for little else . . . which didn't sadden me.

O'Sullevan, Wilson, Lindley, Pitman, Smith, Powell and co., came into their own at the National, Glorious Goodwood, the mid-week Cheltenham Festival and big races like the King George at Ascot, but those were exceptions for the exceptional; there were dollops of bland fodder.

Not sure if they're precluded in the small print, or it's simply to do with the acceptance speech, but an animal has never won *Sports Personality of the Year*; one made it on stage, showing better toilet training than *Blue Peter's* elephant during the Noakes-Singleton-Purves era. It always made the warm-up tape *Lulu* (*"no gold badge for you, young lady"*) trawling her severely hacked-off trainer through the piss and poo.

Red Rum's two-way 'interview' with Tommy Stack in 1977, showed there was more between the horse's ears than blind obedience.
I'd been told on good authority (not Uncle Ted) that a horse would sooner walk round an obstacle than jump it, making Aintree's Chair and the Puissance wall at Wembley, lily gilders (good job the horses never got to see Dick Fosbury flop).

So many were put at risk, week in and week out, in the winter months on BBC Sport. Bryan Cowgill's homily about '*dead horses on my programmes*' (he wouldn't have them i.e. '*always cut away from them*') was a bit rich; don't think altruism was at work there.

Let's lamp the donkey, trot down the bottom field, cover a mare or two—all of them if there's time—then go dip the old rudders in the river. Did you see those crazy bastards at Becher's, risking their tackle—they must think we're all soft. Pass the oats if you're done.

Being 'bred for the job' might not cross a horse's mind, early in the piece, as cold bricks were prepared, nor when its life was extinguished, prematurely, behind racecourse vet's screens. At least the owners, trainers and undeniably brave jockeys have a choice.
Still, they all claim to love the beasts, so that's OK then . . . and gambling, as my Grandpa could testify, is a mug's game.

When *Bambi's* mother died in the forest fire I was in despair. Add that to my Mum's reassurance that Roy Rogers's palomino—with jewel-encrusted tack and stirrup fairings—would always find his own way home, and you'll see from whence my sensitivity came; the singing cowboy would leap from his back onto a speeding train full of baddies to rescue the girl in distress: '. . . *so where did Trigger go, Mum . . . . anything could have happened to him?*' No-one mentioned horses' homing instincts when the cat went missing. My pre-nursery handle on cinematographic licence and grammar was skimpy.

When the A-listed *Shergar* went missing (pissed the Derby in '81) it was of international concern. Wise-guy cracks flooded the market; predictably, Lord Lucan, who'd vanished seven years earlier, got in on the act, and mercurial Ronnie Biggs (kidnapped himself on Barbados in '81) was spotted playing up front for <u>Fluminense</u> in Serié A (Brazil).

Michael Stoute thought he (*Shergar*) was the best he'd trained, and his stud value wouldn't have been lost on the Aga Khan . . . nor his abductors. But what a heartless thing to do; if anyone needed a good 'bricking' it was those dirty rats (*a bullet to the forehead?..Harsh, probably*).

The Great Train Robbers got off lightly.

Arkle's celebrity, rather than my boss' pretention in naming his house after him, meant a trip for the crew and me to Tom Dreaper snr.'s yard in Ireland, there to meet with the grand old man, and to glean an impression or two from the gelding's pilot, Pat Taafe (*not a word of which I understood*); liked his *Guinness* did *Arkle*—Pat and Tom too, I suspect.

Keep an eye on *The Life* around springtime: if there's anything down to run at Aintree that looks as if it's been named after a Scottish mountain, get your shirt on it . . . *Shehallion* or *Ben Lomond* or *Vorlich* something of that order.

Arkle, three-times (on the bounce) winner of the Cheltenham Gold Cup got his name from a Scottish mountain and, stretching a point, so did:

"Trew all this mayhem, Foinavon*'s going on . . ."*

Foinaven with an 'e' is in the same Highland range as *Arkle*—which rises from the shores of Loch Stack—but the connection founders there, for as you'll know, Tommy (and *Red Rum*) is Irish; the Gaels say: *"it isn't a trick till it's done three times,"* reason enough to stake your mortgage in 1977.

In 1984 *Ben Nevis* topped the lot.

Johnny Buckingham—*Foinavon's* jockey in around the 23rd fence carnage that 'amazing' day in 1967 (my first National as a BBC Sport apprentice) was as certain a guest on every subsequent Grand National *Grandstand* as Jenny Pitman (in tears) or 'Ginger' McCain (grinning like a Cheshire cat).

Neither we, nor they, nor *Corbiere*, nor magnificent '*Rummy*' disappointed.

Had he been American, *Desert Orchid* would have been a *Letterman* guest, and his hoof-prints by *Trigger's* on the sidewalk at Grauman's Theatre in L.A.

He was a superstar in the 'Golden Balls' mould i.e. Beck's—the 'entire' Daddy.

No question, Ted Edgar's seemingly uncontrollable grey, *Uncle Max*, was a bit of a show-off—*'Dessie'* however, was something else. Where there were cameras—be they furlongs away on scaffold towers in the country, by winning posts at Kempton, Ascot or Cheltenham, or at pitch level whilst rehearsing on the gallops—a show was guaranteed; our figures were in for a hike.
'Grey' days, with *'Dessie'* and *'Dessie'* on *Grandstand*, were measured and unmissable.

The Philips family were bunched round our mahogany-clad telly for the 1953 Coronation Derby, as *Pinza* (Gordon Richards up) put one over Her Majesty's *Aureole* (. . . and *still* she knighted his little impertinence). Factually, the knighthood had already been conferred; I guess riding over four thousand, eight hundred winners in a career might have had some bearing.
With Dettori breaking his Epsom duck in '07, you sense the little people are in for another audience with the sport's most recognisable punter—cum-swordswoman (*have you ever watched fencing on TV?—quite ridiculous*). Presumably, the 'flying' son-of-a-Sardinian is eligible for 'the full Monty' having already being made an honorary member of the most excellent order—Signore Lanfranco Dettori, Kt, MBE . . . Arsenal fan.

Kop this for a crazy synopsis:

Aintree, Liverpool, England, 1956: a bleak, Spring Saturday, around four in the afternoon—half-times, done and dusted. Manchester United, under Matt Busby, are heading for the league title in England, and, unsurprisingly, odds-on for Scott Symon's Rangers in Scotland.

Thundering into view, a big, bay, boy-racer; atop a little red-faced man in a pale jumper and black cap—its light-coloured tassel bouncing erratically—desperately urges his weary charge on.
The run-in seems interminable—the tank is nearly dry.

What's left of the field, are furlongs left of frame.

Thirty obstacles negotiated, and with less than a hundred yards of a four and a half mile marathon standing between them and National Hunt history . . . . the gelding bloody well collapses!

What's afoot?
Had a shot been fired from a grassy knoll by Becher's b(r)ook and jockey depository? . . . Had he come over unnecessary at the prospect of a seminal win for the House of Bowes-Lyon?

Or was it, 'midst all other conspiracies, that he needed 'to go' . . . Couldn't he have waited? . . . Had he forgotten how boys pee . . . or had ESB, ESP and known all along, that he'd burst, eventually?

Be it a fix, scam or sting, *Devon Loch* and Dick Francis weren't destined to win the greatest betting race on earth.

A whodunit* of 'Mousetrap' proportions (. . . . *it'll never sell*).

P.S. A theatrical non-sequitor: (Devonian) Agatha Christie's play had been running in London's West End for four years already, and *My Fair Lady* (starring Julie Andrews and Rex Harrison) had just opened on Broadway—*that* was Ascot opening day . . . *this* was Day 3 of the Aintree Festival.

P.P.S. *The Mousetrap* is the longest running show in the World—don't take my word for it, check the good *Guinness* book . . . *then go see it*.

*P.P.P.S. (if that is allowed) *The Sport of Queens* by Dick Francis (his first novel) was published the following year (1957).

The '*lege*'—Peter O'Sullevan—began *his* National tv commentaries in 1960 (*Merryman II*); his last was in 1997 (*Lord Gyllene*)—just the one spoiled paper in 1993 (*Esha Ness*) . . . . that's thirty-seven years of research and colouring-in: his race cribs were works of art . . . profiles of every two and four-legged participant with miniatures of each pilot's colours—that remember for *every* race, not just once a year . . .

. . . *e-Bay, here I come.*

How's about *Seagram* winning the *Seagram* Grand National . . . then the sponsor and C.E.O., Edgar Bronfman Snr., waking from his reverie in a sweat, next to Georgiana, his gorgeous, soon-to-be-estranged-if-financially-secure wife, wishing he'd accepted the pre-race offer to buy the beast?

I quit the BBC in January 1991; had I stayed, it would have been my 10th Grand National as editor. *Time out.*
(I just *knew* it would all go to pot without me . . . bomb scares, void races, more dead horses . . . *dear me*).

We'd been very close to Seagram—11th hour saviours of the gruelling, 9 minute trial by attrition—and to their larger-than-life M.D. (in the U.K.), Major Ivan Straker (ret'd).

Blustering Ivan would impose a curfew on his drinking over the Christmas and New Year periods, so that come April (in his frock coat), he'd be in top condition and could give it large at Aintree.

Clerk of the Course for much of Ivan's reign, was John Hughes; the difference between 'Hughsy' and many of the other toffy-nosed Clerks was . . . *he* wasn't.

We got on famously; many nights we had putting the World straight, and sinking reds (mainly), at the Cavalry Club's snooker room in Piccadilly. Not sure how hammered I would have been on a random breathalyser, but when a former army 'chappie' challenged me to an early morning frame for 200 'squidily-dos,' my BAC and BP got in a helluva tangle. My less intoxicated opponent claimed to hold a military championship title from somewhere in Africa.
I kicked his ass.
Like the trooper he undoubtedly was under fire, his cheque came good; an accompanying request for a job at 'The Beeb,' I was unable to fix.

Cheltenham 1973 . . . Gold Cup day . . . strides remain (imagine the voice):

"The Dikler's going to get up . . . I think he's up The Dikler!"
Mr. O'Sullevan, spot on, as ever—*The Dikler*, with Ron Barry up, <u>was</u> . . . up.

Now, there's my little friend, Richard Pitman, at Aintree, on board *Crisp*. ('Pitters'—on *Pendil*—had come second to *The Dikler* in the Gold Cup):

" . . . *he's been out there on his own for so long"* empathised Peter, " . . . *Crisp is getting very tired"* . . . the tone, now, one of resignation . . . *"Red Rum is going to win the National . . ."* premature but emphatic.
Gut wrenching for 'Pitperson'—ecstasy for 'Fletch' (Brian Fletcher).

Crisp had to lug the bad wishes of most of the betting public and twelve stone (including Richard, his gear and the handicapper's forfeit) round Aintree . . . little wonder he lost the plot towards the end.

Dehydration can get to any distance athlete; take Jim Peters in Vancouver at the 1954 Commonwealth Games—the same year Lester Piggott won the first of his 9 Derbies—on *Never Say Die* (. . . *never say interview, more like*).
Only the binge drinkers of Benidorm could begin to understand the marathon man's lack of self-control . . . but a good one for the old folks' home quiz night: Joe McGhee of Shettleston Harriers (*come on!*) won the 'Peters' race.

For another point . . . name one of the half dozen doctors who treated Jim after his collapse?

Here's a clue: not long before, on the same track, the newly-qualified medic had beaten Australia's John Landy over a mile—both men taking less than four minutes, so to do. Landy was the world record holder over the distance, but our good doctor was first (by 46 days) to breech the barrier—in 3' 59.4"—on cinders, three months earlier . . . at Oxford . . . Chrises, Brasher and Chataway, as hares.

OK, OK . . . take the point . . . but who were the other three milers at *Iffley Road* that day? (**philipsjp@aol.com**—Jeffrey Archer couldn't have been one—he was only a teenage fantasist at the time).
Award yourselves a bonus for knowing that the man of the cloth into whose arms the knackered Bannister collapsed, after his epoch making run, was his friend, the Rev. Nicholas Stacey—the rest of you probably aren't that bothered.

Back to the horses.

There was O'Sullevan's own 'little fellow,' *Attivo*: *"The winner of the 1974 Triumph Hurdle is Attivo . . . . ridden by Robert Hughes, trained by Cyril Mitchell, and owned by . . .* (pause, uncharacteristically) *Peter O'Sullevan"* (then a lower lip tremor, perhaps . . . Charterhouse school F.P . . . Dad a colonel? . . . Maybe not).

Show jumping had its share of four-legged characters: little *Stroller* with Miss Marion Coakes astride (*you just wanted to . . . hug her*—well I did; David Mould got luckier) . . . . Dai and Roddy's Dad, Harry Llewellyn (*that's 'Lieutenant Colonel' to you*) on board *Foxhunter* with his crowd-pleasing, trademark, kick-back, which *Vibart* (Alan Oliver) plagiarised, as did *Penwood Forge Mill* (Paddy McMahon—a poker schoolmate).
Round after round he'd miss out on his own name-check, as Tom Hudson's PA announcements were drowned out by the roaring *Forge Mill* claque.

Nothing to do with horses, but an irresistible commentary gem . . . very much in the *Dikler* idiom.

The Dutch girls (you were allowed to describe XX teens thus, in those 'incorrect' days) were winning a European medley final, by gallons, with two relays left.

Their third swimmer was the Olympic butterfly champion—*race over*.

Down she went . . .
. . . set too, Max Robertson, on mic:-

(Touch and) . . . *"in goes the mighty Kok for Holland!"*

That's Aagje "Ada" Kok—gold medalist from Mexico City.

Can't be taught.

Hope Classic Bob

Mention Mecca to a muslim and devotion will be central; for the rest of us, it's to bingo, betting and ballroom dancing we turn. The great pins and bods of the Latin American chicks on *Come Dancing*, with their total covering of fake tan—and no shame—were always worth staying in for, yet—always deferring to Astaire and his synchronised ladies—I never got my head round the genre . . . a minority view nowadays.

Ballroom, strictly, was an acquired taste, that is until a play and film of the same name (strictly, *Strictly Ballroom*) came by to give it broader appeal . . . and then, blow me, the BBC dropped it. What goes around comes back as *'Strictly' Come Dancing*, obviously; massive though the current pro-celeb spin-off is, the immaculate pros are what it's all about, strictly—those dark knights, in baby-grows open to the navel, could turn a dithering man's head.

As their permed partners busied themselves, mums in constant, fussing attendance, unloading sackfuls of make-up, and underskirts by the metre, the principal boys, similarly 'coiffed'—arms in spasm—would take to the floor to test for bounce and 'slidability.' Dapper Joe Loss and his mufti mob laid down the rhythm, and we rehearsed moves of our own.

Lunging, swooping waltzers . . . . quick-steppers on magma . . . flailing tangoists in remotely controlled straight-jackets . . . . wired jivers and the poseurs of the cha-cha . . . . *come* dancing was the way to go (though 'smarties' of some prescription may have been taken prior to, I saw a girl manage it—mid-grinding-salsa—on a nightclub floor in Houston . . . *and she wasn't fakin' it*).

Murrayfield favourite—the very same 'bastard' Peter West—was host of *'Come'* when I started; the show had been running for 18 years, and, in various guises, had another 31 left in it.

Miss World—another Auntie/Mecca collaboration—was a diary must, for upwards of 25 million Brits. Not everyone viewed the female *homo sapien* circus as p.c. Terrorists cells, fuelled by the Pankhurst spirit, lived on.

One such was to make its presence felt at the Albert Hall in 1970, before royalty . . . well, Bob Hope (near enough).

We were rehearsing the great man's patter, and yours truly—one of several assistant stage managers i.e. the lowest of form of production life—was on the very demanding cue cards.

All was going famously as he *blah blahed* his way through high-speed gags and one-liners, while I did a Dylan (in *"Subterranean Homesick Blues"*) with the cards.
Bob (we were insufficiently worthy to call him) began to contort, hideously, giving concern to his minders and our team in the truck.

No panic, the pillock of an a.s.m. had Card 69 upside down . . . . *look, I was nervous, right . . . a <u>real</u> bomb had gone off outside, the previous day!!*

The vaultingly ambitious girls, suppressing their instincts to giggle and flirt, were rehearsed to death by the lovely boys of Mecca, till all was like clockwork:

"Walk, walk, walk, STOP . . . smile . . . TURN . . . smile . . . turn . . . walk, walk, walk STOP . . . smile . . . a-n-d EXIT." Next!

Mr. & Mrs. Morley's drill sergeants were camp as a row of tents, nor would the chaperones—officer cadets from 'Cranners'—offer BBC 'straights' much in the way of competition at the after-show bash; to be fair, the boys in grey/blue were under strict orders. Our crew, on the other hand, were free spirits, able to go directly at the chase (describing the arousing effect of G-force in a death spiral is more of a male thing, and tough to make funny).
Alitum altrix (meaning 'nurture the winged' . . . Cranwell college's motto) could be applied to *les* utterly *vulnerables* who'd failed to make the cut after the national costume section.

One of my colleague's plan for an assault on *Miss Nicaragua* was already at an advanced stage.
Bearing in mind the pre-revolutionary climate in that far-off spot, military precision was paramount. Armed with a seating plan—and the current *Jane's* as a diversionary tactic—he launched the first of several pre-emptive strikes, compounding in their boldness as the complimentary 'shampoo' kicked in. He was dealing with dynamite; unlike Bob's bombs—filled lovingly with self-raising, and stored aloft in a cache for the 'live' show drop—this was the real McCoy.

The following day, when the rakish one sauntered into the videotape area at Television Centre with an ever-so-slightly dishevelled daughter of *La Republica*—facially resplendent, naturally, in a crushed, (*aha!*) canary-yellow ensemble—we surmised a slipping of the *sandinista* bodyguards, and a sexy time—in a suite at the Coburg Hotel, just off Queensway in West London—had been had . . . . allegedly.

A toss-up: had he picked on *Miss Spain,* or *Miss Italy,* or *Miss Israel*, the worst he could have incurred was the wrath of their fearsome mothers. As it was, contracts were issued for his safe delivery to the Caribbean's Mosquito Coast . . . in an unmarked, air-tight box.

Miss Nigeria had a fascinating tale to tell at dinner.
Earlier, during an eliminator in Lagos, one of the contestants had been taken poorly—a dodgy prawn or something in the water. As the close-up camera panned along the line of hopefuls, she let rip the contents of her tightly arranged stomach—in glorious colour; not attractive . . . *quite took the edge off my freebie nose-bag.*
So you see, it's not all tits and bums and ambitious travel plans.

Mr. Hope, out of his golfing cashmere togs at rehearsal, and into the million-dollar tuxedo look, was in full flow when the first of several flour-bag 'bombs' hit the stage—not quite Baader-Meinhof, but a worry nonetheless. Bob's insurance cover was commensurate with a man who could take all his pals shopping till they dropped, without impressing his fortune in the slightest.
He laughed it off . . . a tad nervously.

The winner of the contest was *Miss Grenada* (her Prime Minister was one of the judges—*"Resign!"*) and (black) *Miss Africa* <u>South</u> (*Miss* <u>South Africa</u> was white) came second, stirring the racists, Afrikaners and libbers into a united front.
What a carry on, Eric (Eric and Julia Morley <u>were</u> *Miss World* . . . Julia still is).

Strangely, the next time *Bob*—*old bean, old man*—and I met (in Palm Springs) . . . he didn't remember me.
Now, Johnny Miller was a Mormon (each to his own), an exceptional golfer, and today—in my humble—an outstanding commentator. The long lean Texan, in *Rupert Bear* trousers and red 'pullie,' with a swing that had chiropractors salivating, pre-dated Tiger by thirty years, but there were similarities; 'explosive' wouldn't be too strong for either's arrival on the world's dance-floors. The main difference—apart from the 'wonga' . . . and Tiger's penetrative powers—was Jack Nicklaus, who was still amassing Majors; the year young Johnny wiped out the field in the U.S. Open (Oakmont, 1973) with a 63 in the final round, Jack won the U.S.P.G.A.—his 14th Major title—taking him one ahead of Bob Jones.

Tida and Earl Woods were yet to create Eldrick the Corruptible (*at least he'd be spared the irritation of big Jack, the player . . . and family man*).

Incidentally, 'my mate Bob' was a guest on the *"Here's Mike"* Douglas afternoon talk show in the States in 1977, when Master Woods was first released on the public, aged 2.

Principally because I wanted to see the jewel of Riverside County, I suggested to my *Sportsnight* boss that a film on the sensation that was Miller would fit nicely into our schedule. He agreed, but to give it 'more relevance' (his words), the piece should reflect the contrasting fortunes of Miller and our formidable Ryder cup star, Peter Oosterhuis.

Long tall Peter was dabbling with a career on the U.S. tour, having cleaned up (minus a Major) in Europe.

No disrespect to 'Oosty'—I was a fan and we'd become good pals on the European Tour, twenty years later—but Miller *was* the story; if, however, it meant Harry Carpenter and I dehydrating for ten hours to the comforting whine of two pairs of *Rolls Royce* twins thrusting us LAXwards at three times the lift-off velocity of a teed-up golf ball—his brief would do nicely.

I contacted Ed Barner—Johnny's agent (another Mormonite)—and told him of our plans for his most valuable client.

'Don't waste your time Mr. Philips. Johnny Miller is not available to the BBC' came the stark, business-class-seat-bursting response.

Come on John, think!

Invoking the teachings of Robin Day—guru to inquisitors—my follow-up question would surely unsettle defiant Ed.

'Why not?'

According to Mr. Barner, Miller had been 'offered' to Sports Department years earlier, when the seeds of success were beginning to poke through the cut and prepared. He'd been turned down flat.

(a pox on their short-sightedness, m'felt).

To paraphrase . . . *'no arrogant, second-guessing, dinosaur of a broadcaster, like the Goddamn Bee-Bee-See, would be getting close . . . PERIOD!'*

Clearly not a student of Corporation history . . . of Reith & Baird . . . VERA . . . becoming Elizabeth II . . . Morecambe and Wise—*get out more Ed!*

'Mr. Barner, sir,' I oiled (*manners maketh air miles*), 'every year since the mid-50s (*I was guessing*), the BBC has broadcast the Open to countless millions (*justifiably vague*). It's the greatest golf Championship in the world (*factual, if tactless jingoism*), and one day Johnny will nail it (*he was 3rd that year and winner in '76, so not <u>that</u> patronising*).

In advance of that certainty *(the clincher)*, don't you feel a little responsibility to the masses of British golf fans who'd like to know more?'

(<u>extremely</u> short pause)

'NO!'
(not the time {+ 8hr}, nor place {G.M.T.} for flippancy).

(Mormon or moron—this one had to fly).
I didn't let on . . . even to Harry.

In went the floss and passport . . . alas, the driving licence remained *unpacked*. The heading is *due west*, for Heathrow . . . *and beyond*.

Palm Springs . . . get ready!

Harry—because he was 'a star'—went posh; over eight hours airborne, even 'the Beeb' played fair with the licence fee. I was mid-cattle, fittingly next to one devoid of any personal-hygiene standard, who'd frequently lean into s.b.ds.—*still, if you can't beat 'em* . . .

Now and again, Harry would pop back with a second glass of first class champagne, more to ogle the afflictions on an immodest, black-haired beauty in the row behind, than pass the time of day with me (*bit of a lad, our Harry, but we won't go there . . . just yet*).

With more than a suggestion of *Dom Perignon* on his breath at a rain-sodden LAX, 'H' was less than thrilled to discover that it would be *he* who'd have to run the gauntlet of the *CHiPs* boys en route to Coachella Valley—100 miles due east. My advice—from the navigator's seat—that Interstate 10 <u>West</u> (towards Hawaii) was the way to go, set the tone (silence).

At some stage I'd have to own up to the whole pretence, but for now, stum was best, as producer/presenter relationship was at an all-time low.
We made it, unscathed, though my reporter failed to react, on being commended with a pre-Bruno . . . . "*Nice one Harry.*"

They promised (on cable TV) that the next day would be a stunner; my prospects of an interview remained gloomy to tornado.

I tried Agent Ed again, this time gaining a slightly longer, if, as yet, non-compliant response:

'*NO* (*expletive gerund, to qualify, deleted*) *WAY!*' . . . and *this* a Latter Day Saint (*Harry's going to kill, or shop me, at least*).

'Look, can we come and talk to you and Johnny mano a mano??'

A breakfast meeting was agreed . . . . (*phew!*)

My *driver* took us out to Team Miller's rented house on the golf course, where I'd arranged to rendezvous with the crew . . . *on the off-chance*. Hooking up with that lot had been a bit of a hard lesson.
I'd never had the pleasure of freelance outfit in the States, certainly not one with an assistant cameraman on 'Bob Hope' (however apposite); even in the Golden State, from whence they came, the practice was illegal.

The place: *Denny's*—the popular family diner where 'Archimedes' Atkins might have had his low-carb diet 'eureka' moment.
The time: High Noon . . . the day after our arrival in Cahuilla 'injun' country.

As I sat surrounded by glasses and cups enough for a family of five, and clean answered-out on the menu options, the door swung open and in walked three tall strangers, street-wise and purposeful—Brynner, McQueen and Bronson—magnificent.

I rose, slowly.

Introducing myself in an accent they baulked at, I offered them the run of the house: *this* they fully understood (epic school-boy error by the producer).

At any given time, there are around 150 million males in the United States, and at least three million of them are probably called 'Bill' and half, say, would have fitted the approximate age group of '*Yul*,' the lead stranger (*you know when you're introduced to more than one person at a time, how quickly you forget all their names? Schoolboy error No. 2!*).

Bearing in mind the coffee Americans drink, it's a wonder so many have such brilliant teeth (even the whales at *Sea World*).

Several egg dishes over every-which-way later—plus all available 'sides'—I advised 'the crew' of the call-time for the next day, by which I hoped to have had the better of dogmatic Mr. B.

'Run that *call-time* shit by me again, Jawn?'

'For the Miller shoot, you know, tomorrow, when the light's good?'

Their eyes lit up . . . *Miller Lite* was a positive image even at ten in the morning . . . and Hell, *everyone shot* (one way or another) *in America.*

In the confusion (mine), it transpired they were just drifters, bikers, easy bloody riders on the road to nowhere, now full of my daily subsistence allowance for the entire trip
(. . . *sure, I'd fibbed a bit, but how to explain this to our production manager, she who looked after legitimate expense claims in Blighty?*).
It called for last-ditch P45 protection, so through (off-white) clenched teeth, I took the hit.

The *real* crew phoned in as Harry and I were being introduced to Johnny-boy, in the chintzy, matt-yellow-walled living-room.
Barner had nipped to the kitchen to fix the de-caff and pretzels, so I quickly blurted out the condensed version of my carefully prepared speech—an irresistible, iconoclastic incantation.

It worked . . . or rather Johnny Miller was a shrewder man than the one he was paying to be; we were to be back to the house at 1630 PST for the interview.

"YES!" . . . I punched the air—'*Plop*' . . . my eagle had landed in the tin cup.

Harry hadn't said much in all of this—he was probably saving himself, or was still pissed at having to do the driving (. . . *or was it that cleavage?*); in any event, his chat with Johnny was right on the money, as ever.
Here was a shy, gifted young man, demonstrating that inherent, collegiate ease in front of camera that would stand him in great stead later in his broadcasting life . . . . and we had it all on film.

It doesn't upset me that there's nothing under 'B' for Barner (nor 'R' for Robinson) on my 'Chrimble' card list.

The tournament proper was *The Bob Hope Desert Classic*, a five-day pro-am, attracting those in Hollywood who could swing a little . . . from Sinatra, backwards. Arnold Palmer (who other?) won the inaugural in 1960 and four other *Classics*; thus far, Tiger hasn't any, but had he, there'd be another $5million bucks for someone other than Steve Williams—the richest caddy in history—to get a slice of (*would have been nice if Tiger had been allowed to walk the walk up the 72nd on his own, just once, after all, humping bags, and banging the birdies, ain't the same deal*).
Mrs. Woods Snr., conceived in the summer of '75—big Jack won that Masters <u>and</u> the USPGA, putting him 14 up on her prodigious fetus.

A decade has elapsed since Hope (aged 100) of Eltham SE9 joined Washington State Tacoma's Crosby on the *'Road to Valhalla.'*
Though they've had help from *Chrysler* of Detroit and Hilary Clinton's old man, Bob's *Desert Classic* remains one of the early highlights on the US golfing calendar, raising wads for charity.
Our rights to the recorded highlights came with free rein to film in and around the event, and much was on offer.
Three photographic bimbos, in red micro-pelmets, with *HOPE* and *CLASSIC* and *BOB* emblazoned—one word per pair—across the barrels of their *Tide* whitened T-shirts, were being man-handled (non-pruriently) by the happily married title sponsor.
These were early, post-Jayne Mansfield times; silicone didn't have the grip on the adult channels it has today, so it's a fair bet that Bob's babes were genuinely blessed. Their juxtaposing would form the opening 'tease' to the 'telecast' as mine host deliberated over the conundrum.
I could say that Bob, on seeing me, stopped vacillating, ran across and gave me a hug of recognition (the version for the lads in the pub), but no . . . . as the girls tittered to order, legendary comic actor, Jackie Gleason—a possible 'plant'—meddled . . . persistently. Mid-way through one perfect take, he informed his old pal that he was "flying low," all to the uncontainable delight of a well-primed gallery of *whoopin'* Yanks hanging on his every word. Good stuff, but what a time it took.

The Classic was undiluted show-biz—big-time stars in abundance (none of your Wogans and Forsyths here) . . . Dean Martin, Jack Lemmon and Tony Curtis jawing with the fans . . . old adversaries from Viking days, Kirk Douglas and Burt Lancaster too, plus a host of golfing giants, all of whom gave us the time of day. Doug Sanders, winner in '66, gathered phone numbers from near-hysterical blue-rinses, and the cast of the original *Mission Impossible* were a huge draw: Peter Graves a.k.a. *Jim Phelps* looked on as *Barney* (Greg Morris) hit off (correctly) using a black balata. "Ed-*u-c-a-t-*ed ball . . ." as he applauded a fairway-splitting Scud.

Traditionally—by Hope decree—a 'Classic Queen' was appointed for each celebration: wonder women like Debbie Reynolds, Jill St. John and the lady herself, Lynda Carter; no ingénues of *Miss World* these—nor flawlessly-flossed-floozies—they were proper grown-ups . . . women of substance.

We took the precaution of putting a BBC sticker on our camera which the eagle-eyed comic-master spotted *en passant*:

"Hey, you guys from Scotland, England?" . . . aimed at American geographic insularity.
I told him what we were up to (pointless bringing up the Albert Hall again—he'd had his chance . . . *fuck 'im*).

To my uncontainable delight and surprise he offered to do a bit to camera, promoting the up-coming show on BBC television . . . which he did in one take—pure Gold-Dust (one of the earliest detergent brands in the US).

Had it stuck? . . . Was the sound O.K?
No way of knowing, but <u>what</u> a scoop . . . another one—Jesse Owens and now Bob Hope . . . *come on, you psychophantic, grade A, celebrity chaser!*
To this day I'll never understand why, but my boss decided *not* to show the promo, asking, rather, how we were getting on with Peter Oosterhuis! We weren't; some shots of the affable giant disconsolately lobbing his tools in the trunk—a cut victim—and speeding off to the next tournament . . . but not a lot more.

By the time we met up again, 'Oosty' and I had gone through life-style changes, and a marriage, each. He'd been hired by the Golf Channel to work as 'color' commentator on the European Tour, alongside our most excellent 'anchor,' Renton Laidlaw. He (Peter . . . Renton never did) had re-married and, whenever possible, the redoubtable Ruth Ann would be by his side—lest he became short of ideas . . . about anything. Ruthie was a great 'tourist' and would delight our on-course, hand-held cameramen by turning out for a recreational four at tennis, of an evening.
The sports brassiere hadn't been fashioned that could contain the gifts with which she'd been endowed; I came to the conclusion—from the ump's chair—that the over-use of the lob by the opposition, was more for their gratification than an effective, tactical ploy (Harry would have just loved them/it).
Ruth's rare ability to smell a sub-standard hotel from the airport baggage hall, meant we seldom breakfasted with the 'Oosties.'

Johnny Miller kept to the script perfectly, winning the *Classic*—our story was complete (he'd win it the following year too).

While we were in Palm Springs, my accountant cousin called to say he was flying up from Texas for the night (as you do). He was in oil—wire and cabling, something that didn't involve *Swarfega*—and while not overly flash with it, 'Hughston' loved to pilot his light plane, race his 30m Nicholson (moored in Galveston Bay), alternate between his Mercedes coupés, and stay home in his eight-bed-roomed bungalow—with drive-thru fridge and shower—with his only wife, Maureen, a former collegiate 'Yellow Rose of Texas,' and their boys, Grant Robertson and big brother Hugh III . . . both gingers, like Dad.

Harry made his excuses and took the car (to check out a whorehouse in the desert which, he said, was something of a tourist attraction—'he'd get some pictures for the folks back home'—*yeah, right*).
Cuzz Hugh II and I went legit . . . to *Pal Joey's*, a celebrity bolt-hole downtown in this well-detached suburb of Hollywood.

There was a bit of stir . . . folk were pressing over a group in a darkened corner, causing a mild commotion. As the first wave receded, there, through a mist of *Marlboros*, was none other than Francis A. Sinatra, buddy to John F. Kennedy, anathema to J. Edgar Hoover and agent for Miss Monroe a.k.a Norma Jean Mortenson. Sadly, for bombshell fans, neither she nor Miss Mansfield a.k.a. Vera Jayne Parker . . . were anymore, yet you can bet your bottom dollar the FBI boss had arranged a bug from beyond the grave, for the stranger in the night.
Frank had several properties in town, so *Joey's* would be his 'local.'

Squeaking, near orgasm, like a front-row groupie, I jumped up:

'I *must* have his autograph . . . *quick, quick* . . . something to write with.' (ending a sentence with a preposition . . . forgivable in a crisis).

Hugh threw himself my way as if a bullet spray were imminent:

'Don't be soft, you'll never get near him . . . *look at the Goons!*'

Pinning me to the semi-circular leather bench, he pointed out several of the no-neck brigade—probably 'tooled-up' to the armpits; but hey, I'd had a few bloody good Marys . . . I had an un-transmitted promo by Bob Hope in my bag in the hotel . . . <u>and</u> I'd met Jesse Owens *for Chrissake*
(. . . yeah, and a good night's sleep's coming, with a horse's head, innit?).

'Watch and learn' says I.

I passed the interim interview, then, after what I took to be a body search (you can never be absolutely sure about the side-effects of muscle-enhancers), I was finally escorted to the Godfather's side.

My bar-snack menu duly signed (what a peasant), Mr. Sinatra smiled a kind of smile and I withdrew, genuflecting all the while, back under the stone from which I'd come. Notwithstanding my love of intact horses, I had thought about asking for the closing bars of *"My Kind of Town"* . . . but he seemed so relaxed with his friends.

Hugh Roberston II was my talisman: he'd taken me to meet fellow Houstonian, "Red" Adair, the great firefighter, on board his powerboat-launch-liner; the primary colour—exterior, interior, bar, boudoir, bed linen, bath, bog—of that particular craft was as you'd expect.
Further back—circa September 1967—we were thundering along a freeway in Harris County, in Red Robbo's *Corvette Stingray*, lid down, shades on, *Buds* in the dash, mufflers barking, speed limit (not huge by *Autobahn* standards) flaunted—tripled, at

one terrifying point—when I noticed one of those discreet American roadside signs advertising *The Ryder Cup*, at nearby Champion's Way (*'let's be having some of that!'*).

Greenbacks changed hands and in we went.
Against all rules and tradition, I had an 8mm camera about my person.
I should mention that I was on honeymoon; perhaps this early hedonistic behaviour had been noted by Mrs. Margaret Philips, but she was down the mall with 'Mo,'—one's yellow rose-bud of a cuzz-in-law—and could have cared less about how Alliss, O'Connor, Huggett and co., might be faring. As it was, they were in for a pasting.

Ignorant of the ban, I was filming away happily when a buggy sped past, a middle-aged gent in a white cap at the wheel.
Unprovoked, he gave a Churchillian salute . . .
. . . so I gave it the classic, *gawping-double-take-nearly dropping the honeymoon record so far*—'*what the fuck*'—reaction . . .
. . . for driving (*if I'm not very far mistaken*) was Ben Hogan—*and he was waving at* me!
We'd had "great champions" (as poor Seve often said) in Scotland, but William Ben Hogan—born "not a million miles away" (as the great Alliss says on commentary, repeatedly) at Stephenville, Texas—was a genius.

He was only little, but man could he give it a dunt. Occasionally, we duffers get one to sing from the 'sweet-spot'—the Hogan set was pure Barbershop.

"The most rewarding things you do in life are often the ones that look like they cannot be done," so sayeth Arnold Palmer.
At the risk of being cremated prematurely for doubting the word of God, I submit, assuredly, that no one shall *perfect* golf.
When I worked on the men's tour, two players stood out on the range for being there forever, in all climes, shaping and honing, endlessly searching:—Vijay Singh and Jose-Maria Olazabal.

Firebrand U.S. golfer, Tommy Bolt was quoted as saying that he'd seen Nicklaus watching Hogan practice but he'd never heard of Hogan watching Nicklaus; that's as may be, but Jack (the son of God)—who'd get his first Ryder Cup cap two years later in that memorable sporting tie at Birkdale—consistently said Hogan was the best ball-striker he'd seen . . . . and that included 'Pipeline' Moe Norman (*Google* required)
I await Jack's take on young McIlroy.

Years after he retired—must have been in his late seventies by then—one of the golf mags did a frame-by-frame analysis of W.B.H. swinging the driver; for technicians and emulators alike, it was immaculate.

Hogan was non-playing captain of the '67 team that lamped G.B.&.I.(under Dai Rees) 23½—8½ in Houston. Unlike (Sir) Nick Faldo's ramble at the opening ceremony in '08, Hogan cut to the chase at the pre-match dinner: *"Ladies and gentlemen, the United States Ryder Cup Team—the finest golfers in the world"* (fifteen-love I'd say . . . at least).

The buggy stopped, then reversed alongside.
No-one, not even *"The Hood"* had successfully filmed a *Thunderbird* on location (*any minute my film will self-destruct*).
In his playing days, the wee man in the white 'bunnit' could retire into 'the zone' (right side of the brain on full power) like no-one before, nor since.
I shaped up for a volley.
'Would you like me to do that again, son?'
I was 23, just married, but 'son' was fine . . . *'just fine, Mr. Hogan, your Worship.'*

I was in Year 4 when *'The Wee Ice Mon'* (as the Jocks called him) won the only Open he played in (at the 'Craw's Nestie' . . . by 4), but his was a name in every Scottish household with hickory and persimmon in the hall.

There's a saying in *Mulligan's Laws of Golf* that goes: *'The harder you try to keep your ball from landing in a particular place, the more certain it is that it will go there.'*
Now, legend has it that Ben's drive, at the first of only two par 5s on the Carnoustie monster, landed in the divot created by his second shot from the previous day: *Hogan's Alley* it <u>had</u> to become.
It's a fair bet he was aiming, if not precisely, then within an inch or two of that spot, on the 'tiger' line: that would have been his intention.
The Hawk's positive spin on *Mulligan's* negativity.

Anyone gleaning a modicum of the history of the ancient game, lucky enough to play one of the world's great courses, pauses at Carnoustie's 6th and gives thanks that the little Texan had been fit enough to drop by.
That 'Coronation' year—*four* after a car crash that nearly killed him and his wife—the U.S.P.G.A. (then a matchplay event) overlapped the Open, so Hogan missed out on the Grand Slam proper. Although it was his least favourite form of the game (preferring to *'post a number'*) we 'gave' it to him as a Major 'gimme.' He'd already won a couple—in '46 and '48—so *no big deal, eh?* . . . . *near enough an inevitability* . . . a Broadway ending.

You'll be fascinated that Walter Burkemo—born in Detroit of Norwegian extraction—beat Felice Torza 2&1 in the 36 hole final in 1953 at Birmingham Country Club . . . Birmingham, Michigan
(*Hogan would have walloped either with the left side of his brain on 'low'*). Torza (stay with it . . . and a big thanks to *Wikipedia* here) was known as *Toy Tiger* because he was feisty and small: only his <u>golfing</u> conquests are listed.

New York, New York's response to Hogan's British win was a ticker-tape drive-by, like they'd afforded Bob Jones in 1926 (and again in 1930)—another target *prototype* Tiger may find hard to chase down now.
It rained paper on Jesse Owens parade in 1936, Churchill's in '46 and our Queen's in 1957.

(unshredded ledgers, from a great height—on both sides of 'the Canyon of Heroes'—await the 44th President should he fail to sort out the figures in DC).

I nodded, moronically. Mr. Hogan parked up behind a magnolia, popped his head out to check that I was 'turning-over,' then drove up sedately. When adjacent, slowing to a crawl, he tipped his cap, smiled (in itself a rarity . . . at work, certainly) and drove off, never to be seen again by me at least; no evidence there of the (reputed) cold, calculating ruthlessness that brought him 64 tour wins . . . and just the 9 Majors.

I should point out that the ensuing passage of play—in rugby union parlance—goes through quite a number of phases.

There was always a *compare and contras*t question at school exams, so how's about 'The Iceman' and 'Iron' Mike?
(Tyson is pig-ugly for starters and Ben's brown bread, thus un-defamable)

Des (Lynam), his Rose and I were at *Beauty and the Beast* in Covent Garden, guests of Sam Hammam, the original mini-oligarch and head honcho of Wimbledon F.C. (not sure how big ballet is in Lebanon).
'The Crazy Gang,' of which Sam was a fully paid-up member, were into all kinds of alternative therapy: leading scorers offered camels as bonuses . . . poor performances rewarded with trips to the opera . . . and there were boot camps to endure, with 'R.S.M.' 'Harry' Bassett cracking the whip.
Taking into account their reputation and style of play, quite why they'd taken to basic ballet lessons was confusing: *was it to do with corners and set-pieces?* Who knows, but you wanted to be there when the initiative was put to Vinnie Jones.

Mid-performance, the curtains slid to a close.
Caffuffle.
The 'lads' were just in front of us, in the best of the stalls.
Out came the artistic director, all of a flutter. The principal, male lead had 'done an ankle' mid-*jeté* or *saut,* and had to be subbed. Vinnie stirred needlessly; the tights he <u>could</u> fill, being one of the longest in the showers according to 'Fash' (no slouch himself, apparently).

Make-up and wardrobe for *The Beast* was *Thriller* length, so while the understudy was being readied, we repaired to the bar.

We were bandying *pliés* and *entrechats* with alacrity (and no knowledge), over large 'voddies' and diet, when some*thing*, or some*one*, ethereal passed at speed.
Goose-bump city . . . and that *gorgeous* smell?
A Blairwitch moment.

With the instinct of a *papparazza*, I spun (*fouetté*) and there, being spirited through the throng to her box, her divine face partially obscured by a flowing shawl, was the Princess of Wales (couldn't do the scent . . . *but I'd known a man who could*).

Segue.

The only other time, prior to the release of the students' woodland movie, I shivered similarly, was at ringside in Las Vegas, as 'Iron Mike'—murderous intent in those dead eyes—came within inches of Lynam and me on his way to a blinding date with big Frank. Just as he reached our seats, the ferocious heavyweight champion whipped off his sleeveless, towelling robe revealing the full, awesome, target area Bruno would have at his disposal should an unguarded moment arise . . . no, make that "moment" (unqualified)—Tyson didn't *do* guards . . . . *heavies*, yes.

Spooky . . . once the beauty—then the beast . . . *brrrrr.*

Encores complete—bouquets in water—off one went to Joe Allen's to take wine with Sam and his enlightened entourage. Cast and players had discovered an unlikely bond: the dancers were as grounded as we imagined ourselves to be, though head-to-head, we'd probably nick it on bar experience.

There was a good deal of rubber-necking going on. Anita Dobson (*Angie Watts* of *The Queen Vic* . . . and *Queen's* Brian May) dropped by to say *"Hi"* with an air-kiss or two for a fellow performing seal.
Innocent enough . . . but there *was* history (Des and *Dirty Den's* girl had met in public once or twice . . . *Shock! Horror!* . . . *but let's run with* THE NEW MAN IN ANGIE'S LIFE *header, anyway*).
Garbage of course, but lawyers were contacted as a precaution.
At the time of that particular smear on the anchorman's fine reputation of being devoted to anyone (Rose) who could be bothered to de-bone his barbecue-grilled sardines, we were mid-way through the Commonwealth Games in Edinburgh (predictably, whistling the *Eastenders* theme tune was popular amongst office piss-takers).
And the boy himself . . . shaken but not stirred unduly.

Off we go again . . . on another mazy run, like David Duckham in his prime.

Orwell gave no warning of it, but I fell victim, properly, to the 'popular' press in 1984, and poor old Des got sucked in by being there.

I was 'stepping out' with a young lady from Wales, then domiciled in Hampton, Middlesex. She was beautifully put together, if on the short side, so my stride pattern (a track and field clue) had to be adjusted on country walks to the pub.

Sue Barker and the lady from Wales were close friends—I mention that because *'what happened next'* would settle the relationship once and for all . . . and Sue's is a cracking name to drop.
I'd all but gone from BBC Sport when the flighty 1976 French Open champion joined, though, unbeknown to me, we did have a famous mutual friend: not Martina, nor Chrissie, Billy Jean, nor Evonne Goolagong—she'd whacked them all . . . no, this animal was shiftier by far, a predator with a helluva kick, graceful as a gazelle (*the clues just keep coming*).

I was up to my parts in the Los Angeles Olympics, working round the clock; any kind of social activity was off the agenda, so she (the vamp of the Valleys) would 'go away' for the duration, and leave me to my insomnia—considerate little poppet . . . *not*.

One morning I heard the letterbox crack shut; I wasn't expecting anything other than junk, so I left it till I was ready to go to work.

Armed with a bulging file of what we could expect from L.A. that day, I bent to collect a postcard, face-up on the hairy mat by my front door . . . *'Funny, a shot of The Coliseum . . . hmm . . . must be from the tourists, trying to stick it up us.'* In more recent times, the whole shooting match of BBC Sport's Olympic operation is conducted from 'site,' but because of the time difference and astronomical air fares, it was decided to run the programmes from London in '84—which didn't stop the perennial Press slaughtering . . . *wastage of licence money, huge piss-ups in Los Angeles, massive over-staffing, etc.,*—unadulterated, poorly-researched bullshit, basically.

My mind was awash with images of the Games; I paid no attention, stuffed the pc in my folder and hopped on the bus. Notice the use of the term 'bus'; as programme editor, one could, legitimately, have had a taxi 'on the firm', but for the fifteen minutes it took to get to Wood Lane from my flat in Castelnau (Hammersmith Bridge end), it was good to see for myself that life went on (not in Richard Burton's case), that not everyone (anyone) gave a shit about the Olympic handball results.

Here's an idea of my 1400-0930 self-inflicted schedule (I liked the handball, and the small bores).
There was a peak-time, evening highlights show reflecting all the best bits from the previous day's events—which Des hosted—then the start of the next day 'live,' which ran through the night (Des relaying, safely, with Steve Rider at a convenient point in the early morning, and he, less assuredly, with David Icke, about 6.a.m.) A

breakfast show, incorporating national, local news and weather, followed, seamlessly, but predominantly it was Games material on 1 and cartoons on 2.
Brain-dead, I passed the torch to others and got the bus home.

After a week, cracks began to appear.

I remembered the card as I was making my way to the office.

'Don't contact me again, I'm here with Seb.'

Apart from my name and address, and a brief history of The Coliseum, there was no other writing on the card—*the handwriting, I did recognize!*
A bit unexpected—*not* that she was at the Olympics . . . where better to be with a couple of weeks spare . . . but the 'Seb' reference bothered me.

!!!BOTHERED . . . me?!!!!"

There weren't too many of that name with whom I was familiar; the one I did know—quite well, as it happens—was being tipped by most (other than Brendan Foster) to win the 800 <u>and</u> 1500metres in L.A.

One of my assistants (*"secretary"* as the Pub Landlord would have her) had been emotionally embroiled with Peter Coe's 'athlete'—as he somewhat bizarrely described his progeny—so by our first meeting I'd already formed a pretty good impression of him (girls can't hide their moods as well as we boys—mine were about to be put to the test).

It was a gloomy day at Loughbrough, and out of season, but (my) Patsy's ex agreed to do a couple of half-lap sprints for us, with the camera tracking him from the open boot of my big Peugeot.

The old man wasn't happy, but good as his word, the 'athlete' appeared, stripped for action, and proceeded to explode round the track in that inimitable, effortless, flowing style, hardly breaking sweat; like many others, I was a great admirer of S.N.Coe—'style councillor.'

We were invited into the labs at the University.

Various masks and pads were attached to his slight personage, monitoring and measuring everything that worked: the exact position of his feet on landing/stride and body position/heart-rate/breathing patterns/*who* he had for breakfast/his political ambitions . . . . the lot
(unless he's planning 'a Douglas-Home,' Downing is a street too far).

After all the data had been digested by computer, the unanimous conclusion was that he was a fucking good runner.

I was lucky enough to be working at many of his record breakers—in Zurich, Florence, Oslo and Lausanne—and I remember us hugging (clumsily, as boys do) trackside, after his astonishing 1.41.72 WR that looked like lasting forever (unlike my relationship).

Sir Alec Douglas-Home—by dint of being a knight of the Order of the Thistle—had nothing to do with Scotland, really; the family seat was *The Hirsel* at Coldstream, in Berwickshire . . . . *but the cad had played cricket for Middlesex!*
Harold McMillan still had his stuff in No.10, but was having prostate trouble, so he handed in his notice at the Palace.
After much to-ing and fro-ing, Lord Home (as he then was) got the nod from the Queen, kissed hands and looked set to take up station at the Despatch Box—camera left of Mr. Speaker's chair . . . *or would he—could he?*
Uneasy lay the head of the kindly P.M; the ermine and knighthood in his closet, brought no guarantees, so, jumping into a three-piece country-person's tweed suit, fastening up a stout pair of brogues, he marched North . . . on Kinross and West Perthshire—"*Unionist*"—for a by-election a sack of spuds could have won.

Willie Rushton—"*Death to the Tories*"—a candidate with a snowball's chance (the Returning Officer declared only 45 votes for him), was well known through appearances on *That Was The Week That Was* with David Frost, Millicent Martin, Lance Percival & co., and, eternally, as co-founder of *Private Eye*. Although he was nuisance value in the 'hung' affair that was the 1963 Kinross and West Perth by-election, the searing wit from the fringes kept the centre light and airy. Screaming Lord Sutch—"*The Official Monster Raving Loony Party*"—polled much better, numerically, whenever he sacrificed his deposit . . . *but he couldn't do the satire, luv.*

A feast *The Beatles* had within the constituency (in the restaurant of *The Four Seasons* hotel, over-looking Loch Earn, at St. Fillans in glorious Perthshire) would command the entire spread of *The Strathearn Herald* (our family paper). Even had the boy Christ—a lesser light in Mr. Lennon's book—returned unexpectedly for a third term, he couldn't have been more fervently reported than the Home quest (he had to have somewhere to sit at Westminster—*he was the bloody Prime Minister after all*).

Eagerly, my Dad's reporters viz., his brother Gordon, and cub, Iain Sutherland (formerly, the pipe-major in our prize winning school band) joined the voracious press corps.
Hell, it was exciting, even for a spotty 19 year old: a motorcade of loyalists in *Land Rovers* and 'journos' in bangers, hurtling down country lanes—where sheep had absolute

rights—screeching to an orchestrated halt, as the lordly knight whistled-stopped his way through the shires.

He got in of course—in Kinross and West Perth and Westminster—but it didn't last. The previous Tory regime, under 'Supermac,' hadn't been helped by the Christine Keeler-Mandy Rice-Davies axis, and by Lord Profumo not being able to keep it in his pants. Anyway, lurking in the wings—in a *Burberry*—a mysterious little man—with pipe attached—was itching for sets to the big black door . . . for himself, Mrs. Wilson and Marcia Williams, if overtime were required.
What a cracking time to be a satirist.

On the plane home from Switzerland, air traffic had taken us in over south London. I spotted a deserted athletics track and nudged Seb to look down:
"Do you realise, you can run round a track like that—*twice*—faster than any other son-of-a-bitch on the entire planet?"
May have seemed pedestrian to the world record holder, but it helped my perspective.

The L.A. revelation had traumatised me, I was strung out like a runner-bean. The potentially addictive 'meds'—*not to be taken with alcohol* (in a tiny font), prescribed for short-term relief by my uncle George, an eminent, Harley Street shrink—gradually restored the balance.

Orcas/'salties'/reporters on the red tops are apex predators, charged with maintaining their eco systems: being ahead of the game, teeth and radar *razor* sharp, knowing where and when a kill was on, they kept their respective food-chains ticking over.

As if sensing my vulnerability, one from the Sundays managed to bluff his way into the flat. Can't remember the initial yarn he spun but, unsolicited, far too much of the personal stuff came blurting out. *(Brian Leveson hadn't even taken silk yet)*
Surreptitiously—as expected by his editors—he'd whipped a picture of my two-timing, erstwhile companion from my 'gallery' wall.

Come publication, that week-end, out flew the cat . . . across several pages—*fronts* mostly—but I was merely the crust on a plumb pie.
Des (pictured) got a mention for his support (of me), which was right (the cunning positioning of headline and his 'concerned' image was surely designed to attract and mislead) . . . the inference that the runner had nipped off with my *wife*, wasn't . . . tho it had crossed my mind.

Olympic success for Coe would mean pictures of the 'happy couple' and more holes in my bleedin' heart.

Brendan's re-assurance that Joachim Cruz would win the 800, brought respite from the prescription-drug induced imaginings (the Brazilian missile did him in the eight—in one lungful*—but Seb won the perfect race over 1500 . . . . *magnificent*).
*Cruz would hold his breath while running—presumably nothing over 800m.
One cartoon (of several) had me chasing after Peter's 'athlete' in a BBC van, wielding an axe, the accurate implication being that without horse-power, I'd never catch him.
Every new mark he set meant headlines to be reported, but there was no shirking from my end.
The dastardly duo were often seen (pointed out) at big sporting events we were covering like Wimbledon, the Matchplay golf at Wentworth, at a post Olympic hockey match, and for some reason or other, the World Snooker (not that I was looking . . . much). I even spotted them at one of those *Evenings With* . . . jobs on ITV.
That year's *Sports Personality of the Year* show would be more of a test.
I skulked around backstage with Des during the taped inserts, measuring the damage I'd do to my career (and freedom) by launching myself at the Olympic champion during one of the anchorman's live links (Delboy had enough on his plate without having to police old psycho-drawers in the wings).
Plurality ruled: Torvill and Dean got the big camera . . . the enemy came 2nd (shame) . . . the Scottish curmudgeon was appeased, temporarily.
Having kept it under control, just, my fury—fuelled as the meds and booze-taken collided—got up to around manslaughter when *he* and *she* sauntered into <u>our</u> after-show party at *Barbarella* in Fulham Road—very much a favourite haunt for *she* and *me* in the good old days prior to the Grand Deception of '84. No arrests were made.

A line had to be drawn, however, when my boss hired Coe as a studio 'expert' for an upcoming major Championship I would be editing.
I was on holiday at the time, so I resigned when I got back.

Petulant? . . . perhaps, but it felt right.
It got a bit lary, but good sense prevailed and I was re-instated.
Seb eventually married Nicky . . . I married Ann . . . and Jane—the scarlet woman—married Steve . . . and then we all divorced again—*splendid*.

(by the above precedent, Ryan Giggs should accede to First Minister anytime now and begin spearheading the Welsh Olympic bid for 2032).

Sixteen years later, I was mugging up on some stats in the Sydney offices of *Channel 7*, when Harold Anderson—a BBC old boy (now their Head of Sport in Australia)—came to the door:

'John, I think you know each other.'

It was the white Baron, who, I'd been forewarned, was also seconded to 7's athletics team for 2000 Games . . . *and this was the moment.*

'Looking forward to working with you' he lied.
I nodded, then regretted the gesture . . . *recognition, John, not homage.*
Not even a peer of the realm who, as a commoner, had run that definitive 1500m final in Los Angeles, not even he could read *The Blue Riband* in Sydney. Like everyone else—except Noah Ngenyi of Kenya—Channel 7's illustrious pundit 'gave' the gold medal to the Moroccan maestro, Hicham El Guerrouj, from the off—but then again, *we all make mistakes.*

That was Los Angeles . . . . back to Las Vegas, where we were.

Frank Bruno's much manipulated relationship with 'our' Harry meant unlimited access for us to training sessions. Tyson, in contrast, was *'a demmed, elusive Pimpernel.'* Only by way of a late-night call from our man on the inside—the blow-dry-kid, Mickey 'The Mole' Duff—did we get into Johnny Tocco's gym to film the champ's workout.

"How was that?"
Conversationally, I asked an enormous, Bruno built-alike for his thoughts after two minutes of disproportionately remunerated provocation of the unencumbered man-in-black . . . boots, shorts, moods, intentions.

"Hellish! . . . D'ya wann a go?"
(no need to be prickly, Goliath): of senses lost, humour hadn't been one.

Our hearts went out to Frank, but we were there to speak to 'Iron Mike' . . . . sympathy, in that establishment, wasn't conducive.

Not long previously, Harry and Tyson had turned in a piece for *Sportsnight,* looking back over the great clashes in fistic history, about which Tyson knew . . . *everything*. I was banking that the respect he'd shown for our little man then, would be re-kindled, yet remembering, in 24 hours he'd be defending his Heavyweight Championship of the World. Daily meat rations had to be poked through the bars . . . he was at best, tetchy; *'hellish'* was right—*was he ever a scary boy?*

Tocco's compact gym brought you right up close and personal: that squint of anticipation before looping, murderous blows connected, each producing a delayed shock-wave as it whistled by.
A boxing ring, with Mike Tyson in it, was the epi-centre of the worst place on earth, even for the well-prepared; no one-hand-off-the-bounce/fingers crossed/pansy school-yard shit here.

It had its own reverence: no applause, just a few gasps . . . the occasional thud, as six foot of stunned fodder fell to earth . . . the merciful sound of the 2' bell . . . the ambient walloping of other aspirants at heavy bags and speed-balls . . . the rhythmic tapping of feet and rope to a favourite track, fed privately to mutilated ears.

More in hope, than genuine belief of grabbing a word, we set our camera up in the door of Johnny T.'s 'titchy' office, and threw some light onto the worn, leather chair inside.

I wanted to be able to inter-cut an interview we'd already done with Frank with the one I prayed we'd get with Mike; there was a series of common topics, so by editing the questions out, we'd be left with a verbal joust between the two. *What genius.*

We'd shot Frank against a black drape—his big, glowing profile (right) filling the screen, benignly menacing . . . if that's a possibility; Mike, against a similar backdrop (left), looked . . . *evil,* people.

The respected 'Mr. Carpenter' asked, and got the nod (of approval) from Tyson.

Surely he'll go for a quick shower, or towel down at least.
Not this dude: he bore down on the *Mastermind* chair, filling it, and, taking a heavily bandaged right hand that had spent much of the last hour in several unfortunates' faces, used it to sweep his, like a windscreen wiper in a sweat-storm.

Wide-eyed Don King—he of the electric hair—brushed past, announcing that *'the Champ won't speak on the following:'*

    a)   RELIGION
    b)   WOMEN

We ran up to record, as Harry squeezed on top of a camera box.

All predictable stuff, until, risking death by electrocution, I slipped a note to Mr. C. with *RELIGION* scribbled on it.

'And you've found God, Mike?'

Blimey, look out!

D.K. grunted, but a broad, kindly, child-like grin—revealing his gold implant—spilled over Tyson's countenance, one that bore malice to earthlings of either gender for most of its life.

'Has that made a difference to you?'
(the look would have sufficed)

Yes he had . . . yes it had, in reply to the first of the unmentionables . . . *he'd made the skies bright and sunny . . . he'd brought peace and joy* . . . (sure)
Prudently I kept my own counsel
Was this the same bully who, moments earlier, had nearly decapitated a 250lb sparring partner and would gladly have finished him off but for the intervention of a corner-man with judgement and a flying towel?

I wanted to buzz Frank . . . '*whisper God's name in his ear, just after the bell for Round 1 . . . then clock him with a big right!*'

(good time to get on to the other taboo . . . WOMEN).

Fearlessly (*he would never strike a man in glasses, would he?*) Harry broached the second 'no-go' area, bringing Cus d'Amato's prodigy back to type, instantly . . .

. . . *maybe Frank should know this too, in case of an indiscriminate sledge about Robin Givens—or worse, her mother—at the ref's briefing.*

As dramatically as he came, he was gone, unwashed, in a flurry of minders' fedoras, costume jewellery and barking mufflers.

We'd been working on the fight preview for weeks—at home and on location. Not far out of heartbreak city, we found a converted fort where stunt men put on wild-West shows for the tourists—falling off roofs, crashing out of saloons, guns blazing (the stuntmen)—not quite Warner Brothers, but a perfect stage for us.

The Cooper/ van Cleef look, boys?
Nah, that's naff.
Civvies . . . but we'll do the whistle, for sure.

Lynam championed the Champ, as line by line the tale of the tape unraveled; Harry parried with jingoistic, if hugely optimistic, bluster.
The pugilists were at the height of their destructive powers, each with 31-by-KO previous, and the winner would, for a time, unify the whole peculiar Council/ Association/Federation business.

A week previously we'd shot a studio scene in Television Centre, with a croupier from *The Sportsman* club in London's Tottenham Court Road dealing blackjack, from a customized deck, to Des and 'H.'

On top, they were tuxedo-ed up with nowhere swanky to go; the prop chandelier, shot through a star-filter, lent authenticity (no matter that their shoes were brown and they had work pants on).
The card-playing conversation got us in and out of archive footage revealing—in time-honoured fashion—*'how they got there'* . . . *there* being the three-thousand-roomed Hilton—the largest hotel in Grandpa Conrad's group—at 3000 Paradise Road, 'Lost Wages' (in whose county jail Paris did a little porridge once upon a time . . . . and where she, like Mike, 'found' God—*Beauty and the Beast II*).

"*LET'S GET READY TO RUMMMMMBALLLLL*" (on my 45th birthday too).

Pictures of the two big guys were plastered on one side of giant, home-made, loaded dice, spinning and settling, once on one, then on the other . . . three painted *Franks* and three *Mikes*, replaced bells and lemons on barreling, fruit-machine cylinders . . . . golden coins spewed from its coffers: hideously contrived, but it worked pretty well when edited.

The colour temperature at the old fort was perfect; tumbleweed drifted (or, rather, one pushed it) through shot . . . Lynam ripped *WANTED* posters, offering rewards for Tyson's head, from the walls of the Sheriff's office and trampled them, dismissively, in the dirt.
The boys hammed it up like the 'luvvies' they truly aspired to be.
We closed with a backlit, wide angle, sunset shot of the two mentors, staring wistfully at the horizon as ever-so-slowly, the fighters' close-up images broke through to echoed predictions.
In the valley below, the lights of Las Vegas flickered into life . . . *John Ford, eat your heart out.*

Everyone knows what happened in the fight—Harry lost it . . . so did Frank, and 'Hannibal' Tyson lived to dine out another night.

It was a strange place to be, backstage; never mind the massive physical pain of being battered by a force like Tyson, to witness the haemorrhaging of emotion by Laura—mother of his children—was to intrude on something very personal . . . . but she knew the game, and Frank. She gathered herself, dabbed her eyes, then defiantly laid out a convincing defence of her champion's effort; he didn't need to know that she was confident he'd win next time.

'Christ, there's to be a <u>next</u> time!'—Lee-ave it out Harry'.

Explaining the concept of pantomime as a retirement option, to anyone in America, never mind someone who'd have willingly killed you, would not have done the image much good; in any case there was still plenty fight left in Bruno. He wouldn't make

Tyson that angry again for seven years: and that *"my lords ladies and gentlemen"* would be the end of it—Frank could dress up at will.

The biggest cheer of the night was for the future governor of neighbouring California.
Sporting a bottled tan, and modest calico suit, *The Terminator's* progression to ringside, tracked by spotlight, was interminable.

Earlier in the trip, Des and I got tickets for the fabulous *Siegfrid & Roy* show on The Strip—a while before Siegfrid (or was it Roy?) was chewed by a cast member. Being so close to regular Bengal tigers and their albino cousins, you realised that unarmed man, however trusting, was feckless in the presence of wild, magnificent—albeit cosetted—beasts (*someone should have told Frank*).

Oh, did I mention . . . Bo Derek—the perfect '10'—and her old man, John—aka "Beau Derek"—were a few rows along, but clearly hadn't spotted us.
(*"Of all the gin joints, in all the towns in all the world"*). John was exceptionally pretty too, unlike scar-face legend Humphrey Bogart—once a co-star (or in the same movie, rather)—who told the young upstart that looks weren't enough. (. . . *for what, pray?*) Regardless of the shit he 'appeared' in, and the dross he directed, John did OK . . . marrying Ursula Andress, 2nd, Linda Evans, 3rd, and horse-loving Bo, to the death (his—she's still a 10, midst the over-50s).

Here's *your* choice . . . go to London's famous York Hall in Bethnal Green on a wet winter's night to watch some rank-less Mexican mis-matched with one of our rising stars . . . or be ringside for the Marvin Hagler v. Thomas 'The Hitman' Hearns Middleweight Championship of the World in Caesar's Palace Las Vegas . . .

Based on the 'herograms' and accolades received after the '84 Olympics, Des and I—his tank of cute rejoinders on empty (temporarily), my heart smashed (temporarily)—we went to the bosses with a cunning plan . . .
. . . *let us go to the big fight, and forget the bonuses you had no intention of paying?*

Boxing promoters are masters of hyperbole, but their best endeavours would fall way short on this one—it was as raw as a baboon's ass.
Des was sat next to a Nevadan connoisseur (I was nowhere, but grateful, back in the bleechers). Sensing his companion favoured the former Light Heavyweight world champ, the ever-gregarious Lynam tested the waters:

'How do you think the Hitman's doing?'

Collecting his thoughts for a nano-second, he snapped back:

'The Hitman? . . . He's shh-hit man!'
A bit hasty, and a tad unfair as Hearns—one of boxing's most prolific title holders—had broken his right hand in the opening round, and still Hagler's head was a bloody mess.
What a division the middleweights were: like the 250cc bikers, they were nimbler than the heavies, and ferociously competitive.
Hagler's cut wasn't apparent (but for the different coloured trunks, I could tell jack-squat from my seat, save that 'The Hitman' was getting battered and Hagler's corner were in need of a withdrawl from the blood bank); there was a fair chance their man could lose by exsanguination, such was the torrent from his wound.

No time like the present—The Hitman must fall.
And fall he did, after a further eight minutes of merciless mauling by 'Marvellous' Marvin.
Hagler went on to beat our own Alan Minter, and his fights with Sugar Ray Leonard—accurately categorized as legendary—matched anything the big boys (Ali, versus whomsoever, excepted) could come up with, in the skill and ring craft departments.
Sugar Ray put his well-preserved good looks into booze, drugs, dames, TV and a good marriage, eventually; Ray Robinson—Ali's idol—made some poor choices too and fared less well in the end.

Some years back, one of my oldest pals (my male 'date' at the night of the ballet) had a landmark birthday 'do' in Putney; never one to shy from a photo-op himself . . . *guess who he persuaded to go on the door as a playful minder-cum-meeter-greeter?*.
None other than Hagler, M².
Having rendered all but ten of his 62 opponents 'sparkers,' imagine the spectacle had Chris's 50th anniversary bash kicked-off and 'his bouncer' been obliged to weigh in with more than reason?
Typically, my mate, Mr. Lewis, had pulled off a master-stroke, just as the firm did when they persuaded magnificent Michael (Johnson) onto their track and field team; having Hagler as a BBC 'color' man, cosied up to fightin' Irishman, Jim Neilly (Harry Carpenter's successor) ringside, was another.

The J.P. McEnroe take on Henman's chances at Wimbledon, or Barry Richards' (for *Channel 4* at Lord's) on Michael Vaughan's loss of form, or Butch Harmon on Phil Mickelson's state of mind, did wonders for the broadcasters' cred.

Now, set yourselves for another curve ball.

The inaugural Las Vegas Grand Prix in 1981 was a risky old attempt at bringing Formula 1 to the U.S.A.

Miles of concrete blocks were shipped in to prevent the cars spinning off into the casino, as the track wound its way up and down and around the gloriously spacious car park of Caesar's Palace—two hours of hell for the drivers, pulling Gs in a centrally-heated tunnel: not great viewing for trackside punters, nor, particularly and pertinently, for those at home.

Alan Jones, the straight-talking Australian, in a Williams-Ford, won the race, to a mixed reception from the locals and the ratings-mad television networks with their hyper-analytical advertisers. They tried again the following year, when Michele Alberto won, but it 'bombed.'

Anti-clockwise 'one bending' was the way to go, Stateside.

The Indy 500 is billed as *"the greatest spectacle in* (motor)*racing."*
On the day, some 400,000 petrol-heads squeeze into the Motor Speedway, yet only five million or so watch it on telly; the ratio stacks up against Monaco's returns . . . *but where would you rather be?*

Brits Dario Resta, Jim Clark, Graham Hill, Dan Wheldon and Dario Franchitti (from Bathgate, West Lothian . . . like Resta via somewhere in Italy, at some stage) mastered the high-speed art in Foyt and Unser's own Brickyard, but there was no corollary, from either U.S. dynasty.

We—the classic racing team of Murray Walker and James Hunt, plus a few friends of *Marlboro* McLaren (a dazzling red-head amongst them)—went for a post-race drink in one of Caesar's many bars.

James had just nailed a commentary deal that would keep him in the seat next to Murray for 13 years, a partnership that sustained both—our glue on *Grand Prix*—so were an excuse needed . . .

McLaren had dangled an even bigger offer in front of the 1976 World Champ, but he was 33, in love, and living in Spain with fashion model Jane 'Hottie' Birbeck; life was OK for *Le 'unt*.

It was a no brainer really; whether the zest had left him following the death of his close friend, Ronnie Petersen (former flat-mate, Niki Lauda, was nearly burned alive in Germany), finding a truly competitive car wouldn't be easy as his extremely posh pal, Alexander Hesketh, was back being a Baron and Lord-in-Waiting.

James packed it in (driving) after the 1979 Monaco Grand Prix, appropriately, where F1 began for 'Bubbles' Horsley, Harvey Postlethwaite and Master Hunt, then of the unsponsored *Team Hesketh*.

The horn playing pianist was definitely on something; his trademark cut-off jeans and denim top, bare feet and flashing green and red toy ear-rings—*"being road-tested for the hot one"*—confirmed my suspicions as we struggled to hear ourselves over craps enthusiasts. Neither did he go unnoticed, by hotel security, nor a rowdy party of 'one benders,' some way off our port bow (James's left light).

Mr. & Mrs. Stewart and their glittering party, eased through the tables, Jackie nodding to his public as he progressed, regally, in our general direction . . . *only to veer off, suddenly, as if down an escape road*, when beckoned to attend by James. I seem to remember the words, *"you wee Scottish whoor,"* somewhere in the midst of an indiscreet summons.

The next bit was in ultra slow-motion.

A fat guy—beer in hand—stood up, and lurched towards us; his willful glare wasn't convincing—he must have been put up to it.
James . . . *'all lit it with fairy lights'* . . . was somewhere between sublime oblivion and Hottie's legs.

In fairness, the contents of the glass tankard did no immediate damage to the illuminations.
The race driver, however, instantly refreshed, was out of his pit like an exocet: here was one fit mother, strong and quick on his feet for a big guy, with me, recklessly in pursuit to ensure fair-play . . . which it could never be.
We bowled off into a throng surrounding the giant million-dollar one armed bandit

Now utterly focused, James ducked out of my slipstream, taking out a few innocents along the way (*me* on cursory *'sorrys'*), and pinned the bolting dare-devil right under Joe Louis's nose. The casino's life-size bronze was there (not as *Employee of the Month* recognition as one of its 'meeter-greeters') as a reminder of the Brown Bomber's outstanding contribution to boxing. Big Joe had been front of the house at Caesar's for an undignified time. He died in April that year after an extraordinary career . . . racism, war propaganda, drugs, tax debts, gangsters. You name it, Joe did it, amidst 65 wins out of 68 pro fights, 51 by k.o., all the while maintaining a reputation for fairness and sportsmanship—some guy.

Was Ali greater . . . and does it matter?

In 2010 they unveiled an 8ft bronze of Joe in his home town of La Fayette, Alabama, where proper homage could be done.

"*He can run but he can't hide*" was one of the Louis maxims; the right cross James was about to land on the captive, anti-F1 fan, would have done him proud.

I wasn't wholly sure of what my next move should be (*'I want a good clean fight, no low blows, break when I say . . . touch gloves and come out fighting'*) when the unmistakable shape of a hand-gun altered the rules of engagement. Security had seen all, and the nutter was led away . . . his fate, I fancy, being less traumatic in his countrymen's hands.

James could have gone down for manslaughter and possession, so not a bad result in the end.

One is unaccustomed to having a gun pulled on one at work—not your everyday occurrence in west London (back then)—but we were now in the state of Georgia . . . on our own 'Cannonball Run.'

Peter Alliss, bald Fred (one of the other BBC golf producers) and myself, were *en route* from Atlanta airport to Augusta for the Masters (*without spoiling anything for you, Sandy Lyle would win it*), when we were invited to pull over by a deputy sheriff, in one of those Gleason-style trooper's cars (all doors intact).
Moments before, Peter, who'd taken full advantage of the complimentary fare in First Class, urged my mate Fred to *'bash the pedal to the metal'* lest we were to be denied our apple cider (on the rocks) and a sniff of magnolia, that evening.

It's doubtful if the bold Alliss knew which country we were in, never mind the mandatory 55mph speed limit on Interstate something or other; certainly he was unaware that we'd been in violation and were about to be 'welcomed' to Georgia by two extremely pissed enforcement officers, in wide-brimmed hats and shades, and, crucially . . . *packing*.

'Get out the car, boy.'
(remember Fanny Cassidy of the forbidden boobies in the sauna . . . well this *'boy'* was her boss, Fred Viner, who'd be in his mid-40s at the time).

Alliss whispered something abusive, from the entire back seat.

I tried to quell and distract the commentator from his exacerbations whilst checking on Fred's interview in the rear-view mirror; assuring me he'd be good, I started from the passenger's door:

'Not you, boy—back in the car,' supported by the barrel of a pistol.

You know the moment you've transgressed . . . it's instinct, or conscience, or soiling, whatever, but there's no finer leveler than the gleaming lines of a Colt. Knives and bottles I'd seen before, but this was a Clint Eastwood thing: I assumed, all Southern law enforcement officers would not hesitate to discharge a couple, if provoked, by trash of any hue.

I was back on my bum, with the door closed, quicker than a desperate man in braces—who'd forced a buffalo *phaal* down the night before—could get his drawers off; I only <u>nearly</u> shat myself.

Once upon a time there was a cheery, be-spectacled attendant in the 4th floor loos at Television Centre; always wore a fresh(ish) flower in the lapel of his brown overall as he went about his business, mopping and cleaning. His chat (behind closed doors, generally) was to do with the weather, but responding—mid-peristalsis, as you wrestled something unpleasant into the porcelain—called for precision timing.

Reminds me of a sponsor's dinner in the open-air terrace restaurant at Wembley arena, during a *Benson & Hedges* final between Ivan Lendl (*Terminator II*—<u>he</u> *wouldn't win Wimbledon, either*) and J.P. McEnroe (*three-times the Champ*).
China plates (with knives of the finest Sheffield) meant every incision on a Maris Piper accompanying the tournedos Rossini (medium-rare) had to be made well in advance of Ivan's languid toss; 'lip syncing' to the smack of gut-on-*Penn* was fanciful at that distance.
The dish could be fully in—<u>and</u> di-gested during the subsequent McEnroe rant about "QUIET!" (*rich, coming from him*).

US Golf again.
I'd been on a bit of jolly to their Open Championship in Chicago—won, after extra holes, by Hale Irwin (Nick Faldo just missing out on the play-off . . . *and being very hacked off about it . . . . for hours*). I say 'jolly,' but we were working, not as hard as our hosts—the American Broadcasting Company—whose award winning, and oft-times volatile producer, Terry Jastrow, was at full throttle.
'Tel' had a private thunderbox at Medinah (venue for the 2012 Ryder Cup), parked within peeing distance of their enormous production truck. Health warning : TERRY'S JOHN—KEEP OUT!

At close of play, T.J.'s wife would sweep into the compound in their chauffeur-driven stretch, slip a smoked window, enough, to offer the unwashed a glimpse of her famous face, then—as her less celebrated other half climbed in alongside—off they'd whisk to grander accommodation than any on the crew could ever aspire to.
(by close of play on Sunday, the communal boxes were indescribable)

Not to imply there's money in sports television production, for the face in the slit was Ann Archer's—the tormented wife of cheating bastard Michael Douglas in *Fatal Attraction*, amongst many other lucrative roles.
(full marks to Terrry for judicious use of producer's choice)

Wimbledon meant a rise from bog to high standard, mobile dunnies: plumbed in, wooden seats, pastoral prints on the walls, double-strength soft 'n' gentle, company-green dyed water for the flushing of, ozone-friendly fragrances to spray—i.e. quality cans.

I was hard at it in Trap 5—the orange one (there's no All-England green in greyhounds). Luxurious though the block was, it was transportable, thus the tremor produced by the incoming desperado, shook it to its temporary foundations . . . yet *nothing* compared to what followed: an applause-worthy feat of synchronized evacuation and hollered exultation at having made it in time—braces/drawers/pants down/ knees bend/fart/go . . . . *fwho-o-ah!*
("I know that accent . . .")
I felt moved to speak.
An eerie silence as we paused for the pong to hit: 3 off the tee i.e. out of bounds.
A second, more terrifying cry . . . as though in the throes of death-by-gagging...shook the print to my right:

"SHHHIT!!" (mother of all onomatopoeias).

The traditional, wire toilet-roll holder has much to commend it where decisions have to be made in a rush; alas, for the punter in the striped jacket—Trap 6 (rejected)—his was one of those enclosed jobbies with the little window on the side . . . and no one was home (hard rule No.1 for a fast No.2—check *before* delivery).

My business completed without undue stress, and with reams in reserve, I separated a single sheet and slid half-a-gossamer under the partition, in genuine appreciation of the entertainment, thus far.
There was a permanently-plumbed toilet under Centre Court where I could complete my ablutions, so I tip-toed out, leaving my cell-mate time to implement and execute a plan.
It'd be a case of . . . sliding the bolt . . . checking for strangers . . . taking pants and strides in both hands . . . hopping next door . . . . and praying no spillage occurred on the journey.
(*if ever my wee man with the wilting flower were needed*).

It's a busy place, the production office at Wimbledon, where commentators and producers meet between stints, executives, with nothing better to do, posture and pontificate, and *bon fide* guests congregate for the crack.
(*créac* being Irish for 'arsehole')

Some were sobbing, uncontrollably, as I walked in.

"So what did you do next, Cliffie?"
Unmasked . . . the outhouse unfortunate was the BBC's Royal Liaison officer—former British Lion, and now Head of Sport and Outside Broadcasts—C.I. Morgan esquire; we were good mates but maybe not <u>that</u> good.

Steve Heighway's Cup Final accomplice, Bob Wilson—the Arsenal and Scotland keeper, and as decent a bloke as you'll come across—had regaled us of his own, quite moving, toilet encounter.

The very last droplets of his no.1 had hit the sterilizing crystals, when, out from the only stall for 2s, came a peerless rendition of *MISTY* (written as an instrumental, originally, by the iconic pianist, Errol Garner).

"Shut the f _ _ _ up. Who the f_ _ _ _do you think you f_ _ _ _ _ _ are, you f_ _ _ _ _ _ g w _ _ _ _ r," Johnny f _ _ _ _ _ _Mathis !" roared two erudite uncouths, as down the row, the big custodian tucked his gun barrel away.
(not a classy establishment, clearly—old Highbury, probably).

'*Engaged*' in red went green for '*vacant.*'

Bob's close friend, the imperious Johnny Mathis took a bow.
(. . . *spot the wankers now, dick-brains*)
Autographs were out of the question.

There've been a few stuffed-shirt execs at the BBC, but on Bill Cotton (Jnr., to "*Wakey Wakey*" Billy the bandmaster's, Snr.,) the 'Harveys' (Proctors) fitted well.
As was his wont and prerogative as Controller of BBC 1 (*to go where he 'kin well liked*), he'd joined us on that gun-running trip to the Masters. (*Augusta is very likeable*)

Controllers, and royalty, travel separately, in the decent seats; he didn't have to justify himself to anyone other than the Governors and the more mischievous members of the popular press who weren't there for the birdies altogether.
Air-conditioned media facilities, with databases to take leg-work and research out of the equation, and television monitors accessing all areas, weren't around in (Bernard Darwin) the father of all golf writers' day. Personally, I was more of a (Peter) Dobereiner man myself.

Our local convenience store, on Washington Drive—a couple of clicks from Magnolia Lane's corridor of uncertainty—had a huge figurine of *The Jolly Green Giant* in the doorway, promoting crunchy corn-on-the-cob niblets—'*3-for-2 . . . on sale within*' . . . so the slim Controller of 1 decided to hire it for the night.

As branding slogans go, the one a little further on—just before our turn off—was humming:
Domestic Bog and Drain Specialists
"*we're No. 1 in the no. 2 business.*"

Hitching a ride in a brand new friend's pick-up (he'd talk to anyone), Bill got *T.J.G.G.* back to our rented house, unscathed and in one 8ft piece.
Incidentally, 'Fred the Bald'—our driver at the previous day's civil infraction—got off with a stern warning from 'Dirty Harry' and no official censure from the chief executive of the parent corporation.

Most nights, when the weather was clement, we barbecued: Alliss did most of the cooking . . . we mucked-in with salad and stuff. Stevie Rider tended to look after the booze, keeping him away from all culinary duties, much to our temperamental cook's chagrin.

That night big Pete—never one to stay in the neutral corner—launched into our guest commentator . . . not *specifically* for coming from Scunthorpe, more for not looking after his success better, and for failing to get the knighthood Peter, in particular, craved for his beloved game of golf.
Maybe he hadn't made 'Sir' Tony, but 'Jacko' was a great Ryder Cup player and captain, and his back-to-back majors, with that "corker" of a drive—as Henry Longhurst would describe it—down the last at Lytham in the first of them, is one of the great treasures of the BBC's golf archive.

Fred caved in first, as one by one, we fell off the perch.
The roar from his room was Clooney in *Burn After Reading*.

Imagine it: he's made the bedroom, well-bladdered . . . ignored the house lights . . . opened his closet to hang up his hankie . . . only to have a hoofing-great polystyrene monster tumble down on top him.

Through the door, camera in hand, came Eric and Ernie's biggest fan.

You can take the Controller out of the comedian . . .

I came across Sir Henry (Cotton)—no relation—a few times; he did some commentary for us at the Open, very much in later life, and though he was a little off the pace, and rightly petrified by the climb to the commentary box by unguarded ladder, hearing him describe a four iron off a tight lie on a links course, alone, was worth the licence money.
(we 'staffers' paid that particular levy under threat of emasculation, in the boys' case, and in the girls' . . . of two nights out with Julian Wilson)

The much-debated licence fee works out at under 40p a day, which is fantastic value (even without *Grandstand*); masochists still get *Strictly* and *Newsnight Review* (and Ann Robinson), and for the rest of us there's *The Tudors*, *Spooks* and *Deadly 60*.

As a schoolboy, born and bred into a golfing community, there was no escape. My old man had some pretty questionable gear—spoons and brassies and cleeks—but he could get it round, regularly, under the required amount.
Christy O'Connor Snr., and, later on, Neil Coles—two who could do many things with a golf ball, effortlessly—were his favourites. 'Senior' nearly won the '65 Open at Birkdale (losing out to Peter Thomson's fifth title), and Coles would take the points from both his Ryder Cup singles in that 'honeymoon' hammering in Houston in1967.

Unavoidably late for a golfing dinner in Dublin (during the Irish Open), I eased into my seat next to 'Himself'—Christy's seemly sobriquet—as first course plates were being cleared:

"Would you ever mind yersel on the soup, it's boilin' hotte."

Expecting third-degree burns, I sipped gingerly, as advised.

The ample bosom, across the way, easily contained the jet-stream of gazpacho.

As a treat, Dad had taken us to a Masterclass at Gleneagles, four years after Cotton had stopped the competitive stuff; having topped the variety bill at the London Coliseum, preaching to us converts was candy for him.

"To be a champion you must act like one."
Henry was a sturgeon's roe and 'shampoo' man, for sure, not averse to pitching up for work in a Roller. He won a massive £350 (in total) for winning the Open THREE times, and while it may not be about the money, Darren Clarke got the Champion of Golf Trophy and nine hundred grand for 2011 alone.

'Volunteers' were invited to try Cotton's wrist-strengthening exercise (*"educate the hands"*) by thrashing an iron into the side of a tractor-tyre.
Harry Weetman—a Ryder Cup shoo-in for G.B. & I.—preferred chopping wood.
Arnold Palmer, whose limbs were huge at birth, won the 'British' twice; but for the War, Cotton would have improved on his tally, though anything 'major' Stateside eluded him.

He'd have forgotten one so inconsequential, but I recalled our previous encounter when we met—by chance—at Royal Mid-Surrey golf club in Richmond, towards the end of a long life.
He feigned rememberance, then—a slender bag of wands draped over a rounded shoulder—he set off for a few holes.

Plodding after a three-wood he'd nipped off the top at the first on the 'little' course, he didn't react to any of several:
"I say—*you* there!"
A bumptious blimp-of-a-member—the embodiment of golfing pomposity, an anathema to swithering juniors—had stormed on the tee from the old clubhouse, waving agitatedly, demanding that the lone figure return immediately as singles were "*not allowed*" at that time on the Inner.

I enjoyed putting the arrogant dinosaur straight: all exchanges ceased.
I forgot to mention that Cotton had been instrumental in getting the Golf Foundation started; central to its brief was to encourage youngsters into the game . . . *and to avoid like the shank, pricks like him.*

". . . and the name being . . . ?"

(. . . . similarly, the jobsworth on our compound gate at the tennis)

"Bjorn Borg."

"Not on *my* list, sunbeam."

A timely intervention by Miss Penny Wood, mistress of all things BBC Wimbledon, effected entry for the five-times champion.

As schoolboys—out of shorts and into grey slacks—we'd graduated from golf to girls, but, several failures later, it was decided a 'Boys Only' trip to sunny Portugal, sticks in the hold, would restore confidence.

As the Earth moved us—and several empty jugs of (illicit) sangria—slowly towards twilight, we watched 'Toots' (<u>Lady</u> Cotton, to be) and *'Pacifico'* (the trusty donkey) trudge across Penina, stopping along the way for 'Maestro' to tilt at a limp flag on one of his immaculate designer greens.
Target found with an elegantly finessed fairway wood.

BUMP! (here come some more names)

The organisers always kept a few pro-am spots open for the BBC at events we were televising.
I partnered Jose-Maria Olazabal in one such at Gleneagles, some time before the nightmarish injury saga that almost brought on his premature retirement.
The second shot to the 3rd hole on the King's course is blind, the green tucked away below a huge hump. His approach skelp, with an iron, took off like *Polaris*, and in it

had gone for an eagle, sight unseen, consigning 'Chema' to his back on the fairway, bicycle-kicking like he'd won the Jug (*not to be, it seems*).

The golfing world wanted Jose-Maria back. Talk was of a deteriorating mental state . . . . of crippling arthritis . . . of amputations, but the fact was, his back was the problem.

A return to winning ways, culminating in the Masters in 1999, was miraculous . . . *Hoganesque*.

When I joined European Tour Productions—part of Trans World International, the TV production arm of Mark McCormack's International Management Group—Tony Ball was a technical, financial, mover and shaker with a title that probably included a vice-presidency—most of them did.
Tony knew *zip* about programme making, but always took a keen interest in how we were spending the firm's investment.

In a move akin to Mo Johnson joining the Rangers, he changed strips: *gone* the polo shirts and loafers of McCormack's E.T.P.—*in* the pin-stripes and Windsor knots of Murdoch's BSkyB . . . it was 'mobile' or 'cell,' depending on the conversation or currency.
(the in-vogue 'sunnies'—for added mystique—didn't work . . . way too flash)

'Antonio'—a Pilat in pants—would sit in judgement at the head of the conference table, as I fell out with *Sky*'s Head of Sport over how we should cover golf (with their money . . . not a great move, but why say one thing, when <u>not</u> doing the other would make <u>him</u> look much better?).

The BBC had all the really good tournaments (including the Ryder Cup) in those days, but things were about to change. European Tour Productions would produce most of the events on the circuit, ostensibly for *Sky*, with *The Golf Channel* in the States, piggy-backing the deal, lobbing in fistfuls of dollars and getting masses of air-time for the 24 hour service they were providing for insomniacs in the U.S. and Japan.

The feeling in some (hind)quarters at *Sky* was that T.G.C. were getting more of our attention than their contribution warranted; not the case, but Tony took himself, and his snazzy briefcase, to the Spanish Open in Madrid, to see for himself.
He arrived unannounced, like a Michelin Guide rep, and proceeded on a tour of our various areas of operation (*his* more than *ours*), checking on who was doing what for whom.
Wasted effort really; we were there to cover the golf to the best of our not inconsiderable collective abilities, and to have 'Get Smart' agent Ball floating around

asking questions as we tackled complicated things, wasn't conducive to team spirit thus created.
Directing and producing golf, over four long days (if you're doing it right), is taxing, mentally and physically.

It was a 'moving day' visit—the Saturday.
His chuntering and pontificating was getting on everyone's tits, so I asked him, politely, to step outside in order that some sort of protocol could be established.
Alas, the story was to end in disproportionate merits.
'Bally' became the grandest *frommage* imaginable at Grant Way, Isleworth, and at *Fox* in the US . . . *and I got the sack* . . . six fabulous years down the track, mind.
What was I saying about not making money from sports television, for fuck's sake.
It was reported that Tony Ball made around £30 million while at BSkyB.

We were back in Portugal, covering one of the many tournaments in a constant, year-long schedule. After we'd checked all facilities, one of our trainee operators, Ian Macdonald, asked if he could take a camera back to the hotel to get some scenic shots for the following day's show . . . by way of a bit of practice.

Beached, traditional fishing boats, nets splayed to dry in the sun . . . a tapas bar, nearby, with fish soup to die for . . . the paraphernalia of Iberian coastal life . . . old trainers . . . out-grown prams . . . mangy, barking dogs with stamina to last the night (*every* night) . . . that sort of idyll.

Ian went higher to capture the Atlantic swallowing the Sun, as a final, moody image.

His finger hovered over the *STOP* button, as a lone figure entered the bottom-left edge of frame.
There, in T-shirt and shorts, fully functioning feet splashing in the shallows, was the very private, Jose-Maria Olazabal, seen little since his enforced exile . . . and <u>never</u> like this.

That image, and an understandably tearful close-up we got a few weeks later on the 72nd green of the Turespaña Masters in Majorca, as the impact of his first comeback win consumed him, told the heart-rending tale in two.

Our mate shouldn't have been allowed to die so soon.

And one last golfing anecdote (for now).

Startled out of my reverie by an angry bedside phone at 170 Castelnau, London—a one bed-roomed pad shared with two devoted girls, upon whom much love was lavished (Daisy was the bigger cat . . . her tiny, long-haired, half-sister, Rose, by far the greater attention-seeker)—I made a spot-check to ensure my head was still attached to its engine housing.

"Philips? Walford"
My old chum from various pubs, clubs and playing fields—infuriatingly chipper at sparrow-crack. His course management of the hangover was second to none.
"*Cocktail bar, Wizzers, 1000hr; tardiness and an absence of the 'A'game, will have grave consequence."*
Dial-tone.
From bitter experience, to roll over in the face of a Black Rod summons, would have been foolhardy.

De-and re-vesting quicker than Naomi on a catwalk shoot, my rather dandy, metallic sky-blue company Mercedes—sticks 'n' spikes in the trunk—was soon at cruise on the 316 West.

My playing partner and I embraced, customarily, if a tad awkwardly, at the grand entrance of Wisley Golf Club: Mrs. Colin Montgomerie's decision to become a member, would have a galvanising effect on male members.

Several bloody Marys later (skirting anything solid), *Team Walford* headed for the range to prepare.

The five hours it took us to acquire 39 commendable, better-ball, Stableford points—and the druth (thirst) of a Bedouin—had little to do with *our* speed of play.

We were old school: Christopher Edward "Snake-Hips" Walford's was English and public, and mine was an aspirational Scottish academy, frustratingly single-sex, but adjacent—both heavily into sport.

Don't spoil a good walk by playing at Kenny Brown's pace, yet had we been half as deft on the greens as the former Glasgow Open champion (Hagg's Castle 1984-*14 under par for God's sake*), our tally would have caused haemorrhaging amongst the tournament handicappers.

Surreptitiously, the fearsome club secy., slid my leader to a quiet corner of the lounge bar, as the recorder cross-checked the pencil work.
An animated discussion followed, Chris dismissively swishing his hands in disgust and disbelief, like a mime artist 'doing' table tennis.

With a final, defining toss of his black mullet, he returned, at a clip, with the tablets . . . still glowing.

We were to receive a red and white sponsor's brolly, each, in return for our silence; there would be no further recognition at the prize-giving, and certainly not on the James Capel champions' roll-of-honour board.

The verdict:
"Walford is not a *full* member of the Club, therefore his pick is ineligible."
Null and void.

As Billy Connolly would have it, on being advised as to the methodology of the prostate examination . . .
"FUCK, THAT!"
We'd won, fair and square, and if golf is known for anything, it's fair and square (*and* Mrs. Montgomerie I).

Latin swots at Morrison's Academy told me our school motto—*Ad Summa Tendendum*—was about striving to reach the heights . . . and, as every Reptonian knows, *Porta Vacat Culpa* means *'the (school) gate is free from blame.'* i.e. *flunk and it's your problem, mush.*

Far from flunking (mottoes both, honoured) . . . *tomorrow to St. Andrews and the Royal and Ancient Golf Club's Miscarriage of Justice Appeals Committee.*

A quaff or two of red consumed, we relented, applauded the phony winners, and left in a dignified manner (seething) with our rolled brollies.

James Capel—the title sponsors—were among the first stockbrokers in the city of London, back in the 1770s . . . *so I hope they're proud of their fine traditions.*
Bastards!

Potentially, several RTOs were on offer on the way back—speeding, and driving while *slightly* over the limit in my case, and driving *at all* in my partner's: due to repeated misdemeanours and a loss of patience from the bench, the Walford permit was in safe-keeping . . . at the DVLC in Cardiff.

My good buddy lost out to cancer; no . . . fuck *that!*

"... Now, Bugger Off"

Editors—be it news or sport—have to earn the title by never losing their nerve; caving in in the face of Internet 'ghoulfests' is to cop out today.

A player's leg is hideously broken in a vicious tackle . . . *do you show it again?*
No you don't.
What if a Korean soldier is captured shooting another in the street at point blank range . . . *do you show it at all?*
No you don't.
There are pictures to prove they assassinated Gadaffi and hanged Hussain—and that bin Laden was shot three times in the head—*but would it help to show them?*
I doubt it.

We certainly don't have to see those who opted to jump, to prove how depraved Al-Qaeda are . . . or watch Le Mans decapitations to highlight safety standards at race tracks.

The difference between the mountains of emaciated and dead bodies in Richard Dimbleby's report from Bergen-Belsen in 1945—which we as kids could never understand (still can't)—and that distant view through a car windscreen of Concorde going down with all hands, is that <u>one</u> was an accident.

Someone has to make the call.

Ibrox Stadium, Glasgow—Saturday 2nd February 1971—66 fans, including a teenage girl, are killed at an Old Firm game.
Celtic had been leading with minutes to go. Hundreds of home fans were already making their way down one of the exit staircases, when Rangers equalized. A child stumbled. In the chaos, crush barriers collapsed. Dozens suffocated.

Hillsborough Stadium, Sheffield.
As chance would have it, I'd scheduled myself off editing *Grandstand* that Saturday—April 15th 1989. The gruesome reality of what had happened was obvious right away to John Shrewsbury, my producer colleague directing the game for *Match of the Day*. Like so many, he'd just gone for the football.

Despite massive overcrowding in the central pen at the Leppings Lane end of the ground—accessed by a narrow tunnel—more and more Liverpool fans were allowed in. There was nowhere to go.

John told me afterwards that he'd been instructed not to let John Motson (at the ground), nor Bob Wilson (in the studio), mention any deaths, until they'd been confirmed; dozens of covered bodies, lined up right outside his mobile control room, was confirmation enough.

Heysel happened in mid-week—Wednesday May 29th 1985—so the *Sportsnight* team had charge of that harrowing transmission. As Coleman had in Munich all those years before, Barry Davies—our match commentator in Brussels—handled his responsibilities in a humane and measured way; nothing prepares anyone for that.

In Glasgow, Sheffield and Brussels, thousands of folk, brimming with passion and expectation, had gone out to support their respective teams . . . . 201 of them died.

Despite having one of the best jobs anyone could wish for, these reality checks were round the corner . . . reminders of our remit, tests of character.

Death was never far away in motor racing.
Recently released footage of the horrendous crash at Le Mans—11th June 1955—when the burning wreckage of Pierre Levegh's Mercedes tore into the crowd, killing him, and wiping out dozens of spectators, personally, I could have done without seeing.
I worked on *Grand Prix* for a few years with Murray and James, and not a season went by without tragedy of some kind; the Lauda fire, Berger's, Villeneuve killed in practice—Murray's obituaries were far too frequent.

By the time the F1 Championship had come to the Nurburgring for the German Grand Prix in 1976, James was well shy of Lauda's points total.
The Austrian was on his way to back-to-back titles when, inexplicably, his Ferrari spun out of control and caught fire: his injuries were horrendous.

Within a couple of months, and with just enough plastic surgery to let his eyes open sufficiently, he was back racing.

We'd been given permission to talk to him, on camera, at Watkins Glen; his account—and appearance—beggared belief, but he'd been given another chance, which most of us would have interpreted as . . . *time to get back to Austria and start planning an airline business* . . . not Lauda.
(James would win that championship).

The two commentators and I were at a John Player Special bash in Monaco, on the eve of the '81 race. Protocol and team orders demanded that both drivers—Nigel Mansell and 23 year old Elio de Angelis—be there to press guest flesh. Nigel wore a functional, tweed sports jacket; the suave Italian—in a Brioni, or one from Armani's range (Giorgio was the new kid on the fashion block)—fitted the ambiance of Hôtel Hermitage perfectly.
Moored in the bay below was his powerboat-freak Dad, Giulio's mother-and-father of a yacht.
He appeared to have the lot.

De Angelis was only 28 when he was killed testing the new Brabham in France; he'd raced in more than a hundred Grand Prix—eight more than James, whose own big heart gave out, unassisted.

Murray's agony in putting that obituary on tape was testimony to the special bond they had. An inadequate documentary, some years back (one I'd liked to have done, *properly*), fell wide of the mark. James was a different kettle of fish to 'The Flying Scot'—or the extraordinary John Surtees—but make no mistake, Murray adored the bloke.

The 'publish and be damned' theory, spelled out in an early (prescribed) work by Hugh Cudlipp (prior to his after-burn into the executive stratosphere at the Mirror Group—and subsequent baronetcy) didn't always work in sport.

When Emily Davison made her purposeful dive in front of King George V's *Anmer*—as the field tore round Tattenham Corner in the 1913 Derby—newsreel editors had an option: it was film, which meant processing . . . time to view . . . . to consider what to show of the carnage.

Why, if she'd bought a return rail ticket, would she want to kill herself?
Was it a highly dangerous stunt to draw attention to women's suffrage?
(. . . *there were easier ways, Em, old thing*).
But the presence of scores of press photographers, and thousands of eye witnesses, made it more a case of not missing out, than of good taste. Davison died a few days later from her injuries.

By gruesome comparison, I was directing at the British Motor Cycle Grand Prix at Silverstone, when a mass of 250c.c.riders broke out of the high speed Hangar Straight and into the most God-awful crash: the question was *how many fatalities?*
Race coverage continued for a while—there was nothing else you could possibly show. I didn't replay the incident—a call that wasn't accepted universally. Within minutes, the door of our truck was thrown open and a small delegation from other

world—and I mean *other* world—broadcasters(?) were questioning why the BBC replay wasn't happening.
Cursorily, I told them, it wouldn't:
' . . . now, *bugger off.*

After *they* had, another figure appeared—apparently from the circuit's medical team—asking for a copy of the crash, in order . . . *"to assess the immediacy of the incident team's response"*—I sent him away quicker than the rest, in fact, he might well have *been* one of the rest, so desperate were they to review the mayhem; even had he been *bona fide,* he wasn't going to see the tape. Subsequently, my guv'nor, Cliff Morgan, locked it away in his office, and knowing him, probably destroyed it.

When Giles Villeneuve was killed practicing for the 1982 Belgian Grand Prix, television news producers went to unbelievable lengths, circling his already dead body as it flew through the air (in slow-motion).

I instructed that we cut away from the host broadcaster's coverage of Gerhard Berger, as he sat motionless, trapped in his flaming Ferrari, by the Tamburello corner at San Marino in 1989, where Senna would die, five years later. Berger, who was Nigel Mansell's team mate by then, survived, but quite what the TV race director was expecting to have us watch as he encouraged his cameraman to zoom *in* . . . . makes me shiver.

That Le Mans was allowed to go on after the carnage in '55, was just mad—that the drivers shunned seat belts, doubly so.

Present day drivers—and fans—owe Jackie Stewart a big debt of gratitude for making his sport sit up and address safety, on, around and off the world's tracks.

Despite the damaged caused, I'm pretty well *pro-*boxing in sport's longest running debate, and am definitely *pro-*helmets in cricket. Jerky pictures of Harold Larwood & co., felling one Australian after another on the 'Bodyline' tour—1932-33—made me wince. Nowadays, hundred mile-an-hour, potentially fatal missiles from the 'quicks', cannoning off protected heads, are reviewed in hi-motion without another thought . . . . *but what if?*

What if Abraham Zapruder's view had been a 'live' camera in Dallas—22nd November 1963—instead of on 8mm film . . . what would the producers have replayed of the death of a President?
(it was 12 years before the public got to see all that infamous footage)

To an 11 year old kid, the Munich air crash just seemed so unfair; the idea of someone being killed <u>playing</u> football, must have been impossible.

There were four photographs of the incident in 1931 that led to John Thomson's death: the first showed Thomson—the 17 year old goalkeeper Celtic had signed in 1926—(now 22) diving for the ball as Rangers' Irish striker, Sam English prepared to shoot . . . the second captured the instant Thomson's head impacted the forward's standing knee . . . . the third was of an anxious English looking on, as others milled around . . . the fourth, had Thomson being stretchered off Ibrox by St. Andrew ambulance men.
He died later that night in hospital.
The jeering would follow a traumatised English around for years, and he gave up playing at 28.

Had I been a newspaper editor back then, with those four images in front of me, I'd have left the second one out as being gratuitous—grossly so . . . . *and ended up being sacked, no doubt.*

There was a near mirror-image, 50-50 moment at the FA Cup final in 1956. Manchester City's German 'keeper, Bert Trautman—named Football Writers' Player of the Year that Spring—was badly hurt when he and Birmingham's Peter Murphy came together.
There were no 'subs' in those days, so Trautman—constantly clutching his neck—battled on and finished the match (which City won 3-1).
Not till the following day did X-rays show there to be several displaced vertebrae, which, in other circumstances, might have killed him.

In 2001, Sergey Perkhun, a Russian Premier League 'keeper, died of a brain haemhorrage after colliding, head-to-head, with another player.

In hindsight, we shouldn't have shown it, but unwittingly, *Grandstand* viewers witnessed the after-effects of a heart attack from which former Everton manager, Harry Catterick died; our cameras spotted the isolated figure in the director's box at Goodison as we reported on their FA cup quarter-final match with Ipswich, but no one could have known the extent of his condition at the time.

Only a few months ago, my son Grant was directing at White Hart Lane when Fabrice Muamba suddenly collapsed, and effectively "died" on the pitch during the Spurs-Bolton match.
There are something like 30 cameras on the modern football rig and there was no escaping the seriousness of what was happening out in the middle; with great care and judgment, Grant and his colleagues at ESPN were able to report on what to all intents and purposes was a public tragedy, with the minimum of distress.

Mercifully, these are rare occurrences.

THE XX AND XY FACTORS

Once upon a time—when there were funds to burn—I came close to membership at Royal Mid Surrey golf club, mainly because it was close to where I lived; but it only takes a couple of misfires to put you off your game, and we—a lady friend and I—were about to blown back by one of them (combustible talk around Richmond . . . *you'll be telling us next, the clubhouse would be razed by fire in 2003*).

Prior to her grand deception with the famous half-miler, I had taken Mrs. Williams—an enthusiastic amateur—to play golf at the scene of the Cotton buffoonery.
At the end of our 'good walk spoiled,' we slipped into something appropriate and headed for the bar.

'Oh no, sir . . . not today.' (Jesus, not another one!)

If I can borrow from "The Pub Landlord" . . . they had more rules at Old Deer Park than unified Germany. The handsome bar-steward was condescendingly polite, but my companion wasn't worthy of a glance, making me wonder if all was as it seemed . . . *"as a little peach she was"* (© the diminutive Jedi master).
Ladies weren't allowed in that particular bar on that particular day: be you gay (my suspicion) . . . black . . . a Surrey member of the Klan . . . a closet socialist (*steady on* . . . this is the Richmond and Barnes of Jeremy Hanley—"*Conservative*") . . . or had you been rumbled for a transgression with the leather wedge—and/or failed to declare a double hit—unless you played off 'the whites or yellows,' you weren't getting in (application duly withdrawn).

Labour (the Party) was disproportionately represented in the *Grandstand* office. One declared member—with hellish bad breath (which the mother of his children <u>must</u> have come across)—wore the same hue of political and football colour on his sleeve. There was the 'odd' BNP supporter and one proven golf cheat (we'd have spotted Elephant men in white hoods). 'Outing' wasn't huge in the 70s: the *spot-the-gay-in-five* ratio was much higher than today . . . *but, frankly, my dear, who gave a damn?*

Our 'token' black man was 'accepted' in the late-Eighties, twelve decades after Lincoln's death, and one after *Kunte Kinte's* creator, Al (Alexander) Murray Palmer Hayley had his *Roots* done (Hayley pulled every big brother for *Playboy* magazine . . . Martin Luther King, Martin X, Cassius Clay—the works).

Maybe our new recruit's own celebrity swung it with the appointments board, for the excellent Ernest Obeng was the AAA's 100 metres title holder in 1985, just ahead of the first of Christie's run of eight.
'Good to have you on board, young Obeng' (when the athletics contract came up again . . . not that that had anything to do with letting him in of course).

Though there were women scattered about the place, an Alabaman black had a better chance of making producer.
Machismo rules . . . this was sport, OK?—man's work.
Tosh!
Girls in ties could run the country . . . warble about what they really, really wanted . . . go down on a President in the Oval office . . . plate up cold peas for a grey, rubbery Prime Minister . . . but edit a half of football on *Match of the Day* . . . the hellish Shed at Chelsea would freeze over first.

I've been breast-fed, cleaned-up, infatuated with, married to, bitched at, divorced from, wrung out and fascinated by the ladies . . . at * *"work, rest and play."*
*That slogan had nothing to do with Murray Walker but *"Trill makes budgies bounce with health,"* and *"Opal fruits, made to make your mouth water"* were down to the Masius whizz-kid in leathers (you can imagine the crack when he and parakeet fancier Hunt were put into the same cage).
The one, in the Sixties . . . about the *Mars Bar*, the blonde and the rockers, did the rounds, but the blonde always strenuously denied it . . . and what a waste of a delicacy anyway: dip it in batter, deep fry, with a poke of chips and welly on the sauce—*yum*. Not one for Delia's cheats, but you can see erotic Nigella having a crack at one.

The TV cook is no 21st century thing, it's just that there are more of them—and Matt Dawson (only a matter of time before he gets own show: <u>Peter Kay's *Britain's Got the Pop Factor . . . and Possibly a New Celebrity Jesus Christ Soapstar Superstar Strictly on Ice*</u> could be adapted to suit the scrum-half's seemingly inexhaustible versatility. Dawson's agent was the busiest in the land for a while, with Graham Norton's an expensive second, and in grateful third, he of Phil Jupitus *(what's he for?)*.

We'd always quote Philip Harbin on family pasta nights—*"I like good food, macaroni for instance, Marshall's macaroni"* . . . from an early TV ad
(add thin, brown toast with lashings of butter, and a glass of full-cream milk and you'll see where Mike Myers got *Fat Bastard* from).
Mum's mince and tatties—and Irish stew, falling off the bone—couldn't be taught, or resisted; she was a Do (Domestic) School graduate . . . and please, don't get me started on Granny (on Dad's side)'s broth, or Mum's Mum's snake and pigmy pie.

Ms. Smith was 'huger' in the 70s than she is now at Carrow Road, and crazy, wine-slurping Graham Kerr—*The Galloping Gourmet*—was a must watch in our house;

the Craddocks—culinary forerunners of the Hamiltons (Christine and Neil)—(Fanny doing the cooking . . . Johnny getting in the way) weren't.

They even got my old mucker from *Channel 4* cricket, 'gorgeous' M.C.J. Nicholas (Hampshire and England 'A') in the TV kitchen . . . to host *Britain's Best Dish* (that's the food, Markie).

Wives, mothers, mothers-in-law, mother-fucker line managers, scary secretaries, power-dressing department heads were gradually seizing control, so you needed to know when to keep your muscle to yourself.

If you needed your 'creative' expenses signing, be sweet to awesome Joan Zoller, admin guru at our Kensington House offices. Joanie and I sat on a few appointment boards together . . . at either ends of the table; any female aspirant wearing anything above the knee, heels higher than pumps, or 'lippie' louder than flesh, had no chance—*a Geoff Hurst (first) in Media Studies, notwithstanding*—should it come to *Zee's* casting vote . . . hence the dearth of outstandingly fit babes (babes in general) in the department, for a time.

That house of ill-repute I mentioned a while back, where some of our senior execs—under pressure to make snap foreign exchange calculations in their heads, and frustrated further by the effect their casual approach to German lessons at school was now having on potential deals with the local contractees—was in *Höhennzoller Strasse*; Joan would *not* have approved . . . nor signed, however carefully worded the receipts were.

Tablets came down from on high that having helped her intended, and the rest of the GBR equestrian team, to a gold medal in the three-day event at the 1972 Olympics, Princess Anne, would be calling at our meagre workplace.
Only best behavior from us worker ants would be tolerated.
Our leader, Paul Fox—still only a *Mister* and a cunning one at that—showed the royal jockey in to our corner of the broadcasters' hub in Munich.

It's common knowledge—*or* commoners know—that the Queen's only girl is worldly . . . not "street" exactly, but pretty clued.
A vast array of expletives would be attributed to her from future skirmishes with the media (*know where they came from, Pops*), but what greeted our guest of honour—a lady of 22 . . . yet to have a ring on it—as the sliding door separating our chamber of horrors in videotape from the seeming order of the production gallery (must have been some serious acting going on in there) was rolled back, was unbridled profanity.

Because of ambient noise levels, we operated with headsets on, amplifying our 'unutterables,' but H.R.H.—soon to be plain Mrs. Phillips of Gatcombe Park to the postman—took it in her stride.

Nice of her to drop by, but you needed to have seen some of our guys trying to be cool and correct and succeeding only in making total dicks of themselves.
P.S. Two years later, in the streets of London, Anne told an armed man that his attempt to kidnap her was "bloody unlikely to succeed" as she didn't have the two million quid he fancied as a ransom—*a little bit of a porky that, Ma'am, if I might be so bold.*

Memorably, in the bowels of TV Centre in 1978 (Montreal), Prince Andrew (or was it Edward? . . . *memorable, huh?* . . . could get the drop for this)—a mere lad anyway, (with a snowball's chance of bagging the top job)—did the rounds.
He was perturbed that no one was doing anything about *'the chappie on the track with the gun—look, there, in the corner of the picture'* (guffaws from Royalists, and bodyguards). Our shift leader, 'Jefferson' Goddard—sporting an unsightly, black ink-stain on the crotch of his trousers—dropped like a stone before the regal child to explain, unnecessarily, that it was . . . 'Mr. Starter.'
What a jolly jape.

Neither was there a glut of women in our commentary boxes.
Mary Bignal-Rand didn't last long (*did she jump, or was she pushed?*)despite being coveted by every man Jack—and David—on the premises; randy Mr. Coleman—it's alleged—had her top of his fantasy league.

The first woman to carry the flag for Britain at the Olympics (1964) was (two years previously) the first XX to win *Sports Personality of the Year.*
When she ceased being Olympic, European, British Empire and Commonwealth breaststroke champ, she started banging on and on about swimming in *The Daily Telegraph,* and on BBC Radio.
Quite why she'd then go gaga for a pedaler from Wolverhampton, I'll never know (the thighs, probably), but by 1965 Anita Lonsbrough was Mrs. Hugh Porter.

Britain went gaga for cycling in the wake of Hoy xiānshēng & Co's exploits in China, *but remember, Sir Christopher, non-aerodynamic Hughie P., was a four-time world individual pursuit champion . . . four times!*
(*"catch me if you can"*—Anita beat 'Shug' to her M.B.E. by a whole decade).

Mr. Fox arose as 'Sir Paul' in the late 90s, and Baron Coe of Ranmore (Surrey) got his at the turn of the millennium . . . having got out of FIFA's ethics commission before the shit hit the fan—*toot your horn ma man.*

On the strength of all *his* golds (m' Lordship managed the three), what price Sir Kit making 'Lord Hoy of Hoy' before the Old Man is finally consumed by the Atlantic?

Be warned, all who'd invest (*www.bet365.com*), according to Orcadian law, only those who have climbed up—or bungy-jumped down—the 450ft sea stack can lay any sort of claim.

Technically, all British passport holders are m.b.e.s, but how many mermaid models are there in your street?
Doubtless the yards and yards of Sharron Davies's muscular limbs were factored in to her recruitment as post-race inquisitor on the Beeb's swim team.
Talking to athletes can be unrewarding, as Ms. Davies MBE (poolside) and Ms. Gunnel OBE (trackside) were to discover, but neither received much in the way of media training (. . . *like bugger all*).

'Shazza' the siren—now an accomplished and respected BBC squad member—had to contend with suspect East Germans in her racing days, so overcoming perceived inadequacy was second nature (there was never anything 'respectable' about the accomplished back and breast stroking duo of Jamieson and Moorhouse MBE . . . her co-conspirators up in the commentary position).

Quite where FISA—the incorruptible body politic on matters swimming—stands on boob jobs, is murky: silicone floats, so they could be deemed 'outside agencies.'
Her competitive (swimming) days may be over but Sharron (known throughout her three marriages by her maiden name) is in fantastic nick; if you can't catch her in the flesh, there's a post-enhancement likeness of her top half, by the sea wall at Cowes—on the rocks, in bronze, right outside the Royal Yacht Squadron's clubhouse (the bottom half is disappointing and unrepresentative).
Bearing in mind they're supposed to bring bad luck to sailors, it's an odd choice of sculpture for the RYS's HQ . . . . *or do they know something we don't?*

Thus far, no mermaid has managed to give FISA the slip at backstroke.

"Barker" (MBE)—as my little friend from Wales was close enough to call her (*until they fell out . . . apparently, over a bloke*)—was the best female tennis player in Britain . . . for years. She had a natural, bubbly way; the notion that she once did things to Cliff Richard and Greg Norman, is none of anyone's business.
She certainly got my licensious studio director at it with her short skirts. Prior to her signing, the linking position on sports shows was from behind a desk; it was no surprise when an uncomfortably low sofa was ordered for the Commonwealth Games interview area.

But *baby, look at her now* . . . and Balding, and Irvine, and Logan and Perry, and Gow, and Douglas and Cates and Sky's blondes (and Kirsty Gallacher) and ESPN's Rebecca (BBC's Chris Lowe's girl) . . . a veritable pandemic for misogynistic male "seals" to endure, and, perhaps, an equal rights issue.

How could any credible outfit like Auntie—synonymous with Wimbledon for almost as long as it took Dan Maskell to tell us his tales of Suzanne Lenglen and Jean Barotra between commentary stints—fail to enlist former British champions like Angela Barrett (née Mortimer—more famous than her cack-handed husband a.k.a. the splendid 'J.B.') . . . junior champ and Wightman Cup star, Christine Truman . . . Ann Jones (née Haydon . . . *what a chest* . . . what a ping-pong player . . . *what a handful, Pip*), or Jubilee girl, Virginia Wade: Lawn Tennis and Croquet Club members all?
To question that these gals don't know their onions, would be a challenge wasted.
In the male half of the draw 'Danny Boy' and 'J.B.' were an unforced-error-free, gentlemen's double . . . dandily-dressed Lynam and 'Geraldo' Williams (*'The Bishop'*) hit it off a treat on *Today at Wimbledon* . . . but as a watcher and minor contributor (I once got to the semi-finals on Centre Court—directing), I craved more bite from the 'booths.'

Early in 'the noughties,' the BBC delivered subjectivity-plus, in Shriver, Evert, and 'good Queen Marty' (on the rare occasions she wasn't re-writing history).
If the boys didn't 'show up' on court, they'd have J.P. McEnore, 'b'-B. Becker and ballroom dancer (his *American Smooth* 'needs work' according to Arlene Phillips), rogue (GMTV) breakfast presenter and all-round good egg, A.N. Castle to deal with . . . supplemented, from the chair, by the excellent Mr. Inverdale.

Though the price of strawberries rose higher than Sharapova's hem, cosy, refined, twee, old Wimbledon 'wasn't getting away with nuttin' no more.'
Any in 'Mac' the hirsute gamekeeper's range got the lash, and Pammy was just as tough on the dames.

I know his wife will stick by him—some of them do—but I'm hoping my ex-boss has owned up to his 'love' for Virginia (in a J.M Barrie kind of way . . . wistfully—he *Peter*, she *Wendy*). We less-smitten admirers knew that within her effortless flirtation lay a juicy, long-term commentary contract.
Alas, infatuation can cloud even the sharpest mind.
I was instructed by *Peter Pan* to make a VHS copy of one of *Wendy's* matches, but with millions sat poised for *Sportsnight* that Wednesday, it was *my* head and not *his* heart on the line . . . so we got the show ready first.

He wasn't having it—Virginia was a "priority."

When he abused me, using the deeply offensive 'C' word, I became a red-eyed, Celtic monster; my shirt burst open (revealing not a huge amount), and the desk—with my leader attached—was driven into the wall of his office, till an apology was offered . . . not the kind of tactic Lord Sugar or Karren 'The Hammer' Brady might appreciate, but I was up to here (or there) with his banality . . . *it was time for bigger balls.*

Virginia got her video, and the *Sportsnight* opening titles ran at 21.24.50.
(*my promotion, I fancy, was on hold*)

Channel 4 approached Sybil Ruscoe—a lady with a decent record in broadcasting (radio, mostly)—to, metaphorically, *'break the door down'* at Lord's. In a blaze of publicity—mostly in Black's *Telegraph*, for whom she wrote—Syb became part of the all-male team of cricket broadcasters on *4*.

Jolly Rachel-Heyhoe Flint had done a bit in the past, with box *in* . . . in the middle, and *out* . . . on the box; inappropriate to say she was England's best 'batsman' with no lower-half protrusions to protect, but she had a record 179 to her name . . . she'd scored the first ever 6 in a Test match . . . she was captain of England when they won the inaugural Women's World Cup in 1973 . . . *and she had great connections at La Manga on Spain's Costa Cálida for cut-price holiday breaks for the boys* . . . so you can see why it was impossible to resist her incessant overtures to show more of the women's game on *Grandstand*.

Botham, alone, knows what champions of chauvinism like Boycott, Trueman, 'Chappelli' (*'none of that shit on my face, mate'*—'mate' being our studio make-up artist), bullfrog E.W. 'Jim' Swanton, or the cricketing ghosts whirling round the long room at H.Q., made of Sybil Ruscoe; for my (and her) liking, she was handed rather too many of those no-price, arouse-the-crowds-at-Test-matches, group interviews to do.

Can't say I was a great believer in Hazel Irvine's long-term future.
She was on the fringes of national exposure, but I felt her (*very*) Scottish accent and (*very dodgy*) dress-sense might hinder her progress; good job the man who employed Bill McLaren didn't have the same stupid inclination.
Whether she was trying to make Davis and Parrott sparkle, or bring the viewer up to speed on the life and times of faceless alpine snow skiers (as forgettable as Karl Schranz was to me), Ms. Irvine is the consummate pro and always looks like she's enjoying herself . . . *and why not . . . she's doing the golf, Gary.*

It's not my business to mind, but were I to pick one to fit all criteria from the current crop of female sports presenters, Clare Balding would be that dame.

Her Dad's dog once pissed on my trousers at the Lambourne gallops . . . . *which doesn't make her a bad person, right?* . . . and yes, she's saddled (*ugh*) with daft Willie at the races, but you'd want her on your table at quiz night.

If ever a presenter embodied the passion for, and total understanding of, her specialist subject (and many others besides . . . including orthodontics), it's the well-bred, former head-girl of Downe House school in Berkshire.

Hart (Miranda), whose old man was aide de camp to the Queen for a time, and the Middleton gals—Pippa (the younger) the longer (big sis Kate only did a term) are also FPs, which is no guarantee . . . but *haven't they all done well?!*.

"Where have all the young men gone?" They'll never learn.

The latest, in a long line of women presenters to take many fancies, is Mrs. Kenny Logan (née Yorath), daughter of hard-tackling Terry, of 'undamned' United (amongst others) . . . and Wales. Logan made her (married) name on ITV Sport, where she ought to have been coveted; but whilst Messrs Townsend and McCoist did battle with the fans at an extraordinary, pitch-side lecturn, Gabby sat aloft, often alone in her studio, trying to pretend this wasn't anything other than *'Coventry' unbefitting (*for whom her father 'crunched' on 99 occasions . . . scoring three times, from mid-field).

She must have been tittering all the way down the High Street after signing for BBC Sport. The lady has looks, charm and brains—and won't be led . . . even in the ballroom (*what must she have said to the judges for her not to progress further than her old man on* Strictly?).

I only ever worked under one woman, so to speak—Karen Brown, at Channel 4: no one pushed K.B. around. If the boys at Crecy had no problem getting it on for Jean d'Arc, we certainly hadn't for Karen of St. James.

Across the ever-widening broadcast way, BBC1 and BBC 2 were dominated by women, and Messrs McCormack and Murdoch's female progeny continued to keep eyes on their Daddies' balls (dynasties).

Heterogametically and unusually, *the XY FACTOR* is struggling to hold its own; of the new'ish' generation on telly, Adrian Chiles, Colin "Buddy Holly" Murray (née Wright . . . with ambitions to be Knopfler, really), Dan Walker and 'Markie' Mark Nicholas are stand-outs *"for me, Kevin"* (© Gerry Armstrong on La Liga duty).

If I can single him (M.C.J.) out for a moment, I imagine Britain's best dish gliding to the shaving mirror first thing in the morning—in satin, monogrammed p.js. and slippers of chamois—to quiz himself as to the whereabouts of the other six Wonders of the modern World

But he's good.
Hugely clued on his chosen subject—the life and hits of Bruce Springsteen—with an encyclopedic knowledge of the great game of cricket, M.C.J. is aloof, pompous, erudite, scrubs up beautifully . . . but dwells overly long on two-foot putts *"for me, Gerrry."*.

He and I were thrown together—and clashed almost immediately—on *Channel 4*'s cricket highlights shows.
What had his old mate, Gary Franses (Executive Producer) *done, giving him a philistine Jock as his runner?*

Hampshire's handsomest wouldn't bother to find out about our school First XI's (two-year) unbeaten trot under my faltering guidance as captain, and the canny tutelage of J. E. 'Jack' Walsh; but for the intervention of the pugnacious Japanese, our coach might have played many times for the Baggy Greens. He spun the ball so violently it squealed like a *snitch* at *quidditch* (another popular sport, conceived in Scotland, never to catch on with *Grandstand*).

'Buck' Ryan was one of our English teachers at school in Crieff, and he was . . . *English*.
Loved his cricket did 'Jimbo,' and, like many, pre-lottery punters did *Littlewoods Pools*.
The stiflingly hot summer afternoon that year—having set us an unfathomable comprehension—he disappeared behind his broadsheet (probably, for a spot of nose-picking—*aren't men disgusting?*) to ponder his selections.
Suddenly the door burst open and—flowing gown trailing—in swept J.E.G. Quick, the Rector (headmaster) . . . unannounced.
The class rose.
Shut went the paper, *up* went the coupon, *down* at spinner's pace, in super-slow-motion—at a catchable height—came his 8 from 10.

Comprehensively snared.
Around the classroom, little index fingers were raised in unison.

Mr. Ryan had the most enormous arse which, when bowling his not indecent off-breaks, stuck out so, even 'straight' boy-batters at the other end, could be turned, fleetingly . . . out of curiosity.
During a visit to Morrison's by the great Learie Nicholas Constantine (for reasons I forget), fat-assed Buck was given the honour of bowling an over at the mighty West Indian all-rounder—whose powers of concentration were, as you might expect, greater than ours.

After the fond farewells, the six balls Ryan had used were retrieved from the roof of the school building.
({Sir} Gary Sobers didn't manage his televised feat for seven more years).
(Sir) Learie became a member of the BBC's Board of Governors, Rector of the University of St Andrews, and a life peer in 1969.

I had hours and hours of Test Match cricket under my editor's belt, and plenty from Sunday League cricket . . . *so why so nervous, my dear?*
I guess because he was flung together with a 'lateralist.'
A super-slow-motion of a fast bowler's foot pounding into the return crease, intercut with lingering shots of the batsman's eyes, peering stoically through his helmet grill, in hesitant anticipation of a reverse-swinging cherry, aimed directly at his conk, painted a thousand words.

But Mark Charles Jefford preferred it head-to-toe . . . and in Mitford's English (at first), this on a new show, which, on many hotly-disputed occasions, ended up in early morning transmission slots, where wife-cheating, cricket-loving Premiership footballers and prostitutes—on the pull and hook—might catch it.
The show was called *TODAY* (get it?) *AT THE TEST*.

Nicholas, and cricket, deserved better than that, and I, better than the sack.

Despite the mystique schedulers (viz. of the critic and wasp families) surrounded themselves in, nothing got up the sports fan's nose more, than having to chase a favourite show round the listings.
David Coleman battled constantly with the 'box-fillers' on *Sportsnight's* behalf . . . and prevailed: Wednesday 9.25p.m., without fail . . . the footy on—post embargo—@ 10p.m. sharp.
Des fared less well in his campaigning for a regular spot for *Match of the Day* . . . so he left. The fact that ITV made a culchie from the south of Ireland an offer he couldn't understand, is irrelevant; with declared homes, investments in Icelandic banks, dogs and swanky cars, and an incurable craving for those sardines *á la diamond* (Rose)—and one, straight drive—how unhappy could *he* be?

Where were we?
The Talent. I wasn't alone in liking smooth-talking, slow-walking David Sole (writs may follow); the former British Lion, and captain of Scotland, commanded subject matter <u>and</u> mother tongue, if not peerlessly, then a damn sight better than many other trialists: to my untrained ear, he had perfect pitch, not in Karen Carpenter's league, but just right for the little speakers on my telly, *and* I believe, he sang well in the big boys' bath. He didn't last long on the network.
Keane (on ITV) and Souness (BSkyB), I like, and if ever there was one to bring studio punditry up to revealing, it's Harry's boy, Jamie.

Many don't take to the radio/television transfer market, but John Inverdale swopped codes as effortlessly as John Surtees had on wheels.

The belief was (*his*, possibly) that Julian Pettifer was too handsome for radio, but *who cares what you look like on TV if your stuff's good* . . . as sex-bomb Andrew Marr would surely concur?
Widening crows' feet and a 'turtle' neck on *any* woman under daily scrutiny—worth it or not—would normally spell the end; *best give in to the process, before the Tweedy or Mrs.Rednapp Jnr., take to reading the News.*
And while we're there, I defy anyone to come up with better than Huw Edwards at that game . . . . *bloody brilliant, bach.*

Jonathan Agnew—the man who reduced dear old 'Johnners' (*'oh, do stop it Aggers'*) to a mess on the commentary box floor at St. John's Wood—still prefers 'steam.' He and I worked together—at some distance it has to be said—during the 2007 World Cup of Cricket—him in the sun-drenched 'Windies', and us back on Satellite Way at *Aqiva* . . . a ground station somewhere in the sticks, from where they now do the BBC *Lottery Show*, <u>and</u> a bit of spying, I suspect; they've more dishes than MI6, pointing sky(as in *Milky Way*)wards.

Mr. Murdoch's people descended on the islands like something from a Coppola blockbuster, setting set up Camp Cricket by a beach, with D.I. Gower in charge of links and drinks.
Down the other end—in association with the TV licence payers—was our team, led by the redoubtable Simon Wheeler, a long-time mate from the heady days at BBC Sport, and now a stalwart at Trans World International.

We had one camera (well, two actually) and one cameraman—ubiquitous Des Hymers—for linking our shows, and a couple of island hopping crews to chase matches and stories.

The tournament proper threw up six sixes for Herschelle Gibbs (against the Dutch), and 14th ranked (of 16) Ireland had beaten Pakistan in the group stages.

With all that sun, sea and testosterone flying about, someone was bound to misbehave.

But a suspicious death . . . a murder possibly . . . at a cricket fest?

Asphixia by manual strangulation was put forward . . . some believed in a mafia hit . . . others that the Pakistan team were involved . . . *or was it more straightforward—hadn't their coach had a history of heart problems?*

Sport has to be pretty scandalous to make quality front pages—magnitude Woods, the brothers Giggs, or this year's Boat Race, at the very least.

Were the Brazil national team to fail to qualify for the World Cup . . . moist (predominantly Catholic) eyes (in Rio) would turn on *Christ the Redeemer* for probable cause.
A cameo appearance by Sachin Tendulkar at a Mumbai takeaway would get a higher rating than any episode of <u>Kaun Banega Crorepati</u> (*Millionaire*, in Hindi).

But it was hard to explain how slowly UK news moved on the Bob Woolmer story.

Our reporters in the field—there, ostensibly, to deal with playing matters—had to service various news and current affairs shows, until re-enforcements arrived . . . *for pity's sake, it wasn't Tristan da Cuna—drag your asses out here!*

Had that real tragedy not happened (the jury in Jamaica would return an open verdict on Woolmer) Andrew Flintoff's fall from grace—and *pedalo*—would've seen an EWCB task force deployed to St. Lucia, by RAF 2 Group, with NJP (Non-Judicial Punishment) powers.
A groveling apology followed, but he was stripped of the vice-captain's pips (*still, the boy's a fucking hero, right?*).

Barry Ferguson and Alan McGregor—the boozing Rangers and Scotland duo—were felt to be letting the side down, and they got a 'life' (for a while) . . . that is until big "Al" turned in an heroic display of his own in a European qualifier at Hampden (the naughty boy remains our No.1).
Ferguson (also reprieved in the Levein amnesty) is currently loving it by the seaside in Blackpool, and has told Scotland where to stick it . . . *in the nicest possible way* (for a Member of the British Empire).

Just prior to that Cricket *World* Cup, I was working on the *World* Darts Championships, at the 'world famous' (if you're into darts) Lakeside Country Club, Frimley Green, Surrey, South East England.
Somewhere in the scent/smoke/alcohol/aftershave/chip-fat mix, a fall, of sorts, was certain.

When giant Andy Fordham failed to show for his match one night, alarm bells started ringing, for real; Fordham was far from match fit—the worst was feared.

Bearing in mind we were broadcasting the event 'live' to millions who'd probably care, the organizers diligence in keeping a lid on things wasn't helpful . . . but it worked out fine; paramedics swooped and whisked the big lad off to hospital (just in time, apparently).

The stellar job Simon and his somnambulists did in the Windies was a throwback to the pioneering days of outside broadcasts, when radio signals were as reliable as Northern Rock and grid references were needed to follow football matches on the wireless.

For the most part, our links were 'live,' with one presentation camera, a satellite up-link truck and the Wheeler *Blackberry* on 'hot.'

It was a miracle—a tribute—that nothing went wrong.

In and around the action, dramatic West Indian backdrops at twilight, fine homes, harbour bars, the sounds of Marley (and Ambrose), rum and coke, flying-fish 'butties' and cricketing memorabilia, and it was fantastic, for we cricket fans back home, to have Sobers and Richards and Richardson and Garner and Walsh and Ambrose 'guesting' on our shows. You couldn't imagine that the Curtly sat jammin' on guitar with the boys in his band—in jeans and t-shirt—was the tormentor of Mike Atherton and four hundred other Test batsmen during the Ambrose/Walsh axis of speed.

The 'white' West Indian, Tony Cozier—commentator and writer, who knows more about island cricket than Sir Trevor McDonald (the UK's first, black news-reading, cricket nut and Gooner)—was a generous host.

Never professing to being totally comfortable in front of camera, 'Aggers' was, on sparkling form nonetheless, and so's not to miss an opportunity to replay his *piece de resistance* with Brian Johnson at Lord's, we set the former Leicestershire and England quick, off along a deserted beach.

Prompting him (without getting his feet wet) was our front-man, and now *The Football League Show* host, Manish Bhasin—formerly of BBC Radio Leicester and a committed Fox (*chacun à son goût*).

The under-layed sound tape made even those who'd never heard of the principles, lol (try it, on *You Tube*—with Naughtie and Hunt the . . . . to follow).

We re-enacted the Cleese/Barker/Corbett skit about the class system—from *TW3* (. . . or was it *The Frost Report?*).

In descending order, Joel Garner—like a good 'un—played big Basil's character . . . looking *down* on Agnew (the regular Ronnie's character) for only taking 4 Test wickets @ 93.25; 'Aggers' looked *up* to 'Big Bird' for his 259 Test wickets at 20.97, but *down* on Manish (tiny Ronnie) for compèring *Football Focus* . . . . Manish '*knew his place.*'

Nothing like a bit of plagiarism if the actors can pull it off, and in Garner, Agnew and Bhasin, we had an accomplished am-dram cast.

The cricket was 'all right,' in bursts . . . if a week (or three) too long.

Meanwhile, on Antigua and Barbuda, Texan banker, Allen Stanford, was hatching a devilish plot—a 20/20 series between England and an all-star West Indian XI, to be captained by Chris Gayle.

Rumour had it that big Chris had dallied (in the past) with the organiser's bird, and she was president of his board of directors.
She got the bullet . . . Gayle's team won millions . . . England were eradicated . . . and he (Stanford—currently in nick and denying any fraudulent behaviour) will stand trial eventually.

Meanwhile *in England*, three Pakistan players were done for a spot of fixing, and unceremoniously booted out of the game; perhaps they'll show up again playing college basketball, like Marion Jones, or coaching in Libya, like Ben Johnson did when the madman was in charge.

None of it's cricket, but 'Freddie' falling off a pedalo, pissed, is pretty small beer.

The night D.C.S. Compton C.B.E.—of Middlesex and Arsenal (clues therein)—was asked to leave his hotel room in Manchester in the middle of the night (wankered), I'll leave for my next bestseller.

"... IT'S AN EeeNOROMOUS ONE!"

Unless you were caught *in flagrante delicto* in the broom cupboard with a *Blue Peter* presenter (thereby hangs another tale), the chances of being sacked from a staff job at the BBC were remote; people were dismissed in the heat of battle, only to be re-instated as tempers abated. I recall a colleague in Glasgow being removed, permanently, for putting a 1 in front of his expenses claim for £11.10s., but that was crass (parliamentarian) . . . desperate for the rent though the boy was (. . . *and no, he wasn't*).

There are reliable witnesses—who may now be on the run—who claim to have seen the unmistakable face of a 'famous' sports commentator (there's evidence in the preceding 215 pages . . . . and more ahead), through the steamed up windows of a parked car at a popular sports venue in southern England, being administered to, and clearly deriving pleasure from, a person equally well-known in other areas of the media. But that was private misconduct—if in a public (*always do a spell-check*) place; unlike either participant, my lips are sealed (the super injunction wouldn't have covered it).

Presenters—or 'talent' as they are grandly described in the U.S.—were less well-protected than us scruff. John Motson had a rock-solid contract that spelt remuneration even if he broke wind, but fall from that grace again (who never *was* a *Blue Peter* presenter), and you could be replaced.

Frank Bough was almost suicidal when he was stood down from the Winter Olympics in 1984 (Mr. Coleman fans doing the pushing); I never got to the bottom of it, but understandably, 'Frankers' took it very badly.
A few of us took him to a quiet boozer in the West End—with the best intentions—but when he tumbled in the open (fully practical) fireplace—completely out of it—signs were that our therapy had been misconstrued and overly indulgent.

At Cup Final time, Barry Davies and 'Motty' would stand microphone to microphone, while the hung jury played on their emotions.
John had a run like Jock Stein's Celtic, until one day he was seen heading for Hammersmith Bridge—lead boots in hand—having learned that Barry had 'done a Rangers' on him and taken the Wembley title.

Ron Pickering could, and did, protest . . . at every juncture, but it was tough (as in, *"too bad"*); Coleman's experience, accuracy and sense of occasion would always win the day. He was the best for the job, hence, for four decades, up to and including Sydney (a bridge too far), *his* was the voice of the track: *Hobson's*.

I asked Stuart Storey to call the 110m final at the Weltklasse in Zurich in 1981, not as a mould-breaker, nor to create internal strife, but he'd toiled away at the field events (with Ron) for years, and being a former Olympic high hurdler, I thought it fair to give him a go at this one.
You can imagine his glee when Renaldo 'Skeets' Nehemiah not only won the race, but became the first man to run the distance in under 13 seconds . . . epoch busting stuff; ask *'Stewpot'* about it . . . *you'll need an hour.*

To save any in-fighting, the producer or editor, at any kind of meet, would go through the events and apportion workloads; they'd all been there before and knew what was coming.
Chairing an informal commentators' briefing, just before the European Athletics Championships in Split—before the split . . . if you get my drift—I asked the others to take on some of Ron's duties, especially early heats and interminable field event qualifiers; worryingly we'd been told the towering Eastender was having mild, heart murmurs.

I nearly killed the old boy—his face went ashen, he puffed out his not inconsiderable chest and protested vehemently that he was "*OK*," and *would I kindly hold the sympathy vote.*

It was a massive loss, some years later, when big Ron died of his condition. He was devoted to athletics, as are his wife Jean and son Shaun.
He had deep knowledge, not least of the sport's big issue (drugs).
The enthusiasm he showed during the long hours of London Marathon transmissions, brought his passion and commitment to the fore.
He was terrific company; dinner at a posh London eaterie, with him and a ravishing (make that 'ravenous') decathlete of his choice, made spectacular reading on my expenses form.

Ron *loved* Lynn (Davies) but he *adored* Daley (Thomson) . . . so you could forgive the hyperbole:

"That's big, that's <u>very</u> big . . . *it's an <u>EeeNORMOUS</u> one!"*

Call it jingoism or a temporary suspension of BBC journalistic impartiality in trying circumstances, but it was 'Pick' the fan, as Mary Peters set off on the seventh leg of

her quest for Heptathlon gold in Munich 1972 . . . urging her to: *"Come on Mary, get those legs going . . ."* with the whole of Germany on her back.
Mary was born in Liverpool, but regards Northern Ireland as home.
(best that we're accurate)

Believe this or believe this not (and why on earth wouldn't you), but Jeffrey Archer—the great imaginer—reflecting on a personal moment of Olympic history (which we were filming for a mini-series), claimed he'd been in the stadium amongst a loyal and vociferous British crowd, camped behind the high jump pit, late into the night (when one's mind tends to wander), as Mary leapt higher than ever before and into contention for day two . . . by then, just a couple of hours away.

P.S. Mary is a revered Dame, and Lord Lieutenant of Belfast City.

Big guys, and gals, turned Ron on—here was classic proof:

". . . and (Alberto) Juantorena opens his legs and shows his class . . ." *
. . . as the powerful Cuban blew away the opposition in a heat of the 400m in Montreal.
Ron on testosterone o.d.
It's been put down as a blooper, but it summed 'White Lightning' up to a tee.

*Coleman even denied him <u>that</u> honour, being quoted in *Private Eye* (and elsewhere) as being its author—without correction.

Good on ya, Pick

Coach Pickering was fascinated by the infrastructure of Cuban sport, especially athletics and boxing, whose twin embodiments, *El Caballo* (Juantorena) and the mighty Teofilio Stevenson, featured in one of his many filmed trips to Castro's lair (it's quite possible that he spotted Alberto's 'class' in the showers . . . they were *that* close).

It wasn't Split . . . though it might just as well have been . . . but a drug scandal had broken: *surprise, surprise*. Some duped, persecuted, rising star of athletics, slightly off the pace, had been caught with naughty elements in his/her wee-wee.

'Call, Big Ron . . . big Ron . . . big Ron . . . *big Ron.*'

Chances were that he'd been out the night before, mediating, as the strident "Voice of Athletics" ripped into one of us production types; Coleman would protest his purpose was 'complacency prevention,' but the attacks—more frequent than athletes' denials, and always verbal, lest the plot be lost—were ferocious.

Smile, patronisingly, and the intensity control would be wound up to savage. As befits the bully, it was seldom a private chat.

Ron sounded drowsy, but as soon as he heard my inept stab at the chemical name for the foreign body found in urine sample 'A,' he was already mumbling his introduction as the phone clicked off.

Twenty minutes later he was on camera.

Other than calling a world record decathlon by D.T.—having inwardly conceded the glamour events to D.C.—this was R.P. at his best. Even the pretentious tossers in documentary features would steer their investigative units to Ron, first, for *his* thoughts, rather than to faceless chemists with letters after their names.

Our outside broadcast director had positioned the big fella by the finish line, taking the shot from a camera high behind what would have been the right hand goal . . . had we been doing the football (not that drugs, and complicated sex, are issues there).

Looked fine in the wide shot, so we stood-by to "throw to the talent"
(that, after all Will Shakespeare had done for us).

As Ron gathered momentum, the camera began zooming.

That morning, presumably whilst still dark, he'd decided on a casual, grey ensemble: a hooded sweatshirt with matching cotton 'trackie-bums'—the uniform of humanity haters with a habit for hallucinatory brands of illegal substances; putrid performance enhancers would only make the chase through dingy avenues and alleyways, hopeless for less nimble, arresting officers.

Hood down (it should be said), Ron's delivery, as ever, was word perfect and, one assumed, technically and clinically accurate; he could reel off the syllables like a Sri Lankan cricket commentator nipping through the home side's batting order.

Why is it that drugs—like flowers, and birds—come with such complex names (I blame the Italians); not as tricky as Warnakulasuriya Patabendige Ushanta Joseph Chaminda Vass (bowler), or Denagamage Proboth Mahela de Silva Jayawardene (batsman) . . . as it seldom says on the team caption . . . but others manage with Cliff or Bey or Ali or Bono or Tiger or Giggsy.
I say *keep it simple* . . . like *nandrolone* (19-nortestosterone) . . . or Baxter's *Vick*.

Similarities between Ron's figure in the 80s, and Freddie Ljuhnberg's in *Calvin Klein*'s in 'noughtie' 4, were confined to a region, not even the most dedicated anti-drug campaigner could have failed to 'pick' out, or be sucked in by . . . a mouthful of *Shreddies* ready to launch.

By the time the 'end frame' was reached—the size of shot when zooming ceased—Ron had been cut off about an inch below his crotch; quite acceptable were it cheeky Andrew Marr, at Westminster, in his Sunday coat, or gorgeous George Alligiah in Beirut, in safari shirt and cargoes—but the difference was, Ron's adequate bottoms were from a time when he could have given Stuart Storey a run for his money . . . . but his waistline wasn't. You expected it from Nijinsky or Nureyev, but there was something about the unflattering cut of his jib, the hang of the limp, grey material that accentuated his endowment arrangement.

I cried out (sub-consciously) for a flashing arrow to be superimposed, on or about the nether mounding, thereby grabbing back the attention of those who may have strayed into a chemical minefield.

I registered my dismay to the field director over a talkback circuit already cluttered with sniggering.

Ronnie P. had heard:

"*That*, boys and girls, is where the <u>action</u> comes from."
Bless him.

Ron's manifestation may have been pre-meditated, but what should a director do when someone consciously wants to hang it all out . . . say, at Lord's in front of a full house, or, as Miss Roe did, seminally, at Twickers?

The first couple (of occasions) you'd show, for originality and novelty (and the archive), but since Jordan cornered the market, the judicious course is to ignore the attention seeker—abhorrent to the reality show producer . . . but you can live in hope (*better still, don't watch*).

With so many simultaneous points of interest during a golf tournament, one little prick is easily avoided. It's trickier in the confines of Centre Court or the Crucible; perish the thought at the darts, or boxing where angry wives and free-fall parachutists have acted in the past.

You need to know your audience: streaking is a fresh-air phenomenon, vital elements being . . . a good run up . . . room to manoeuvre luminous pursuants in jailer's boots . . . and a pre-set point of egress, should you skin them.

Following a pitch invasion in 2002—and a subsequent, serious, can-throwing incident—cricket clubs threatened offenders with an instant £1,000 fine for crossing the boundary ropes.

Didn't stop them.
A couple of weeks later, at H.Q., a fully dressed male cad—neatly arranged (deception in itself)—marched, unchallenged, to the middle to 'escort' the magnificent Tendulkar from the field at the end of an unfaltering display.
There he was, an arm round India's most treasured soul since Ghandi, breathing something vile-smelling in his face, as we looked on helplessly; were this not an amoeba who'd drunk too much . . . had he had a knife (Monica Seles) or a gun—like the pistol-packin' footie ref in South Africa—and done the little man damage . . . even the unthinkable, before a 'live' T.V. audience . . .

The master batsman appeared unperturbed by the knob-head.
K.P., or Sir I.T.B. would have given him a tougher time—Brian Clough (or Jock Stein) would have slapped him.

Barring Erica—the inspiration for the cosmetology phenomenon —exhibitionists are neither entertaining nor newsworthy
(*tell that to a 'boobs' man*).

As you'll know, on the golf course the responsibility for getting you 'in close' at tournaments falls on the handheld, radio cameramen; they need to know the rules and etiquette of the game, and where best to position themselves to get the optimum view, whilst not upsetting the players; a fluffed or mis-directed shot from one in the frame with a short fuse . . . and *have your buggy handy*.

Try this hypothesis: 'Monty' is driving off the 72nd in 2000, needing a four to win his first 'Major' (*stay with me*). At the top of his languid backswing, a naked citizen (tough as granite in Ayrshire) breaks cover, causing Mr. Montgomerie Snr.'s progeny to hook one into the *shuch* (literally the crack in one's arse . . . *videlicet,* the shit, or rough . . . a dropped shot, more than likely)—*Never Land* being Royal Troon, where Colin's Dad had been secretary.

DEFCON 1—maximum readiness—'Monty' ablaze and back-drafting. But this was linksland . . . nowhere for spectators, nor lensmen, to hide. Gannets on Ailsa Craig, struck by irrepressible flatulence, simply explode; further west—on the Isle of Arran—mating butterflies withdraw, ever so gently.

Magma tears through his blood vessels, in every direction, as a provisional is prepared; holing his second skelp is now the requirement.

"*Wake up, Monty!*"

'Big Coe-lyn' (as in car-restoring, ex-four-star general and US Secretary of State, Powell) wisely married a school chum of my niece's, Gaynor Knowles; Gay (as in Bey) is loaded too, but shed-loads off Mrs. Jay-Z's rating.
Where others have failed (or not bothered), Mrs. Monty II appears to have calmed the big teddy bear down, so much so, that the live-wasp sandwich—a long-time favourite of our last Ryder Cup captain's—is now off the supper menu.
Spread the word: *"Ejaculating lepidopterans, he's cured—shout out loud!"*

We had good relationships with most of the players on the European Tour, but flare-ups were unavoidable. You wouldn't expect their management to side with us, but some of our boys were pushed to the limit; verbal abuse in any workplace isn't on.

Tampering with Her Majesty in the rushes—heinous, treasonable.
Mess with legendary names in broadcasting—approach gingerly; beware the second-guesser, and vitriolic, audience backlash.

Some presenters and commentators wield frightening power—I'm thinking Oprah and the former Andy Gray.
The seals (performing) know their ground, their marquee, their value to 'their' shows, their support from on high, so, amelioration can only be achieved through the spineless, chicken-shit approach (*unless you've something on them to sell*).
The tendency might be to opt for the quiet life and watch egos, and salaries, grow completely out of control.

I remember 'Kit' Lewis (Hagler's pal) telling me about an incident on the floor of the *Parkinson* show, way before 'Mikey' became a 'national treasure.' (*p-LEASE!*).
He (Chris) was floor managing when the holy host suddenly went into one (this would be around the time Billy Connolly and Muhammad Ali were doing their best to make him famous).
As he helped to untwist an ear-piece lead, petulant 'Parky' hissed:
'Tell those w_ _ _ _ rs upstairs, this is MY show, these are MY guests—it's MY way, or NO way!'
(the poor love).

Hate to hear talent 'directing' from the floor, on air, as Judy Finnigan's husband does, incessantly, and Coleman did for fun (his).
The great golf instructor of the 70s, 'Doctor' John Jacobs would too, during live broadcasts on ITV, advising the director (correctly, in his case) that . . . *rather than watch so-and-so on the 17th at +4, we'd be better switching to what's-his-face on* the 5th (who was probably six under).
But there are ways and means; monkey and grinder need to work together; sure, Lynam and I fell out, but it was only sport on the telly . . . *deal with it.*
(deep down he knew I was <u>always</u> right)

The time would come when Maskell or McLaren or Coleman or Carpenter or O'Sullevan or Alliss would have to go . . . for good—you just wished they'd take the hint (*or you were at the dentist*) first.

The shelf-life of the 'color' commentary is shorter—unless, like Hunt with Walker, Brookes-Ward with Williams, Critchley with Alliss, Barrett with Maskell, yours was a highly-respected ticket.

No room for fanny and wool—the great impostors—in swimming; it's technical, so knowledge of the mechanics is paramount; whether the unfancied Irish, in Lane 8, waxed* or shaved would have no bearing on the outcome of the race, but (*his*) split-times, tumble-turn-technique, hyper-extension-high-arm-recovery, six-beat-leg-kick bollocks, might.
(* 'Girly' claims about the pain of a *Brazilian* . . . *mere bagatelle, chaps**)
The hairy pits of lofty Ms. Davies's rivals might have turned East German boys on, but it was an oversight by the lab technicians.

One of my 'charges' as producer at Sydney 2000, was former Aussie rules goal-kicker—the *naturally* deep-voiced and very decent—Dennis Cometti.
Channel 7 had assigned the big fella (and me) to the swimming; Cathy Freeman (in her space-suit) apart, *this* (as big Ron might have put it) was where the action was going to come from—Australia-wise.

The German commentary position was one along from us.
When the identity of their 'color' was made known, disapproving stares headed in our general direction. Couldn't make out the pitch of her voice, but the ex-Eastern blocker wasn't amongst friends.
Water under the bridge . . . I think not.

There's a movie you might like to avoid, about track-cheat Marion Jones, restoring her as the mis-understood victim who fell amongst thieves and glory burglars . . . . *but hey kids, she too broke the fucking rules*—knowingly.

But for some 'out-of-the-blue' performances by lesser lights to his left and right, 'Thorpedo' might have done even better in Sydney, but think of the sugaring time he saved by wearing "Mr. Condom," the frog suit.
(* the werewolf-look—still favoured by some Premiership love-cheats—wouldn't do for a swimmer)

Cheery Duncan Goodhew's alopecia was a stigma put to good effect.

I'd be pushed to find a more punctilious commentator than Hamilton Bland (Murray, maybe . . . da stats Daddy, 'Motty,' definitely . . .

OK—Bill McLaren and O'Sullevan—*shit, they all were!*).

With half an eye on Hammy's notes, Alan Weeks did the build-up—swimmers' idents and so on—and between them they'd call the race (with Bland on World Record watch!!).
'Piggin'' was more than capable of handling himself . . . and the job, alone—not a view shared by the pro-Weeks lobby (David Coleman carrying the banner). Alan had been a founder member of the BBC commentators' club—the doyen in many ways: done every sport . . . football, gymnastics, table tennis, snooker, you name it . . . and when we re-kindled interest in the fastest game on earth on *Grandstand,* in the late eighties, 'Weeksie' was in a sty of his own; his affair with Brighton Tigers—the champions of Britain in 1930—lasted to his dying day.

"The Voice of Ice-Skating" and "the Voice of Athletics" were inseparable on foreign assignments—in all but the hotel sauna; before the V.o.A. would bare his bits, the V.o.I-S. would be sent scurrying to suss out the occupants.

Theirs was a Jeeves-Wooster sort of arrangement, or, more appositely, a Taylor-Clough collaboration.

We (Al and I) were standing in one such lobby when Coleman burst from the lift; he was exceptional at making a drama out of a crisis.
None was apparent.

"Here, Weeksie," he commanded, *"hold this"* . . . handing him his suit jacket.
Alan draped it over his arm and we continued to chat.
"Not like that . . ." barked the V.o.A., grabbing the V.o.I-S. by the hand and extending his index finger like a human clothes hook . . . . *like this!"*

Weeksie—bizarrely—took it . . . ignoring my gesture.

I mention their curious bond because the two ended up being principles in another difference of opinion that would threaten my great Winter Olympic initiative of Sarayevo 1984.

With deference to Puccini and Ravel, anyone hearing *Nessun Dorma* and *Bolero* (apart from red Robinson) would immediately think . . . World Cup football and Torvill & Dean . . . *right?*

The Yugoslavian host broadcaster offered overseas clients a 'world feed'—a package of pictures and international sound i.e. sound effects + music—on which, in normal circumstances, Alan would commentate.

Months in advance of the Games beginning, better-off 'clients' would secure postions for 'unilateral' cameras, and because of the enormous national interest in the Olympics, the BBC always went into these bookings with plenty of foreign exchange.

Having discussed the logistics with my studio producer, communications experts and the girls and boys on site, I decided we'd cover Jayne and Chris's performance on our rink-side 'uni' camera.
If I'd got it wrong, some of our 23.9 million viewers would let me know.

Be done with the Safety Curtain!

The Failed Assassination of the Archduke Ferdinand

A melodrama in one Act—music by **Ravel.**

(cast in order of appearance)

Gavrilo Princip, the assassin . . . .   David Coleman

**The Archduke Franz
Ferdinand** (*what a band!*) . . . .   John Philips

'Weeksie's 'agent'—the studio presenter—didn't concur with my scheme (not that I was particularly interested) . . . . "*in fact, Philipo, that picture alone, will disorientate him and his commentary will suffer—you're a prat.*"
Cobblers! What commentary?
All Alan would <u>ever</u> say was . . . *who were next on the ice / where they were from / what expectations they might have / what bearing, scores carried forward from the compulsories and short programme would have on the free dance / a couple of moves to look out for* . . . not a lot more.

As the music started, I wanted commentary to stop.
What is amiss . . . afoot . . . askate, even?

The inevitable ovation would be the trigger to begin speaking again . . . with flowers and replays and huggin' and kissin' and smilin' and wavin' and the drama of the judges' marks to follow.

It wasn't rocket science: under the rules, couples in ice-dancing have to stick together, so no point in cutting away to other angles . . . close-ups of skates or faces, or wide shots showing their rink position . . . that would be the basis of the World Feed—the coverage everyone got—which we'd record as a back-up (*cameras have been known to fail, nose-pickers—circa 1972 and those missing Owens' moments*).

If Timberlake or Flatley or 'Jacko' or Kelly or O'Connor or peerless Fred dance, *show us*—they are, after all, masters of their craft.
Slap-happy directors can vent their frustration making videos.
Two and a half minutes of unexpurgated Beyoncé shaking her tush in master-shot is priceless instructional for wannabes and anthropometry students . . . . *may not help sales, but it's a great watch.*

In T&D's less sexed-up case, it told the story; artistic impression and technical merit in a single, intimate, 2D image.

As Jayne and Chris spiralled to a dramatic, gymnastic, body-cooling finale, I spotted them squeezing hands.

They could scrap like mud wrestlers when rehearsing, but they'd just pulled off something outrageous—*this* was *their* confirmation.

Quickly as resources and Miss Brincat—our dexterous vision mixer—would allow, the digits were zoomed up and circled, the background luminance taken down and the whole thing made frame-by-frame slow through the pressure point . . .

(Gulp)

"Don't speak, Weeksie."

I felt a prick as the "V.o.A." drove another pin in my doll.

A private moment of elation—a personal postscript to <u>the</u> perfect performance.

"... Kissing The Cox of the Oxford Crew"

The circuit breaker in my cousin's 'other' Mercedes soft-top barked into life: *"This is Cadillac, cruisin' and dry, on Griggs and Mykawa—got your ears on Dimps, good buddy?"* Soubriquets first—*'Cadillac'* given at boarding school in Scotland because he'd lived in the States for a while . . . and *'Dimps'*—clear impression when smiling.

Hugh Robertson II, found earlier in this tome (could there be a Henry Tudor IX, lurking in the US somewhere?) was a WW II concentration camp survivor—reasons to be grateful to his resourceful, courageous mother—and, since his eventual citizenship, a darned near dollar millionaire.

The two flash motors—one silver, one maroon—pulled up outside an unprepossessing, four-storey building; inside was buzzing with upwardly mobiles. It was only 5.00p.m. of a Friday in Houston, Texas, but that meant business shutdown for the week-end. *Winnebagos* were packed and fuelled, de-mob happy kids in deck-shoes, Levis and Ts, were well up for the bay—or Grandma's at worst—and Mom Maureen, the embodiment of organization, had all boxes, except *husband* and *cuzz-in-law*, ticked.

The discos on floors 2 and 4 were in full flow, as friends of *Jack Daniels* got intimate on the odd levels. Therein lay potential for casual after-work/before-home (and Gulf coast with the family), liaisons *dangereuse*. My purpose, however, is to draw your attention to the plethora of built-in backgammon tables. Providing you could play the ancient board game, and I knew the rudiments, it was a belting ice-breaker, with your stake money going towards the next round of *J.D.s*, or *J.&B.s*, on the rocks.

Was there potential here for the next, big money-spinning televised leisure activity? Uncle Sam's make-a-buck-culture attacks the ambitious like a virus—receivership and suicide are the only known cures for failure.

Bridge and chess had been tried, but even with the tape speeded up, they made dressage look break-neck; backgammon was cooler. Good players trying to make points (and dates) raced their counters round the board to the constant rattle of dice and provocative calls of *'double'* from the supremely confident, and idiotic novices like me.

Entrepreneurs and ratings monitors were always on the look-out for a game, or gadget, that would make them rich, smug and obnoxious.
So . . . how's about the World Y.U.P.P.Y. Backgammon Championships from the penthouse at Canary Wharf, Chippendales on the door, Park Lane Playboy bunnies doing whatever they do best on the floor of the house, David Vine on commentary, Omar Sharif on colour?
Sounds a winner . . . fire in a proposal.

When my *Pernod*-swigging buddy, Mike Begg, took over as producer of *Miss World* (one of OB Events Department's unusually progressive appointments, considering his dedication to the sickly dynamite), we talked about 'sexing it up' . . . way before Gilligan and the September dossier.
Get the girls to ditch the high heels . . . shoot the swimsuits in the Maldives . . . go on safari to the Earth's hottest place, near Addis Ababa for the biographical wallpaper thereby keeping day-clothes to a tantalising minimum . . . give the Versace boys (loosely speaking) *free rein with the evening gear . . . and watch the numbers soar.*

Beggie bottled it . . . and in downtown Houston, I had one more *Coke* and hit the road, in the maroon car.

If you think backgammon's a daft idea, next time Hazel Irvine and the gang rack 'em up, wind the colour out and try commentating on snooker in monochrome; due to some bad planning that ended with his commentary position being miles away from the baize, Max Robertson—another of our pilgrim fathers—had been set the task. He was fine on the black, and providing the cueist was chalked up and ready to fire, the yellow wasn't a problem.
'For those watching in black and white, the blue is behind the brown' sort of thing.

Robertson was a Max of many strands, from *Panorama* and the British Grand Prix to George VI's funeral and his eldest's Coronation.
He's probably best remembered for his ball-by-ball radio commentaries at Wimbledon (which may have given rise to Eminem's global superstardom).
An orchestral conductor has to be a nano-second *ahead* of the action to give the boys and girls half a chance with the dots, but Max would always be that much *behind*, rapping out his lyrics like an auctioneer on *Going for a Song* (which he also compèred, with daft old Arthur Negus).
Sometimes you'd fear for the boy's safety . . . . till the winning point ovation beat him to the breath he was about to take.
It's 'lemon squeezy' with today's base-line game, but back in Rod the Rocket's time they'd chip and charge and volley and lob and smash, with the ball pinging about like a pinball on flippers.
Ventilate, and off he'd go:
'The Laver serve is . . . <u>good</u> to the backhand . . . cross-court return by Rosewall . . . the champion gets it back, on the run . . . top-spin return, forehand, dips inside the baseline . . .

Laver blocks . . . in comes Rosewall charging (thunderous applause), *he volleys . . . it's wide'*—"15-love."
Well you got the point, but try doing that for five sets . . . or a game, even; trouble was, every rally sounded the same, so Christine Truman's job would be to tell the listener *what the devil was going on out there*.
Not a lot of people may know that Max's second wife created *The Wombles*—eco-warriors of Wimbledon (*Common* that is)—modeled, possibly, on the 1967 French Open champion Françoise Dürr . . . she of *le grand 'ooterre*.

En passant, my fourball partner—from that debacle of a golf tournament at the Wisley which James Capel & Co managed to cock-up for us—Christopher Edward Walford, had fallen into a taxi in the City, so pissed that balance and words failed him, but as brother Steve was opening the batting for their club side in south-west London that evening, he was keen to be there, even if the action would pass him by altogether.

The driver asked, customarily:
"Where to guv?"
Much as "Bertie" Windsor had to do every Christmas Day, Chris stole himself to reply, believing a couple of manageable vowels would make sense of the spate of . . . "nine consonants and three vowels please, Carol."
"Wannagowmldn."
The cabbie slid his little window wider:
"You what?"
Chris grew impatient:
"Wmldn, take me to Wmmbldn!"
The cabbie tried one last time.
"Oh fuck it, takemeto Putney and I'll walk!"

Max was swimming commentator at the first ever 'British Commonwealth Games' in Edinburgh in 1970.
Should you be fascinated so to do . . . take the inaugural *British Empire* Games in Ontario, Canada, add a *Commonwealth* when Vancouver's turn came around in 1954, now take away an *Empire* for Edinburgh in 1970 <u>and</u> a *British* by Dehli 2010—and there you have a potted history of Imperial Britain circa 1930-2011.
So what's next . . . *The* (naked) *Games?*

Alun Williams, Max's opposite number on the wireless (in the row behind), was—as you'll have deduced—Welsh . . . a magnificent tenor (one after another), who knew the words to the five anthems used.

"Hen Wlad Fy Nhadau"—*Old Land of My Fathers* (Alun's *pièce de résistance*)
—was a bit of a rarity, Welsh swimming being in one of its many tapering-off periods—indeed, Alun only got into wide-open-throttle-mode once, when Mike

Richards took the 200 backstroke title, and a heavily starched *Y Ddraig Goch* could be raised in his honour.
(broad-jumping Lynn "the leap" Davies was the Principality's only other winner)

Didn't pay a huge amount of attention, but I think it was *Land of Hope and Glory* for Diane Lansley of England in the 100 fly; other than that, *Advance Australia Fair* (20 plays), and *O Canada* (11) . . . till *everyone* poolside was fluent.

I remember struggling to applaud our clever-dickey school sports champion, as he stepped forward—*à plusiers reprises*—to get the winner's red rosette; even his parents wearied of the loyal, ecstatic reaction when his smart-arse name (which I've forgotten) was called (the type of wanker *The Apprentice* attracts).

Time after time, the golden girls of Aussie swimming—Denise Langford, Lynn Watson and Karen Moras—climbed to the top step; add Mike Wenden's four podiums to those, and only minor-place flags would be required for poles 2 and 3.
In three successive 'British Commonwealth' Games from 1966, Wenden would win 9 finals . . . a record equalled in two 'celebrations' by Ian Thorpe, and topped (eventually) by Susie O'Neill's 10.
(Michael Phelps' parents may not even have been dating).

By 15, Shane Gould—the next 'wunderkind' from *'Ss-try-lia*—held all five world freestyle records from 100 to 1500 metres . . . she'd won five Olympic medals in Munich, three of them gold . . . and by 17, she'd had enough.

The life of a swimmer, eh?
. . . *school from 5-17 . . . pay a bit of attention between training . . . aim at being Olympic Champ by 15.*
Done that, got the gold, time to put a stop to the early-rising rubbish.
Right, hire a 'ghostie' to do the autobiography . . . catch up on lost time by cramming-in several guys at once . . . plump for the most (seemingly) reliable one (with prospects), marry the sucker, have kids and teach them to swim slowly.
Fight and separate, leaving room for post-divorce custody hassle . . . get a degree from the O.U . . . . make a packet from public appearances . . . ship in a live-in toy-boy . . . fall out with the family (who sacrificed so much) . . . take an overdose, die in your sleep . . . leave your stash to philately.

(nothing like the Gould fairytale)

As far as anthems go, we Jocks concede that Princess Anne (of Edinburgh) has nominal, if distant, rights to sing along to *Flower of Scotland,* but perhaps *La Marseillaise* would have been a more fitting send-off for 'Marie' Stuart (Queen of Scots)—<u>and</u> Boleyn for that matter—at her (Mary's) final public appearance in Fotheringhay.

One clean, defining swipe by the axe/swordsman, and they'd sing no more (in French) of . . . *fields of red, steeped in tainted blood* . . . *of treacherous slaves and false kings* . . . . years before the deification of Platini, Cantona and Henry.

Our stunning win over the French (Hampden 2006) had structural engineers (and health & safety) racing along King's Park Avenue towards Queen's Park F.C.'s unnecessarily large stadium, as our synchronised pounding (60,000 of us—to the brothers Reid's *500 miles*) put the whole, re-modelled thing at risk of collapse.

Hearing the massed pipes and drums, augmented by an even bigger mass of brass-bands-persons, letting rip with *Scotland the Brave* (a sillier number than *Flower*, by far . . . if easier to march to), in front of a packed Meadowbank Stadium at the opening ceremony of those 1970 Games, was to empathise with a tearful Dallaglio in Sydney . . . and that self-conscious moment for our whistling 'Superman' in Los Angeles.
Regardless of whether individuals compete for themselves or their flags, the anthems can set bottom lips a-trembling, female hearts a-fluttering . . . and boys' gonads a-tingling.

Picture us in Cordoba, Argentina 1978 . . . streets bedecked with Saltires (the white cross part of the blue and white flag of St. Andrew) and Lions Rampant (rearing lion, in red, on a yellow background—officially, the King of Scotland's banner . . . *no, not Dalglish*) . . . folk in their thousands lining the route, clapping in time to a local arrangement of our (former) anthem.
Not many knew Cliff Hanley's lyrics (none of *us* there did), but we could *la-la-la-la-la-la-laa, la-la-la la laaa-la*—or *rum-tee-tum-tee-tum-tee-tum, rum-tee tum-tee-tum-tum* . . . . as 'The Big Yin' had instructed.

The team bus—Kenny, 'thighs' Souness (*the answer was there all the time*), Joe Jordan with his teeth in, wee Archie (*"beautiful goal—Archie Gemmell!"*), Willie (*never take sweets from a stranger*) Johnstone, & co., on board—crawled through the throng towards the Town Hall and a civic reception; stirring enough, but when the entire populace broke into their *Himno Nacional Argentino*, you'd have handed over the Falklands without fuss.
(*OK, so we cocked up the tournament . . . but at least we were there, Ron*)

A Johnstone in '78, a Johnson in '88—fortunately for the good name of one of our oldest clans, Bobby (Hibs) and 'Jinky' . . . and Michael (USA) and Martin (ENG) . . . were/are good, clean-living boys; Ulrika (SWE) can't help herself.

If backgammon didn't appear to have a future on the tube, snooker (in colour) had . . . and a past, epitomised by the cheery, round face of Joe Davis, whose picture—alongside 'The Don' (Bradman), 'Sugar Ray' (Robinson) 'Slammin' Sam'

(Snead) and 'The Galloping Major' (Puskas, largely as a result of his dumping Billy Wright and England on their asses)—adorned my earliest scrapbook, aged 9.

William Ambrose Wright was one of the bosses—'one of the boys'—at ITV Sport; I'd bumped into him at dinners and golf days, yet never, extraordinarily, with any of the devoted Beverley sisters . . . not Joy (Mrs. Wright) not Teddie, nor Babs.
Charming man, Billy; what would surprise you was how vertically challenged he was for a centre-half, nothing like the musculature of Sol Campbell, nor the towering presence of Rio Ferdinand, still, he must have had something to get 105 caps for *The Auld Enemy.*
That said, our strikers (née forwards) were mostly 'wee yins.'

Another regular at the annual *Grandstand/World of Sport/Sportsman Club* golf match, in north London, was Mick McManus—professional wrestler. Depending on the opponent (and 'script'), Mick 'played' good or bad cop in *World of Sport's* hugely successful Saturday afternoon wrestling shows, synonymous with the mis-leading North American tones of 'Mr. Grunt 'n' Groan' himself, sexy Kent Walton (born in Cairo, educated at Charterhouse).

In the flesh, Mick was tiny alongside contemporaries like 'Giant Haystacks' and 'Big Daddy' (he'd be dwarfed by present-day World Wrestling Entertainment superstars 'The Big Show' and Mark Henry), but there was something about his jet-black, dead eyes, the cute turned-in ears and the east-west nose that prevented you drawing attention to it . . . . or the aforementioned 'script.'

Tacit: *"Rey Mysterio kicks out at two-and-a-half!"*

Where Mr. Vincent Kennedy McMahon, WWE Smackdown, and RAW, have taken the 'sport' now, is a media phenomenon; they call it entertainment (not to be tried at home, school or in the playground), but these are very large people—athletes, performers, gymnasts rolled into one—with very deep voices (the divas too), who must have skeletons in there somewhere midst the muscle and blood (and unnatural mounding).
Wrest the remote from the kids and take a look at Bobby Lashley or Batista or Randy Orton or Mr. Cena—bods to marvel at . . . even if you're not into protruding veins and shaved chests (the divas too).

For nothing, another quick *Colemanballs*:

"Christie has a habit of pulling it out when it matters most."

(Seconds back out)

Reg Gutteridge was to ITV's boxing, what 'Carps' was to ours—obviously we believed 'H' to be better; any man to whom this quote could be attributed (from his Boat Race commentary days) did it for us:

"Isn't that nice . . . . the wife of the Cambridge President is kissing the cox of the Oxford crew."

None of us cared to spoil it by trawling the archives for authenticity.

Reggie loved his golf; despite an artificial leg (he "mis-laid" the good one during World War II . . . and made plenty light of it), his consistently high, if suspect contributions to the opposition's combined Stableford points tally were taken with a pinch of salt . . . providing we—the BBC—won.

Golf is tough enough, until you've seen Douglas Bader.
It was my first experience of the professional game—a pro-am in fact—and leading Bader's squadron was golf's little Welsh maestro, Dai Rees; odd when 'golf' (Welsh golf) and 'little' and 'maestro' are mentioned in the same sentence, images of Rees and Huggett and Woosnam pop up . . . must be the lack of sunlight.
Former Walker Cup star (and now ex-pro) Philip Parkin, one of B.Sky B.'s on-course commentators on the European Tour, is Welsh too . . . but a <u>tall</u> one; not only can he could *hit* the thing like Álvaro Quirós, he can *throw* a golf ball 100 yards . . . on the full—a skill not in great demand, but incredible to witness.
As we stood on the 3rd tee of the Emirates course in Dubai, he launched a highly compressed missile, straight up—out of sight, literally.
Like everything else in those hallowed parts, the tee ground was well watered, so on its return to earth, the scud created a little *Titleist* 'grave' on the grass, the headstone poking out much as in Connolly's career launching, childhood tale from Glasgow . . . about the bum and bike-rack.

Never mind 'leather' wedge infringements, imagine, were you one of those rare birds, the golfing cheat (*we all know one*), being left to your own devices in the woods, with that kind of arm, following a wayward drive?

After a respectable time searching, thank and dismiss your partners for their efforts with:
'I'll have a quick look myself.'
Moments later, probably well outside the time allowed (5 minutes):
"Got it!"
. . . then, following an improbable birdie, created by a highly-suspect recovery:
"3 for 3 for me"
(cheating bastard)

I desperately wanted to get back home to tell Dad about seeing Bader.

Undulating links courses are quite hard on the legs—if you've got any—and climbing down the steep face of a greenside pot, when you haven't, is unimaginably difficult . . . plus he got *it*, and *himself*, up and down.

Were there an image to inspire and give perspective to the petty irritations of life, it was the guy with neither legs nor arms, crossing the line in the London Marathon; that's not to patronise him—he was doing what he felt capable of, given the cards he'd been dealt.

David Vine was the ideal man to front up the snooker—ideal, because it meant he was out of mainstream sport viz., football and athletics, where certain established names demanded he be kept. David was a highly competent performer who could fill any chair, hence the jealousy amongst some other 'seals.'

Everything young Vine touched turned up the ratings.
Snooker took off, and with *Rothmans*, *Embassy* and *Benson & Hedges* as sponsors, and green-rooms stocked with his favourite tipple, David settled in for a very long stay indeed.
Between times, he adroitly fronted our show jumping . . . compèred *A Question of Sport*, *Superstars* and *The World's Strongest Man* . . . and at Olympic and Commonwealth Games times, he'd do anything asked of him—providing it was weightlifting.

D-Vine took a fair bit of stick for his *Ski Sunday* work from the (get this) legions(?) of British officiandos . . . types who drove round Home Counties South in their fuck-off 4x4s—*Thules* still attached in mid-summer—who did Chamonix, annually with the kids and nanny . . . who'd use honee wax on their skis, to keep up appearances . . . and write home of "Kaiser" 'Clamour' like they knew him.

"Viney" adopted the Austrian Express's approach—get it down the hill as fast as you can. Peak at split-times, add a line on waxing, and enjoy genius at work.

Quite what Ingemar Stenmark—the slalom-*meister*—was doing between the poles was an appliance of the science, no one knew anything about.
The more agile of the great Swedish 'Ingos' (the other being Johansson of the 'dingo' . . . with which Floyd Patterson would become embarrassingly familiar) didn't know David Vine from a bar of saddle soap, but intelligent questioning elicited respectful answers from the Scandinavian icon, giving David (and me) a real exclusive, out on the piste, in Orë.

The number of fans well worse for the drink, first thing in the morning, was human cultivation of the Norwegian lemming's recently disputed take on life . . . and death (they're not as dumb as first thought), and neither did the dexterity of our taxi driver, on the hard-packed stuff, come as a shock—*the Knowledge* at break-neck pace, sideways, in chains.

Before leaving snooker, despite the massive audiences it attracted down the years, Stephen Hendry never won the democratically elected *Sports Personality* award . . . and he's been World Champion <u>seven</u> times; he won the Scottish version a few times, *but a BAFTA ain't an OSCAR* . . . . or should that be the other way round?

Editing videotape in the Dark Ages (circa 1970) could bring on angina, and *our* family had history; mistakes waited in queues, to happen.

Saturdays meant *Match of the Day* for we underground Luddites; there was a separate *Grandstand* team, but the *Sportsnight/M.O.T.D.* crew, considered ourselves mustard (*Coleman's* . . . with an 'e').

I won't mention him by name (you can't defame the dead), but an absolute howler from the basement got the phone ringing to '*the men in the darkened room*' (as Richie Benaud calls videotape and its pallid inhabitants).
Manchester United were playing in our featured game—Law, Best, Charlton *et al* . . . not that they needed the *al*s with that lot strutting their stuff.
There are other blessings at being a post-war baby . . . I got to see George in the flesh . . . I've played golf, and football, with Bobby, and I've been handbag shopping with 'The King' in Argentina.
Don't care . . . *it were great.*
(the handbags* were for Mrs. Law).
*There couldn't be a more inappropriate metaphor to associate 'the Lawman' with, bearing in mind one particular tackle on England's Ron Flowers (W.A. Wright's fellow *Wolf*) at Wembley in 1963.
It was up there with Gascoigne's career buster—smack in front of the Royal Box.
Denis got away with a caution.
We won (it goes without saying . . . *oops*): Baxter two, Douglas one.

Two senior production assistants were assigned to Man.U.'s game; programme editors were very particular about who should be given charge of match 'cut-downs' (women—as previously stated—need not apply).

With an accompanying number from a tiny, calibrated clock, set below an in-built 14" monitor on the recording machine, anything that would provide a point from which one passage of play could be joined, seamlessly, to another, was noted: crowd shots . . . . players' and managers' close-ups, etc. Nowadays, time-code (to the hundreths of a second) appears 'burnt in' on a hoofing great HD-ready flat-screen number, so one's eye need never leave the screen (*don't know they're born*).

Incidents to be included—goals, fairly crucially—were given stars for quality and replay potential. There were no dedicated player or manager cams, so geography was crucial, nor was there time, nor machinery, to show everything twice (up to six, nowadays . . . *if the director's quick, and brave enough*).

There was nothing 'instant' about the 'replays' on highlights matches . . . but more of that anon.

The 'main match' was ready—or at least the 1ˢᵗ half was—and whilst the rest of us scratched around preparing bits of analysis and closing titles, the others sat back to watch their efforts hit the fan (airwaves).

United had taken a quick throw-in, just below our main camera rostrum, sending them off on yet another raid (the beauty of edited football).
A God-awful yelp burst through the control-desk speakers, like someone had been shot (or was about to be).

Sensing a cock-up—and, therefore a volley from 'Fat Sam' (Leitch)—we wound up the talkback. Sam was editor of *Match of the Day* for years, and also fronted *Football Preview* (father of *Focus*) within *Grandstand*.
He was Scottish and quite round—like a *Diddyman*—and you always knew when he was nervous: beads of sweat would seep through the make-up, just under his bottom lip, usually brought on by an 8 second, 24 word, countdown into a telecine (film) insert—a feature on Derby County perhaps.
You'd see him bluster from his Saturday morning taxi, scribbling last minute facts on scraps of paper, perhaps plotting which call he'd make come the next month's coin-tossing session with his opposite number at ITV, Gerry Loftus; that was how they decided who'd bat first in the televised match selection process.

Generous to a fault was Sammy—first to the bar, last to leave.
When I had a family emergency in Scotland, he stopped me doing my *Match of the Day* shift, peeled off 200 'oncers' from a wedge in the back pocket of his ample trousers, and ordered me north.
The loan became a gift.

We gazed at the 'hotline' phone—a red hand-piece, tucked down the side of the control desk, from where all videotape inserts for the show were selected and routed to the production gallery, at the push of a button.
It was the co-ordinating production assistant's job to man the desk, field all calls initially, and buzz his little buzzer if a conversation were unnecessary.

"V.T. (videotape) . . . ON THE PHONE!"

Not having physically done any editing, Martin Hopkins knew the bollocking wouldn't have his name on it, so he permitted himself a sly, trademark grin.

"Yes Sam . . .
(he paused as Leitch ranted)
. . . no . . . not with you, sorry."

The level went up a notch:
"No one noticed <u>anything</u> down there?"

Unsatisfied, yet confident, Sam demanded to know who had edited the 1st half of the match.
"John did."
(*ratted on us, hadn't he?*)
I was one of three '*Johns*' working that night.
Sam fumed on:
"Well, when this match is off the air Martin, get bloody John to go back to 12 minutes from kick-off, and see if he notices anything . . . and then get him to F _ _ _ _ NG RING me!!"
BANG!
May the soul searching begin.

Had we left a goal out?
Had there been an audible 'F' word?
What <u>could</u> it be?

By simple process of elimination, we knew the 'John' in question . . . and we also knew *he* would not be fazed.
Best form of defence . . . *full-on attack!* Coleman would be loving this.

We spooled the tape back . . . witnessed the horror . . . then ushered John McNicholas to the red phone.

"Look Sammy, we absolutely <u>hated</u> it down here too" (brazen sarcasm).

"It" the sequence, as it happened 'live,' went like this: a United throw-in on the left . . . George Best, spotting a runner in space, takes it quickly . . . the 'runner' deftly controls and speeds off towards goal.
Sadly, for our immediate futures, the way the incident was edited—and thus purveyed to the great unwashed, millions and millions of them, glued in armchairs—runner and shy-taker were the same . . . i.e. *Best to Best* . . . with commentary to compound it . . . an historic, gargantuan balls-up . . . show-boating at its zenith.
Even Coleman (who may have been the commentator) saw the funny side of it . . . in the end.

(*some player that Best, eh?*).

Now those replays: to make it simple, each 'main' match (we did two most Saturdays in edited long-form) would be recorded on a couple of 60 minute, 2" magnetic tapes—a half each, obviously. When Sam had decided which would lead, and his preferred durations for all the others, the assigned P.A.s went forth and, quite literally, *cut* their highlights to length.

Unless it were the Cup Final or an important international, there would be no replay facility on site; that meant the commentators had to remember moves leading to goals, or other dramas, in detail, and recount them, as though they were watching the slow motion—not easy, but Motson and Davies were brilliant at it . . . and if they weren't, they could send us the words at the end of the game: that meant matching sound levels and intonations, which was a pain as the enemy ticked by, but it didn't happen often.

Those 're-caps' would be assembled on to the master tape and their position noted on the edit log.

Then you waited your turn on the Video Disk—a great big shiny thing, the size of a kid's bicycle wheel, encased in a perspex box and mounted, horizontally, on top of the gizmos that made it work.
(*a little knowledge . . .*)

It may have been *Diplodoccus* to a modern CD's humming-bird technology, but the HS 100 Video Disk was a ground-breaker; reminded me a little of our family *Dansette Major* record-player in the 60s, though, as far as I know, it didn't do Bill Haley and the Comets.

'The Disk' was on duty all-day Saturday, providing replays for *Football Preview*, *Grandstand's* outside broadcasts, and now, *Match of the Day*.
There was only one Video Disk (to be sung to the Cuban *"Guantanamera"*) for the entire Corporation, and, very occasionally, the responsibility would bring it to its knees.

When you got the nod it was your turn, your goals and incidents would be played *out* from the edit machine, recorded and stored *on* the Disk—one at a time (it's capacity was 36 seconds)—then, at the videotape editor's behest the slowed down passage would be replayed *in* to the slot he'd prepared earlier on the master . . . guided by those pre-laid lines of memorised commentary—clear enough?
The trademark 'BBC Action Replay' graphic would be superimposed—from a caption scanner in the Disk room—on the first, frozen frame of each insert, then, with a hold

for a couple of seconds, off it would go, as if by magic, as the ubiquitous George Best dribbled goal-wards.

With two or three matches being edited at once, it only needed a handful of netbusters—plus a few penalty-box scares—to cause a jam outside the disk room like junction 2A on the M25 on Good Friday.

The affable *Thin Controller*—a.k.a. Nick Bayston, autocratic ruler of the videodisk booth, blessed with technical knowledge to rival any of the doctors *Who*—contrived a stacking system with which Heathrow's tower would gladly have been associated.

Nick was indispensably a television boffin, and where his beloved disk was concerned, more fastidious than a silver-backed gorilla with a family flea infestation.
He was always tweaking and twiddling . . . *it drove you feckin' mad.*
You could try to jump the queue by bribing him with tea and 'bickies' from the catering trolley (a highlight of Saturday nights in VT . . . *"when you're down in VT, with a cold cup of tea, and the wheels are continually turning"* etc., etc from a Christmas in-house poem competition)—or offer to take his bladder content to the loo, by hand, in order that the flow of maintenance went uninterrupted, but unless 'Nick the Disk' said so, nothing happened.

Keeping the transportation analogy going . . . there then followed an almighty train crash; how it happened, one's God alone knew.
Amongst us, we'd contrived to get the replays for three of the seven goals in one of the matches (therefore, all of them) 'not <u>necessarily</u> in the right order.'

In itself—with so many eyes and ears on the job—twas a feat worthy of comment . . . and public enquiry.
The road to the labour exchange would have been littered with good intent had the mess not been rapidly obviated . . . with Masonic stealth.

But some things are best laid bare for generations to come . . . which brings me on (or back, rather) to Jimmy Hill.

Lynam exuded confidence, it was his hallmark, you could stake your bricks and mortar on him; *The Beard* was less of a banker, which—those of you who never <u>could</u> appreciate him, will spot—rhymes, readily.

Everyone knew something about Jim . . . from his playing days at Brentford and Fulham . . . to the P.F.A. and the abolition of the minimum wage (*what have you <u>done</u> Jim!*) . . . from Coventry's Sky Blues . . . to London Weekend Television (thence, to us).

Unsurprisingly his good mate, Eric Morecambe (of the Variety Club, *SPARKS*, and other mutual charitable involvements . . . including supporting 'The Hatters' and 'The Cottagers,' respectively) was leagues ahead when it came to improv . . . Chaplin to Jim's Gielgud.

He'd try to allay our fears:
"If anything goes wrong, at any time, just cut back to me, I'll cope."
Good show, Jim.

Anti-smoking laws weren't stringent in the UK, despite the wartime efforts of that great social campaigner, Adolf Hitler . . . who never came . . . never saw . . . and never got the chance to change our habits; you could still go for a night in the pub and come back smelling like shit.

We'd recorded some links for that night's edition of *Sportswide*—including one into a longish football item—but, as things mechanical have a habit of doing, the tape broke.
Without waiting for my instruction, the vision mixer (who operates panels of buttons controlling sources like studio cameras, videotape, graphics etc.,) cut up a 'live' shot of Jim at the desk . . . where he'd been, a few minutes previously.

You know those 'spot the difference' puzzles in kids' comics, with two seemingly identical pictures, each with a tricky little nuance or six?
Well, here, the set and lighting seemed identical . . . the bearded one's clothes were the same . . . but a 3 year old would have spotted that Jim's feet were now <u>on</u>, as opposed to <u>under</u> the desk.
Instead of the look of intense concentration moments before the crash, the bold boy was having a *St. Bruno* moment, meerschaum ablaze, dreaming of making birdies and how to explain his method without boring us rigid.

Bloopers abound (to give the redhead more work . . . she must *love* the sporty ones): as you'd imagine, the weather has produced some stonkers.
Way back in the 70s—when Jagger and the Stones ruled the world and 'The Big Yin' was in banana wellies—Michael Fish was heading for a fall.
The in-vision weatherperson had been with us for 20 years, but with 'British' motorways stopping at the Border, BBC Scotland couldn't afford the luxury. So it was down to a bit of meteorological DIY; we had all sorts of printed strips to attach to a stand-alone map of Scotland . . . . RAIN mostly.
The network had more cash and used posh magnetic maps and strips.
FOG's initial letter fell off, on air, didn't it, prompting linkman Julian Pettifer (I think) to apologise *"for the f'n fog."*
Anonymous female presenter: the previous night the forecaster had promised heavy snow, but it didn't show. Thinking on her feet for a natty handover, she went with:

'So Bob, where's that eight inches you promised me last night?'
Not sure the boy ever recovered.
One that still sends its creator into signature whoops of laughter came during the Scottish Open golf championship . . . Kenny Brown on mic:
'Some weeks Nick likes to use Fanny . . . other weeks he prefers to do it by himself' (the Sunnesson/Faldo axis lining up the putts).

"Botham, in the slips, legs wide apart, waiting for a tickle."

The heroic Botham's expletive wasn't deleted during a Test match pitch report; not his fault . . . they put out the wrong take. Whilst regrettable, a single use of the 'F' word at ten-thirty in the morning made Chef Ramsay appear 'Laraesque' by the end of service (the West Indian master batsman was 501 not out for Warwickshire against Durham at Edgbaston 1994—match drawn).
(Sir) "Beefy" (who left Durham C.C.C. in 1993) was *Pipe Smoker of the Year* in 1988; alas (like Stephen Hendry) J.H. never got the recognition he deserved, but Eric Morecambe held the (now defunct) title in 1970, and—quite interestingly—it was Stephen Fry * of Norwich City F.C., at the death.
(* *what more can a poor boy do . . . surely he's due for the blade soon, Ma'am*).

Everyone makes mistakes on air—even extraordinary Mr. S.J. Fry—but 'spoonering' Jim Naughtie—representing gorgeous Milltown of Rothiemay, and *Radio 4*—remains on pole . . . *for me, Jeremy*.

Good value though he's been down the years, George W. Bush (a particular favourite of Lily Allen's) would be booed off stage at the UK Comedy Store awards.

Look, whole parts of programmes have been repeated . . . goals have gone in twice . . . . *tries have been missed out* . . . .

Cut right THERE!

"... Here Comes The Assistant Manager of Leeds United."

On Saturdays I always look for the St. Johnstone score—for auld lang syne—and so, I'm certain, does Ken Schofield—30 years grand vizier of the European Golf Tour—because we're Perthshire folk . . . like draper William McGregor of Braco, who first had the idea of a football league in England (again, *Q.I., no?*).

Kenny—currently applying his structural skills to the great game of cricket—was my sister-in-law Margaret(also from Braco)'s badminton partner for years, and though he (from nearby Aberuthven) has flown higher than a balata off Phil Mickelson(no connection with Perthshire, whatsoever)'s lob wedge (other than he's played *Gleneagles* a few times), he's well aware of his humble beginnings (and iffy golf swing).

One wouldn't choose to take issue with Mr. Fry on a 'fact' of any record, but it's generally believed the first-ever feature film, made at turn of the last century, was about the Irish-Australian baddie, Ned Kelly . . .
(no countermanding racket and flashing caption . . . so, press ahead).
The first film I made with Strine-talking Greg Norman, when he was as rough as a croc's back, did nothing for his status as one of the world's great golfers, but it kept you interested, as if, somehow, you were part of the unfolding story (utterly fanciful of course); you need only look to his lifestyle, his Midas touch in business, his amazing consistency at play, to appreciate his singular thirst for success (and the flimsy analogy with Master Nedward).
(by the way, how good was that attack by 53 year old Norman on the 2008 Open . . . if only to be upstaged the following year, at Turnberry, Scotland, by super "Mac" Watson?)

Greg is not a miserable man, but no ex-world No.1 (for 331 weeks), let alone a big strapping Aussie bloke, would laugh out loud while imploding at Nick Faldo's feet (. . . or *"Dick" Faldo*, as one American commentator had him early on—the same, insular, dyslexic who battled with *"Liam Wooseman from Wales, England"* for most of that week in the States).

John Motson had suggested following two young football managers from the lower divisions, as they went about their business, as a film feature for *Sportsnight*; the charge of making it fascinating fell on me. The names put forward were: Alan Durban, the manager of Shrewsbury town—ex-Welsh international (27 caps) and Derby County player (under Mr. Clough)—and the Lincoln City boss, Graham Taylor, a childhood fan of Scunthorpe United . . . two wholly different characters with futures that wouldn't match.

The relationship between the Football League and television wasn't always (ever) harmonious: they blamed us for dwindling gates and we thought they were greedy bastards. ITV's regional policy meant they could cover twice as much as we, yet, despite contractual obligations to cover games outside the top flight, many clubs never saw the light of day . . . other than the occasional cameo within a strand programme; any exposure was seen as a bonus.

Generally, our cameras were made welcome wherever they went, though we did get locked in at the Hawthorns once; I think it was a mistake . . . or maybe Gubba had upset someone.

Graham (Tayor) and his wife—lovely Rita—gave us access-most-areas, even looking on as the ex-Mariner and Lincoln Imp wrestled with home-school French: perhaps his ambitions lay with Monaco and France—grace and élan—rather than the pop-rock and turnips of Watford and England.

"Motty" and I were to make (son of) *Young Managers II, the sequel*, based on the phenomenal success of *YM 1*, and Graham in particular, who'd done wondrous things to Elton's Hornets, hauling them up three divisions in almost as many years; Alan was just about managing Stoke City F.C..
(we could, conceivably, complete the trilogy, if asked—everyone was gagging for The Return of the Kings, *if you recall)*

Brian Clough—a name that should appear in any book, about practically anything (because he'd have an opinion on it)—was on the box more than Arsene Wenger is today, and with good reason . . . his club sides were outstanding: 'The Rams' in white . . . with Durban, Hector, Hinton, McFarland, O'Hare, Mackay & co.,—First Division champs in 1971-72—and 'The Reds'—astonishingly, <u>twice</u> Champions of Europe—among them . . . Shilton, Anderson, Clark, McGovern, Lloyd, Burns, Bowyer, Birtles, Woodcock, Robertson and Trevor Francis.
Ajak, whom Forest beat in the semis of their second win, in 1980, had scored 30 goals in six matches up to that point . . . their prolific former pupil, Cruyff J., was a Los Angeles Aztec (out of Barcelona F.C) by then.

While girlies tend to remember the lyrics of songs, and read books and stuff, being able to reel off a favourite football team didn't qualify you for intercourse of any kind at parties. My old mate John Helm can do all 92 football league clubs (not the squads you understand) in the time it takes *'The Bolt'* and his mates to run a lap . . . *now that (he) <u>is</u> impressive, ladies.*

My seldom requested party pieces were: Simpson, Craig, Gemmell, Murdoch, McNeill, Clark, Johnstone, Wallace, Chalmers, Auld, and Lennox of *'The Lions'* . . . Younger, Parker, Caldow, Evans,Young, Docherty, Smith, Johnstone, Reilly,Turnbull, Ormond of *'The Bravehearts'* . . . and Sprake, Madeley, Cooper, Bremner, Charlton, Hunter, Lorimer, Clarke, Jones, Giles, Gray of *probably the best English team on telly at the time.*

Forest had agreed to pay Birmingham City £999,999 for Trevor Francis when they brought him to the City Ground—Clough insisting they keep a pound back, lest it went to his (Trevor's) head . . . a bit rich coming from the prototype.

If Forest's captain at the turn of the (20th) century, Sam Weller Widdowson, is to be credited with inventing shin-pads, <u>and</u> flood-lighting (*bit dubious that one, Stephen*), then Brian could claim to be the first of the TV friendly—or, impossibly intolerant, depending on the tenor of your questions—football managers.

The medium suited Ol' Big 'Ed'—interesting to have seen what *Newsnight's* formidable striker would have made of him, and fascinating (and quite by chance) that Jezza's long-time partner is one, Elizabeth Ann Clough.
Who do you think you are, Liz?

Even Ali was shaken: "Clough . . . I've had enough," said the great rhymer.

Rio Ferdinand, today's most celebrated wind-up merchant, has much to learn from the former Billingham Synthonia F.C. centre forward:
"I don't mind playing you at ping-pong Tony (Gubba), *but I won't be coming on* Football Focus *to talk to <u>you</u>, young man."*
He did of course, but "Gubbs" bit like a hungry pike . . . and they'll chew on anything; you had to prepare for a kiss as part of the make-up, or a slap, were it meant and on-going.
He'd spar, vigorously, with Barry Davies and John *la Motta* at the grounds, before and after games, but Coleman was a prime cut:
"Look, here comes the assistant manager of Leeds United"—an off-camera reference to the approaching Coleman's affinity with Mr. Revie; like many purists, D.C. appreciated *The Don's* men-in-white (and yellow), especially *"Norman Hunter, David."*
Norm's on-pitch battle with "Franny" Lee of Derby County—which "Motty" commentated on—was not one of football's best adverts (even our director missed the telling punch from "bite yer legs").

Leeds United F.C., in the 70s, were spectacular—a gritty version of Real Madrid of the Bernabéu—in the mud of Elland Road.

But they needn't crow at the Baseball Ground—their pitch was rougher than the infield at Yankee Stadium, and yet, most times (from where I was logging) both sides played the game as Pelé (and Andy Gray) would have wished . . . *"beautifully."*

Even Brian would concede that comparing his efforts to the mighty Brazilian's would be a gross impertinence, but career strike-rate-wise, it stacks up OK:
Clough got 251 goals in 276 games (2 for England, without scoring) against the boy Edson's 1283 in 1276 games (77 in 92 for Brazil).
Brian's crook knees stopped him (as a player) at 29—*O Rei Pelé* was still up for it at 37 . . . so we'll never know (*Oh YES WE WILL*).
The scale of little Nottingham Forest's astonishing back-to-back European Cups, weighed against Pelé's three World Cup winners' medals, brings the curtain down on any further debate.
(*not even on his best day, would Michael Sheen make a good Pelé*)

Lady Jane Grey (*"her only vice was virtue"*) was Queen of England for nine days . . . . Cloughie (*"you're a bloody disgrace for missing the target from there . . . you want bloody shooting!"*) would be King.
Alas, it never happened, but at least *he* kept his head . . . sort of.
His reign at Leeds lasted 44 days, and though the exit polls probably had him ahead through most of the campaign, it was some irony that Revie—a fellow Boro native—was coronated.
"Seconds out!"

That *"bloody shooting"* rant came in a filmed piece at Forest's training ground; Brian was like Desert Orchid—put the cameras near and watch him perform:

"Oh, that's bloody rubbish . . . I didn't buy you to take corners!"
Don't call the recipient of that one, but the cap would have fitted perfectly had it been Britain's first million pound (with tax) player.
Trev got the message and nutted in the winner against Malmo, in Munich, for European Cup No.1 . . . . though Brian always maintained he wouldn't have played him, had all his regulars been fit (*yeah, right*).

Alan Durban's old boss was the denominator in our *YM* re-make, when Watford visited the Clough lair; to talk then of *"Taylor for England"* would have been preposterous . . . but not for "The People's Champ."
(*similarities with snooker's 'Hurricane' wouldn't end there*)

Whenever Graham made the news—which he could hardly avoid at Watford—"Motty" and I would hook up for a knowing chat; were he to make it to the top job, we'd muse, he'd look back and thank us with handfuls of Wembley 'comps.'
(*"Motty" had his face—I wasn't that fussed*).

The crew journeyed to a recording studio in Surrey, where short-haired (and thinning) Elton (on lyrics and keyboard), long-haired Davey Johnstone (on lead guitar) and the boys (on something) were working a new album.
The distinct smell in the band room wasn't *Woodbine*.

The piano player tinkered away.
I genuflected and told him what we were up to; immediately, he launched into a self-accompanied, stop/start burst of *Part Time Love,* professing to have forgotten the words and asking for 'a few moments' . . . . *Granted, your bi-Sexualness.*
Bit by bit, the boys joined in, and ere long we had a private audience with one of the best acts in the business—ever.
This time, we checked the recording.

Graham's 'hornets' reached the Cup Final in 1984, remembered—at Vicarage Road anyway—more for the Chairman's tears at *Abide With Me* (his brand new missus, Renate, by his side), than the two-nil score line to Everton: Glaswegians, Andy Gray (actually, his Mum is Hebridean) and Graeme Sharp (32 national caps between them . . . *not enough, say a lot of us*) with the goals.

Neil Martin, who played for Scotland three times (3 goals) at centre forward, scored the winner in Clough's debut as Forest boss (against Spurs in an F.A. Cup replay), having already become the first player to score a hundred league goals in Scotland <u>and</u> England—Ton 1 coming from Alloa, Queen of the South and Hibs—Ton 2 from Sunderland, Coventry and Forest.

I was always on the look-out for relevant, showbiz catalysts for our pre-match build up; comedians were favourite, and most of the teams would be disposed to a bit of light relief, given that Wembley Stadium and its pressures were four to five hours away.

In 1984 we had Michael Barrymore with Watford—causing havoc in the players' hotel at breakfast—and 'Toffee' fanatic, Freddie Starr, causing havoc all day, wherever he went, dressed as Hitler in wellies.

If Spike Milligan—Irish rugby fan, and frequent visitor to our *Rugby Special* recording area on Five Nations days—had a penchant for taking the piss out of the deeply unpleasant Nazi, then Freddie was no less enthusiastic . . . . and equally unpredictable.
No-one was safe . . . from his rantings on the team hotel balconies, to our gantry studio with Des and his 'normal' guests . . . in the team changing rooms as the opposition's numbered shirts were re-arranged to suit Everton's game-plan . . . or out on the pitch, stirring partisans into a separate, neutral frenzy.

"*Aye, aye Yippie . . . the Jerrmans bombed our chippie*" sang 'Scouse' comic, Stan Boardman as he led the crew and me across an 'unrestored' site in Liverpool, towards a bar and disco, following a tribute night for Ian Rush. Stan wasn't exactly a closet 'Reds' fan, but if the money was right, he'd try to kid them on, across the divide, that blue, in fact, was his colour; that night poor "Rushie" didn't know if he was Dixie Dean or Trevor Ford by the time Stan had done with him.

The Monday following the '84 final, Rocket Records were due to release the video of *I'm Still Standing*—the Chairman strutting his stuff along the seafront at Cannes, in white coat and boater, giving it plenty to another Taupin/Dwight collaboration. Recognising the massive launch-pad audience they'd be getting on BBC 1 (we'd pull around 10 million), they gave us permission to air it first, on Cup Final *Grandstand*.

We were always walking a commercial tightrope; Wimbledon and the Test matches clung to their all-white images as best they could, but sponsors were lurking in the shadows to try it on wherever they could.

Take the billboard to end all billboards—Formula 1 motor racing.
In terms of value per square centimetre, the drivers' fireproof 'dungies' were territories to be coveted, but for 'BIG' value, perimeter advertising was the ticket.

In the name of good public relations—and the prospect a *Marlboro* baseball cap, or a *Longines* umbrella (*'no watches left, mate'*)—we'd invite sponsors' representatives into the truck to check out our camera angles. Boards and banners could be moved a couple of feet either way, for maximum effect, without offending anyone.

More importantly, their hospitality suites were well stocked, and 'beautifully' staffed, by the evenly-tanned and high-heeled.

We'd gone through our rehearsal at Brands Hatch, on the eve of the British Grand Prix (it may have been the Race of Champions), and everyone was happy with the way things looked.

The Kent circuit was steeped in all of them—Moss, Clark, Brabham, Prost—and for the best view in Britain, the Indy sector was the one to watch.

It came as a bit of a shock, therefore, on my early morning stroll round, to see a giant *John Player* advert painted on the inside run-off of the first corner, at Paddock Hill Bend . . . the price, perhaps, of letting them (the sponsors) buy dinner.

Number 1: it was in neither head, nor tail, of our signed agreement.
Number 2: it was a spook-like, slimy manoeuvre in the dark.
Number 3: it was a contravention of the advertising laws of the land.

Number 4:   we were going to pick up the ball.
Number 5:   we were serious about not giving it back—a stand-off.

(*Number 6: were their fags . . . and my steak was rare—I'd ordered medium*)

Advertising wasn't permitted between the camera and the action, where this one certainly was. A meeting was hastily convened with the circuit boss, Mr. John Webb, and *J.P.S.* spin doctor, Peter Dyke (*what a pair*).
John was the autocrat (*dear me, just spotted that one*) who governed with acerbic fist and clenched tongue, who wouldn't step down, despite the enormous clout F.1 types wielded, even then. There were plots and scandals (nothing in the Mosley league), but at Webbie's place, the wee hard-man with the crippled legs was in charge.

During one of my spells between jobs (. . . *or was it marriages?*), John generously offered me the run of *Le Castellet*—his magnificent gaff in Barbados—for a spot of r. & r. (nothing in the Blair league). The villa took its name from the town near Marseilles where the French Grand Prix used to be held—at Circuit Paul Ricard (Elio de Angelis was killed there in 1986).

Never one to waste *John Player's* hospitality budget, Peter Dyke had Murray and me* up in First Class for a 10-hour champagne-tasting, on the way to Kyalami for the South African Grand Prix, around the time 'Lord' Ecclestone's turbo-charged Brabhams ruled.

(* James's posh seat came as a super sub-clause in his contract)

Perhaps Peter's graffitist's wanton act at Brands was a marker being called in, but the black masking-paint fell short of anything like efficacy, indeed, your eye was drawn to the cover-up.
It had the makings of a *cause célèbre* (not in the Brand-Ross league).

Amazing that it could create such a furore, when you look at how circuits and stadia are dressed-up these days.

Baths were re-filled, babies lobbed back in, and the race went ahead.

A couple of years later, Silverstone became the permanent home of the British GP—Nigel Mansell capping both eras with a win, but as far as F.1 was concerned, there'd be no more *Hawthorn* and *Dingle Dell*, *Druid's* and *Pilgrim's drop* . . . shame, cos it was a cracking circuit for television.

I hope Boardman and Starr don't get wind of this, but *Hugo Boss*—one of Hamilton and Button's sponsors—used to make uniforms for the SS in the bad old days; the founder, Hugo Ferdinand Boss, died shortly after the War, but his company survived.

When their (*Boss*) representatives came to TWI's production offices in London, in search of a cheap commercial, I was 'volunteered' for the job.

There were all manner of possibilities and permutations—*Boss* . . . *Hugo Boss* . . . a firm for clothes . . . a firm for 'smellies'—but not many Deutchmarks put aside; *Baron von Cheapskatehausen* was after a low cost, high impact production . . . and I was just the very fellow to give it to them.

Herr Langer and Seve Ballesteros were their most recognizable clothes-horses, so I concocted a multi-image storyboard, using recurring oblong frames (which we'd fill with action images from our library, and footage they'd provided from a fashion shoot)—all in keeping with 'the look' and grammar of their cologne and perfume ranges. With a burst of the techno-house-acid-raving *Boss Drum* (by the *Shamen* . . . from Aberdeen, Scotland) to wash it down, I was confident their account manager would be bowled over.
There was no movement for the company purse; the commission was lost . . . 'too dated' was the thrust of the critique, so much so, that a year later, they ran a campaign that looked hellishly similar to my poorly funded effort.

Well I liked it, and so did the boss—*my boss* (Bill).

Alan Minter and his *DAF* trucks sponsorship caused another stir.
We were huge Minter fans, from the time he became Olympic champion, in Munich, through some pulsating nights in London, as he crafted his way to a (successful) crack at Vito Antuofermo's World Middleweight title—seven years later—in Las Vegas.

'Boom Boom' had his fair share of wins . . . and controversy.
The Marvin Hagler affair of 1980 was something else.
Never mind the racist undercurrent at Wembley (Minter's doing) . . . the seven-and-a-bit minutes of southpaw savagery . . . Alan's cuts (Hagler's doing) . . . our man Harry being hit on the head by a can <u>and</u> a beer bottle (unattributable due to the absence of adequate lighting and CCTV) . . . and half a dozen men of the Met having to man-handle Hagler to safety . . .
. . . Alan Minter's reign as champ of the world was no more.

Viewed against the brawl in Porthcawl, twenty years earlier, it was mild mayhem. The post Brian London/Dick Richardson family free-for-all—a bonus for ticket holders at Coney Beach Arena—was played out, more or less to the rules, though one unfortunate did appear to take a few, while down.

As in the Minter fight, stoppages due to cut eyes—and proclaimed illegal use of heads (by Hagler and Richardson)—were the triggers.

In his post-match interview with Cliff Morgan, 'The Blackpool Rock' described the champ as "a novice"—a cleaned-up version of the stuff he'd been roaring at him during the fight.
'London' (real surname Harper) took shots from some of the greats: Ingemar Johannson, Floyd Patterson, and the man himself (Ali stopped him in three, in 1966).

During one of Minter's 'qualifying' nights, big Neville Allcock, our Jaguar-enthusiast, stage manager (*top* of the expenses pops), had gone to the dressing rooms to check the fighters for advertising; that which was visible seemed to be in order—his trunks were 'clean.'
Whether *DAF*'s all-night tattooist had burned a two-tonner across his back, we'd find out in due course, but in the time it took "our Nev" to get back to the ringside commentary position, a fresh pair of branded trunks had appeared . . . *as if by magic.* Threatening to pull the plug normally did the trick.
We were serious, <u>we</u> were the BBC, so off they—or *it* (*DAF*) rather—came, and on went the approved *GOLA*.

What a time for boxing, British boxing at that . . . Minter, Conteh, Magri, Buchanan and Watt . . . governed by the B.B.B.C. and televised by the B.B.C.'s bad-boys.

Dave 'Boy' Green and John H. Stracey were to get it on at a Barrett/Duff bill at Wembley, in 1977; Stracey had won the world welterweight title from Jose Napolés in Mexico City in 1975—a fantastic achievement, having been down early in the fight—but, subsequently, he'd lost the title and now the boy Green was in his face.
Davie's style (may I be spared) was agricultural, awkward . . . and jolly exciting, but <u>he</u> was the pretender—the doubters needed convincing.
John Henry had to be 'eliminated.'

Having driven old man Stracey round his manor, flogging tickets, by way of the greasiest spoon in north-east London (the 'Full English' was *afloat*) we ended up at the gym in time for sparring; it's fair to say they saw us coming.
The only part of the boxer's upper body, devoid of *GOLA* sponsorship, were his eyes.

(*Not original—we used to do it at Murrayfield*) when my first born, Grant, was little, he was a ball boy at Hampden; didn't take him long to suss out that if he rushed on to the pitch at the end of the match to pat Kenny Dalglish on the back, there was a fair chance he'd get on the telly

GOLA did similarly by kitting out physios and trainers in heavily-branded tracksuits, their 'cure-all' bags placed precisely—logo side up, facing the cameras—when assisting the fallen and distressed.

The nifty Loftus Road legend, Stan Bowles, apparently turned out for England (v. Holland) wearing one *GOLA* boot (Made in England) and one (German) *Adidas* number—*GOLA* claimed he scored with *theirs*, naturally; and when Liverpool won the Cup in 1965, the entire team wore *GOLAs* with *Adidas* stripes painted over the top (allegedly).

Stracey jr., had advertising on his T-shirt, across the upper chest, shoulder-to-shoulder; the blood-red head-guard, protecting chin and eyebrows, were perfect sites; more *GOLA* on wrist and waist bands, *plus* at mid-calf where the shorts ended and the *GOLA* tongued boots began. *The soles were opportunities missed . . . a thought I kept to myself.*

If the BBC had the money, he'd take it all off . . . pointless trying to get heavy—suicidal, in truth—but we weren't into appeasement.

A couple of shots of his eyes did for our *Sportsnight* preview, and Davie did for John on the night . . . after 10 rounds.
Funnily enough (were you not involved), it was the splendidly named Carlos Palomino who accounted for John Stracey <u>and</u> the Fen Tiger; Green said he (Palomino) was the hardest puncher he'd ever crossed—handsome bugger too (Carlos) . . . did a spot of acting, before trying an ill-fated comeback . . . (<u>that</u> old chestnut).

Bags of scope for billings writers and promoters when champion, Sugar Ray Leonard and challenger, Dave 'Boy' Green were lined up for the world title in 1980.
Seldom, it was reported, *had the boxing world seen a left hook like it*—Davie didn't, for sure . . . in round 4.

In my days on outside broadcasts, one tier of perimeter advertising was permitted; now, they're stacked like playing cards. In posher stadia, like the Emirates or the Ethiad, motorized affairs revolve and animate brand names, in scientifically tested colour schemes; for a stipulated number of seconds, airlines and internet sites alternate with banks that want your money, and *Hill* and *365*, who'll probably get it . . . but search me how their effectiveness is quantified (the megastars remain grateful).

An observation test for next time in the boozer:
'Name five advertising boards round the ground during the match—*you may confer . . . losers get them in.*'

Even supposing '*a Mars a day*' could help you '*work, rest and play*' and '*Lucozade*' did aid '*recovery*' (which I very much doubt), slogans weren't allowed.

Booze and fag companies had budgets, and style.

Johnnie Walker was the classiest sponsorship act out of town, and at home, *Dunhill*—notably at St Andrews—would feature in a photograph with *Seagram's*; my old sparring partner, Peter German, of TWI, was tournament director at the first two.

The *Johnnie Walker Classic*, in Thailand—which we covered as part of the European (?) Tour—was . . . classic; having local boy, Eldrick Woods, blast a sub-par final round to win the title at the Blue Canyon Club in Phuket with his Mama and Papa looking on, and our pictures going to millions around the World, was just the way *Johnnie Walker* would have wanted it—a bit like Monty winning the Open at Troon (same dream), with *Irn Bru* as the official drink and the spirit of Arthur Havers (1923) manifesting at the 19th during Lineker's closing link.

Twelve months previously, Greg Norman—the World No.1 . . . if (pre-Westwood and Donald) you can remember a time when Tiger didn't dominate—had kept to the script, rising from his sick-bed to win in Phuket . . . thereby exonerating that year's casting director for shelling out so much appearance money, and for paying the heavy duty on cases of coveted 'black,' being shipped home to Florida—east or west . . . depending on the route filed by the Shark's shuttle commander.

Whenever the tour went seriously foreign, to a place starved of sporting publicity—like Thailand—the commercial people's hunger for exposure was insatiable, be it for club, town or country.

In the weeks following one of the *Classics*, we received stern words on Blue Canyon headed: quoting their contract, they'd calculated that after adding up the number of stipulated seconds they had on air—that's interior and exteriors shots of the building and its environs, plus verbal mentions by the commentators—we, European Tour Productions were 12 whole seconds light . . . . in short, 'we owed them' (*someone gets pay + expenses to do this!*).

When there are 156 professionals battering it round off two-tee starts, on days 1 and 2, and many of the survivors in contention at the week-end, that fine detail had escaped the attentions of both the director and myself; even 'the suits' at E.T.P. were ruffled.

I managed to put it right during the transmission of that season's final event, contriving a spurious competition from which the Blue Canyon emerged as *Clubhouse of the Year* (despite Sunningdale doing the best roast lunch . . . in the world—and St Andrews, being there).

Somewhere along the line, the men in black bartered with the local Tourist Board and obligated us to show some of their dodgy, holiday footage: *soft-focus shots at sunset* . . .

scantily-clad '10s' skipping along flotsam-free beaches . . . others showering their size 8 bods in secluded jungle waterfalls . . . bird-life, of extravagant hue and plumage, frittering in the canopies . . . carefree, if alert, fauna grazing the forest floor . . . out on an unnaturally blue ocean, local fishing craft bobble, alluringly—all to the hypnotic strains of an ethnic melody . . . . when really . . . .

Irritating, is it not, in traffic, when a sponge is hurtled, unsolicited, onto your windscreen as you wave fecklessly from behind the glass?

The Phuket version was to slap a babe in swaddlings on the *Triplex*, the mother thrusting her free hand through the open window urging you to read from the card. <u>We</u> stared ahead . . . <u>she</u> at us, imploringly, putting our humanity and generosity to the test; it certainly made that evening's sponsors' bash appear extravagant in the extreme . . . *but everyone went.*

One year the *J.W.* people hired a fort-cum-castle downtown, lit it with flaming beacons, and staged the most spectacular dinner/party/cabaret imaginable; superstar divas from other cultures were jetted in to entertain over brandy and brand *Walker*.
The Sultan of Brunei—a man not light in BNDs—regularly lures the seemingly 'un-lurable' to a relative's birthday, or simply to break the monotomy of being filthy rich, but this was the Kingdom of Thailand—king cobra country—and for the majority, *bahts* were tough to come-by.
I'd followed *The Shark* round in practice, the year of his Classic win; though our subsequent meetings were sporadic, he always seemed happy to see me (*personally, I didn't give a shit*).
We'd taken wine the night before, going over some of my memorable moments at Fleet golf club (more anon), and ranking the string of babes he was able to produce over a comparatively short stay in England . . . but it was like he didn't know me at all next day, as I moved in to show him where his drawing drive had landed on the 1st at the Canyon.

Looked right through me—*the bastard*; it's called focus, apparently . . .
"fuck you," more like.

After the usual exchanges with the scribes at his press conference, he sought me out, in an indescribably poor Scottish accent:

"And <u>your</u> question, Jimmy . . . yes, <u>you</u> with the burned face?"

Ever mindful that the invitations to the 'glam-bash' hadn't yet reached the TV compound, my reply, on behalf of E.T.P.F-L.A. (European Tour Productions Free-Loaders' Association) was measured:

"After hours on the range, practicing those towering, soft-landing 3 irons, and your trademark, exploding trap shots—which indeed are things of beauty—how do you unwind . . . a stiff 'Black' on the rocks, perchance?"

Worked a treat . . . *what a gig!*

Minus the sunshine of the Far East, the annual *Dunhill Cup* at St Andrews was every bit as distinguished: adequate showers in the public loos . . . punctilious, pooper-scooper action on the sands . . . daft buggers paddling in the freezing shallows . . . shitting seagulls hovering above—but no beggars.

St Andrews (the course) is what it says on the tin—magical to see, the stuff of any golfer's dream to play; whenever there was a window of opportunity, Murray, Critchley, Brown, Barter, Hutchison, Parkin, Castle and I, were through it, like burglars . . . a selection of clubs over the shoulder . . . ever mindful of pre-Middleton history, and—in my case—not much in the way of course management (according to Bruce).

I'd tangled with the Old Course many times in the late 50s, when it was ten bob a-go . . . . *shillings, farthings, florins, tanners and thru'penny bits* (under-40s may have to look them up), but now, in my professional capacity, I was being allowed to play round it with old pros (and Bruce) . . . *for free.*

Having survived the ballot, it'll cost you a few quid for the privilege, but for the hours and hours spent trying to work out what to do next—whether to pitch or putt on the double greens, deciding how many seem fair on your partners, and those behind, before calling it a day at the road hole bunker—it's great value . . . in any currency.

Soft-spoken, wine-slurping Frank Nobilo was our pro-am team leader one year. My opener—in full view of the members' lounge (the whiff of singeing ears filled my nostrils, doing little for the nerves)—made it to the temporary toilets to the right of *the* most generous of 1st fairways.

"RE-LOAD!"

A distant cry pierced the air from a balcony of the Rusack's Hotel, (renowned for its seafood and game) . . . a full 200 yards to my left.

It was Alliss, trying to make me feel better.

"FORE LEFT!" . . . I was able to reciprocate, as my third hooked, devilishly.

The great thing about St Andrews—apart from the courses, the University, the student fashion shows, Tom Morris and son, the Cathedral, the R. & A., the Kingdom of Fife, Laurie Auchterlonie's, the best fish and chips this side of Anstruther, and the *(Irn) Bru*, is . . . *that* beach (if only the water temperature were 30 degrees higher, the married man would get away with two rounds a day).

When the tides out, you could land a jet on it—dead flat and unspoiled—as trainee pilots doing their 'circuits and bumps' at RAF Leuchars airbase, just over the estuary, keep in mind.

An ideal spot, you'd be right in saying, for Hugh Hudson to film that glorious scene in *Chariots of Fire*.
Call us predictable, or lacking originality (*which would be harsh in the extreme*), but we took to more plagiarizing of Puttnam & Hudson's initiatives (*look, the bloody film bagged four Oscars in '81 . . . pillage on*).
The Great Court Run round the quad at Trinity College, Cambridge, has to be completed in 43.6 seconds, or so; there are proper corners, it's 367 metres long, and before the college clock strikes 12 (two rings per hour + the quarterly prelims) you need to have your educated ass over the line (students—*possibly pissed*—have a go at Matriculation Dinner time: one, Sam Dobin, did it in 2007).

To be fair Dave and Hughie were only messing with history themselves, with chunks of poetic licence: the real Lord Burghley (*"Magdalene, reading . . ."* politics, I assume) who'd won gold in the long hurdles in Amsterdam (1928), and was the only man to have done the court run in the prescribed time (1927), got the hump and refused to allow his name to be used in the film; so the lads invented "Lord Lindsay" and had Harold Abrahams beat him round the quad—*nice one*: alas, that never happened for real, hence the ignobility.
Where TWI—the event organisers—did score heavily, was that this was *yer* actual Trinity College: for reasons best known to the Academy award winners, they'd shot theirs elsewhere.

Seb Coe, still world 800m record holder (1.41.73) but coming to the end of his career, played himself, as did Steve Cram, recently deposed World 1500m champion. Seb and Steve could do a 400, on tartan, in around 46", but this was about as forgiving as the TT circuit on the Isle of Man. Daley Thompson lay await in reserve.
The American, Butch Reynolds had run 43.29 for the 400m in Zurich that year . . . a NWR, *apropos of precious little relevance.*

At first sight, it seemed Seb had made it: the clock showed 42.53. Now, Steve and Seb were arch rivals in the '80s but I doubt Crammy would have been behind the referral. It transpired that the (Lord) Coe had been 12 metres short of the line when the last chime tolled so the committee said "No." Still, charity got a few quid out of it, and Lord Burghley a chuckle, from on high. *"Don't mess with the Exeters!"*

The fight we staged in the *Grandstand* studio, one Spring Saturday, was an unconventional way *into* the show; it summed up the blind faith of our staff that, come Monday, we wouldn't all be looking for other work
(*. . . based on what, exactly?*).

The dress run was 'hammy' compared to what's in the archive.
The guys and gals in the back of shot were graphics and voice-over artistes, news sub-editors, typists and runners.
As we went on air, there was a moment when things looked 'Porthcawlish,' so good was the acting . . . *or were these secretly harboured, workplace grudges?*
Either way the switchboard lit up.
What on earth is the BBC coming to? . . . Has Lynam no control of 'his' staff? . . . This is <u>not</u> *what we pay the licence for . . . What sort of example is it for our children? . . . Unacceptable behaviour!*
It was after noon—so a bit of rope—but it <u>was</u> April Fools' Day.

A tuneless, Barber-shop sextet (same stable as 'the fighters') joined Des, on Twelfth Night (1230 actually), for a *Twelve 'Sporting' Days of Christmas* routine, peaking round the *Grandstand* set, boaters raised on: *'five go-o-old 'rings'* (for the Olympics, you'll appreciate), and thence to: . . . *'a partridge in a pear tree.'*
No objection raised by the religious police.
Neither episode would have amused the founding fathers (*Faith, Hope and Charity*—a.k.a Dimmock, Fox and Cowgill—*"the French hens"*) . . . but did we give a monkey's?
Ratings were good, Lynam was a star, all was well in TC4 (the sports studio) so . . . *'back in your prams, ladies.'*

(Mel) *Smith* (Oxford) *and* (Griff Rhys) *Jones* (Cambridge) agreed to go face-to-face on *Boat Race Grandstand*; what with coxes and crabs, and strokes and oars, and bow-balls and gimps, I feared the worst, but their 'script' just made us laugh; *it was my head on the block, people.*

The day Everton played Watford in Elton's Cup Final, they debated the risks of having '*heavy, bevvy, Nevvy'* (Southall) in the Toffees' goal; their concerns were unfounded—the great man was seldom troubled.

Rory Bremner still hadn't perfected his 'Lynam,' so he'd pop in from his studio next door, to brush up. Des let him 'throw' to the cricket at Lord's—in the 'Benaud' voice—which Rich completely blanked unusually . . . maybe he hadn't heard, or was struck speechless by someone 'doing him' properly at last.

People were taking notice; Lynam's window cleaner was a big fan:
"What was you doing running round Wembley with that Cup then, Des?"
. . . referring to a cunning stunt we pulled one Cup Final day.

Doubling for the anchorman, Derek Martin—an aerobically fit *Grandstand* assistant producer—was sent haring round the running track in a grey wig, holding a cardboard trophy aloft, like a crazed (we sped the pictures up) winning skipper . . . bursting, eventually (now Des), through the dressing-room door and stepping, fully clad, into an empty bath from where he linked to our set-up montage (hence the Dimmock bite from page 4).

The rewarding thing about these occasional diversions was, we were up for it, audience figures got better and better, so really what the Board of Governors and the rest of 'the dinos' thought privately, was wisely left unsaid—it was working for them, and we were enjoying ourselves.
However, they did come down, harshly, on my cryptic, off-the-wall *Radio Times* listings for *Grandstand*:
'Who, what, where and when, stop trying to be a clever dick'
. . . was the thrust of it (*took me bleedin' ages to come up with them*).
Within a week of my admonishment, the billings writers on *WOGAN* were doing the very same thing, with glowing endorsements.

When the BBC and I parted company, others got to 'benefit' from my shortcomings . . . like my dear friend and *Golf Channel* commentator *extraordinaire*, Renton Laidlaw; be it at work, or downstairs at *Langan's* celebrated restaurant-to-the-stars (near Green Park tube on the Piccadilly line—*the bangers and mash are the biz*), he is a joy to be with—a proper gent.
Paramedics might not put the lowly haggis at the top their list of potential life-savers, but Renton owed his (life) to one of the Bard's *great chieftains of the puddin' race*. As a result of nearly choking on a mouthful of the indelicate Scottish entrée, Renton was rushed to A&E.
The prognosis, without surgery, wasn't great.
In went the blades, and out of the sleepy stuff, scarred and minus a few vital bits, came the old boy, apparently, as good as new.
The *chieftain* was cleared of all charges.
Of the many things in life the former golf correspondent of the London *Evening Standard* enjoys, food—*soup* in particular . . . *any* soup—ranks higher than a West End musical, or the view from his Fife home at Drumoig overlooking the St. Andrews peninsular . . . even a blether with anyone, anywhere, anytime, about golf, or (to spoil the imagery) Hibernian F.C.
When the Professional Golfers Association of America think you're pretty good at you do, and say so on parchment, and everyone else in the U.K. sporting media establishment knows it already, then who am I to tell you how big a star he was?

Thinking back to his hernias and by-passes, the wisdom of asking him to jump in a freezing cold, outdoor swimming pool at the (golf) *Club Naçionale* near Paris, from which to deliver his opening *mots* to the French Open, may be questionable-to-malevolent.
They're playing the Ryder Cup there in 2018, by which time the Americans should have a handle on where France is . . . and a little of its history, after all, had it not been for Frenchie guns and stuff, the American War of Independence mightn't have

worked out the way they wanted . . . and what would they have done for a *Chevrolet* or a *Gillette* razor.
(even Elvis had a little bit of French in him . . . from way back).

We were alluding to the fact that the relationship between *les Francais* and *les Anglais*—separated by *la Manche*—had not always been an *entente* of the most *cordiale* type.
The Scots (present on Elvis's Dad's side) could boast of a stronger, older alliance: Mary Stuart—Queen of the Jocks—had done much of her early conspiring in France (Ste*w*art was the Scottish spelling).
Mary loved *gowf*, but—courtesy of the Tudors—she was heading (in her ruff) to an unplayable. Her father banned the game because his archers had developed fades, when the further-flying draw was required.
Leadbetter—*David,* to the practice range born, not *Margot,* to the Manor—would have had 'a fix' for that, but his advice (at today's rates) would have cost the King of the day—James V of Scotland—his ransom.

It would have been simpler, and a deal less risky, to have used a map of Europe with: '*Welcome to the French Open from Club Nacionale, near Versailles*' (. . . but we could do better).
Having my man emerge from the depths to explain the proximity of the two super states—by way of Captain Webb's 22 mile 'Sleeve' crossing in 1875—was to make plain to the Americans, especially those struggling with what exactly Versailles was, from whence, precisely, we were coming.

"*Sai-ling, sai-ling, over Niagra Falls,*
"*Captain Webb lost a leg and a shark ran away with his balls.*"

Couldn't do the derivation of that stanza from my kindergarten playground, but for accuracy's sake, Webb had both legs when he drowned in the rapids (at the foot of the falls—never having made the giant 170ft foot leap for man, or mankind) and, to the best of my limited knowledge, steelhead trout aren't man-eaters.
Sharks?—*Behave yourself child!*

Who wouldn't be fascinated by feats of controlled madness like Blondin's?
Whether his manager was wild about the offer of a piggy-back across Niagra on a tight-rope is hard to tell from the photographs.
One thing's for certain—Philippe Petit's 'coup' in Manhattan, is, tragically, unique.

We're drawn to acts of so-called "derring do" like most are to the seaside.
I didn't have the balls or powerful leg-kick for it, but I remember watching, gob-smacked, as my cousin Hugh swam across the River Spey at Grantown, during a family holiday; he'd been a lifeguard at college in the US, but the Spey—like the Tay

in Perth—flows at a fair clip, and is several degrees cooler than Lake Michigan, where his watchtower was.

There have been no reports—post the Permian period—of salmon attacks in Highland waters, and as there are no navigable links from the Spey—or its tributaries—to Loch Ness . . . . *she* wouldn't have been a threat.

Kids seldom escape a dare, at one time or another, be it with a yard of illicit ale to impress the girls, or a boob-flash for the boys.

I was the youngest amongst some seasoned thieves in a raiding party on *Woolworths* in Perth. In those days, sweets—priced by the ¼ lb—came in jars, so the easy pickings of today's (well, yesterday's) open-plan *Candyking* pick 'n' mix, wasn't an option.

While my accomplices lifted transformers and domestic appliances, without hesitation or fear of detection, I hovered by the costume bells display—*4 for 1d*—until the coast was clear.

In my panic I only managed a farthing's worth.

Not a great start, and nothing for the Great Train Robbers—some ten years down the line—to take notice of . . . but I'd broken my duck.

Tinkling bell safe in my shorts' pocket, I sped off down the town vennels, never looking back (as our sports master instructed at primary school sprinting practice), and never—to date—having been brought to justice. Only time will tell if the crime of the 20th century can be prosecuted fifty years in retrospect . . . *but what a rush, "Biggsy."*

We had Renton and Warren (Humphries) arriving for the Cannes Open by stretch-limo, dressed as *The Blues Brothers,* as fans (extras from the crew) hustled for autographs . . . he (Renton) read Shakespeare (*As You Like It*) in the Forest of Arden prior to the English Open, and Topaz McGonagall (*who?*) in Carnoustie, before the Scottish . . . we linked from a Spanish galleon in Cadiz, and from the Bernabéu in Madrid with Seve, Cervantes and Columbus as catalysts.

One of our more expensive shoots ended with the camera sinking, irretrievably, to the bottom of a deep lake at Slayley Hall, County Durham (*oh dear*); the shot of *Excalibur*—the putter—rising from a mist-strewn pond (fishing rod and dry ice), didn't please our equipment suppliers (*Ping*) nearly as much as I thought it would (*no freebie blade*).

Ewen Murray and Andrew Castle were complicit, lending idiocy . . . . and, when the knives came out, encouragement.

Toasting the viewers, and the champion, with pints of the sponsor's drop, at the end of the *Murphy's* Irish Open, didn't go down too famously with *Ofcom*, but considering a 30" spot on some shows can cost up to a quarter of a million nicker, little wonder the brewers were delighted.

We'd had a long week.

We went to a French version of *Legoland* with Renton and his stalwart partner at the mic, Peter Oosterhuis, who remained game, if bemused, throughout. I sent him crawling on all-fours (he's nearly *deux metres*) along the model *Champs Elysée*, poking his head through the *Arc de Triomphe* to joust, verbally, with Renton from the portals of mini-*Notre Dame* with *La Tour Eiffel* in the background—famous landmarks for every tourist's album . . . with great golf nearby.

Le Nez (the tester-in-chief) at a perfumery in *Le Midi*, picked out fragrances to suit the reputations of the greats of French sport . . . . we were captivated by Dali's museum near Barça, and Goya's exhibition in Madrid; everything was designed to give 'travelling' Americans a jolt to . . . "*get packin', hon.*"

As tourist board money kept the Schofield empire's heart beating, we'd get good marks—at a stroke—for history, geography, maths and English, (and golf packages), such was the diversity of venue, language and culture, on a circuit fast becoming global.

One year, seven U.S. players entered the *Trophée Lancôme* at St. Nom La Bretèche—not far from Disneyland Paris—so I pinched my 3 year old son's porcelain statuettes of *Sneezy, Sleepy, Dopey, Doc, Happy, Bashful, Grumpy* and, via composite images of each, parodied the characters to suit . . . and would you believe it, *Happy* (Mark O'Meara) won the bugger.
Critchley—representing *B.SkyB*. and traditionalism—wasn't amused (not that it had anything to do with him . . . other than *his* employer—*our* principal paymaster—was gathering the tabs).

My indulgent nonsense had been noted: I was pilloried by the Sky chiefs, but then when you look at recent Ashes promos and the like, we weren't so stupid after all.
I think it's fair to say, we enjoyed coming to work.

Tangentially (the ethos of this entire thing), were I a petrol-head (and 40 years younger), I'd be applying for a job with *Top Gear*; no team of presenters were better cast in a classy, high octane production—attitude, egos and a *lorra* laughs . . . and how much fun must it be to work on *QI*?

If sport makes the newsreaders smile (and they always do—unless it's "Giggsy" or John Terry leading the way), it can't be that deadly serious.

The European Tour was integral to the start-up success of *The Golf Channel,* so that part of our responsibility had to have its own identity—ours to Sky, was never compromised.

From the Swiss Alps to the deserts of Dubai, via Loch Lomond and Royal Jersey, we had something other than baseball caps, flat white 'traps' and unnatural contouring to offer . . . nor were European golfers ever seen to spit *(poor show, Tiger)*.

Every programme—from 1992 to 1998—had a novel beginning and a complimentary end . . . and the bit in the middle (the golf) was spot-on too.

Then they fired me; there's absolute, corroborated evidence of who loaded the gun, and who pulled the trigger, so when I came down from the ceiling and saw the look on my pregnant wife's face, I sought my copy of Dumas' *Le Comte de Monte Cristo* . . . and made a plan.

Amidst the frivolity was an enlightened approach to covering tournament golf, be it on Tenerife's volcanic piste, or Wentworth's green and pleasant.
The knobs on were extra.
Our leader, Mr. McCormack—who knew a thing or two about golf <u>and</u> TV . . . and making a buck—was never disappointed and, understandably, would tout ours as the best coverage of the game in the World.
The only great sadness was that when we were in with a chance of the television production (E.T.P.) or commercial rights (TWI/IMG) for the Open, the pragmatic M.H.M. opted for the earner.
(as you read, big Mark is probably drafting a World rights deal for the *Elysian Masters* . . . assuming magnates go that way, and his God is a fan)

The mention of whom . . .
McCormack's greatest client, A.D. Palmer, and a US entrepreneur from Birmingham (Alabama), Joseph E. Gibbs, were the men behind *The Golf Channel*—a 24 hour-daily service that threatened to take US divorce and unemployment figures to unprecedented heights.
We—European Tour Productions—produced their first ever 'live' event from Dubai in 1995.
The re-designated *Golf Channel on NBC* is now a major player.

There's nothing to beat 'live' sport in my view, no matter how clever the packaging; with the voracity of internet services and digital channels, little escapes these days: avoiding the football results until *Match of the Day*, is impossible for all but *The Grinch*.

BBC television outside broadcasts group did unprecedented work, but their resources were stretched in so many directions, that something had to give. As a consequence of the 'Iron Lady' spending too much time on the range with 10-gallon Ronnie Regan, competition was deemed to be the method; the market was thrown wide open—even the independents were given cake. It wasn't *who* could be trusted, but who had *the dosh.*

Enter stage right (running), Mr. Murdoch, pockets bulging, to join Mr. Packer, closing his palms round the audience, centre stage.

Football went to the highest bidder, even cricket went a bit daft (not in the Stanford league) but it was altruistic extravagance. The Australians upped their game. Short-form cricket, with loud clothes, loud commentary, and louder music, shattered the village-green idyl; the cemeteries of Marylebone would soon reverberate to Jacko's THRILLER.

Presently, liveried hard-hats—in MCC 'egg and bacon'—will greet hesitant members at the Grace Gate.

"Whatever next, Charles . . . pink balls?"

"Oh, they wouldn't go that far, Sheridan!" (with thanks to *Harry & Paul*)

Yes they would/have.

Horror upon horror, Test Cricket had gone to Channel 4 . . . but they'd been cute: the No.9 shirt had Benaud's name on it . . . destiny beckoned for Hampshire's 'gorgeous' midfield general, M.C.J. Nicholas (at a price) . . . a couple of overlap-dancing full-backs were brought in in the window, in the contrasting (hair) styles of ubiquitous Dermot Reeve of Warwickshire and England (ODIs mostly), and Simon 'Yozzer' Hughes of Middlesex and Latymer Upper School, a.k.a. *The Analyst*—a balding, cricketing mercenary, soon to be an award-winning author, courtesy of *A Lot of Hard Yakka*—a funny, sexy read (try *Amazon* if *Waterstones* are out).

It wasn't that others didn't know how to cover cricket, that would be daft, but there was something about producer Gary Franses's package that stood out (if you're covering my point).

'Gary the Gooner,' and my night nurse, Dylan Jane (highlights producer, and supreme 'Hammer' optimist) went up, repeatedly, for industry awards: the Channel, Mums and Dads, Wenger and (Harry) Redknapp duly thanked, they'd return to 4's table to get stuck into any trampled grape left by Sheerlock, Keen, Normington, Scovell, Barber (now Darke), Waters, Reeks & co.

The Cricket Roadshow helped dispel the mystique and bunk that had weighed the game down for years; it was prescribed viewing, not perhaps for antideluvian club members with Long Room berths, but for true lovers and, progressively, for new kids in boxes.

Tradition was upheld and history revisited, with relish: Gary and Richie *loved* a bit of black and white—*Bodyline*, the Ashes of '53, Wes Hall and Charlie Griffith—innovation was positively encouraged . . . *whoopee, I'm in.*

Cricket is a fabulous game to play, and watch (unless you're a Yank); at Test level, it's fast and sublime, cunning and creative, technical and subtle, and positively dangerous at times. Those elements were exposed, exhaustively, by fine minds at *Sunset+Vine* and their state of the art kit. The commentary team gelled in aspic, and with copious helpings of the deified Barry Richards, ex-Kiwi gloveman, Ian David Stockley Smith, who'd re-trained on magnificently (he'd hung them up by 1998 when New Zealand became *The Black Caps*), and old stone-face Atherton (who's anything but), they had it cracked.

Throw in *Hawkeye* technology, see-through red zones, the snickometer (*not sure about that one*) super-duper slow-motion cameras, stump microphones and brilliant technicians, and there you had it—the epitome of the independent sports production.

Golf and cricket were done; whether football can look after itself, totally, without toppling over under the weight of expectation, debts, fees, drugs and egoes, is debatable, but there's no going back.

In the 70s, when footy equalled Brazil, ITV Sport spawned 'the panel.' Depending on the grandeur of the occasion, three or four sage counsellors would sit in judgement, at half and full time, prognosticating, analysing, infuriating. There weren't the myriad of toys available to Gray, the great enthusiast—who, as a player, boldly put his head where his mouth used to be on Sky—but it made for lively exchanges.

Forty years on, the format remains but the characters don't: 'Cloughie' and Jimmy Hill—together or alone—could take entire families to the brink of a group ASBO.

Malcolm Allison—a buddha in sharp whistles (and flutes = suits), very noisy shirts and huge, matching kipper ties—versus the cantankerous Irish wolf, Derek Dougan (Wolves and Northern Ireland), versus smiling, sinister, Paddy Crerand (Man. United and Scotland), versus 'double' Gunner, Bob McNab of England . . . potential for red cards everywhere.

Courteous Brian Moore, nervously discouraged peace.

Not a lot of people know that Ken Wolstenholme—D.F.C. and bar (against *"the Jerrmans"* of all people)—whose assumption that some of the 100,000 fans at Wembley on July 30th 1966 had already settled for a 3-2 win for the lions over the bears (just as 'the boy 10' was ramming in his undisputed 3rd past Germany's Tilkowski), was sat a few feet along the media gantry from BBC Radio's Brian "Binsy" Moore (soon to be the subject of a defection to west London) . . . well, *they do now.*

As it happens it was Alan Clark—not "Mooro"—who was on mic as Hurst buried any doubt the opposition had; 'Sniffer' Clarke—with an 'e'—(Leeds United) would play for England in Mexico four years later (. . . *which might just make another for quiz night*).

On TV, big Ken—bomber pilot and lifelong Bolton fan—brushed Arsenal's Walley Barnes (his co-commentator) aside; he would <u>not</u> be denied his bite of the century.
The hat-trick hero was (denied), however; as big Jack sank to his knees and Englishpersons everywhere went mad, Helmut Haller—scorer of West Germany's first—half-inched the orange leather.
According to some records, Hurst wasn't sure whether his third had gone in <u>before</u> the final whistle, so why would he bother to seek out the match ball?
Some years later it ended up in a museum in Preston, and I believe Sir Richard Branson now owns a piece of it . . . or the firm does.
The rest of England's class of 66 got winners medals—albeit 43 years after the fact—and it was good to see Manchester United helping out Nobby Stiles out in his time of need.

Could you imagine that happening again—not the World Cup for England, as such (. . . preserve us), but, in the unlikely event of that catastrophe, any of its winners needing a financial leg-up?

Maurice Edleston was the third member of radio's strike-force in '66.
I played alongside him in a charity match at Crystal Palace—the first time I'd been on the pitch with a proper pro. Eddleston was a GB veteran of the Berlin Olympics, and had played for England during the war years. The little man conducted us useless wannabes round the pitch with precision, and a knowledge of the principles of the old game we'd never really given much thought to.

At one terrifying stage he urged me into a 'hospital' ball with former Charlton Athletic enforcer, Derek Ufton—an England international (once . . . against the Rest of Europe, in 1953)—the effects of which I can still feel on a cold night.

'Uffers' was a good friend of both broadcast camps and drove our triangular golf tournament from his office at *The Sportsman* club and casino in Tottenham Court Road, London . . . . where we were also made most welcome to lose our ill-gottens.

Jimmy Hill poached Brian Moore from BBC Radio, just before the Mexico World Cup, and (typically) Barry Davies went the other way (ornery not gay).

While I'm on about hat-tricks, and keeping things, when the 1970 final was all over, Brazil—victors by 4-1 over Italy (the Germans were 3rd if anyone cares) got to keep the little 12" gold trophy.

It's about and joining the dots, but I believe a Gordie Howe hat-trick in ice-hockey—presumably after the player of the same name—is when a player scores a goal, gets an assist, <u>and</u> gets in a fight, in the same game,
The Old Firm records would surely support claims of this kind.

In '66, having negotiated the 39 steps, and, under other circumstances, irritating slaps on the back, 'captain correct,' Bobby Moore, spotted the whites gloves his Monarch was wearing (wonder if she kept them—*e-Bay, if tough times persist Ma'am . . . or Branson perhaps*), wiped his 'shaking' hand on the cloth covering the Royal Box ledge, and graciously accepted the Jules Rimet trophy.
The tenancy would be for three years, eleven months and a few days.

Go on *You Tube* and watch Nobby Stiles on his parade lap, skipping round Wembley like a 10 year old . . . you'll see Bobby Moore ruffle the wee man's hair then immediately wipe his hand on his shorts . . . *nits, perhaps, or germaphobia?*

As to the identity of the patriot with 'BBC for Sport' painted on the back of his shirt, I await your letters, but his was a priceless cutaway, albeit in black and white. (*Pathe* did the final in colour . . . *and no, the whole ball <u>wasn't</u> over the line!*).

The other 'cup'—the FIFA trophy—which I think should have been named after the world's best player (Pelé), looks dumpy (Maradona) against the svelte (Cruyff) original, but (should we ever wake from our reverie), we Jocks would accept it, gladly.

Were the yellow shirts (or Argentina) to snatch it back in Rio, the Federation will need another creation for 2018; not certain *unified* Germany qualify, but again, don't be shy to write in (somewhere else).

For most of my spell at the BBC, my running mate was the thoroughly excellent, Christopher John Rowlinson—a Shrewsbury School-boy and graduate from one of the Light Blue colleges *"reading history."*
Served him well, when, in collaboration with John Walker Motson of Culford School, Suffolk (*"memorising Rothman's"*), they put together the magnificent *History of the European Cup*, in hardback.
You needed to know the two to fully appreciate the quality of this near biblical work . . . the perspicacity . . . the passion . . . the price (mine was gratis).

'Rowley'—a.k.a. 'Arthur' as he became known to us . . . Arthur Rowley, player manager at Shrewsbury Town . . . 'Rowley' therefore 'Arthur' . . . *aw, forget it*)—was a helluva winger until his left knee stopped bending properly. And while I empathised with his hopeless designs on Olivia Newton-John, his delusion over Crewe Alexandra F.C.'s potential was untreatable.

Post an unsavory end to his BBC life and times, John sat comfortably enough, for a while, on the front bench at the All England Lawn Tennis and Croquet Club, near Wimbledon village in south-west London (meaning he was good for a tap in the rainy season).

He's now consorting, and hoping to deliver, with Lord Coe, so I've put in an early request for 'a pair of briefs' for the 100m final, the 4x1, the men's 10K, all evening sessions at the pool, velodrome and head-bash, and a front seat season (single) at the beach volleyball*.

Nothing, so far.

(*I'm imagining a small raiding party, heavily disguised, leaving Buck House, making its way, stealthily, through St. James's Park for Horse Guards, pausing along the way so its leader can catch his breath).

The Johns were suckers for the archive-based feature, histories of this and that, and they'd come roaring into their own—and programme editors' offices—when it was FIFA World Cup time.

It'll be lost in translation, but picture Bremner or Culshaw (Lynam even) in a sheepskin coat, in the pissing snow, shoulders hunched, eyes boring into the lens, stick-microphone with BBC Sport cube, in hand . . .

. . . but more than that, think *voice*—Motty's voice:

"He hid the World Cup . . . under his bed!"

Quoting a Motson original, without legal representation, is risky, but he was referring to David Corbett, whose dog *Pickles,* just months before the '66 final, had discovered the missing trophy under a hedge, and, for safe keeping, (Corbett) hid the priceless pot—correct—"under his bed."

The incident (and voice-over) became integral to all World Cup preview shows.

Wolstenholme begat Coleman begat Motson, though the new order of succession is unclear. Under the (refuted) ageist policy at the BBC, "Mots"—via the commentators' Hall of Fame—will soon be sliding towards the knacker's yard . . . but then who'll do *Young Managers III* with me?

When football was for fans who could stand up for a couple of hours, take a punch, and sing club anthems in attainable keys, half-time meant a cup of something hot, a pee—if you could get through—a read of the programme notes, and an analysis of the first 45 with anyone who'd join in without resorting to A.B.H; the outcome of lively forums in 'The Jungle' at Parkhead, or amongst 'Sheddites' at the Bridge, often involved stitches—straying into either pit, by mistake, *was* one.

Everyone is a football expert, from the fathers of the Under 11s Youth League of a Sunday morning in the park, to the beautiful team of the 70s—Garden, Brooke-Taylor and Oddie, a.k.a. 'The Goodies.'

In one episode, called *Football Crazy,* they concluded (following in-depth analysis) that football violence was caused by players' shorts being too short.

Solution: one fan per match with dozens of police on crowd control.

It didn't work, so football was cancelled altogether.

To vent their frustrations, violent fans turned on ballet—some backing primas in pointes, others, super-enhanced men-in-tights . . . and football socks; for credibility, Ken Wolstenholme was invited to commentate.

The beauty of the occasional shower in England is that it affords cricket experts acres of space in which to pad about. Endangered species like Arlott—deceased sadly . . . a full-bodied claret man, and Benaud—alive and well, at homes in Australia and the South of France, and sustained by foie gras (*never put anything in your mouth you can't get past your nose*), and brutally chilled Sauternes, were breast-fed on *Wisden.*

We were astounded by Mike Tyson's knowledge in our filmed chats with Harry Carpenter: he'd be aware the second Jack Johnson's left-right-left combinations were due . . . of who'd been responsible for Carmen Basilio's on-going facial disfigurement . . . and of the battles and perils that would bedevil and account for Benny Lynch in the end.

Tyson knows his stuff . . . *the voice though . . . be fair Mike, isn't great.*

(This is unrelated) but of course there were gays in boxing . . . why wouldn't there be, but you needed to tread carefully.

After he'd stopped bowling people over in the 60s (Minter beat him once), the legendary Emile Griffiths wrote openly about his sexuality:

'I keep thinking how strange it is . . . *I kill a man* (Benny Paret died after their fight in 1963) *and most people understand and forgive me. However, I love a man, and to so many people this is an unforgivable sin; this makes me an evil person.'*

Like the man said—in the film and play of the same expression—*'they shoot horses don't they'* when they break a leg; so what happens when an active sporting life comes to an end—the playing thereof—apart from *Strictly Come Dancing* and *Celebrity Chef?*

Of course the cosiest option is the media. There are cupboards full of willing 'ghosts' to help pros with the prose—the life story they might never make entertaining, alone, and radio and television's appetite for 'names' is as insatiable as Lloyd's.

Coaching becomes a less, well remunerated option; touch-line close-ups on TV are rare, and marginalized by a dominant boss aware that the big spending boys of today can dedicate a camera to them for the entire game . . . plus pay them shed-loads for a platitude or two in the breaks.

Way back, before the digital revolution, when George Best was using the liver he started with, we devoted a camera to his genius.
As they say in the north: *Maradona* good . . . *Pelé* better . . . *George best*.
Not that day, he wasn't—must have got up on the wrong side of someone else's bed, cos he hardly got a kick (not even a Best-to-Best moment to savour).

And then there's (Sir) David Beckham—the ultimate fusion of world and oyster—top bloke, fit face, ugly tats.
If Sid Waddell can make a career in broadcasting, then 'Becks'—should he feel the need—is nailed on . . . Sky being the only one with sufficient funding.
E.A. do Nascimento ticked ambassadorial boxes for both 'beautiful' games—football and (safe) sex . . . a sanitised Maradona would have been sanctified, but he messed up . . . loquacious Cruyff keeps talking his own brand of sense to anyone who asks . . .
I.T. Botham probably watches more cricket now than he ever played (the pay's better and his golf handicap has tumbled . . . and still he finds time to walk for leukemia).
The Atherton-Hussain axis has added hugely to my understanding of the game, even if they refer to the pitch as the wicket now and again.

Crippling arthritis, brought on by expediency to keep the best team playing, takes its toll on many darting soccer stars, but age is of no immediate concern to the golfer. Do-it-yourself plastic hips are available over the counter on the seniors' tour, where the newly turned 50-somethings have a year or two to blow lingering pensioners off the gravy train; the (Robert) Maxwell factor doesn't apply . . . in the main, they're minted.

Mentalist Harvey Penick—the "15th club" in Ben Crenshaw's bag when he won the Masters in 1995—wrote his philosophies in little diaries, full of gems, whilst fellow guru, long, tall Leadbetter, charges about ten grand a day . . . despite not making it as a player.

What Braid, McKenzie, Colt, and Tyre Jones started, the Trent-Jones family built into a course designing dynasty. The less prolific and, I suspect, more argumentative pairing of Peter Alliss and Dave Thomas, gave us—amongst others—The Belfry, most famously.
Arnold Palmer, designed the K Club, near Dublin and Jack Nicklaus did the Monarchs at Gleneagles . . . for when Scotland takes its biggest commercial break (*never took to* the Polaris World *ad, Jack*).

The game's all over the place nowadays: appearing like postage stamps from the air, the made-man oases in Palm Springs and Dubai prove the will, and the way, and if you can stand the mosquitoe—a distant and much dirtier player than the Loch Lomond midgie—you can play a form of the game on the edge of the Arctic circle . . . after midnight; we were the dummies who tested it, when *Volvo*—perennial backers of the European Tour—generously invited a party of media folk to Lapland.

Journalists have the reputation of being good in and around alcohol, and were confirmation needed, that charter flight would provide it.
Spilling from our private jet, we were helped into a coach and driven up Longtitude something or other, towards the top of the world.

Fighting booze-induced comas, most were barely awake when the bus pulled up at the side of a lake; *'pee' break, we thought—we prayed*—but the urge was placed on hold, as there before us, resplendent in what we assumed were his picture-postcard day-clothes, fully-antlered stag by his side, was the local Chieftain . . . the Boris Johnson of the area.

The (pre-ordained) ruse was this: one of our number (nominated by the Deer Handler) would be 'thrown' into the icy waters of the lake, like a sacrificial beast, in a rid-you-of-ever-shanking-again ritual.

The *less* inebriated saw through it immediately . . . the *more so*, might have welcomed the shock.

An oily substance, in a solid stick, extracted (or excreted) from an unspecified part of the reindeer's anatomy, was administered to each forehead and nose (those with broken vein-patterning were attached to the heavier drinkers).
Through an interpreter, 'Lars the Lap' explained immunity from the 'mozzy' bite was now guaranteed.

There are more than the obvious perils to playing golf in a land of perpetual daylight.
Two other drunks and I were slotted in, in front of Mickey Britten (think that's how you spelt it) and his three-ball. Mickey was a small man, with I suspect, most of their hang-ups, and being a *hack, hacker, hackest*, his approach, and writing style, were confrontational.
I didn't take to him one little bit.
He looked as though he was up for a fight, but Dad always advised against bullying, and cocky-fuckers.

As I prepared to launch one into the western sun, my thoughts turned country, to Bowling and Wheeler's *Coward of the County* . . . . well, to Kenny Rogers' version with my spin, anyway:

Promise me, son, not to do the things I've done (get pissed now and again?)
Walk away from trouble if you can (watch me, Pops)
It won't mean you're weak if you turn the other cheek (hmmm . . .)
I hope you're old enough to understand, (43, yeah, I think so)
Son, you don't have to fight to be a man (or a better golfer than Britten)

Better that Team Philips beat Team Britten over 18 holes; any blood-letting would only have alerted more airborne fans. The course had lots of mosquitoes, and undulations, but in general you could see everything before you, even if the light meters suggested play be abandoned.

We were about to putt on the long par 3—uphill (3 iron for me); into a zephyr, it was at least a driver (and a prayer) for little Britten.
Well, he caught the driver (and the top man) on a good day, because in around shin-level came a balata, with serious revs on.
It wasn't the first time we'd been violated, but being gentle country folk, we'd ignored previous etiquette breaches, putting it down to the fading light and bad manners, rather than mischief and luck.

Not this time . . . enough was enough.
I knew who it was, if not from the distance achieved, then from the attitude and absence of the customary audible alert.
Whether the word has anything to do with the 'fore' caddy of old, or infantrymen advising (from the rank behind) that their mates (in front) should duck, thereby avoiding close-range, co-lateral damage . . . a simple rendition would have sufficed.

Fortunately for Mickey, I caught my return 3 iron, even better than the first, three-point stager that lay at my feet.
His errant missile flew back (with interest) to its launch-pad, whistling over his unpleasant head and thudding into the gorse behind the tee.

I left Lapland with all 'O' group pints intact.

A couple of days after breaking up for our school summer holidays I'd gone to play a few holes with my elder brother, while our parents packed for the annual trip to Aberdeen.

The old 16th at Crieff golf club (now the 8th—*if you get the chance*) was a reachable par 4, and in his attempt so to do, David—'the willy crusher'—had come off his driver, big time, sending strike 1 into the copse to our right.
I stifled a snigger.
"Hold on . . . . I got the line . . . I'll get it."
A charitable, brotherly act . . . so he reciprocated.
Imploring me to wait awhile, he re-loaded using an undisturbed peg.
By now, I was between a rock and a hard place; I'd strayed beyond the tee, no question, yet (notwithstanding that first wild effort) I felt I was out of the firing line; this wasn't Spiro Agnew . . . *this was my brother—off 8.*

As I dropped to the ground, clutching what I thought was my empty, left eye-socket, the green-keeper approached on his tractor. Several stitches and two clips later, my flapping cheek had been skillfully closed up; the eye, I thought Siamese-twinned to Davie's provisional 65, was back in place—not that I could see out of it for bandages.
Though postponed, Aberdeen (butteries and cones) was still a possibility.

One of my school pals was less fortunate; he'd taken refuge from his mother's tee-shot, behind a huge oak tree (on the 5th of the Ferntower course—now the 7th on the wee course—*if you get a second chance*).
It was a bit like doing your passport photo in a booth at *Woolies* (deceased): the money's in, you're ready, but the machine appears not so to be, so you do a *Rab C. Nesbitt* and . . . *FLASH!*
In my mate's case, the 'flash' was his Mum's ball—his eye was out!

We'd come across the Australian hard man, Jack Newton, several times in his heyday, most notably in 1975 when he lost to Tom Watson in a play-off for the Carnoustie Open. Newt's subsequent brush with the propeller of a *Cessna*, cost him his right arm, eye, and the use of some other organs, but like my glass-eyed schoolmate, Richard Philp, he played on.

Take time out between chapters and/or coitus (or whichever way your predilection takes you) to check out the CV of Doctor Haruhisa Handa, the only man (other than Greg Norman) to have been made an international ambassador of Golf Australia. Amongst a raft of degrees and appointments, the good doctor was instrumental in the formation and funding of the International Blind Golf Association.

If they could package that stuff we got from 'the Lap of the Lake,' and send it south-west to Caledonia, there'd be a surge in visitors' green fees . . . not to mention the eradication of one of nature's less welcome creations: on a one-to-one basis they're manageable, but, like pirranah and shark, midgies—mob-handed—are a right pain.

And, making good use of sharks, Australians, sponsored charter flights and golfing wildernesses, let me tell you of a visit we media types made to an embryonic Norman design on mainland China, during another trip to Singapore.

The craft used for the journey in no way resembled the custom-built G. Norman Inc., airliner that would be added to his collection of personal transporters in later years, yet, to see the grand designer, threading his way along the aisle of an ageing jet, dispensing champagne to we non-paying customers, was like officers' day in the sergeants' mess.

Some notables have been accused of merely adding their names to projects they've probably never visited, far less drawn plans for, but *'The Shark'* was hugely visible, trudging through the broken earth in his *Timberlands* . . . maps and mini-bin(ocular) s in hand.
An entourage of consultants and engineers of various national persuasions were rather more keen to rub shoulders with the great man, than heed his urgings for greater speed in realising bunkers and water hazards. Subtle changes to the topography of greens, barely discernable, in the rubble and dust, to the untrained eye, were dutifully noted by draftsmen and surveyors.

Greg spent hours there, on design and diplomacy, and later that night, having scrubbed up to a fine polish, was guest of honour at a dinner in Singapore; he was becoming an accomplished ambassador.

Posh's old man has taken on Pelé's mantle for football, globally, and like it or not, Jonny Wilkinson had to for rugby in the UK after the World Cup . . . and that perfectly struck drop-goal; if they haven't already, Murray (*'after winning Wimbledon, sometime soon, Andy, eh*'), massive Hoy and tiny Trott, Jenson & Lewis, Daley the diver, Adlington the swimmer, Jenkins H., and the Brownlee brothers, not forgetting magic Mo Farah, shall have it thrust upon them, respectively, for a time in the future . . . medals on ribbons to follow no doubt.

Geoff Duke, John Surtees, Mike 'the bike' Hailwood and Phil Read carried the banner for British motor cycling throughout the 50s, 60s and 70s—as did Carl Fogarty in the 90s and Joey Dunlop, continually, on the Isle of Man—but the shattered embodiment of the daredevil, two-wheeled flyer was Barry Sheene, a real diamond geezer on wheels, and a familiar face at ERs round the world.

Whether he was taking time out to give arch-rival Kenny Roberts 'the V' sign as they blasted out of Copse Corner at Silverstone in 1979 (a race Roberts won by 3 one hundredths of a second), or mischievously setting off airport security alarm systems with his re-enforced skeleton, 'Bazza' was an icon . . . a media Godsend (very much in Clough's league . . . brazen as Boycott . . . horny as Hunt).

He literally broke scores of bones: at one time there were metal plates in his knees, dozens of screws in his legs, and a bolt in his left wrist.

Like the good Cockney boy he was—fag in the mouth—he'd tell it straight, in his own unaffected way; he'd race till his Suzuki begged for mercy, or his rivals sat up from his slipstream and conceded to No. 7, be it on a 500c.c. Yamaha or, more successfully, a red and black Suzuki.
Were he into early Grecian mathematics, he'd have known the component parts of 7 (4+3), and their sum total, were considered lucky.

Sure, he fell off, that's what bike racers—even the great ones—do, but the Sheene crashes were epics, most notably on the slopes of the Daytona speedway and on Farm Straight at Silverstone during practice sessions.

Having cheated the Grim Reaper for the umpteenth time, we made our way out to Norfolk, where we'd arranged to do a 'will he/won't he retire' piece for *Sportsnight* . . . could have saved ourselves the trip, but none of the fun, by phoning the question in.
He wouldn't retire, not while the bike had more metal in it than he had.

I had offended coach Coe by asking his 'out of season' "athlete" to *"Run Like the Wind"* (our backing track—by Mike Batt of *The Wombles* and *Bright Eyes* fame), but Sheene wasn't answerable to no organ grinder: he'd do our film, but we'd have to go with *his* flow.

"Life in the Fast Lane" by the Eagles, requisitioned from our 'gram' library (*gramophones, remember them . . . they're on the way back . . .* Eagles *too*), was looking to be wholly inappropriate—Barry could hardly walk.

As if bench-testing *Twister*, he manipulated his re-enforced limbs into the front seat of our car and pointed us towards a business deal in Norwich.

We'd reached the city limits when I was instructed to turn into the forecourt of a garage, its showroom gleaming with pristine road bikes.

Having exchanged courtesies with his salesman pal, Barry emerged, gingerly, astride a great big, beast of a thing—a state he often found himself in . . . according to corroborated information.

We occasional subscribers to *Penthouse*, knew (quite well) of the future Mrs. Sheene (36-24-35).
By 1976 Barry was World champ for the first time, and, understandably, happy with Stephanie McLean.
Life in the Fast Lane came out the following year.

They had one thing in common, they were good in bed
She'd say, "Faster, faster . . . the lights are turnin' red."
Life in the fast lane
Surely make you lose your mind, mm

Helmet-less, he nodded on being cautioned to take care of himself and, from his mate's career point of view, the brand new 500.
Barry wasn't buying either.
For all the world, he looked like a rank beginner learning the basics of balance and throttle control as he poodled off into the road . . . and out of our sight.
I'd asked the cameraman to keep 'turning over' throughout; you had to have the instincts of a fly when the Freddie Starr of motorcycling was about . . . not that he was a clown (nor a fantastic Elvis impersonator), but he did have his moments.

I nearly dropped the clapperboard into the rep's gaping mouth when Barry re-appeared, camera right, with enough revs on to lift the front end of his bucking machine clear of the tarmac, as it roared back across the forecourt and off down the street . . . the pilot maintaining the mother and father of all wheelies (reminiscent of his start at the 1979 British Grand Prix) . . . his doctor's note fluttering away on the tow.

Cue the music.

The Roberts/Sheene battles brought tens of thousands into Silverstone, as Nigel Mansell did, Damon Hill would, and Jenson and Lewis shall, you'd expect, for the foreseeable.
Sheene was good . . . you didn't become back-to-back World Champion by being 'gangsta' altogether.

Steve Parrish—biker, lorry driver, pilot and author (and seriously clued foil for the excellent Charlie Fox on BBC *Moto GP* commentary) was Barry's pal and *Suzuki* teammate in the 70s. Barry had been best man at the Parrish wedding, but many playboy instincts remained.

As discussed, we'd pre-rigged Sheene's flying machine (chopper) to do some filming over Silverstone, but in the rush—possibly to A&E, or a chemist for fentanyl—he'd forgotten our appointment.
Unceremoniously, he and Steve chucked us, our gear and our exclusive, out onto the infield as they made off on a pressing mission.

We'd crossed over early to the Northamptonshire speedway, to cover the big boys—the five hundreds—on *Grandstand*.

Kenny Roberts was having all sorts of mechanical trouble with his yellow *Yamaha*, but knowing a good thing when they saw one, the organisers were giving his mechanics an inordinate amount of time to put things right.

Sheene v. Roberts, be it a sideshow or the main event, was a foregone attraction worth making every exceptions for . . . but *catch this for embarrassing* . . .

Just as the grid re-formed after the warm-up lap, with tension reaching deep into Murray's pants, he announced, in his inimitable, over-stated sort of way, that it was *'time to leave Silverstone, and hand you back to the Grandstand studio.'*
(shades of Gooch at Lord's).

Not Murray's fault, but the gaff detectives made a career out of 'Walkerisms.' The bloke was thoroughness personified, but fast-moving things have a habit of making a dick of you . . . *re*-action is a doddle.

Hypothetically, had Britney Spears's limo run out of petrol on the way to Nice airport, with just 20 minutes before the flight home, *she* wouldn't be offering to trudge—can in hand—to the nearest gas station.
In our *actual* instance, Murray was that man . . . . a gesture Hunt and I applauded, roundly, as we guarded the hire-car.

Hands up—my fault entirely, but on another frenetic, airport run I'd inadvertently gone for the unleaded pump to top-up our diesel *Hertz* rental—normally a terminal act that would draw the sharp intake of breath from the garage mechanic and a least an overnight for the car.
Don't know how much made the tank, but James managed to limit the damage by banging on the window, miming . . . 'fucking tosser,' I think.

I dropped a five franc note on the pump as Murray and James did a *Le Mans* style changeover up front. I'd barely made the dunce's chair in the back when the tyres squealed into life under the Shunt's accomplished right foot, and off we careered, slaloming down the motorway towards the airport—the theory being, that by sluicing what little *essence* had made it into the tank with the remnants of the *gazole*, neither spark plugs nor engine would be any the wiser, and progress could still be made.

With a few blue farts, and swearing consistently, we made it to the periphery of the 'Rental Returns' multi-storey, and hoofed it to check-in, without signing any kind of affidavit.

We (the BBC) could never afford to employ Jackie Stewart as co-commentator on a regular basis . . . but the Yanks could.
It might have been the Indianapolis 500—it was certainly a 'one bender'—so we'll let *them* pay the Flying Scot . . . and *we'll* buy the race in, minus VAT.

This grown-up version of *Scalextric* came with a health warning . . .
IT COULD DEFINITELY KILL YOU . . . . driving, watching or working the pits.
Jackie alleged, in commentary, that he'd seen one of the wheel-nuts loosening on a lead car on a previous lap.
The man we couldn't afford to hire for such 'instincts' alone, then predicted, in that two-stroke, Scottish whine of his:
"I think a terrible accident is about to happen . . ." (. . . lo and behold)
The perils of post-produced commentary.

<u>Sir</u> Jackie (*excuse me*) is no stranger at court, in the houses of Windsor, Grimaldi and Ecclestone. Murray probably mentioned it in his autobiography, but of the men he admired most in Formula 1, Fangio probably got the nod as <u>the</u> driver, but John Young Stewart was held in highest esteem for his skill and enterprise.
Both their Dads had been into bikes: Stewart snr., was a flat-out racer and Murray's old man Graham, a regular on the Isle of Man had several high places (1 win) in the TTs to show for his courage.

Hosing it round the island against the clock, between—and sometimes into—buildings and trees, getting airborne at 130mph (without a working speed camera in sight for ten days), wasn't for Barry Sheene.
(*blimey, if <u>he</u> felt it was unsafe . . . .*)
The figures don't lie, sadly, but that said, it's a helluva spectacle . . . in hi-motion or in the flesh . . . and no-one <u>has</u> to do it.

I guess cos he and his Dad had done a bit in the past, Murray came over a bit unnecessary when he and I went to shoot a 'sensible' trials event for *Grandstand* somewhere in Wales. Though the machines and liveries had changed a bit, the principles and rules were basically the same . . . balance, throttle and machine control *and* . . . "*no putting your foot down or you lose a point"* i.e. dabbing or prodding with one's foot (nothing to do with speeding). A five pointer was considered a "fiasco" though I'd put it at a "pity" rather than "a humiliating disaster."

The extreme end of the sport, as exercised by the freestyle 'bampots' of today with their somersaults and twists off ramps, sides of buildings, edges of cliffs, their ludicrous insurance premiums, their babes and 'biker-speak,' is on the wild side of sanity, but balls of steel are required.

The odds against Jackie Stewart may not have reached the same levels as those stacked against the equally bashful, camera shy, *Virgin* boss, in his bid to save *Concorde*, but the little man with the squinty eyes from Dumbarton, was not about to rest the Stewart family name on his numerous laurels as a driver. He campaigned for, and won, on many safety aspects of the sport . . . he formed his own racing team with his son, Paul, and took it all the way to the premier league . . . all the while pushing me to buy clay-pigeon shooting for *Grandstand* (at 'knock-down' prices, Royals included) . . . at which he was also a bloody expert—*tedious isn't it?*

When Mr. Stewart spoke—quite often in the first person singular—Formula 1 listened, even Bernie, who is fractionally smaller (if richer, by quite a few flying laps).

As photo opportunities go, big sporting occasions are made for Royalty. The Queen's Dad opened the London Olympics in 1948 . . . the lady herself, as you know, handed over the Jules Rimet to Bobby Moore from the very same spot . . . her daughter jumped Captain Becher's brook for *Grand National Grandstand* (rather well, if one remembers) and her Granny was regularly at the races.
And then there's 'amazing' Zara . . . (*"give it a rest will you, or I'll send my old man round"*).

All of us staff 'lackies' got involved in the manual vote-counting for our Sports Personality award in 1971 (the year Steph McLean was *Penthouse* Pet of the Year); they'd been for a drive on the Moon by then, but the little *Radio Times* coupon was still the only way to go.

Doublet's royal jockey—a couple of years off becoming Mrs. Mark Phillips—was in the hunt, early doors (the Zara making process, a further decade away), but the veil of secrecy had to be of sackcloth . . . no one must know; this was hush at 'Harry in Afghanistan' or 'Kate's dress' level.

Alas, as in things where trust is a must, someone's hoof ends up in the gob, followed, smartly, by another's boot up that very same contortionist's arse.
He who'd knowingly leaked the result—prior to assuming the leap-frog position in order that the Head of Sport could plant one, dead centre on his quivering rectum—was the BBC Information Officer, Alan Kingston.
(*nice enough bloke*)

We were accused of flushing 'non-royal' votes down the toilets at 'Kensington House' (the compounding name of our offices in opulent Shepherd's Bush), but they were all Republican lies, I tell you.

Mum (or Ma'am), closing in on two decades of reigning over us, had just received news of a staggering five hundred and five grand hike to her wage packet (to £980,000p.a.) . . . . girls in hot pants had been let in to the Royal Enclosure at Ascot . . . and Celtic and Arsenal had won their respective doubles.
All was hunky-dory in Britannia.

Princess Anne won without reference to the Serious Fraud Squad, and got her hands on a trophy she'd once presented to Henry Cooper (whom she succeeded) . . . just as her brother had to Steve Ovett in 1978.

Her 'amazing' daughter won in 2006.

Ray Winstone will give you the odds on Princess Kate doing the honours . . . . at some stage . . . "*NOW!*" (Olympic year, perhaps*)*

(*"I'm thinking Nigel Clough and Brendan Rodgers for our re-make, Motty."*)

And so ends this particular circumnavigation.

"Arnold and I are Playing with Jack..."

When I first confronted the Great White Shark, he was just plain Gregory John Norman . . . well, not plain exactly, he was developing all kinds of skills, not many of them social.

Lurking in the shallows were the Marshall brothers, unmistakably, twins: film producer John, the uglier, was behind *The Greatest*—an early, feature-length account of the life and times of . . . *The Greatest*—entrepreneur James, in yellow socks and shiny brown loafers—patently county—was into patenting . . . anything.

I came across the affable brothers at James's lavish (rented), baronial hall out in Gloucestershire's sticks; we'd gone there to profile the rising young star from Australia—blond, unquestionably, and showing predatory signs, but some way off being great. Greg did the golfing, James did the deals. They had big plans . . . and *Ferraris*: one penal extension for the boy racer, who probably didn't need extending—at his age, the other should have known better.

Chez Marshall, there were non-tax deductible peacocks, a moat and servants. The early morning mists lingered over the big ditch as our car wheels crunched across the drive; the noisy cocks were noted by Fred, the soundman.

Lingering behind the liveried footman, his eye on our heavy gear, stood the elegant Lois, Mrs. Jas. Marshall—Bette Davis and Lauren Bacall in one—cool and prepossessing.

'I always keep a drink handy, in case I see a snake . . . which I also keep handy.' (W.C. 'Bill' Fields); Mrs. M. was never far from her sleek, black cigarette holder, clenched between sexy teeth, à la Terry Thomas.

She ushered us into a vast dining room. At the press of a secret button, freshly ground coffee was at hand. To the side, in a rank of spherical silver basins, a be-deviled feast of eggs (various), bacon, kidneys, mushrooms, tomatoes, sausages, smoked salmon, toasts and breads. James, resplendent in blue toweling, sat at the far end of the table. We'd only ever spoken on the phone, but rather than offer a hand, he revealed a far from arousing calf and upper thigh for our appreciation . . . . daft as dressage he was.

The unmistakable slap of flip-flops, on finely buffed oak, betrayed oncoming guests. Two identically clad figures, in white toweling, wandered in, giggling the kind of giggle that would suggest something of an intimate nature had recently occurred in the garret of the west wing. All but in the golfer's arms, was a very 'beautiful' looking person (apposite use of the adjective—an albatross pales when you've seen Mike Samuelson's daughter. *Emma Samms*—the name she took, most famously, on the *Dynasty* set). She shouldn't be singled out, but she would not be a future Mrs. Norman, but an enduring beauty, unequivocally.

When the opportunity arose Greg and James and I golfed at the Northants Club in Fleet (where Justin Rose is a venerable member).
One Sunday—on the par 4, dog-leg-left 2nd—my very best skipped past the Shark's by several yards (*talk about swollen penal extensions*).
No glint of recognition, no exchange of words.
As the deal-maker prepared to baby one down the right, I looked across: Norman had three fingers flush to his cheek, which slowly animated to the middle one—*his had been a 3 wood*.
One thing he never did, at work, was short change anyone . . . . but the boys didn't need to know.

Inevitably, separate ways beckoned; manager and client fell out, big time (where the latter remains to this day), and James and I lost touch.

Now, kop this for an opportunity missed.

1986 was incredible for *The Shark*: he came second in 3 out of the four majors, winning the Open by five shots at Turnberry—on even par . . . as the Championship Committee ordained.
No question, he was the *BBC Overseas Sports Personality* of that year, and yours truly—the self-styled 'Florida correspondent'—was off again with the factor 20 and a replica trophy.

It gets pretty steamy down these parts in summer, even for the gators, so having a family home there in winter is ideal . . . assuming there are plenty beans in the tin.

A.D. Palmer sat in *his* office, overlooking *his* Bay Hill Golf and Country club, barely visible behind a mountain of *his* golf gloves (with the little umbrella brand), which he was signing, in permanent marker, for *his* 'Army' members, scattered round *his* globe.

Greg lived seconds away (by *Ferrari*).

Maybe, at 23, I was getting on to be autograph hunting, but I did get Colin Meads—New Zealand's secret weapon of mass destruction—to sign my programme (*the bone-crushing handshake, I could have passed on*) before the Scotland game at Murrayfield in 1967
The Blacks' No.5 weighed in at around 16 stone—light by modern standards for a lock—but he wasn't 'Pinetree' for nuttin' . . . to be avoided, ball in hand, in a short charge for the line.
Le massif central was sent off for damaging at least one of our boys.

With knowledge aforethought of A.D.P.'s vice-like grip—from an earlier introduction by Peter Alliss in the bar of Gleneagles Hotel—I took the initiative, thrusting my hand deep into the power booster. In the belief that I could reduce its potency, I'd overlapped his wrist with my fingers 1 and 2, and, as prescribed, the '*V*' was pointing over my right shoulder. We inter-locked hands and eyes, as golfers do, whatever the differential.

'*As much by skill, as strength*' . . . is the English version of Troon Golf Club's Latin motto; Arnie's win there in 1962, would do as my ice-breaker . . . while he signed on, and on, *and on*.
The commander had used prodigious strength (and not a little skill) in retaining the Claret Jug he'd won at Birkdale, tugging battalions of Scottish recruits around with him.
Incidentally, the future design partners of Alliss and Thomas were joint 8th in '62; Dave had come 2nd in 1958 behind Peter Thomson, and did it again eight years later, behind Jack, at Muirfield (*his* 1st of 3); in 1959, Gary Player won *his* first Open (of 3) at the Honourable Company of Edinburgh Golfers' place, at Gullane, in East Lothian and of course Sir Nick bagged a brace there too . . . and we all know what he did to Greg at Augusta (*on, and on, and on, the connections go*).

I'd walked the fairways during filming of a very early episode of *The Big Three* viz., Palmer/Player/Nicklaus (lest you're heading down *Nessun Dorma* way). The immediate impression on the ground was of power . . . like nothing I'd seen or heard, before. These were persimmon days, but even then, the compression was awesome. Gary launched (no other word for it) some kind of mid-iron shot into the stratosphere, albeit from an uphill, dune-side lie: it disappeared (back then, I could see really well).

Quantum leaping to the mid-80s, the forces applied to Tiger Woods's bullet, perched, unsuspectingly, atop a high tee on the 3rd hole of the Blue Canyon course in Thailand, defied description.

The huge gallery, gasped as one. A sand wedge was applied, deftly, for the remaining yards and the inevitable birdie opportunity was duly converted: easy game.

In February 2008, Tiger—still a boy in the life-span of the successful professional golfer—went past Arnie's record number of wins on tour; some folk transcend the bare facts—there are two.

Throughout his playing career, 'The King' always knew where the cameras were—which to best catch the extravagance of the follow-through, or the intimidating trouser-hitch . . . where best to grimace for maximum effect, and personality points.

Arnie and Greg agreed to do a synchronized 'lash' for us, off the first tee at Bay Hill. Greg would appear to thin his . . . smash the camera lens and then, with a promise to honour the repair bill, accept the BBC's Overseas award (*audacious, hilarious* . . .); they were media savvy so the whole thing took just a few minutes.

"Arnold and I are playing with Jack this afternoon . . . do you want to make up the four?"

(A-GAIN?!)

I went through the whole performance . . . the double take, gawping eyes out like organ-stops, pointing to one's own chest . . . full-on incredulity syndrome, with a final, mimed:

"Me?"
(not even Archer could make this one up).

Let me just make you absolutely clear about what <u>exactly</u> had been said:

"Arnold (PALMER) *and I* (GREG NORMAN) *are playing with Jack* (NICKLAUS) *this afternoon . . . do you* (Philips) *want to make up a four?*

This was that 'final question . . . final answer' moment, the cacophony of thoughts on leaving the pillion at speed with only trees ahead and no lid on: . . . *could my flight be changed—no, shit, the rushes <u>had</u> to get back to London . . . what about the filming we'd still to do at Greg's house and around Bay Hill . . . and be honest, could I face it with no change of trousers?*
Jesus (CHRIST) . . . . *wouldn't you want to die already?*

"Fore, please—John Philips now driving."

The year the Alan Bond syndicate won the America's Cup with *Australia II*, I was back in economy again, hand-carrying a BBC trophy charged with fixing up a 'live' two-way segment into the show.

These annual expeditions were fraught with complications—technical mostly, but the humans could be a pain in the ass too.

Australia II had been shrouded in mystery during its racing life, its revolutionary 'winged' keel kept under wraps any time the hull was out of the water . . . . but how to you lose a 75ft boat?

'Look, someone must know where you left it!'

Someone remembered.
We dragged ourselves down to an out-of-town hangar, in the early hours of a Monday morning, Australia time, for the 'inject.'
Don't recall if Bond . . . Alan Bond . . . was there, but designer Ben Lexcen, skipper John Bertrand and most of his crew, were.
The hottish, old American streak of a hundred and thirty-two years, had finally come to an end.

The raising of Greg Norman was quicker, but not without its moments.

That *'to be a champion, you must act like one'* mantra of Henry Cotton's, was written for young Gregory John. He'll probably sue (and certainly win) but the edges were a touch on the rough side when he landed in the U.K., on his ancestral tour. He was a big strong boy with the looks (and buns) of a Bondai beach-bottom, a wild, extravagant golf game, and a wild, extravagant zest for life in general, and girlies' bits in particular.
He got up noses, and did his fair share of 'spoiled-bratting,' but the self-confidence(and the birdies) set him apart.

He blasted his way, from side to side, down the 15th on the King's, at Gleneagles, during *The Double Diamond*, 'Uncle' Peter huffing and puffing away on commentary about course management and Henry Cotton . . . only for Greg to chip in from the latest gorse plantation, for par.

He's done books and vids on everything, from basic grass-growing to the futuristic fake stuff, and there's Midas dust over all of it. Apart from his 'squillions' (*he might easily have forgotten our first film*), what irritated me most about him were . . . Emma Sams . . . his unerring accuracy with a 12 bore on agent Marshall's front lawn, as we gathered material for our biog . . . . his charisma . . . and oh . . . his *Ferrari*.
Why couldn't he just be good at golf (in Australia)?!

The astute woman behind Greg was Laura Andrassy; the 'marriage' with his management was heading for *D-I-V-O-R-C-E* (not a happy time). Lois Marshall had been like a mother to young Norman, but there's only ever room for one woman in a lasting relationship, Rhodri bach.

After 25 years with Laura, 'Chrissie' (Evert-Lloyd-Mill) acceded; Laura had to settle for about a hundred million dollars of pain . . . .
"*Wow, Wow, Wow, Wow!*" as another Aussie superstar might have put it.

"*I don't think he'll never win another major, do you, John?*"

Forlornly, James (Marshall) wanted re-assuring . . . or revenge, but you knew the G.W.S. wasn't destined to fall on those rugged chops. Sure he lost at Augusta a couple of times, but, like he said (as he winged it back home to his mansion in Florida aboard his customized jet liner, dollars gushing down a dedicated pipeline to off-shore accounts), it hadn't made him <u>that</u> depressed; he was top of his pile for years . . . and had more friends than Faldo.

Should his early detractors and embittered colleagues need evidence of his *corps diplomatique* status, his respectful exchanges with the 1932 Champion, Gene Sarazen, on the 18th green at Sandwich in 1993—after he had indeed *"won another Major"*—suffice.
Any bets they talked about the sand wedge (Greg was a master with it)? The first (active) Knight of golf came second, for a change.

Decades on, an Ivor Robson-type announcement rings in my ears, as *The Fantasy Four* prepare to hit off:

"On the tee—winner of the 1961 and 1962 Open Championships . . .
ARNOLD PALMER.

"On the tee—winner of the 1966, 1970 and 1978 Open Championships . . . JACK NICKLAUS.

"On the tee—winner of the 1986 and 1993 Open Championships . . .
GREG NORMAN

"On the toilet . . ."

That destiny by-pass, that *Dynasty* moment, have had a profound effect on my game . . . and the TV I watch.

Do **Not** Try That at Home

Hemingway alluded to it in *Death in the Afternoon*, but a huge gulf exists between professional sport and what we enthusiasts regard as our capability and potential. Marveling at the ambi-dexterous genius of Ronnie O'Sullivan and my wiping the floor with my 8 year old (albeit on a slow table, with dead cushions and slight gradients due to the un-evenness of the living room floor) is to amplify the notion. It's like the kid from Equatorial Guinea swimming in the Olympics—he shouldn't really have been there, and predictable comparisons with Eddie Edwards, doesn't make a right. Forget the "taking part" bullshit—wee Charlie Philips isn't ready for the Crucible.

How do you honestly think you'd fare against a Federer serve . . . tangling, mid-air, with Nemanja Vidić . . . being paired in a foursome with Sergio (pass very *quickly* on Calzaghe)?

There once was a girl in Scotland—around about the 11+ mark—who came in my school uniform (not the skirt, obviously), who out-drove me, out-thought me, out-played me and outraged me—a Babe Didrikson in the making . . . *good at every-bloody-thing*.
Carly Booth's Dad, Wally, was British Middleweight wrestling champion in 1966 (didn't get huge media attention that year) and in '67; several lb later, he took the super-heavyweight title . . . *but the gear, Wally—that sleeveless baby-grow, with the bulging crotch*.
Carly's older brother, Wallace, got it round a marginally slower Augusta (*almost* the one), in 78 strikes, on debut.

My brother David (off 6—in the Stone Age), son Grant ('Jesse James'—on 7), Carly (then 5—and tumbling) and I (suffering, with an unfathomable lob wedge) went to play Carnoustie: Walter Hagen thought it the best golf course in the World . . . they all say that if they've won there—makes the natives feel good and the hotel porridge smoother, but Hagen never did.

A few pages back I discussed a hypothetical scenario which allowed for a "Monty" win at Troon—and by rights, he should have done it by now. The tablets show that the fat chap's 64 at Carnoustie is a course record, one he shares with genial club pro, Alan Tait. Once upon a posting, big Al would wake to the glories (when it's not lashing rain) of Spey Valley, at Aviemore in Inverness-shire, and proceed to relieve wishful-thinking members of as much tax-free cash as he could, reasonably.

When Aberdonian Paul Lawrie won the Open in '99, it was a 'Scottish' thing for us patriots, compounded by his becoming 'British' on BBC News (Faldo was never anything other than 'English'); no worries for Paddy Harrington on that score—southern Ireland never gets a mention on the weather forecast . . . *yes, I know why,* but it's weird, especially on Six Nations days.

I managed to persuade the powers that be to let us incorporate the (one o'clock'ish) week-end weather summaries into *Grandstand,* arguing that it might have a bearing on what to expect at Wimbledon or the Test match . . . whether to take a brolly to Wentworth, or stay in and watch us.

She (Carnoustie) was dressed in her winter coat as we introduced the girls to one another.
Armed with infuriating, turf-preserving mats, off we set—*how long, I wondered, negatively, before that accursed wedge would be needed?*

Hogan's Alley looked the same, even off the forward tee, and we paid homage (Carly was too young to remember . . . or care).
The Spectacles—twin fairway bunkers on the par 5 14th (of the same name . . . which Gary Player 'eagled' in 1968)—were definitely in range.
The Barry Burn at the 17th and 18th, with its three obvious crossings, had embarrassed Monsieur van de Velde, in Lawrie's year, and ruined ordinary cards down others—as fearsome a finish as you're likely to find, anywhere; *Home* it's called (the 18th)—*like you're looking forward to it!*

Carly was far better than most of her age, better than her elders, a multiple Champion at three separate clubs in Scotland, an international winner, an accomplished gymnast, a Junior Ryder Cup player and the youngest ever—at 15—to play for *us* in Curtis Cup; *The Big* (Michelle) *Wiesy* (for *them*) was 14 on debut. She too started out with all manner of firsts, and continues to dazzle, amaze and coin it . . . not quite up there with 'Shara'(pova) the buck guzzler, who, single handedly could take the US out of recession if she continues winning (or even if she doesn't)—and that from a daughter of Cold War Russia.
But Carly's getting there; as a golfer she has time on her side, providing she sticks in and some horny bloke doesn't go and spoil it by distracting her; with that last bit in mind, Miss Booth has much to do.
Thus far, the Leadbetter school experience hasn't borne the same kind of juicy fruit Faldo and Nick Price enjoyed (or Ms. Wie), but she's a feisty lady, and—knowing her folks—she'll not want for drive.

As we waited for *Home* fairway to clear, I went, for the umpteenth time, to my ball compartment, having littered my way across the burn to a double figure return on

Island, the 17th at Carnoustie; seen from the air on my *Strokesaver* (there's a laugh), the hazard looks like half a lap of Silverstone on wets.

As I glanced sideways, hurtling past—Tourischeva in a storm; my playing partner, utilising her wait-time with an impromptu flick-flack and somersault routine 'The Hoff' would have loved, but you can't imagine the secretary at Muirfield putting her through to the next round.
Carnoustie is altogether more laid back; their trade in hooky(slicy)lake(burn)balls . . . ferocious.

Carly's wedge into the green reacted as commanded.
Her birdie was twice as good as Pádraig Ó hArrachtáin's closing effort in regular play in 2007, but he went on to win the Jug . . . *and the next one, for Jack's sake!*

When I was growing up, Jessie Valentine was the most celebrated woman golfer in Scotland—in Britain. Like me, Jessie (née Anderson) was born in Perth; unlike me, *she* could play. A cert at Curtis Cup time, her record of six Scottish amateur titles was only improved upon by Isabella McCorkindale (Belle Robertson to you and me) from Southend in Argyll.

For the last five years or so, I've been very close (in a business sense) to the ladies of the professional tour (we did the TV—*extremely well, if you don't mind me saying*), rubbing shoulders with Annika Sorenstam and Laura Davies, veritable giants of the game (in either gender).
My particular favourite was Gwladys Nocera from France (not for any prurient reason—she bats for the other side), but she was my pro-am team mate at Chart Hills prior to one English Open, and though our time together was curtailed by a lightning storm, I was stunned by her effortless power and grace (can/will do moody if the putter turns ugly).

On completion of their rounds, women pros go for the one-armed-raised, banging of (different sized) chests, with repeated shoulder/back tapping; should they be anything other than British, a butterfly peck on either cheek is de rigueur—some do three, four (par) if needs be . . . <u>with sound</u>.
We were always taught to doff any headgear ('bobbles' in Scotland, September thro May . . . longer, sometimes), look opponents/partners in the eyes, and with a 'well played, enjoyed it' kind-of-a-half truth, shake bare hands firmly and proceed to the 19th to buy, if successful . . . to bemoan the greens, if miles over, or cuffed 10 & 8.

Snooker players do a self-conscious, lurching, insincere sort of wet-fish coming together . . . but what about all that glove-touching in cricket—they've even got some notoriously non-conformist Aussies at it.

Don't know which is more bizarre on court, doubles partners' motivating rituals, or singles' 'towelling' between every *point.*

Whatever beach-volleyball girls choose to do is fine by me.

On the subject of multi-tasking, if I'd wanted a better golf swing (*why wouldn't anyone off 10?*), or to learn to tap, there's a unique sequence in a Fred Astaire film (we're back in post-Wall Street Crash USA) where the featherweight legend does both, simultaneously, tapping and spinning his way along a line of teed-up 1.68s, skelping each and every one . . . *right down the bloody middle, Ronnie.*
Up until 1990, the 'beautiful British' ball was 1.62 inches in diameter.

Nowadays your balls can't weigh more than 1.62 ounces and must be at least 1.68 inches round the waist . . . not that anyone checks.
Paula Creamer's are pink, and for a while, Becky Brewerton—from Wales—used a ball for the visually impaired, with football markings, which, they claim, helps your putting:
. . . *to* Nevada Bob's, *and don't spare the horses!*

It's a one-shot scene—as was Fred's wont—no fakin' it.
The Astaire mantra was: "*Either the camera will dance, or I will.*"
Hogan's was: "*I don't like the glamour, I just like the game.*"
. . . two philosophies music-video editors might like to consider.

I'm not going into a story about meeting the great hoofer, though I was in the same room with him, once (and three hundred other guests). Slight as he was, you'd easily spot him gliding through the crowd, beaming that practised smile . . . *then sashaying up the wall, and over the ceiling.*

Neither Hogan nor Astaire is the issue . . . Leadbetter and Forsyth *are*; as far as being nice guys to do my business with, I'm happy to waive any lingering colonial right to the Fifth Amendment.

Leadbetter had just produced a well-illustrated instructional book called *'Faults 'n' Fixes,'* around the time Nick Faldo—his star pupil—published another . . . *with exactly the same title.*
Oops!

They were in the huff with each other.
Nick had won all the Majors he was going to—as a result, 'Lead' was now loaded . . . if surplus to requirement.

So, off to Florida, yet again, to one of the guru's Academies, to try to turn his book—or some of 'the 80 most common problems in golf'—into a video.
The catalyst was gentleman Nick Price, a childhood pal in Zimbabwe, a wonderful player and universally acclaimed as one of the game's prized ambassadors.
He and *The Shark* jointly hold the course record at Augusta National (the slick one)—63 shots . . . but not a jacket between them.

The coach made it clear, on a less than gracious first meeting, that he was in a hurry (probably had a date with some fishing pals); we could have two days of his time (that's about 20 grand, in dollars—if *The Golf Channel* audit is to be believed) in which to do our business.

It felt like a fortnight.

Not sure Leadbetter was any more confident of my credentials, sight unseen, than Mark Nicholas would be a couple of years later, which is pretty arrogant of them when I think about it—I *had* done a bit.

Fiscally, times were good for me in the mid-Eighties, so I plunged into a campaign that I hoped would bring me at least country membership of the mighty Wentworth Club at Virginia Water—a tall order, with a high maintenance tag; every conceivable string would need pulling if I were to get through the 'qualies.'
A couple of guys have escaped *from* Alcatraz, but here was I trying to break *in*, metaphorically.

I'd had enough rejection slips from the BBC—and other potential employers—to paper a room, so *"The Spanish Inquisition"* held no fears. For the most part *I didn't blaspheme*—unless Celtic had a late winner chocked off by a Proddy 'lineo' . . . there was no history *of witchcraft* in the family as far as records went, and whilst I'd known of a couple of bigamists in town, *sodomy* had never taken much of a hold in 20th century Perthshire; if asked, I'd have to own up that Grandpa Grant was a freemason, but surely they wouldn't be so petty.
Nope, all things considered my application seemed pretty well fireproof.

We were in the grand hall of the old house, which, funnily enough, has historical links with Spain (and the Duke of Wellington)—"we" being *me* and five, sated (through the card + brandy) adjudicator/inquisitors.
Shafts of sunlight leaked through an overhead window, as gentle twists of post-luncheon cigar-smoke slowly diffused, depositing faint stains on a creamy, ornate ceiling.

'Come in Mr., eh . . . ?
. . . 'Philips,' I prompted (*good research, chaps*).

Not the start I was looking for; even at this early stage, something told me they were less than disposed to grant me full privileges.

The interrogation went along the lines of: *Did I know anything about golf? . . . Had I had any kind of handicap? . . . What did I imagine I could bring to the club? . . . . What sort of job did I do, and was it well paid?*

"*OBJECTION! . . .* relevance?"

We'd barely begun my only driving test, on a hilly track in Crieff (circa 1961), when one of the back wheels mounted the kerb during the obligatory reversing manoeuvre, thereby removing (I thought, mistakenly), any chance of a pass.
Bollocks—just go for it.

So here I went again, my conviction doubled by case history.

I hit the pompous old f _ _ _ s (as 'bum-face' Will Carling might have wished he *hadn't* said about his RFU bosses)—in their ties and tweeds—with a burst of name-dropping that rocked them like stuck extras in Joffé's *Killing Fields*:
. . . *Hogan, Palmer, Price, Norman, Nicklaus, Miller, Seve, Player, 'Mr.Longhurst,' 'Petie'* (familiar) *Alliss, Sanders, Thomson, McCormack, Schofield, Cotton, Jacklin, Sarazen,*—rained down on them from my filofax (all the rage for upwardly mobiles and pretentious TV tossers).

Just as they appeared to recover the few remaining senses unsullied by booze and bombardment, I pulled the switch on the bullshit bays of my B52:
. . . *20 years in BBC Sport, the Open, the Masters, the Ryder Cup, the PGA and World Matchplay* (dumping a smelly couple on their own doorstep), *Crieff Golf Club, Jessie Valentine and a handicap of 5 . . .*

"*YOUR witness*".

Attitude (mine), and a black polo-neck (*dashed smart . . . with matching slacks, socks, shoes and blazer*) were probably my undoing.

I was proud of my *curriculum vitae* which, by the early 90s, had several World Cups and Olympics in the *'Career so far'* section, so to be treated like a no-mark by a failed ex-pro like Leadbetter, and, subsequently, by an unexceptional act like Forsyth, was rude, frankly.

As we prepared to be guided through another part of the shoot by the man in *very* long trousers and ribboned straw hat, one of the backers of the *Faults 'n' Fixes* video came close to whisper in my shell-like:

'*Stand your ground*' . . . he too, less than impressed with the palid guru.

Amelioration would be down to Nick Price; watching—on day two of two—as he repeatedly crunched fairway wood bullets through a stiff left-to-righter to the heart of a green protected on three sides by water, was to make the nasty man . . . *go away and fish*.

Leadbetter and *The Surrey Inquisition* could stuff their beach-balls and 'stogies' where gay boys go for fun.

DO NOT TRY THAT AT HOME.

I've always liked the purity of sport, and getting to places I'd dreamed about, in shorts, was pure J.M. Barrie.

Go up, and left a bit, from Carnoustie, you'll be at Kirriemuir from whence James Matthew Barrie <u>and</u> the four and twenty maidens came (repeatedly).
J.M.B. attended Academies in Glasgow, Forfar and Dumfries, but, as far as I know, was more into cricket than golf . . . . but I digress.

What I couldn't bear were pretentious arseholes who tried to fuck it up with their own self-importance.
Toilet talk, granted, but it leads me on very nicely.

(Game-show pilot).

'*All right my loves . . . the next game is called, ARSEHOLES.*'

(the action cuts to a big close-up of the grimacing host)

'*Bring on the bums and turds*' (helps if you do the voice)

(the pouting, twirling assistant, all-of-a-tingle, does as bidden)

'*Thank you my luv . . . line them up there . . . fine.*
'*Now, all you have to do is to work out which turd came from which arsehole . . .*

(yet another idiotic close-up)

. . . your time starts . . . . now!'

The plot for video number two—starring the former *Generation Game* host—was this: he'd been invited to play in a competition at the magnificent Swinley Forest

Golf course, Coronation Road, Ascot, Berkshire, not far from his actual home at Wentworth
(*ah, first the Membership Committee, now a country member to remember*).

Very kindly, Bruce Critchley—a 'lifer' at nearby rival Sunningdale G.C.—had invited me to play Swinley, a privilege, as its address might convey, few are afforded.
The third member of our group was Arne Naess Jr., avid mountaineer (he died in a climbing accident in South Africa in 1994), explorer and shipping magnate who, at the time, had his own island in Tahiti
(. . . so <u>that's</u> why 'The Colonel' asked him along).
Mr. Naess was his own man of course, but having Diana Ross as his missus (for five years) meant there were few inter-shot questions about bongs 'n' buttresses and the *Plimsoll* line:

"Will 'Ross the Boss' be joining us for bangers and champers at half-way, Arne . . . unlikely, right?"

To the video.

In the highly imaginative script, Bruce F., playing himself (who, of his many piss-takers, would want to?), is led to believe that the event is being run by the London Tap Dancers Association.
As a more than capable exponent, he agrees to attend.

A black cab arrives to take "Brucie" and his big bag of clubs to the course.

Instantly, as is their propensity, the cabbie engages his fare with a fusillade of rhetorical questions.
Civility exhausted, 'the fare' drops off.

(fade and cue the dream sequence of birdies holed and trophies won)

Jolted awake as the cab comes to a standstill, he finds to his horror that the L.T.D.A. aren't dancers—they're the London Taxi Drivers' Association on a routine society outing; he's right in it . . . *lump it*.

I'm no Danny Boyle (and Forsyth ain't Astaire) but 'the star'—aged about 70—and the director—a lad, 20 years his junior—clashed on set on a couple of occasions (*I could have made it more, but why stoop?*)
I'd make the dopey video as good as I could, but I wouldn't be screeched at by a hacker I could whip any day over 18 holes.
Childish, I know—*his* behaviour, *my* thoughts.

Fair play to the old boy, he *was* game to do a little tap routine on one of the tees, in his spikes, but denied ever having seen Astaire's seminal cinematographic moment—"bitchy" will suffice.

My first on-site experience of the Open Championship was at St Andrews in 1970—Sanders' year . . . or rather the year that should have been his.
A few months before he died, I had the privilege of working on another masterpiece with the Crown Prince of mirth, Peter Cook. Between us, over liquid breakfasts, marathon lunches and hazy soirées, we contrived four characters, each with a theory on how the great game should be addressed.

Player 1
An inadequately handicapped Floridian—off the max (24)—in 'sunnies' and Hawaiian top. The radio aerial on his baseball cap neutralised the strobing effect of his loud top and acted as a route-finder should bearings be lost at any juncture.
There was a transmitter in the back pocket of his *Ruperts*, which, were he not to make it in before dark, would automatically send out distress signals.
We'd borrowed a giant display bag from the pro-shop. Housed therein were his S.C.U.B.A., for retrieving lake balls . . . a mobile barbecue should play become unbearably slow . . . . collapsible table and chair, as seen in English country lay-by Easter break holiday newsreel footage . . . and a free-standing saline drip, on a pole, in case of seizures.

Player 2
The smoking rooms of posh clubs were full of them: blazered old codgers, kicked out by the memsahib first thing in the morning . . . who *may,* if it's clement, stab at a putt before lunch . . . who *will* catch fire through carelessness of pipe or cheroot . . . . who *shall*, forever more, bore for Britain—an amalgam of *Arthur Streeb-Greebling* and *E.L. Wisty*.

Player 3
A 'Cherman' scientist, in white lab coat, who believed more could be learned about ze golf swing from studying ze suppleness of ze fish, than from any of Herr Leadbetter's teaching aids (*him* again).

Player 4
The perennial, craggy, canny caddie (Scottish), sat by a roaring fire in his bothy, stuffed dog at his side, with whom he kept constant counsel, even tho he'd passed over, long since.
There's always a hare on the loose during major tournaments, but every effort to restrain his best friend from chasing it onto the putting surfaces failed, much to the caddie's embarrassment.

As budgets were tight, we chose the back room of a pub in Hampstead, near Peter's ancestral home, to shoot his scenes.

We had the full monty, viz. camera, sound, lights, wardrobe and make-up . . . but no script, as such. Although in the presence of a "world-class" ad-libber, I confess to have been a tad nervous about his sustaining it over the long haul—between drinks . . . no worries.

One night, the spirit of the royal and ancient game, on top of a wet lunch and some afternoon delights of the nippy sweetie variety, got the better of us; armed with gutties and putters, we tumbled into the mews.

Peter demanded the honour (*the last he'd get*), and prepared to launch:

"Aim for the green door down there."

The line was left to right, downhill, cobbled . . . unreadable.

Showing his many years of being an irritating-bastard-of-a-neighbour, he shot off a pissed effort, bobbling towards the target.

Onwards! . . . as if being swept by electrocuted curlers.

The yellowing gutta percha cannoned off several walls and panes, finally coming to rest by a plant pot, fully thirty feet from its intended destination . . . at which point the irate owner appeared through it, to foreclose, prematurely, our 'nearest his green door' competition.

Player 4—the caddie—claimed to have been on Sanders's bag in 1970.
If you haven't seen the ghastliness of that missed putt . . . '*where have you been?*' (the second half of a famous 'Barry Davies-ism' I beg to borrow from the Seoul Olympic hockey competition—GBR v IND, I think . . . but an absolute gripper, not to be missed ideally).

Angus explains that at the precise moment Sanders struck the putt, an army of angry worker ants (which we later superimposed, graphically, on the archive original) had started up his trouser leg, and bitten him in the gonads.

'Mr.Longhurst,' commentating on the real thing, from his eyrie by the railway sheds, reflected everyone's frustration—and Doug's apprehension—giving an exasperated grunt as the man-in-mauve lurched out of the address position to remove 'something' from his line.
Henry wasn't to have known about the creeping infestation.

The Championship, contended 'his' man, could have been Doug's had he worn Nicky Tams (tied at the knees), or plus fours . . . '*instead of those ridiculous purple troosers.*' We hadn't bothered to research whether ants were colour blind.

I was beside the 18th green at the actual time of the awfulness, with Mark McCormack. We'd been instructed to get interviews with both Sanders and Nicklaus.
Little could *I* have imagined—or *he* given a damn—that 20 years on he'd be paying my stamp and pension, as an TWI employee.

To pass the time of day, as the two golfers made their way to the green (Doug had over-shot the flag slightly, but *"only needed a 4"* to win), I respectfully asked my future employer if he had a preference:

'Don't care . . . they're both mine.'

Rrr-ight.

We were back the following day to interview Jack.

Amazing man, McCormack—the prototype agent—not a bundle of laughs, nor one to dwell in casual conversation, but mention golf, tennis, TV rights, barter deals, marketing and distribution strategies, or the minutest detail from the travel schedules of any, or all of his IMG clients, and you'd have him in the palm of your hand . . . for a second or two.

I was ferrying some non-alcoholic drinks—save for a favoured quarter bottle (0.2 litres) of champagne for Mr. Longhurst (*"avoids me having to offer any to my wife"*)—to the commentary box, perched high above the 17th tee at the Old Course, wherein lay a *Who's Who* of golfing faces.

At the far end, by a solitary camera, stood Harry Carpenter with his blown-up map of the course and reams of paper, poised—at the flick of a switch—for 'in-vision' updates, scores, news of ant attacks etc.
In front of him, at a long desk, overlooking the most famous out-and-back links lay-out on the planet, sat 'the voices' . . . . daily-disinfected, numbered, lip microphones at the ready.
Peter Thomson, who'd had a pretty good Open record, winning the jug just the *five* times (including a hat-trick between 1954 and 1956).
Next to him—*the pupil*—old 'electric hands' Alliss, 8 times a Ryder Cupper, who'd missed a tiddler or two in his latter days, but *'a great champion'* nonetheless . . . alongside and hanging on the every word of . . .
The Master—Henry Carpenter (would you believe) Longhurst—another who, indubitably, would have felt the cold steel on his shoulder . . . had he lived.

Then 'His Highness' Arnold Daniel Palmer—if not beheaded exactly, then scalped by big 'Petie' in their Ryder Cup singles in '63 (*we* lost).

. . . and, finally, far post, his best buddy M. H. McCormack, bringing up the rear; with many of the players, the R& A and BBC Sport in his pocket, we can forget *'the rear.'*

The first golf instruction book I'd laid eyes on—my brother was very possessive about his things—was called *'Hit It Hard'* by Arnold Palmer. One of the pictures was of the author and agent Mark, in a short, white Mac—briefcase, no doubt, stuffed with air-tight contracts, caveats and crippling clauses for any who'd fail to fulfil.

Alan Mouncer—my mentor at 'the Beeb'—had managed to sell an idea to the Controller of One for a series of golf-related chat shows: I would co-produce. We toyed with all possible permutations, and after what seemed like minutes, came up with a highly original title,

The basis of the *A MAN LIKE ALLISS* shows would be a dinner party, at Moor Allerton Golf Club in Leeds, from where Peter had previous convictions.
It was a while ago, but I recall the guest list included a leftie, Henry Cooper . . . an unusually *large* Welsh golfer, Dave Thomas . . . a record breaker, diminutive Tommy Campbell, who'd held *The Guinness Book of Records* world's longest drive mark for years (it's now about 515 yd on grass) . . . a double Major winner—at Hazeltine and Lytham—Scunthorpe's own, Tony Jacklin . . . a club pro, Hugh Lewis (not *Huey* of the *News*), who could, and maybe should have been a stand-up comic . . . and my nemesis-in-waiting, Bruce Forsyth, in a tartan tux (*just to piss me off*).

Our idea was to film the get-together from pre-food cocktails to liqueurs, and break it down into six episodes, the working headers as follows:

Hors d'Oeuvres
Potage
Poisson
Entrée
Dessert
Fromage

We didn't need to worry about converting 'working' to actual . . . nor translating from the French.

Two schoolboy errors:
i.   the booze wasn't 'prop' tea, it was real, free . . . and pernicious
ii. the plates were made of china—the cutlery, Sheffield steel.

Engaging though the chat was, the noise was deafening; the early stuff was all but inaudible . . . . the later stuff, indecipherable.
The Controller demanded a re-think, so we started on some features.

Doug Sanders had known Peter for yonks, so when he came across for the Open, 'His Flamboyance' agreed to a couple of days filming.
Prior to the shoot, a fourball was set up—Peter, his son Gary, Doug and me. I could play 'okay,' but these guys were bananas from the top of the cluster; neither was the venue too dusty . . . the Ailsa course at Turnberry.

The R&A were still four years from staging the Open there, but even off the 'whites' it was way too good for me.

No wind.
You could see puffins on the giant plug, <u>and</u> Goat Fell on Arran . . . the portents were exceptional.

Peter pinned me to the floor to try to stop the shaking:
"You'll be fine, Philipo, it's just a quiet Sunday morning friendly."
(*easy for him to say*).

Sartorially, I'd chosen modest dark blue, with black shoes; I make mention of this only, as there, at the top of the hotel steps, overlooking the Irish Sea, on a beautiful Scottish morn, stood . . . . *TANGERINE MAN*.

Christ, talk about drawing attention to my nerves.

Doug was in character for an *Outspan* ad: matching shirt, jumper, pants and patent shoes—I prepared myself not to be shocked by the glove. Slipping past him quietly, as several autograph hunters poked pens and papers at him (*'a crowd already—it's only 7.30 in the pigging morning'*), I belted down the long staircase that leads to the haven of the clubhouse (*maybe I could turn an ankle in my spikes . . . or concuss*).

The pro at Turnberry was Bob Jamieson, who'd gone there from his job at Crieff golf club, so I guess if anyone was responsible for my excellent swing, it was 'Mister Bob.' He looked just as he had, all these years ago, testament to the efficacy of *Grecian* products (denied).

One of his commercial ploys (back in his 'natural' days)—never reported to the Ways and Means Committee at St. Andrews—was to stand on the 1st tee of the Ferntower at Crieff, with a box of new balls, a knowing look on his handsome face and some small change as we lads set off, bleary-eyed and poorly stocked on the Sunday assault course; to the right was jungle i.e. OB . . . 3-off-the-tee country.

When you looked back down from the cussing and cap-throwing, a black-wrapped 65 was winging your way.

"Still pouring iced water on the till, Robert?" . . . Peter opined, cheerily
The takings from the Turnberry shop were legendary; American tourists could clean him out of cashmere, quicker than lesser establishments could shift those round tins of dusted, fruit boilings.

A gallery was now lining either side of Ailsa's 1st, as *Outspanman* made his way through, to a roar of Ayrshire approval; they knew their golf down there—Prestwick and Troon were just round the corner, and all manner of hidden gems were dotted along a majestic coastline.

To have any kind of handicap on a links course, suggests an intimate knowledge of the mechanics of the golf swing in wind, and, in the 'colorful' American, the wary fans had a soul-mate.

Doug's opener (you'd have needed slow-motion to detect the backswing) landed within 8 iron range of the first green, smack down the *James Ryddelle*.

'How's the slice, John . . . cured it yet?'

Oh, nice one Bob, cheers . . . don't we have a good memory.

You're right, it went wildly that way, but my recovery landed three inches from the stick . . . and a winning birdie it was.
What unfolded isn't worth reporting, suffice to say that I was utterly humiliated and vowed to drive back out to the 10th tee and consign the lot to the North Channel, or, depending on the tide, the rocks.

We'd been filming a pro-celebrity event at Turnberry—I think Tom Watson and Lee Trevino were the pros that year—and my crew was assigned to follow that man Mathis round.
Johnny had been a bit of an athlete in his college days, and was a regular on the 'celeb' golf circuit.

Talk about an impromptu performance money couldn't buy . . .
The crooner walked to the edge of the cliff by the lighthouse and burst into 'On a clear day (which it was), rise and look around you.'
Gents' toilets and extinct volcanoes did that kind of thing to him.

Having decimated my spirit in front of my kinfolk, Sanders owed me; the next day we took him out for a 'master class' round Troon, where the '73 Open would be enacted.

The shot Doug played from a downhill, plugged lie in the coffin bunker at the Road Hole during the 1970 Championship was inches short of genius . . . . <u>pure</u> had it gone in, as it so very nearly did.

Four times he was bridesmaid in Majors (not a patch on Norman's 7—"Monty" has 5) which would be tough enough to bear; add torticollis to the mental anguish, and that's tough . . . but he never moaned.

"OK Jaawn, let's do some *bunker* shaats as you guys call them."

(for fashion followers, his shoes today were of white leather, with a tartan strap, matching piping on his dark pants and half-sleeved top to complete)

In a cascade of sand, Doug's first ball staggered out, teetered on the lip and then, agonisingly, rolled, back to his feet.

'*That's* how you <u>high</u> handicappers do it'
(*I was off a drifting 10 at the time—cheeky bugger Georgian*).

Actually he is George (Douglas) Sanders by birth . . . same as the legendary Russian-cum-British actor, who himself was a peacock with an eye for the ladies having married and divorced both Gabor sisters. Quality.

Ball 2: less sand, a bit of flight and a landing six feet or so from the stick viz. the single-figure version.

". . . and <u>this</u> is how we pros do it."

You've got it . . . . holed the sucker.

Dutifully, I raked away Imelda's footprints, as the caddy slotted the magic wand back in the bag, and Mrs. S.—the scrumptious Scotty—marched her man onwards towards the *Postage Stamp*.

Doug had a stinker of a 79 in the first round proper, and ended up 28th equal, a couple of shots ahead of 44 year old Peter Thomson, and my china-in-waiting (. . . to be Open champion of Zambia 1980), Ewen Murray.

Even eventual winner, Tom Weiskopf—to whom Dunbartonshire's midgies should be eternally grateful—was overshadowed by events on Day 1
(*don't' be put off, Loch Lomond G.C. is a wonder of the old and modern worlds*).

"Big Tam" known, early on, as the "Towering Inferno" on account of his height and temper, would also build Troon Country Club at Scottsdale, Arizona with his design partner from the Loch Lomond project, Jay Morrish.
(*look, the Arizonan desert is full of 'rattlers' . . . and <u>they</u> can kill you!*)

My function was to 'direct' (that should really be 'supervise') a single camera, fed into a remote scanner, parked out at Royal Troon's 8th green.
During the four days, every tee shot would be recorded on the off-chance of an eagle; on the surface, not one of life's more fascinating or taxing assignments . . . . *but wait up*.

In 1935, Gene Sarazen holed his second shot at the par 5 15th at Augusta—*Fire Thorn*, the one over the lake they make a nonsense of today . . . or not.
(Gene would win the jacket after a play-off).
Alarm bells rang all over the golfing world.

Compared to that from his seminal act of 1973, the resonance was merely a dull *clink*.

The splendid old man—inventor of the 'get out of the shit' sand wedge—was grouped with Fred Daly and Max Faulkner for the first two rounds at Troon: *now Max <u>was</u> a snappy dresser*. At 57, he was the baby of the trio—Open champion in 1951 at Royal Portrush (Fred's home track) and a non-scoring member of Dai Rees's winning Ryder Cup side in '57.
Fred was Open champ at Hoylake in 1947, sixty years before the loon Padraig did it again, in Angus.

71 years and 4 months young, with a career Grand Slam, and a bridge named after him, Sarazen was the oldest *ever* competitor in a Major at Troon . . . plus he'd won 7 of them—3 USPGAs, 2 US Opens, 1 Masters and our one at Sandwich in 1932.

Without instruction my cameraman zoomed in gently to the tee.
Sarazen, in what looked to be a nifty pair of 'nicky-tams,' was first up.

The ball-follow, against a blue sky, was immaculate . . . . looked bang on line as it hopped on a green many before (and since) have had extreme difficulty hitting.

PLOP . . . . in she went.

I shouted something of no value to the cameraman, but he'd already whipped back to the tee to get the reactions.

The other thirty-five cameras on the course, Alan Mouncer was directing, and I mean *directing*.
Calmy as I could, I advised him that:

"We have a hole-in-one at the 8th."

(God, I hope we have).

"Denis?!"

Denis Kelly was operating the 'Reithian' recording machine—a VR something or other, powered by steam.
No reply.

My level went up a notch:

"Denis, have we got it?"

"Hold on" came the dismembered voice from a speaker in front of me.

Hold fucking on . . . is he a bloody sadist or something?!

Alan had taught me to be aware and measured in the truck; his methods were under strain.

"Seems to be OK," said Denis, laconically, with history spinning round before his very eyes ('The Kelly' was more of a racing man, *but seriously* . . .)

"J.P. get the tape on a buggy, soon as you can," 'Mounce' decreed.

Ere long, the most famous ace in history was on the air.

Sarazen holed from the greenside bunker the next day for a two, but my camera had been deployed to do back-up reaction shots of Johnny Miller and Tom Weiskopf on the adjacent 7th fairway—anyway, as Doug had proved, pros did that sort of thing all the time
(*there WAS a difference*).

We were very lucky to get spots in many of the pre-tournament pro-ams.

I played Gleneagles (where the Ryder Cup idea began) with Ben Crenshaw (4 caps) and Jose Maria Olazabal (7) . . . the Blue Canyon in Thailand with *'The Shark'* . . . St. Andrews with Frank Nobilo . . . Valderrama with Ian Woosnam . . . Turnberry with Christy O'Connor Senior 'Himself' . . . . Majorca with Lee Westwood (who I was grooming to be World No.1) . . . Chepstow with Wayne Grady . . . . Woburn with Jane Geddes—and shall happily continue to brag about the lot of them (and wee Gwladys).

I'd come by my invitation to play in the pro-am at the PGA Championship at Wentworth, through Iris Au, a lady of oriental extraction, who looked after the courtesy cars at all *Volvo* sponsored events on Tour.

Spotting the big blue logo on the envelope in my office mail one morning, I nipped off to the gents for some privacy, being in no need, at that point, to put pressure on.
I was like a British Lion waiting in bed for McGeechan's team sheet to be pushed under the door.

I carefully opened the missive, advising me that I'd been selected to play: *pairings and tee-off times, overleaf.*

You may think this is juvenile—and it was—but I folded over the covering letter to make a sort of mask, and began to reveal the names of the players, one by one . . . adding all the while to my building erection.
The BBC boys were normally given early starts so they'd be back in time for rehearsals, but as I got to midday on my list, still no sign of my name.

Maybe Iris has made a mistake . . . plough on.

My little game was now reaching idiotic proportions.
I'd created a second mask, which would only reveal the tee-time and the pro, and since I'd have donated reproductives to play with the Spanish Master, I scrolled down to 1225 and Team Ballesteros.

The first two names didn't ring anything other than alarm bells at the single figures in parenthesis . . . but *PH*—for starters, had me standing up in my cubicle and checking the *Andrex* . . . .

. . . *I-L-I-P-S.*

I'd selected a grey pullover, in an attempt to offset my ashen complexion.

I'm thinking of a moment when I was more nervous . . . . Nope.

Look, I came in at a couple of holes, O.K!

Our playing partners weren't in Seve's league, or mine . . . they were miles better than I. The cocky, smaller of the two was sporting a brand new set of Seve *Slazengers* he'd won in a newspaper competition—easy way in for him.

Pro-ams aren't high on the professional's wish list of things they'd want to be doing on a Wednesday, but it's part of their duty, and some people pay good money to be humiliated.

Upholding my sycophancy, I was following Team Norman over the closing holes at St Andrews one year. As they walked up the 16th, coming towards us, and going a deal slower on the adjoining 2nd was Fuzzy Zoeller, Greg's old mate from Winged Foot . . . and the white handerkerchief of surrender.

It must have been around five in the evening.

Greg called across to ask the 1984 US Open champion how he was doing: Zoeller rolled his eyes and threw his head back—there in a cacophony of sand and clicking *Nikons* was one of his team members, wrestling with a fairway bunker.
Fuzzy held up 8 fingers.
It takes about five hours to get round the Old Course under normal conditions.

Back on the Burma Road, Team Ballesteros was doing reasonably well. Me and 'my mate' Seve were down the right, and tighter side, of the 18th fairway—the other two were centre left, with better, if slightly longer lines, into the green.

The vertically challenged person pulled out a now less than pristine iron.

'*Whatuplay?*' asked our leader in an Anglo-Iberian mix.

Mini-Me's choice of an iron, to lay-up, was summarily dismissed by the future Ryder Cup captain as he stormed across to deliver 'team orders.'

The revised five-wood shot towered and drew into the optimum spot on the fringe, bounced thrice and rolled up absolutely stiff for an amateur eagle that would earn us each a very nice travel case—*thank you very much*—and a flashing smile from the legend.

"Get Out of the Water!"

Bobby Robson and Jock Stein (his second turn on tiller) were the men in charge in *Nineteen Eighty-Four ("duck!")*; assuming George Orwell had miscalculated, British was still deemed to be best.
No one in England or Scotland with any sense of Wembley '66 or Wembley '67, could be thinking that by the turn of the millennium we'd be sucking up to a randy Swede, or building bridges with 'a Cherman' for our national salvations . . . well, football futures, at least; Eriksson & Vogts had decent CVs, but we'd had the wheel for about five thousand years.

The den clock showed a quarter of five a.m. (swimmers' families can't do duvet munching) as we began filming . . . . obviously, back in the US of A.

At 20, Tracy Caulkins was getting on a bit for a swimmer; missing Moscow through the U.S. boycott, it seemed every time she pressed on goggles and knifed into the shallows—be it on her front or back, legs together or legs apart, arms up or arms down—she'd break records . . . world records.
Her coach at the University of Florida at Gainsville was one Randy* Reese (**could only happen in the States*), who was to swimming what Rinus Mikels had been to total football, and Dave Bassett was to the route one game at Wimbledon F.C.—i.e. different.
(*I was liking him already*).

Hamilton Bland told me all about Randy's methods: upstream river training (fully clad) . . . restraining weights and belts . . . arm paddles for perfecting technique . . . and strange dry-land drills for amphibians.

When we bumped into Don Talbot, the Canadian team's Australian coach, on the deck at Gainsville, the coaching gibberish was enough to send the crew scurrying in search of GVs (general views) of campus, and me after 'Miss Versatility USA.'

Brother and sister, John and Ilsa Konrads—Wagga Wagga's finest—had a spot together in my well-thumbed, all-sports scrapbook, alongside Bobby McGregor and high-diver Peter Heatly: they qualified for a 'glueing,' not by being Scottish, but by being extremely good, in, out, above and below the water-line.

The Konrad kids' flight from German occupied Latvia during the Second World War is well documented—what I didn't know, was that Don Talbot, had been behind their successes at the Rome Games.
(Ilsa won a relay gold in, but I stuck her in anyway).

The enormous differential between numbers one and two in all-time Olympic swimming medals (USA 353 to 111Australian) would only be affected by fractions were Randy's pupil to live up to expectations in Los Angeles, but, psychologically, every win sharpened the rivalry.

Only by mitigating on her behalf for her late arrival—a crime punishable by a fearful rollicking from Reese—was the mighty motivator appeased; not even his star pupil was immune from a dressing down—in front of the others, for maximum effect.

Tracy was *"a floater"* Don explained—Hammy knew it, being a former GB swim coach—so, checking no one was watching, I looked closer: her bum—the most opponents would get to see of her in three Olympic finals—surely did stick high out of the water, as though she were doing her miles in the Dead Sea.
Fit, and built for particular purpose . . . like Ed Moses and Seb Coe.

I thought back to R.B. McGregor—the pre-decimalised, world 110yd record holder—and his adamantly held view, that style and technique were the speed-keys in swimming, borne out, duly, by Mark Spitz and Ian Thorpe (having webbed feet and being 20 metres long were bonuses for the Aussie missile) . . .
. . . *and then there's Michael Phelps.*

Certain factions of the nose-clip and floss brigade—'synchromesh' swimmers, as Lynam tagged them in a nocturnal link during the L.A. Games—don't like to be associated with Busby Berkley and Esther Williams
. . . *what's wrong with that, they were iconic?*

'Perfect 10s' were awarded to a synchro duet recently—eight of them in all—at the World Championships, and just as the Chinese have in spring and high-board diving (and trampolining, logically), the Russians have taken synchro skills to another level; it's hugely complicated.

Synchro didn't command any kind of priority with the schedulers in '84, *but I liked it*; maybe it was Esther, who was what Beyoncé is to the teenager of today—buff—with great choreographers behind her, and, in Miss Knowles's case, a great behind.

Make no mistake, synchro girls are finely tuned athletes, anaerobically and aerobically; with their hair down and blow dried (at the opening parade) right 'lookers'—a point not lost on our most celebrated spear chucker, Steve Backley.

Not only did Hamilton Bland do the graft on the racing side of swimming, he took the lead on diving and synchro.

"Here's a test for you non-believers," he said as we began a live session of synchro from the McDonald's Swim Stadium at USC, "try holding your breath with the girls from the start . . . and make like you're swimming under water"
(the nation arose, as one).

The five minute routine began in a flurry of underwater egg-beatering, sculling and power-boosting, arms, legs and bodies in fine lines, above and below the waves . . . eyes open, ears tuned (to the water music) and (as in trials motor cycling) *no touching the bottom* (of the pool) *with your feet* (points deducted). The water was about 9ft deep . . . breathing was mandatory . . . the smiling, cosmetic—they could hardly be *enjoying* such huge effort.

Boy swimmers and divers ditched the *Speedos*, bunched their wigs, slapped on lippie and mascara and put on a show at their end-of-games gala in Sydney 2000; the entry was more spectacular than precise, as they 'bombed' in from 10 metres, yet even in jest, their performance highlighted the degree of difficulty better than any cynical blob in an armchair.

The girls struck their final pose—the marks were punched in:
'OK to take a breath now, Bland?' (pause)
The commentary line went silent—corpsing in progress.

Minutes before we were due on with the first event from the European Championships in Split, our main commentary circuit packed-up altogether.
If there's anything you need to know about TV 'plumbers' (engineering department) they *l-uhve* a problem . . . *'bring it on'*—the more complex and seemingly terminal, the better . . . *'keep the those production numpties on tenterhooks.'*

Dave Warton's day and night job was to look after incoming satellite and land-line circuits at the International Control Room, but he liked to get away from TV Centre now and again, and being an A-level technophobe, I loved having him along . . . . on this occasion, it bordered on homosexual.

I looked across to see Dave dismantling our life-line . . .
Jesus, man, what a time to be messing with the phone.

What he was doing of course (*numb-nuts*) was hooking Alan's microphone to the telephone line, so there'd be some kind of commentary—albeit, sub-standard quality—getting back to London.
Time for one of those continuity captions, much loved by presentation department:

'*We apologise for poor quality sound. We are trying to put things right as quickly as we can.*'
They used to compound it, in the old days, with: '*in the meantime, here's a little music.*' . . . or, if they thought it was going to be a long un, the potter's wheel or the windmill (cracking entertainment).

We 'numptiess' beatered and posed like swans—serene and poised on the surface—as 'English-only' speaking Davie and the duty engineer from Yugoslav TV, huddled under the desk, pantomiming at each other; exposed wires, dodgy connections, steaming soldering tools—quick-fit heaven (for them).
It worked, of course, Thomas (the incredulous).

We'd upgraded our coverage of the synchro: our girls had a good chance of a medal—in fact, we were in for a clean sweep. Carolyn Wilson had already won individual European gold <u>and</u> the duet, with Caroline Holmyard, and now it was the troupe's turn.
Ann Clark, a former GB coach, was on hand to help Bland with the technical stuff.
N.B. (*I did*) Esther Williams did the 'color' at the synchro in L.A. for US tv (1984), but the boys didn't even think to take a picture for me.

I can attest, with impunity, to our crew's designs on Wilson and Holmyard—embodiments of fitness and muscle-tone, in figure-hugging one-piecers, with the lung capacity of blue whales: should our blokes be so lucky, the C.s would leave them gasping in the lingering kiss stakes.
Next time you drop the kiddies off at the pool, go in and try power-boosting your tiny progeny in deep water . . . and see if you don't both half drown.
To have a chance of being a 'synchroette,' you needed to be a swimmer (crucially), a runner, a gymnast, a dancer, a weightlifter, a free-style diver, and a beauty therapist (specializing in water-resistant creams and lotions), plus, you had to remember:

a) to have packed a spare clip
b) to appear charming on the surface
c) to retain a sense of humour if Lynam wanted an interview.

Water up the old hooter is the bane of the submariner's life; surely, in this day and age of human cloning and 'moob' reduction surgery, someone has to come up with a less disfiguring device than the nose-clip . . . based on the contact lens principle, some sort of removable valve in the trachea . . . . *come on girls, get down the Den—big 'Jonesey' is a sucker for a pretty face* (his own, primarily).

Up came the last set of marks for team GB . . . they'd won gold . . . another one!
Incapable of containing her glee, *up* jumped Annie C . . . she was, shall we say, of greater density than Zola Budd, and, understandably, ebullient. Encouraging Hammy to share a bit of ecstasy (delight), she elbowed his ribs on the way back down, bowling

him out of his seat to the very brink of the deep stuff, as he battled to confirm a clean sweep for our ballerinas.

Elsewhere in Split, the women's events were dominated by East German cheats: all fourteen available golds (plus nine silvers) went to their women; their men didn't win one . . . . *how sexist is that?*
Swimming legitimately for 'the West,' the Albatross (Michael Gross), came first in the 200 fly (Phil Hubble GBR got silver), and they also won gold at polo—but something was seriously amiss . . . in Yugoslavia . . . at FINA . . . and in the labs of East Germany.

Breast-strokers, 'Suki' Brownsdon—she of the bubbly personality and explosive recovery—and pugnacious 'Ade' Moorhouse—now twinned with fly-boy 'Andy' Jamieson (European silver medallist in '85 . . . behind Gross, no less)—were our only other 'podiums.'

Four-time Olympian, and former City of Coventry favourite, Susannah B. now lives in Oz; Adrian M.—the golden boy of Seoul—replaced Bland in the BBC commentary box, after he ('Hammy') had been fired following an alleged bribery scandal.
I'd make this analogy: commercially British swimming was a liver in need of a detox—Bland was the *Andrew*'s. Case closed.

The diving board at our school baths was a solid structure, the launch platform about six feet off the ground; add a foot to the surface, plus six more of anti-varruka, eye-stinging, chlorinated *sin* gas, and your were on the tiles.

Were you long and skinny, like I was when the voice started to break, pitching yourself headlong, even from that modest elevation, through a very basic swallow manoeuvre (no time to elaborate), towards what you hoped would be a ripper (unprotected, adoring parents in the 'splash area'), without first adopting a pre-set, upturned hand-position akin to the toes of baldie Brynner's slippers in the *King and I*, was to invite a skull fracture or possible paralysis.

Astoundingly, no more than the occasional split forehead, a mild concussion or two and the odd pike (dive) were ever reported.

I learned to swim in the modest pool at five-star Gleneagles Hotel; you could, as an ordinary punter, pay 2s.6d.—half a crown, or an $\frac{1}{8}$ of the incorruptible pound—and pee where the rich did.
It was around the time of the *Million Dollar Mermaid*, starring the gorgeous Ms. Williams in a golden one-piecer. The film was called, imaginatively, *The One Piece Bathing Suit* in the UK—so, as much to do with that as my not being able to stand up

in the pool, my best early work was *under* water—grandpa Grant on guard duty; big breaths and along the bottom, like a European plaice, one slithered.

Those formative sessions were invaluable when I produced/directed the swimming for 'The Beeb.'
Thunderously powerful and streamlined as you have to be in the sprints, racing over the longer distances can be processional; observation windows offered a gloomy, restricted view of the tumble turns, while tracking shots along the deck meant our riggers pushing dolly+camera+cameraman, back and forward, thirty times over 1500m . . . and their renowned senses of humour, to the limit.

We were allowed to take roof panels out at Coventry baths for the smallest lens-person on the crew; the view of the developing echelon was as good as it got—an unmanned 'hothead' wire-cam was as unimaginable as hi-tech swimsuits and a sub 47" for the 100 metres.

The ASA—the sport's governing body in the UK—weren't 'Leesom school' i.e. high-risk takers; my suggestion to have a camera-frog-person swim upside down underneath the racers, proved colder sick than the hovercraft notion at the Boat Race . . . *still, nothing ventured.*

The daredevils of Acapulco had been part of schoolboy legend—mis-timed leaps into the frothing brine, meant death by rock, a hundred feet below . . . *muy riesgo!*

Don't know that anyone has ever died doing it, but . . . *how come, where do you rehearse?*

Here's the drill: (i) pray our exploding star, the moon and earth are on the same page, tide-wise (ii) cross crazily at the shrine of the virgin of Guadeloupe (iii) take a finger-licking check on the wind (iv) wait for the swell (6ft *poor* ☐16ft *max*) (v) fart at will (vi) *'loup' for all you're worth* (30ft out)—shit or bust (136 feet down).
Some travel firms offer voyeurs night time, *al fresco* supper packages at El Mirador hotel, where one can enjoy the divers of La Quebrada to black bean burritos and something red from the famous Chateau Camou vineyards, nearby.

Our best 'piker 'n' twister' in Split, was Christopher Snode, a veteran of two Olympics and heading for a third in the States. Chris was the latest in a line of hard-of-hearing British divers, like Liz Feriss, Peter Heatly and the extremely disturbed Brian Phelps.

So familiar (friendly) had we become, that just as *'Christopher Snode, Great Britain'* was going to take one of his high tariff dives in the Championships—*'reverse three and a half, somersaults, tuck'*—he looked across to the commentary box, gave a cheeky little wave (*slightly outside the bubble, if I were to be critical*), then nailed it.

Competition diving dates back to the late eighteen hundreds—the days of Jack *the Ripper* (entries of a terminal nature)—when head-cases dived off John Rennie's New London Bridge (the one that went to Arizona—not that upon which William Wallace's head was shamelessly impaled); there must have been some bad stuff in the river in those days—*boala weil* (vial's disease) for starters. *"Call David Walliams to the stand!"* When they introduced it to the Olympics in 1904, in St.Louis, it was called 'fancy diving,' which probably attracted 'gorgeous' (male feedback) Greg Louganis to it in the first place.

Four score and sixteen years on, in Sydney, couples were at it—openly—in the 'synchro' events; be they piked, tucked, free or straight, millions, worldwide were in for a treat.
(*'free' wrestling—George Hackenschmidt and his Greco-Romans—seems a curious thing for regular blokes to be doing*).

Gregory Efthimios Louganis you might liken to Georgios Kyriakos Panayiotou for his . . . Greek name; the boy Snode was more in the Beckham mould—a bit of a falsetto, blond hair, six-pack, and great feet.

Be very clear, George Michael is a wonderful singer, and Louganis was a wonderful diver; his back-to-back 'double' golds in L.A. and Seoul, would almost certainly have been a 'triple' had the Yanks been in Moscow instead of sulking at home.

Everyone knew Greg was gay, but few that he was HIV positive; fewer still, in Korea, knew what that meant.

The day he cracked his head open on the way down—inwardly—from the 3m springboard, ignorance surfaced . . .
"We're all doomed!"

What a recovery . . . *what an athlete*; when he retired, Louganis got into breeding dogs—the "pretty police" got after Michael on the heath.

Sensible divers do much of their training on trampolines (*how else would you imagine . . . trial and error?*), strapping themselves into harnesses Harry Houdini might struggle with, as a trusted man (not a love rival, preferably) controlled the flight, by counter-weighted pulleys and ropes.

If you've never seen competitive trampolining in the flesh, nip along (if you survived your synchro rehearsals) and have a look . . . it's fantastic.

England's Stewart Matthews and Carl Furrer were—at one, and different times—singles and synchro World champions.
We'd signed up to cover the World Cup, somewhere in Surrey.
After practice, I asked our scaffolders to build a camera rostrum so that the lens height would be level with the top of the bounce . . . about 30ft up. Even though the cameraman's head was rammed into the ceiling of the leisure centre, he managed to get some stunningly intimate shots—empty frame, then . . . *boyng!* . . . big face of the flier, searching for the optimum height from which to initiate his aerobatics—*mustard*.

You'd know, if you've ever come a cropper in the tramp-cages at the end of the pier, or watched any edition of *You've Been Framed*, it has its dangers; good sport for kids, who seldom show fear, and recover quickly from fractures.

We'd filmed Chris doing his dry-land contortions in the gym at Florida State uni. The following morning was a beauty—clear blue skies—as we, lensman Ian Kennedy, daft Fred Clark, our sound man in headphones (. . . *what high speed express?*), Hammy and I, went poolside to watch Chris unraveling in free-fall.

?A boat . . . that's the ticket!

As in most things American, someone, somewhere has what you want. Although the device we ended up hiring was more like a Dunkirk landing craft, than the simple inflatable we'd had in mind, it did the job.
Duly delivered—*"inside the hour"*—our Duck was sturdy and spacious, enough for the crew and me . . . and, at a push, a squad of marines.

(*surely Chris couldn't miss it from ten metres up . . . could he?*).

Ian, the sarcastic perfectionist, wasn't satisfied with the first dive:
'Nice try Chris, but can you get a bit closer to us?'

I swear, by the great insurer in the sky, the diver had the faintest of paint smears on his shapely ass with the next effort: he hit the water, fists first, like a failed exocet.

'Perfect . . . a few more like that' . . . exclaimed Kennedy.

(*shoot, we'll kill the sonofabitch*).

I conjured the headlines:

SNODE TRAGEDY . . . BBC STUNT GOES TOO FAR.

. . . or, in the 'Reds':

DISHY DIVER, DUCKS AND DIES.

The opening slow-motion sequence of our film—to a haunting, building track (*'risvegliato'* innit?)—was superb . . . 30" of Olympic prospect, seemingly suspended in dexterous animation, re-aligning finally, and knifing through the surface at 40m.p.h., like a booby at breakfast.

Later that evening, we went lakeside for more interviewing and stuff; word was that the local alligators had a weakness for marshmallows
(*the freshpersons must have been pissing themselves*).
So, like many of the shell-suited 'fat squad' around these parts, we armed ourselves with far too many bags-worth, and set up: Chris, foreground, profile . . . lake and potential background-interest, predominate.

If you've never seen *Crocodile Dundee I* or *II*, or a Steve Irwin show on telly, I can assure you these ancient critters get out of the blocks on four short and stumpies quicker than Ben Johnson on *stanozozol*.

One of the brothers nipped a prize poodle from the front lawn of a lakeside garden, as big Kev—my erstwhile brother-in-law—and I walked between holes on a West Floridian golf course. The perfectly groomed, pink (and no doubt 'adorable') pooch was hoofing it for the cat-flap, when *Tick Tock* caught up with his aperitif; I left my big hitting 'relative' (who was several up at the time) to search the reeds for his own ball.

Having survived the diving, how ironic were he (Chris) to perish by death roll . . . but we needn't have worried; ten bucks worth of pink and white softies later, the waters' calm hadn't been troubled
(the sniggering *Bud(weiser)* brigade needed a Glasgow 'sorting').

Snode was 5th and 7th behind Louganis in springboard and platform.

Not too far away, at Winter Haven—all things American being relative—was Cypress Gardens, home of water ski-ing, a sport we'd been into back home in Scotland and one that would be 'demonstrated'—without adoption—at the Munich Olympics.
Some years before, BBC *Sportsnight* had sent a film unit north to Lochearnhead, in Perthshire, to do a feature on Jeanette Stewart-Wood, who was attempting to become the first woman to jump over a 100ft on water-skis.

If Cypress Gardens* was the Daddy of *world* water skiing (* it's now owned by *Legoland*), Lochearnhead would be a distant Scottish cousin . . . and Ruislip Lido, its English twin.

The grandly named David Nations was the driving force down south, and Jeanette was his star pupil. David's best mate was Donald Campbell who died in a 300mph crash on Coniston Water (he was never allowed to drive the tow-boat).

In stark contrast to immodest Nations (name like that you could afford to be), the head honcho in Perthshire was Ewan Cameron—mine massive host at the Lochearnhead Hotel (at the head of Loch Earn, patently). Permanently kilted Ewan scaled at 22 stone—a latter day *Geordie* who could toss the hammer, the caber and any would-be rowdy from his bar, with alacrity (lock-ins for the favoured few—including the constabulary—were standard).

The clashings were irresistible: Ewan . . . educated privately, and worldly—David . . . well-heeled, a bit flash and headstrong. In the title race for 'Heavyweight champ of British water ski-ing,' Ewan was immovable.

Both clubs contributed to the GB team of the day: Duncan Croll was the leading Scottish light—Jeanette and Robin Beckitt, the pride of Ruislip, and developing at a remarkable pace (suspicion of growth hormones in his *Frosties* were unfounded)was Nation's prodigy, Mike Hazelwood.
Little Mike (he was tiny when he came to our club) would become World jump champ, pinging off a 6 foot ramp at speeds you'd get a ticket for in the States.
Dad Maurice (Hazelwood) had the same kind of parental determination the Williams sisters and Tiger Woods would 'benefit' from . . . nor was he averse to getting his hands dirty.
One evening, in a *don't do what I say* . . . *do what I do* display of parental folly, he stripped to his *Speedos*, strapped on a life-vest and went for a tow behind the club's big, horny *Boesch* boat.

Alas, his *p.s.i.* to *m.p.h.* ratio on arrival at the slippery slope wasn't right—the key being to relax, momentarily, as ski and wood first meet, otherwise it's not going to work out as shown in the brochure.

Miraculously—some said commendably, for originality—Mo contrived to half execute a somersault in the 20ft of available ramp, bashing his helmet-less head off the top edge—Louganis style—and crash-landing in a heap of skis, blood, and embarrassment.
What a silly old Maurice.

Another great talent of the era was Jack Fulton, a puny, bespectacled waif-of-a-thing from Paisley*, where William Wallace studied subversion, a boy, David—the retiring *Doctor Who*—was born to the Tennants, and from where Paolo Nutini's *Pencil Full of Lead* probably came.

Wee Jack was asthmatic—chronically so—but found the sport efficacious to the point of becoming British champion and, in an act of biblical flourish, was able to cast off his inhaler for good; any of you cursed by 'the wheezers' could do worse than give it a shot . . . it's one of sport's real thrillers (there is no known cure for supporting *St. Mirren F.C.).

In stark contrast to the warm, shallow waters of Ruislip lido, Loch Earn is deep—very deep—and full-length protective rubbers were advisable most of the time (what one did of an evening was entirely at one's own risk).

At its west end, the waters were sheltered from the prevailing winds by hills on three sides, making it an ideal venue for competition . . . hence Jeanette's presence at the 1965 Scottish Championships.

The film crew were out of London: I mention it because their first act was to sink their hired *Land Rover* up to its axles on the pebbled foreshore, smack in front of a big Scottish crowd—the *BBC Sportsnight* sticker on the side of the truck had been an error.
No question, they were jeered.
Fierce Hamish MacGregor (Rob Roy country)—not a fibre between his (rumoured) prodigious manhood and the inside apron of his kilt—brought a tractor to the rescue and pulled them free, to a good, if sarcastic hand.
The Sassenachs won the day . . . or Jeanette did, as she soared to splashdown 101ft from the edge of the ramp.
The world record, currently, is almost twice that for girls—the best man is in the two hundred and forties.
Two years on, Jeanette Stewart Wood became the first ever *British* World water ski champion; a decade later bionic Mike did the same.

Lochearnhead 0 Ruislip 2

One of the judges at the measuring table—as Jeanette flew by—was Lewis Drysdale, an eccentric lawyer from Crieff, whose bright red (Alpine air and gluvine), four-eyed (NHS bins) 'visog' could be seen peeking out of the starting hut at all the major snow-ski races in Europe during the reign of King Klammer I of Austria.

Lewis was a regular at our local . . . *'a warm welcome awaits you at the Murraypark, a small friendly hotel where personal service is assured. Guests can enjoy full access to Crieff Hydro's Lagoon leisure facilities and daily entertainments programme, all within a five minute walk!'* (best they do their own publicity).

One night, having arranged his briefs in a shambles at the office, he dropped by for a swift half.

As he approached the bar, he produced a shelf-rattling fart:
"*Sorry,*" by way of a half-apology *"I meant to cough . . . large Gordon's and tonic, Maisie, if you please"*
(the owner's formidable Irish wife gagged as she steadied the bottles).

Propped up at one end of the tiny bar was another long distance drinker—and avid Rangers' fan—Bruce Watson.

An American couple, swathed in cashmere, cologne and *Coco*, slipped in for pre-dinner cocktails.

"Evening" said Bruce confidently, displaying non-malevolent effrontery, ". . . you folks' first time in Scotland?"

(*'don't get involved'* we begged, silently, of the house guests)

"First time, yeah."

Mrs. Crawford fixed the *Martinis*.

"What line of work are you in?" pursued our man in the boiler-suit.

Politely, the abundantly affluent tourist replied:
"I'm in oil."

"*Me too*" exclaimed Bruce extending a weathered hand to his new pal.
(Bruce delivered essentials to businesses and farms in the Perthshire area . . . by *Shell* tanker).

Down the east end of Loch Earn, at picturesque St. Fillans, *The Urgle Gurgle Water Ski Club* ruled—founded on 'heavy' beer, chasers and good social intercourse.

Not only did we kop most of the bad weather, we had to run the gauntlet of the local sailing club and their stern commodore, Major Campbell-Lamerton (r'td) . . . or was that the rugby player? Yes . . . Campbell-<u>Crawford</u>—'Admiral' Campbell Crawford, that's the very commodore.
(*'water, water'* every day, lest all his boats should sink)
Giving way to sail was tricky, as you screamed through regatta traffic into our bay and jetty; some cross-bow swearing and fist-waving, but no accidents.

When the weather cock on Crieff's South kirk steeple swung to the east, we 'scrambled' the cars; twenty minutes later we'd be at the club, suited up, with ideal, mill-pond conditions for ski-ing.

P.C. John Wilson of Stirling County's motor cycle division, had a caravan on site, kept neat and trim and amply stocked by wife Ida.
Most Sunday mornings John could be seen flying over our wooden clubhouse—from a handy incline behind—on his trials machine, as Mrs. Wilson made crispy bacon for the 'eggie' bread.

Shed jumping wasn't called for much in the force—*but, in an emergency, we knew a man who could.*

I was hugely disappointed to learn that my hero, Steve McQueen (*Virgil Hilts*)—a.k.a. "*Thomas Crown*" a.k.a. "The King of Cool"—had <u>not</u> been on board during the fence-jumping stunt in *The Great Escape* (based on the true story of *Stalag Luft III*). Being the world's highest paid movie star at the time, the producers probably felt their no-claims was at risk.
Top Gear petrol-heads would know that McQueen *was* at the wheel of the Ford Mustang GT 390 during much of the seminal car chase in *Bullitt*, and I say hats off 'Stevo' for saving Fred {Astaire}'s ass in *Towering Inferno*, and for giving sexual meaning to chess.

It's not a festival renowned for tolerance, but P.C. Wilson had been 'volunteered' for an away day shift in Glasgow, one 12th of July—Orange march day, the annual celebration of the Battle of the Boyne, circa 1690: William (*"Protestants"*) v James (*"Catholics"*) . . . 'King Billy' getting the point (*"away win"*).
Trouble was expected—and, most times, delivered—so *'all hands, horses and bikes on deck.'*

Patrolman Wilson edged his way through the throng, towards the ranks of marching bands. Just as he drew alongside, the man setting the tempo—the big drummer—let him have one, smack on top of his skid-lid, without missing a beat, as the columns processed towards Glasgow Green for the traditional skirmish; inwardly, John applauded his technique.
Some arrests were made . . . and the band played on.

None of us made it to international level, but we could all slalom, trick and jump enough to have a great time on the water. Few who came to us as debutantes failed to conquer, and it was thrilling see others crack the basics with little instruction.
The newsreader is probably not related, but the family Rayworth came to the club during the summer holidays and one of the daughters was 'Sophie' (*suppose I <u>could</u> ring after the Six* . . . *but what if it's not?* . . . *"Love your work"* I guess).

Our heavyweight A-lister was handsome, tanned, strong (as a bleedin' ox), Andy Robin, the British wrestling champion; any talk of 'fixing' would find the perpetrator in Andy's famous leg lock:

"What happens next . . . *I* dive backwards . . . *you* break both legs—tap out, sucker."

Were you prepared to have copious amounts of calcine gypsum plastered to your broken limbs in A & E, you might describe Andy's wrestling of a fully grown 54 stone grizzly bear, as '*a cabaret act*.'
Discard the idea of a cuddly koala—very possibly with Chlamydia—or a lugubrious, sex-starved panda on triple strength Viagra . . . this bad boy was fully practical.
"*HERCULES*"—or '*Sir*,' were you not a family friend—stood 8ft 4in in his bedroom slippers, and was like a son to Andy and Maggie—a greedy bugger admittedly, but house-trained and respectful.

How many loo rolls and jars of bee-processed flower nectar fit in a cash and carry trolly?

'Herc' often joined 'Mum' and 'Dad' for a drink down the local in Glendevon.

When he went missing in the Outer Hebrides, during a film shoot for two-ply, luxury *Andrex*, he apparently lost 20 stone in three weeks—*now that is a diet* (according to *Wikipedia*—in whom we trust . . . and to whom all should make contributions—we in the UK use enough *Andrex* each day to stretch one and a half times round the world).

He of the sweet fang and devastating claw played alongside *007* in *Octopussy*, and 'caddied' for another of my mates, Bob Hope, at Gleneagles . . . but he never did master water ski-ing; it would have taken *Bluebird* at full pelt.

'GET OUT OF THE WATER!'

"Have You Heard . . . Josh Gifford Died?"

As surely as the silvery Moon has nine phases—and *The Rain* would become *Oasis*—it'll be lashing in Manchester.
Never a problem at Old Trafford, you just reached for a cricket standby—the BBC archives were bulging.

Naturally, the US does bigger storms, electric light shows Mr. Disney could only have dreamed about. One such postponed the World water-ski Championships in Florida, and nearly cancelled out the crew—a tree, a few feet away taking the hit we could not have survived.

As a rule of thumb: *were you to get caught in a storm, make yourself as small a target as possible and steer clear of tall trees and water.*

Thunder and lightning are carefully monitored on the golf tours; portable detectors, on site, give early warnings that perfect conductors—like clubs and 'brollies'—should be dropped 'smartish,' balls marked where they lay, and players do whatever they believe to be the best thing in the circumstances . . . *LEG IT!*

On a recent ladies tour event in Europe, we had a barometric breakdown; ominous skies, sudden drop in temperature, stillness in the air . . . but no hooter to evacuate; there was nowt wrong with Laura Davies's instincts as she left all in her wake in a sprint to the clubhouse.

Having survived a lightning strike, Lee Trevino was asked what he'd do if the storms came again: *"I'd take out my 1 iron and point it to the sky—not even God can hit the 1 iron."*

Lightning kills more people than practically any other 'natural' occurrence, yet for we carefree teenagers, the danger signs were often ignored. Giant gashes rent into massive trunks, scarred black by the ferocious heat, and crippled branches left to suffer in silence, was proof enough—for idiots—of unimaginable power.

When 'The Ghost'—a.k.a. John White—was killed on the golf course it was surreal . . . *by lightning*? He was 27, at the peak of his powers; his was a priceless talent, orchestrating 'the double' wins for Spurs in '60-'61, and bringing order to

Scotland's eclectic mix—the original 'mid-field general' and perfect foil for the extravagances of Denis Law.

Valderrama looked just as its eccentric owner would have wished—'Augustan'—as we at European Tour Productions rolled up for Ryder Cup 1997. Southern Spain, in September, gets its fair share of rain, but you trusted Jaime Ortiz-Patiño to have had a word; his connections far outstripped those of the many fugitives-from-justice living it up along the coast. For a man once seen trimming ambitious grass shoots from an otherwise uniformly shorn putting surface, *with a pair of nail scissors*—by torchlight—attention to detail was paramount . . . worthy of a syndrome, and possibly a visit from the men in white coats.

His course was 'Sotogrande New' when we first played the Sherry Cup there (an annual trip by British worthies to take on the might of amateur Spain). Many nights were wasted in *Jimmy's Bar* (he was an Irish 'Jimmy') at Porto Banus, discussing handicap irregularities; not that we had absolute proof, but we did overhear the 'oppo' talking of 'winter' handicaps (you *what?!*).

'Jimmy' P., took over in 1985. He was into mining on a large scale, and his plans for Valderrama were vaultingly ambitious; top of the wish list . . . *bring the Ryder Cup to Spain for the first time* (it went 'European' in '79—not that Garrido and Ballesteros did much to help on that occasion), . . . *and have my good friend Seve elected captain*.
The mercurial one was at the old man, constantly, to change this and that . . . a bunker here, an entire green there . . . and it'd get worse.
The Augustan identity became an obsession: there were similarities . . . lush grass, 'linoleum' greens, an abundance of water and trees (pine—like Ike's—in Augusta, cork in Andalucia), but the Yanks (make that 'the southern boys') had history on their side, not all of that, prejudice-free . . . even now.

Mr. Robert T. (for Tyre) Jones converted the former Georgian nursery into a stiff exam for *The Masters*, and Mr. Robert T. (for Trent) Jones (no relation . . . *no comparison*) was similarly charged:
. . . *'if necessary, move mountains.'*

Way back, Canadian actor, Bernard Braden, hosted a game-show on TV called *The Name's the Same*—simple formula, nicked from the (generic) Yanks: celebrity panel . . . 10 questions . . . guess the contestant's famous name. In the US version it could be an actual person, a place, a thing or an action ("Will Kiss" or "I. Draw"—open to all sorts of abuse).
A few years ago, BBC Four produced a revival edition, *but the patient didn't recover*.

Willie Fernie was part of the highly successful Celtic and Scotland teams in the late '50s-early '60s. He was in the Hoops' 'double' side with Charlie Tully, Bertie

Peacock, Bobby Evans and Jock Stein, and played for Scotland in two World Cups (Uruguay—the holders—did us seven zip in the first of those, in Switzerland. *Have mercy . . . it wasn't all Fred Martin's fault).*

It's not a milestone Rangers fans like reminding of (*so here goes*), but Willie was among the scorers in the 7-1 battering *we* gave them in the 1957 League Cup final at *Hampden in the Sun ('Come On!').*

Willie's namesake (Willie Fernie, by deduction)—the Open Champion over Musselburgh's 'forgotten' 9 hole links, in 1883—was allowed to fiddle with his home course at St Andrews—<u>and</u> Royal Troon—but takes full credit for Turnberry's twins, *The Ailsa* and *The Arran*.

'The (White) Ghost' was a Musselburgh man—as were Willie Park Snr, Bob Ferguson, 'Deacon' Brown, Mungo Park and Willie Park jr., Open champions all, integral to a glorious heritage we Jocks dine out on (in the absence of anything comparable in fitba or rugby, nationally).

'*Of Astronauts and Artisans*' was the working title of my ambitious plan for a series about golf in Scotland.
Here, in two dimensions, the ultimate compendium—enduring, alluring, entertaining, informative, further reaching than any glossy brochure, or 60" Tourist Board ad on telly . . . OK, so the delegation would miss their annual jolly to the golf show in Florida, but what potential for the Scottish economy (*it said here*).
Anything anyone would ever want to know about the game and its diversity; no turgid chronology this—a crofter's glen-side lay-out, sheep on agronomy, tin cans for cups, an honesty box for maintenance, juxtaposed with Muirfield's impregnable fortress, home to chauvinism and dastardly challenges by the (all-male) Honourable Company of Edinburgh golfers, in pink . . . with their royal and ancient rivals, in waiting, up the coast. Mrs. Campbell's B&B at Dornoch, with tattie scones and black puddin' to start the day, against five-star room-service in the presidential suite at Gleneagles, where caddies are patronised, and laced haggis, spuds and neeps are musts for lunch in the Dormy House.
Sandy Lyle and Paul Lawrie to show you round . . . students and historians to make it precise . . . 'Perthite' Ewan Mac(Gregor) as mine Hollywood host.

It was to have been my legacy; this rubbish will have to suffice.

What do 18th century 'Planter John'—4th Duke of Atholl—and John Brown's shipyard have in common with persimmon and low density titanium?
All would have been connected, had I been given the means.

Take away shipbuilding and herring (which they did), whisky (which many do) and the Old Firm (*they wouldn't dare*), and what's left—tourism, Frankie Boyle, and a quarter of a million golf club members.

As part of the ill-fated project, my cameraman, business partner (and 3-handicap golfer), Davie Maxwell and I went to film *The Musselburgh Challenge*—a hickory competition (in period dress)for clubs in the area—the glue in a day-long celebration of their five Open champions. Surviving relatives came with memories and memorabilia . . . from Massachusetts a distant relation of Musselburgh born Willie Campbell, who'd helped design the famous Brookline Country Club . . . a grand relative of the Parks talked casually of "an old club" she'd found in her attic—imagine grinning Arthur Negus getting his teeth round that evaluation on *Going for a Song*.
Not the majesty, nor dimension, of Mount Rushmore, but likenesses of the *Famous Five* (previous page), mounted on the clubhouse wall, were unveiled to a haunting pibroch . . . then everyone got 'pished' at the céildh.

Scottish business, from airlines and hotel chains to mineral water bottlers and highland distillers 'endorsed' my plan . . . the R&A gave us their 'blessing' . . . but no one coughed the requisite 'wedge.'

Imagine my surprise when both Ireland and Wales beat Scotland to the Ryder Cup.

Bob Jones would need a pin to exact a signature hole from the ponds and ericaceous plants of *Amen Corner*; but at Valderrama there was no debate . . . *Los Gabiones* was Jimmy's baby.
When we played it, the 17th was the no-less-impossible 8th, but Patiño figured swopping the nines around would make for a sterner test; 10 out of 10 times he got what he wanted. Dynamiting cliffs to build motorways and essential access roads to his dream-world was stock-in-trade for a miner; if he wanted the water in his lakes to be unnaturally green, the residents would have a choice—comply . . . *or die* (a bit harsh perhaps, as Snr. Patiño would become a guiding light in conservation).

Beauteous as many courses are to the beholder, certain factions remain unconvinced that flora and fauna are receiving their full allowance.

Our TV planning had taken months but everyone was pleased and ready to go.
Europe were holders . . . *just*, and favourites . . . *just*.
Seve was just hyper . . . *and he wasn't playing*.
We had all 18 holes covered; fleets of buggies were poised to move cameras, microphones and technicians round the course on a continuous conveyor belt—there would be no visible joins.
Until it were dusted, we'd hardly be coming off.

Studios were lit and 'guested' . . . then, with minutes to go, the heavens opened.
That rain in Spain seemed mainly to be falling on our gigantic truck. Inside were rows and rows of monitors, and a sprawling mixer-desk hooked up to all manner of visual inputs—toys to shape and distort the images, to add captions, to split screens, to froth the *cappuccinos* and mix the *mojitos*—a very sophisticated, highly technical, ludicrously expensive bit of kit, powered by electricity, which, as we know, doesn't do rain.

Autumn leaves clogged the ducts, so the water, at its most resourceful, found weakness . . . *directly above* the aforementioned ludicrously expensive, highly technical, very sophisticated, electrically driven mixer.

The producer (me), director Mike Wilmot (who'd planned, meticulously, for things not to go wrong), and our unflappable switcher, Jackie Watkin, leapt backwards as *'la cascada'* viz., 'the waterfall' (hole number 4 / par 5 / a 516 yarder . . . . *'one of the best I've done,'* said Trent Jones . . . two huge belts if the *Levante* blows) hit.

Were you thinking of a night out in the 60s, nowhere better than the Whitehall Theatre in London for a farce, starring actor/producer Brian Rix (very possibly with his trousers down at some stage in the evening) and his Invernesian wife, Elspet McGregor-Gray (now Baroness Rix).

Where farce is afoot, timing is at a premium . . . doors and windows opening and closing on cue . . . . marks being hit, unfalteringly . . . controlled chaos.

And thus it was at Valderrama; engineers from adjoining sound and vision booths burst in with receptacles . . . and intelligence.
One climbed on the roof and cleared the ducts, stemming the flow . . . . *but it could 'blow' again at any moment.*

Out of work-clothes, megastar footballers are seldom far from their i-Pods and hairdryers, but Jackie's odd decision (or premonition) to bring hers to work was a huge blessing—it (the hairdryer) became central to the mop-up.

Handbags and glad rags in and around changing rooms are integral to the modern game, but when handsome dog Franz Beckenbauer was leaner and darker, they might have raised an eyebrow or two.
He was more of a suit than sarong man, more into Baselitz's than body art.

The amiable giant came to Scotland for a Dalglish testimonial (*be very surprised—it was hosing*) and as any excuse to talk to him was a good one, we made a date to meet in his hotel room later that evening.
'Der Kaiser' was as popular in Munich as 'Becks' was in Manchester;

"the whole of Scotland," as Bill McLaren would (if asked) have said *"loved Dalglish."*

The German and Beckham the 'Pom' were archetypical alphas—they'd skippered their countries . . . scored a few (Franz Anton 14, David Robert Joseph 17) . . . they'd had long tours with one club (Bayern and United) . . . each invaded America, one landing in the east (Cosmos), the other lured—perhaps steered—west (Galaxy); yet differences remain: David is monogamous, in most senses of the word, and has tats to remind him, but he hasn't won 'The Big One' . . . as a player nor boss.
Beckenbauer has been married three times.

Some cheek asking a man with 103 <u>caps</u> for West Germany, who'd been in 3 World Cup squads (2nd in '66, 3rd in '70, and 1st in Munich in '74), to take a turn with the hotel's hairdryer, but the inner workings of our camera had fallen foul of the tempest at the match, and blowing hot air was its only salvation; we had a room to set and light, *ich bin Ihnen sehr dankbar*, indeed.

I had to know about the goal that wasn't . . . and how he felt about the hosts (the 'home' team) picking red for the final.

The Springtime of '66 . . . . an expectant crowd gathers on the tarmac at Heathrow, not far from the wartime Heston aerodrome, as a small jet liner—a distant relative of Geoffrey de Havilland's Comet—rolls to a standstill.

Smooth as a dalek, a mobile gangway kisses its fuselage.

The forward door is punched open, and in the archway looms Harewood, President of the Football Association.
A cabled microphone is rushed to the top of the stairs.

Flashbulbs pop as the 7th*Earl—George Lascelles—produces a single sheet of paper.*

'My good friends, for the first time in our history, a British team has made it to the World Cup Final

(applause*)*.

'I've just come back from West Berlin with some great news for all hard-up parents of England—they've agreed we can play in white!'

(hearty cheers ring out . . . hoo-rah!*)*.

Peace on our terraces (disaster for the merchandisers).

V-ery interrr-esting . . . but had the 'Chermans' been telling ze <u>whole</u> truth?

It would have been a *"pick up the baw, we're no playin'"* moment had it been Scotland (a longish shot for 2018) and East Germany (Olympic Gold medalists in 1976) who'd made it to Wembley that summer; 'Slim Jim' Baxter and the boys wouldn't have come out to play in anything other than dark blue . . .

. . . still, they did OK in red, I guess.

In Sotogrande, the clock ticked by.
We got on air on time, but Richard Keyes, having his first taste of 'live' golf, had to fill for an eternity. Predictable guests—including three time skipper Bernard Gallacher, by right, and Prince Andrew, by private jet—were rolled in and out of Sky's battered studio, as mouth fatigue and golf starvation took their tolls.
Eventually José Maria Olazabal and Costantino Rocca got the fourballs rolling, and by Sunday afternoon 'Monty' (*who else*) had sealed the deal.

My old Devonian 'china,' David Vine—the dental amalgam when serious filling was required—had a mind powered by word association, and a vast knowledge of sport. Like Ted Ray, Bob Monkhouse and 'Doddy'—comedians with total recall—'D'vine' could go on endlessly.

No one was laughing at Badminton on day 3 of 3.

I'd just completed an edited version of the cross-country stage of the horse trials, down at the Duke of Beaufort's bijou in Gloucestershire—green-welly/shitting-dog/silk head-square country. The sequence we'd put together (through the night) would be transmitted prior to going 'live' for the decisive show jumping phase.

Frank Bough introduced *Sunday Grandstand* from the middle of the arena; say what nasty things you like about 'Frankers'—and plenty did—he was exceptionally good on the job (*leave it!*).

His opening link was delivered effortlessly and immaculately.

'Badders' producer/director, Alan Mouncer, stood me and my edited package by.

Without warning, the machine took off, careering past the 10 second cue point to God knows where down the tape . . . and they were big suckers—once in high-speed-spool mode, pulling the *QE II* up at Southampton harbour lights would have been easier.

You know the fairground ride that leaves you hanging against the wall of a spinning cylinder as the floor drops away . . . no gravity no centrifugal anything?

This was it . . . shock, panic, horror . . . . the D.H.S.S.

"You'll have to fill, Frankers . . . the V.T.'s not there.
("Viney" would have loved this)

Windy-stainers hit my boxers.

Mouncer embodied cool—Frank too; all cameras were on alert.

At the entrance of the parade ring, the Master of Foxhounds, horn at the ready, sat high astride his bandaged steed, as below, sniffing detectives 'hoovered' for clues.

Obvious things to fanny on about, had been . . . too quickly for Frank's liking: size of the crowds . . . the uniformity of *Barbour* and chameaux chasseurs . . . the results of the dressage—*but whether to give away the cross country too?*

"What news J.P?"

There was none, to be frank, Frank.

The cry went up: *'Release the hounds!'*

In at pace came the Hunt . . . well, the Master and hounds anyway.
In group sessions, these puppies can make one helluva mess of a cornered fox (in the name of pest control—*bollocks!*).
Naked Ape zoologist, Desmond Morris, would have an explanation, but anything excited dogs can cock a leg at . . . *they cock*, be it territorial marking, flashing their bits to bitches, or pure desperation to wazz.

The anchorman was besieged; subconsciously pleading for some
'It's On Cue' relief in his ear, he blethered on about this and that, as queues for the loos—as long for the boys as the girls, unusually—intensified. A riot seemed likely.

But what a trooper! (* *any cheap remarks about men in women's underwear would be inappropriate at this stressful time).*

Instead of good news, 'Boughie' got bladdersful of *Hampden's curse*—'the feeling' I'd had when toilet-trained 'animals' surrounded me in Glasgow.

Clare Balding would probably have been snoozing in her pram in Dad's yard at Lambourne during my other (previously reported) soiling-by-dog. *Channel 4 Racing* was still a decade away, so perhaps the family growlers were just happy to see us BBC types at Kingsclere.

Doused in pungent uretha juice, the hour and a half journey back to London from Berkshire, in a packed car, was mighty unpleasant; at least Frankers had a fresh pair of knickers to change into (* *OK to do it here*).

It wasn't <u>whether</u> *Mill Reef ("owned by Paul Mellon, trained by Ian Blading and ridden by Geoff Lewis")* was going to win the 1971 Derby, but by how many lengths.
A few days after his (two-length) win at Epsom, the pilot and I ended up in a heap in the lobby of the Ariel hotel at Heathrow. Having built up a considerable head of steam through several circuits of the revolving door, he hit me like a ten-pin bowling ball, choosing his moment of release as precisely as in 'the closing stages' of any of those other fantastic finishes that year—at Sandown for the Eclipse, the King George at Ascot and the Arc at Longchamps.
The wee guy was shit-faced. No steward's . . . . no usable quotes.

Julian Wilson, whom Clare succeeded as BBC Racing Correspondent in 1997—not without a snipe and a bitch or two—was champagne to the lofty O'Sullevan's caviar; neither was much good for a tip, though there was a 'Whitehall' moment one Royal Ascot when Peter let slip his 'nap of the day. Several staff were unseated and crushed in the mass evacuation . . . *and* it won.

My office, in Shepherd's Bush, was on the ground floor of Kensington House from where *Sportsnight,* and *Match of the Day* were produced and administered.

The door flew open.

A distraught looking "Jules"—hair 'gelled' tight to his skull, in waistcoat, clashing Harvey Proctor and pin-striped, braced trousers set to the optimum atop poorly-buffed Chelsea browns—pronounced, in his best Harrovian:

'Have you heard . . . Josh Gifford died?'

Jesus! . . . obit . . . no time . . . get Aldaniti stuff . . . the Hennessy . . . champion jockey quotes . . . who can do it?

I needn't have panicked.

'*Josh Gifford*' was Julian's Jack Russell.
Apparently a racing pal had come to lunch with one considerable larger than wee Josh, and promptly had him for his (lunch).
The surviving Gifford—the four-time national hunt champion jockey—never fell off in the Grand National in 30 rides and would live to train on. Olympian eventer, Tina Cook's Dad, Josh, died in February.

Several things needed doing at the Grand National (apart from my buddy Richard Pitman winning it, and the finish being shot from the inside); I mentioned my straight-face notions for a hovercraft at the Boat Race, and a frogman at the swimming—both committees had said "*NO.*"

Would National Hunt take a punt on a helicopter?

'No, absolutely not . . . . it'll spook the horses.'

"*Objection—leading the witness.*"

"Sustained."

Using the not inconsiderable influence of wily John Hughes, Clerk of the Course at Aintree, we ran tests at a mid-week meeting at Chepstow, with encouraging results: *only four horses were lost* (I jest).
The 'bird' caused no distress whatsoever, to horse nor jock.
We showed the tape to those who must be obeyed in Liverpool . . . at the Jockey Club . . . G.C.H.Q . . . MIs 5 & 6 . . . Parkinson . . . and Buck House, and got the nod.
The rest is . . . *excellent.*

A combination of isolated recordings at the 1st, Bechers, the Chair, Valentine's and the Water, plus the helicopter camera and a few unmanned expendables in the brush, produced the definitive visual account of the race.
The massive audience of occasional punters on Grand National day wanted to know how *'theirs'* had fared . . . *had they fallen . . . if so, why?*
At last, we were able to provide most of the answers.
Within minutes of the winners making it through hordes of neck and calf slappers to Lynam's lair—next to the unsaddling enclosure—'Pitters' and Bill Smith were poised in the parade ring commentary box with the tale of the tape.
It was a cracking complement to our 'live' coverage, which had been tinkered with and honed by race directors and producers down the years; the debate about the best siting for the Canal Turn camera, in man-hours per spoken word, outstripped the reformation of the House of Lords issue, by a distance.

Our great relationship with Aintree, and *Seagram*—through "Hughsie," and Ivan the terribly nice—was underpinned by the head honcho.
Just as *"Jock"* is inoffensive to us hairy arses—and "nigger" is to Afro Americans—*"Yid"* (providing it rhymes with deed) is acceptable to most Yiddish speakers.
The *"yeed"* in question was Edgar Bronfman who ranked alongside Einstein, Golda Meir and Antony Sher, at the top end of the world's-most-influential-Jews league table.

A select band of us were invited on a booze cruise to Maryland, U.S.A. for the Hunt Cup—'booze' in the sense that Edgar's private jet was laden with the stuff, and 'cruise' as at 30,000 ft and steady (ish).
Amongst other tax-deductable company activities, Mr. B. used the jet to fly his kids back and forth from Canada to private school in England.
It was his crate, to do with as he bloody well liked; for shorter trips, there was a twin-engined chopper, and on the ground—to avoid pollutents and the proletariat—a fleet of stretches.

So what if it's one of the deadlies, envying how the other half live is a neat way to self-assess, without the repeated 'none'-filling in empty boxes on your annual return.
Not having a yacht in Monte Carlo bay was nothing to get depressed about when one's mortgage only had thirty-five more years to run, and gap years were about to begin.

James Hunt ran a dispensary of sorts, off the back of one honey-of-a-thing during Grand Prix week; it would shock you (and infuriate, to be teased thus) to know who his customers were, especially in view of the average speeds around the tricky streets of Monaco.

Team crews, on compressed air, sprinted for the pits—*we were all set.*
Murray, legs akimbo (he preferred to stand), revved up.
Every available Grimaldi was present and correct.

No Hunt.

"GO!" Sainte Devote here they come—Standby with the crane.

As befits the perspicacious, Murray had the commentary position furnished precisely: meticulous notes and charts placed strategically, high and low, to suit his vari-focals; a swift turn in any direction would have him face to face with a priceless stat. Little of today's minutia was available to commentators, so it was DIY for the most part, and Murray was an expert.

As the slowest qualifier tore up towards Masenet and Casino square, a bottle of the finest rosé arrived on the desk . . . *James was in the house* (more of a cage in truth, right by the pavement, with Rainier Louis Henri Maxence Bertrand Grimaldi, His Serene Highness The Sovereign Prince of Monaco in made-to-measure earplugs, a couple of boxes along, en famille).

"Stuck in traffic, old boy"—a *'sorry C.J.'* moment *Reggie Perrin* would have been proud of . . . bearing in mind there was none.
Murray pressed on.

Like Barry Sheene—his good buddy, and fellow lothario—James would have a fag and/or shag prior to, and immediately after, racing; now that he'd retired (from driving), he got down to honing his other playboy addictions.

"Fuck it, Philipo (me), *I'm out of here* (James) . . . *he* (Murray)*'s hogging the bloody mic again."*

Kyalami, South Africa—during the sliding skirts/FISA-FOCA wars era. James and Murray had already been at the centre of a pay dispute with the host broadcasters, but there was no need for such petulance from one so normally measured and confident.
Murray cracked on on his own while James hunkered down, outside the commentary box, to a mega spliff . . . returning, after a couple of laps, as if nothing had happened (which it hadn't, fairly typically).

The job took me to all sorts of exotic places bank clerks could only dream of:

Brazil 1978.
The big goalkeeper reached up and pulled back the curtains in his 16th storey bedroom overlooking the Sugar Loaf; the beach below teemed with talent . . . barefoot ball-skills . . . babes in bikinis (or better) . . . even the occasional male cheeks in a thong was forgivable on . . . *Copa, copa-cabaaaa-na*.

Unashamedly, we hugged each other—*what a spot . . . what a job!*

Bob Wilson, who'd kept for *us* (and 234 times for the Arsenal), who'd won 'the double,' who'd married magnificent Megs, who was pals with Cruyff and Mathis, who'd grow to dislike Ken Bates almost as much as the rest of us, was thrilled to be in Rio de Janeiro.
Along with Barry Davies and our film crew, we'd gone in advance to get training footage and interviews with the Brazilians, before heading down to join the rest of the BBC team in Buenos Aires for the World Cup finals.

Poor old Barry got the trots 'early doors.' While he sat on a rock contemplating suicide, Bob and I went for a (no pun intended) run.
Bob pounded effortlessly through the soft sand—I was timing my stitch for the girls' volleyball court.

In order to fully appreciate the tactics involved, it's sometimes necessary to frame the front players ass, in huge close up, on telly, in order to pick up the signals: wiggles and flashes need capturing, just as the catcher's crotch code does in baseball. It's just the nature of things.

After an ass-dragging climb into the mountains by minibus, we came upon Camp Brasilia.

At one end of the pitch little Zico was bending balls round six metal defenders, hitting the corners of the net, unerringly.
Up to that point, Roberto Rivelino had scored forty times for Brazil—they tended not to be tap-ins; he's also supposed to have scored the fastest goal in football history, catching the opposition keeper at pre-match prayer . . . begetting Pelé's nearly-effort in Mexico, the 'stoater' by young "Becks" at Selhurst Park, and Luis Suarez Diaz's 3rd, 'back-pedaler,' at Carrow Road.

Through our interpreter we asked if Bob could go in goal to *"experience the power of his patada atomic."*

Fred Clarke, our sound man, taped a microphone to Bob's hairy chest as John Walker set up the camera—in comparative safety—behind the net.

"*Rivelino's left foot* . . . (pause a second) . . . *and that's it!*"
Coleman's commentary as another bomb flew past Ivo Viktor, Czechoslovakia's goalkeeper, during the 1970 World Cup.

"Willow'" didn't have to move for the first one—it hit him flush on the mic, destroying it . . . but we did get a "*WHOAAAH*" to go with the ball-on-chest audio, and half an apology from the great man in the bushy moustache.

A couple of nights later, Brazil played a friendly in the Maracana; at one point in its history they got nearly 200,000 fans in for a match, but by the late 70s they'd cut the capacity in half (*Health & Safety*).
No trouble filling that baby . . . . TV or no TV.

We got permission to work our camera on the touchline.
Prior to kick-off, the public address announcer introduced 'our man' Bobby Charlton to the delirious masses. Game as ever, Bob—in his walking shoes—joined a 'keepie-uppie' session in the centre circle with the amazing *Coca Cola* kids; they could do what they liked with the ball. Our Bob was a two-footed, long-range specialist, with winners' medals from the World and European Cups, 106 caps for England and 49 international net busters to his name . . . even Brazil fans knew it.

No sooner had one in yellow and blue scored, than portable lights on a myriad of hand-held cameras came on, like shoals of angler fish on the prowl. *TV Globo*'s touchline reporter was in with his questions.
No one seemed to mind, and play re-started, eventually.

Claudio Countinho was the man with the World's best/worst post: head coach of the Brazilians. Exclusive one-on-one interviews simply weren't allowed, but Barry D., (now fully restored in the bowel department)—never one to be marginalized—grabbed him for a word on the sub rosa.
TV Globo had spotted us.

There was hell to pay.
Globo is one of the largest commercial channels on the planet, and they didn't take kindly to being upstaged . . . especially by the godfathers of sports television from whence their *jogo bonito* (beautiful game) came.

Pelé dedicated his book—*My Life and the Beautiful Game*—to those who *made* the game beautiful . . . a different thing altogether to commentator Stuart Hall's generic assertion. Stuart's undying loyalty to Manchester City could soon see them earn riches commensurate with their inexhaustible funding, though watching Nigel "the lawnmower" de Jong 'asaulting' Xabi Alonso in South Africa (not to mention the diving comedy turns of *La Liga*) might cause *5 Live*'s lyricist to think again about *his* 'beautiful' game.

Our sense of propriety precluded us from following *Globo's* crews into the showers, but we'd already nailed our exclusive . . . *anyway, who wants to look at fine young Brazilians in the raw?*

Getting to the later stages—even playing in the final—wasn't on . . . Brazil <u>had</u> to succeed.

Alas, Argentina did (*could it be worse?*).

Needless to say Countinho's effigies were burned in the streets . . . *and you think Graham Taylor got a bum deal?*
Sexy Sven got cash—and the girl(s); you'd assume, decent Steve (McClaren) got to keep the 'brolly.' *Need a blindfold, Roy?*

They put three bullets in the side of a taxi, just outside our hotel in Buneos Aires . . . . the guy must have jumped the lights, *but then who didn't?*
Our admin folk had wisely turned down self-drive hires.

The night Mario Kempes sealed it for the hosts, no one, for miles around, slept; the city was gridlocked—what celebrations, *what propaganda for the Junta.*

Roly-poly Vincent Hannah—on our team, with special responsibilities for anything bordering on political—was granted permission to interview Jorge Videla, the

President of the Federal Republic, for *Panorama* or *24 Hours*, or whomsoever . . . there were chunks of it.

Wrongful imprisonment, disappearances* and murder were rife.
It was the time of the 'dirty war' when millions fled the country.
Vince had best tread lightly—not easy, bearing in mind the strain on his knees, belt and lower back, nor was he renowned for a cautionary interviewing style . . . nearer the Muggeridge/Levin school of riling, than the tender entreaties of Larry Grayson on *The Generation Game*.

Countinho would view his predicament as career-threatening, but even failed football coaches tended not to go missing (presumed drowned) in Brazil, high though the Iguazu falls on the Argentine border are.
Across the way, Eva Peron and her old man were gone, long since, but Juan's third wife, Isabela, had only just been dislodged by coup d'etat.
The truce with the people was mighty fragile . . . *ask that taxi driver*.

Our questions had to be submitted in advance—Videla insisted on doing the interview in Spanish, though he understood English perfectly well.

Choosing civilian clothes, rather than the resplendent army uniform with its scrambled egg, sashes and medals, the General couldn't have been more charming; the same couldn't be said for his ever-present military escorts, who were packing . . . and sensitive.

I prayed wild-man Hannah would stick to the pre-ordained questions (much as Harry *hadn't* with Mike Tyson).

Gradually—the flannel smothering him—off he strayed down the **desaparecidos*, kidnapping and torture dead-ends.

We could die here, Vince, you crazy, Irish son-of-a-bitch.

The sound of collective gulping from behind the camera would need editing; the President declined to comment of course, got to his feet (cutaway to the goons) and retired; we were shown the door . . . nicely, mind.

Subsequently the two-faced bastard would own up to all manner of horrors during his term in office, and they locked him away.

An outing to a ranch on the pampas had been arranged for all UK press and TV folk, as part of the pre-tournament, hands-across-the-water-but off-the-Falklands build-up.

We watched as teams of gauchos adeptly caught and branded steers (*Christ, that must hurt*) . . . we played an impromptu game against some of Diego Simeone's distant relatives, in the yard, and got a right kicking (no Scots was sent off) . . . then it was *dinner time!*

The barbecue came with a promise-cum-threat that all parts of the animal would be served for our pleasure; save for the really hard bits, everything was edible—that's <u>everything</u> . . . *the good, the bad and the unmentionables.*

Never cute to offend your host when you're miles from home in an unstable country . . . and that host is the spit of Clarence LeRoy van Cleef Jr. *("all whistle together")*

Huw Jones—one of my oldest mates from the halcyon days of Coleman's tyranny—got one . . . *you know* . . . one of <u>them</u>.

He looked my way and shook his head.

Just as he was about to ping it on the grass, he spotted big 'Lee,' chewing on a cheroot, at the end of the table. Without looking up, 'Angel Eyes' tapped his holster in a precautionary gesture (I don't *think* he would have used it . . . this was pre-Thatcher).

Prudently, the chastened Welshman closed his eyes, thought of the Rhonda and swallowed.

Dexterously, the cheroot changed sides—no hands involved.

'*Curiouser and curiouser!*' cried Ally—he was so much surprised, that for the moment he quite forgot how to speak good English (. . . or *pick the right team*).

(Ally) McLeod and the Scots had failed in their bid for World Cup gold, early on. Despite Archie Gemmill's 'wonder goal' in our third group stage match against Cruyff-free Holland, we were *out of there*.

(Cruyff's reasons for his 'no-show' in Argentina wouldn't surface for thirty years, but everyone missed him, especially those with tickets for the big one).

How the hosts managed to beat Peru by the required six goal margin in order to make it to the final, will go to the grave with Videla . . . and only the High Sheriff of Mid-Glamorgan (aka Clive Thomas) knows why he blew when he did, as Brazil's corner was speeding into the Swedes' net—via little Zico's head—in their Group 3 match, but then where would a major sporting occasion be without a bit of controversy?

The phone rang by my bedside . . . . 0130 . . . my pillow was still cold.

Had we gone too far with Videla?

Mike Murphy, one of the editors:

'Get the crew, J.P . . . . there's a helluva story breaking.'

Finding my 'fast response unit' in Cordoba at night was one thing, getting them out of the clubs in a fit state, another.

We'd just had a caning from Peru in our opener, and as the Jocks seldom did things by half, there was now a drugs rap to face. Willie Johnston had been caught popping pills he shouldn't have.

In the end, the S.F.A.'s special forces gave us the slip and 'Bud' Johnston was gone . . . spirited through various airports, out of South America and into international oblivion, even before the full impact of Teófilo Cubillas' Peruvian brace had registered back home; like Rivelino, the kid—*'El Nene'*—regularly 'put his foot through the ball' (whatever that means) with devastating effect.
Our drawing with new boys, Iran, was laughable.

Next time round—Spain 1982:
Northern Ireland and England made it to the second phase, but once again Scotland didn't, losing out in their group to Oleg Blokhin's Soviet Union (2nd) and Brazil (1st)—Zico, Eder, Socrates and Falcao, amongst some decent-to-brilliant players.
New Zealand were laughable.

Nothing against Spain . . . I've been there dozens of times, for *golf, sevillana, y cerveza* excesses *por favor*, and Madrid is one of my favourites towns, but Bilbao, where the England camp was—and, incidentally, where the Spanish Civil War started in 1936—is neither my first, second nor last choice of holiday destination.

Denis Law, who'd played his only game in the World Cup finals, against Zaire eight years previously, had signed for our radio colleagues to do feature work and colour commentary in Spain.
We had Bobby Charlton on telly.
Georgie B.'s whereabouts were a mystery as ever . . . . pity, because their three countries were there, for once.
Hard to take for Best (and Giggs and Law) that he never got to do perform at the World Cup, but at least they saw Bobby centre-stage.

Despite the very real possibilities of torn 'hammies' and hernias, no one declined when 'Our Kid' masterminded a media team to take on some Bilbaon lads.
ITV stalwarts, including Bob's big brother Jack, slim(ish) Jim Rosenthal, and Martin Tyler, joined up with us BBC boys.
None was in any condition to last against the Spaniards.
Were spice needed, in the *real* event, England and Spain had been grouped together in the second round—in *Madrid*—with West Germany.

Bobby played it like it was '66 all over again, albeit in a dustbowl, with just a home-boy ref, and no one running the lines.

Where was Tofiq Bakhramov—the man from Azerbaijan—when our best effort was chalked off, following an horrendous mêlée in front of their goal?

It was score-less in the end, just as the grown-up, group match meeting would be at the Bernabéu.

Bobby was Messaniac on our evening walkabouts; a nod of his well-*kent* (known) *heed* (head) was as efficacious as lacquer on an unruly mullett.

He and I dipped into a tapas bar, empty, save for an old fella, past caring.
No sooner were the landlord's eyes back in their sockets, than in swept 'Senora Equallygobsmacked' with *jamon Serrano y cerveza* . . . on the casa.
The patron disappeared to ring a friend.

Within twenty minutes the place was heaving—Bobby was engulfed in bad breath and fawning Basques.
A swarthy, be-suited gent came to his rescue and ushered us through the throng, to a backroom, and thence out into the street.
Sheepishly, we followed, across dimly lit cobbles and down some stairs to a cellar room.
I should point out that **E**uskadi **T**a **A**skatasuna—the separatist group—had been particularly active in the lead-up to the World Cup.

A rustic table had been laid with goblets and metal plates.
Darkened shapes shuffled by . . . elderly men, dressed the same, in somber suits and regular black ties, their white shirts piercing the gloom.

Was this a last ETA supper, a pre-cursor to the ritual killing of the great Bobby Charlton and his anonymous, expendable companion?

I was liking kidnap more—*Man. U. would pay fortunes for him/us, surely.*

Hadn't been that scared since the Cuban missile crisis of 1962.
Back then I'd just started dating my future wife, though no bases of significance had been reached; the prospects of never seeing her (or Airdrieonians F.C.) again—<u>and</u> World War III (nuclear)—were overwhelming for an 18 year old.

Scented pillar candles were lit.
Taking the lead from our abductor, we sat.
At each place setting, goblets brimmed with blood-red wine.

(*Should I try to warn Bobby . . . OUR DRINKS MAY HAVE BEEN SPIKED . . . he was too far away . . . would it be quick . . . who'd tell our kids?*).

After much mumbling and sly glances Bobby's way, the head of the table stirred. Solemnly raising his chalice (*oh my God, it's sacrificial*), in as near an English accent as he could achieve, he snapped out the order:

'BOBBEE SHARLTON'

The only casualties were occasional chairs clattering backwards as the company rose in response.
Amid several variations of the toast, down went the contents, followed by the syncopated hand-clapping of flamenco backing singers.

The man's revered everywhere.

"Game On!"

Flying in the face of a barrage of scepticism, my crusade to make squash TV friendly only attracted the converted. Experts consistently put Jonah Barrington at the head of the personal fitness league, which he was immodest enough to corroborate; his showing on *Superstars* compounded the belief. He was in disgustingly good shape. Added to his dexterity round the world's cream-coloured boxes, Jonah was the ideal role model and ambassador for his sport—a positive perfectionist.

Viewed from the narrow balconies, the normal, black squash ball—once called a nigger ball (*dear me!*)—propelled and finessed by practitioners of every skin-tone, was imperceptible. The effort expended to produce a rally, numbering scores of strokes, only to be summarily struck off as "*let*", would break your heart . . . that's supposing an attack, as an ill-prepared amateur participant, hadn't already done so.

Angling was similarly treated i.e. badly . . . *how come so many did it, and we 'telly Johnnies' couldn't find a way of putting it on successfully?*
I did make a little film for BBC Scotland about Peter Anderson—'The Kilted Kingfisher'—when he was world fly-*casting* champion; now *that* is a thing of beauty—timing, finesse, pin-point accuracy . . . golf with a spot of over-head racquet work on the side. The tiny lure didn't know if was Arthur or Martha as it careered one way, then the other, alighting . . . I was going to say, *like a Mayfly on water*.

The prettier of the Marshall bros (*The Shark's* man) and I had discussed staging a pro-am angling competition in the freshly-stocked lake at Brocket Hall, in Hertfordshire, with the owner . . . but the idea sank, much as Lord Charlie B. and his Ferraris would in an almighty insurance scam; the 3rd Baron did two and half years of the seven handed down.

We must be able to do better with squash.
A fan, a player, a dentist by trade, came up with a ball coated in reflective cells which, under T.V. candle-power, glowed like Kamikazi fireflies. A custom-built, transportable court was already in production, its glass-paneled sides affording spectators 360° visual access, and players, a matt finish to hit against . . . . a massive police interview room, open to the public. By painting the floor deep blue and regulating the colour of players' clothing, we had it cracked. The lighting had to be spot-on, and the balls replaced regularly, as the little cells gradually attached themselves to the walls, but it

was a million times better than before—if only the rule makers would adapt and put the players on the clock. Games could take an eternity.

The rules of rugby union are changed on a daily basis; anymore preliminaries to a scrum being formed, and refs will need a crib: *"Crouch"* . . . *"touch"* . . . *"pause"* . . . *"blow a kiss"* . . . *"engage"* . . . *"spit"* . . . *"apologise."*
In my day, front rows would rush to get down *first*, hookers used to *hook*, and we never heard the ref warning us against breaking the rules in mid-play—*whose side is he on?!*.

If the Yanks had gotten their way, there would have been time-outs at World Cup '94. Knowing FIFA's fondness for an inducement, they could have pulled it off, but Fergie would have gone *completely* mad (had he been our manager . . . and we'd qualified . . . *which we most certainly would have*).

A tiny tinker with the rules of squash could have saved it from broadcast extinction; ultimately, BSkyB would come to its rescue with cash and airspace, while lobbying continues for Olympic recognition (quite right).

We looked into *speed rock climbing* . . . and out again as insurance quotes came in; *backgammon* was more suited to reality TV for beavering yuppies, and I had to draw the line at *log-rolling* from Canada, which one of our more respected suppliers kept trying to flog me.
Unless Bobby and Boris (Spassky) finally came to blows, *chess* was beyond redemption.
Boris (Becker) was still in his whites—and Mr. Hearn in his snooker-boxing period—so *poker* didn't get a mention.

The first artificial course used in the Olympics (1972—Fischer, now champ of the world, was beginning to hear voices) for white-water canoeing—at Augsburg, West Germany—was an odd-looking structure when the tide was out.
Must've been something in the water, cos the East Germans bossed the kayak and Canadian slalom.

"Motty"—our man for all seasons (before signing a contract that effectively committed him exclusively to football for the rest of his life, and, very possibly, the thereafter)—had agreed to commentate at the canoeing.
Better the devil you know, mush.
Don't recall the operating arrangements as they set out, but our hapless paddlers spent much of their defining run *upside down*, banging helmeted heads off man-made moundings.
Rocks, in your regular river, will kill you.

Cautiously, 'John-boy' summed up: . . . *it's fairly safe to say, as we watch the British pair battling to right their upturned craft, that their medal hopes have quite possibly receded—I hope they don't mind me saying that* . . . or words to that very well qualified effect (duly logged for the 'funnies' film).

Shortly after that "Motty" went monogamous and pre-nuptial, swearing never to cheat on football again; Hall's (generic) beautiful game was having none of it . . . no cheating, no swearing, one spouse at a time . . . tush.

We took units to Bala (with an 'a' for Atlantic) for the World Canoe Slalom and White Water Racing Championships—on the Afon Trewyrn (a.k.a. *Shit Creek*)—a category VI, nightmare test of nerve and bouyancy, in North Wales. One had to know one's *K*s from one's *C*s, but fundamentally, it was gutsy men and women in crash-hats and P.F.D.s (personal flotation devices—or *Mae Wests*), taking to thin-skinned boats—on their 'jack,' or accompanied—'boofing' the life out of angry waves and undertows . . . with sticks.

Previously, our coverage had been on film, but I wanted to put outside broadcast cameras in to make it, if not 'live,' then as close as (without being a total oxymoron). The support we got from the devotees who risked life and limb for the rush (and recognition on *Grandstand*) was as with any who'd vie for a little air-time—huge; that said, certain *key* elements, they kept to themselves.

Plotting cameras positions on the slalom course was straightforward, but the white-water race could take half an hour; strategic points were difficult to identify. If you can imagine the Head of the River race on the Thames during a *tsunami* (doom-merchants say it's better than a distinct possibility), that's how unstable the Trewyrn was—not for the faint hearted . . . the top-heavy . . . or antihistamine addicts prone to pewking on water.

We had a couple cameras on cranes, for geographical reference; several low level jobs close to the banks, conveyed the power of the river and the temerity of the nutters, brave and skillful enough to take it on.
Should the pictures fail so to do, David Goldstrom, our commentator, would . . . ably.

I'd boobed . . . much as Jack Hawkins and Bill Holden had in Mr. Lean's *Bridge on the River Kwai*.

Having built several substantial scaffold rostra for water-level cameras—based on a reconnaissance trip a month or so previously—you can imagine the horror when, with 24hours to go to 'the off,' I found them all but submerged.

You're a pure goon,man! At 'recce' time, the river was in its natural, gravitational state . . . by race time, it was a torrent.
The volume of water could be raised from a dam upstream turning it, if not into the madness of the Colorado, then certainly to a frothed-up and wild-looking challenge.

These cameramen were my pals.

Nearly every Christmas (BBC 1 having seen to it), the shot of Alec Guinness—*Colonel Saito*'s pal—gaping, incredulously, at the exposed fuse-wire on the tidal *Kwai*, reminds me of the Trewyrn (minus the fictional train crash and appalling loss of life).
That was Kitulgala in Sri Lanka (Ceylon that was)—our factual account was from Bala in Snowdonia (which still is).

No one died.

It's something about having to *pay* to get in that makes you think twice about visiting Welsh Wales, but we were on expenses. We handed over a Prince's ransom to the man in the Severn Bridge toll booth, and with an exchange of '*bore das*' (plus receipt), we sped off towards the Rhondda . . . . World Darts Champion territory.

Here's the time-line *(the what?)*.
It's more than thirty years since Leighton Thomas Rees of Ynysybwl *(where?)* won the first world professional Championship. That season *(when?)*—1977-78—the rugby union team of Edwards, Bennett, Williams, *et al*, were Grand Slam winners . . . Tredegar's finest, Ray Reardon, was world snooker champ, for the sixth time . . . Shirley Bassey and Mary Hopkin *(who?)* were selling lots of records . . . but unusually, 'Tom the Voice' wasn't *(why?)*.

Tom's mate, Elvis was in, and doing, serious shit—born 1935 . . . died (no question)1977.

Actor, singer (fantasy footballer), Dennis Waterman was the highest paid thespian on British TV—courtesy of *The Sweeney*, and his own creation, *Minder*.
The latter had been retained for a second series at the behest of my old pal "Ginger" Cowgill, then managing director at Thames TV . . . and on and on and on it went to huge audiences, and a 10th series.

Dennis's second wife Pat (Maynard) had recently given birth to Hannah, but still, midst all that responsibility, he would not forsake his pals,.

We'd done our high-speed film shoot with big Leighton in our local—*The Turk's Head* at St. Margaret's, near Twickenham—and despite a detectable unsteadiness brought on by 'voddies' and slimline,

D.S. George Carter (by several other names) had agreed to do some links and voice-over:

'GAME ON' . . . and all that other stuff Sid Waddell makes such a meal of.

Diesel's movements were unpredictable, at best, as he was deeply into a blue-label binge. Lest the next episode of *Minder* was to become a George Cole monologue, he had to be tied down.

Our attempts at producing a dart-receptive, transparent covering for the unattended camera lens, failed miserably. Leighton was precise and accurate, but the consistency of the jelly-like substance our props people had come up with, wouldn't support a tight group; one dart was fine, but the weight and impact of the others made them all go limp.
To film at such speeds meant using yards of stock; the sound of the celluloid tearing round the special camera's innards was terrifyingly expensive.
We got some great images of darts, barrelling like bullets, Leighton's customized flights guiding the business ends, consistently, to treble 20.

Arrows—as in 'good arrows,' the understated acknowledgement of a *'one hundred and EIGH-T-EE'* maximum—was growing in stature . . . and so were the players.
My view was that the 'game' of darts would be better placed in its own, late-night slot on BBC 2. *Grandstand's* founding fathers believed the show was about 'sports and events as they happen, where they happen' but I couldn't make a case for it; darts and alcohol didn't mix with testosterone and risk—in any case, we already had a separate events department.

Having negotiated a long-term contract with the British Darts Organisation, my boss didn't concur . . . nor would Olly Croft, their heavyweight secretary.
Pinning me against a wall with his not inconsiderable frame, the Hon-Sec of the BDO pointed out the error of my ways . . . but I wouldn't budge—*I couldn't*.
There was no escaping the boozy tag; fine for the legions of fans, but when John Thomas 'Jocky' Wilson, due up at the oche for his next chuck, suddenly disappeared from the stage after re-fuelling, the game was up (great stuff for *Alas Smith & Jones* though).

Leighton was a mighty lad, a smashing guy, cheery and generous; I still have a set of L.B. branded flights.
Like Bill Werbenuik and a few other notables from the darts and snooker worlds, he hadn't gotten to those proportions without beaker-upon-beaker of amber nectar—the dartist's calorific *aqua vitae*.

What it did provide was a substantial launch pad; the occasional list to port was testament to the dangers of mixing one's drinks, and the difference between 60 and 15.

We filmed and drank and missed our doubles at the Ynysybwl working men's club: Leighton was their hero—the first pro Champion of a comparatively small world. His celebrity didn't stretch to *Ferraris* and film premieres—nor *OK* and *Hello*—but a more honest cove you couldn't wish to meet.

N.B.—for Americans, and those without GCSE geography, or Welsh—Ynysybwl is a village in the Clydach Valley quite near Cardiff, not far from Merthyr Tydfil, and a stiff walk—in sensible shoes—from Pontypridd (the pronunciations were probably appalling).

No thanks to my narrow mind, darts went ballistic after that; the ratings for such an unpresumptuous game—phenomenal. Great characters and champions emerged in Bristow and Lowe and George . . . <u>and</u> wee Jocky.

A bit of that early craziness may have been lost in the sanitised version, but the standard of play remains outstanding. More than 60 countries take part in each version of 'The Worlds' today; unification is still some way off (*there's only one Phil 'The Power' Taylor . . . one Martin 'Wolfie' Adams*).

Throughout, the support has been extraordinary . . . even if they have to go outside nowadays for a gasper.

Drop a fag-end at Augusta National and it's up and away and in the trash, quicker than you can say 'shank'; their intolerance of litter could be measured against the history of racism in that part of the US.
Whilst it's policed as diligently as it is in Singapore, the punishment for the lout is less Draconian in Georgia—'you da man' or 'go in the hole,' however, should mean lethal injection (still an option in some States, Georgia among them, I believe).

What goes around comes around.
Twenty years after my tiff with Olly, I found myself co-producing the 2007 World Darts Championship for the BBC, as a self-assessed, independent in TWI's employ. Olly didn't remember me, fortunately.
In all that time he'd lost a pound or two, but none of his enthusiasm for the game.
My old buddy, Tony Green, was still calling the shots: the *maximum* effect was unchanged . . . *foundation shaking*.
There's no atmosphere like it at any indoor activity; every session is sold out . . . there's dry ice, flashing lights and splendid, over-the-top players' walk-ons . . . be it to *Quo* or *The Kaisers*.

To start one of our shows, Ray Stubbs—still in favour at the BBC and with the gag writers on *Mock the Week*—went walkabout, eulogizing about champions past adorning the corridor walls, and hyperbolizing about the atmosphere within:

"Have a listen to <u>this</u>" as, demonstratively, he threw the arena's double doors apart.

The hall was dark . . . empty but for a cleaner with a hoover (or was it a *Dyson?*).

The *re-wind* effect had 'Stubbsie' going backwards at high speed, arriving at his mark to decelerating garble.

Take 2

This time, at the point of entry, all hell was let loose, as the masses got at it to Rossi & Parfitt's *"Rockin All over the World."*

The Lakeside Country Club is a must-have experience—like Augusta National (*kind of*).

Bobby George—the old 'King of Bling'—still commands attention.
The bones may be creaking under the weight of his chain of office, and assorted rocks and bangles, but when he strikes that scorpion-like pose on the oche, barrels spin, triggers cock.

"BEST OF ORDER . . ."

I was on a mission to George Hall, Bob's 18-room mansion on the Essex/Suffolk border (*yes, he built it himself*),.

As Marie—peachy Mrs. H.—prepared supper, the lord of the manor warmed-up with a couple of *Courvoisiers*.

Think, Bobby George—showman, flashing smile, snappy dresser,
(pre-Marie) ladies' man.

Now, conjure an apposite opponent from the world of Light Ent—tall, snake-hipped (in the 70s), swarthy, cultured gnashers, tonsils to throw knickers by . . .

Got it?

Englebert Humperdinck the Second.

Just prior to us moving into the 'home of darts,' "Humpy"—as he described himself—was playing Frimley Green as part of his anniversary tour. Farewells by ageing crooners tend not to fulfil their promise, so for this old fella to be still hauling them in at 61, said more about his talent, than his critics.

If the mountain will not come to Mahomet, Mahomet must go to the mountain.
Take that anyway you like, but it was he, who's used to Las Vegan excess, who made his own way to Bob's gaff—*OK, by chauffeur-driven limo.*

Englebert played the great venues—the Palladium, the Royal Albert Hall, Caesar's and Dunes—but the sports room at George Hall was unchartered territory . . . and darts was not his specialist subject.

Bob had commissioned one of those forgiving, square-bottomed, cover-all, darts player's tunic tops, in black satin with *The Humpster* in silver printed on the back.

Down the years, the girth had expanded beyond Bob's good intention, so we put his livery on the wall as set dressing.
(I"ll come to his liver, proper, in a second).

Bobby Dazzler's signature tune is *Queen's "We are the Champions"* which the faithful continue to give plenty to, as the grinning old favourite strides towards the middle for diddle.
Alas, the crown, cape and candelabra are no more.

Englebert's man called to say they were without.

"*Release Me*"—which Eddie Miller and Dub Wilson did, originally, in 1962—was a No.1 for Humperdinck five years later, selling over a million copies and keeping the Beatles off top spot. Lots covered the song, including the Everly Brothers, Jerry Lee Lewis and Elvis (before he got in serious shit), but Gerry Dorsey's version was the guv'nor.

First checking that the boy George had a gramophone (which, by phenomenal luck, he had), I took an LP of Engle's greatest hits—which I'd unearthed (receipt) in a charity shop—on set.

It took us a fraction longer than Bob Hope in Palm Springs to get Bobby to mime his opening line:

"Pleeeese release me . . .' le-ette-me go-o-o"
. . . (in close-up, as the stylus grooved through vinyl furrows at thirty-three-and-a-third revs per minute)

"For I-I-I-I don't love you . . . any m-o-o-o-ore"

. . . came from *behind*, and then *through*, the opening games' room door, the great balladeer making his 'surprise' entrance.

Same key, bang on the money—*what a pro!*

A knicker-soiling moment from the 60s—just the *print* we needed.

We frigged the match a bit (a dangerous practice had proper Royalty been involved) and left Bob and the mighty crooner to finish several sets.

Our excellent host reported later that he and Englebert were 'legless' by the end.

"Good darts!"

"You Look Like a Heavyweight"

The lots at a boxing auction, in north London, ranged from jock straps (soiled) and foul cups (concaved), to signed gloves and depictions (on canvas) of some of the ring's great battles . . . "*but not <u>necessarily</u> in the right order.*"

The man with the gavel was more Sadam than Sotheby's; holding aloft a *Litesome* support—an early version of the cheeky cheese grater, favoured by Peter Stringfellow on his hols, and, more appealingly by his staff on the meter—he pointed, directly, at a weasel in the front row:

'*Thank <u>you</u> sir—an Ayrton Senna it is . . . every little helps.*'
The weasel nodded vacantly, ruing the loss of his only tenner.
In stark contrast—but still themed—a 'Bernie' is a million (after Mr. Ecclestone of F.1) and a 'Maggie' (the £1 coin) after Mrs. T.—"small and brassy and thinks it's a sovereign" (*like that one*).

Thousands had been extorted, for some very good cause, as two brown coats staggered on stage with the final lot—a huge work, mounted in the sort of ornate frame millions of Tretchikoff's *Chinese Girl* prints could be found—but here was an original, a shocker . . . but an original shocker.

"Now gents . . . (the smattering of augmented ladies in risqué outfits were assumed kept, and off limits) . . . tonight's top piece you'll not be able resist, right? A diamond water-works of Casheous Clay and the three geezers he done over to win the World title back again.

"Do I have a pair of big ones anywhere?" A moll tittered.

Smokin' Joe's image, in the long baggy greens, was to the Champ's right, by dint of their first, momentous 'Fight of the Century' in New York, and there too, the far from dopey George Foreman being 'roped' in Zaire; the seemingly indestructible Sonny Liston was to the left.
These were fights everyone remembered, but clearly the titling on the auctioneer's sheet was wrong, for, as everyone knows, Ali won it back *twice* . . . once against barbecue George, and the second time, somewhat meaninglessly, from Leon Spinks.

'Retained' 'regained' . . . . semantics in the great scheme of things Ali, but when your mates came round for dinner, best to get bragging rights right.
I was buggered if I was getting involved.

Amidst a forest of raised hands, a number of heads ducked and dove for cover; either they'd spotted the factual discrepancy, or, like Joe Frazier, they'd already given their all.

Whether he was Clay the irascible Baptist, or Ali the Muslim extremist, he was media gold dust, yet for his efforts to spread the word, he'd get as good as he gave—the U.S. Government, Smokin' Joe and Ken Norton saw to that—plus, his treatment of the ladies was questionable-to-poor.

Whether she was just being nice, or she was genuinely interested in Don Cockell's fate, my Granny made room for me in her bed in the very early hours of 17th May 1955.
The great, white, British hope was eight hours behind us on the Granny's alarm clock as he came together for the last time, peaceably, with the even greater, white, American Champion of the World, Rocky Marciano. As far as my hard working parents were concerned, sleep was the greater priority, and my elder brother had literally begun his 14th year.

There was a bit going on back in the UK: Joe Davis had cleaned the lot away on TV for the first time . . . somewhere in the Lake District, David Nations's mate, Donald Campbell, was getting *Bluebird* ready for a crack at the world water speed record, and a General Election was looming.

But for 20,000 fans packed around the sixteen and a half foot ring in downtown San Francisco, countless others glued to their radios, and me, the Cockell-Marciano clash was the business . . . . one to risk lines for:

I must not be late for school.
I must not be late for school. (x 100—a mindless punishment)

The bedside radio crackled that familiar inter-Continental hiss, adding safe distance to the unpleasantness that would occur in earthquake city. Eamonn Andrews—years away from the sweaty brow, the big red book and *"This is Y-oo-er Lyfe"*—was the ringside commentator, with Barrington Dalby on inter-round summaries; only the one between the 2nd and 3rd gave us Brits any hope.
No one gave Don a prayer, but neither had they fancied anything other than a pounding for Tommy Farr when he took on the mighty Joe Louis in 1937—the last time, prior to Cockell, a British (Welsh) fighter (from Tonypandy . . . or 'Tonypanda' as some US journals gave it) had fought for the top title. Farr went the distance; had it been a

'home' fixture (instead of Yankee Stadium), "The Terror" might have won, narrowly, it's said.

Farr and Cockell fought a few times, and Don went down a weight to have a go at Turpin; if Randy had been several steps *up* in class for him, his, with the 'head of the heavies,' would be a full fire escape worth in power and menace.

It was a harsh introduction to the richest prize in sport for Granny, never mind portly Don. It's fanciful to suggest that the challenger from London might have won, but subsequent newsreel footage confirmed all was not 'Queensberry' in California that night.

Marciano was deemed invincible, and in Eamonn's account there were clues as to why; plucky "*DAWN CAW—KELL*"—as the pre-fight announcer would have him—was hit in the kidneys, elbowed, butted, belted when he was down on one knee, and, using the philosophy of the picador, hammered relentlessly on the upper arms to reduce potency. The stuff Marciano hit him with in the latter stages, even on radio, made me bite down on the bed clothes. *Brutal, brutal, brutal* . . . but that's what they do.

Forty-two of *The Brockton Blockkbuster's* opponents hadn't made it as far as Don, though by the 9th of 10 scheduled rounds, technically, he was spark out and might have been spared earlier . . . *much earlier.*

Rocco Francis Marchegiano died in a plane crash, a week before his 46th birthday; brave to the end, D. J. Cockell died of cancer aged 55.

Every kid had heard of Jack Johnson, and Dad used to tell us about how Benny Lynch had dragged himself out of Glasgow's infamous Gorbals to become world flyweight champion (1936), but not until Sonny Liston came on the heavyweight scene did boxing grab my attention again.

We <u>had</u> to box—sick-notes weren't adequate at Morrison's Academy.
While we stalked the girls, the more pragmatic put their testosterone surges to better use *(says who?)* by joining the boxing club, in sure and certain knowledge that the end of term, inter-house competition wouldn't go away.

I just about recall the punch with which Tommy Hogg—the school champion (if you don't mind)—knocked me out; I heard the count from 8 . . . but *"fuck that for a game of soldiers."*
It came on me, big, within seconds of the bell to start proceedings . . . thus preserving what Mum attested were my boyish good looks.

Dad and J.E.G. Quick—the school Rector—had front row seats . . . *and history*: the deadlines he'd try to impose on my father's printing works for the delivery of the annual school magazine, put their relationship at *permanently fragile*. Thus, my triumph over young Donald (Quick) in my second bout was doubly sweet, though tempered by the threat of parental backlash.
'JEG' was a sadist with the belt—the efficacy of which is still debated, despite the abolition of corporal punishment in schools in 1986.
The first two (of six), you'd definitely feel.
By doing one's utmost to avoid a repeat performance, suggests there was method in the madness; a damaged wrist (blood) in the maths class sealed the fates of cane and belt.

Eventually they banned boxing at school too, after best friends had lost it and battered the living kidneys out of one another (cracking fight, though). If its re-introduction in UK schools helps with knife crime and bullying, *then bring it on* . . . for lippy, stroppy tarts too, *innit?*

Despite the good guy/bad guy hype, there was something to like about Floyd Patterson—there was absolutely nothing about Sonny Liston. We used to get the tape measure out and compare our puny fists and chests to the ugly jailbird's . . . . then join the rest of the planet in prayer for *The Louisville Lip*.

When Clay whipped Liston and *"shook up the world"* (in somewhat mysterious circumstances), the heavyweight roller coaster was off and running.
By the time *The Rumble in the Jungle* and *The Thrilla in Manilla* came along, you'd have had to have been frozen in suspended animation to have missed out on Ali.
And what a time it was for us at the BBC; access to these two fights alone—never mind others stage-managed, promoted and starring the dancing master—was justification for hiking the licence . . . without Her Majesty's seal.

Much as Calzhage, Khan, Lewis and Hatton are respected at home—and Pacquiao and Mayweather are ubiquitous—the Clay/Ali era was/is transcendental: from Zbigniew Pietrzykowski (Rome 1960) to Joe Frazier (Manila 1975), it was something else . . . a phenomenon.

My late friend and colleague, John McNicholas, 'produced' most of the Ali fight previews for us.
I'd never defame the old boy—he was a toff of a bloke—but his brief was pretty simple: take lots of stock, keep the camera and sound recorder *on* from 'imm' to 'em'igration . . . then soak up the plaudits.

Following a dazzling work-out at camp Deer Lake PA., an aide throws an inflatable gorilla in the ring. Acting like it's a great big surprise, the champ suspends his beautification and begins to shuffle round the unfortunate dummy, pummeling it with the fastest hands in the trade:

"*There he is now, Joe Frazier, Joe Frazier . . . . he's so ugly . . . get him out of here . . . he makes me nervous!*"

Smokin' Joe—the real deal—got his own back, many times over, but not the last laugh.

The ring was no place for basking; out of it, there was oodles of reflected glory, for all . . . and Parkinson; he got uncomfortably close to the great man's dark side during an early interview (monologue).

Don King had been right—best not to question a man's faith if a) he can knock you down by blowing on you, and b) shout you down in a rhetoric storm.
Sad a disease of that name should afflict his greatest ever guest.

Like scores of others, Ali fought on long after it was sensible; many of the greats made come-backs—some paid the full price of pride . . . but again, *that's what they do.*

In 1976, Joe Bugner 'de-retired' himself, having been the distance with most of the big guns: now he was to get it on with the current British, European and Commonwealth Champion, Richard Dunn (*who?*), for all those titles, at Wembley.

Ali was in town, so he decided to 'turn-up' at their press conference.

BEDLAM IN PICCADILLY.

Dunn didn't last a round at Wembley against the mighty Magyar.

Joe once tried to hit (metaphorically) on one of our BBC assistants—quite rightly . . . . *she was* (is) *gorgeous,* but way too street-wise to be compromised. Standing six-foot-four and heavy, Joe had been a dab hand with the discus at school though the encrusted dinner plate, thrown *Oddjob* style—his reward for any extra-marital lowering of the *Litesome* had mighty Marlene (Mrs. B) found out—would have been harder to handle . . . mind you, a glimpse of those two super-bantams going at it, nails out, in the mud, would have been worth the entrance money.

The Hungarian-born-Aussie adonis was a good technician for one so large, and always game for a laugh with the media, despite their criticism (in print) of his lack of killer instinct; nor was he top of the UK charts in 1971 when referee Harry Gibbs awarded

him those very same British, European and Commonwealth titles at the expense of the nation's pet, Henry Cooper.
Our 'Enery decided on golf as his preferred sport, thereafter, and Joe ended up rumbling in the Australian jungle with Ant and Dec.

Twice—both on BBC television—Bugner went the distance with Ali: in Las Vegas in 1973, and, for the world title, in Kuala Lumpur in 1975, which tells you a lot more about Joe's lack of a finish than Ali's (he also failed to shut down Frazier).
The truly big stars made the division a vintage collection, the like of which we may never see again.

Richard Dunn was knocking over any daft enough to stand in his way.
If Cockell had been plucky, Dunn was crackers; he'd be the only* British boxer to "fight" Ali for the World title (he was dropped five times in Munich, before referee Herbert Tomser stepped in—not one of the sport's classics).
*N.B. anoraks—Cooperman's bloody night with C.M.C. was 'a friendly.'

No point in joining the media scrum, I would have to negotiate a labyrinth of go-betweens and minders to get to Ali with my request for an audience with Harry on that Wednesday evening's *Sportsnight*.

Choose your moment, then set the chain reaction in motion, via Mickey Duff, promoter, fixer, scrounger, charmer extraordinaire. He'd probably manage to squeeze his face into the shot somewhere along the line, in part payment, but Mickey was legend; everything was "a problem," but most times he came up with the goods, even if some of the asylum seekers he produced from his broom cupboard to fill the mid-week bills at the Royal Albert Hall verged on the ridiculous.

I'll liken this next bit, pretentiously and ostentatiously, to *Lawrence of Arabia*, and David Lean's masterful introduction of Omar Sharif's character.

Like Cassius Marcellus Clay had for his own reasons, Michel Demitri Challoub (Omar al-Sharif, in bridge playing circles) converted to Islam for the love of his first wife, Faten.
(by strange co-incidence, Sharif's character in the film was *Sherif Ali ibn el Kharish* . . . well I think it's strange)

As I leaned, casually, on a Mercedes at *Quaglino's* restaurant car park in Central London, a lone figure appeared, some way in the distance . . .

. . . but this was no shimmering mirage in the baking sands of Egypt . . . no red carpet stroll at the *Odeon*, Leicester Square.

Ethereal, nonetheless.

I removed my shades to check . . . . and re-check.

Ali.

I kept my head down, hoping it wasn't a trick of the light . . . that it would last . . . that everyone would stay away . . . that I would have him one-on-one, to do my inviting in person.

The sound of footsteps grew louder
(*no, it <u>wasn't</u> 'a shuffle' . . . let me tell it!*).

An inability to retain my cool overtook me so, sheepishly, I raised my eyes.

It might sound like Mike Tyson and 'his God'—or David Icke at 'a happening'—but I swear there was a blue aura outlining this be-suited form. Maybe it was just my imagination in overdrive, but it's as clear to me now as *Nessie* is to bed and breakfast owners in Drumnadrochit on the banks of peaty Loch Ness.

There wasn't time to take it in because something was flashing in and out, blocking my light, then dazzling (Mr. Lean would have loved this).

Ali was shadow boxing (*and yes, shuffling*) . . . and I *was* that shadow.

"You look like a Heavyweight."

You'd remember that; I didn't argue, but the cut of my jib would have me down at least one division.

I'd prepared a statement about my professional intentions . . . *but you know when you've been desperate to meet someone, dreamt about it, rehearsed it over and over?*

This was that 'first date' moment and I didn't want to blow it.
I had to say something intelligent, something low on sycophancy.

Drawing a deep breath (he feigned to the left) I launched into my speech about . . . being 20 on the <u>very day</u> he fought 'Big Bear' for the first time, and how petrified we'd all been for him—OK, bordering on oily, but it was fact—Sonny Liston was a terrifying prospect.
(sensing further Philips family anniversary coincidences may not have fascinated, I edited mention of the 1955 Marciano-Cockell fight occurring on my brother's 14th)

352

Ali interrupted me with a quote we'd all used at the time:

"If you wanna lose your money, bet on Sonny."

Unnecessarily, I summarised . . . . running down the clock on my exclusive: the pre-match bear-taunting, the hysteria at the weigh-in, the blinding liniment in his eyes, the mysterious shoulder injury that kept the Champ on his stool at the start of the 7th, and the new man's rantings to Joe Louis—the bemused TV interviewer—after the fight.

"I shook up the world."

That's a fact.

Right after that astonishing night, Clay had given up his 'slave name' to become the man I saw (*and was beginning to bore*) in front of me (*quit while you're ahead, Jake*).

He offered a manicured right.
I muttered my thanks, holding on for as long as was respectable . . . then he was no more.

When I was sure the coast was clear, I did my own little shuffle.

Ali turned up (to the appointed second) with our programme already underway, yet everyone on the studio floor stood to applaud.
Only Mandela (and Beyoncé) would be thus capable.

If the first Frazier fight at Madison Square Garden had been massive (Sinatra in the ring . . . Lancaster interviewing in the dressing rooms) their third and final meeting in Manila was X-rated; the one in the middle, in Jamaica, with no title at stake (George Foreman had become champ by clubbing Joe into submission) was a bit of an anti-climax by their very high standards.

Joe and Ali had been friends, once, but the battering they gave each other in the Philippines came perilously close to double murder.
After Ali had refused the draft, Joe apparently had loaned him money to tide him over during his enforced exile; what was to happen thereafter, turned into hatred—at least on Frazier's part.
Ali's antics, which he'd claim in retirement, were designed only to promote their fights, were enduringly offensive to Joe.

Ali was properly feted for his contributions to boxing, and much else besides, but for Smokin' Joe to end up in a flat above his gym in Philadelphia with little other than his memories, wasn't right.

He was a fantastic, courageous, ferocious fighter.

"CUT! . . . CUE DES"

John McNicholas, who I just mentioned as being the producer of most of our Ali previews, was the Clement Freud of the department: his lovingly crafted, off-the-cuff one-liners were eagerly anticipated.

The upcoming University Boat Race—a priceless piece in the department's firmament—was top of the agenda at our production meeting; any inference that ITV would wrest it, ultimately, from BBC Sport's grasp, was to be scoffed at . . . *a national event* (however marginal) exclusively *on ITV* . . . *remain serious* (. . . so, they had the Derby).
Ever since it was mooted in 1829, it's had its critics, but recent races and worldwide audiences are proof of its enduring popularity. Sometimes it was over before you could down the first pre-race pint—or, if you were *really posh,* a *Pimms*—at Putney. There were sinkings and once a slightly 'inaccurate' dead-heat, but more often than not it was processional, punishing for sure, but hardly an edge of the bar stool number.
What nobody wanted was 'easily' against their name.

We needed *'to spice up our coverage'* according to the then editor of *Grandstand*, Alan Hart, an angular, *Basil Fawlty*-like figure with gait to match, who trained on to be Controller of BBC 1, and—if we're to believe *his* publicity—was responsible for *Eastenders* getting its start.
He fancied himself as a bit of a wit, with little justification: it was an acquired taste, like *Guinness*, or Phil Jupitus.
He'd laugh heartily (*oops*) at his own stuff, so smart-ass ripostes had to be timed perfectly.

Hart's voice was deep and forbidding . . . in the Vin Diesel range. Amplified by the 'hotline' connecting the studio gallery to the video tape control desk in the dungeons of TV Centre, it made greater men than I run for cover; providing you indulged his sarcasm, he'd forgive and forget over a post-programme glass

How was this spicing to manifest itself?
I was keeping the hovercraft up my sleeve. A two week stint on the video disk during the French Open tennis would be the punishment for talk of in-board engines and head-starts.

We all looked away as McNich got to his feet.

"Here's a thought, Al: hire two helicopters . . . paint one light blue, the other dark . . . race them up the river . . . and film it from a rowing boat?"

John spent the rest of his career on *Sportsnight* and *Match of the Day*.

The sanctioning of my great hovercraft idea—by referee Rankov*—may be some way off (*won't catch me whining about plagiarism*), but in its own silky way the Boat Race has come a long way innovation-wise, since 1938 (Oxford by two lengths) and the BBC's first 'live' showing.

Hawkeye and *Hot-spot* have transformed the coverage of tennis and cricket; catch technological crabs slowing Varsity rowing down. Nowadays, coxes have cameras and mics and there's GPS lest either goes missing . . . we know exactly how far and fast the boats travel between bridges (clearly of enormous interest to those who would man them, and the g.p.at large) . . . heart-rates, fuel consumption and impending bowel movements are monitored—and brain scans are on their way to check for commitment. Pretty scientific stuff . . . *but in the end, David, it's a game of two boats.*

Question: Do oarspersons prefer travelling backwards on trains?

We prayed for a close one—a leak, a paddle war, a mid-stream boarding, a Thames bore . . . because for millions of sober, neutral, tabloid-reading, *Butlin's* holidaymakers, that was what it was (till 2012 . . . *o.m.g!*).

The previous weeks had been taken up filming all manner of cameos and vignettes in preparation for the great day—little time compared to the year-long blood-letting of those occupying the two yellow 'blue' boats.

The 'Jenny Pitman' of Boat Race day (in that he always *on* it) was spiffing Dan Topolski, who'd steered—or coached, rather—Oxford to 10 wins in a row between '76 and '85 (shouldn't count '78 really cos some rat—perhaps reading Burgess and McLean—let the plug out on the Cambridge boat).

'Toppers' the oarsperson triumphed a couple of times in the '60s, but nothing compared to *Boris Rankov's Rule of six-on-the-trot (*how many degrees is one allowed?*) from 1978 . . . or (*be fair, ref*) '79 to '83.
In the year before the first of those, the Oxford boat was coxed by m'future-Lord, Colin Moynihan (and coached by 'Danny' Tops), and he—small Col—would also be steering and calling the shots, in a squeaky voice, from the back of the GB eight in Moscow, as they tried, blindly—to everyone but aforesaid rudder-man and boxing blue, C.B. Moynihan—to haul in the gold medal winning East Germans; they did see the Russians coming 3rd.

Rankov really is a professor (of Roman History), whereas *Dr. Gregory House* is made-up—a state Hugh Laurie would have found himself in *a)* when *House* became the most watched TV show on earth in 2008, and *b)* more recently, when *L'Oreal* rang to ask if they could use his 'boat race' on their ad campaign: they considered—quite rightly—that for his work on *Fry and Laurie*, the *Blackadders* and *House M.D.*, plus the acclaim his musical renaissance attracted . . . not to mention the commendable 2nd—for the 'filth'—in the 1980 river race . . . he was indeed worth it. Cambridge, with the as-yet undiscovered J.H.C. Laurie in the 4th seat, were pipped by a canvas. The closest they ever came to drawing was in 2003 when Oxford sneaked it . . . by a foot.

Bred in *Oxford*, Laurie honed his manners and comedy at Eton and *Cambridge*. His buddy Stephen Fry—a man you'd love to have for dinner (non-cannibalistically)—is a Norwich canaries fan and darts lover; if you can think of a finer connection between Deila and Sid Waddell—other than eggs and bulls' eyes . . . and their diverging views on how to broadcast . . . . you're better than I *(but then you'd know that)*.

Dan joined wee Harry Carpenter (an ideal coxsworth), and that rascal of an Olympic double sculler, Chris Baillieu, in keeping the BBC boat balanced.

The rowing of the Boat Race takes anywhere between 16 and 22 minutes, and the Grand National is around 9 minutes, at best . . . so your actual happening had better deliver, given the hugely disproportionate amount of time and effort spent on the build-ups.

Well for starters—the sinkings, the dead-heat(ish), the great races and the *Foinavaon* fiasco notwithstanding—there was the *false* one in 1993, when *Esha Ness* won 'the race that never was' (Mrs. P. was the 'wretched' trainer) . . . and the bomb scare in '97 (O'Sullevan's swansong) . . . . but a R(river).T.O. on Boat Race day?

In the year George Orwell predicted it would end in tears, Peter Hobson, the little man on the pedals at the back of the Cambridge boat, crashed their £7,000 rig into a barge—easily done when all you can see in front of you is a long ton-and-a-half of educated "muscle and blood and skin and bone."

None of the President's men—not even bow man Reynolds—thought to take a peak, each having being 'in the zone' for about twelve months: no sex . . . no fizzy drinks . . . *no fun really.*

We didn't capture the actual collision—it happened under Putney Bridge—but there was no question of failing to stop, or reporting the accident. Reputedly, there are around six million TV viewers in the UK alone.

Barge crashes happened a couple of times in the eighteen hundreds, when river traffic was dense . . . this one was *parked*.

Hobson's was a minor issue when you consider that Iraqi crews training on the Tigris have to put up with rocket attacks and floating bodies as part of their Olympic preparation.

Postponing a rowing race on the tidal Thames isn't simple for the authorities; the Moon would have a say . . . there were media difficulties to ignore . . . and—dilemma upon dilemma—*what to do with the Saturday night ball?*

For cox Hobson, double jeopardy was still an option.

Up to that day in March 1984, there had been 129 lung-rupturing rows between the University Boat Clubs, most from Putney to Mortlake, though they *had* done it the other way round (as it were) in the early days, and once from Westminster to Putney.

Fittingly, they'd also duelled at 'Henners' upon the self-same Thames.

In races won (1 very dodgy dead-heat), Cambridge hold the edge over the Dark Blues who might be considered the 'home team,' given that the Thames doth run thro' Oxfordshire (and Middlesex and Surrey).

The only time I directed the TV coverage, there was an early evening 'blade-off,' which meant back-lit shots of clashing oars and spectacular wide shots from our tracking helicopter of the tiny waterboatmen—'triumph' and 'despair'—leading the armada of scarves and posh accents, West . . . towards Chiswick and resolution.

In a downhill ski race, the slightest stumble out of the hut may only cost fractions of a second but will result in a huge drop in the final standings; in rowing, demanding, but not getting eight giants to strike it right, as one, from the off, could mean the difference between forgiving one's cox by hurling him/her in the river, or trudging home in wellies too knackered for a long overdue shag of choice.

BBC Sport was never huge on change, but there were vantage points and elevations, as yet untried, for our cameras. I shouldn't have bothered; never mind my bosses, the minefield of red tape you had to negotiate in order to book a spot on the toe-paths (tideway) was more complicated than Chaucerian English. Each bit of real estate I coveted, came under a different local authority—*there weren't enough hours, Geoff.*

Of eventualities factored into our planning, Hobson's choice wasn't one of them; none of the crew publically blamed the 'swain, but when they came back next day, in a borrowed boat, and heard of Oxford's storming effort (in record time) to win by three and three quarter lengths, inwardly they'd be cussing . . . just a Sloane fraction.

The rivalry between *Grandstand* (we did the really important stuff), on the second floor of our Kensington House block in Shepherd's Bush, and *M.O.T.D.*, in the basement, persisted to the day they scuttled the old flagship, though the shop had long since moved to Television Centre

David Coleman transcended all: he presented *Grandstand* and—to use a golfing metaphor—'his signature hole' was the teleprinter, the on-screen electronic typewriter that brought the fastest football results service (courtesy of the Press Association), right into your pools coupon. Coleman was a master of it, remembering a complimentary stat for every significant result that clicked on the page, in any division, north or south of Hadrian's; it was his *piece de resistance* and he hammed it up accordingly.
'Lyners' cracked it too—good job, because I was editing most of his shows and I was buggered if I wanted to learn when Kiddiminster last scored an away goal against ten men in injury time in the Conference (*not to cast aspersions on the fine traditions and history of the mighty Harriers, you understand*).

Frank Bough's reign (1968-1983) bisected Davie and Dessie's; without maligning the old footie Blue (from Cambridge), his knowledge of, and passion for 'the beautiful game' didn't match D. or D.'s. Where Frank was magnificent was in his ability to take 'talkback'—the editor (Alan Hart)'s (deep) voice in his ear—then blurt out given facts with an imperceptible delay; keeping up with the incoming line on the teleprinter, under those circumstances was nothing short of genius.
Coleman extemporised: you could ping facts at him which he'd store like a hamster preparing for a cold snap, then, as you were about to remind him, out they'd come with his own interpretation and, latterly, a stumble or two too many.

All things considered, Sky's Jeff Stelling (a BBC old boy) is peerless. Should he forget in the drama and excitement of a late winner for Hartlepool, Messrs Nicholas, Thompson, Merson and Le Tissier—plus all eye-witnesses at grounds round the country—are on hand to remind him that he's *"Jeff"* to his friends.

If *Grandstand* were the leviathan (steady as she goes), *Sportsnight with Coleman*, and, to a lesser degree, *Match of the Day*, were destroyers with cutting edges. No one escaped, from politicians with sport in their portfolios to the earliest form of chavvy, football agent.
Stars queued up to get on—some would regret the wait.

In the show of his own name (changed from *Sportsview* in '68), Coleman was ubiquity personified . . . he'd dream up and impose his ideas on the editor . . . use his black book to secure studio guests . . . write his slick *Pick of the Week* action sequences . . . commentate on a match kicking-off at 7.30.p.m . . . nip down to front the start of the live show at 9.25 (the football embargo was 2200hr) . . . and, as self-appointed head oligarch, issue bollockings, routinely.

A couple of features—a big fight preview or a 'live' studio debate—would precede forty minutes of football, which we'd be editing well into the transmission. When almost all was said and done, he'd round up the day's news and results, pretty well off the seat of his shiny pants.

D.C. was exceptional for his time—not easy, but exceptional; you felt the rough edge of his tongue on a regular basis—a bom-*bast* and a bit of a <u>bast</u>-*ard*, in truth. During that reign of considerable terror, when screaming and shouting was the chosen way, he was the ideal catalyst.
That changed, thankfully, when smooth-ass Lynam took the reins, following a half-hearted 'comeback' by the old hack.

'Them old uns' had their moments, but I'd defy any of those (moments) to top this one.
Tony Cornell, our senior sub-editor—a man of Fleet Street, Wapping, and a million gags (*some* were funny)—leaned on my shoulder: he was breathless having flown up the metal staircase to the production gallery from his seat by the agency machines—*Reuters, Associated Press, The Press Association* and the like. Tony wasn't known for 'flying' anywhere.

The subs' condensed stories would be passed up to the editor for possible inclusion between the action, and this one had a better chance than most.

Unusually, the sheet he thrust in front of me was an original, unexpurgated . . . and HOT!!. I took several stabs at reading the words, handed the paper back to wide-eyed 'Cornelli,' and asked that it be taken down to Des, pronto . . . *if his heart could stand it.*

WOW!

September 27th . . . . around three in the morning.

We'd been at it for hours; if our star presenter was to be seen with his feet on the desk browsing the early editions, it wasn't disinterest . . . . we were in the middle of a recorded package and knew the outcome.

Tony slid the bombshell under the anchorman's *Daily Mirror*—a publication Tony contributed to, in his day job.

Lynam stirred.

A joke now would be inappropriate.

Uncharacteristically, big Des appeared excited as Martin (Hopkins), the studio director, geared himself and those about him, to crash out of the tape.

"CUT! . . . cue Des" he snarled.

This isn't verbatim, but it went something along these lines:

"If what I have in front of me is true—and it's an unconfirmed report from a French news agency—it is the biggest story of these, or any other Olympic Games."

The gist of it was, Ben Johnson had been cheating and they'd caught up with him: 1988 South Korea.

(time to think)

. . . run the 100m final again . . . even with replays and post-race interviews, not long enough . . . we need breathing space . . .

Ron Pickering—the man from *Superdrug*—was poised; in the great scheme of performance enhancers, *stanozolol* was a relatively easy one to get his teeth around.

There were press conferences to get to: remember the portentous I.O.C. lady with her accusatory *"Ben Johnson, Canada"* . . . and the subsequent shots of the haunted, hunted runner being bustled through Seoul airport?

Cupboards rattled with accusation and denial—the fall-out would last for years and years . . . . forever.
(my 'mate' Jesse would be turning in his grave).

What a moment.

Four years earlier, Lynam and I were collaborating on the Los Angeles Games, when the ground began to shake . . . in a manner of speaking; not the Canadian this time—he'd only managed 3rd in the hundred behind his all-conquering nemesis, Carl Lewis—no, this was a *white* American tale . . . with a *white* South African twist.

Mary Decker had fallen over in front of her own folk, lusting—as is their jingoistic wont—for gold.

Metaphoric guns were leveled at Zola Budd; the personal implements marketing men were raising to their temples would be real deals.

For team Decker-Tabb, this was a rhino crash.

We've all mis-used the word down the years, but the "disaster" the US media were ranting about was just an unfortunate accident.

Coleman steered clear of hyperbole, but was adamant: *Budd had tripped Decker*. The little, barefoot 18 year old—with the awkward running style—(in the British vest) from Orange Free State, was to blame . . . *said Dave*.

I glanced towards Des on the monitor . . . his face contorted with mine: "surely that's Decker's own fault" I opined . . . he nodded.

Fully prepared for vilification, I ventured in the commentator's ear: '*it was an accident, David—Budd was in front when it happened.*'

He'd heard alright, but ignored me. He stuck to his guns; indeed, he kept on and on and on about where he believed, unequivocally, the blame lay.

We came back to the London studio to do our own analysis with 'color' man, Dave Moorcroft (not too shabby himself over 3,000 metres); he concurred with Des and the rest of the planet (bar the U.S.A.).
A few phone calls later—to athletes' shop-steward, Derek Johnson, and several of his members—the UK jury came to the unanimous verdict: *Decker had tripped over Budd's legs*.

It was galling for Des to have David dismiss our findings after we'd handed back for the next event; he could have acknowledged his teammate's stance, even if he felt it to be tosh. Fuelled by other fundamental differences, that was the catalyst for a career-long feud of near silence between the two giants of sports broadcasting—respect, but nothing else.

Moorcroft and Lynam were outstanding at the Olympics and World championships; Davie took to it instantly, insisting he had production talk-back in his ear so he wouldn't miss out on the banter.

Carpenter and mutiny-buster Topolski only locked rollocks once a year.
Dan's internal war with five American 'students' over who should or should not be in the 1987 boat was the stuff of a good read though some critics did question its accuracy (*and here's another, sports fans*).

What joy for little 'H' when I re-positioned the Putney com box to a spot where he could actually *see* the start of the Race. More often than not, the defining strokes to Hammersmith Bridge were clues to its outcome, and now, at last, he could see some of them; prior to, he'd been stuck in a back-street room with no view of the University stone or the lights of Craven Cottage.

Hunt and Walker started shakily: James's sporadic absences, at *Prix*, for substance inhalation (residuals making their way into their shared lip microphone) . . . the odd bottle of rosé to lubricate . . . bare feet on the desk to nauseate—none of it helped, but they worked it out.

The line-up for rugby union was a moving feast.
We did two games on international days with the *A Team* picking itself: Bill McLaren, and the Dada of scrum halves, Gareth Edwards—lynch-pin of the invincible Lions in South Africa, and master at the Arms Park for Cardiff R.F.C., Wales (53 times) and the Baa-baas . . . *"What a score!"*

Northerner William Macall invaded London society in the late seventeen hundreds and created the exclusive *Almack's Assembly Rooms*—a Victorian version of *Scribes West* (without Venables on karaoke); if *Almack's* was tough to get in to, so was the 'Voices Club' at the BBC.

Coleman, Carpenter, O'Sullevan, Maskell, Benaud, McLaren, Walker and Alliss had vouchers and ties; in Peter's case, a personalised number plate—*PUTT 3*—on his 'Roller' added a nice, if self-deprecating touch (*not one to nick with your car door, ideally, on alighting at Ken House car park*).

Don't imagine by storming the border, bearing *Hawick Balls*—a confection akin to the golden humbug—that spurs would be awarded willy-nilly; bring an informed, thrilling, deeply researched, unbiased approach to rugby commentary and the chair could be yours for as long as you chose to stay (49 years in big Bill's case).

The admirable Nigel Starmer-Smith of Oxford, Harlequins, England and the Baa-baas, plus an ex-player, like Bob Hiller, who'd banged a few over for Quins and England in his time, might commentate on the other game. 'Starmers' handled *B Team* status with dignity; no one could usurp 'Hannibal Bill' from the *A Team*, so the tough little scrum-half dug in, made *Rugby Special* his own and set about coping with some awful personal tragedies, his gutsy wife, Roz, a constant on his outside.

Bill Beaumont's immaculate playing credentials—Lions and England captain and 'Grand Slam' leader in 1980—meant his non-chavvy if pushy agent, John Hockey (quite a decent, pre-metric 'right-half') had little to do but negotiate ridiculous fees with my boss, Jonathan Martin.

'Hocks' did similarly on 'Motty,' Desmond and Alan Parry's behalves, while indirectly helping to consolidate my marriage plan for Ann Upright (now *Philips* in name only)—mother of magnificent Jamie David and Charlie John from that second innings—by providing us with an apartment on the Algarve wherein to examine our deepening feelings; Richard Shepherd's heady wines and stimulating fare at his bistro in Quinta do Lago, did the rest.

If Peter Cook's (anti) *Establishment Club* in Soho was *the* place to go in the 60s for piss-takers and pianists (Dudley Moore did both, superbly), *Langan's*—named after co-founder, 'Hell-boy' Peter (Michael Caine and chef Shepherd being his fellow *co-s*)—cannot be improved upon for nose-bagging and rubber-necking, these last thirty years.

Grace Kelly and Marlon Brando probably sat on or near a table my pal Renton Laidlaw (the haggis survivor) and I have used on many visits to Mayfair . . . *not many people know, or will be interested in that.*

There wasn't the same hysteria about whipping ex-athletes into commentary boxes, or onto our screens as ill-prepared presenters, as there is today. There was no divine right, but 'live' TV is closely scrutinized and unforgiving. The chosen needed to know that theirs was a privileged position; being able to express highly qualified opinions, coherently and consistently was the 'must' part of the deal. Our aim, behind the scenes, was to be as professional and properly prepared as the athletes on them were, whilst retaining a sense of fun and occasion.

No one, of sound mind, would question Gareth's right to talk about the game he commanded, universally . . . but like it did—and shall—for lots who go 'unproduced,' it got a bit cosy; chinks in his identification and knowledge of emerging players began to appear.

Pointing the finger at G.O. Edwards M.B.E. (now CBE . . . ought to be 'Sir Gareth' really) would have been impudent and imprudent and I wasn't blessed with Trump or Sugar's arrogance.
It wasn't an easy conversation—*'Christ, he's the best rugby player of all time.'*

In a later life, Mark Nicholas accused me, jokingly (I think), of being a 'star fucker' (*don't mince your words, will you*).

Look, I confess to believing Barry Richards and Gary Sobers and Jonty Rhodes and Malcolm Marshall and Jack Russell and 'Lords' Viv and Ted were the business; against the tree in our school grounds I was 'Barry' with the bat and 'Garfield St. John' with the ball . . . . but then to get to <u>work</u> with them . . .

Guilty as charged, Markie Mark.

Rugby League was staple to *Grandstand*; it fitted perfectly into the 'live as it happens' ethos of Saturday afternoon sport, even though it had a 'regional' tag up till Cup Final day. ITV's *World of Sport* fed off the higher ratings their wrestling produced . . . *but was it sport, strictly, and what business was it of ours?*
As I mentioned, the established League combo was Eddie Waring and Alex Murphy; you couldn't take issue with Eddie's enthusiasm for one of sports tougher pursuits, but Ray French would be my man for all seasons and tours.

My wee guys loved Jonathan Pearce on *Robot Wars* but, like brainy Sid Waddell at the darts, he was attracting the attention of psychosurgeons and lobotomists: both needed help—their commentaries could give Murray's a good run for it, hysteria-wise.

JP—perhaps with an eye on the fading Motson/Davies dynasties—toned it down a little, and willingly succumbed to treatment. Waddell remains terribly well paid by Sky and appreciated by millions.

O'Sullevan and Wilson I've touched on too, and whilst never a team in the sense of sharing the 'lead' (commentary), they dovetailed supremely, seldom treading on one another's toes, professionally; what they didn't know about on any given day at the races wasn't worth wasting money on.

Maskell and Barrett were the embodiment of good manners and fair play. J.B. was a mischievous lad out of his All England Club livery . . .
Dan was just Dan, untouchable, an "*ace*" . . . not easy to say with a mouthful of ill-fitting *wallies* (dentures).

The Grand Match—the annual piss-up between former Ryder cuppers and forgotten heroes of the Walker Cup—was the brainchild of respective old boys, Alliss and Critchley: fierce encounters were enacted over the impossible links at Deal, near Sandwich.

The Pete and Brucie partnership lasted 14 years before 'The Colonel' decided to jump ship and join 'electric hands' Murray at Sky . . . for loads more money and <u>hours</u> on mic.
Post-schism, Alex Hay—'The Silver Fox' of Woburn—was on alternate shots with gorgeous Jackie Alliss's bloke, but however incestuous their relationship became—and it did—it had nothing on Gray and Tyler's.

Kenneth Wolstenholme, Alan Weeks, David Coleman, even 'Boughie' were our main footie strikers, but eventually they made way for Motson and Davies, the synonyms '*for me*' . . . utterly different personalities, with a shared passion for a game neither could play:
'Motty,'—the living embodiment of *Rothman's* (in a very silly coat)

'Bazz'—a wordsmith, a pronunciation freak (of foreign players' names).

Evergreen (for a *Reds* fan) Tony 'Gubbalavic' and Gerald Sinstadt (the best script writer to film, I ever came across) did sterling service—Tony being the shorter, and feistier.

When I joined, borin' Jim Laker was on pole at the cricket: 19 for 90 in the '56 Ashes was bloody remarkable + . . . *but how did he pass the audition?*
There wasn't one.
John Arlott still called televised Sunday League matches, but 'steam' was *his* thing, so when Benaud accepted his Queen's shilling and came on for the ex-off-spinner at the pavilion end, I for one gave thanks and praise. The bells of St. John's Wood rang out . . . smoke billowed from the Long Room—for the next 40 years or so 'His Loyal Aussieness' would keep all ends up and cricketing nations enthralled.

Oddly, in a game of partnerships, cricket commentary on TV isn't conducive to their formation—it's too long . . . like a Gavaskar innings (bar for 1.2 billion Indians); who sat at Richie's side was immaterial.
Along the way the *TMS* team of 'Johnners,' Tony Lewis and 'Aggers' would whet everyone's appetite for lunch as the obligatory over of spin, just before one (p.m.), proved there was nothing to be gained from risk-taking.

Duck is never served to batsmen, but Nicholas M.C.J., took to broadcasting much as they do to water—quite rare.

Good broadcasters on television have generally done the air miles on wireless. The success Lynam had translating his unique style to the telly made it difficult for wannabes.
Guess where urbane, new boy Adrian Chiles did time? . . . the (former) *News of the World*—same as Richie (and Brooks and Coulson) . . . and radio too* of course *i.e. as well.

They call it 'the comfort factor' . . . .
Does he/she know what they're on about? . . . Will they tell me something I don't know? . . . Are we in good hands?
It's a bonus if you're fit like the Brook (singular), or handsome like Clooney, but most folk would prefer to be driven *well* in a banger, than recklessly in a Silver Cloud.

Motty got there on criteria alone.
If it looks like a duck and walks like a duck, it is a duck.

There are so many channels on the dial that presenters are in and out like fiddlers' arms as the public, and advertisers, lose faith; yet, looking back, it'd be tough to deny the contribution made to sports broadcasting by the original BBC 'rat-pack'—they set a pretty high bar.

But no one lasts forever . . . the trick is knowing *when* to go.
Virulent "prima donna" virus/fading eyesight/ brain-mouth-co-ordination-meltdown/more than one guest appearance on *Loose Women* are vital signs programme makers ignore at their peril.

Watching expressly articulate John Barnes struggle, early on, in his role as presenter of *Channel 5's* football, brought back a poignant memory; J.B. was another thrown to the wolves without reference.

You may well say that by going to Malvern College and Cambridge, Jeremy Paxman had a head-start: but could he rap like 'Barnsey' (on *"World in Motion"*)?
Could he ever dream about scoring a 'wonder goal' against the 'Brazzos' (at the Maracana in 1984)?
Could he raise a family five-a-side, plus two subs, without batting an eyelid?
NO!
Still, it was a bit of a nightmare for the old boy—not in affable Ortis Deley's league, for his was, without debate, a "world class" sports broadcasting disaster (Daegu 2011 on ITV . . . and *You Tube*).

Even connoisseurs of the cleavage have to admit that Kelly Brook was pretty dire when she started out on *The Big Breakfast* with Johnny Vaughan; happily it ended well. She went off to Hollywood and was eaten alive by a piranha in 3-D, whereas London's *Capital Radio* and children's charities are grateful Johnny stayed home.

Helen Rollason caught my boss's eye at the Commonwealth Games. She'd come to us from Radio Essex and BBC *Newsround*, but her life's ambition lay in sports reporting. She was determined and confident enough to take on anything, as she would subsequently prove.
I didn't see her as a *Grandstand* "anchor," much as the p.c. lobby clamoured for a breakthrough.
The pressure to "give her a go" turned into an order from the man on the rung above.

Helen's debut: 1990.
(*Grandstand's gallery assistant counts down the final minute to "On Air"*).

"Oh, *shut up* John!" she hissed.
Blimey, there was me thinking I was helping with my idle banter, getting her to talk back, limbering up her lips and vocals: unlike *Veronica Cornerstone* in *Anchorman*, she was consumed by nerves.

However difficult that had been, no one deserved to endure what she did. I'm glad I knew her a little.

Helen presented lots of diferent shows thereafter, including the 'golden' nights of athletics from Oslo, Lausanne, Zurich etc., where Coe and Ovett swopped 'blue ribands' and world records to raucous crowds in packed stadia (*yes, athletics . . . British middle-distance superstar athletics . . . honkies, at that*).

In his pre-purple-shell-suit passage, that position was also held by David Icke (*need to be careful here—he could bring down the wrath of a force greater than defamation*). Apart from David, no one knew what was to come to pass, but for now he was keeping his own counsel; perhaps he saw me as repitilian humanoid (*might explain those long silences during the '88 Olympic breakfast shows*).
Then something equally far-fetched came to the old goalkeeper—he was struck by a thunderbolt . . . the heavens opened, books and conspiracies theories rained down on us in *The Illuminati* and *The Elders of Zion* . . . . a spiritual haemhorrage, the like of which we may never see again, hopefully.
Whether he was a tad too close to his Maker, or it simply scared him shitless, the bold Icke wasn't a great flyer and had to be physically restrained on one occasion; doesn't explain everything, but those doing the restraining appeared to get enormous satisfaction.

The Dutch Master, Denis Bergkamp, and Dad's favourite golfer, Neil Coles are aerophobes (pity, because Neil would certainly have given the Yanks a good run for their prize money).

In 1976, we took our cameras to Southampton docks; our film would feature a man capable of changing the tyres on a Jumbo, on his jack . . . had airports and Geoff Capes got on.
Forcing the big bobby to do anything he didn't want to, was asking for it. Some said he was a gentle giant, but boys and girls advocating crime as the way forward, should *grab their beads and worry . . . a lot*. '*A good kick in the bollocks and run for it*' wasn't the answer, for massive as his thighs were, he could power them over a hundred metres at county sprinter standard—*and when he caught you . . . .*

Tooting impatiently at that particular caravan enthusiast, on the road to Cornwall, would be to miscalculate on a gargantuan scale: the parties unknown who nicked an earlier model of his will be shitting themselves for the rest of their days will be.

Geoff would go to Montreal by sea . . . *and that was dandy with me*.

His friend and coach, Stuart Storey—not averse to a (black) shell-suit himself—came along as reporter-cum-chaperone, lest all on board was not to the large one's liking.

A chain of butchers had helped with rations, there was a gym of sorts, but the cabin didn't exist on that level of ship that could house such a giant—a badly slept, 20 stone shot-putter isn't worth thinking about.

At the point of testing his bunk's worthiness, his waters broke and the cameraman and I were offered a trip over the side in return for continuing to film; we were still in dock and the pier-side, to port, was the closer . . . *so we stopped*.

Udo Beyer from East Germany won gold at the Games, by a couple of centimeters, but nothing doing rostrum-wise for P.C. Capes. Four years later he turned pro, was measured for the kilt, conquered the Highlands and Islands without help, became the World's Strongest man (as if it were in doubt) and grew large in recessive pieds (i.e. breeding budgies) . . . the personification of 'soft hands.'

James Hunt, as we know, was also into birds—budgies, parrots and blondes, mostly.

En passant . . . apart from Juantorena's 'class,' Viren's 'double,' Comaneci's '10s' and Wilkie getting Britain's first Olympic swimming gold medal for 68 years at Montreal '76 . . . there was this Italian in the heats of the 400 metre hurdles.
Filling the frame, in the killer outside berth, our man in azure had prepared for years; gilt-edged dreams of Jupiter and *Il Canto degli Italiani* would have kept him up permanently, during the long months of winter training.
(*you can't fail to have noticed how Italian male athletes love to show off their equipment at meets {and two veg}, in lycra huggers that once fitted*).

As bade by the starter, the swarthy one went to his marks.

'Set' produced no further movement.

The gun went—*he didn't*.
Looking all around, appealingly, in that 'Italian' way—shoulders hunched, hands and jaws at the droop—you felt for him . . . . *then cracked up*. There was no recall.

Hauling the qualification standard back to *schoolboy*, there was a similar occurrence at one of our sports days.

Denis Carr, nailed on favourite for the four hundred flat, had been drawn in the hare's lane:

'*BANG!*'—off went Denis.

Pissed up, didn't he? . . . unopposed!

Alas for Carr D.—in the yellow of the house of Campbell—it'd been a false start, and the poor wee man was running without his crucial hearing aid; he was too far gone for the re-run, but being a good spud, he took one for the deaf guys.

Whether or not it was at that very same meeting, it sits nicely here.
The school spear-chucking champion would have had something in his porridge that morning because, first up, he unleashed 'an<u>ee</u>-normous wunne'—as big Pick often said—a Jowett javelin . . . a zinger . . . a Zelezny—*on and on it flew*.

Don't know if he would have won, but John Cameron—in the blue of the house of Drummond—was felled within 150 yards of the half-mile finish.
Had the javelin impressed the grass, rather than John's neck, it would have been a school record.
Miraculously, no lasting harm was done, but imagine the 'Camster' out on the pull:
". . . *seriously, how <u>did</u> you come by that mark on your neck, was it a bullet?*"
"*No, actually . . .*

The Italian hurdler was a must for our end-of-Games music sequence, which Doug Hammond—a cameraman pal who'd come south from the BBC in Glasgow after a highly successful stint in studio and outside broadcasts ('successful' as in tugging birds at *Songs of Praise*—*may he be forgiven*)—would compose. He plumped for Gerry Rafferty's *"Get it Right Next Time"* (*"Baker Street"* was a couple of years away . . . next time would be in Moscow, in four).

Rafferty & Egan (*Stealer's Wheel*)'s *"Stuck in the Middle with You"* would have worked well for javelin-kebab-man 'Mr. Blue' and my mate Denis: *"clowns to the left of me, jokers to the right . . . here I am . . . .*

Way back in this load of disconnected nonsense, I mentioned that Rafferty and Connolly—*The Humblebums*—had been regulars at our folk club in Crieff, and that Gleneagles Hotel—and its fabulous cream teas—was just a few miles away.
Join the dots.
We were on the 1st tee of the King's course at the Glen for a pro-celebrity golf match, featuring James Hunt—who *had* a clue, and Peter Cook—who definitely hadn't.

Lee Trevino was one of the pros; his opening shot went:
"If Heaven is as good as this, I sure hope they have some tee times left." . . . more of less guaranteeing his country membership for ever.

James brought along his long-haired Alsatian, *Oscar*, a veteran of showbiz events, and a regular at many fine dining tables. Unprompted, he took up station, in the prone position, just outside the tee marker, as James prepared to let one rip; though the front paws were 'in the water,' they were not deemed to be interfering.

Oscar pulled off the classic 'eye-follow' as Shunt's ball bulleted right towards the gorse. Politely, he waited as the others teed off.

Peter was up last, in every sense . . . arriving a trifle late . . . characteristically unkempt . . . and with one dog-breath-of-a-hangover.

Not to be outdone by Hunt and pooch, 'Wispy' stepped forward holding a mysterious cloth-covered object in both hands, like a magician about to dazzle and amaze.

Dramatically, the covering was whisked away to reveal a tiny goldfish, aimlessly wandering his glass enclosure *(might that, I vunder, have been the inspiration for his German professor in the video we were to make together twenty years later?).*

Peter apologized for being late: neither he nor the fish had had a great night—*not that his pet ever slept . . . due to an absence of eyelids.*

Very precisely, the bowl was positioned next to *Oscar*, whose gaze remained steadfast . . . . locked on the co-ordinates of Shunt's errant drive.

The circling motion of Pete's fish indicated that his master's ball had survived the opening couple of swipes.

Nor did time improve his form: the green work, however, was markedly better than the rest, testament to those hours on the tiles (cobbles) back home.

Oscar was used to long stints in the car and yawned as James and I made off into a freezing December night, to attend the *Sports Personality of the Year* show at Television Centre.

We were chatting, inconsequentially, at the drinks reception afterwards:

"Let's go Philipo . . . *Oscar*'s got something for us in the car park."

It'd been snowing heavily: a couple of inches had fallen and stuck, as we trudged back towards Hunt's left-hand drive Mercedes.
I deferred to Oscar, in the off-side front, and slipped in the back.

Presently, out came *the* most enormous spliff; the co-pilot nodded his approval . . . .
I offered to drive (wimp).

Scooby, barely discernable in the fug, was evenly covered in a neat blanket of white powder (snow) as the sunroof slid open . . . . couldn't be having the fuzz stopping us

en route to the after-show bash at the Cricketers' night spot downtown now, could we?
(*can a canine have its licence endorsed for doing drugs?*).

In warmer climes—Hertfordshire, if I remember—we were feeding another habit-of-the-trade, necking large G&Ts on the Liggetts' lawn, prior to the Milk Race—of which Phil was the mastermind, and his missus, Pat, the masseuse—starting.
The *Tour de France* is clicks longer and does better scandal, though on one occasion Phil did manage to stub the UK peleton into a cul-de-sac having missed his jerk with the route map. There were no recriminations; Phil got on with everyone—even Hugh Porter!

The very mention of cycling gives me a pain in the wallet.

There was no Chris Hoy around at the time to stimulate and excite a British audience. Sean Kelly's heroics in the Alps, and on the roads, notably between Paris and Roubaix, received little attention from the BBC, and the great tour of attrition and urine testing was never in sports department's portfolio during my tenure.

But we did have rights to track meets at Leicester, and in 1982 I was given the World Professional Road Race Championships at Goodwood to direct and produce—Phil and Hugh on commentary.

None of us drones was wealthy; Phil's spread in the country came from the proceeds of unsubstantiated cocaine and gun-running deals with the Bolivian cartels and the Welsh nationalists . . . but he also kept an eye on the markets.

His advice to sink what little I had into **A**lan **M**ichael **S**ugar **T**rading—a newish electronics firm in Essex—fell on deaf ears. I'd no interest in how fortunes were made in the City—bulls and bears could've been grid iron teams for all I knew.

Without any investment from me, AMSTRAD grew to a point (in 2007) where B.Sky.B. felt it a snip at £125 million, sending the unshaven founder and former beetroot salesman soaring up the Forbes money list. Eventually he'd become, in the UK, what Donald Trump was to the nauseatingly ambitious in the US on *Apprentice* . . . a right shit-head.

The road race part of the 'Worlds' was staged at Goodwood, in the lea of Lord March's place, bound, on high ground by the grandstands of the glorious racetrack, and on the low, by the equally famous and all but defunct, aerodrome motor racing circuit, where Fangio, Farina and Hawthorn plied their early trade (and Bernie Ecclestone). It was still being used for testing, but fell millions short of the standards demanded by the big boys of Formula One.

We were invited to Goodwood House for cocktails—a motley production crew and Pat and Anita's husbands.

The butler ushered us into the drawing room.

After a suitably correct passage of time, the strikingly elegant Lady of the manor made her entrance; she'd been a ballerina before moving into the big house—*'poise and deportment, Louie . . . you never lose it.'*

We made small talk and sipped on the cellar's finest—maybe not the *red and green apples, meadow flowers, fig with a dash of nutmeg of an Armand de Brignac*, but a decent drop nonetheless . . . . more of a *Louis Roederer*, or a *Deutz* perhaps.

A tinkling of a drained flute made way for the briefest of briefings by Lady March: "My husband will join us shortly . . ." then cautioned . . . "he has an unsightly blemish on his cheek which one would prefer not to have mentioned at any stage, but do enjoy the rest of your evening."

There's a scene in Disney's *101 Dalmatians* where Hugh Laurie's oafish character *Jasper* cautions his gormless sidekick *Horace* (played by Mark Williams) **not** to comment on the hideous scar *Skinner* (the fearsome mute charged with providing dog pelts for *Cruella's* latest creation) had on his face.

For *Horace*, read my co-director and occasional golfing partner, Huw Jones, who was anything but gormless being a MENSA member with an intelligence quotient up around his personal best gross score at Pinner Hill golf club.

Huw, if you recall, was the buffoon who'd baulked at the bull's ball by the barbecue in Buenes Aires . . . but who'd brilliantly saved BBC blushes at Birkdale.

Goodwood was just the start of another error-strewn passage in 'Jonesy' life and short times.

Right on cue:
"What's that horrible mark on your face, Lord March?"

Reminds me of the 'Mansell-Murray moment' at Monza, in 1991.
Nigel had just collected a huge bump on his forehead after colliding with a low bridge on his lap of honour. Interviewing him afterwards, Murray—lest anyone be in any doubt as to what he was referring—gave the throbbing mound a good old poke.

Refresh your memories as to how good Mansell was: Senna came 2nd that Monza . . . 'Professeur' Prost was 3rd . . . . and Martin Brundle 13th.

Were you anything other than Latin, in trying to escape the track, you'd not need reminding of how fucking rude Italian drivers are.

The official line in his Lordship's case was: "it's a bumble-bee sting."
It appeared as though the little furry bugger had gone deep inside to recover his weaponry, and left his arse sticking out, but really . . . *not the kind of thing one would say, Huwie.*

'Bepe' Saronni of Italy won the race after blitzing the field just before the finish. Reportedly, there were 65,000 punters scattered round the course with the customary nutters edging perilously close to the riders as they wound it up for the finish.

Greg Lemond—Lance Armstrong's old buddy*—who four years later would become the first American (the first non-European) to win the Tour de France (he won it three times all told) was 2nd at Goodwood, but not before he'd stitched up his team-mate Jonathan Boyer by dragging the best sprinters onto his tail in the closing stages . . . which is not done in cycling apparently.

*Lemond's beef with Armstrong was/is all about drugs and stuff and makes the Haye/Klitschko pre/post fight shenanigans look pat-a-cake.

Phil's post race interview with Sean Kelly, who was 3rd, was unintelligible due in part to exhaustion (Sean's) and his (Sean again) broad Irish accent.

The World Track Championships in '82 took the same gang and me to Leicester's velodrome in Saffron Lane—the Cycling Federation's H.Q.

Probably due to early line-dance leanings, back in the Sixties, the madison was particularly appealing on the track . . . that gripping hand-launching amongst team mates, proper use of 'men in tandem.'
When the ominum and points races came along I was *such* good friends with the commentators, graphics operators, and dear old Barry Davies . . . who was 44 at the time. *Over to you people.*

The pursuit—Hughie Porter's forté (when he had the legs for it)—is not the easiest event to cover on television, with starts on either side of the track . . . like there was a bad smell or something. The possibility (in a poorly matched race) of one team or individual pursuing, catching and ignominiously (for the 'passee') pissing past the other, meant the coverage had to be flexible.

A split-screen shot is the only way of making sense of it. The traditional method was for a horizontal split—team A on top, team B on the bottom, with their clocks ticking away and freezing as they crossed their respective home stations; the time differential automatically registered on another part of the screen.

Being a clever dick, I thought by mounting two high cameras, head-on, down the straights—one an on-coming view, one going away—and splitting the screen vertically, you'd get a better geographical reference with more of the run-ups to the time-lines.

As producer/director you had to punch your own buttons (which camera should the viewer see at any given time); the timing of the cuts was crucial and quite tricky, even with the split outputs of the two high cameras pre-set (ergo . . . coming up at the press of a single button).

My fear was that as many expert broadcasters were there . . . from Holland, Italy, France, Spain and Germany, where cycling is endemic . . . this somewhat revolutionary approach might not go down too well (there was also my boss to ignore).

I needn't have worried: most were delighted and vowed to impose it on their people when they got back home . . .

. . . that was, until 'Brains' struck.

With so many events on the track, we had to divide the load, or share it, at least; the Welsh wizard would do some as I looked after the highlights show, and *vice versa*—the 'vice versa' lasting as long as Huwie's first crack at the pursuit.

I kid you not, apart from when they adopt that slightly suspect position with their handlers at the start, the cyclists never appeared during the race.
As Huw cut to the split-screen, they had already careered off into the bends, and were well into the straights before he got to the corner camera.

In its own way, 'twas a thing of beauty—vociferous clamouring of the board-beating fans . . . frenzied commentary . . . but not an aerodynamic wheeler in sight . . . *sur-fucking-real*.
Fortunately, the commentary boxes had a good view of the track

The verdict from a hurried post-mortem amongst European Broadcast Union commentators was unanimous . . . . 'Jones should only do the sprints.'
I threw in the Kierin to keep my dejected pal sweet.

Huwie's addiction to the bottle killed him in the end; I couldn't have wished for a more genuine and loyal friend.

Cycle racing on grass was common at Highland gatherings, where most battled for cash prizes. In the running races, "Purry" McGregor was the local hero at our Games. He was a stalwart of the New Year Powderhall Sprint, which dates back to the 1870s and years before the Modern Olympics (1896); by the time he'd begun using the bus pass, "Purry" needed only fall over to win, such was his handicap in the 100 yards.

Before Geoff Capes marched on Scotland, fellow shot putter Arthur Rowe—an Olympian in 1960—came to our annual celebration in Crieff's Market Park. Not only did he master the rigid-handle Scottish hammer throw, the stone put, the weight throw, and the sheaf toss ('Granny bashing' was a Monty Python creation), he could land the caber—in the prescribed twelve o'clock position—like a native . . . of Barnsley.

The *seann triubhas*—a traditional Highland dance dating from the Jacobite rebellion of 1745 (when the English banned Scots from wearing the bloody kilt)—would only be attempted when 'bladdered.'

Highland Games are a big deal in Scotland . . . at Cowal, in Argyll, where pipe bands converge from across the world come to compete . . . . at Braemar where Elizabeth Windsor, Queen of the United Kingdom and other Commonwealth realms, presides in Royal Stewart tartan (a band of which F1 'royalist' Jackie Stewart wore on his skid-lid when racing cars).

Ewan McGregor and his brother Colin—a retired veteran (30'ish) of the Gulf war and RAF Losseimouth—have both been Chieftains of Crieff Games, as has my mate Jim, their Dad (the bastard).

Perhaps the most impressive of those who've processed to 'let our Games begin' was Ewan Cameron, the water-skiing and hotel boss at Lochearnhead . . . 22 stone of Scottish beef, cromach in hand, kilt swinging—everything below in perfect working order.

'Heavy' athletes, of which Ewan was a very successful one, wore hoofing great Boadicean shoes with a single spike sticking out the toe-ends. They were driven, with purpose, into the sod prior to launching the rigid handled hammer, lest all ended in a flash of true Scotsman.

SPECTRE agent, *Rosa Klebb*'s lethal booties in *From Russia with Love* (the new sign on FIFA agent, Sepp Blatter's office door) clearly had Caledonian roots.

Killin's chieftain was the splendidly named Sir Gregor MacGregor of Macgregor—great name if you're stopped by the polis with a few on board and asked to identify yourself (like Boutros Boutros-Ghali, or any son of Iceland).

If legend is to be believed—and why would anyone besmirch the good name of Pierre de Coubertin—some Highland events were 'adapted' for the modern Olympics . . . among them, the shot and hammer; the caber tossers weren't invited to demonstrate.

'Geordie' MacTaggart, a puny Scots lad who got his oats every morning, was selected to represent Britain in the hammer at the Melbourne Olympics in 1956 . . . .
Stay where you are!
. . . . a mere figment of Gilliat and Launder's imagination—co-authors of the film of the same name ('Geordie') in 1955 (starring Bill Travers).

Grass tracking—speedway, in its earliest form, as practised by notables including Murray Walker and Bernie Ecclestone—was a weekly treat for us on the village green at Methven, in Perthshire; lots of mud, blue smoke and those distinctive, intoxicating two-stroke fumes—habit forming . . . if you let them.

My first trip to a BBC outside broadcast in an official capacity, was (excitedly) in 1967: Wembley stadium—floodlit and heaving.

Back then, Ove Fundin, Ivan Mauger and Barry Briggs could probably have afforded similar housing to Greaves, Hurst and Charlton—they were the superstars of their sport . . . . *and what an atmosphere.*

Fans went crazy, even if it was a 'foreigner' (Fundin—of Manchester Belle Vue Aces and Sweden) who came out on top (the last of his five world titles). Mauger (a six-time World champ, and Briggs (just the four) were Kiwis.

After each race, the cameraman who'd been 'stuck in the middle' throughout, needed unwinding—he was like a Masai tribeswoman, with yards and yards of fat, black, camera cable constricting the life out of him, head to toe . . . . *and* the poor bugger did the greyhounds.

The Patents Office will probably be on, but one of our videotape editors, Mike Moss—a subterranean from the bowels of TV Centre—claimed to have invented the mechanics for the electrically-driven hare.

"Cut, cue Harry."

"OK Son . . . When You Like."

Another man of boxing whose wrong side you didn't want to get on (wee Harry couldn't have hurt a fly) was Hugh McIlvanney; were you to close your eyes and invite both he and his brother William to speak, you'd struggle to pick the writer from the novelist—both had almighty Ayrshire accents.

It's acknowledged globally that we Brits are lazy dogs about learning other tongues, so it was a real leveler to be amongst the Dutch in 1974—Cruyff, Rep, Resenbrink, Krol, van Hanegem and Neesekns—'total' footballers in lots of senses.
On 'open days,' the media were invited to sit around the pool at their team hotel. It was relaxed and informal.
Both sides of the German press got there early, and we—representing the only British qualifier, the Poles, the Aussies, Italians, Spanish, Bulgars, Swedes and Slavs etc., followed on, but no obvious signs of any from the South American contingent (Brazil, Argentina, Uruguay and Chile); either they didn't rate Netherlands's chances, or were cool with press releases; the Haitians and the Zairians were thrilled to be there.

You didn't see McIlvanney scrimmaging with the pack much; his disciple, Ken Jones—of *The Mirror*—was a constant companion: *Holmes & Watson*, on the sniff.
When Cruyff had done turning the Swedes inside out, he'd shuffle across in his flip-flops to the Italians, conducting his interviews in the language of his hosts—pretty darned impressive.
'Jinky' Johnstone was hopelessly ill equipped linguistically . . . *but was he ever a wizard with a football*—the embodiment of the *keep your head down and let your feet do the talking* self-analysis.

Hugh's stuff, these last thirty years, exposes an arrant passion for football generally, and the life and times of Jock Stein in particular
(he'd be torn between loving football or boxing the more, but unequivocal on the dram).
McIlvanney's magic was at turning casual managerial "bites" into ten columns of deathless—and he was just as comfortable writing to film. Such was his compass, that he beat the entire UK branch of 'The Fourth Estate' to a *Journalist of the Year* award, and that hadn't been done before—nor since—by a sports specialist.
By not reading him, you were missing out on how to tabulate prose . . . and, very probably, an evolving, between-the-lines exclusive.

A summons was issued by the Head of Sport to discuss how best to approach McEnroe Snr., for a 'warts and all' film with his eldest—the current US Open and Wimbledon champ (1984).
McIlvanney or Wooldridge were glaringly obvious candidates to put up as writer/presenter, but I was over-ruled; the top man felt David Coleman embodied BBC Sport, so he would be joining me on location.

Christ, what a pair!

Neither we, nor it, flew . . . . something to do with the 'warts and all' clause, I fancy.

Some time before Ross & Brand took broadcast English to new heights, Greg Rusedski put pressure on 'Mac the Mouth' with his infamous outburst at Wimbledon, during a big serving clash with Andy Roddick. Daytime viewers heard every last 'F' word, but, in defence of my mate Paul Davies, who was directing at the time, you could have heard the sonofabitch over a late breakfast in Montreal.
McEnroe you could laugh at: his could have been motivational or part of the act—or simply a way of winding-up strutting super-brat Jimmy Connors—but our "British" Number 2 wasn't known for losing his marbles (nor, it transpired, for his membership of the 'innocent' nandrolone gang).

"Oh, I say" wouldn't quite have covered it, had Dan Maskell been commentating (rather than chewing celestial fat with Fred Perry . . . Dan having *gone up* the year before), so Paul asked Barry (same spelling, no relation) to say "sozz" on Greg's behalf, as it were, and the beak (affable Alan Mills . . . the ref) fined him a paltry, fifteen hundred peanuts.

If, at several strokes, Greg's profanity had taken the g.p.'s perception of p.c. Wimbledon and gentlemen's professional tennis to a new level, the inspirational Davies (Paul)—and my good friend Philip Bernie of the *Nessun Dorma* franchise—blew *Sports Personality of the Year* into another league of excellence altogether.
"Smithy" Corden's state of the sporting nation address could not have happened during the Fox-Cowgill dynasty . . . *but why stop there?*

Maybe 'the Beeb' should look into a *Foul-Mouthed-Rude-Bastard of the Year* award (everyone else seems to get one)—Howard Webb MBE doing the honours on officialdom's behalf—and perhaps a worldwide *Cheat of the Year* presented by one of the many reprieved.

Reprehensible though some recent intrusions by the *News of the World* have been, where do you imagine the lurid tales of adulterous footie stars and management scandals come from . . . . research?

Was it ever news . . . occasionally—was it muck-raking . . . every week, yet once upon a time, one-in-six willingly sucked it up on Sundays.
(a Commons majority . . . let's get on down to Rupe-baby's birthday bash).

The irresistible, dentist's coffee-table mags use better quality paper (*Andrex* quilts to bracken leaves, when caught short orienteering)—and probably pay better—but how often does it go sour for those therein who'd willingly lay bare their <u>good</u> bits for a big fat cheque?

If only the sayings of Sepp Blatter and Max Mosely were more uplifting, sport could consign rally 'driver' Henry V—on the barricades for Harry (?Rednapp?), England, and Saint George (fail) . . . and Mel Gibson—on *"hold"* for eye-white, and freedom for émigrés, in the Scottish Wars of Independence—to a box marked 'clichés, no longer fit for the purpose of hyperbolising sporting events.'
Evert v. Navratilova, any Calcutta, Solheim or Ryder Cup, Ali v Frazier, (Fischer v. Spassky) Liverpool v Man. Utd., or the Old Firm, huge affairs, none in need of literary fortification . . . . bloody tempting though it is.
'Faster, Higher, Stronger' translated thousands of ways, or the parental empathy slogan *"it's not the winning, dear, it's the taking part,"* shall have value if their integrities aren't compromised in 2012 (some chance), but Kipling's *"If"* (by any who'd 'voice-over') should never be allowed out again.
A pot pourri of the good, the mad and *FIFA* (assign at will).

Grinning Greg always seemed to come out second best to 'Tiger Tim' in UK(?) exit polls—certainly in the Mitcham and Morden constituency; a similar fate would have befallen Lennox Lewis had his and big Frank's careers co-incided, yet neither Frank nor Tim won *Sports Personality of the Year* (Lewis—as you'd know—and Bruno were born in London).

Delusional, Oxford United fan Henman's rise to single-figure ranking in world tennis was a fantastic achievement; Murray's done more (and rattled more cages) in a shorter space of time, but he'll be aware of our national propensity to assault what's wrongly perceived as 'under-achievement.'
Wonder what Fred and Dan are making of it from the hereafter (if you believe in that stuff)?

Tough for any professional sportspersons not to make dreams their master . . . because, Rudyard old love, that is what they do.

How preposterous to ridicule our top downhill snow skiers—compared to what . . . *the flights of Eddie 'The Eagle' Edwards and Hans Weisflog?*
Kon Bartelski and the Bell brothers getting it down the mountain within a couple of seconds of Pirmin Zurbriggen was way better than 'useful.'

And so should it have been for Tim—failure and the Wimbledon semis ain't the same impostors; triumph enough getting there, time after time: one of the best four on the planet isn't good . . . it's feckin' brilliant.

Tim was billeted at 'Lady' (she wishes) Jane (Coe)'s house in Hampton, on the capital's fringes . . . quite near where Henry Tudor played 'real' tennis . . . and that two-timing Boleyn woman got hers.

Henman and Jamie Delgado were of the 'chosen' David Lloyd/Slater boys
(Jim Slater had the dosh—"Lloydie" was about to get *his . . . and some*).

If Denis Law and David Beckham were considered skinny striplings, tiny Tim barely moved the needle on Mrs. Williams's bathroom scales, yet there was something about him . . . he was a cheeky bugger for starters, and I was liking his expertise with the pitching wedge.
When the landlady was out on manouevres, we'd practise chipping balls against the drawn living-room curtains, or cutting them up into a waste-paper basket. In the absence of Roddick verocity, that hallmark deftness could easily have turned him into a champion golfer, I'd be bound (he's a scratch amateur already).

Leadbetter & co.,—gurus inc.,—argue that there's a correlation between the golf swing and the driven forehand, but in all my years I've never seen a racket on the range . . . though I did see a lad, down my local, being trussed up by his Dad in something Houdini might have struggled with . . . *"it's not the taking part, son . . . it's the bloody winning."*

We were trying to put material together for that series on Scottish golf for *The Golf Channel* in the States.
Sandy Lyle had agreed to be our 'touring pro.'
He, Yolande and their kids live in a big house overlooking the Braes o' Balquidder in Perthshire—"Rob Roy" country—a remote spot, far removed from the fast lane life-style of most modern professional golfers. The kids go to the village school, and while he's not tearing across the hillsides (some of which he owns) on his quad-bike, he's banging wedges off the front lawn to a makeshift green by the loch-side (in truth, were he to 'bang' a wedge from that tee, it'd be irretrievable—Scottish lochs go down, forever).

Pride of place . . . correction . . . *stuck* in a golf bag in the corner of the front room, amongst many other tried, tested, rejected-but-kept-just-in-case, drivers, irons, and normal length putters (when the hands could be relied upon) was an ordinary looking 7 iron.

"That's the one" he said with an understated flicker of pride.

There were three of us on the crew—devotees of the ancient game, and the exploits of Alexander Walter Barr Lyle, M.B.E.,—craving a waggle, imagining that some of *Excalibur*'s magic would rub off (*nope*).

On one wall hung a blow-up of Sandy, under-lit by the bleach-white sand of the 18th fairway bunker as he clipped his 280th shot towards the 72nd green and a winning 10 foot birdie putt at the 1988 Masters Tournament; on another, a 'semi-official' study of the bold boy in kilt and Green Jacket, and on the other a giant, group shot of family Lyle.

Seve described Sandy's as the greatest God-given talent in history:
"If everyone in the world was playing their best, Sandy would win and I'd come second."

A couple of weeks later he was off on his own—back to the States and the dollar trail—leaving Yolande to the school-run and the rest of their lives, which, fortunately (for Sandy), she was particularly good at organising.

You remember your first <u>real</u> kiss—none of your old Auntie's slobber—that *'oh my God'* moment when you make full-on contact with the juicy labiums of one you fancy enough to risk rejection, or a slap, for—thus, also, you'd remember your first hole-in-one (*stay with me*).

When I began in sports television, no European—far less a Brit—had won the Masters: in 1961, Gary Player had broken the 'home' run of 24, and would win again, twice, before the advent of Seve & Co.

John Pilblad was golf department's senior on-course cameraman; a giant, poorly manicured thumb, slightly out of focus, rammed against the lens, signaled he'd made it to the optimum position from which to offer the next tee or fairway shot.
By the time I met up with Graham Goldstone (ex-BBC)—Pilbad's slighty more solid (in mass) equivalent at European Tour Productions—Seve had hosted dinner at Augusta three times, Faldo twice, Langer, Lyle and Woosnam once apiece.

Graham was a legend on the links—well, he was to us anyway, and to the pros on the European circuit; they knew they were playing well if G.G. turned up behind them. Boring though he was about his own mediocre game, Goldstone was right on top of etiquette; even Howard Clark kept a barrel back when Graham was about, partly because he was a big mother, and seldom, if ever, to blame for a mis-cue.
"Monty" was still fine-tuning kindergarten petulance into his game.

Without the intimacy of the radio camera some of the Spanish Master's greatest moments would never have been recorded: at Lytham, from the car parks . . . lensman Peter Cook (not *Wisty*)'s view of that fabulous pitch at 18 . . . frantic R&A boss Keith

MacKenzie and press officer George Sims trying to separate the hugging Ballesteros brothers so the heir apparent could sign his card and tell the world about it . . . . the *"I know your nervoose—so am I"* moment at Wentworth . . . countless on-course rule 'negotiations' with referee John Paramor, most memorably (with home support) at Valderrama (not that there was a difference) . . . the beaming matador at St Andrews . . . . and of course Crans Montana, 1989.
Seve was in big trouble (for anyone else); he'd been on the charge, but the five-straight birdie run looked to have foundered with a blocked drive at the last.
The cameraman's picture of the ball, the wall and forest ahead confirmed it—he didn't have a shot . . . going forward.
We were taken up-close as caddy Billy Foster and the great escapologist discussed their options—not so much a discussion, more an explanation of what was about to come to pass.
Billy took the flea in his ear, aside, and left Seve to it.
Well every follower knows what happened . . . he knocked a wedge through the eye of a needle, five yards short of the green and chipped in for birdie no. 6 and a third European Masters/Swiss Open title . . . . as if it had been in doubt.

We set up for a shoot on a grassy knoll behind the 8th green of Royal Golf Dar Es Salam—King Hassan II's course in Morocco.
Downwind, Alexander Cjeka—a man with more passports than Lee Oswald—took dead aim; a full 7 would have taken us out.
Goldstone checked his back-focus and prepared for ball-follow number one zillion and plenty; he was almost cavalier about it—he'd never missed . . . *why should this be different?*
Cjeka smashed the face of his 8 iron at the object-ball.

Off it soared into a deep blue, (monochrome) viewfinder-friendly sky.

Down went the panning handle, *up* went the camera, nailing the balata like a clay in Jackie Stewart's eye-line; a spot of hang-time (*zoom in, if you dare*) . . . then, all *down* together . . . two hops . . . *IN!*
An ace, an eagle . . . a 3,000 to 1 shot . . . Graham's first hole-in-one—virginity lost in Rabat.

One year, at the British par 3 Championship which pre-dates (1933) the Augustan version (here endeth all similes), an amateur golfer managed two aces in the same round; the odds against that are about 60 million to 1, apparently. Sadly, my cameras were elsewhere at both moments in time, but I did get Tony Jacklin*—the guest of honour at Nailcote Hall . . . on the 40th anniversary of his Open win in 1969—to interview the hot-shot afterwards, and pass on some bubbly . . . a paltry return for such accuracy.

Little wonder tournament sponsors get the strength of the insurance companies around them, especially when there are flash cars on offer.
The 125,000 dollar 'condo' (*how vulgar*) at Gleneagles Isao Aoki of Japan won, by holing his tee shot on the 2nd at Wentworth, during the World Matchplay Championship in 1979 (against David Graham of Australia), was a bit of kick-in-the-teeth for the eventual winner. In addition to the apartment (*that's more like it*), the Japanese superstar also got forty grand for coming second; Bill Rogers, the winner—only there because Tom Watson had turned down Mark McCormack's invitation to come out to play—won a mere $65,000.

Because there's so much golf on telly, holes-in-one aren't that rare. "Howie" C.'s seeming disgust at his effort during the Ryder Cup at Oak Hill in '95 (the least productive of six he played in) stands out if only for its conclusion, and fitting that *Tony Jacklin's—on the 16th at Sandwich in 1967—should be the first 'live' one on British television.
There were two there in 2011—by Dustin Johnson on Jacko's hole, and Tom Watson's career 15th on the 6th
It's irrelevant, but Tom was 61 at Royal St. George's—Gene Sarazen was 71 on the old course at Royal Troon . . . *and Howie Clark says to mind your own business*.

Why is an "albatross" so called in British golf?
Search me (philipsjp@aol.com).
Maybe it's something to do with "diving in" or, perhaps, the big bird's renowned footwork prior to getting his skinny leg-over.
Notwithstanding having to push the boat out on an unusually busy day at the 19th, it can't be anything other than *good* luck for the shootist.

I never had the experience, but when we were slapping it round Crieff, there were hole-in-one possibilities at the 2nd, 8th, and 14th (par 3s), and, should you cream one and get a whoor-of-a-bounce on the switchback (par 4) 12th, one there too.
If authenticated, a fashionable Golden Goose putter (by John Letters), and a very smart h-i-o tie could be winging their ways, courtesy of *The Sunday Post* (*a bit of reverse swing/psychology, there . . . a putter for a hole-in-one*—not sure Sir Alan would have approved).
No doubt with today's improved communications and the apprentice's eye for a lucrative marketing ploy, one could *order* the club (assuming the offer remains) that caused such joy (and pain in the wallet), on line.
How many 'proper' putters have you had in your careers so far?

Once upon a time, *The Post* (*Oor Wullie* and *the Broons* cartoon strips, included), out of Dundee, Scotland—jam, jute and journalism country—was in the *Guinness book* as having the highest per capita readership in the world . . . *so stick that in your pipe and smoke it, Murdoch*.

Its publishers, D.C. Thomson, were also responsible for other best-selling titles like *The Beano* and *The Dandy*, prescribed reading for all Scottish weans into *Desperate Dan, Dennis the Menace* and *Minnie the Minx*.

'*El Mecánico*' (Miguel Angel Jimenez) had negotiated his tee-shot at the 1994 Volvo Masters into the dilemma zone—slightly left-side of the 17th fairway at Valderrama. The approach is not one to fanny with: either you lay-up short of the lake, or go 'balls out' with anything down from a driver. A 'pure' 3rd with a spot of backspin, and add one for luck.
Seve would tilt at it from anywhere, but his future Ryder Cup 'vice' was circumspect.
He was in spot *numero uno*, with little or no wind, other than the head building in his caddy's shorts should he be consulted over club selection.

Our 'follow' camera was on a hoist, parked between the 11th and 17th fairways. As Jimenez prepared to let rip, the vision mixer selected the output of Goldstone's hand-held camera viz., golfer foreground/soft focus green, lake and flag in the distance.
Stunt-kite enthusiast Martyn Porter, strapped into his cage 200ft in the air, got the ball-in-flight, big as a baseball . . . *but could it clear the water . . . . and should it, would it hang on?*

Answer in two . . . . *albatross*—start the dance.

Goldstone rapidly re-postioned himself to capture the measured elation.

Bernhard Langer won the event by shooting a 62 . . . . "*and that, Richard, is why we love this game so much*" (Gray to Keyes on any *Monday Night Football* prior to the coup . . . . or "cowp" as we Celts say).

God-fearing Herr Langer would be the next European <u>not</u> to steal a green jacket from Augusta National (Seve and Gary couldn't stop themselves).

We were shooting a pro-am at the Blue Canyon Club in Phuket prior to the Johnnie Walker Classic; there was the usual banter and play-acting on the pros' tee; the 'ams' were wetting themselves (in the shitting sense), but enjoying the reflected glory while they could.

As Langer stepped forward to tee-up, Graham snuck in beside him: his start-frame would be a nifty two-shot of ball-on-tee and the German's black and white *Adidas* booties. With a press on the 'hammies,' Graham raised himself and arms to a point where the camera was two feet above his head (a counter-weighted boom-arm couldn't have done it more smoothly) . . . a pose not dissimilar to Louis Oosthuizen's after his 'double eagle' at this year's Masters: "WOW" said Butch . . . not for the first time.

Langer was never a quick player, but spotting the power-lifting cameraman's end-pose, he began a *very* deliberate pre-shot routine, safe in the knowledge that eventually our man would begin to suffer and burn.

"*Hurry up will you*" Graham shouted, much to the amusement of the gallery.

"In Ordnung" said Bernhard . . . and began his routine all over again.

Golfers on tour were "one big family," said Seve; I'm sure he'd have included our girls and boys in that too . . . *God knows, he took us to some weird and wonderful places.*

"Slim" Hewitt was a much sought-after 'stringer' cameraman, an original from *Candid Camera*—Bob Monkhouse, Jonathan Routh and cars with no engines—the seed from which so many have spawned.

The BBC had finally lost patience with Alan Mouncer and fired him.
Now a freelance producer/director, he'd been commissioned to film *The Melton Mowbray Ride*—a hybrid of the cross-country phase of a three-day event and a fox hunt, minus the mutilation.
Our film would be for general release in cinemas.

We hired a helicopter and the best camera crews available: four were down to me—the 7th, 8th, 9th and 10th unit director.
At the briefing to unveil the grand plan, Hewitt appeared to pay scant attention, sitting alone in a corner, in his trademark raincoat, with a fag on: *he'd be one of mine.*

I took him to the spot Alan and I had decreed/agreed would be best for that section of the ride; without comment, he made for the roof of a horsebox, nearby.
The racers would pass each camera twice, so we'd tried to offer crews alternatives; with Slim stuck aloft, that option had gone . . .
. . . *Oh, well.*
(Danny Boyle would have been firmer)

No sign of the raincoat . . . no giveaway smoke signal, as I went to gather the tins of film when all was settled.

I shouted up . . .

Momentarily, Hewitt appeared by the guard rail:

"OK, son, when you like."

I'd fallen (briefly) for the *'ready when you are Mr. de Mille'* routine from the days of the Hollywood blockbuster: his 'parting' of the Red Sea could only be done once, and there were thousands of extras to drill.
What we were at in Leicestershire was not related to any of the miracles.

Slim's rushes were outstanding.
The movie *had* to open with his irresistible shot of a fox (the County symbol) on a church spire, silhouetted—as if on the move—against the pulsating incandescence of 'the currant bun.'
There were de/re-focusing shots of dewy, spiders' webs, unraveling like candy floss as they billowed gently across a uniformly ploughed field . . . there was flora and fauna none of us had spotted.
The Hewitt alternatives of the race itself—*different class* . . . a second unit director's dream.
(*Am I good, or what, Cec?!*)

Quantity means quality has sometimes to defer, but the mystique of the cameraman remains; their prurient power to isolate babes in the crowd is hard to avoid, and folly to stop.

Since our vision mixer and production assistant were 'laydees,' I came over all p.c. on a tennis gig, inviting a few in-between cutaways of tasty looking men; to be honest, it wasn't the same.
Seeing how many serves the directors at the French Open would miss, as their crew got stuck into some classy broads at Roland Garos, was infinitely more entertaining than the interminable baseline rallies.

You never quite knew what you were going to get when you 'dry-hired' crews abroad—the wild bunch I'd had on the Bob Hope shoot had conditioned me.

Ark Production—owned by ex-Commonwealth Games hurdler, Mark Fulton ("*Scotland*") who I mentioned way back, running in Ed Moses's dirty air—was, until recently, the chosen supplier of all things TV on the Ladies European Golf Tour.
Mark loves his life, work and fast cars; like McIlvanney with boxing and football, Mark can't separate his mobile and i-pad.

Not for want of trying (he was educated by monks), he finally made it with the dames: three came at him at once, like buses . . . . Angela Towers—a jewel of a production manager, calm and efficient as Yolande Lyle (if several shoe and dress sizes smaller) . . . . her successor—the equally organized and charming "Harry" Holloway who, amongst other less vital duties, was in charge of the firm's *per diem* scatter-gun . . . . and Lesley from Scotland, who makes him happiest of all (Mrs. Fulton II).

Like the men's pro tour, the 'European' tag has, of expediency and sponsor's generosity, gone way beyond its nominal boundaries.
We were heading for Singapore and one of those 'new' events.
The minimum requirement for half-decent coverage was five crews.
Mark Jerome, an old pal from our days at Tour Productions, came attached, umbilically, to his soundman: Jerome & Gabrel were mainstays . . . the first two on (and between) the sheets . . . socially, *formidable (Fr.)*, bordering on rakish.
Swarthy, cloth-eared Lee would wow them in the world's karaoke bars and at cocktail hour, Jerome—on mane alone—scored heavily; 'His Blondness' could look as bad as *Iceland*'s Catona in an unguarded morning moment, but, should the evening's activity require, as rich and fulsome as Miss Nordegren . . . before the genius sleazeball got hold of her.

The post 9/11 ban on liquid products in one's hand luggage had near catastrophic impact on Mark's ability to 'coiff' consistently on a long haul.

'Big Kev' Townsend—another stalwart of E.T.P . . . . with licence to fly fixed wing—completed our home boys, so three 'locals' were needed.

Golf is huge in the Far East, and spreading . . . as the LPGA tour in the States can vouchsafe; not a week goes by without a Park or a Choi or a Kim or a Yang to test the graphics team.

Broadcast standards demanded in the UK are extremely high, and while two of our eastern colleagues were more than able—the third guy's early stuff was rubbish . . . useless.

Director Fulton sent him to cover one of the par 3s.
Rather than set up *behind* the green, he went to the point of sale, thus the outcome of the tee-shots remained a total mystery . . . nicely framed though his close-ups of the hits were.
For one reason or another (the on-course logging of scores was abysmal) the entire morning's effort had to be dumped, putting us under pressure to make our 47' minute show by the 1900hr (local) satellite slot.
But it came good in the end: unusually, the early starters fared less well than the 'lates' (*that's how we made it look, anyway*).

One of our inter-Continental sorties (on the men's tour), took us to the cradle of civilization (and apartheid).

I was at the wheel of a mini-bus, en route to the PGA Championship, a few miles outside Johannesburg. To my left, in the passenger's seat was "Hoddy" Wood (as a toddler, his baby sister had coined this curious, phonetic compromise from his given name of Algenon), and lounging in the back, the 1980 Zambian Open champion—Sky's long-standing golf commentator, raconteur and wine expert—Ewen Murray (his locker may have more facts and jokes than Tour titles, but *he* works *every* week-end . . . for plenty).

As we neared a complicated inter-section, I indicated right, which would have taken us under the overhead motorway, and merrily on our way. Must have mis-read the lights and filters, for, half-way across, four thousand pounds (lb) worth of 4x4 hit us amidships, impacting, fortuitously, at a sturdy point on our hired machine's superstructure . . . exactly between where Hoddy sat, and Ewen lay ablaze (smoking).

Some prang . . . some *bang*.

I knew 'the Hoddster' was OK (or hallucinating) when he enquired of our illustrious passenger as to the state, or fate, of his brand-new, unmanageable 3-wood which he'd placed lovingly in the back window. Ewen was quick to console . . . and mitigate: the oncoming car was going like a bullet, and he was certain the driver had been phoning.
In any event, 'the feds' were on their way.

You didn't need hidden cameras to expose racism in the Johannesburg police department—*it had just shown up* . . . in black and white.
The 'whites' first . . . in a shiny, green machine, all spotlights and gleaming hub caps, dude cops with well-honed bodies in tight, neatly pressed uniforms—four-wheel chips off the old Californian block.
No 'white' was injured in the fracas, so they were cool, declining to take notes; with a tinge of bitterness and resignation that times were a-changing in the Republic (Mandela had just been freed and was losing faith in Winnie, by the minute) they assured us that:
"*The real cops will be along any minute.*"

The blacks' car wasn't worth shining . . . hub caps long since nicked.
They compounded things somewhat by mounting the pavement, pretty clumsily (perhaps in the absence of decent brakes), but somehow you knew which car they'd be driving, ere long.
Needless to say, the middle-aged honkie who'd hit us gave them a hard time, pointing fingers and shouting his own instructions, showing intrinsic intolerance . . . . possibly for the last time.

We co-operated fully with the 'real cops' who were charm personified.

Contrite and reconciled, the dudes offered us a lift to the golf course; we were already late for rehearsal, so we accepted, but we could have done without the disingenuous mitigation for taking the piss—*too late for that . . . <u>and</u> they knew it*).

Ewen's commentator buddy on our various trips to South Africa was Dennis Hutchinson—no mean player in his time . . . . *great voice, deep knowledge, total empathy*.
Amiable "Hutch" came to Britain in the 60s, always acquitting himself well at the Open: his best finish was equal 16th at Troon in 1962, the year in which all four majors were won by one of the Big Three viz., Palmer (Masters and the Open), Nicklaus (US Open) and Player (USPGA). Despite their phenomenal, combined haul of 34 big ones, it only ever happened *once*.
Peter Alliss and Dave Thomas were equal 8th at Royal Troon.

No surprise that Arthur D'Arcy Locke—nine times the Open champion of South Africa—was Hutchie's hero. He'd regale us of stories from all corners, as 'Bobby' (winner at Troon in 1950) took on practically everyone of note, and beat the lot (except Hogan): Locke had 'slammed' Sam Snead 12 times in a series of 16 matches in South Africa . . . local knowledge playing little part.

Short games and putting they had in common . . . if not the method (Locke's was unique) definitely the result: from a 100 yards out you could call it in advance for Dennis . . . *stiff* as his favourite tipple—cane (rum) and coke.

Jill and "D.J." live in a little bungalow on the outskirts of the country's most populated and volatile city. Vast houses nearby had security fences, guard dogs and very nervous owners—Chateau Hutch in Jo'burg had an open door through which we poured, worse for the wear, on many occasions.

The damage would be done at Kensington Golf Club (alas, no more, to our friend's eternal chagrin—there's no sentiment in property development).
The old boy's bar bills made choice reading and, were an explanation needed as to how, down the years of plying to and fro, he managed to escape death by hanging, just follow his banger back from the club to School Road: it was as if the thing was on rails . . . . manual cruise control set at 30 m.p.h., nothing untoward for cops of any hue to get suspicious about.
It's painfully ironic that the Hutchinson home was burgled recently.

As any regular to Sky's golf coverage will have answered correctly by now, Dale Hayes is '*the youngest ever winner on the European tour*' and a proper giant of the game in South Africa, standing six feet and as many permissible inches before the next one.

Dennis, Ewen and I had been invited to play in an opening-day competition on a course Dale had designed, some distance out of town.

There was nothing memorable about the golf—we did OK.
Omari, however—my caddy—played a blinder: a good looking kid from Soweto, dressed in white shorts and tee-shirt, a pair of clean, worn, trainers about his plates of meat, and brimming with moral support
Having had an early glimpse of my lack of potential, he clubbed me perfectly throughout (the execution was less than exact).

The pros looked after themselves, though Ewen did get very stressed with his man, who, we suspected, was a bit of a dipso in need of some of Dennis's extra strong mints were his denials to have had a chance.

Omari was polite and well-spoken; had he still been playing for real money, Ewen said he'd have had him on his bag any day (*not necessarily a great career move for the lad*).
Some white members, fearing inflation, discouraged tipping, but Ewen and I ignored them, emptying our bags of balls and gloves . . . even the E.T.P. golf shirts off our backs; my '15th club' said everything would be 'pooled' when they got back to the township, and there was no reason to doubt him, having cleaned all four sets of clubs as part of the package.

The Dimension Data pro-am, at Sun City, was a cumbersome event for television (much as the current Dunhill Championship in Scotland is).
It was played over two courses, with the amateurs (annoyingly) still there on Sunday . . . that is unless ancient, thick-skinned reptiles at the 13th on the Lost City course hadn't already done for them (*Lacoste* branded players were treated to quicker deaths).

The television camera—even in pre-digital days—could do wonders with natural light, but our moon is no match for the yellow dwarf when it comes to key-lighting; as we rolled towards darkness (January 1997), there was nothing for it, but to listen.

Gentleman Nick Price—'Mr. Persistence'—was the eventual winner . . .
I think (*looked like him*).

Sun City was a phenomenon, developed ostensibly as a casino resort—in the middle of nowhere—by Sol Kerzner (now he *can* throw a million dollar party for you). It didn't matter to the moral, pro-apartheid government that long-legged ladies showed off their naughty-but-nice bits to out-of-town gamblers; conveniently, Sun City was in independent Bophuthatswana . . . so they could do exactly as they wanted.

It's part of new South Africa now, and thanks to the little man in all black (or all white, should the mood take him), it's as well-known for the Gary Player golf courses as for its casinos, fine hotels and horrifying zip slide.

At night, you can easily lose your shirt on the tables, yet in several subsequent visits (for the Women's World Cup of Golf), I never saw a pole-dancer; some of the LPGA/LET members—given the right blend of cocktail—could do a pretty good job of it, I'm damned sure, but they'd certainly lose their cards and privileges in the process.

The long journey from Johannesburg was hazardous, pronouncedly so in the dark; despite frequent warnings to reduce speed due to straying farm animals, it came as a mighty shock when a huge side of beef suddenly filled the arc of your headlights.

The year of our crash in the city, a people-carrier with some of our South African crew members on board came off the road home, and a talented, young cameraman was killed.

What a pisser.

They Shot Off His Legs,
So He Laid Down His Arms.

Tony Gubba's creative thinking would have me believe that the direct route from Shepherd's Bush to Kent, was to head west towards Heathrow, hang a long left at the end of the runways and keep circling till you spotted the turn off for Brands Hatch.

The most celebrated, all-expenses-paid trip of significance by man, was a Route 1 affair from Cape Kennedy, Florida, in 1969 to the Sea of Tranquility on the old Harvest Moon (actually, it was July so a couple of months before crop gathering in the UK). At the BBC rate 'Gubbs' was on (8p per mile), that's a giant nineteen thousand, one hundred and eight pounds and 56 pence, roughly (before tax).
I sent the wee man back *tae think again*.

John Lennon and Yoko had just got dressed after a week in bed, and Ronnie and Reggie were already three months into a long stretch for murder. Their turf-war with the Richardsons of south London was one of extreme violence, and whilst it didn't have a direct affect on us at W12 8QT (*read twice*), it had the perennial fascination of seriously bad boy behaviour.
Rod Steiger's *Al Capone* (he used to own greyhounds—*Al*, not Rod) and Robert Stack's *Elliot Ness*, I remember from the flea pit; names, dates and places like the St. Valentine's day massacre (1929), the Lexington in Chicago, the Untouchables and the Rock at Alcatraz rivaled anything *Grand Theft Auto* and *Bully* offer to *X Box* and *Playstation* addicts today . . . and *they* were real.

We had no such violent influences in my childhood; sure, there was corporal punishment, and certainly Indians removed cowboys scalps with blunt tomahawks, and a flaming arrow in the eye wasn't pleasant to watch, but my time (between fruitless forays into the mysterious world of women) was spent studying the past . . . . and a good deal of that meant *war*.

God knows the time our history teacher, Johnny Williamson must have spent, class upon class, handwriting his notes in white chalk on his rolling blackboard; you wanted to take a polaroid before he wiped it off, not just for cramming purposes, but altruistically, knowing the years he'd been at it before you reached his advanced class. He was a proper gypsum junkie.
Significant dates would be highlighted in a colour viz., 1933 Shaw's cats-eyes; 1314 Bannockburn; 1928 The Wembley Wizards (actually, nearer a quarter-to-five by the

time 'Alexes' Jackson and James, Hughie Gallacher, Alan Morton and the wee boys in blue had hammered the might of the English forces—Dixie Dean and all—5-1 . . . in their own backyard).

'Pluch' Williamson had retired by 1975—Connolly on Parkinson.
(Billy's a global superstar, so how come it's Sir Michael, by the way?)

He sold the piano to the lady with carved legs

One of those modern English usage tips from Buck Ryan's class—down the stairs from History, first left on the main thoroughfare, where arm-numbing, knuckle-punches were administered by school bullies to passing 'weeds.'

And here's another:

They shot off his legs, so he laid down his arms.

It's sobering when you look back at the cessation of hostilities between Scotland and England, that it's only four hundred years or so since we laid down ours (arms); a mere nanosecond in the great scheme of the planet's creation (according to wondrous, keyboard-sensation, Prof. B. Cox), and our evolution into Champions League fans.

There's a handball Champions League in Europe—not that many in the UK give a tinker's.

We in sports television had our own turf-wars (not in the Krays' league).

During the period when we shared FA Cup final rights with ITV, Wembley was the venue for annual clashes. The two sides had come together at World Cups and Olympics (e.g. Moscow 1980 with Coe and Ovett), and though no permanent damage was done, the odd skirmish kept us honest and our bosses on guard for signs of defections—*us* to *them*, oddly (for money).

At the 1974 World Cup in Germany, the two rival camps were dug-in in Frankfurt. Our billet—funded by the state—was modest compared to John Bromley (ITV Sports' head boy) and his foot soldiers' more lavish quarters, but we were best friends on tour, often taking steins of lager together.

Our aim was always to peak by the Cup Final.

'Fraternising' was frowned upon by our leader, Mr. Cowgill . . . but we pressed on regardless. Covertly, a match was arranged with ITV, and for posterity, as much as irrefutable evidence of our expected victory, we drove one of our mobile units in to record the carnage.

Time can play tricks on the mind—they may have sneaked a draw, or forgettably, a lucky win—but the post-match analysis in the bars of Frankfurt, when dubious line decisions by partial officials (one per flank) and refs (a half each, for balance) always got a bit fruity.

The upshot was a *'No more fraternising with ITV'* edict from above.

Stuff and nonsense . . . *or was it a cunning plan for Wembley in May?*

Number-crunching Catholic priests in sectarian Glasgow believed in 'getting in early' much as our schedulers did on Cup Final day.

'If ITV plan an eleven o'clock start, we'll come on at ten . . . . if it's ten for them, we'll go for nine-thirty' . . . and so on into breakfast time.
A *three o'clock kick-off*, remember!
Though our relationship with affable Ted Croker of the Football Association—nurtured by fine wines in haute cuisines across the Capital—was of an enduring quality, he wasn't about to sanction a mid-day bully-off.
We had clout in those days, but nothing to Sky's present power of 'fixing' matches . . . *in the determination of dates and kick-off times, you understand, Sir Alex.*

Our infantrymen—over the war-torn period—were remembered 'vets' like Wilson (Bob) . . . *"Heighway!—one nil"*; Davies (David) . . . soon to be called to the Erickson school of scandal at Golden Square); Parry (Alan) . . . *his* Reds were on the brink of an extraordinary run; Gration (Harry) . . . on the off-chance Don-less Leeds would make it to another final; Gubba (Tony), Sinstadt (Gerald) and Stubbs (Ray), above the need to qualify.
They dug in on one side of the goalmouth nearer the tunnel (which came as a great relief to Bob), while ITV's marquee—with free bananas and isotonic drinks—was on the other. They'd always bring more troops than us (something to do with the unions) but we were prepared and tactically savvy.

As Barca of today demonstrate—five goals at a time—size doesn't matter.
If not by nationality or ability, then certainly by height, Parry and Gubba would not have stood out amongst *The Wizards* of '28, whose tallest forward was 5'7".
Unleashed, and wired for sound, 'Al' and 'Tone' terrorised the opposition.

With the main event still an hour off, the uniformed protagonists emerged to 'smell' Empire Wembley's 'flowers.' . . . still the hint of Billy the horse . . . of Stan the man's shirt (murder getting rid of fag-niff) . . . of Harry Gregg's shorts as the "Lion" (of

Bolton) closed in . . . . and listen everyone: *"that ball was on the line, chalk flew up—you can not be serious, Hurst."*

At once, respective snipers set to work.

The fans were too far away to spot jacket-tugging, or pick up sledging.

It grew in risk in the rain; liveryed umbrellas became vital ordnance, as prizes were closed down and dragged before the inquisitors.

How very silly parallel broadcasting was.

When the rights to Wembley field (wide players should be aware that the new pitch is slightly narrower than in Matthews's day) finally became our 'exclusive'—quite properly . . . *we* were better—embellished tales of battles lost and won were consigned to folklore, and books of no significance.

"Porterfield! one-nil" . . . . Cherry and Lorimer denied by Montgomery's wonder save(s).
Whether *our* man Alec Weeks, cut to Soton's manager Stokoe, or his goal-keeper, *first*, on the final whistle in 1973, was only of interest at post-mortems for in-breds.
Actually, ITV chose the wrong option and went to Bob first: albeit, they caught him in mid-rain-dance, but Montgomery was the story . . . so, *good on you "Weeksie."*

Following his outburst in the wake of the Bilbaon affair in '82, any chance Cowgill might have had of being even quoted in the short-list of candidates for the post of manager of the BBC Commentators XI, was fanciful.
Here was an amalgam of disparate spirits and loyalties—some players, some dreamers—altogether tougher than anything big Phil (Scolari) encountered in his six months midst the Chelsea egos and toilet bags.

Ours was a flag of convenience; the natty sky-blue strip was donated by Coventry City F.C. (under Mr. Hill's auspices).
Depending on the quality of the opposition, the 'ringer' had as much right to a shirt as any from the broadcasting houses.
Sundays, at Motspur Park, '*was all about winning, David.*'

Now the team news.

In goal, the future Chief Executive Officer of the Television Corporation i.e. Sunset + Vine—Channel 4 cricket, *Gillette World of Sport* and all those nocturnal sports shows from around the globe: JEFF FOULSER.

Ex-ITV *On the Ball* / *World of Sport* producer and drinking partner of the legendary Mr. Bromley (*weren't we all?*), Jeff stands head and shoulders above most at the TV Corp, markedly over his vertically-challenged M.D., John Leach—step-Dad of Sophie Ellis Bextor, hubby to Janet (*Blue Peter*) Ellis and eternally grateful to Olly Slot (sister of Owen of *The Sunday Times*), his perspicacious production manager . . . whom he <u>could</u> look in the eye.
Neither did fame and fortune change 'Foulse'—like Fred Martin, Stewart Kennedy and Alan Rough, he is leg end.

Our No.2 was seldom guaranteed the full 90 minutes; now one of B.SkyB.'s leading football commentators, he was leagues ahead of 'Scholsey' when it came to the late challenge: ALAN PARRY.
The scything tackle he used to fell a huge, black, nubile, dancing-master-of-a-left-winger at the *Decca* sports ground, just outside London, one Sabbath morn, was later than the 33 from Fulwell to Hammersmith.

A brief exchange followed, then a dazzling right hook . . . *our little right back was no more*—not dead, but he might as well have been. An aggressive, ginger, Scouser (if that's not a triple negative) was Al; Sky even let him to do Liverpool games now, so clearly he's calmed with age and hair loss.

In at No.3, former marriage counsellor, and mentor to at least a couple of old has-beens: JOHN HOCKEY.
John's cheery demeanour belied a ruthless streak, which surfaced at intransigent contract negotiations in various Heads of Sport's offices; our right back, right half and right winger—amongst others (Lynam, notably) have reasons to be grateful.

Tall boys at the centre of our defence—a pugnacious, former Corinthian Casual . . . and a BBC 'lifer' (*well, that was the plan*).
My centre-back partner: STEVE HAYMER.
He and I embodied Glasgow's notorious enforcers, 'Hoderim' and 'Heederim' . . . "*you ho(l)der him, and I'll heeder him.*"
The great Brazilian doctor and mid-field thinker, Sócrates Brasileiro Sampaio de Souza Vieira de Oliveira—"*Sócrates*" to any with hamstring niggles—'guested' for the Casuals when they toured South America.
'H' was equally rugged . . . *and Welsh*.
There was no right of passage with him; though I could give him a few years, he'd encourage me to ". . . *go on <u>son</u>, it's yours*" . . . which it seldom ended up being.

Get a picture of Beckham—the blond Adonis—raking 40 yard balls to Cantona's feet . . . plopping one on Ronaldo's head to nod in . . . bending it past the Greeks (thereby saving England's ass, again): JOHN MOTSON couldn't do any of that . . . 4 yards at best, often with insufficient pace to prevent hospitalisation . . . that was our right half's distance. *How*-ever, he could run *for*-ever (*'not always an advantage when you're three-zip in arrears and the right side of midfield is collapsing, Lawro'*).

Fusing the whole sorry lot from centre-field, *our* Sócrates : STUART JONES. Like the tall Brazilian (Stuart wasn't tall)—and Stoke and Blackpool's 7—he liked a smoke, assiduously passing on half-time orange segment nonsense.
"Jonah" was a star amongst the public schoolboys of Shrewsbury, progressing to correspond for *The Times*; the weekly (sackable) challenges we set—to include some impossible phrase or saying in his column—taxed him more than his midfield responsibilities for 'the comms,' but seldom did he fail either.
Stuart was an unlikely member of the football writers' rat pack—not that his grasp of the Queen's, or knowledge of roasting and adultery, were lacking . . . it was more 'the look'—the long, flowing, curly, tresses, cutting a dash for our front-men *on* the pitch, but with bundles in reserve, pitch-*side*, for WAGs who'd bothered to wake & make-up: very early Beckham, but quite a lazy Salopian.

Dad Peter—a founder member—smooth as silk on BBC Radio Sport (*Welsh, isn't it?*) was our free-kick specialist—Zico's skill and Beckham's charm.
Sunday mornings in winter were for to lying-in with the rags, so his appearances were sporadic, if invigorating.

Left mid—when his dodgy 'comics' (*comic cuts = guts*) allowed—*Grandstand* editor and bookies' friend: MIKE MURPHY.
Murph's game was inaccurately modeled on Bobby Moore's; he (the amateur) could play a bit, in short bursts—both packed all manner of things into short lives.
Stomach ulcers saw to it that eating wouldn't be a priority, but neither was alcohol on the banned list . . . so it was given large. Calvados—over marathon lunches at *Langan's* in Piccadilly—was his favoured tipple (*bit poncy for a Paddy*).
Mrs. Murphy I—aka Sue Green . . . epée in hand, her pretty face hidden in a wire veil—fenced with distinction for Great Britain, so it was a brave husband who ran that particular gauntlet; staggering into the marital home in Barnes, the worse for several huge measures of apple brandy, was neither courageous nor foolhardy: Susie was/is a peach.

Who, would you imagine, could have a nickname like *The Assassin?* Answer . . . our man at 7: JIM ROSENTHAL.
Where our right back was just late with every tackle, 'Rosie' meant it; had he been playing for the opposition, he would have been a 'dirty bastard,' but he suited our purpose perfectly.
A Us man (Oxford United F.C.) through and through, Jim's playing style could be likened to an ox on undiluted testosterone.

On the other wing, *another* Salopian would you believe—Cheshire born, now living in some style at Lambourn, my running mate and great pal . . . . *Woodward* to Motson's *Bernstein*: CHRISTOPHER JOHN ROWLINSON.
Education—from Shrewsbury and Cambridge—made it all the way down to his wand of a left peg . . . *"a sweet left foot"* by any other name.
(*"sweet"* with footballers' trodden feet . . . not apposite—rhymes but doesn't go)
John's falsetto cries for more effort from the rest of us were wholly justified by example. Little 'Arthur' (I laboriously gave you the derivation a while back)'s devotion to the Railwaymen of Crewe is his only weakness.
The former assistant Head of Sport left the BBC acrimoniously—in a hail of litigation which only his solicitor wife could make head nor tail of—for that very nice number at Wimbledon, and thence to another with his pal Lord Coe . . . he of the spiraling budget and spinning mitigating interview.

Last (and least), our super centre forward, who even at this very, very late stage of his life claims still to be playing (turning out) . . . a voice that all listeners to B.SkyB.'s 'super this' and 'super that' would recognize, but whose face you might pass in the street, without so much as an *"alrite Zapper?"*: MARTIN TYLER.

Sky's premier (best) out-of-vision man-on-mic is a student of association football, and Hieroglyphics, another former *Casual* and occasional *Times* correspondent (like Haymer and Jones . . . none of whom, you'd be well advised, should be left alone with your wife or girlfriend) who believed in the Martin Chivers (Tottenham and England) method . . . probably because he looked a bit like him.
Analogies—and 'super long' qualifiers—stopped at kick-off.

"Let's hear it for The BBC commentators' XI, ladies and gentlemen." (silence)

Now, the Barbarians Rugby Football Club don't have a clubhouse—nor did the Dennis Waterman XI—the *Turk's Head* at St. Margaret's, a couple of (Bob) Hiller punts from 'Twickers' was our H.Q.
The Flying Squad needn't know, but we'd meet there *before* opening of a Sunday morning, and leave, in an orderly fashion, long *after* closing, depending on the extent of the hammering we'd taken, on and off the pitch.
W.P. Carpmael's vision for the Ba-baas was pure and simple: *the player's football should be of a good enough standard and he should behave himself on and off the field* . . . . perhaps we shouldn't search deeper for comparisons.

Our leader and dashing front-man had aspirations of emulating Peter Osgood's feats at (their) beloved Stamford Bridge.
They remain aspirations.
Dennis wasn't short of enthusiasm and could, if his close control let him down (his *what?*), get quite aggressive for a luvvy (sibling Pete was British Welterweight champ

for a time) . . . it's just that he was bloody hopeless at '*sticking it in the back of the net, Alan.*'
Where the skipper was '*World class, Gary*' was in the pre-match build-up.
I can only describe his capacity for "large Blueys" (vodka) and slimline (tonic)—the prescribed team livener—as 'Bestial' . . . nay, 'Gascoignesque.'

Ours was a charitable firm, raising wedge for any who'd invite us; the opposition were seldom thus disposed . . . kicking the shit out of a celeb* seemed central to many ambitions; *most were on some list or other.

Surviving against Liverpool F.P.s—including St. John, Callaghan, Smith, Lawrence, Lloyd, and Brian Hall—was arguably our finest hour and a half. We'd drafted a few 'ringers'—obviously—but class 'outed' . . . *they slaughtered us.* 'The Saint' was sent off for disputing a late penalty—his competitiveness, if not his knees, living on.

All sorts played: Anglo-Scot Bruce Rioch—Scotland's first ever captain to be born in England; flanker-turned-stopper, John Taylor—born and schooled in Watford, made in Wales, *lovely*; bald, smiling Terry John (*aha*) Mancini (who was Irish and a one-time Hornet); handsome Hotspur, Mike England (who was Welsh); gentleman John Hollins (gloriously *"for St.George"* . . . once).

With 50 caps for Scotland, and hundreds of showings for West Brom and Man City, Asa Hartford's heart could be said to have been in the right place, most of the time; he was able to slot into our sophisticated game plan with consummate ease.
We had a Reptonian and a Salopian for gala evenings and acceptance speeches should our captain be embarrassing . . . plus some very skilful players on the cusp of a good scouting.
I wandered the middle of defence alongside hard-man Taylor; took a bit of getting used to, he having kicked a last minute penalty from wide out right at Murrayfield to deny us a famous win in the Home Internationals in 1971 . . . . yet without the "Brush" our spine would have been brittle.

It's only recently been revealed that Seb Coe's decision to run in Moscow—in 1980—was not as his leader would have wished. Mrs. T. didn't believe any good would come of Britain's going, and 65 other countries concurred.
Three decades on, the Russians have '*England*'s' World Cup to look forward to; it'll be interesting to see who takes the moral high ground there.
Depends what's happening in Afghanistan, I guess.

When the Lions of '74—under Willie John McBride—went on tour to South Africa, "J.T." dissented and stayed home, arguing that the Lions presence would only fuel apartheid.

Edwards and Bennett and J.J. Williams were immense with ball in hand, and overall our rugby was terrific—unbeatable—but the ugly-to-criminal brawls, in between times, did little credit to the game
(*'gadzooks W.P., some of those were Ba-baas!'*)
The segregated blacks in the crowd were in the Lions' corner for sure.
"J.P.R."—a dentist by trade—did his level best to re-arrange some Springbok jaw-lines, for free, but wee "McGeech" and the rest of the backs were right to hesitate during "99" call-ups.

The Ashes in Australia, three years earlier, had deteriorated into an unsightly mess too, with Ray Illingworth deciding to clear his troops from the pitch after some Aussie fans turned typical. John Snow—arguably England's best *ever* fast bowler ("*call, FRED TRUEMAN . . . Fred Trueman . . . Fred Trueman*")—became embroiled with a pissed blob in the crowd.
Later in the game Snow would break a finger on the boundary fence while trying to head off a catch—*better that it had happened on the fat bastard's nose.*

I can't be absolutely accurate with the order of events, but our Waterman XI team secretary, C.E. "Snake Hips" Walford—a gifted Reptonian on the pitch and fierce defender of all that *The Boro* put him through, off it—claimed that the Sussex quick had nipped off with his girlfriend (breaking his heart, obviously) . . . then, blow me, if it didn't happen again when funnyman Mel Smith stole/whipped lovely Pam from under his nose?

They went and told the sexton, and the sexton tolled the bell.
Not sure either of the 'scarlets' was quite as keen as my mate, but when the dust settled so did Chris . . . . with sassy Sal and <u>her</u> two gals from a previous knock.

There was never any dissent when actor-cum-feckless-midfielder, Patrick Mower (lovely hair, and chin gouge to rival Kirk Douglas) brought *gf* Suzanne along on long away trips, by coach.

History now that 'La Danielle' moved on to make Sam Torrance (an early John Letters' signatory) a very happy chappie, but those aboard the Waterman bus remain grateful for her mercies . . . and outfits.
One of my particular favourites was a shimmering, silver, satin top with embossed thru'penny bit protrusions; the butt-enhancing, skinny jeans and high heels made the whole experience a delight . . . *little things, but they <u>never</u> leave you.*

Our W.M.D. was at right back—the yet-to-be-created, warm, sensitive, groin-scratching Superintendent Andy *Dalziel* . . . foil to Colin Buchanan's non-smoking, university educated, vegetarian D.I. *Pascoe*—back editions of which you can catch on *Dave* (or is it *Gold?*).

On the pitch, and seldom out of some character or other, Warren Clarke was very, VERY loud . . . *oh yes*.
It's seen more on the long leg/third man boundary, but such was the man's poise and awareness, that autograph hunters hadn't to wait for a break in play to get his cross in their books . . . *it's all about timing, Alf.*

Warren's man+ball+crowd+pet+children+WAG+corner flag+'lineo' sliding tackle was a thing of wonderment.

Alan Peter Pascoe whose red-faced, bum-numbing attempt at proving there was still life in his legs after winning the 400 metres hurdles at the Commonwealth Games in New Zealand in 1974 . . . when, patently, there wasn't . . . came to a birthday 'do' at *The Turks* for one of our ladies-in-waiting.

Jill Clark was a dancer on *Top of the Pops* with *Legs & Co* (the really pretty, petite blonde), and that night she was unequivocally the best hoofer/looker in the room. Her ginger-Tom boyfriend Chris (Marvin Hagler's pal)—ever-present in team Waterman's goal—went by the apposite moniker of *The Plunging Carrot:* his very best plunges were saved (*uh*) . . . reserved for pre-match phot-ops i.e. no angry-fucker forwards boring down on him.

If only I'd lasted.

'Wazza' and I were trying to follow one of Clarkie's complicated steps, on the floor of the Church hall adjoining our boozer (Chris could spot a free venue from his front room; in a sprint, Pascoe could have beaten him back there in about 49 seconds).

Happens regularly in discos—I blame my expensive, if slightly suspect, grey 'court' shoes for the ensuing broken ankle
(*quite how Bey does it in those heels is a mystery I can live with*)

Selflessly, Alan got me to Chelsea and Westminster A.&E., where I spent the rest of party time *in* as opposed to *getting*, plaster(ed).

I expected hyperbole from "The Carrot" . . . he was famous for it . . . *but nothing like this.*

Shortly after my attention-grabbing mis-fire, an unexpected guest had shown up . . . the type you'd ask, but never expect to show.
They'd jammed the night away: Mick Moody, former lead guitarist with *Whitesnake*—a veritable wizard with one or two hands on; from the less-famous *Meal Ticket* . . . Willie Finlayson, a right old Scottish rocker with a *Nickleback/Capstan* full-strength-kind-of-gravelly voice (and a more than capable inside forward, in the Bobby Lennox mould);

and the 'Waterperson' himself, who could sing a bit (*"I Could Be So Good For You"* as we know, was down to his missus Pat, and composer/singer/ song writer Gerard Kenny).

The latecomer was *Yardbird* and *Cream* old boy, GOD . . . Hosanna in Excelsis
. . . and I'd missed him.
The Slowhand played all night apparently.

While we're on the subject of star-fucking, one back for M.C.J. Nicholas; not only did Jagger text him, regularly, at work, but once, on the eve of a test (at Headingley), he flew to New York for a Springsteen gig, and was back the next day—red-eyed, yet magnificent—to open up Channel 4's transmission: *touché, sweet-cakes.*

I used to see 'Tall Hall' (Mick's ex) most days at my son's school by Richmond Park; oddly it was <u>other</u> Mums of the parish who'd doll up to be noticed.
Ibstock Place fees are about four grand a term (*I know . . . I <u>was</u> that overly ambitious parent, living way beyond my means*).

But now that I've started on the superstars . . . I'll finish.
MC Hammer was huge, and Kirk's boy, Michael, was right up there.
Both agreed to take part in our mini-series on favourite Olympic memories, in which 'Arch-Bish Bazz' had already featured.
(Hume to Hammer . . . *what a leap*)

'Hammer Pants' was in Monaco for one of his extravaganzas: his *"Turn This Mutha Out"* had been selling in millions . . . even the Monégasques had heard of him.
As we checked in to the Loews Hotel (by the bendy bit of the Grand Prix circuit), his huge troupe of dancers and backing singers were doing an impromptu show in the lobby, as their master's voice boomed from a giant 'tranny' by reception.

Piers Morgan, there for his showbiz column, and Jackie Brambles for Radio 1, had helped me pull the boy for interview.

Punctuality wasn't a strength—he was hours late, purposely . . . *it's what they did.*
Some cool dude, tho . . . tightly gelled hair, strip-of-a-tash, white shirt crisp as a poppadom, multi-coloured braces and red patent shoes (you'll have to imagine the strength of the cologne).
The 'conservative' bedroom decorations were incongruous as a backdrop . . . *but at least he was there!*

He spoke excitedly about the U.S.A. v Russia basketball match in 1972 in Munich, which ended in a rumpus and the spoilsport Yanks not showing for their silver medals;

Stanley Kirk Burrell hadn't been impressed as a 10 year old and M.C. (yes, *Master of Ceremonies*) Hammer wa'nt neither, bled.

Michael Kirk Douglas opted for Frank Shorter's marathon win in '84—an odd choice . . . *but who's the megastar?*
A profound feeling of unworthiness engulfed me as I attempted, meekly, to 'direct' the man from *The Streets of San Francisco* through a less than taxing, one camera shoot, in his L.A. office.
The nervous, courtesy-car wench, who'd driven Jackie Stewart to his hotel in central London, after recording *Superstars*, came to mind.

Mr. Douglas was as delightful as I imagined his darling Katherine to be; much as I prayed the office door would open at any moment, affording me the chance to "cut" her old man off mid-sentence, Z-J was a 'no-show.'
Just as well really . . . the gas station flowers weren't up to much.

Jeffrey Archer's soliloquy on Mary Peters winning the heptathlon in Munich, was accurate and word perfect . . . *but very long*; maybe he was hoping for a mini-series.
We had *"irrefutable, photographic evidence"* of Jeff's own athletic prowess at Oxford *"your Honour,"* which we'd use as introductory material (possibly with a clip from KANE AND ABEL . . . if he could swing it for us), but none of us on the crew was fooled into believing that his insistence we each took a (free) paperback from the bookshelf of his South Bank penthouse, on departure, was altruism.

The archive-based programme is pretty easy to make, and 'sell' to broadcasters . . . in the give it air-time, non-profit making sense; should its trunk be Olympian, settling rights is slightly more complicated.

To give you some idea of the IOC's rate-card, Comcast agreed to pay $4.38 billion for the United States media rights to four Olympics from 2014 to 2020; that means, if you want to use a clip of Usain Bolt's prodigy progeny pissing the 100 metres in 8.97 seconds—be it in Rome, Madrid, Tokyo or Istanbul . . . . or, in a moment of supreme optimism, Inverness, Scotland—then you'd better start saving.

Nova producer Peter Brown no doubt referenced his boss, Brendan Foster's desktop carousel in gathering an eclectic mix:
John Major spoke of Lilian Board . . . of her courage and Mexico '68 when she was overhauled in the finishing straight by Colette Besson of France (the P.M. had terrible trouble knowing what to do with his hands, until an aide stepped in).
As foretold, David Puttnam had ulterior motives for choosing Ann Packer as his 'fav' Olympian.
The leader of the H.M.'s Oppo, the Rt. Hon. Neil Kinnock was most hospitable in his private rooms at the Palace of Westminster as he waxed lyrical (as only *he* can) about

Daley Thompson. I resisted mentioning Cardiff City as he'd already made quite a hole in our stock.

Japanese-born-Hawaiian-Miss, Marie Helvin's was not a heavily researched contribution on the life and times of Carl Lewis—but the camera loved her (as did David Bailey, whom Puttnam 'managed' for a while, incidentally).

Unwittingly, Dr. Roger Bannister gave me an idea* when he plumped for David Hemery's high altitude/low hurdle win in Mexico (we did the decent thing and came out of Coleman's commentary at . . . *"Hemery takes gold for Great Britain"*. . . as Gerhard Hennige and John Sherwood trotted in, on 'empty').
*I had my *title (here goes).*

Amazing that in a year when Bannister broke the four minute mile (1954), the first BBC Sports Personality of the Year should be Chris Chataway; true, he'd smashed the 5,000m world record by wiping out the holder, Vladimir Kuts, in front of 45,000, under floodlights, on White City's cinder track—plus he'd done his fair share of pace-making at Iffley Road, Oxford that June . . . *but which one do you remember?*

Despite Celtic's triumph in the Scottish Cup final that year—a seminal moment for yours truly, amidst overwhelming family bias Aberdeen F.C.'s way—the four of us in the Philips household voted for the good doctor (he'd become) by flushable *Radio Times* coupons.

Of course Celtic F.C., won the team award in 1967 . . . lest kilt and wode sales rocketed again north of Hadrian's.

Cooper motor racing—back-to-back Constructors' Champions . . . with Jack Brabham their main man—were the very first winners in 1960; BRM would follow, the year Graham Hill 'arrived' at Zandvoort . . . and the World breathed again—post Cuba, i.e., circa 1962.

Sports Illustrated named Roger Bannister *their* first *Sportsman of the Year* in 1955—the UK vote was for Gordon Pirie.

Tell the sexton.

Me?
I'm phoning the bookies to get a price on Mo Farah for 2012 (*assuming he hasn't already won it*) . . . Jamaica's 4x1 team (*it's still a Commonwealth realm, is it not?*) . . . Lord Coe for a life-time achievement award (*what's next up from a Lord? . . . a Strictly Come Dancing judge?*) . . . and the odds against my other two 'initiatives' being adopted, anytime in the future.

"So, It's Goodnight From Me . . ."

Front-room faces like Michael Barrett, Frank Bough, Sue Lawley and Bob Wellings formed the hub of *Nationwide,* an early evening magazine show on BBC 1, amalgamating national and regional news and current affairs, out of creaking studios at Lime Grove in London. It wasn't high on Mrs. Thatcher's list of favourites, having been taken to task by a viewer over the infamous sinking of the *Belgrano* during the Falklands war, but when our sports section came on, on Friday nights, perhaps hubby Denis seized control (*unlikely*).
There was always the chance of catching up on son Mark's whereabouts, in the main show. Journalist Carol, his twin sister, whom I'd come across during her dalliance with one of my producer pals, was launching her own celebrity in Australia (to be revisited), so at least mother knew, roughly, what she was up to.

We were allocated the last fifteen (negotiable) minutes of the programme, which meant our running time moved, unfalteringly, *down*, as the parent company took liberties; we were constantly chopping and changing, often on air, with Jimmy Hill presenting (*O-M-G!*).

The emphasis was on Saturday's football fixtures, but we'd promote upcoming events due on our mainstream programmes: the English Greyhound Derby, for one.
Five-time classic winner *Mick the Miller* was already well mounted and stuffed in the Natural History Museum in London, but winning it back-to-back in '29-'30 meant he was always worthy of a mention, as was *Westpark Mustard*—another serial winner.

Our piece was with the owners of the most fancied dog for the following week's race . . . to be shown on *Sportsnight* (with Rider), direct from Wimbledon stadium (with *'Harry Commentator the carpenter'*).
The two Ronnies were on later, so I thought we'd finish with a Corbett/Barker closer/promo—*not original, but worth a shot.*

Jim—the *'me'*—assured us he'd "got it," which was a worry; the *'him'*—the flying canine—got his recorded part, bark-perfect . . . in close-up.

Roger Moody, the director, prompted 'The Beard' into his wrap:
". . . . *so it's goodnight from me* . . ." (slight pause, with trademark snigger from 'The Chin' . . . then cut to pre-recorded shot of open-mouthed growler, in close-up, as stated) ". . . *and it's woof-woof from him.*" . . . Jim's words, drowning out the barking altogether, thereby ruining a perfectly stupid idea.

I'd never pick on him, because 'J.H.' is annually in a European spot in the league of top blokes . . . *but here's another of his absolute belters*, this from *Match of the Day*, which he presented, prior to Lynam acquiring the taste, well into the '80s.

('Jimbo' reads out the address where entries should be sent for *Goal of the Month*—again, 'doing' the voice helps, but if you can't do his, do Forsyth's)

"Send your answers, on postcards only please, to Goal of the Month, BBC Television Centre, Wood Lane, London W12 8QT READ TWICE"—*thus the autocue operator had typed the instruction, omitting the brackets round* READ TWICE . . . . *a* "Go Fuck Yourself San Diego"/ *'Anchorman' moment.*

In my limited view, the object of the football co-commentator is to avoid the blindingly obvious, and not try to baffle we Hillmans (Hillman Hunters=punters) with jargon and gibberish about retaining 'shape' in formations that can't vary that much, given the basic principles.
Provoke debate through subjectivity . . . and at that, Jim was masterful. Sure, he'd have spouses fleeing in blue clouds of invective, as 'expert' husbands prepared ashtrays for launch . . . box-wards; but everyone listened—some 'saddos' even bothered to write in.

Jim's pal, Lynam, only 'dried' once that I can recall. He was linking from an international match somewhere in Europe, when, midst the pre-match hullabaloo, he lost his place. Had the director been smart, he'd have cut to one the 'match' cameras which the host broadcaster very kindly supplied us with . . . . *but he wasn't* (smart), so big Irish was left 'up' to make his own way out of *his* crisis; one knock-down in thousands of appearances ain't Calzaghe, but it's a pretty darn good record for a 'live' presenter.

The job doesn't come with parachutes, as Peter Alliss discovered at *The Masters*; he wanted to go on to a play-off, when everyone else was happy that further action was unnecessary . . . but we're all human.

I contrived to have all three *Sport on Friday* presenters—viz., Lynam, Ron Pickering and former England cricketer, Peter "safe hands" Walker—turn up for the same show one morning ("afternoon"—talent never rush anywhere), due to a clerical (mine). What a cataclysmic coming together of egos that was . . . Pick's particularly. Lynam could have cared less (on the surface), and Pete was forever the gent.

As *El Presidente* he would have been thrilled when the EWCB acknowledged the 'W' therein, by awarding test matches to Glamorgan CCC and Sophia Gardens, where many of Peter's seven hundred-odd, career catches were taken.

I awakened from a partial 'overnight,' on a bench in Paddington station (due, indefensibly, to a very late session). Having missed the last train home to Reading, and, subsequently, the start of a vital rehearsal for *Sports Review of the Year* . . . by a distance, editor Alan Hart's concern was touching . . . *but hey, big guy, shit happens* (I can safely say, now).

A colleague—since granted immunity and a new identity (and now having to live with a partially-leaked secret)—went missing altogether in Argentina in 1978.
Nothing unusual there; thousands vanished during the Dirty War . . .
. . . *but no political dissident he.*
The Mothers and Grandmothers of Plaza de Mayo's concerns were grave, and thirty years from justice/closure.
My man just disappeared for the day . . . with a hooker, leaving us to cover-up.
YOU <u>KNOW</u> WHO YOU ARE!

Frankie Bough presented *The Review* for nearly two decades, when Jackie Stewart and Graham Hill handled the comedy, and a *Lotus* was the car to be seen in.
Prior to, we'd often slip into the Paynes's gaff in Shepherd's Bush for a 'livener,' before assuming point duty at Television Theatre on the green. The father and son caterers were munificent hosts—sure, they had much of our location work sewn up, but Gus and Alan were great party people; you could easily forget your public duty over a glass or two of Payne's pernicious potions.

We lowly production assistants (they're called assistant producers these days) acted as usherettes (you *know* what I mean), showing the clean and polished—and sometimes unrecognisable—to their seats.

Post-match, we'd offer canapés and dry white to our guests as they battered away at our hospitality budget.
The boxers were always last to leave, as any wanton female staff member, (rare) with a notch in mind, was quick to spot.
YOU <u>KNOW</u> WHO YOU ARE.

As I stumbled on stage, reeking of tic-tacs, to wish my old mate 'Frankers' well, he appeared less than gracious; bearing in mind the complexities of the two and a half hour 'live' show he was about to embark on, getting a *'fuck off'* was probably as good as I could have expected.

On the subject of sexual preference, lesbians were never much of an issue during my early years; they must have been out there, doing that increasingly popular thing, but save for a rumour about one of the local ladies' outfitters in Crieff, dykes in my world were free-style, dry-stane (stone) boundary-markers.

Cousin Hugh Robertson was in Mexico, vacationing with his troupe, when he heard an English accent at an adjoining table. Never one to hide his light—nor spare his wife's blushes—he spun round and clocked a couple of blondes, deep in trivia and iced Piñas.

Infuriatingly invasive as Americans tend to be, particularly on their hols, he enquired if the girls were from England—a generic term for "Britain" that makes Alex Salmond go pink and Andy Murray fans see red.

Hugh was a Scot himself but, for Green Card purposes, he'd taken the oath and become a naturalised 'septic.'
The uninhibited fitter of the fitties * replied in the affirmative, narrowing it down to London (England) . . . which kept the door ajar for more mindless interrogation; by the time Mrs. Robertson got him to the privacy of their hotel suite, it had escalated to "shameless flirting, Hugh."

"*Hell y'all* . . . ma cuzz's from London-England."

Transpired that not only was the *u.f.o.t.f. from 'London, England,' but she knew John Philips (*quite well, actually*).

. . . . of all the bars and colada joints in Cancun, eh?

Depending on your stance—or preferred position—here's the *disturbing* postscript. My North American correspondent had spotted the girls kissing, intimately (tongues—confirmed). Worse (or better), as they left hand-in-hand, giggling, my 'ex' tossed her sumptuous mop and signed off with a sarcastic, hurtful, yet somehow conclusive:
"Give Johnny *our* love when you see him next."
I console myself that only another woman could measure up.

Stephen Fry's 'elves' (researchers) on *QI* are charged with getting the facts right, making for a fascinating, informative, funny show by the time the resident comedians are done with shooting themselves in the foot . . . and accumulating negative equity on their scorecards, as they might put it after a glass too many of the black stuff in Dara O Briain country.

But why (Jeffrey) let the truth get in the way of a good yarn?

Everyone knows that Idi Amin wasn't the last King of Scotland—how could he be? After William II came Denis the first and the incumbent, King Kenny the one and only . . . His Excellency President for Life, Field Marshal Alhaji Dr. Idi Amin Dada, VC, DSO, MC, CBE was just a crazy bastard who fancied the title, and slaughtered

anyone who got in his way (it's no co-incidence that John Lloyd's *QI* came on air in 2003, the year big Dada croaked it).
Imagine a phone conversation between 'His absurd Brutalness' and an 'elf' in pursuit of a few biographicals, for series 1.

There is no doubt (is there?) that Napoleon I was, at one time, exiled on Elba, and confined on the UK's St Helena (smack in the middle of the Atlantic) in his latter days.
I was more of a Dickens than Dostoevsky man—never having made it through his *Crime and Punishment*—but it did occur, as I was stealing that farthing bell in "Woolies," back in a day, how awful it would be to spend the rest of one's life in Bass Rock nick (out in the Firth of Forth). I'd heard about (Al) Capone on Alcatraz (fact), and seen Burt Lancaster and his birds in the Frankenheimer classic (*bit of bender that one, Johnboy—Alcatraz was for human 'animals' only*).
The chilling sequence when wrongly convicted *Edmond Dantes*—Alan Badel (BBC), Jim Caviezel (Hollywood)—is taken out to Château d'If by rowing boat, in the dead of night—on a cheap day single, as it were—during Bonaparte's Hundred Days, is not only a deterrent to any who may have seen it and would break the law, but a classic fusion of historical fact and poetic licence . . . a bit like Dumas's man in the iron mask—*Christ, what a way to go.*

Nelson Mandela's story is appalling . . . irrefutably.

Africa seemed like a good place to escape the slings and arrows of Television Centre, after another year of long knives and good ratings.
I'd been steered towards a Masai-style hotel on the coast, near Mombasa, by my friend John Hockey . . . sun, sand, and, at that time, no evidence of Somali pirates, incoming.

We—the lady from Cancun (before her 'conversion') and I—arrived at registration. As I turned to her for our passports, she collapsed in a heap at a hotel porter's feet. Not ideal, but I could cope.
The interminable journey by tube, plane, airport bus, taxi and tuk-tuk had taken its toll, clearly, but a swift cat-lick and brush-up later we were off to dinner . . . right as rain.

The dining area was modeled on a tribal long-room, with the emphasis on ivory (disgusting) and Masai gears of war, (non-iron) masks, spears and shields, and tubes for the launching of poison arrows . . . should your neighbours in Uganda become intolerably loud.

Each table had dedicated, low-level lighting, isolating diners in pools around an otherwise darkened room.

Sensing we wanted some privacy, our waiter showed us to the farthest corner, populated only by one other couple.

"Hallo boy!"

Mother of God . . . talk about gin joints . . . there, in safari suit and Stewart Granger neckerchief, wife by his side and a massive *Delboy Trotter* concoction in front of him, was . . . only *Match of the Day* producer Alex Weeks (from "Stokoe's Wembley"—amongst countless other Cup finals, Internationals, European Cup ties and English football league matches)

Alec bloody Weeks—*I don't be-leeeve it!* (Hockey, you bastard)

Fortunately they'd done the safari, so we'd be spared a jolly fourball in Tsavo National Park, and to be fair, we didn't see much of each other, but what were the odds on that encounter, I wonder?
Hockey denied any culpability . . . it was just one of those things.

We decided against the 'tourist' safari and went instead for the self-drive hire-car experience. Others returned boasting of lion, giraffe, rhino, brontosaurus and pteradactyl sitings . . . but in seven hours, we managed a solitary water buffalo, at about five hundred paces, in a reserve "teeming with wild-life."

In a roundabout way, the point I'm making is *Match of the Day* was a fortress and 'Dada' Weeks its warden; I never saw him strike a man in anger, but like Mr. Amin, he'd been a decent boxer in his army days, so the bark loomed, constantly, should you fuck up on your match coverage or editing.

It's more of a trial by ordeal at Sky with Mr. Melvin nowadays (I'm told), but odd that both 'wardens' should have martial arts qualifications.
(not sure Andy M. ever directed a 35 camera OB, but he sure as hell can talk it up)

"Kick his fucking head in, Johnny."

Not me: this "Johnny" was Johnny Johnson on pitch-level camera 3, with special responsibility to never miss the apposite close-up, following a raid on goal—successful or otherwise—or a card-warranting tackle.
You might imagine Oliver Stone directing thus, but this was only a fitba match. The "head" Alec wanted stoving in, belonged to an innocent ice-cream vendor, just doing his best by the fans, prior to kick-off of a friendly (*huh*) match of little consequence at Old Wembley.

Weeks seldom wavered from his format. Strange though it would seem today, he'd call the crew for rehearsal at nine in the morning, and expect the cameramen to have familiarised themselves with every participant (via specially prepared miniatures) by the 3p.m. K.O.

In the weeks before the Cup Final, he'd arrange for his 'match' camera crew to meet the finalists at some sort of social get-together, in order that their identification, on the day, would be spot-on.

Gordon McQueen was easy to pick out, in or out of a lounge suit, but the boys might struggle with Arthur Albiston in a goalmouth scramble.

The 'true' boss of *M.O.T.D.* was everybody's friend, Sam Leitch (with his secretary, Audrey Adams—one of the pioneers of Ceefax—a close second). But cross big Alec by hiring a car, or dining a manager without prior permission of his trusted assistant, Julia Anderson, and be prepared to go a few rounds with the senior director/producer.

My son Grant <u>does</u> direct 35 camera OBs (brilliantly), on a regular basis—most recently in Dublin, when Mr. Villas-Boas' Porto won the UEFA Europa League final . . . which made Mr. Abramovich very excited, not about the match which was tedious, but their manager . . . so he bought him, as his, as you do.

Probably because it was an awkward ground to cover, I frequently found myself down to direct at Loftus Road. The angle of attack for our master cameras, nearside—1(wide) and 2 (tight), mounted on scaffold poles on the TV rostrum—was extremely acute, so much so that occasionally (at corners particularly) 1 might catch a glimpse of 2, or vice versa . . . unless 3 was available.

"Yours <u>boy</u>"—he liked that, did Alec . . . none of us did.

The programme's opening titles were in need of a re-vamp. Archive shots relevant to the day, would be worked in subsequently, but I needed something to kick us off, dramatically.

We were given access to a QPR training session on their plastic pitch: the surface would be of no consequence. I wanted a close-up, through the top corner of the net, with a ball heading that way . . . only to have it plucked from the sky by a pair of hoofing great goalie gloves—*Cue the music!*

The background blue was perfect . . . we had a bunch of pristine leathers, and two excellent actors; neither was particularly handsome, but that too was incidental.

With our framing set, Stan Bowles—Rangers' dazzling inside forward . . . with the skills of Rodney Marsh (whom he succeeded in the No. 10 shirt), and the temperament of Antonio Rattin (whom he missed by 13 years in an England shirt—32 caps 3 goals)—got ready to shoot.

In goal, with the aforementioned hoofing great gloves (and mullet to match Stan's), was P.B.N.F. "Phil" Parkes (1 cap v. Portugal, 1974).

This is not a lie. Take 1: ball to corner of net—keeper saves. Done.

Nowadays, the OB match director may have a helicopter/airship camera, a spider wire-cam, four on the main gantry, two high behind each goal, two on the 18 yard lines, two high on the goal lines (lest the 5th official loses his bottle), two low behind the goals, eight chip-cams in the nets, two steadicams patrolling the touch-lines, two manager-cams, two reverse angles and the irreplaceable camera 3 on the half-way (with licence, if instructed, to kick heads in). Throw in three in the gantry studio, and a couple for interviews in the tunnel, and there you have the standard rig for a Champions League game.

I had <u>three</u> at Luton in 1985: one wide, one tight and one centre below.
I was editor of *Grandstand* at the time, but the M.O.T.D. boys (<u>only</u>, remember) were stretched on FA cup week-end, so I agreed on a comeback . . . *you never lose it, Al.*

What was it with me and plastic pitches?
I remember little of the clash, other than David Pleat as manager, and a cracking shot of one of our staff members, in mid-celebration, as the home boys tore into the lead in their astros.
Emma Josling—who, unless I'm confusing her with someone less, played a mean trumpet, between *Grandstand* shifts and dressing-up in orange—is a mad Hatters' fan . . . pretty, and a charming with it (thereby covering every sexist base).

(Non sequitur)
Seeing one of television's most recognizable outlines (can't do that *'you know who you are line,'* again), hunched over the bonnet of a parked car in Shepherd's Bush, in the wee small hours, trying to avoid injecting new life into a willing, if utterly trashed (female) colleague, is to count *his* blessings that even 'paps' sleep sometimes.

Parked on the very spot, later that same morning, was the coach we'd booked to take a load of sports folk—including the dastardly shagger—to northern France, to celebrate my predecessor's D-for-departure-day.

Mike (Murphy) had decided to strike out on his own and join the ever increasing number of sports producers and directors trying to make it big in the independent sector.
Warren Buffett might have struggled.
The Oracle of Omaha is consistently listed in *Forbes* as World No. 2 to Bill Gates (Ronaldho to little 'Leo,' or Kelly Brook to 'Chezza' . . . in the 'real' world); were

'Wazza' B. to give everyone on the planet ten bucks, he'd need a tiny overdraft facility to tide him over . . . for an hour or so.

The sun was visible but his shades weren't about 'cool'—they were hangover diffusers: Mike + mornings? . . . not pretty.

One or two other 'stars' were in the party, notably "Jules" Wilson of Harrow school and Burrough Green cricket club, Newmarket, where he foxed no one with his left-arm spin. Indeed, legend has it that he was once hit for six sixes in an over, just as Sobers had done to Malcom Nash, and Learie Constantine to Buck Ryan at my alma mater.
To add insult to injury, a bounder batter hit a maximum off the "Wiz" which landed flush on the bonnet of one's car, quite startling the life out of the memsahib, snoozing therein (not a fan, clearly).
I suspect 'Josh Gifford'—the Jack Russell—had been eaten by then.

Through his French connections Julian had arranged *le déjeuner* at a beach-side bistro, with great views of *La Manche* . . . and, possibly, a cross-channel swimmer association member *"ooh aah*-ing" over the rocks.

The coach was adequately fuelled for the journey.

Typically, ubiquitous Cliff Morgan, top man-manager in our department, had taken the trouble to see us off.

(*Enter, painted lady, in fur coat and high-heels* . . . that's all folks).

Sleep deprivation, even for the heavily protected Mr. X (above), was no longer an issue.

"*Morning boys*" she cooed "*is Murph the Smurf ready for a little boarding?*"

Mary and Joseph, it was six-terty in the feckin' mornin'!

Locals making their way to tube and bus couldn't fail to notice the commotion outside BBC Kensington House; around these parts, cameras and commotion were commonplace, with *That's Life's* Esther Rantzen 'vox-popping' anything that stopped (old Annie Mizen, without fail) on a wide range of topics—from package holidays and talking pussies, to unusually-shaped vegetables and unreliable contraceptive devices.
On one occasion, while filming, Est was grabbed by the fuzz
(I was going to add . . . *and swung by the tits* but that's just gratuitous).
According to the law she was obstructing the pavement, so they nicked her.

Karen Wilmington—Murph's confidante, and our organiser supreme—had a quiet word to tip Cliff off about the next phase, though he seemed to be getting into the spirit well enough, on his own. With a respectful nod, *en passant*, to the lady in fake fur, firey gloss and 4" stilettos, he took his leave (wouldn't do to have the Royal Liaison Officer compromised thus).
We promised to show him the video.

The dappling effect dried foam had given his fly region would need careful explanation when we got back to Sue at 0230.

'Murph' knew his place, but it didn't stop him boorishly barking out orders whenever we came to call (the bacon rolls had been prepared earlier . . . she was that kind of girl). Whether it was a macho, Victorian parental control thing, he'd insist that the 'saucepans' (saucepan lids = kids) were removed until business had been taken care of (fancied himself as a bit of gangster, but he was a pussycat, really).

Unarmed, pissed or sober, her old man was a pushover for Ms. Green compared to two-time world champ and four-time Olympic gold medallist, Elena Belova-Novikova, whom she'd stabbed, repeatedly, in Vienna one year.
Don't know that our school ever produced an Olympian (letters may follow), but sport was encouraged, not as an academic by-pass, but as a *vitae* part of the *curriculum*.

Sprinters fascinated me, bursting reservoirs of male testosterone, and those fast-twitching ladies. I once made fourth in our senior cross-country—which was <u>not</u> an invitational—but I never felt comfortable over long distances; too much pain, too little gain—short spurts were the future.

More senior elements at school had fashioned a peep-hole in the floor of the army cadet-corps hut. I was the lowest form of juvescent voyeur, so I had to wait my turn, much as a spawning salmon, bursting with milt, desperate for a crack at the rapids and the abundance of eggs awaiting fertilisation upstream, might.

"Sarge"—the school janitor (ex-army)—regularly attended to the magnificent limbs of the girls' sprint champion, Barbara Fraser; it may only have been a massage, but for a 10 year old, desperate for knowledge, it fitted—in the playground, at least—as soft porn, about which I knew little (hence the research).

Years on, at a school reunion, I spotted Barbara drifting regally through the mists of boring *"d' you remember"* stories . . . and *"God you haven't changed a bit"* lies.

Those legs . . . had they withstood the rigours of heels and motherhood?

Risking cardiac (and judicial) arrest, I contemplated and bottled asking for a flash. Even with time being the great healer it undoubtedly is, I still couldn't bring myself to own up to our pre-pubescent prying (*expect she'd known we were there all along . . . bitch!*).

Burning up the tartan, in later life, was little power-house, Sonia Lannaman—shorter of leg than caucasian Babs, but she'd got it to the line in under 11 seconds once, and, but for injury, would surely have 'medalled' in Montreal—black, fast and 'Brummie' . . . and a good laugh.

My brother's missus-to-be, Margaret Bradley, was quick at school—and she could run a bit (. . . *joke, bruv*). My second wife, Ann, regularly won the Mums' Race on the lawns of Ibstock Place and Sheen Mount Primary schools, but just as she went off me, I went off really fast women; Flo-Jo (allegedly) and Marion Jones (guilty) had undone the honest work of Wilma Rudolph, Wyomia Tyus and Evelyn Ashford—we'd known all along what the East Germans were up to.

Owens was 'the man' of course, though seeing Peter Radford finishing fastest in the 1960 100 metres final in Rome, made me and my sprinter brother mad at how poor his start had been (not as mad as he was, I guess, with the bronze).

I was standing in the bar at Crystal Palace with a well-known sprinter (*no way*) who told me—in confidence (*as if I'd use it*)—that a dab of Bolivian marching powder on the gums did wonders for his start.
Armin Hary who'd pipped Radford and David Sime to the gold in Rome could 'beat' the gun apparently, so was in no need of temptation.
Ben Johnson's start in Seoul, regardless, was astonishing.

Those Friday night meets at the Palace were a gas; the house was always full, and though Coleman was never a joy to work with, he relished big-time 'live' affairs, and that infected us all.

I was stage-managing for producer John Shrewsbury, a placid man, even in the face of relentless denunciations down lazy-mic 1.

"Shrews" and his 'right hand'—assistant Jean Pointing—endured terrible verbal poundings for their mortgages, but as their equities slowly turned positive, the desire left them, and Martin Webster and Sharon Parker inherited an unenviable, and unnecessary, legacy.

The job was tough enough. Martin contracted something horrible, some years back, which nobody—especially one of the good guys—deserved. He didn't make it.

Working with Channel 7 in Sydney during the 2000 Olympics, restored my long held belief (despite the Cowgill/Coleman axis of fear) that not everyone in sports TV needs to behave like a raving loon. I had a great time alongside the excellent, well-informed and civil Bruce McAvaney (even if I did have to grin and bear it when Seb 'baby' joined us for the middle distances).
Helping in the box for the sprints was Raelene Boyle, who'd recently been diagnosed with breast cancer (from which, I'm delighted to write, she has recovered), and by Rob "Deek" de Castella, who is to marathon running what Eddie Izzard is to *Sport Relief*—outstanding.

Boyle won stacks of medals, at two Olympics and four Commonwealth Games, and it was hard to tell who was the more delighted—Raelene for Cathy Freeman, when she joined us upstairs after winning the 400 metres gold, or Cathy for being able to share it with another great star of Australian athletics.

I'd arrived early to sort out the commentary box at the Palace, with places for David, Ron Pickering and Stuart Storey. David had to be bang-in-line for the finish of the sprints, and his monitor no more than a squint away.
After much deliberation and re-adjusting of chairs and kit, I'd cleared the first hurdle . . . everything in its place, and a place for everyone . . . . *perfect*.

Wrong!

David loved an entrance . . . volume on 'max.'

I began work on a revised plan.

Coleman was exceptional at the old track and field—or "athletics" as it was known when running was fun (circa the Foster-Pascoe-Wells-Lannaman-Cook era), probably out of frustration at never having progressed from the Manchester Mile.

What David didn't know, his devoted, long-suffering 'stats' man would provide . . . gingerly: an ill-timed presentation of some priceless, handwritten crib from Stan 'the Man' Greenberg would be crushed into a ball and hurled at an unsuspecting spectator, or back towards its beleaguered author. Stanley didn't like it, but he stuck to the task; for any National Union of Track Statisticians member, *this* was the best job in town.
NUTS!

Pre-Greenberg, Norris McWhirter—the quicker of the twins, and co-founder (with Ross) of *The Guinness Book*—was our track and field analyst; occasionally, he commentated too.

Rather like Mark McCormack on golf, Norris knew everything . . . about everybody.

In 1954, after Roger Bannister had done *that* mile at Iffley Road, corroborated word came through to the public address announcer.
The small crowd was on tenterhooks.
Having spun the pre-amble to the brink of student riot, Norris declared:

"As a result of Event Four, the one mile, the winner was R.G. Bannister of <u>Exeter</u> and <u>Merton</u> Colleges, in a time which, subject to ratification, is a track record, an <u>English native</u> record, a <u>United Kingdom</u> record, a <u>European</u> record, in a time of *three minutes* . . . (crowd go bananas) *59.4 seconds*."

D.C. was brave for one so slight; cracking the lazy microphone on big Pick's wrist—either to demand silence, or afford 'Goliath' a turn on the airwaves—was to have implicit faith in an uncorroborated biblical story.

The chances of a boost to your self-worth when Coleman was around were nil to gale force . . . and worsening.
We all had a job to do; next to golf, athletics was the mightiest of challenges for the OB producer/director—sure, the commentators had plenty on their plates . . . but *we* didn't shout at <u>them</u> . . . . <u>and</u> their cars (and homes) tended to be much flashier.

Saveable students in Scotland came away from school with a few Highers and Lowers, depending on your gene allocation, sporting commitments and the quality of the after-hours social scene; none of your 47 GCSEs tutored wunderkinds of today can flush out.
Science was biology, physics and chemistry in a 'oner' . . . algebra trigonometry and calculus came in a bumper bargain-of-the-week advanced maths combo . . . with fries, and any two sides.

And thus athletics was what it said on the tin.
You had to have eyes in the back of your head with so much simultaneous action going on. Such was the demand for places in asylums, that the module had to be broken down into . . . *running* (with a spot of high, low and water hurdling) . . . *throwing* spears, shots and balls-on-chains (and the occasional wobbly) . . . and *jumping*, broadly, in stages or off one leg, or up in the air, with or without leverage.
Each 'discipline' has its own gear, director and recording facilities, yet in the final analysis, the big cheese in the track truck carries the can.

As I mentioned, David did every potentially meaningful race, but the 100 metres was his pet. Gradually, as the years rolled by, his mouth and brain became strangers;

concise identification became more of a task, so he implemented Plan B., i.e. say less . . . narrow the margins.

BOOM!

He could make *"C-H-R-I-S-T-I-E"* last the entire 9.9 seconds, and leave Pickering, or Storey, to sort out the minor places.
L-i-n-f-o-r-d won a lot of races.

Coleman's rantings had lost their repeat value by the time we got to Split for the 1990 European Athletics Championships.

Even then, rival factions weren't speaking, as we found out when our Croatian interpreter-driver failed, utterly, to secure desperately needed breakfast, at a local café (the owner's Serbian cock in our cappuccino was NOT for contemplating).

Most of us hoped Yvonne Murray would come away from the Championships with something to show. As Paula Radcliffe endured many times in her early career (before switching to green unleaded), Yvonne would be leading her distance race to the top bend, only to see her rivals pour past on the outside. The look of resignation at that moment . . . . and then at the line, as she sunk to her knees in despair having missed out again . . . would make you greet (weep).

Not this time: with a hundred yards to go, the Musselburgh leveret, in the white headband, was away and clear.
Coleman revved up for one of his emotive, super-charged finishes.
The host broadcaster switched, briefly, to the Soviet runner, Yelena Romanova, as she clawed her way up to the leader.

I asked Martin (Hopkins—our BBC director) to take the head-on shot our unilateral camera was offering, as, gradually, it began to dawn on Yvonne . . . . *no-one was beating her this time.*
We held the shot through the line . . . and there the full impact of her achievement, for all to behold—except my boss in London; he was on the 'dog 'n' too fast not be pre-meditated, demanding why we hadn't seen the Russian's position as Murray approached the golden moment.

For once, Coleman baled me out—firstly with his commentary, suggesting that race was already won (the margin was sixty-two hundredths of a second—*so good on you, Wavey*) . . . . then with his personal greeting to our leader in the London studio gallery, on overhearing my end of the telephone conversation.

Strictly speaking, the gentleman to whom David had suggested such a well-nigh impossible, physical act, was right . . . but the moment had been irresistible—to replay it would have been antediluvian.

I enjoyed being rebuked . . . as any masochist might.

Following the Korean debacle, it took two decades, and a thunderbolt, to re-kindle my love affair with sprinting.

Alchemy is years off finding an enhancer that'll bring anybody into a photograph with Usain.

'I Must, I Must Improve My Bust'

Chad Rowan was born in paradise, and from the dawn (a hint for Japanese speakers) of his creation, his Hawaiian mom was a 'breast-is-best' subscriber (I'm guessing here).

Ere long, he'd completely outgrown his surfboard, so he began to look west for his big break.

Twenty-four years of gorging himself later, he'd made it . . . he was *Yokozuna*, in with the grandest of Sumo cheeses.

As a 97lb schoolboy weakling, I was led to believe that Angelo Siciliano was the strongest man in the world (west was best for him too—Acri in Italy to New York, New York . . . . in pursuit of happiness and the American Dream).

For young Rowan there was no choice . . . Japan, or bust.

Mickey Duff—charmer, fixer, smoothie . . . BBC spook—was Prager the boxer, in the east, and Duff the boxer in the west; Rocco Francis Marchegeano tweaked his vowels and consonants slightly, into the easier-to-announce Rocky Marciano.
It's always been Joe Calzaghe.

The other two heavyweights made dramatic changes: Angelo Siciliano grew into *Atlas* . . . *Charles Atlas*. Apparently (we believed anything), he could lift the world on his shoulders, and for years we mistakenly took him for 'gongman' on the Rank Organisation movie bumper, when actually it was 'Bombardier' Billy Wells (amongst others)—a former British Heavyweight champ from Stepney, London . . . . a man with real gold in his Lonsdale belt.

In Nippon, Chad Rowan became Akebono—literally, *dawn* (see top).

I bought a tiny version of the trunks Angie Atlas wore in his publicity shots, but try as I might—with 'dynamic tension' and everything legal—my chest remained like Twiggy's (always had the legs of a Lowryman).

"Hey, Skinny! Yer ribs are showing!"

The school bullies feasted on those early Atlas commercials; sand from the long-jump pit became the stuff of relentless taunting of the pigeon-chested. Our corner shop didn't do over-the-counter steroids, so all manner of devices were ordered by mail: chicken-wire expanders, which, on careless contraction, trapped and rooted out priceless, early chest-hair . . . sickly, milk-of-magnesia-tasting 'wate-on' potions, swallowed, surreptitiously, before breakfast and bed . . . even girly propaganda like *"I must I must improve my bust"* caught skinny buggers' attention—could it work for us?

Moobs and cellulite weren't the worries they are today, so when I saw *rikishi* in the flesh at the Royal Albert Hall, my simple mind wandered off towards their massive thongs—what on earth lay within the *mawashi* (sounds like a baby who's just shat itself—no offence chaps)?

One of my mates at school was hung like *Dumbo*, but he was jibe fodder.
There was nothing untoward about our P.E. teacher—he was married to a pretty little woman, into whom many of us bumped (accidentally-on-purpose) at the school dance—but for some reason he always insisted we change out of our swimming stuff at poolside, before showering. Instinctively, eyes down on "Dumbo"—imaginations on overdrive.

Could this be classic, inverse proportion at work—disappointing for load-bearing gals with designs on fuller-figured partners (to be rolled in flour—*aim at the damp bits*) from the glamorous world (in Japan) of Sumo.

The recalcitrant Carlos Tevez (and Ballotelli), the league's leading liability, should know that when these lads are at training camp, it's not unusual for the bigger amongst them, to give trainees who fall out of line, a good hiding; their top pros make around fifteen grand a month.

Throwing salt, prior to giant *sumotori* getting down to that stomping and staring business, has nothing to do with superstition, or "let's step outside" bravado—it's a purifying gesture, and the kelp, cuttlefish and chestnuts placed by the ring aren't inter-round, pang-killing munchies . . . . they too go to the religious root of this ancient activity.

My first job as a freelance person—aged 47—was to make a film of the film of the Sumo invasion of London in 1991, i.e. the off-*dohyo* activities which, ultimately would be amalgamated with the 'live' coverage.
Masterminding that, a former BBC colleague, Piers Croton (also hung like *Dumbo* by the way . . . I've heard), who'd joined *Cheerleader Productions* with *Grandstand* old boys, Charlie Balchin and Derek "Brains" Brandon.

Our paymasters—*Channel 4*—were always on the look-out for good, sporting "alternatives" (*oh, yeah . . . like horse racing, cricket, snooker and athletics*—and *the Olympics!!??*).
OK, they 'fannyed' around with basketball and badminton and stuff, but for my money, the best of their dead-ends was city-centre cycling.
While they were at it, they'd hurl words like "staid" and "moribund" at the BBC, and they had a point . . . not a great one, but a point.
4's big hitters, Jeremy Isaacs and Adrian Metcalffe, were like Robert the Bruce and the Prophet, sat waiting in caves for inspiration, from any<u>thing</u>, any<u>one</u> . . . . while Mr. Murdoch accentuated the positives of multi-channel broadcasting by eliminating the competition and teaming up with British Satellite Broadcasting.
The rest is an on-going phenomenon.

At the height of their powers, Sumos can put 7,000 calories away, a day without alarming the medical staff.
Many fine London hotels had to bring builders and scaffolders in to modify bedrooms and bathrooms . . . and increase larder capacity; there wasn't a shower-rose in town to adequately douse such massive bods.
At ramming speed, Akebono and countryman, Konishiki, packed seventy-three-and-a-half stone of turbo-charged menace, so porcelain trombones had to be prepared for some serious bum action.

Cheerleader had been offering Japanese-based sumo to UK viewers for years, but it was new to me, *so the smart move would be to follow the Nipponese crews around . . . they'd been there a thousand times . . . but which one to choose—they had London surrounded?!*.

Truck-loads of clay, scooped from pits near Heathrow, were dumped on the floor of the big dome; by way of a time-lapse recording, the *dohyo* was to be seen rising from the dust, in a flash, into a hardpan fighting surface, two and half feet above floor level.
The boundary rope of *tawara* laid . . . battle could commence.

One month on, that very space would echo to the marching feet of British service-folk at The Festival of Remembrance . . . Clapton's claque having made way (. . . *if only I'd worn sensible shoes, instead of those gay, grey numbers*).

We did some up-close (. . . well, not <u>that</u> close) and personal shooting with 'The (human) Dump Truck' near the Tower of London; Konishiki was never alone . . . cocked Nikons, everywhere . . . coals to Newcastle syndrome, but with the signature back-drop of Her Majesty's Royal Palace and Fortress—their hero dominating—it was *kanpeki* or (picture) "perfect" . . . as the world's top sports photographer, Walter Iooss jr.—"Mr. *Sports Illustrated*"—might say.

Caption: *'The Tower in London'?* (. . . well *you* think of something).

We were privy to the referees and judges's dressing rooms as *gyoji* and *shinpan* laid out their ornate kimonos and head-gear (*what* <u>would</u> *Harry Gibbs have made of it, Harry?*); we tangled, perfunctorily, with the laws (there are 50 or so <u>moves</u>, but few rules); we watched as the *yokata*—the ceremonial canopy, shaped like the roof of a Shinto shrine—was lovingly unpacked and hoisted above the *doyho*; and a final touch . . . the big bass drum—*yagura-daiko*—was set at ringside . . .

"Seconds out . . ." or . . . "On your marks . . ." . . . "*Haakyoi*" ("*get intae him*") . . ." Tachi-ai ("*Charge!*")

Prince Albert's giant cake-box had been transformed into a little piece of the Orient for the first-ever *basho* to be staged outside Japan in sumo's two thousand year history . . . and it was a sell-out.

That's ancient—darts, comparatively, is infant.
If you can believe anything Ann Boleyn said (or did), she's supposed to have given her Henry a 'prezzie' of a set of "arrows" back in 1530 (*Christ, I sound like Waddell: need to be right tho—history's Sid's bag*) . . . and a lot of good it did her.
The Yanks got to hear of our strange board-game via the sailors and pilgrims on *Mayflower*.

Several beheadings later—including adulterous Ann, and that of buccaneering weed importer, Sir Walter Raleigh MP—*Embassy* fags were prepared to back the game on TV in the UK (1975).
It would be another three decades before the first darts 'Open' in Japan.
On the flip-side, we now have a UK Sumo Federation: large British boys (and slightly over-dressed girls) compete in the World Championships. Furthermore, should you go grappling in the annals and origins, you'll find evidence of sumo wrestlers at Covent Garden at the turn of the 20th century. (*so now you won't have to*)

Two years after the London basho, Akebono became the first foreign-born wrestler to make it to *yokozuna*—the J. League Division 1 of Sumo.

Televised sport's balance of trade wasn't . . . balanced.
Channel 4 sucked on Grid Iron till it was dry: every play was 'analyzed' . . . every stat dredged . . . every hyperbole murdered in the name of conversion, but it was never going to be massive here, any more than soccer would be over there.
Football, soccer . . . call it what you will . . . was our thing; they could drop fridge freezers, hulks in helmets (with unnaturally deep voices), and scatter little yellow flags all over Wembley in protest, but 'Chopper' Harris and Tony Currie, at full tilt, with 'shinnies' in, "*is what it's all about, Brian.*"

Give me gnat's piss tea and a warm pie at Parkhead on Old Firm day . . . cod and jockeys' whips (chips) in the Sun (newspaper) at Chelsea v Liverpool on Champions League night . . . caviar on melba toast with 'The Invincibles' of Highbury, anytime . . . or a nice drop of claret with Sir Alex., past, present and future . . . and the Yanks can keep their monkey nuts and multi-colored candy floss.

"*Who-o-o's the wanker in the black and white stri-pes*" (see, even that doesn't scan), and 'trash talk' is against the rules for players in American Football . . . *no future there for our Wayne, then.*

My eldest boy Grant, who is the best television football director on the planet (say quite a few . . . other than *moi*), was showing promise in the midfield for Burnside Monchengladbach F.C.—a local team of scruffs from just outside Glasgow, until he snapped a leg . . . so I kept on reproducing, in the hope of a glorious and comfortable retirement in the St Andrews area.

Charlie J.P.—living proof of my ability to fertilise successfully at 54—was a top striker for Sheen Lions Under 10s, before Roehampton <u>Rangers</u> (not easy to write for a 'Tic' man) paid out telephone numbers in last season's window.
Jamie D.P.—his blood brother—has van Persie qualities yet to be scouted . . . if only he'd leave the babes (and <u>Facebook</u>) out.
Both are committed 'Gooners,' but when their big brother-from-another-mother is around, the 'goss' is about the only head-to-head in town, in which *we* trail 156 to 141 (at the time of writing) . . . and (*whisper*) his good pal "Coisty" and the travails at Ibrox.
Big 'sis' Amanda (also f-a-m) supports Scotland, Queen's Park and 'The Bhoys' in equal measures, while Gordon (Hart), her husband—father of twin babies, Drew and Jamie (the <u>much</u> Younger), and little cutie-pie Alex—is a Rangers fan; they co-exist in comparative bliss . . . for now (the bairns are still deciding), in a smart, three-bed-roomed-semi, equidistant from those sporting cathedrals . . . *so you see, it <u>is</u> possible.*

Following in parental footsteps isn't always a bad thing.
Grant did it on his own . . . via the Melvin school of martial arts at Sky, then ITV, ITV (On) Digital, the (too) fast-growing Setanta (R.I.P) and Disney's ESPN who've taken the Premier League to their hearts . . . much as the good folk of Massachusetts did with darts.
Grant and I talk about things but he's his own man, much more comfortable with authority than I ever was . . . . but then, <u>he</u> never met Jesse Owens . . . *na-na, na-naa-na!!!*
His (Grant's) "bairns"—Luca John Lee (0, with uncontrollable bowels and bladder) and Ben Alexander (5)—I fancy, will be groomed to shoot with both feet, thereby increasing their chances of national honours . . . *but they could just as easily be dancers.*

Nepotism is a label: if you're any good at what you do, class will out.
The Graf-Agassi children are obliged to give it a shot, if only to satisfy our curiosity; and where would Indianapolis be without an Unser or a Foyt or an Andrettit or a Mears?
In F1 there are Rosbergs, Villeneuves and Piquets.
Graham Hill's boy listened to what Dad said (when he was home), and though he never won over the rich and famous at Monaco quite like the old man, Damon was the best in the world for a time—he certainly made Murray gag with pride—stopping *him* for that long, took some doing.

Coming with different philosophies and styles, the Pesoas, the Smiths and the Whittakers played their own show jumping generation game.
Smokin' Joe's, Marvis, made a good fist of his inheritance; unfortunately, for the vendetta, Ali jr., is a girl . . . albeit an extremely tough one.

It was never going to work out for Jack Nicklaus junior (*how could it?*) . . . and pray, what else would Young Tom Morris have done living in that house?
Liam Botham had to be a sportsman, end of.

Superhumans apart, young Matt Lorenzo started with us in the *Grandstand* office; his Dad was BBC Sport's scrounger, much as James Garner's character in *The Great Escape*.
Pete 'the Greek' (Lorenzo) could fix anything, and was closer to Alf Ramsey than David Davies (or Ulrika) was to Sven.

Of course Mancini's beef with his moody Argentinian striker made the back pages and headlined on the (sports) web . . . but dally with a News of World columnist, Sven, and see if you don't end up on billboards from here to Sunne, Sweden.

Why it comes as such a great surprise that footballers can't keep it in their pants is difficult to fathom—they've been at it for years.

Quite by chance, I came across this passage from a website—while researching the origins of the trial by ordeal—and I'd like to share it with you:

In the presence of the temple priests, the woman would be required to drink water mixed with the dirt from the tabernacle floor after calling upon God to strike her with sickness if she were guilty of adultery. If she grew ill from drinking this contaminant, and her womb swelled or she later lost muscle tissue in her thigh, this was considered clear evidence of her guilt, and she would then be stoned to death. (No similar testing method existed for testing adulterous husbands, however.)

My, how times have changed.

On big England nights, Peter (Matt's Dad) did everyone's bidding, and—having crossed over from ITV without fuss—he'd call games on *Match of the Day* . . . occasionally:

"Hodge scores for Forest after 22 seconds—totally *against the run of play."*
The ever-smiling 'Greek' told the joke against himself.

In his absence, I had to ring the Ramsey 'estate' in Suffolk to fix an interview—my very own trial by ordeal for the new boy.

"Sir Half ain't eearr" . . . came the incongruously refined reply, I presumed from one of the staff.

"Sergeant-Major Posh," as they called him in '66, didn't suffer fools: he was a Cockney boy who'd worked out his own way of *speakin'*—*"I don't want no dinner"*—much as he'd changed the way his winger-less England team played . . . *"most certainly, we shall win the World Cup."*

I had a picture of earnest Alfred Ernest when he was ranked much higher: 'The General' (*nice eh, after all he'd do for St. George*)—pristine kit with just the right amount of white to the tops of his black stockings, jet-black hair plastered-down (with *Brylcreem*, probably)—had just hit a spot-kick:

Bryl-creem, a little dab'll do ya,
Bryl-creem, you'll look so debonair.
Bryl-creem, the gals will all pursue ya,
They'll love to run their fingers through your hair . . .

"The Black Panther"—Gyula Grosics of Hungary—went the wrong way.
The 'pen' made it 3 for England (6 against, alas), and they lost 'the return leg' in Budapest 7-1 (. . . . *oops-a-daisy*), the same year we were pipped 7-0 by Uruguay in Switzerland.

No argument, Ramsey was the best Englishman to have managed England, so maybe us Jocks should go for Pep G. or Mourinho next, and give Fergie a few more years to start delivering at Old Trafford; by then, my Charlie and Jamie (perhaps even the Hart twins, if they get a spurt on) will be ready to 'Save our Scotland' from this shocking run of non-qualification.

Where are Jock and Willie and Ally, when they're needed most?
(. . . *"deed"* that's where).

When Grant was trying to anticipate Melvin's next move at Sky, one of his running mates was Jason Ferguson—a son of "God" (no argument—<u>the</u> best football manager . . . in history).

For long enough, 'Papa' Alex didn't like 'Auntie' . . . Jason rattled plenty cages at Sky . . . I argued the toss, constantly, with my 'Beeb' boss . . . and my eldest—no debate—is amelioration personified.

We come in all shapes and temperaments, but none of us would trade places with an estate agent, or a North Sea diver.

"Don't Put Your Daughter On the Stage . . ."

Love is a powerful word, but—save for the latest opponent to come in contact with his famous left hook, fractionally before lights out—most who knew of him, felt that for Henry Cooper.

It was more for his personality than intimate knowledge of Korean amateur flyweights that we signed him as 'our man at ringside' in Seoul 1988.

At one evening session, Henry got himself in a terrible tangle with a little guy called Y Kan. Invited for his inter-round thoughts by Harry Carpenter, everybody's pal trundled off down a cul-de-sac:

"... no, eez big, alright, 'arry ... he can hurt you .... eez what you'd call a little geezer for a flyweight ... but 'e can punch, Y Kan ... yup, eez's a good fighter, oh yeah ... but eez taken some bangers ... don't fink Y Kan can win this one 'arry, nope!?!"

Whenever you passed Henry in the corridor at work, you wanted to say ...
'Hi Henry, how's it hangin'?' Sure you'd seen him fight, many times—our 'Enery was public property, a hero—yet propriety, and a liking for the conscious state, forbade. A *nod of recognition suffices, and is reciprocated, genuinely.*

The heavyweights were the crème de la crème, seemingly infallible celebrities, paraded like trophy brides by those who'd bask in their kudos; some, like Jack Johnson and Ray Robinson were oxygenated by media and public attention, but my favourite, Floyd Patterson—he of the lightning combinations, "gazelle" left hook .... and (some dared say) "glass jaw"—was happier in the crowd.

Let me pinch and embellish a story you may not have heard, unless you've done Henry after-dinner.

In the blue corner ... 'The Gentleman of Boxing,' Patterson, now a former heavyweight champion of the World (Sonny Liston, Ingemar 'Ingo the Dingo' Johansson, and Ali having sussed out his weakness) .... and, as if to be colour co-ordinated, in the red, opposite, Cooper—his neatly-bandaged, gloved *Hammer* (approved by the Board as legitimate weaponry), primed and ready to take on another proven hooker.

The read-out at the weigh-in might suggest Patterson's poundage was better suited to the light-heavies, or (with wasting) the cruisers, but light for the top division or not, he proved too good for 'Cooperman.'

Some considered Henry and introspective Floyd too 'nice' to be great fighters, but there was nothing apologetic about the looping right-hander that all but ended their night together—and with it, Cooper's lifelong ambition.

As soon as referee Wally Thom had counted *our* man out, *my* man moved in to try to help him back to his feet, genuinely.

That's the curious thing about boxing none but the brave can comprehend. They prepare with gladiatorial intensity, and intent, for an occasion that deep down they must know could result in personal injury—wishing it or dreading it—but when oblivion comes, for one or the other, one or the other is first to console.

I likened the middleweights to the 250cc bikers, for their nimbleness, and the competitiveness of their divisions (skill and courage, being 'givens'), and in Chris Eubank, Nigel Benn and Michael Watson boxing fans in Britain, in the mid-eighties, had dazzling embodiments.
Not for one with so little knowledge to extrapolate their individual qualities—you need only have been there, or seen the tapes—but in the immediate wake of happened to Watson, these guys proved they were honest brokers, *genuinely*. Had he died from his horrendous injuries, instead of getting up to fight his corner on ring safety and walk a marathon, then the finger-wagging campaigners might have had a dreadful pyrrhic victory to use against the sport's continuance (*which it shall . . . rightly*).

That period, for us media types, was as glorious, domestically, as the Ali years had been, globally, and while it's natural to compare and contrast eras, my view is (*ours* was best), that of *all* sports to benefit (Sir Alex) from TV money and exposure—boxing isn't one. Aficionados will pour scorn no doubt . . . but the sheer anticipation of Ali v Frazier or Benn v Eubank or Leonard v Duran—those *extra* special *occasions* . . . regardless of the hype—can't be matched by show-biz window dressing on pay-per-view . . . but maybe I'm dwelling, unnecessarily, in the past. It's just the way it is I guess.

In his post (Cooper) match interview, Patterson—whom World champ Ali had branded "The Rabbit" before *their* first fight in '65—hoped *this* win (1966) would help him to a re-match with "Cassius Clay" (aka "Muhammad Ali" since '64 . . . so not helping the mood much).
It took another six years for it happen. Ever courageous, and incredibly fit for a 37 year old, Patterson was stopped with a badly cut eye in what was only the third happening of the second coming.

Patterson's best was behind him . . . the "spark" he believed good fighters needed to be great, had gone.

That would be his last hurrah.

(This, perhaps, is the point at which fact and fantasy need separating).

Driving home from the Patterson fight, with his mentor and manager Jim "the Bishop" Wicks, cornermen Danny Holland and younger, identical twin George, Henry's car came together with a cyclist . . . by accident.

The all-time mis-match when a car hits you on your bike—*makes you mad as Hell*—but this had been the faintest of touches.

When the lights went red, so did the wheeler; his opportunity to remonstrate got the better of him.

Henry rolled down his driver's-side window to enquire, politely, as to the effects of the impact, and was greeted with a straight right, on the exact same spot the former Heavyweight Champion of the World had spent most of the early part of the evening featuring, with palpable success.

"If there weren't four of you, I'd f_ _ _ _ _g have you!"

Imagine the moment, seconds later—his undamaged bike retrieved—when the raging pedaler's sub-conscious caught up with his conscious in an horrific flash of recognition . . . and relief:

Holy Jesus Christ . . . . that was Henry Cooper!

It's not a great bet (even for fellow 'sawff' Londoner, Ray Winstone), but I'd wager Henry appeared on BBC Television more often than any other sportsperson in the '60s and '70s; Graham Hill and Don Revie would feature in a photograph for ***second.*** "Cloughie" was gathering himself.

Cooper remains one of a trio—Nigel Mansell and Graham's boy, being the others—who've twice been voted *Sports Personality of the Year*:

In 1967, the team-of-the-year was easy . . . as it would be, twelve months and *their* European Cup later, for Mr. Busby's boys . . . but individually, it wasn't looking great for British sport: Fred Perry's Wimbledon record remained intact, though big Roger Taylor did get to the semis; Billy Jean Moffitt beat Adrianne Jones in the ladies—she (Anne) wouldn't add the senior version to her junior title (while Miss Haydon) for a couple of years.

An Argentine—Roberto de Vicenzo—won the Open at Royal Liverpool, all by himself, and an Australian jockey—George Moore—cleaned up the Derby with *Royal*

Palace, both Guineas, on *Fleet* and *Royal Palace*, <u>and</u> the King George on *Busted*. None was going to beat Celtic, so they gave *him*—George—the overseas award.

Had Donald Campbell managed to keep the nose down on *Bluebird*, as she screamed across Coniston Water at more than three hundred miles per hour, he'd have won the little camera, hands down.

Sports producers love a bit of culture when they're shaping and preparing their features: a burst of classical music and/or a stanza from a laureate's quill + some apposite images, and standby for a BAFTA nomination.

I was for sitting Francis Chichester down in a dubbing suite with John Masefield's *"Sea Fever"*:

I must down to the seas again, to the lonely sea and the sky,
And all I ask is a tall ship and a star to steer her by,
And the wheel's kick and the wind's song and the white sail's shaking,
And a grey mist on the sea's face, and a grey dawn breaking.

(circa 1962: *"I'm going to work that into my Higher English exam paper, asked for or not"*)

Archive footage of *Gypsy Moth IV* (and the welcoming flotilla at Plymouth, as she came to the end of her 119 day trip round the blue planet) . . . a graphic of the Queen's *'well done Chichester . . . see you at the investiture'* note (plus one for P.M. Wilson's greeting), and the old dog would have amassed oodles of coupons; never mind that Henry C. had gone unbeaten all year (the Bodell fight was a cracker), and was probably the most popular sportsman in the country.

In 1970, from where I was sat . . . as an ineligible voter (staff, no fee), avid golfer (9) and bit of a "feartie" (coward) . . . was that "Jacko"—Tony, that is (12 year old Michael was *still* the cute-looking one in the family's fantastic Five)—was more deserving than Henry, having done the Open "double" at Lytham and Hazeltine, thereby ending all kinds of statistical runs.

A year later Joe Bugner, and Harry Gibbs, brought the Cooper boxing chapter to a close . . . . *and yes, Fabergé still make it*: twas a toss-up between that and *Old Spice* when the dames came on heat. So compromise: shave and pits . . . *Old Spice*, then splash handfuls all over. They'd be gagging *at* it—<u>man</u> that *Brut* was strong.

The truly fabulous, food-throwing, former street footballer "Dusty" (as in 'not too dusty in the tackle') Springfield had been making records since she was 12; now 31, having blown away all-comers in the UK, she was out and about, conquering the States. Coming the other way (direction) . . . the spiritual leader-elect of world sport's

lesbian movement, 25 year old Billy Jean Moffitt, who'd already won Wimbledon three times.
I mention these big-haired, iconic, in-vogue figures in relation to our pro-celebrity golf series which was in dire need of a lift—someone to break the repetitious nature of the 'celebrity' end of the cast . . . a dyke in spikes would get tongues wagging.
The circuit wasn't littered with great exponents of the golf game, and those that were, were straight, and male: angry Connery, *Sean* Connery . . . the smaller of the Ronnies . . . "Tarby" . . . the perennial Forsyth, and Henry—albeit, round the wrong way.
(*whether B.J. or Dusty could play is unclear . . . and inhibiting*).

Lynam was commentating at the fights for BBC Radio, with Henry on inter-rounds; by decree, Phil King—Dessie's mate/best man/valet/producer—was at his side.
As the fighters headed for their stools, "Hank" got the nod to summarise.

Throughout his 30" soliloquy, he sounded unusually strained, as though struggling with training weights, or a urine sample: something was amiss.

Henry had been resting *The Hammer*, casually, on the canvas by one of the corners (television had prime position, ringside—*radio took what they were given*), as the protagonists rallied for an eye-catching flurry on which to end the round . . . . but his normal lightning reactions had deserted him.
As the bell went, a 14 stone second, armed with smoothing-iron, spit-bucket and baby-buds, piled one size 12 down on the summariser's prized possession:

"I couldn't talk proper, Des, nope . . . the geezer was standin' on ma bleedin' 'and!"

Ring-babes with long legs—and big cribs—were Henry's cue to wind up, as those not involved were 'shooed' clear of earth's loneliest place by "your" timekeeper.

In by-gone early mornings, 'seconds' (the d'Amato and Clancy of medieval dueling) were also allowed to have-a-go, should the mood take them.
While gentlemen charges endeavoured to resolve questions of honour—by sword or pistol—the seconds got stuck in too . . . a tradition not lost on the bare-fisted Richardsons and Londons at the 'Brawl in Porthcawl' in 1960.

Being part of a fight-night audience was akin to being on the terraces in Glasgow or Liverpool: the crack was keen and direct.

We were recording an early encounter at a Barrett/Duff promotion, prior to going 'live' for the main event. Any part of a boxing ring is not a funny place to be, less so when those assembled on its periphery appear not to *give a toss about the outcome of your hard-earned night under lights*.

After two rounds of near pointless (as in scoring) activity, a frustrated fee-payer had seen enough:

"*Stop this senseless slaughter, ref!*"

In recorded scenario, you, as TV fight director, were obliged to judge a good and bad round as you went along (the aforementioned non-event was never assessed, nor considered as standby material).

Harry 'Carps'—or whomsoever awarded the main microphone . . . Jim Neely or Des perhaps . . . even 'Motty' on occasion—would do the build-up, atmos, odds, biogs, tales of the tape, etc., but should the duetists then let them down by not laying on any kind of meaningful leather in the opening three minutes, they'd have to set it all up again . . . in Round 2 and so on—a bit of a drag.
Having ploughed through hundreds of fights—from York Hall to Kinshasha, via Bethnal Green and Las Vegas, not to mention hours and hours of Olympic qualifiers—Harry, in particular, was professionalism personified; problem was, as subsequent rounds were dropped to make the fight fit, some of his 'pearls' perished.
I'm as big a sucker for a 'good line' as any journo or spin doctor, but given our (pre-digital) editing constraints, you had to be prepared for a huffy commentator.

An erstwhile, and, it has to be said, arrogant junior colleague (he's selling time-share now) once edited bits of <u>two</u> rounds together, thereby reducing his package by a couple of minutes . . . *but a four and a half minute round?!*

In the 1860s Jack Boughtanis, John Douglass and the good Marquess of Queensberry set out boundaries beyond which pugilists should not stray; bare-fists and interminable rounds (sometimes to the death) were things of the past.
Time allowed: 3 minutes, with a 60" break for a rest and a chat (*what were these . . . men or well-hard men?*).

Another almighty figure in our boxing firmament was Harry Levene *The Merchant of Menace*—not a tough one to work out, taking account of his professional and religious persuasions; you'd probably get up to offer him your seat on the bus, so frail did he look, but that was to be deceived by appearances.

Levene waged a concurrent promotions battle with Jack Solomons—*The Sultan of Sock* (do that one yourself)—the man behind the Cooper-Clay clash at Wembley in 1963 (amongst hundreds of other top bills). Appositely—bearing in mind Cuban passion for the fight game—he loved chewing on a large *Havana*.

The story goes that as a fresh-faced young fighter in the capital, Mr. S. had been forced into a corner . . . by his fiancée:

'What's it to be, Jack . . . the ring or me?'

"Kid Mears"—his fighting name—chose the wedding ring, and with his good looks pretty well intact, went on to become one of the great promoters. Death doth them part when Fay—his wife of 25 years—passed away just after the Second World War.

Solomons promoted the first-ever bill in Israel: between 1910 and 1940, there were 26 Jewish world champions, "already" . . . many of them living in New York.

Were you to lay *Sock* and *Menace* end-to-end—the way some vanquished contenders might like to have seen them—Solomons and Levene would account for the lion's share of what was good about British, and World boxing, for almost half a century.

I won't pretend to remember the actual fight—I was still pooping in post-war, re-usable *Pampers* equivalents, with the life-threatening safety-pin—but when Jack brought Gus Lesnevich to London (in 1948) to defend his world light-heavyweight title against England's Freddie Mills, the trade route to the booming booths of Britain was thrown wide open. American scrappers came east, in droves.
Transatlantic television and mega-rights deals were a decade away, but the lure of London's night-life would certainly have helped convince the great Sugar Ray Robinson to book a passage.
His fight with Randy Turpin, I do remember; it was at London's Earl's Court in 1951, the year Marciano came to the throne, via fading 37 year old Joe Louis.
What names . . . and Solomons's was right in the middle of them.
Such was the publicity that even a little squirt of seven, battling with joined-up writing in Primary 2, got in on the role play.

It wasn't a tough one to sell: Robinson, the dazzling World champion—and odds-on favourite—was the Ali of his day . . . a handsome, dandy of a boxer . . . and Randy was the very best of middleweight Britain.
(imagine the field-day promoters and headline-writers would have had, had Turpin's trainer/brother, Dick, been more of a contender.)

Talk about value: the fight went the distance—Turpin won.
I couldn't wait for the pictures in my brother's *World Sports*.

Alas, the effects of *The Leamington Larruper's* post-match celebrations had barely worn off by the time the Rolls Royce of challengers was ready to take back what he knew was rightfully his . . . 64 days and 10 rounds later, in New York, New York.
But Turpin had been Champ of the World, and he'd beaten the 2nd best fighter there's ever been to do it (make that "3rd" . . . . *I'm a Frazier fan*).

Pound for pound, "Sugars" Robinson and Leonard were about even in skill, 'marketablilty' and pulling-power (dames); the late 70s/early 80s version was cannier with his winnings . . . by a stretch.

Freddie Mills didn't fare too badly, winning, if not the richest prize in sport, a world title (at light-heavy), nonetheless.

Seventeen colourful years later, Mills—buddies with the Kray league of criminals—died mysteriously, providing us garrulous twenty-somethings with our first conspiracy theory.
A slightly bigger one was just around the corner . . . by the book depository in Dealey Plaza, Dallas, Texas . . . . gun(s) involved again.

Randolph Turpin shot himself in the end.

I'd been aware of Jack Solomons—an Hitchcockian figure—flitting in and out of our offices, long after his deal-making days were over, and there was something of a "Puzo" feel to the corridors when Mr. Levene and his party dropped by for tea and contracts: if either needed 'a favour' doing, we became amazingly compliant—*fear? . . . ratings? . . . intimidation? . . . family* (ours)? . . . take your pick.

Roger Levett, an East End spit of David Suchet's *Poirot*, viz., slicked-down hair, pencil 'tache and grey spats . . . plus some of *Hercule*'s cunning, descended on my editor's office with an offer I couldn't (shouldn't) refuse—a long term deal for Lennox Lewis, emerging as a global force.
Frank Maloney, and a pair with non-speaking parts, came along too, lest there was any hesitation.

There was a superfluity of 'head-bash' on the BBC—*you pay for the big ones, you swallow the dross*
Albert and York Hall bills on Tuesdays brought us the big prizes at Wembley on Wednesdays, or at week-ends.

We had obligations to other promoters—Mike Barrett and Mickey Duff, mainly—so like the Lewis proposal (as I most surely did) or not, I was over-ruled on cost . . . and no small measure of politics, I fancy.
The future (British) Heavyweight Champion of the World took his plans elsewhere; the public knew of him from the Commonwealth Games in '86, and the Seoul Olympics . . . *but what an opportunity missed.*

Frank Warren—another of our fistic associates—didn't just represent the game's honour, he embodied its sinister side.

Cheery bloke Frank—a survivor—but you can never be absolutely sure when someone pulls a gun on you on your way to work (in *England*?)!

I'd been shown the entry and exit wounds from a bullet a friend of my cousin's had taken for buggering about with someone else's wife in Houston, Texas . . . but this was Barking (the town)—a little too close for comfort. One of Frank's fighters, more used to aiming hoses and dousing fires, became prime suspect, but Terry Marsh was cleared, completely; the cartoons endure.

Back to Wembley Pool.

Not many (other than family) will remember Walter Ris from the USA. "Walt" won the 100 metres freestyle at the 1948 London Olympics, under the very boards many of you will have 'danced' upon—to *The Beatles* or *Britney*—and where World Middleweight Champion Alan Minter and Marvin Hagler (his successor) did brief and bloody battle in 1979.

I was pretending to assist the resident stage manager, whose job it was to ensure Harry C. had everything he needed . . . producer in his ear . . . . right pictures on his monitors . . . last minute tit-bits from the dressing rooms . . . a dirty mag or two—the bare necessities.
This was a highly emotive, volatile boxing crowd, so casting me as Harry's 'minder'—should it all kick-off over a marginal decision—was preposterous.

Suddenly, a dead hand dropped on the wee man's shoulder.
The assailant must have stood on the headphones' lead, because Harry's head jerked back, violently, as if he'd been garroted.

(. . . right J.P., the dreaded moment is upon you)

More adverse headlines:

LEGENDARY BOXING COMMENTATOR KILLED AT FIGHTS
Carpenter lynched at ringside as chicken-shit colleague looks on.

. . . *not on my watch he wouldn't*; I clenched the right hand that had done for our school Rector's son, and prepared to swing . . .

FREEZE!!

Stopping simultaneously at the point where the supposed assassin became recognisable as *The Menace*, I'd briefly visited that Cooperman-with-the-bloke-on-the-bike moment.

Mr. Levene had just wanted "a word" with Harry about the size of the crowd, and knew little (and cared less) about TV's prissy rules of engagement.

Whether or not the Levene green-room at the Empire Pool was the same one Walt Ris and the 100 metre Olympic finalists used for changing into their hairy trunks, it was *the* place to be for post-fight analysis.
Here was an informal session of boxing's Cabinet, the inner sanctum—"the Rt. Hon. Member for Wembley, presiding"; managers, agents and the night's showered and patched-up winners would drop in to pay their respects and amass good-manners points from the promoter . . . "*a moment of your time, Mr. Levene*"—no bad thing to strike while the iron was hot.

We put microphones on 'tame' trainers during the A.B.A.s—same venue, different dress code: no money changed hands, visibly. We'd hoped to enhance the theatre and drama of amateur boxing's gala bash by eaves-dropping the inter-round huddles.
<u>Not</u> one of our smarter moves.

In 1970, I asked Doug Sanders if I could "mic him up" during the Open (*what a scoop, eh?*), but even before approaching the R&A for their tacit refusal, Doug put the mockers on it; this was *his* workplace, and what went on between his caddy and him was 'for their ears only' (*they hadn't worked out a code word for 'miniature'*).

So frustrated did Ali become with his cornerman/foil, Bodini Brown's constant urgings, that he let him have a backhand clip as a reminder of *who* was having to parry the bombs, and *who* was watching from a safe place . . . . *the butterfly's creator had been stung by the bee.*

We were looking (and listening) for something more constructive and informative from the amateurs, and it began well enough. The volunteers didn't appear inhibited by their 'wires,' but, as it tends to, with a career-changing title in sight, and just three of the nine minutes remaining to *stick* it, push rapidly turned to shove: off, metaphorically, came the gloves and profanity ruled (with heartfelt, official, BBC apology to follow).

As a mini-sequitur of sorts, Chef Ramsay got his third Michelin star in 2001, the year Mary Whitehouse passed away.
He's never looked back.

Now, fancy this for a joust.

Mr. Churchill—the former PM—is confronted in the Commons by battling Bessie Braddock ("*Labour*") from Liverpool:
"Mr. Churchill you are drunk."
Nice shot, Bess . . . but cover-up.
"And you Madam, are ugly; I shall be sober tomorrow."
Ouch!
Henry Cooper's alleged conversation with another famous abolitionist—Baroness Edith Summerskill—about the brutalities of *his* sport, went along these lines:

"Mr. Cooper, have you looked in the mirror lately and seen the state of your nose?"
Relaxing *The Hammer*, Henry counters:
"Madam, have you looked in the mirror and seen the state of <u>your</u> nose . . . boxing's my excuse!?"
Mr. Churchill—not known for misogyny—came up against another female opponent . . . the Member for Plymouth Sutton ("Astor . . . *Unionist*")—prettier, by far, it's said, than the Member for Liverpool Exchange:
"*If you were my husband*" Nancy said, staring down Churchill, "I'd put poison in your coffee."
Hardly what one would expect from "a laydee," finished off at school in the Big Apple.
"And if I were your husband,' replied the great man, "I'd drink it."

2-and-oh to *The Motivator*

'Beauty, like supreme dominion is but supported by opinion.'
'Speak not but what may benefit others or yourself; avoid trifling conversation.'

In words other than Benjamin Franklin's, lay off the booze, and keep your gob shut.

One of the more delicate, sensitive, thought-out, boxing quotes came from Mike Tyson on the eve of his clash with Lennox Lewis—(to be on the safe side, this is <u>attributed</u> to Mr. Tyson):

"I want to rip out his heart and feed it to him. I want to kill people. I want to rip their stomachs out and eat their children," cooed Mike.

Hannibal Lecter had <u>some</u> sense of propriety:
'A census taker once tried to test me. I ate his liver with some fava beans and a nice chianti.'

Having Dr. Edith and her righteous band banging on, incessantly, was too much to bear, even for the ambivalent; there's cock-fighting, bull-fighting, dog-fighting, binge-drinking fightin' gals, punch-ups in schools, scraps in the home, handbags at football, hitmen at rugby, realistic digital weapons of mass destruction in the hands of the barely responsible . . . . *so what's the problem with a bit of controlled brutality in the boxing ring . . . it's a great night out?!*

The Prager family (the old man was a Polish rabbi) had skedaddled out of the Republic when Hitler started to get 'arsey' in the late 30s. Following a trip to the deed pollster's, little "Monek P." became Mickey Duff, and, subsequently, a handy boxer. However, the lure of continuous bright lights, the dry ice and fanfares, occasional appearances on the box—by chance or design—plus weekly hair and beauty sessions (deductable treats), turned his handsome features (in a Terry Downes sort-of-way) towards management and promotion.

Mickey was Max Clifford in tux and (fake) tan; he knew every mother-fucker and, vitally, he was on *our* side. Some folk (*not me*) swore he was permanently made-up, on the off-chance of a word 'in-vision' on this and that—a match to be made/a title to fix ('arrange')/a chance to buy into an "un-missable war" he had a piece of, Stateside (where he also held considerable sway).

Those kind of aspersions could earn you a visit from the boys; as well as Terry D., he looked after Jim Watt, Lloyd Honeyghan, Alan Minter, big Frank and Maurice Hope, and, more recently, the mighty Joe Calzaghe, and whilst <u>they</u> didn't do home visits, he knew someone who did . . . . *be absolutely certain.*

And then there was Mrs. Lawless—the redoubtable Sylvia—whose husband looked after her extended family of boys at work. In boxing corners, Terry was almost as famous as Mr. Dundee—certainly over this side—and though not as prolific, high-profile and controversial as the American, "Tel" had his share of world champions to hone and cajole; the rest was down to Sylvia.

Were heads to drop, Mother Lawless was always on hand, an ever-present ringside, permed and immaculately turned out, ready to trade verbal blows with any who'd dare doubt or denounce her lads.
She'd a soft spot for wee Charlie Magri—but then we did too, having been party to most of his tales from the Montreal Olympics in 1976, to 1983, when the wee man from Stepney (out of Tunisia and Malta) took the WBC Flyweight Championship of the World from Eleoncio Mercedes of the Dominican Republic.
Like Turpin's, Charlie's reign on top was short.
His net profit and loss were recorded within months of each other at the Empire Pool, Wembley.

Under lights, Frank Bruno could be relied upon to perform, but get him on a bad day in training with a question about the dubious quality of the opponents he was flattening regularly en route to Tyson—and, as a consequence, the value devoted punters were getting for their money—and have a clear escape route mapped out.

Des interviewed the big fella, on a park bench, one nippy Spring morning, at Highgate Ponds in North London—a favourite haunt for fighters 'on the run.'
The lack of response to the question, and stare of raw foreboding, were early indicators that we were heading down the wrong road; continuing to film the silence was to waste valuable stock, everyone's time . . . and endanger lives. Fearless interrogation by Lynam, on the surface, but down below wind was building. He warned me—during a (fleetingly) tense passage in our working relationship—of his fighting ambitions as a youth, on the trot round the bogs of Ennis (*in his dreams*), but *this* menace was a potential Heavyweight Champion of the World (*in his dreams*), so best not to bullshit anyone.

Even with the recordist, cameraman and sparks on board, our combined flab at Highgate would hit around the 378lb mark; a hideous mess for the parks superintendent to clear up.
As makeshift referee, I took *'a long hard look at the Irish challenger,'* cautioned him about low blows (and Bruno's head-to-heads) and suggested a question about . . . *his kids, perhaps?*

Our tiff wasn't so much a scuffle, as an aberration, a moment when friendship got in the way of perceived status.
The great communicator and I had just arrived in Northern Italy for the European football championships.
It was bucketing . . . we were lost, but jovial enough.

Nothing untoward . . . thus far.

As accreditation was required to go about our television business, the first task would be to find the offices of the organising committee.
We huddled in a doorway, planning the next move . . . when suddenly, without warning, Des snapped:

"*Taxi, John . . . NOW!*"

Woops—we might end up testing our fistic credentials here, ma man.

Over a bottle of *Barolo* (receipt)—mug-shots having been taken and passes issued—he explained that he'd been over-wrought, a late night, a spot of acid indigestion, a hammering for the Seagulls, a shitty 'fan' letter.
I went more for the *not wanting to get the grey mullet wet* sob story . . . but a rare moment in our soft times.

If Mickey Duff looked like an ex-pro, his partner Mike Barrett could have been the family doctor; he was gracious, well-kempt, unflappable—for the most part, and, according to wife Rosemary—the peachy Scottish diva—he had an excellent bedside manner.

They (and Jarvis Astaire) monopolised the fight game in my time.
'Franks' Warren and Maloney were gloved up and waiting to inherit B.SkyB.'s money, and in Ireland, Barney Eastwood ruled—*which was cool by me* . . . . Barney knew a lot of people.

Our producer 'in the North,' Joy Williams, was well-in at fortress Eastwood during the Barry McGuigan epoch. She was a handsome looking woman, jet black hair and brown eyes. On the phone, you might have been talking to *ein* East German heptathlete, such was the depth of her voice.
Mistakes were made but offence never taken—one great dame.

I think we were 'in the South,' Des and I . . . there was a harbour with fishing boats and stuff, and it was a beautiful day, I recall.
My lines could be crossed here (*it has happened*), but I think it had something to do with Barney, or Brendan (from the very large family) Ingle—the former boxer-turned coach-turned manager—anyway, we bumped into 'unbeatable' Herol Graham as he was doing his roadwork (must have been Brendan, then).
I'd heard about his man's 'cabaret turn' where he'd invite members of the audience to try to hit him as he danced about with his hands tied behind his back in that most arrogant and challenging of positions (not that he was in any way a knob-head).
Couldn't get near the mother . . . nor did many professionals, though Julian "The Hawk" Jackson did catch him, clean, in a careless moment—thereby denying "Bomber" a world title he appeared to have in his grasp.
Like Michael Watson, a top bloke.

On mainland Britain, if it wasn't a Barrett/Duff promotion, with Lawless boys top of the bill, it wasn't worth the money—*and sometimes it wasn't*—but as Martin Pipe was to prove with his horses, having a stable full of consistent winners made you irresistible to television.

Put Jim Watt in the Kelvin Hall in Glasgow for a World title fight, and you'd better have a strong constitution . . . . with any kind of ticket.
The frenzied atmosphere at ringside got the better of my cousin George, there reporting the fight for the *Scottish Daily Mail*.
Blood, sweat and tissue flew round the ring, while the fight doctors attended to George, who was having an epileptic fit.
He recovered quickly and was able to drink Jim's health at the bash afterwards; tragically, he never knew when to stop.

Everybody liked John Conteh—my seriously fit (attractive) assistant, Patsy Richards adored him.
It was frustrating that John didn't sustain his promise after landing the top prize in 1974; there'd even been talk of a match with 'brother' Ali, but it came to nothing (retrospectively, maybe a good thing for the boy Conteh).

We were paired in a charity golf match in Hertfordshire; the green we'd just cleared, wasn't visible from where you played your approach shot, so I took my wedge out, to warn those behind:

"Don't ring that!" John implored.
Too late . . . his bag crashed to the ground . . . up went the guard as he wheeled away backwards, circling the green, jabbing and hooking:

"Sorry, it's the bells, mate . . . I did warn you."

'My' Patsy was far, far too young when she died.

There was no sports staff as such in the BBCs studios in Edinburgh, so I was sent (from London, if you will) to set up a two-way interview between Ken Buchanan (in the Queen's Street studio) and Frank Bough (at Lime Grove).
Ken had recently returned from New York where he and Roberto Duran had knocked the living shit out of each other at Madison Square Garden.
So conscious were they about giving value for money (not), they kept it going for a full eight seconds after the bell to end the 13th, during which time the Champion suffered some kind of injury: some said it was a low left hook, others that Duran had kneed him in the groin, in any event it was stopped in the Panamanian's favour.

The only way to avoid controversy at MSG is by knock-out.

A chauffeur-driven limo pulled up outside Broadcasting House and in the absence of any movement, therein, I stepped forward to open the rear door.
Very gingerly, out stepped the former Champion of the World, sporting sun glasses on a cold afternoon in February.
He shook my hand, gently.

As I went to usher him up the steps, he cautioned:

"Don't touch me . . . please."

That, more than any graphic slow-motion image, illustrated what these guys put themselves through in pursuit of notoriety.

The rules of kick-boxing, cage-fighting, ultimate and extreme madness may be harder to detect, but those who abide by the code, proposed by the 9th Marquess, deserve respect—bad-assed hoodies, don't.

Mrs. Worthington was fortunate she had a daughter:

'The profession is overcrowded
The struggle's pretty tough'

. . . Noel Coward advised

'Dont' put your daughter on the stage Mrs. Worthington
Don't put your daughter on the stage.'

"THE BIG GIRL'S BLOUSE."

I read somewhere that Ken Buchanan (66) is still keen on a re-match with Roberto Durán . . . *never mind the sexton, get a shrink round, smartish.*

Notwithstanding the millions of dollars he'd amassed, the loss of the 'vital spark' Floyd Patterson was convinced separated champions from good fighters, was down as much to his finding inner peace with his new wife, as the daily trudge to the gym at 37; on top of that, Ali was getting his second wind.

Meanwhile, on the Clyde . . . . the good ship *Vital Spark* had been given another chance too.
The exploits of *Para Handy* and his crew, aboard the little puffer-steamer, plying its dodgy trade around the Western Isles, was down to novelist and journalist, Neil Munro, a native of Inveraray in Argyll.
It was a floating version of John Sullivan of Balham's *Only Fools and Horses*; the accents differed (widely) but the scams, essentially, were the same—a whisky mack was as close as it got to the *Trotter* cocktail.

Did you hear the one about the hedgehog family who were out on the highway teaching their youngster about road safety? Dad would head off across the street, but as soon as a car appeared he'd freeze and allow it to pass over.
He forgot to warn his boy about Reliant Regals.

(And a literary footnote for you to think on: Roddy McMillan starred alongside Nicholas Ball in the detective series *Hazell,* which Terry Venables is said to have been party to in its early development; when *he* died, Neil Munro was described as "the apostolic successor of Sir Walter Scott.")

In the original series—*"Para Handy—Master Mariner"*—Duncan Macrae played the Capt'n, and Roddy McMillan, his mate.
By the time the second series—*"The Vital Spark"*—came along, Macrae had died, so McMillan was made skipper; the excellent John Grieve missed out on promotion and remained the temperamental chief engineer *Dan McPhail* . . . Walter Carr was the languid factotum, *Dougie* . . . . Alex McAvoy, *Sunny Jim*, the ageing cabin-boy.
It was an all-male crew/cast of mixed gender allegiances, and egos, so moods and tantrums were never far from the surface: keeping the peace, on series 2, was the fabulously named Pharic Maclaren—the producer/director—and keeping <u>him</u> in

check was Margaret Agnew, his dedicated PA, who had agreed, rashly, in 1967, to become Mrs. Philips 'in sickness and in health,' swearing on the good book that she'd change from her maiden name on the credits.

Pharic fell victim to polio in bizarre circumstances, but his enthusiasm for the job never diminished; getting him on and off the boat for the outside shoots was heart-stopping, as he dangled over the quayside in his wheel-chair on the end of a crane-arm, scripts and spy-glass in his lap.
Doris McLatchie, a versatile board-treader, would have seen something of Stewart Granger in her intended's handsome face, and, no doubt, a bright future for an up-and-coming director.

Many years later the BBC brought the formula out of retirement for a re-make—*The Tales of Para Handy*—with Gregor Fisher (*Rab C. Nesbitt* more famously) as lead, and Rikki Fulton (my comedic hero) the mate . . . but *'the spark'* had gone, for me, Floyd.

Another of Pharic's many productions—which included several 'live' episodes of *Billy Bunter of Greyfriar's School* (no way of recording them, sadly)—was a thriller called *Scobie in September*, set in Edinburgh around Festival time; I played a tiny part viz. assistant stage manager on the location shoots—char wallah, essentially . . . and busily.
The leads were Sunderland born 'Glaswegian' Maurice Roëves, and petite, wide-eyed Hannah Gordon. Having checked her credentials in the office *Spotlight*—the casting director's bible—I felt an affinity with Hannah Campbell Grant Gordon . . . . being a (John) Grant Gordon (Philips) myself.
Hannah would star in the hugely popular sitcom, *My Wife Next Door,* with John Alderton, and, notoriously, was the 'woman' who 'killed' *Victor Meldrew*.

One of Maurice's early credits was the film adaptation of James Joyce's controversial book, *Ulysses*; not only was the screenplay nominated for an Academy Award, but it's thought to have been the *first* motion picture to use the "f" word on screen . . . the kind of 'fact' Stephen Fry & co., might dispute/disprove on *QI*. Alas, no Oscar.

Dashing Anthony Valentine, cast as an undercover cop, impressed everyone on the crew with his urbane style and 'professional' handling of a side-arm; his future portrayal of the sinister Luftwaffe officer, *Major Mohn*, in *Colditz*—the long running POW series on BBC—amplified the point.
Tony had a full head of hair back then, and (as I mentioned) 'the hots' for Alexandra Bastedo, one babe-of-an-actress who could—should the need arise—talk dirty in several languages, and who'd once been a translator on *Miss World* . . . an event she could easily have won.

If I'm not to be mistaken *twice* in two sentences, it was the year the German winner had been stripped/'de-throned'/ disgraced, a couple of weeks after donning the ill-fitting crown and walking that faltering, triumphal walk-of-life in the Albert Hall, to a mighty fanfare, and in an 'epilepsy' of flashlights my cousin George could not have survived.

She'd been exposed—in some mag or other—exposing herself (*'in the buff, Eric'*), and Mr. and Mrs. Morley hadn't liked it (or so Julia said).

As would happen to Carl Lewis when Ben Johnson was caught, metaphorically 'with his shorts down' in Korea, *Miss Guam* was installed as head-girl by Mecca, and the tutting could begin.

When I was growing hairy balls, the 'ideal' vital statistics were 36-24-36, probably based on Rosemarie Frankland from Rhosllannerchrugog (*no idea whatsoever*) in Wales, the winner in 1961; the current *Miss World* measures 86.5-61-89 which falls off the tongue like cured anchovy.

Pharic had gone for Anton Diffring as the arch-villain in Bill Craig's *Scobie*; anyone who's watched Alistair MacLean's *Where Eagles Dare*
(a movie, network television ensures, escapes no one) would recognise the face: those ice-blue eyes and long 'Heseltine'* locks . . . the perennial German officer. Diffring bought into the type-casting even though he'd left Gemany before the War . . . the story being that he didn't buy into the doctrine—others had other ideas.

Here's a crazy play on blond ambition (*"we'll be round after we've trussed up Mr. Buchanan, Mrs. Philips"*):

The crystal ball (*"Papa don't Preach"*) showed millionaire status by 25 (*"Vogue"*), a seat on the board by 35 (*"Think of Me"*), pack leader by 45 (*"Where's the Party"*), and royal patronage by 55 (*"Take a Bow"*).

I could be talking Madonna (*"Material Girl"*), but, in fact (*"She's not Me"*), this was the path (*"True Blue"*)
Michael Ray Dibdin Heseltine ("Conservative"*),
M.P. for Henley-on—Thames (*"This used to be my Playground"*) predicted for himself (*"And the money kept rolling In"*).

Another blond bombshell—Boris *"ping pong is coming home"* Johnson, now Mayor of the capital—took over *Tarzan*'s seat by the river (*"Swim"*), when he was called to Lord's—make that <u>the</u> Lords (*"Oh what a Circus"*).

Once more to *Auld Reekie,* dear friends.

Two names would always stand out on the screen credits:

Rostrum camera
Ken Morse
(never saw another soul credited with the work)

Fight arranger
Peter Diamond

Think *Star Wars, Raiders of the Lost Ark, Doctor Who* and any meaningful TV show with danger about it, and Diamond was your man: he'd set out to be an actor but got into stunts as a better guarantee of steady work, albeit in its riskier form.
I'd most assuredly be lying if I said he was involved in *Scobie*, but I *can* say it was my first experience of the peculiar, masochistic world of the stuntman.
On the surface, it wasn't too elaborate—*speeding (four wheeled) car mows down man in street*; not *X-Men* stuff, but someone had to do it.
DIY Harrison Ford had never been seen around the Festival, and anyway, he'd have done our entire budget by breakfast on Day 1.

As powerful arc-light flooded the night-time crime scene, simulated rain from a water-canon soaked our skid-pan of 'death' (imagine, *fake rain in Scotland*).
Huddled in a corner, the stunt crew prepared for their moment.

Half an hour later we were still waiting (*that's the movies for you*).
Girding one's loins to be taken off at the knees by a car travelling at 20mph, cart-wheeling over bonnet, windscreen and roof, and landing—without fracture—via the boot lid, on wet tarmac, took a bit of mental and physical rehearsal.
I imagined we were only going to get one shot at it, and so it proved.

"*Lights, camera—ACTION*"
. . . all that squealing tyre business
. . . then THUMPs 1-2-3-4.

The stuntman lay motionless, way beyond the "*and . . . CUT*" command.

Oh my God, we've killed him!

The edited version was spectacularly convincing; the final shot was held for 'terminal' effect (as anticipated . . . <u>what</u> a pro).

Anton Diffring was already an international star, and, but for a dubious gait when running, was the embodiment of male menace—the women on the crew loved him; in the main, the male jury was out. Valentine we were more comfortable with . . . and so—if I were not being overly jealous at this early point in our relationship—was Mrs. Philips.

Jack Hedley was another who, by association, got on my tits.
Pharic cast him in something or other that kept Miss Agnew at the studios for an unreasonable amount of time during our courtship; the *Colditz* producer, Gerard Glaister—a familiar face in the canteen queue at BBC Scotland—pitted Hedley (as a Brit of course) against the same Tony Valentine, in a series that would run and run (for 28 episodes, over two seasons).

Another useless 'fact': RTE—the Irish state broadcaster—produced a radio version of Joyce's *Ulysses* . . . unabridged and uninterrupted for 29 hours 45 minutes:
"*Fuck*" *that for a book at bedtime.*
(if you think the chapter headings in this load of nonsense are bizarre, take a gander at Irish Jim's—he must have been on the wacky-backy)

Compared to Alcatraz, Colditz . . . or Oflag IV-C (sounds like a primary class at German school), leaked like a colander. Escape plans were submitted, daily . . . even one proposing the building of a glider was given the nod by the committee; it was funny in Lord and Park's *Chicken Run* . . . . but in an 'escape-proof' wartime prison—*they're havin' a giraffe!*
"Where were the Germans, and frankly . . . . who cares?" (© Barry Davies)

Here's another quiz question for you:

What do post-Second World War new-borns, Roza-Marie Leopoldyna Lubienska, and Stefania Zofia Federkiewicz have in common . . . apart from the obvious connection with Poland?
Some clues:
Both are now tall, flame-haired beauties.
The former was married to our super-centre-forward in the Waterman XI (according to her second husband Dennis, she didn't approve of his staying up till all hours playing snooker and drinking with his footballing mates in *her* house, though I never found her anything other than charming when we came to call and over-stay our welcome) . . . .

The latter played *Mrs. Jennifer Hart*, on-screen wife of (lucky bugger) Robert Wagner (*Jonathan*) in *Hart-to Hart*, and—for real—would become an overseas member of the Windsor Park Polo Club . . . .

So, with some of the *Harts'* 'schmoozy' powers of deduction, you can easily work out who is Countess Rula Lenska, and who is delectable Stefanie Powers.

Pretty boy "R.J." Wagner wasn't to know that we shared common interests: not only had he dated the stimulating Debbie Reynolds, but then he went and married 'my' Natalie Wood . . . *twice*, and thence to another of my 'covetables'—the fabulous, Jill St. John.

Now there he was cavorting on screen—and off (allegedly)—with Steph . . . *had the man no shame?*
(just one crush after another).

My constant platonic, heterosexual companion through the very long days on the men's European golf tour was former *Harrod's* cheese salesman, and fine videotape editor, Simon Thompson.
"Tommo"—or "Tom-Oh" as his US employers (during the Open) would have him—is a bit 'mutton Geoff' nowadays, by way of a rare and unpleasant complaint . . . exacerbated, no doubt, by having to listen to the ravings from the American production truck.

US networks would send over plane-loads of key people for 'majors' like the Open and Wimbledon, and "Tom-Oh" was one of several UK bods taken on to staff their not inconsiderable rigs.
Many who agreed terms did so, as much for the talkback, as the daily-rate; it could be all kinds of hysterical, and recognising its repeat value was often recorded, internally, for international distribution (in-house).
By way of resignation, a verbally-abused technician 'shot' himself walking away from his locked-off camera, headphones trailing, with a 'finger' (in perfect focus) to the production truck . . . in perfect focus(you).
Simon knew an *Appenzeller* from a *Drunken Goat* when he smelt one . . . not only that, he was very well-connected.
When he was a lad, his folks would take him to Hollywood on holiday to stay with some A-list family or other.
When he told me about living *in the fame fecking house* as Nats* and Bob Wagner, I fell at his feet like a porn star.

It must have been around the time Mrs. Wagner was contemplating a declaration from her first innings with "R.J."

*Наталья Николаевна Захаренко . . . to her family, or Natalia Nikolaevna Zakharenko . . . to her friends, or 'Natalie Wood' to you, me and Hollywood (she didn't like the screen name, apparently)—was soaring, following rave reviews for her dancing and acting in *West Side Story* (she mimed her songs . . . . *but who cares, Barry?*).

In circumstances similar to *Ján Ludvík Hoch's demise, Wagner's brown-eyed girl died aged 43, having, somehow, fallen off her yacht.
(there was never any suggestion of *Robert Maxwell being in a nightie when he drowned.)

Presumably through the cash and clout of Universal World—the *Colditz* co-producers—Wagner was teamed up on the set of the leaky old castle, with men of R.A.D.A. like Hedley, Valentine, and Bernard Hepton.
Hepton (*Herr Oberst*) played *Karl*, the 'big softie' Wehrmacht Kommandant—no match for smooth-talking *Colonel Preston* (Hedley). Slimy *Major Mohn* could not be trusted.

Glaswegian, David McCallum—'the blond Beatle' from his portrayal of *"Mr." Kuriyakin* in the block-busting TV series *The Man from U.N.C.L.E.*—came home to play hot-headed, Flight Lieutenant Simon Carter.

Even as 20 year olds, we knew about t.h.r.u.s.h., (and that Candida Albicans was no exotic dancer): it didn't come from shagging, which was a huge relief to the more sexually active among us.

Illya Kuriyakin and *Napoleon Solo* (Robert Vaughn) were the good guys—agents of the *United Network Command for Law and Enforcement,* and the *Technological Hierarchy for the Removal of Undesirables and the Subjugation of Humanity* were their sworn enemies.

Hedley was . . . . *quite* good-looking; the quality of his voice was undeniable, as was Alan Badel's—a near contemporary, remembered most for his portrayal of *Edmond Dantes* in the TV adaptation of Alexandre Dumas's *The Count of Monte Cristo* . . . . my favourite book (next to this*, Great Expectations* and anything by James Patterson).

If *listening* to Badel was a pre-occupation, slavering over his character's cracking (if tragic), first love *Mercédès,* (emphasis on the accents) was an obsession: Natasha Parry became another of my 'targets.'

Being Piscean and an early believer in all that astrology bollocks, I prayed they'd get back together . . . that *Edmond* would forgive her for marrying shit-face *Mondego* . . . but he never did.
The film version had a happier, 'Hollywood' ending; James Caviezel was splendid as *Dantes*.

J.C.'s *Jesus*—in Mel Gibson's *The Passion of the Christ*—got more attention, but he (Caviezel) was again on top of his game as golfing legend, Bobby Jones, in *A Stroke of Genius* (*possibly a tad on the tall side, if I were being picky*).

My first love (*or was she just being terribly nice*), the far from tragic Carol McGregor—née Lawson as she was when my first overture was made so clumsily at the school gates—had since produced Colin and Ewen with Jim (the bastard), yet still had time—from walking the dogs, audio describing and hospice fund-raising—to be UK producer (*McDongall Films*) of the St. Andrews end of the Jones movie.

Getting your hands on a copy is difficult; it's as hard to come by as Badel and company in the original1964, black and white TV version of the Dumas classic . . . but well worth the effort.
Sports stories that work on the big screen are rare, but *A Stroke of Genius* did; *Escape to Victory*, with Sly Stallone and Bobby Moore was another exception.

Meanwhile, back in Scotland, in *September* . . .

The scene: a spooky cemetery at dusk—Greyfriar's possibly (when in Edinburgh . . .).
It's haunted, don't you know?
Greyfriar's school in *'Bunter'* was complete fiction.

Maggie Agnew—soon to be Mrs. Philips, and thence mother of Grant and Amanda—was continuity girl, wet-nurse and producer's assistant on *Scobie* . . . all of which should have added up to half a grade, at least.

Her boss grew agitated . . . he was "losing the light."
Hannah (*Judy*) and Maurice (*Scobie*) had a long passage of dialogue to do, on the hoof, in two-shot.

The great man retreated in his chair to start the action.

The paraphernalia for the shoot took ages to set—a myriad of lights and reflectors supplemented the twi-light . . . boom microphones hung perilously close to being deemed 'unacceptable' (or worse) by Norman Shepherd, our irascible cameraman.

The ambient silence was deafening.

Grips had laid fifty yards of track between the gravestones; the camera was mounted on a dolly, the cameraman mounted on that . . . and the riggers looked forward to a single take.

A dozen or so later, we were losing the will. The sound recordist was all for legging it: he could hear a mole fart three feet down, but couldn't account for the squeaking that was causing so many sync-clicks of the clapperboard.
The 'noise' (as it would) had begun on a word-perfect conversation between the stars.
We examined every moving inch of the dolly, re-greased the track, tested dodgy footwear, banned breathing, spot-checked graves—but to no avail.
Pharic was exasperated . . . the performing seals grew moody . . . and, being the junior, it was all my fault—Radar O'Reilly to Pharic's *Henry Blake:*

"Fix it, Corporal!"
"No problem Colonel."

As he tracked alongside the camera—all eyes and ears—the wheels of his director's chair were rubbing against the seat supports, creating a noise low-flying bats would have struggled with . . . . but better to know then, than at the rushes review.

Once upon a time in Glasgow, a videotape engineer loaded a 2" spool on the BULK ERASE machine, doing, irreversibly, what it stated it would on the large warning notice slapped to its cover. In a frenzied instant of de-magnetisation, one of the early studio recordings of *The Beatles* was lost for good (not one you'd own up to . . . . *if there's truth in it*).

And early one morning, just as the sun was rising, I heard my bladder crying "it's time to go and pee." I was putting the finishing touches to a long—some said, excessively so—opening sequence for the Sunday show at the Irish Open golf championship, when nature called. The room had two rocker-switches at the door, one for the bathroom . . . the other (the one I mistook for the bog light) was the master.

Hadn't saved my work on the laptop, had I?

Basic fault of some smart-ass interior designer, still I guess I was spared a memo from Sky about self-indulgence—*"get to the golf, Darwin!."*.

The BBC sports portfolio in the 70s was bulging with goodies: any event worth talking about—apart from the Derby and the Tour de France—was ours.

Long term contracts were rubber-stamped, rather than re-negotiated.

After a protracted dinner in the magnificent Turnberry Hotel, buttering up Keith MacKenzie, the larger-than-life Secretary of the Royal and Ancient Golf Club of St Andrews, we (A.P. Wilkinson, Messrs Alliss, Carpenter, Mouncer and me) knew a flute of champagne, or two, would seal a deal that was never in doubt.

"K-Mac" (as he was *never* called) came as close to omnipotence as the R.&A. finance committee would allow; when it came to TV rights, he was the man to wine and dine, so, having exhausted the patience of the bar staff, we repaired to the lobby and yanked on the night porter's chord.

I've never known a man to take so long in the toilet in the morning as our deputy Head of Sport, A.P. 'Slim' Wilkinson . . . but that's irrelevant.

He scribbled something on a cigarette packet . . . Keith nodded . . . hands were shaken, and, bar the fine print which David Keir and his mates in the Contracts Office would knock out, the BBC had the Open for another five years.

Great work while it lasted.

Eventually the Ryder Cup—amongst many other 'biggies'—went west, down Grant Way, Isleworth; this was BSkyB putting money where their avaricious mouth was, then taking sports TV coverage—the Premiership in particular—to another place.

Don't have a dish? . . . Tough shit . . . . Get one! . . . was the thrust of it.

Imagine 'the Boys from Brazil' in high-def widescreen, with frequency directed, dual driver sound, and the boy Pelé available in hi-motion on 'playercam' at the touch of a button (got to be the yellow one).

Mr.Coleman, in slinky short shorts and baseball cap, added to our envy back home (circa 1970), by bragging from poolside:

'It's so hot here in Mexico, you could fry an egg on the deck'

It wasn't of course, but they were adventurers, prone to hyperbole in the rarified air.

Had it been the high plains of Africa—to where we'd journeyed in 2001—he might have had more success with his breakfast cholesterol experiment.
The Ethiopian capital, Addis Ababa, is miles above sea level and not far from the hottest place on earth.
You'd imagine therefore, that long distance running wouldn't be the first choice Sunday morning activity . . . and you'd be right—it's a *daily obsession.*

The backlash for the curlers after Cousins and Curry and Torvill & Dean had won their Olympic golds, meant a fight to the death with the free-skaters, for ice-time.
The Martin rink's late-night sweep to glory in Salt Lake City in 2002, may have turned a few heads back curling's way.

The box office at *Les Mis* in London's West End didn't need any help from Susan Boyle, but her astonishing debut performance on *Britain's Got Talent*, made you want to rush out and buy *Guitar Heroes* on *Wii* . . . it's one of those magnetic, inspirational moments, and for many uncommitted, lazy bastards, it was the kick-start they needed.
(how good are Ant and Dec, by the way?)

The unparalleled success our sailors have had at Olympic regattas, down the years, has done wonders for the subs at yacht clubs; what Redgrave and Holmes, and Redgrave and Pinsent, and Pinsent and Earle and Redgrave and whomsoever, did to the habitat of the Chinese mitten crab while training for major championships, may yet have to be referred to animal rights groups, but they were inspirational, nonetheless.

Hoy and co., brought new meaning to "*on yer bike,*" and Tom Daley to . . . "S-H-I-I-I-T!," but if you're white, and fast out of the blocks . . . don't give up your day job.

Were you *Raffles* or *Barry Blowtorch,* and burgling your persuasion, Addis was the place to be when Haile Gebrselassie and Derartu Tulu came home from their Olympic runs; everyone was out (. . . . not that there's helluva lot of re-sale value to nick in the majority of homes).

I'd hooked up with Brendan Foster's production company again, this time under the indefatigable influence of John Caine.

These two are responsible for a lot of things.

Among the printable are . . . staging the Great North Run . . . boosting office shower-unit sales in north-east England . . . and, on this occasion, organising and filming the Great Ethiopian Run.

Gebrselassie had a name revered in Ethiopia; through prudent harvesting of the rich pickings available to the modern star of track and field, neither was he short of a birr of two.
In conjunction with Brendan and the British Ambassador in Addis—Professor Myles Wickstead—Haile persuaded the authorities to stage a 'great run' through the streets of the capital, the year following his Olympic 10,000 metre win in Sydney.
Sponsors came forward; many would run for fine causes, not least, Aids awareness.

In its first year, Haile, in his running gear, started the race, nipped down the ladder to join the masses—10,000 of them (many more 'joined in')—and won the whole shooting match, at a canter.
Running twenty clicks to and from school every day made him into a better than your average runner.
Ten gold medals from major championships across the world later, he'd attained god-like status in Ethiopia, right up there with Haile Selassie (deceased)—*The Lion of Judah, Lord of Lords*.

The inaugural race had its problems: the start was a shambles and there was a mini-riot at medal-collection.

Injury prevented the little grinning Master taking part next time round, but he was ubiquitous, shaking hands, organizing, encouraging, being adored.

Richard Nerurkar, no slouch himself over six miles, on the track or across rain-sodden country-sides, was living with his young family in Addis—wife Gail was a specialist at the local children's hospital.

Fortunately for Richard, Gebrselassie was still on the school run when he was competing at his best; by the time Hailie won his first World gold, in Germany, the man from Wolverhampton was wisely doing marathons.

Whether as a result of his religious calling, or his regular work-outs with the elite Ethiopian squad, Richard seemed capable of working miracles in a community, literally, *born to run*.

I think Prof. Wickstead was slightly embarrassed to be living in the comparative opulence of the ambassador's residence, but no doubting his commitment to Africa . . . and running on its behalf, albeit sedately.

On race day, Peter Brown, the producer, and I got to the start early.
I had to check my watch—the place was swarming with runners.
On a terraced, stone stairway behind Meskel square, thousands and thousands of athletes were *warming up* . . . with the race more than three hours away.

The scene was terrifying and awesome; scores of trigger-happy soldiers—others with long sticks, for the good whacking of leg and rump—patrolled the space between walls of human flesh and the start-line.

As in any mass run, the elite runners have priority, but even their protected pen looked under threat as, inexorably (with a beating or two for practice), the lines of runners inched forwards.
Peter had taken a mini DV camera into their midst.
I feared for him as Haile sounded the claxon to release the flimsy dam.
His shots were stunning . . . the scene from the VIP stand, like nothing I'd ever seen . . . the whole of Africa looked to be on the move in a sea of yellow, Aids awareness, T-shirts.

By the time marvelous Madge Sharples would get to Westminster Bridge, in by-gone London marathons, morning paper-boys were delivering the race results to homes across the capital (and organisers could begin calculating her massive contributions to charity).

Some ex-pats—none as old as Madge at debut (64)—had chosen to run for fun in Addis, but in the main, this was about *racing* . . . for fun, sure, but rivalries were fierce.
Down Ababa way, Haile G. was bigger than David B.—by a distance. Local kids, some in 'lapsed' Man. U. shirts, showed a competitive edge as they kicked-about in the warm-up area.
When it came to business end, friendships were put on hold—it was survival of the fittest time . . . *and these guys were phenomenally, and uniformly, fit.*

There was a 'derby' atmosphere at the 2002 race; anything—from border disputes to Olympic gold tallies—stirred passions.
Neighbouring Kenya sent a team (and their Ambassador) to do battle with the homies.

On the day, Ethiopia won internationally—and diplomatically—and UNICEF was eternally grateful.

In no time at all—apart from a couple of guys on stilts—everyone was home safe; don't forget, this is 2400m above sea-level and blisteringly hot.
It reminded me of Manila, the morning of 'the Thrilla', when Ali and Frazier 'went to war' in temperatures up in the 120°s Fahrenheit:
"It'll be a killer and a chiller and a thriller when I get the gorilla in Manila."

After he'd taken an Earnie Shavers 'bomb' to the temple—at Madison Square Garden in 1977—Ali (never one to forget his roots) declared it had shaken his kinfolk in Africa.

A few 'whitees' who'd miscalculated the ferocity of the early morning sun, kept the race-clock ticking longer than Caine & co., might have wished; John was on a tight financial rein.
Only one side of the official timer ever worked that day, and *Timex* spares weren't easy to come-by in the Horn of Africa.

Watching from the winners' podium, race organiser Nerurkar—whose outward serenity belied the knots in his well-honed mid-section—was relieved to see order amongst the masses, proudly queuing for medals.

Wild horses couldn't have separated the runners in Africa from their mementoes, which perhaps illustrates how pissed off Cassius Clay must have been to ping his Olympic light-heavyweight gold medal (from Rome), into the Ohio river in 1960.
The marathon at those Olympics was won by Abebe Bikila (Ethiopia).

Four decades on, local heroes Haile and Derartu (she'd was first among women at the London marathon earlier in the year, and would win in New York in 2009) were handing out the trophies to those in line *who would succeed*.

Scientists and physiologists will tell you why it is that folk from that part of the world excel at long distance running—legends like Bikila . . . Yifter 'the Shifter' . . . and Mamo Wolde, who, incidentally, was one of the stewards at *our* race—but were evidence needed that the tradition lived on, it was there in the faces of three, elated, age-group winners . . . . *lovin' it* they were, and not a *Big Mac* in sight . . . yet.

From triumph, briefly, to a big let-down.

Our school sports day—my big brother, running in the last event of the day: being the quickest of our sprinters, he was on the final leg of the 4x100 yards.
The four 'houses'—the Murrays, the Campbells, the Drummonds and the Grahams—were in green, yellow, blue and red, respectively.
Last, for the Drummonds, Alastair Aitken.
Something had gone down between these two in the past—perhaps David had been disciplined by double A—a school captain with a little bit of a vindictive streak . . . . in any event, needle was in the air.
As the third runners raced towards the final relay—up a bit of an incline—the Murrays were dead last . . . but 'with chances' *if Philips could run to form* i.e., like the wind.

Batons successfully negotiated all round, Aitken was several yards ahead and winding it up for the finish. A crowd of proud parents and partisan house members were packed on the natural, spectator-mounding under the Morrison building, with a complete panorama of Academy Park and the warring factions below.

As one, they rose in anticipation . . . what theatre . . . one race left (one leg of it) *and the House Championship at stake.*

"Come on Wavey!"

Come on he did, gobbling up Aitken in the process.

Stuart Storey would have seen it thus:

"Here come the Murrays . . . Philips floating over the grass . . . . high knee lift . . . arms pumping . . . relaxed in the shoulders . . . <u>look</u> at that head——still, like a hunting leopard . . . . eyes glued on the tape."
(love that '*relaxed in the shoulders*' business—never managed it myself).

That's how you knew when to stop (the tape) in those days, a simple white strip stretched across two poles, with enough 'give' in it so as not to garotte you in your moment of glory.

Inexplicably—in a Devon Loch happening—Davie (race and Championship sewn-up, in the frigging bag) . . . *slowed down.*

What's he doing? . . . He's stopping!

Sure enough.

458

In a flash, bugger-lugs Aitken was upon him.
All was lost to the House of Murray.
Drummond win.
David had mistaken two identical poles, stuck in the ground about ten yards from the actual finish, as *the* line.
I'm not saying he was a short-sighted git (he did wear *Buddy Hollys* from quite an early age) . . . *but come on, run though the shagging tape, bruv.*
The poor sod was inconsolable.
My grandfather—clan chieftain—arranged for a special medal to be struck as a compensatory gesture, but it was gut-wrenching for the boy (I'm only sorry I had to bring it up).

Being a keen biker in his youth, he might be consoled by a recent cock-up in Barcelona.
Were Julian Simon to win the Catalan 125cc Grand Prix, he'd go top of the standings, ahead of nearest rival, Bradley Smith.
As he (Julian) crossed the line, he prepared to 'wheelie.'
ONE LAP TO GO, mush!
He managed to limit the damage to a photo-finish for 3rd (which he lost), but still managed to hold on to top spot in the table.

(. . . and there's more, before getting back to the triumphant in Africa)

I was directing an international meet in the converted aircraft hangar at RAF Cosford, near Wolverhampton, in the west Midlands, where many great champions (including home-boy Nerurkar) had come to do speed across the boards.

It's hard to forget Cornelli Antoinette Harriette Cooman—or 'Nelli' to her friends: she was only little—Surinamese by origin, now out of Holland—but her designers had endowed her with an enormous pair of top bollocks, which, should she make it to the line in a blanket, were a distinct advantage . . . embodiments of the dead-heat in a zeppelin race. Nelli's knockers were often the difference between gold and silver in the 60 dash, and handsome as sports-bra promotional aids.

As ever, Coleman was cracking out a commentary on a long distance race.
Must have been confusing for the 'short-trackers,' counting laps while keeping their balance on Cosford's sloping banks.

Well blow me down if the leader didn't do 'a Davie Philips.'

Like my man, he slowed to a standstill, with half a lap to go; didn't bother to re-start once the penny had dropped—even lapped runners took time to stare in amazement on the way past.

That, of course, led to an enquiry—Coleman style.
My view—the blatantly obvious one—was he'd forgotten where he was and stopped; the huge wall of the hangar, right by the finish line must have been a clue, but over on the 'open' side of the track, with fifty metres to go, his race was run.

Davey C., never prone to let a drama die in peace, went off into one—his own conspiracy theory; somehow *I* was half expecting to get the rap . . . he had that ability.
Despite my entreaties, he wouldn't settle until he'd heard it from the horse's mouth . . . but that particular horse had showered and bolted, long since.

Coleman and Gubba lie deep and inseparable in my psyche.
The hopelessness of his place in the line of accession—somewhere between Prince Charles and the other seven runners in a Usain Bolt race—was amply demonstrated when he took over from David on *Sportsnight* in 1972. It was no more than a crafty holding operation, orchestrated by the producers on Harry Carpenter's behalf . . . . *to let the dust settle.*
Harry moved in after three years—time enough.

Tony's anaemic, albino look, his pallid skin in the pale-blue kit of the BBC Commentators's XI, rendered him indistinguishable out on the wing, on a cold and frosty Sunday morning.

We were doing the 1985 Cup Final between Manchester United and the holders, Everton who were on for a treble of League, Cup and Cup Winners Cup titles.

There weren't anything like the number of replay angles there are today, but we did have a camera in the Royal Box, essentially for the Cup presentation. John Shrewsbury, the match director, arranged that its output be fed into one of his slow-motion machines; although it was 'a reverse'—that is, not on the same side and therefore a different 'eye-line' to the other match cameras i.e. it 'crossed the line,' *savvy?*—it might offer an interesting alternative.

The scoreless game had gone to extra-time . . . the 20th minute thereof . . . when Norman Whiteside, United's attacking mid-field hard-man—a.k.a. *"The Shankill Skinhead"* (born in Belfast, shorn somewhere in Manchester)—fired in a curler, giving his nine team mates left on the pitch, a win over the Scousers . . . Andy Gray *et al*.

Although Kevin Moran had been the first player to be sent off in FA Cup Final history (in the 90th minute of the match above), Kevin Keegan and Billy Bremner's clash, and exit, from the 1974 Charity Shield is a more vivid memory.
"Gazza" in '91 was just lunacy.

Some daubed him "the greatest player of his generation"—enormously talented will do me; wife-beating and alcoholism are big issues, but he could dazzle and amaze on the pitch . . . *which didn't make it alright.*

Whiteside, at 17, was the youngest player in World Cup history in 1982 . . . some days fewer than Pelé in 1958 (thereby ending the comparison).

The main replays of what looked like being the winner done, the director called up a 'reverse angle' graphic and ran in the Royal Box slo-mo.

Were you to look closely, as the ball hits the back of the net, a little figure sat on a camera-box, right behind the left-hand corner of Neville Southall's goal, suddenly topples off his perch in shock.
Unashamedly, "Gubbs" is a Man.U. fan.

That camera's next offering was of Bryan Robson raising the famous old trophy, as his side (of full internationals) waited for their mementoes and a touch of the Cup.

We offered to drive the Great Ethiopian champions home.
Clutching their hard-earned trophies and medals, they leapt in the back of our pick-up, as we set off on a journey far longer than the one they'd just covered in bare feet—some in preference, some of necessity.

At our first drop off point, the tiny athlete's living relatives were waiting to greet her; incongruously, an ancient, flickering TV set—in the only room—did fine for one shiny new trophy.
Everyone was a bit self-conscious, but we got by.
We took pictures, which the man from UNICEF promised to frame and deliver.

At the next house, the boy's mum was out working, but if his other relatives were measures, you knew she'd burst when she got back.

'Modest' would be to exaggerate conditions at our final port of call.
Our third winner, a beaming, slip-of-a-girl, whose ambition—if not to be Tulu (in Ethiopia she was getting on at 14)—was to teach.

We drove our trucks up a narrow track, and no sooner had we switched the power off, than scores of villagers appeared, waving their hands and calling her name.
That, in microcosm, was just as we'd seen earlier in the week at the local TV station, as we viewed Haile and Derartu's rapturous homecomings after the Barcelona, Atlanta and Sydney Olympics.

Our camera crew was swept through a labyrinth of passageways, on a tidal wave of hysterical supporters, the champion holding her silver chalice high above shovels and rakes and sticks . . . anything that could be raised in her honour.
Little ones took our hands, spontaneously—you wanted to give them something, anything, that would make them happier, but really all they wanted was for us to share in their unreserved joy.

The crew, and as many as could fit, disappeared into the girl's house—all singing, all dancing . . . fantastic.

She had little more than her family's support going for her, but you couldn't imagine her lying down on the track, protesting, as John Drummond had, so pathetically, in Paris—*the big girl's blouse.*

It's easy to be sanctimonious when you see what it means to folk with next to bugger all, but how big a prick must Drummond (or Tevez) feel, behaving like that? In the footballer's case does the money immunise?

Integrity, dignity and respect was the way we were taught.

Go back to Kenny Buchanan, a very classy world champion, the embodiment of will and guts, who'd given his nuts, and taken a bit of a battering for the privilege, only to have it taken from him by a foul.
Took it like a (sports)man.

"Cloughie" was right . . . *they need bloody shooting!*

They need to go to Ethiopia.

"... The Big Greek in Lane 8."

Fear not, the end is nigh.

This, the penultimate chapter, will be no more than a flysheet, and your journey across it may only be complicated by a chameleon.

I'd be remiss were I not to devote at least a small part of this jumble to my Scottish roots, and while I've been unbelievably lucky to get to some extraordinary places, shared airspace with many of the greatest sportspersons—loved and been loved by a small and exclusive group of ladies—there's no place like 'hame.'

Like that other great missionary, Columba of Iona—fourteen hundred years previously—William Connolly jr., had leanings towards Caledonia <u>and</u> Erin, but was still able to poke fun at overt patriotism . . . . *why, if we love the place so much, do so many take off and leave it?*

I've lived and worked in and out of London for forty years . . . . case in point.

The extremely adventurous hard-nut, Monty Halls, recently completed a series about his six months of crofter simulation on the majestic, wild, west coast of Scotland (albeit with a camera and a 4 x 4).
His conclusion was, that of the times he'd spent travelling and exploring the world, nothing had been more rewarding than his sojourn at Beachcomber Cottage, overlooking the Isle of Skye; having been approximate to both spots, it's easily understood.

Of course there are other awe inspiring examples . . . in the Alps . . . at Yellowstone . . . in Vietnam . . . on New Zealand's North Island . . . but unless you've been to *Disneyland*, Florida with the kids and ridden *Manta* at Sea World, three times in a row, on a full stomach, you haven't lived.

Augusta National is beautiful, if a tad cosmetic; your chances of playing it are slim-to-none, and should a copy of this find its way there, mine are bugger-all.

So here's my recommendation: get yourself to Edinburgh, take the train across the Forth Bridge, muse some on the life of its perpetual painters as you rattle onwards towards Fife, then, on arrival at St Andrews, see if the spirit doesn't grab you.

Genuflect to Old Tom and his boy . . . or Kate, if you're not playing.

The Old Course will be full. Head on to Kingsbarns Golf Links—you'll not be short-changed; others will claim to have played better . . . those at Royal Dornoch and Cypress Point will have a case . . . but bear with me.

Order a three-ball lunch—one haggis (don't ask), one neeps (turnips), one tatties (creamed like cumuli), douse with single malt, neck the rest, and strap on the soft-spikes.
You'll get extremely lucky if it's warm and clear, but worry not, the test ahead is sumptuous—birdies a bonus.

See . . . told you.

Showered and irresistible (locker-room smellies are gratis), soak up the view, have a stiff one for the road (if you're not the nominated driver), point the sat-nav at KY10 3AB, for Anstruther (prounouced 'Ainster' by the locals—they'll answer to anything), and dream of al fresco, tea-in-a-box.

The Anstruther Fish Bar is to die for . . . well, its fish, chips and mushy peas are; again, there'll be those who claim to know better . . . the queues from London's Marylebone High Street, most nights, into Lisson Grove and *The Seashell* (a metropolitan pretender to Ainster's crown) bear witness, *but where's the backdrop?* . . . no semi-redundant fishing boats . . . no conducive pong-de-mare . . . no marauding, shitting seagulls competing for your supper.

Scotland rules on this one—*Proven.*

(This is a minor diversion)
When intelligent apes gave way to us, and our erect, bi-pedal gait, thumbs had an uncertain future; the Scots and the Dutch, joint claimants to its origins, hadn't begun to think golf . . . or *goulf* . . . or *kolf* (whatever)—that was four hundred thousand years away, and the Vardon grip . . . thumbs and forefingers in Vs pointing at the right shoulder (for all but Bubba Watson and the southpaws) . . . five hundred more.

Hugely important for clinging on during trips across the forest canopy, and half-a-plier when it came to de-lousing or seed-shelling, thumbs had to be tucked in and protected during inter-missionary fist-fights; and as binge drinking wasn't the problem it would become for homo sapiens in 'Glesga' and 'Newkasssle,' crawling on all-fours was not deemed to be a method of self-propulsion out of the ordinary.

Handwriting was simply beyond our primate ancestors; nor was there was any evidence, either in Ken Clark's *Civilisation*, or Doc Bronowski's *Ascent of Man*, to suggest the use of 'thumbs-up' as an indication of their on-going well-being.

Clark and Bronowski's ground breaking series—like *Match of the Day*, and snooker on the telly—were commissioned by social anthropologist and friend of the silverback, 'Controlla' of BBC2, David Attenborough.
His decision to return to a desk job in the early 70s, gave the Corporation a massive lift, but he didn't stay long (call of nature).

With the birth of the short message service—circa AD1990—'Son of the Reformation' had begun (the Yanks claim they invented SMS . . . *but then they would*).
Across the globe, human thumbs stirred and began working out
(less certain were the fates of the Sumatran orangutan, Asiatic dholes and low-fat cod).

Quink-stained index and 'rude' fingers were products of hours of fountain pen practise (with *Parker* . . . if one were really posh).
Budding doctors never bothered with . . . "*thin* on the way up, Class, *bold* on the way down" nonsense; coded messages to pharmacists didn't require copper-plating . . . pissed-spider hieroglyphics, in Latin, got you the necessary pills.
But for love-letters, greeting cards and cheques, handwriting seemed trapped in a time-warp.

Never mind kids, and garlic bread . . . *thumbs were the future.*
Dexterously, they tapped out weird, predictive words and sentences, and sent them hurtling through cyber-space, reuniting friends, who, in many instances, should have been left where they were . . . . having 'moved on.'

When I began on *Grandstand*, fish and chips* was the way forward.
I use the 'singular' verb to describe the practice, not the great British coronary inducer.
By way of large, black velvet boards, with lined grooves and white *Letraset* characters, horse-race betting and results were laboriously and meticulously composed by the appositely named, John Tidy, and his squad of graphics men and women.
So visible, across all areas of our sports production were 'J.T.' and his crew, we (BBC Sport) took them as 'ours'—ex-officio—and often, for granted.
His company—Wurmsers Aids (of German extraction)—continue to be a force in TV graphics, after 65 years of excellence.

A Tidy & Co., mistake was as rare as a Coleman compliment.

*The lateral, fish and chip reference comes from the menu boards found in every purveyor's shop (where batter matters) from Ainster village to London town . . . obviously.

We'd moved on by 1984: the fish and chip was back in its wrapper.

The Teleprinter begat the Vidiprinter (same service but nattier looking), and the Aston character generating company—which grew and blossomed out of a loft in Surrey—had body-swerved 'the Dragons' and gone straight to a Queen's award for industry.

Entries for the Olympic Games had risen to around ten thousand—that's a serious amount of typing and spell-checking.
Modern data bases require that you remember a log-in and password, but twenty years ago there was a lot of do-it-yourself about on-screen graphics.

Early calligraphers must have breathed a sigh of relief that TV war corresponding was still centuries away.

The appointed place: Culloden Field, near Inverness
The date: 16th April, 1746
The match: Hanoverian Loyalists v Stuart Sympathisers
(not going great, at this moment in time, for the Jacobites):

"*Can I have a word, Majesty?*" (Charles III)

Standby . . . (wait for his reply)

Charles Edward Louis John Philip Casimir Sylvester Maria (*hello*) Stuart
Prince of England, Scotland, France and Ireland, Prince of Wales and Earl of Chester, Duke of Cornwall and Rothesay, Earl of Carrick, Lord of the Isles, and Great Steward of Scotland
. . . . *stick that lot on a graphic, if you can.*

Before leaving battle-torn Inverness-shire, let me defer to the greatest ever sports headline—from the Scottish editions of *The Sun*:

SUPER CALEY GO BALLISTIC CELTIC ARE ATTROCIOUS
(following Caledonian Thistle's shock Cup win in 2000)

Had W.P.U.J.C. Vass—the Sri Lankan cricketer—been a sprinter, instead of an awesome 'death' bowler, he'd have been plain VASS Chaminda on the start list, with a tiny golden-dragon-on-a-red-background against his name, denoting the Democratic Socialist Republic of Sri Lanka.

At Olympic time, 'J.T.' had to be ultra-careful: every nation had to appear politically correct—borders changed, regimes collapsed, new territories evolved.
While SRL would seem logical for a Sri Lankan athlete, SRI, in fact, is the one used at the Olympics, though LKA is given in some quarters
(*Mary and Joseph, I hope I've got that right*).
The folks from what used to be Ceylon can do you a spectacular surname—AMIRTHALINGAM, or DAHANAYAKE; one of the early political bosses went by the handle of Solomon West Ridgway Dias BANDARANAIKE.

Thankfully, for Mr. Coleman, and his fellow track and field commentators, 'the little Lankans' weren't huge at the dash.

The Greeks, however—from whence much of it came—often were.

After a few stabs at the line-up for a heat of the 100metres, we agonised that Coleman might find an alternative, before the starter got serious.

Adjusting his manhood, in lane 8, was PAPACATSOULAKTOPOUS of Greece . . . or something equally time consuming—a name that would lay waste to all voluptuous Vorderman's boxes and shelves, but, when taken in stages, wasn't that hard.

Davie wasn't huge on compromise, but even he grew weary of false starting, so Papa'pous became *"the Big Greek in Lane 8"* and, fortunately, that's where he finished . . . 8th of 8.

Early in the piece—on Day 1—the grand master of track spotted a 'typo' in one of the on-screen start-lists; rather than let it pass for the rare lapse that it was, he drew attention to the anonymous (to all but distant relatives and fans in the U.K.) runner's name, making the otherwise impeccable Tidy, cross with himself—*but why would you?*
(Mary Decker syndrome)

Typosquatting (purposely messing with spellings) is a modern malaise which can lead to big trouble, nasty viruses . . . and to some highly suspect Internet sites.

Mum used to proof-read our family newspaper; seldom did the columns pass her eagle-eye without correction, but when I was in Airdrie, one of our Scurrilous, linotype operators on the *Advertiser* managed to get a hot 'shit' past the readers; in my original version, the Diamonds' goalkeeper easily coped with the effort.

We were going on air with a Test match—Sri Lanka against England (LKA v ENG)—on *Channel 4*.

One of the young assistant producers, keen to make an impression, had spent hours composing an animated sequence on video, with swooping maps and bold graphics, pointing the viewer towards the day's venue.

Sadly, for him—and our reputations at Sunset+Vine—he took us off to MAD (Madagascar) rather than the much smaller island of SRI, thousands of miles to the east . . . where they *do* like their cricket.

Unlike in investment banking, our top man took the rap.

There was I banging on about Sri Lankan names . . . .

Claudio Randrianantoanina and Anicet Andrianantenaina Abel are Malagasy footballers, with little chance—you'd hope, as a commentator—of making the big time.

Compared to F1 everything else is Tato Nano, but it might surprise you to learn that one of the quicker 'live' TV sports—graphics-wise—is golf: the action comes thick and fast (if you're doing it right); each image has to be identified with the player's name, country, score, shot, hole number, par and yardage.

On U.S.P.G.A. broadcasts, the graphics operation is as grand as the production, with banks of 'in-puters' firing up all manner of stats, with varying degrees of relevance, for inclusion on the 'telecast.'

Our one-man operation, on the Ladies European Golf Tour, was Matt Ralph. In between texting gorgeous girlfriend, Lizzie (since replaced), and working his strong fingers—and thumbs—to the bone on his Aston Red keyboard (and designing my book cover), he climbed boulders (*he's had all the tests and seems to be responding OK*).

Matt be nimble,
Matt be quick,
Fall on your arse
And you'll get some stick.

Boulderers don't get to any great height, but crash-pads—or bouldering mats—are in place, just in case.

As we awaited our ground transport, taking us to some Spanish airport, at an un-Godly hour, for the early morning *Easy Jet* scrum to Gatwick, we challenged *'Spidermatt'* to scale a sheer wall by the entrance to our hotel—something a builderer might do; there was nothing to hold on to, but, chalkless, in his work-shoes, up he went.

It was as if the entire building had tilted through 90°.

*(isn't it astonishing how quickly they run out of ham and cheese toasties on *Easy Jet*, yet there's a plethora of duty-free and *Pringles* nobody wants?)

Time was when football matches on telly were all but graphics-free, save for an occasional score-line and primitive count-down clock for the dying minutes; having those on constantly, took some getting used to, but you can't live without them now—*animating perimeter advertising, in hi-motion, however* . . .

In Maskell's reign, you had to wait till the end of a game at Wimbledon to find out what the score was; the old boy would go apoplectic were there a delay . . . even for Connors to calm down.
Game-point settled, applause, wait for it . . .

"Nastase leads by two games to one, and by one set to love"—cue Dan.
McEnroe's commentary indiscipline would have given the old Master a seizure, climbing over the umpire as he does, repeatedly . . . *so nothing new there then.*

I'm not sure how readily 'Danny Boy' would have taken to challenges; by the time he got used to *Cyclops*, it'd been lobbed in the don't-bother-to-recycle bin, with male nipples.

There are huge sums at stake in modern pro sport—FIFA and the IOC can vouch for that; technology is the least of their worries.

They hanged Derek Bentley for less, but *"let them have it"*—that's what I say . . .
. . . *but will we been home in time for Horlicks?*

If golf gets the boys and girls of graphics at it, cricket is like a breeding ground; not upsides baseball, or grid iron—or F1—but it's hard to imagine where it can go next.
Apart from the myriad of stats in *Wisden* . . . . the encyclopedic memories of ex-players with total recall . . . what's going on 'live' in the middle, and in hi-motion in between times . . . there's *Hawkeye*, the Red (or Blue) Zone, *Hotspot*, and *Snicko* (not convinced by that one).
Very soon referrals will become part of a changing culture across all forms; no room then for 'precious' umpiring.
Who knows, maybe batsmen will start 'walking' again.

Crawling match stats across the lower part of the screen as the winning footy manager prepares to duck some tricky post-match issue, is a bit rude:

"Was it a penalty and deserving of a red card, in your opinion?"

(. . . hold on . . . just as he answers . . . let's show punters with no interest whatsoever in his predictable bullshit, that his team committed 47 seven fouls, there were 8 yellows, 19 corners and 12 off-sides; the other lot had 72 per cent of the ball, hit the target 3 times and missed the bugger 5; of the 29,336 people in the ground, 64 per cent bought match-day programmes, 15,004 had tea at half-time, and all but 4 believed the ref to be a wanker at some stage in the game)
"Sorry Sir Alex, what were you saying?"

And why does goal difference get equal billing over points gained?
In the first half of the season, it's irrelevant—goals *for* and *against*, fine, but games played and points totals have to be the main focus.

So how do you get a chameleon face the front?.
. . . easy, stick it in front of a Saturday results show—or *Sky Sport News*, any day; obviously it won't know the players, but if anything can take it all in, this little guy has chances: latest scores, full-time results, animating league tables, travel updates, the FTSE, pop-up Lady Gaga dates, drop-down 098 numbers (for the wishful-thinking couch spud) . . . in the swivel of an eye.

Got the remote . . . her indoors is washing the motor . . . Ocaydoakie's delivering the shopping . . . the 'illegal' au pair is seeing to the saucepan-lids . . .

SORTED!

"When's La Liga on, Nan?"

"... AND FINALLY ...
(© ITV NEWS)

Spermatozoa sounds like something Ben Johnson might have swallowed before taking off for a quick one, but, as any straight woman will testify, they're probably man's only redeeming feature. Problem is, where best to deposit these swimming seeds of life for maximum yield?
The perfect host should only apply be she, overwhelmingly fit viz., sexy, lovely, smashing, gorgeous—Cheryl Cole, in essence. Liking football (Celtic, ideally), cooking to my Mum's incredibly high standards, and keeping it local and monogamous, are—in my bachelor, Beeton-driven world re-visited (for a second time)—obligatory ('Ash the Cash' could learn from such Victorian principles).
Furthermore, she (the applicant) should never have qualms about opening the downstairs curtains, and letting the light of her life flood her deepest recesses.

My greatest achievement, other than making it north to Junction 15 on the M40 before spotting an *EDDIE STOBART* lorry, was to generate—at precisely the right moment—enough thrust to launch four, loaded, determined 'atozoons, and send them (midst hundreds of feckless, fellow bathers) careering along two distinct Fallopian Ways—one Scottish, one Anglo-Welsh—towards cell Block O-vum. Re-released by the host, the slithering catalysts breeched the walls, fairly aggressively ... and exploded. *Do your worst, lads.*
Vulgar elements might construe this as a metaphor for four highly satisfactory and successful shags, but—as nutty astrologers would have it—Pisceans are more romantically inclined than that ... *and we can't be burdening the likes of Sir Elton and David F. with the future of the human race now, can we?*

After months of feeding on-line, each of the sightless cargo was ready to quit neutral buoyancy for a life of angst on the outside. Should the now hideously distended egress still prove too tight for a wide load, sharp instrumentation, in skilled, confident hands could create an escape hatch.

(after childbirth, constipation is sheep-shit for mothers)

You never know what you're going to get . . . . an astronaut, a sporting great, Kelly Brooks or Average Joe . . . but in the end, *what's it got to do with you anyway?* You want the best for your babies ... long life, health and happiness, and an early, significant

strike on Euro Millions, before *you* lose control of your bowels, and can no longer break a hundred in the monthly medal.
Pay-back time.

Like Dr. King, I've had my dreams . . . of walking on the Moon . . . of winning the Open, (of being the applicator tip on Kelly's lip gloss doo-dah) . . . of being the first white man since Alan Wells to win, or even to get *into*, the Olympic 100 metres final.

Everyone has them (dreams), and a banker or two . . . a favourite joke for the office Christmas lunch, or for when you're three down at half-time.

Here are a couple of mine:

Teacher advises her primary class that the morning lesson is about telling the difference between prose and poetry.
'If I said,' she began
"*Mary had a little lamb, it's fleece was white as snow,*
And everywhere that Mary went, her lamb was sure to go"
. . . . that would be poetry.'
'Had I said
"*. . . everywhere that Mary went her lamb was sure to wander*"
. . . that would be prose.'
'Think for while' she said, 'and see if you can come up with an example for me.'
A few minutes passed.
Suddenly, Johnny, the boil-sucker, began clicking, frantically, from the back row.
Reluctantly—with sure and certain foreboding—the teacher acknowledged him,
'Yes, Johnny'.
'Yes Miss,'
"*Mary went down to the sea-side, she went out on the front,* (omg!)
She paddled in the ocean, and the water came up to her knees
. . . that's prose (phew!)
'If the tide had been in, it would have been poetry!'

Mum and Dad Balloon were having a lie in.
The door opened, and in bounced their son.
He tried to squeeze in between his parents for a cuddle, but he couldn't fit.
He let a bit of air out of Dad and tried again—still too tight.
Mum next: nope, no good . . . so he let some of his own air out.
Successfully snuggled in at last, Dad turned to him:

"Boris, you've been a huge disappointment; you've let _me_ down, you've let your _mother_ down, but worst of all, you've let _yourself_ down."

A spin, perhaps, on Richard Milhous Nixon's 'confession' to David Frost in 1977 (at the end of their 28 hour chat on his Presidency and the Watergate shenanigan), that he'd . . . *let his friends, his country and the American people* down—no laughing matter.

Genetics, big bangs, the origins of species, faith in a God—we may never get to the bottom of them, so before Sir David Attenborough heads for Bristol and yet another *"how they got there"* series, why don't we end by creating an **identikit super-sports-being**—an eclectic . . . our very own spin on *In Vitro Fertilisation* . . . the ultimate test-tube baby . . . then we can sell the copyright for a stack, live eternally in space, catch *Sky Sports* on the way up, and never have to worry about the licence police again.

Even if the boy Jackson didn't, you'll remember a badly drawn version from childhood: sketch a body part, fold your paper, leaving two stems exposed, and pass it round . . . . *what a ruse!*

My choices come from half a century of watching, doing, envying and admiring.

Let's begin:

HAIR

Duncan Goodhew—the antithesis: not a shred of physical evidence
Mrs. King—when little Miss Moffitt: mullet Queen of Wimbledon
D.C.S. Compton—DSQ: sadly, Denis tested positive for *Brylcreem*
John 'Basil Brush' Taylor—one scary, hairy, flanker
M.C.J. Nicholas—cos he's worth it

'Ssh-sh-sh . . .'

"Gentlemen please . . . my Lords, Ladies and Gentlemen . . . _this_ is the main event of the evening. Introducing . . . and make plenty noise for the electrifying hair of the un-disputed, un-defeated, h-e-a-v-y weight champion of trichology . . .

DON *'LET'S GET READY TO BLOW-DRY'*

KING KING KING"

EYES
generally, have it

Gary Lineker—crisply on to Gazza's blubbing
Phil the Power—20/20's normal . . . what's *phinormenal*?
Merlene Ottey—don't blink . . . start to finish
'Wee Jackie' Stewart—appeared crossed, but how ridiculous is that?
An Olympic fencing judge during a power cut

Marginally less well suited to telly—ice-hockey: Wayne's world of skate-hand-eye-stick-puck-goal-fortune co-ordination
GRETSKY

EARS
(*"Line-acre"*'s eyes—and thighs—were his best shots)

Manly Andrew's on a pair
CADDICK

If you wish, slip on . . .

SPECS

Eddie Edwards—one small leap for the N.H.S.
Denis Taylor—should have gone to Prada
Edgar Davids—dark, Dutch, distinctive
Clive Lloyd—facing Lillee and Thomson . . . *in a cap?!!*

Let's hear it for 'lezzers' in lenses
MARTINA and **BILLY JEAN**—20 single *Slams* between them—*WOW!*

NOSE job

Bill Lawry—for openers: long, slim—a museum piece, like Concorde
Françoise Durr—'*Mon dieu . . . comme Cyrano, n'est pas?*'
Steve Bruce—the perils of a *heed-the-baw* centre-half
Houston McTear—'*dem's ma ret-ros!*'
Alain Baxter—*VICKS* declined to comment
Mike Tindall—get him to the family orthopaedic surgeon
Carmen's affliction commands so much face space through countless bustings
BASILIO

TACHE
the old Brazilian tickler

Mansell's looked painted on—**Groucho's** was—but take **a Cold War, Eastern Bloc female shot putter**, any female, Cold War, Eastern Bloc shot putter, if it's the faintest of impressions you're after, and you won't get done for slander in this court.
Ray Robinson's strip—like Gable's and Fairbanks jr's—was in vogue. Though irrelevant, might *Rinse and Spit*(**z**) have trimmed a hair off his seven world records with some fusion power in München?
"Be—Jaysus begorra . . . would you look at it!"
Prior to its one-off removal (for charity), only contemporary little people from the southern bogs, and a by-now, ancient, Irish midwife might remember seeing this top-lip free of impediment; chafed ladies the world over (*no pack-drill*) still speak the name of
LYNAM

A category omitted from modern editions of this impertinent parlour game, is the **CHEEK** section, sponsored by the John Birks Gillespie Foundation (you may need to look that one up). **Leighton Rees, Emil Zatopek, Kenny Dalglish** and **Matthew Pinsent** may inspire you

MOUTH (as in gob)

Cassius Clay—when ranting, before conversion
Any 'wronged' footballer in close-up (nasal 'spit' to follow. They do it when they're substituted too, then offer the hand to their replacement—*G-ROSS!*
Greg Rusedski—sustaining profanity longer than a rally at the French

Enduringly, in the "*you can NOT be serious/chalk flew UP*" address '*Stand up, if you love John Mac[4]*' (to '*Go West*' by the *Pet Shop Boys*)
McENROE

(**Jim Nantz** of CBS has the sexiest voice in sports broadcasting—fact.
Shelagh Fogarty, on the wireless, back home, sounds sumptuous—fact)

TEETH

Nobby Stiles—the Tooth Fairy would have made a killing on e-Bay
Mike Tyson—'*a word in your ear, Evander . . . "Take THAT, bitch!"*'
Haile Gebreselasse—"*bite together, please, and . . . smile*"

Stunning proof of the efficacy of orthodontics from an early age
TIGER

Make room for a thought bubble, reflecting . . . Ben **Hogan's resolve**, Ayrton **Senna's** concentration, 'Smokin' Joe **Frazier's** bottle, Gareth **Edward's** seeming indestructibility, Angel **di Maria's** theatrics, Marion **Jones'** mendacity, Jonah **Barrington's** ego, Andrew **Flintoff's** dynamism, Ingemar **Stenmark's** rhythm, Roger **Federer's** cool, Byron **Nelson's** consistency, Mike Hailwood's elan, Lionel **Messi's** balance (well, everything really), Alan **Ball's energy**, ambi-dexterous, 'Rocket' Ronnie **O'Sullivan's** prognostications, the **Bryan brothers** telepathy, **Seve's** charisma . . . . and Brendan **Foster's** accent

CHIN

Rusedski already missed out (Peter Beardsley is too much of a gent to take the piss) and J. Hill and Schumacher are earmarked for other categories . . . so a bit of a walkover for Floyd

PATTERSON—fast hands, quick feet—'glass' jaw (relatively)

BEARD

(Mrs. T. hated beards, and *Spitting Image* . . . and Fulham F.C.)

J. HILL—unopposed

NECK

Bert Trautman—on the line for Man City . . . pre Man Sour
Dalton Grant—Masai-esque in mid-arch flop
Will Carling—brass-necked nemesis of the RFU's 57 committee

By football association
POSH—WAG Queen Victoria II . . . . Mum to Harper VII and the lads
(*whose book is this?*)

SHOULDERS
The Charlie Atlas dream in every 97lb weakling

Martin Johnson—broad enough for British & Irish expectation
Mr. Pinsent—what Mr. Redgrave saw, most, of the common man at work
I.T. Botham—all-round shoo-in at the knights' table

No *Dynasty* styling required—Maria and Gabriella's hangers are <u>**прирожденный**</u> and *inherente*

<u>**SHARAPOVA**</u> from the left . . . <u>**SABATINI**</u> to her right

ARMS
mono dexters
Joe "The Blaster" Caggiano—pub-wrestling icon
Tina, Tessa and **Fatima**—the great spear-chucking triumvirate
'Joe Cool'—Montana of the *49ers*
'His Airness'—slam-dunk Jordan of the *Bulls* (and Ryder Cup galleries)
Rod Laver—a.k.a. *'Popeye'* . . . pre-dating the double-hander

Ambi-dexters
Andrianov (gym)**, Kerly** (hockey) **Calzhage** (head-bash)
A.D. Palmer—a.k.a. *'King Arnold'* (big as thighs, they are)
Mr. UNIVERSE 1969—a.k.a. *'Arnold the Governator'*

'Is it a bird?'
No, but Michael's 'wing-span' is 2.13m (the albatross: 3.40)
<u>**GROSS**</u>

ELBOWS

John Fashanu—a near-blinding example for Gary Mabbutt
Bobby Fischer—waiting and waiting and waiting for Spassky to move

Irrefutable evidence of WMD: *"call, DAWN COC-KELLE" to the stand"*
"Guilty," as charged . . . "take him down"
<u>**MARCIANO**</u>

WRISTS
(you may add a sponsor's watch)

Carl Fogarty—the biker's carpals are bound to go . . . just the way it is
Caroline Bradley—strong as an ox, yet lady-like (from the horse's mouth)
A.P. McCoy—controlling thousands, for owners, bookies and Hillman hunters
Sunday-league referees—a.k.a. *"wankers!"*

Should you need to 'spindle and travel' by pommel horse . . . hail Zoltan
MAGYAR

HANDS

Maradona I*—up with his left . . . for <u>his</u> God and country
'Banksy'—down and away with his right . . . a legend denied
'Warney'—*"so it's a . . . googlie from me*
'Murali'—*and it's a . . . doosra from him"*

Bob's were as safe as the Commonwealth Bank of Australia
SIMPSON

FINGER
The Sugar-Trump "get tae fuck" single digit

Billy Bowden—the crooked finger of doom
Malcolm Cooper—breathe and squeeze in three positions
Seb Vettel—on a hat-trick . . . anyway you pronounce it

COWGILL—cheers Bryan, without you little of this would have been possible

NAILS
(*n.pl.* horny plates on the dorsal of fingers)

Any Stirling Albion F.C. supporter in May—bitten to the quick
U.K.s most recent rugby playing ex-P.M.—recession or no recession

In star-spangled red, white and blue and still the world's fastest cuticles
FLO-JO's

You could pop the Joyner phalanges into a pair of **Jack Russell's** disgusting wi'-keeping **gloves** . . . or try tucking Don King's highly-charged barnet under **Dave Wottel 'the Throttle's** incongruous **baseball cap**

CHEST

'Shazza' Davies—saline-filled implants for increased buoyancy in retirement
Mickey Hargitay (Mansfield)—in proportion with his sweet baby Jayne
Nelli Cooman—often the difference over 60m
Ryan Giggs—wax that conventionally, if you dare

('Ping, pong') . . . *"Hi-di-Hi Ann"* . . . all Pip's Christmases at once—a very happy camper
HAYDON

WAIST

(stomach follows, alas)

Denise Lewis—post-Kluft, corrugated, designer-wrapped, girly, six-pack
Nadia Comaneci—two hand-spans-worth . . . a tiny girdle of truth

Wee Jocky's belly of righteousness
WILSON

BUTT

The Lopez-Minogue *Rear of the Year* award

Greg Louganis—multiple entries on, an absolute ripper, still
John Curry—buns-in-tights-on-ice
Lester Piggott—feather-light on colt or filly
Carl Lewis—black & fast
Rafa Nadal—wedgie-prone
The Brazilian Women's Olympic beach volleyball team—de Coubertin's nightmare/Samaranch's recurring dream

Gargantuan *glutei*
AKEBONO

REPRODUCTIVES
"Eyes down . . . it's the erogenous zone"

No CCTV from **The Ladies European Tour showers** . . . nor of **Juantorena's** 'class' (Vinnie's welcome to **Gazza's** balls)

Avert your eyes, kiddies . . . it's the flying lunchbox—in hi-motion

"C-H-R-I-S-TEEEE!"

How about some offal and things?—e.g. Alan Minter's **heart**, Lance Armstrong's **soul**, Roger Bannister's **lungs**, Lasse Viren's **blood**, Ben Johnson's **bladder**, any of George Best's **livers**, Steve Jones's **bowels** (<u>not</u> a post-race interview to be close to at the 1985 London Marathon) Alain Rolland's **nerve**

THIGHS
(this really is wide open)

Anelli Drummond-Hay—a treat for *Xanthos*, a put-down for 'Colemanballs'
Chris Hoy—*'power to yer pedals, Sir Kit'*
Ludmilla Tourischeva—straddling her 4" equipment . . . *"in the <u>name</u> of Valery!"*
Lineker and **Souness**—grown men in high-rise shorts

'Pump dem peerless pistons, Mikey'
JOHNSON

KNEES

Bjorn Borg—on them at Wimbledon, repeatedly
Devon Loch—*'curiouser'* than a Francis mystery
Sandy Lyle—down, but not out, at Sandwich
Don Fox—seeking forgiveness from the Gods of Wembley . . . and Wakefield
Greg Norman—aspic at Augusta

Skip those—*Rhona's in the house*
MARTIN

CALVES
a leg-man's first port of call.

The mother of my youngest two, back-lit, in heels, in Portugal . . . *mmm, nice*

A natty pair . . . *"to die for"* said **Judy Nelson**: a win double for the indomitable 'First Lady' of Tennis
MARTINA

ANKLES

Jonathan Edwards—never fazed (phonetics) under immense p.s.i. pressure
Harold Larwood—tested to destruction in *Bodyline*
Johann Cruyff—a twist of Orange . . . *and then he was gone*
Katerina Witt—only tight-ass judges would be looking at them

By kind permission of *Le Federation Equestre Internationale*, fetlocks and kick-backs (could be a follow-up for *The Manics*)
PENWOOD FORGE MILL

FEET
Several nominees from the in-vogue metatarsal collection

Wyndham Halswelle—(*Google* him)
Budd and **Bikila**—out of Africa (dead-ends for the shoe sponsor)
Phil Bennett—twinkling Welsh Lion in (*baa-baa*) sheep's clothing
Mick the Miller (*'canine'*)—worthy as any equine
Johnny Hancocks—a wandering wolf in tiny, black boots
Michael Phelps—stewards checking for illegal webbing (and dodgy pipes)
***Maradona** II (four minutes later)—*"gie's oor baw back, Diego'"* (a playground chant in most Scottish schools following England's tragic demise in the '86 World Cup quarter-finals)

DANGER—*United Man in Spikes*—*"Bolt's the name . . . Usain*
BOLT"

For anything to develop on the love front, one has to like what one is looking at, so, before unfolding one's final versions, consider

THE OVERVIEW

David Rocastle—handsome cur, late of Arsenal & England (and Earth, sadly)
Meyfarth/Krabbe—fit cop/bent cop of German athletics
Dan Carter—All Black caucasoid—a "10"
Anna Rawson—model Aussie golfer, fabulous dinkum
Valeri Filippovich Borzov—from the boys' showers
Anna Kournikova with **John Newcombe**—double delicious
Wilkinson & Becks—'Butch Cassidy and The Sundance Kid II' (Vic on the 'bars . . . *"but no singing!"*)

Really, there's only ever been one, truly pretty boy, and he <u>is</u> legend . . .

ALI

P.S. Give thanks and praise, daily, for little **'Chezza' Tweedy** . . . and **Bey-Z**

P.P.S. The recently widowed **SOFIA SCICOLONE** isn't sporty as such (<u>and</u> she smokes), but at 70+—in all her eternal Roman magnificence—she still cuts it.

"May la forza be with you, Mrs. Ponti."

On its own, my eclectic is <u>a gorgeous, blow-dried, foul-mouthed, thin-necked, broad-shouldered, thirty-stone, big-boobed, soft-handed, long-driving anthropod, of indeterminate gender, all teeth and nails, who can see like a hawk, swim like a fish, run like the wind, jump like an Afro-American, fart for Hawaii and . . . knock the shit out of anyone who's laughing</u>.

What's yours like?

Reveal all . . .

NOW!

. . . just a bit of fun." (© *Rob Bryden*).

(*encore une*, protracted P.S.)

The business has been a pleasure and a privilege: were I to pick some favourites . . . the bell to end Round 14 of the thriller in Manila, and my sightless kids' initial efforts, would be tops, audio-wise (no need to alert the paedo police, but nursery school playground hullabaloo takes a bit of beating—the tinies being the future, whatever Cern says)
Tele-visually it's harder . . . the clip (on *You Tube*) of the naked, tennis court streaker is up there, comedically, with most of Fulton, Connolly and Kay (and the leaning tower of *Trotter*, of course), but sports-wise, I'd have to go for the Pelé montage from Mexico 1970—*'bloody beautiful, Edson . . . for me . . . at this level.'*

Had Plomley (Roy) or Lawless (Sue) asked, my book to take would be anything by Nigel Slater (to hasten insanity), with Bruno Mars' *Lazy Song* video for us island inhabitants to enjoy, equally.
Assuming there was already a solar-powered DVD player at the retreat, scissors (singular) would be my luxury item.

I'm never going to get the invite, so where to, practically, from here . . . with no *Grandstand* . . . no *News of the World* (and, if the Chinese keep it up, no African elephants).

If the whacky Mayans are right, we'd best get a jildy on—we've only got till December this year.

Were Charles to completely lose his marbles and be devoured by his favourite *Ya-te-veo* tree, and (*BREAKING NEWS!*) Wimbledon go to Sky, we'd need a President, a prophet, a face for our worthless banknotes—Russell Grant, say . . . with Prof. Cox scoffing, uncontrollably, on the bench opposite.

I predict Sir Alex will become Red Baron Ferguson of Govan . . . Edwina Currie will get 'life' for topping Chef Ramsay (*"not fucking long enough"*), . . . and a (very) mature Anne Robinson will give birth to the first-ever, winking *"squeeze-me"*, plastic baby (by A.I.).

Branson jr., will buy the BBC at a knock-down price (Forsyth, and *Dancing on Ice*, must not be retained), and Murdoch Snr.,—a victim of extraordinary rendition by the natives—will die laughing on board a prison ship to Southampton (the boy James having been taken, and eaten, by dingoes).

The only way *Big Brother* will be allowed back (to insult even durr hoodies' intelligence) is if they agree to it being shot in the Danikil.

"Beautiful," "absolutely," and *"epiphany"* are removed from common English usage . . . due to flagrant misuse; further, anyone heard touting *"110%"* as a measure of effort, will be forced to host *Oz Aerobics* in a blindfold, for their stupidity.

By now, rugby union has ceased to exist, owing to the dearth of refs capable of remembering the recently extended, pre-scrumdown routine. Disgruntled backs (on 'the brew') form an orderly line outside Matt Dawson's school of *cook 'n' dance* . . . or learn to give (and take) a high one in the (flourishing) other code.

Superbowl would pass like a game of 20/20 compared to the early FA Cup Final kick-off viz.,1200 BST . . . between inexhaustibly-flush clubs—for non-British nationals *only*— playing to destruction, with legal diving, *carte blanche* referrals and 3rd-eye-replays at a zillion frames per second.

Gray and Keyes would run referee (now 'Dame') Sian Massey's lines; should the crowd not concur with their decision-making, fearless *Al Jazeera* promise to keep their jobs on *Superb Saturday* open, while surgeons retrieve barbed flagsticks from their arseholes.

Ex-WAGS, and Max Clifford, would get concessionary rates in the family enclosure, while in the VIP area (Delia on the dishes, affluent Gordon Taylor on drinks), visiting Sultans, Sheikhs and investment bankers are pandered to (in his own, peculiar way) by President Grant.

Based on occasional trips (under sufferance) to Loftus Road, the "frightfully bored," insanely minted, Ecclestone sisters—invited to do TV, in Q.P.R. hoop tops, heels and suspenders by *Babestation*, the host broadcaster—waive their match analyst fees. Medics rush to assist Mom, Slavica.

A *Best in Show* racist/sectarian chant would be adjudged by Louis Walsh and Sepp Blatter, from their hermetically-sealed box, high above Wembley field.

N.B. The BNP Paribas S.A. *Homme du Match* (in his pink Astros) has to marry Babs Cartland's nemesis and fellow author, Jordan (3 days notice, either side), and sip champagne from 38KKK, onyx, loving cups, at their "live and exclusive" (on *OK TV*) wedding bash.

Should it survive in its long-form, bound similarly to the footie, above, a drawn cricket Test—sponsored by a dodgy firm of Abbottabad bookies . . . played in the dark, at *Green & Cowell*'s ('flat,' as in 'level') amusement park, on the site of Thomas Lord's former cricket ground, in re-developed St. John's Wood . . . using a corkscrew-swinging ball of mad, Jersey cow-hide, tanned by luminous over-the-counter formaldehyde . . . with infra-red, night-vision goggles for all (making thick edges easier to detect, and 'not-walking' even more of a crime against sportsmanship)—would take a month out of our tedious lives.

"Becks"—properly ascribed 'national treasure' status . . . and now entirely covered in indelible ink—gets the proper needle waiting behind various chat and game show hosts for his knighthood, and decides to pack his US Presidential Medal of Honour, La Gran Cruz del Merito Civil (from the grateful Spanish), the key to (parts of) the City of Manchester, and his tribe, off to Samoa.

Following the relative success of the last-ever Olympics, in London, the IOC come clean; back-dated ill-gottens are donated to the <u>Bill & Melinda Gates Foundation</u> and retrospective life-sentences for drug cheats, finally puts paid to sport as we know it.

In its wake, FIFA and the CIA have unprecedented attacks of conscience; all conspiracies (except *Nessie*) are proven: surviving perpetrators are either shot, or have their golf handicaps cut.

Errant priests join cheating-fucker athletes in receiving absolution at a midnight sacrament-of-resolution ceremony on Mount Olympus (in the territory, formerly known as Greece—now a Chinese dependency), before the ubiquitous flame is snuffed forever.
The boy Frayne—aka "Dynamo"—is in charge of separating the rings.

Works stops, as inter-gender hostilities go 'nuclear,' and our patience on fusion power and the hunt for Higgs, runs out; the only way 'up,' is homosexual.

"And finally," the Sun (the star . . . . I mean—*oh, Hell*) will go out, taking orange women (non-sectarian) with fake tits, every species of wasp, and broom-handle putter, with it.

"*Uranus: you've reached your destination.*"

P.P.S. (*how much fun is this?*)

Following the public emasculation of *Top Gear*'s main presenter . . . in front of family Clarkson, and a couple of billion, worldwide, bearing witness) . . . The Big Three (Musketeers, Stooges, Wise Men . . . call them what you will) viz., "DavCam," "SebCo" and "BoJo," perform the seminal, UK bankrupting act of the 2012 Olympic Closing Ceremony.

As the stadium lights dim, there, in spotlight, stands a solid fuel, four-stage mother-of-a-rocket, sponsored by *Virgin Intergalactic* and the *LHC.*, oozing bum vapour.

Sat aloft, in the command module, the suspended bodies of Branson, Cox and "DavAtt" (plus 'the mean winker' . . . for breeding* purposes).

Their mission: *"to boldy go to Kepler-22b to begin the whole fucking process over again."*

* Who cares who's third?'